Aspects of
Indian History and Historiography

Aspects of
Indian History and Historiography

(Prof. Kalyan Kumar Dasgupta Felicitation Volume)

Chief Editor

P.K. Mishra

Kaveri Books

New Delhi-110002

Aspects of Indian History and Historiography
(Prof. Kalyan Kumar Dasgupta Felicitation Volume)
Chief Editor: P.K. Mishra

Edition 2025

ISBN: 978- 81-7479-009-5

Price: Rs. 1500.00

Published by
Kaveri Books
4832/24, Ansari Road
New Delhi - 110 002 (India)
Tel.: 011- 4707 2321
E-mail: info@kaveribooks.com
kaveribooks@gmail.com
website: www.kaveribooks.com

Laser Typesetting by : Delta Book World, New Delhi

PRINTED IN INDIA

Preface

Professor Kalyan Kumar Dasgupta is a familiar name in the domain of Indology. An exhaustive list of his publications has been furnished as Appendix to the present volume to provide a glimpse of the vast panorama of intellectual pursuits of the learned scholar. This volume represents yet another attempt to felicitate him for his significant contributions as an Indologist and man of letters. In response to our request large number of papers were received from various corners of the world in recognition of Professor Dasgupta's scholarship. The papers compiled in this volume represent various aspects of Indian history and historiography covering a wide range of subjects which include popular movements, tribal history, system of education, role of temples, traditions and social customs, trade and ports, India's foreign policy and on historiography. As the papers have been contributed by specialists on the concerned subject, the reader will have the advantage of going through the best in his area of interest. In compiling the papers the Editors have taken pains to ensure the qualitative aspect as befitting tribute to the great savant of Bengal. They will feel their humble labour fruitful if the volume meets the expectations of the students and scholars engaged in historical research.

We are thankful to M/s. Kaveri Books for showing keen interest in bringing out this work with meticulous care and diligence.

Sambalpur University
Jyoti Vihar, Burla

P.K. Mishra
Chief Editor

Prof. K.K. DAS GUPTA

Professor Kalyan Kumar Dasgupta : A Profile

Born in 1935 Kalyan Kumar Dasgupta, the son of Harendra Mohan and Suprity, had his education at the Presidency College and the University of Calcutta. Though the family of Dasgupta hails from Chittagong, (now in Bangladesh) his childhood was spent in Punjab where Harendra Mohan was serving as the Professor of English in D.A.V. College, Jalandhar.

Kalyan Kumar is a recipient of Ph.D. and D. Litt degrees of the Calcutta University. He has spent thirtyfive years in teaching, first in the Government Sanskrit College and thereafter in the Department of Ancient Indian History and Culture. He has led the Kalyani University as its Vice-Chancellor for a full term of four years from 1988 to 1992. Presently, he adorns the prestigious chair of Rani Bageswari Professor of Indian Art of Calcutta University.

Professor Dasgupta has not only supervised Doctoral works but also has made significant contributions in Indological studies. Among his books, *A Tribal History of Ancient India : A Numismatic Approach* and *Wood Carvings of Eastern India* are considered fundamental having broken new ground. His writings on Indian iconography go beyond the descriptive and belong to the realm of iconology. That his studies on art bear ample evidence of deep and fresh insights can be gleaned from *A Comprehensive History of India III*, (edited jointly with R.C. Majumdar) and *Ananda Coomarswamy : A Centenary Volume* and *Sastavarsher Aloy Rakhaldas Bandopadhyay* (edited by him). Besides providing an editorial model in them he maintained a high standard of research methodology in his articles contributed to the *Dictionary of National Biography* (ed. S.P. Sen) and *Supplementary Dictionary of National Biography*, (ed. N.R. Ray). His analytical study of nineteenth century Bengali literature is represented by his papers contributed to *Renascent Bengal* (ed. R.C. Majumdar) and *History of Modern Indian Literature* (ed. S.P. Sen). The elaborate notes appended to the Bengali version of Kissory Chand Mitter's *Memoirs of Dwarakanath Tagore* and in the Sambodhi Dushprapya Granthamala series are indispensable works to scholars. The annotated edition of his father's pioneering work *Western Influence on Nineteenth Century Bengali Poetry* is also a product of profound merit.

It is interesting to mention that Dasgupta is a noted modern Bengali poet whose poems have been included in anthologies like *Ekaler Kavita* and Sahitya Akademy's *Bangla Kavya Samuchhaya*. He has recently participated in the Asian Poetry Festival held at Dhaka where he presided over one of its sessions.

Dasgupta had presided over the 71st annual Conference of the Numismatic Society of India (1983), the Cultural History Section of the South Indian History (1985) and the Ancient India section of the Punjab History Conference (1986). He delivered the Sarbeswar Sharma-Kataki lecture at Mangaldoi (Assam) in 1991, N.N. Law Lecture at the Iran Society in Calcutta in 1992 and Alice Boner Lecture at Varanasi in 1993. He gave a lecture as the special Guest in the First International Seminar on Mizo history and Culture and Aizawal (1992) and presided over its academic session. He was the Chairman of the Numismatic Society of India (1985-88 and 1988-91) and Treasurer of the Asiatic Society (1972-74). He visited Japan in 1986 as the State Guest.

A Fellow of the Institute of Historical Studies, Dasgupta has received the Nelson Wright and Akbar Medals of the Numismatic Society of India.

Dasgupta's scholarship encompasses a vast area of Indology including the study of numismatics, (Journal of the Asiatic Society, 1961, 1965 and 1966) and *A Tribal History of Ancient India,* 1974); *Wood Carvings (Wood Carvings of Eastern India,* 1990 and the *Catalogue of Wood Carvings in the Indian Museum,* 1981); Sculpture, Art and Iconography (*Bharatiya Murtikala,* Hindi, 1995; Indo-Iranica, 1995; *Comprehensive History of India,* III & IV; *Studies in Ancient Indian History;* Journal of Ancient Indian History, 1976-77 and *Vajapeya*) and Historiography of Ancient India (*Historians and Historiography in Modern India,* Edited by S.P. Sen). He is highly admired by his students and colleagues as a soft spoken and hardworking scholar who prefers to work in silence rather than seek Image building publicity. Though not very prolific as an author he entertains no regret on that account as he has already bequeathed to us an enormously rich treasure of research work. He is currently busy in the publication of 'Nataraja in Bengal Art' and the 'Pratimasilpe Hindu Deva Devi' in Bengali is in the anvil.

All his works are distinguished for the clarity of thought and lucidity of expression combined with brevity and precision. Being free from rhetorical jargons and plethora of footnotes his writings reveal the deep insight of an analytical mind.

Contents

Preface iii
Profile v
Board of Editors ix
List of Contributors xi

Section I

1. Petty Peasant Production and Agrarian Capitalism : A Recent View on their Relationship in Colonial India/B.B. Chaudhuri 3
2. The Congress Ministry in the Central Provinces and Berar, 1937-39 : The Communal Problem / K. Mojumdar 22
3. Civil Disobedience Movement and Women in Midnapore District / Niranjan Ghosh 48
4. Nature of Agrarian Discontent and the Origin of Peasant Movements in India During the Pre-Nationalist Era (1757-1857) / Debabandya Kabi 53
5. Protest Movement in Manbhum Against its Merger with Bihar, 1912 / S.C. Mukhopadhyay 60
6. The Indian Reform and Awakening of the 19th Century : A Study of its Impact on Bihar / Sumanta Niyogi 64
7. The Quit India Movement and the Tamralipta Jatiya Sarkar/P.K. Maity 76
8. Western Poligars in Madras Presidency/Anies George 86

Section II

9. A Living Tradition of Tripura : An Ethno-Cultural Probe/Sumangal Sen 101
10. Endowments to Temples in Northern India (Early Medieval Period) / Puspa Niyogi 112
11. Modern and Secular Trends in Muslim Social Thought in Nineteenth Century Bengal / A.F. Salahuddin Ahmed 124
12. Tribal History of Ancient Bengal / Bhaskar Chatterjee 133
13. The Cōḷa Army and the Royal Temple of Rājarājēśvaram / Geeta Vasudevan 147
14. The System of Education in Ancient Orissa (6th Century A.D. to 13th Century A.D.) / Sanghamitra Dasgupta 155
15. Widow Burning and the Madri Episode : An Analysis / Ashvini Agrawal 164
16. Glimpses of Social Condition of India in the Aṅguttara-Nikāya/ Gayatri Sen Majumdar 167
17. Medical Science as Known to the Chinese Pilgrims / Sukumar Sengupta 173

18. Medicine in Ancient India : A Review / Rakhal Chandra Nath 178
19. Orissan Chronology: An Epigraphical Study / P.K. Nayak 188

Section III

20. Jagannath Cult of Orissa and the Rajas of Nepal / P.K. Mishra 197
21. Indians Around the Pamir Plateau in the First Decade of the Nineteenth Century : A View of Contemporary Russians / Surendra Gopal 203
22. India's Foreign Policy in the Post Cold War Era: Can it be Reconstructed to Build a South Asian Community? / Jayanta Kumar Ray 211
23. Origin and Development of Arakanese Settlements in Bangladesh: A Study of Arakan-Bangladesh Relations (1760-1825) / Abdul Mabud Khan 215

Section IV

24. Craft of History Writing : An Early Indian Perspective / Sukla Das 225
25. A Lost Book on Politics in Ancient India / Pratap Chandra Chunder 236
26. Perspectives of Pāli and Buddhistic Studies and Bimala Churn Law / Dipak Kumar Barua 240
27. Some Illusionistic Thoughts in History Writing / Rasesh Jamindar 250
28. Swamikannu Pillai's Indian Ephemeris : A Reconsideration / Mahesh Sharma 259
29. Voices of Protest and Dissent in the Works of Bāṇa / Shankar Goyal 269

Appendix
List of Select Writings of Prof. K.K. Dasgupta / K.K. Chaudhuri 275
Index 287

Board of Editors

Contributors List

1. Abdul Mabud Khan
   Professor, Deptt. of History
   University of Rajsahi, Bangladesh.

2. A.F. Salahuddin Ahmed
   Retired Professor of History
   Dhaka University, Bangladesh.

3. Anies George
   Lecturer, Govt. College of Arts
   Karsagod, Kerala.

4. Ashvini Agrawal
   Department of History
   Punjab University, Chandigarh.

5. B.B. Chaudhury
   Retired Professor of History
   Calcutta University.

6. Bhaskar Chatterjee
   Professor of History
   Burdwan University,
   F/5, Tanabag, Burdwan 713104.
   West Bengal

7. Debabandya Kabi
   Reader, Deptt. of History
   Sambalpur University, Orissa 768019

8. Dipak Kumar Barua
   Professor of Pali
   Calcutta University
   B-I/LI/140/1 R.N. Choudhury Road
   Calcutta-15.

9. Gayatri Sen Majumdar
   P-17B, Ashutosh Choudhury Avenue
   Flat 205, Calcutta-19.

10. Geeta Vasudevan
    'Akshoya' 6, 7th Cross Street
    Karpagam Gardens
    Madras-600020.

11. Jayanta Kumar Ray
    Professor of Political Science,
    Calcutta University,
    Calcutta.

12. K. Mojumdar
    Retired Professor of History
    Nagpur University, Mangalam Aptt.
    241-242 Lendra Layout
    Ramdespeth, Nagpur-10.

13. Mahesh Sharma
    Fellow,
    Indian Institute of Advanced Studies
    Rastrapati Nivas, Simla-171005 (HP).

14. Niranjan Ghosh
    Principal, Tamralipta Mahavidyalaya
    P.O. Tamluk, Midnapore, 721636.

15. P.K. Maity
    Reader in History
    Tamralipta Mahavidyalaya
    Tamluk-721636.

16. P.K. Mishra
    Professor Department of History
    Sambalpur University
    Jyoti Vihar, Orissa.

17. P.K. Nayak
    Reader, Sambalpur University
    Jyotivihar, Orissa.

18. Pratap Chandra Chunder
    24, Nirmal Chandra Street
    Calcutta-700012.

19. Puspa Niyogi
    Retired Professor of
    Ancient Indian History
    6-7/C Lower Circular Road,
    Calcutta-17.

20. Rakhal Chandra Nath
Professor of History
Kalyani University,
Kalyani.

21. Rasesh Jamindar
Retired Professor of History
B-10, Vasu Aptt. Naranpura
Ahmedabad-380013.

22. Sanghamitra Dasgupta
536, Jodhpur Park
Calcutta-68.

23. S.C. Mukhopadhyay
Professor of History
Vidyasagar University
Midnapur (West Bengal).

24. Shankar Goyal
41-A, Sardar Club Scheme
Jodhpur-342011.

25. Sukla Das
Reader in History
Jadavpur University
Jadavpur (West Bengal).

26. (Late) Sukumar Sengupta
22, Rajanikanta Das Road
P.O. Haltu, Calcutta-78.

27. Sumangal Sen
East of Circuit House
P.O. Abhoynagar,
Agartala-799005.

28. Sumanta Niyogi
Professor of History
Patna University, Patna-5.

29. Surendra Gopal
Professor of History
Patna University,
Patna-5.

Section I

Aspects of Indian History and Historiography
Editor : P.K. Mishra
Kaveri Books, New Delhi, India.

Petty Peasant Production and Agrarian Capitalism: A Recent View on their Relationship in Colonial India

1

B.B. Chaudhuri

I intend this essay as a critique of a paper[1] by David Washbrook arguing; with reference to Colonial India, that persistence of petty peasant production impeded the development of 'agrarian capitalism'.

Washbrook's argument, elaborated later in this essay is as follows. The archaic system of petty peasant production, which the Government sought to uphold, primarily out of political considerations, tended to frustrate the 'free market mechanism', and 'the potential capitalist development of agriculture' in British India. Two consequences followed. Indian agriculture, though grossly undercapitalised, continued to be so, despite a plentiful availability of capital, since the persistence of the old mode of production discouraged transfer of capital to agriculture. On the other hand, some modes of employment of this capital—such as rentierism, usury, and commodity speculation further undermined the peasant farming.

A necessary precondition for a rapid agricultural development, Washbrook argues, was either the elimination of small peasant farming or providing capital with instruments to subordinate production.

This point has been debated earlier too. The debate still continues, to which we briefly refer.

We would first analyse Marx's ideas in this regard. Marx has not systematically analysed peasant economy as a specific economic system. His method of analysing it was largely influenced by his basic categories for explaining the modern capitalist society—bourgeois and proletarian, the former living by their capital and the latter by the sale of their labour power. These categories were essentially based on the difference between those who owned the means of production and those who worked within a mode of production. The peasant combined both the properties. To some degree a worker and partially an owner of the means of production, he falls in between Marx's vital categories. Marx thought it possible to understand a peasant society by looking at the peasant as a combination of 'two persons: as owner of the means of production he is capitalist; as labourer he is his wage labourer'. He seems to have ignored the methodological problem involved here. This indifference was partly because of his conviction of the negligibility of the role of the peasantry in the momentous economic transformation of his times : the growth and consolidation of the capitalist system. Marx thought the peasant had a basically negative role to play in this process. 'Peasants were most interesting to him when they were ceasing to exist as such' [2] their expropriation from land, constituting 'the prelude to the history of capital' seemed most relevant to him.

Marx exposed the ruthlessness of the process of this expropriation, but had no regrets. The perpetuation of peasants upon their lands seemed to him perpetuation of 'universal mediocrity'. Both the material and cultural bases of a peasant society were fixed and narrow, while he thought, capitalism created conditions for an enormous expansion of the productive forces and an immense broadening of the cultural frontiers. Marx, though aware of the frightful social costs of the capitalist development, did not, therefore, bemoan the gradual extinction of the peasantry as a class.

The perspective of Marx's study of peasant societies was not invariably an incipient capitalism. His analysis of the 'economic development of small peasant property' was evidently influenced by his conviction about the technical superiority of the capitalist mode of production in both agriculture and industry. In Volume 3 of *Capital*[3] he analyses the circumstances, mostly connected with the organisation of peasant farming, which tended to undermine it. As a specific historical case, he had earlier studied the decline of small peasant property in France, particularly during the first half of the 19th century.[4]

He was emphatic about the narrow base of the productive forces in a peasant economy. Of its characteristic features he particularly noted 'free ownership' of land by the farmer, consumption by the producers of 'the greater part of the rural product', and rudimentariness of capitalist production. 'Small peasants' property excludes by its very nature the development of the social powers of production of labour, the social forms of labour, the social concentration of capital, cattle raising on a large scale, and a progressive application of science....Concentration of capital moves in narrow circles in the other lines of production, and dissipation of capitals predominates'. Given the narrow capital base of peasant farming and the negligible growth of productive forces, any thing that further depleted the capital availability tended to weaken small farming. Marx notes in this connection usury, taxation, and particularly, 'the expenditure of capital in the price of the land'. Free ownership of the land necessarily involves frequent changes of ownership. The capital transferred to land purchase 'has nothing to do with the capital invested in agriculture itself. It forms neither a part of the fixed nor of the circulating capital employed here; it merely secures for the buyer a title to the annual rent'. Such a transfer, therefore, 'is a proportionate deduction from the capital which the small farmers can employ in their own sphere of production. It reduces to that extent the size of their means of production and thereby narrows the economic base of their reproduction. It subjects the small farmer to the moneylender's extortion, since, credit, in the strict sense of the term, occurs but rarely in this sphere'.[5]

The study of the post-Revolution (1789) French peasantry indicates some of Marx's ideas about the decline of small peasant property in an economy where capitalist production had considerably developed. The growth of capitalism had not, however, brought about any marked change in the organisation of peasant production in general. 'The small-holding peasants form a vast mass....their mode of production isolates them from one another....Their field of production, the small holding, admits of no division of labour in its cultivation, no application of science and, therefore, no diversity of development'. On the other hand, developments tending to corrode the base of small peasant property had been taking place. Notably, 'what is now causing the ruin of the French peasant is his small holding itself, the division of land, the form of property which Napoleon consolidated in France'. This happened because 'the economic development of small-holding property has radically changed the relation of peasants to the other classes of society'. Marx thus describes the process : 'in the course of the 19th century the feudal lords were replaced by urban usurers; the feudal obligation that went with the land was replaced by mortgage; aristocratic land property was replaced by bourgeois capital. The small holding of the peasant is now the only the pretext that allows the capitalist to draw profits, interest and rent from the soil, while leaving it to the tiller of the soil himself to see how he can extract his wages....The bourgeois order, which at the beginning of the century, set the State to stand guard over the newly arisen small-holding and manured it with laurels, has become a vampire that sucks out its blood and marrow and throws them into the alchemistic cauldron of capital'.

Marxian ideas have evidently influenced a recent study by Brenner.[6] He attributes to petty peasant tenure a crucial role in impeding the growth of agrarian capitalism. He compares in this regard England and France. The failure of the small peasant property to consolidate itself and its gradual elimination ensured a systematic enlargement of holdings by landlords in the context of favourable market conditions.[7] The landlords, controlling by the end of the 17th century, about 70-75% of the land, were free to create large farms and to lease to substantial tenants capable of making capitalist investments. 'This was the indispensable precondition for significant agrarian advance, since agricultural development was predicated upon significant inputs of capital, involving the introduction of new technologies and a larger scale of operation. Such higher levels of agricultural investment were made feasible through the development of a variety of different leaseholding arrangements which embodied a novel form of landlord-tenant relationship.... The capitalist tenants were assured that they would take a reasonable share of the increased revenue resulting from their capital investments, and not have them confiscated by the landlords' rent increases'. The resultant growth in the agricultural sector was large enough to stimulate the economy as a whole. This, Brenner thinks, was the reason why the widespread 'crisis' in 17th century Europe only marginally affected England.

The agrarian structure evolved differently in France. Its central feature was the growing strength of the peasant property. The landlords had steadily lost the battle with the warring peasants. A crucial factor in this was the consistent support of the French monarchy for the peasants. The monarchy's motives were not altruistic. It had been developing as a class-like phenomenon, as an independent extractor of rural surplus. Ever increasing taxation made it a 'competitor with the landlords'. Stability and security of its income necessitated limiting the landlord exactions as far as possible.

Hence the failure of the French landlords to create large farms out of petty peasant holdings, and the weakness of the enclosure movement in France. They continued to regard rental income, rather than the profits from a reorganised agriculture, as the most important source of their income. 'Given the strength of peasant property, supported by the exploitative state, the landlord could not usually take advantage of increasing prices for land and agricultural products by improving and by increasing output, because this usually entailed the very difficult task of consolidation. The landlords therefore took the only course open to them: to try to obtain an ever greater share of a constant or even declining real product'.

Peasant production, Brenner does admit, was not altogether 'incapable of improvement'. It particularly suited certain types of agricultural production—viniculture and horticulture, and also dairying. However, 'this sort of agriculture generally brought about increased yields through the intensification of labour rather than through the greater efficiency of a given unit of labour input'. The spread of this type of husbandry resupposed moreover, growth of basic food production elsewhere. 'Improvements, in the productivity of grain were best achieved on large consolidated farms with major capital inputs'.

Incompatibility of petty peasant production with rapid agricultural growth was a typical argument of a powerful group of English economists writing about the pre-Famine (1846) Irish agrarian situation.[8] On the assumption that Ireland should seek to maximise the social product as a goal they argued that the country must get rid of her petty peasant farming (cottier system). They viewed economic development in terms of the comparative rates of increase of population and capital. Since population growth in Ireland tended to outstrip capital increase employment opportunities were few, and money wages were extremely low. (The Irish people could still support themselves, because of the comparative ease with which land could be obtained, through subdivision, and a sufficient quantity of potatoes raised from it. The system provided no incentive to produce more.) The minutely subdivided land precluded capital investment in land. In order to enable capital to grow faster than population, the cottier system must therefore be replaced by English-type middle and large farms, held by capitalist tenants under lease from improving landlords and worked by wage labour. The improved agriculture would absorb a considerable section of the displaced cottiers and small tenants. Emigration would drain off the rest of the redundant labour, where other employment opportunities were not available. The two aspects of the Irish agrarian scene, capital and population, were thus related: stimulating capital investment in the land required that the improvident cottiers encumbering the land must be cleared off, and the petty holdings be regrouped into more efficient farm units; and employing the displaced farmers and raising their real income necessitated a large capital input.

A rival point of view, developing after 1848, regarded the welfare and security of the existing Irish population, and not just maximization of the real product, as the goal for Ireland, and conversion of cottiers into 'peasant proprietors' as the main means of realising the goal. English-type contract tenures, it argued, were inconsistent with the Irish social system, and were all the more undersirable, since, as continental examples showed, agricultural growth was not necessarily predicated upon the existence of large tenant farmers.

In the Indian context a considerable group of British officials anticipated Washbrook in some ways. Their reasonings would be cited later. Curiously enough, some nationalist leaders similarly argued, particularly Ranade,[9] evidently under the influence of the land legislation in Prussia in the 19th century. The small farmers of India, he thought, were incapable of regenerating agriculture. He, would not, however, want them eliminated altogether on this score alone. In order to enable them to play a worthwhile role in the economy, they must be made 'free and independent ryots', 'unencumbered in every way', and holding their property 'in absolute possession'. The crucial role in any plan for agricultural improvement would be that of large farmers, similarly owning an 'independent property', unfettered by an excessive revenue demand and restrictive tenancy laws. This group, though a tiny minority, monopolised in 'all old and backward countries like India... all the elements of strength. They are socially and religiously in the front ranks, they possess intelligence, wealth, thrifty habits, knowledge and power of combination'. He identified the 'Banias and the Brahmins' as the 'saving classes', and wanted all restrictions on transfers of their savings to land purchases removed. This would ensure the natural 'gravitation' of all 'property, whether in land or goods, towards that class which has more intelligence, and greater foresight and practises abstinence'. He was particularly critical of the restrictions on transfers of peasant holdings to non-agriculturists since this would' check' the inevitable tendency towards 'concentration of the landed capital of the country' and 'undo' the 'the legitimate influence of the saving classes'.[10]

Washbrook's seems to me to be the best exposition of the theme that the intervention of the State, in the form of tenancy and debt laws, toward protecting the social base of petty peasant production and its failure to build a 'modern' administrative structure, necessary for underpinning 'free market relations', 'kept landlord and mercantile capital at a remove from the productive base', and caused a considerable dissipation of capital. Not that the colonial state opposed throughout in principle promotion of a free market. Its own interest necessitated the promotion. However, this policy was not consistently pursued to its logical end. The government 'was not bent on creating a free market economy, sustained by the rule of law'. Its attitude 'towards a hypothetical capitalist transformation of agriculture was notoriously ambiguous'. The attitude was not the same throughout. Washbrook identifies three phases in its evolution : 'the mercantilist state'[11] 'the high colonial state'[12] and 'the incipient nation state'[13] the approximate periods being 1757-1850, 1850-1900 and 1900-1947 respectively.

The 'mercantilist state' did not show any real interest in 'making market competition, under the rule of law, the dynamic behind agrarian society'. Some of its public laws did create conditions favourable to a market system, for instance, the 'Permanent Settlement' of 1793.[14] The Settlement 'envisioned a society whose prosperity was underpinned by a free market in all commodities, including and especially land'. It created a private property in land. The fixation of land revenue precluded for ever encroachment by the State. Transfer of properties became nearly free from all constraints.

However, the State hesitated to go beyond a certain point. It carefully defined the 'personal' or 'private' law of its subject.[15] The public laws sought to 'free the individual in a world of amoral market relations', the personal law entrenched prescriptive status—caste, religious and familial. 'The personal law was meant to limit the sphere of 'free' activity by prescribing the moral and community obligations to which the individual was subject'. It conceived of property 'as a trust rather than right'. Its implications were conservative : to 'keep society in the structure of relations in which the colonial authority had found it'.

Even the permanent settlement did not ignore the traditional and 'customary' rights of peasants. The compromise inevitably restricted the private property in land which the settlement aimed to uphold. Absence of a clear definition in the law of 'custom' added to the complications. Recognition of the village brotherhoods of northern India was another instance of the state's reverence for tradition and custom.

On the other hand, certain other activities of the 'mercantilist state' partly counteracted the role of the public laws in the development of a free market relationship. For instance, the excessiveness of the revenue demand[16] hindered the growth of private property in land. The existing state monopolies, by shackling commerce, weakened the base of a free market system.

The attitude of the 'high colonial state' much better suited the needs of a market system. Significant agrarian changes partly explain the change in the attitude. 'Conditions of market competition now touched the agrarian base', and a kind of 'property revolution' nearly happened. The value of land was fast rising, the decisive factors being the increasingly unfavourable land-labour ratio, the widening of the grain market, the rising grain prices, and the increasing commercialization of agriculture. On the other hand, the monopoly control of the state over certain areas of the economy had been weakening. The declining value of the old staples, such as opium, together with the expansion of commerce in areas outside state control, reduced the weight of the residual monopolies (salt and *abkari*) in the economy. 'More significant than the liberation of commerce was the easing of the land revenue burden', mainly as a result of the rising agricultural prices. 'It was this which marked the real 'property' revolution in the Indian state'.

If these conditions were to transform agrarian society, 'the sphere of amoral market relations assigned to Indian capital must needs be greatly expanded'. The state now became far more aware of its responsibility in this respect. The law was altered 'to beat back the frontier of the personal laws and the free private property rights from the trammels of ascriptive status?. It recognised 'competition rents' and permitted rent increase on the ground of rising agricultural prices aimed at facilitating rent collection by landlords, and, made land transfers easier. Revision of the usury laws strengthened the right of moneylenders to acquire ancestral land toward realising the unpaid debts of individual joint-family members. 'Much land locked up in status—and role-specific *inam*[17] tenure' was converted into freely alienable private property.

The law, however, 'did not move very far or fast to accommodate the social imperatives of market capitalism'. While eager to guarantee to mercantile and rentier capital a certain level of returns, it was anxious to contain the resultant pressures on the traditional rural society. The legal recognition of 'occupancy right'[18] of peasants severely limited landlord rights. It prevented landlords from adjusting their rent demand to the growing demand for land and gave them only a conditional right to dispossess 'resident' cultivators. New usury laws constrained the old freedom of creditors to enforce debt contracts. Law courts could now question their validity and propriety. Urban money lenders suffered worst. Land transfers to them were nearly banned, mainly in the Punjab.[19] The 'institutional shelter' provided by the Court of Wards to ancient and prestigious families, now more methodically and on a larger scale, artificially excluded a vast amount of property from the normal land market.

As a result, 'large accumulations of capital' found it pretty difficult to gain access to, and control over, agricultural production. An effective control meant having the ability to dispossess resident cultivators. Without it why should landlords invest in improving the lands? Inadmissibility of 'completion rents' would also weaken the peasant initiative. 'What forces', Washbrook asked, 'drove peasants to increase production'? The usury laws distorted the market mechanism : 'If urban and mercantile capitalists did not possess the ultimate sanction of being able to seize their defaulting debtors' lands, how could they impose the rhythm of the market on production?'.

'Landlord and mercantile capital' was thus 'kept at a remove from the productive base', and perforce diverted to unproductive uses: rentierism, commodity speculation and short-term usury. Landlord rights 'tended to drift off into further rent rights and urban property speculation'. Mercantile profits circulated within a narrow groove : moneylending, commodity speculation and acquisition of revenue rights.

The attitude of the 'incipient nation State' was determined by a significant development : the gradual breakdown of the attempt of the 'high colonial state' to conserve, as much as possible, the social base of petty peasant production, while sustaining some market dynamic. Ambiguities in the state policy became more pronounced.

The background to the development was the intensification of the conflict between landlords and peasants. The rate of population growth caught up with the possibilities of the quantitative expansion in cultivation. 'The force of competition was making the landlord and mercantile capital increase their pressures'. The heightening of the rural conflict was reflected in the large increase in litigation and the widespread peasant agitation. The depression brought about a qualitative change, convulsing the old rural order.

The state now intervened on a far larger scale. It was not any longer simply manipulating the terms of the civil law to provide protection from the potentially disruptive effects of the mercantile and rentier capitalism. It became more deeply involved in the regulation of the uses to which property could be put and of market relations. 'Rental rights and obligations were fixed down to increasingly small details and taken further out of the market context'. The administrative apparatus was brought closer to society, a process facilitated by the devolution of the law and of agrarian administration. The crisis of the depression necessitated an unprecedented degree of intervention. 'The chaos of unrecoverable rents and debts left in its wake suspended the operation of the market over large parts of the rural economy'. Cancellation of a large amount of debt 'overrode the legal conventions of property rights'. In general, between the two world wars, the state was trying to isolate the wealthier members of the landholding community'. The burden of taxation was consciously shifted off landownership. State finances increasingly relied on customs, excise duties and taxes on non-agricultural incomes. 'The Raj was directing its income and capital towards landholders. 'Co-operative credit movement provided at least the large landowners with a privileged credit status, and means of taking over local-level credit systems from outside financiers.

However, the major beneficiaries of the generosity of the state, Washbrook argues, were not equal to the task of reorienting agricultural production to the new needs of the market. The protected interest 'represented that of wealthier, village-based landowners and members of the dominant castes....These agrarians had little ability to develop agriculture along lines suitable to the external world of capital'. He cites the German case as a contrast. 'In German industrialization the agrarian interest of the Junker aristocracy at least had been able to improve production by sponsoring large-scale farming and to drive labour off the land and cheapen its supply to industry'.

The Government, though aware of the rapid expansion of market economy, thus failed in the long run to 'provide capital with instruments to subordinate production'. This resulted, Washbrook argues, from a conscious policy of relationship. This was after all a political choice. 'The Raj saw the agrarian problem much more in political than in immediately economic terms. Its policies of social conservation and peasant protection flowed from the fear that if competitive capitalist relations were allowed freedom to take over the countryside, the resulting conflict would destroy the raj's own institutions of government and security'. This fear crystallised into a conviction with the growth of nationalist movement, which, the Government felt, was being strengthened by peasant participation. The softness towards the petty landowing interest was part of 'Government's political struggle with nationalism'. In Bengal, Punjab and most of Madras the Raj was 'inclined to identify nationalism with urban groups among the intelligentsia or commercial classes', and its programme of political devolution was designed to 'exclude or weaken' them. The shock of the depression reinforced to political imperatives to protect agriculture. Its worst effects were felt by those most closely involved in market production and commerce, including at least the wealthier village landowners who invested in commercial crops.[21]

In what is primarily a critique of Washbrook we briefly referred to some similar ideas—Marx's formulations in regard to small peasant property; a recent debate, relating, among other things, to the nature of comparative agricultural growth in England and France in the 17th and 18th centuries; the contemporary economic thought on the economy of pre-Famine Ireland and Ranade's ideas about the means of regenerating Indian agriculture-in order to show that Washbrook's is not an altogether new idea. What is novel was its exposition in the context of British India, with a particular emphasis on the role of the colonial state.

A brief note by way of indicating the usual criticisms of some of these formulations seems relevant in connection with our examination of Washbrook's reasoning.

In evaluating Marx's formulation in regard to specific historical societies, we should note their context. Marx (unlike Chayanov, for instance) was not interested in the peasant economy as a specific economic system. This context largely determined the way he choses to analyse the peasantry. His account of the extinction of the English peasantry was intended as an exposure of the stark reality behind such phrases as 'primitive accumulation', while in general 'in the tender annuals of the political economy the idyllic reigns'. 'The strength of Marx's account is his emphasis upon the connection between technological advance and political power, and the social costs incurred in raising productivity'.[22] The specific perspective of his analysis precludes any judgement on the role of the yeomen or other peasant groups in the agricultural development in England. His study of the French peasantry was secondary to his analysis of a political phenomenon: the rise to power of Louis Bonaparte with a massive peasant vote. The event puzzled him since Louis was, by any standard, a small man. He ridiculed Louis, and since the peasantry had backed him they also came in for a fair share of his derision. One, Marx thought, represented the other : Louis 'clumsily cunning, ... a cleverly stupid anachronism, a world-historic piece of buffoonery and an indecipherable hieroglyphic for the understanding of the civilized-this symbol bore the unmistakable physiognomy of the class that represents barbarism within civilization'.[23] This mocking characterisation of the cultural traits of the numerous social class is scarcely based on any sober analysis.[24] His interpretation of the decay of the French small-holding peasantry is only partially valid. Relating the decline to the small holding itself and the increasing burden of mortgage-debt ignores the complex elements of vulnerability in the French small peasant farming.[25] His assumption about the technological superiority of large-scale capitalistic farming leads him to the inference that small holding *per se* necessarily precluded 'application of science'. The forms of this 'science' widely varied from one historical period to another.

Critics of Brenner[26] disagree with his assumption that 'the petty peasant tenure was in itself an obstacle to the development of capitalism and that this explains the French tragedy'. They have questioned his method : choosing a long period of about three centuries and generalising from the existence of large farms. The role of middle and small farmers tends to be underestimated or ignored altogether as a result. Some plans for agricultural development, particularly large-scale reclamation schemes, did require a large capital input. 'Other improvements, such as manuring, new crops, and even convertible husbandry could be undertaken on any-sized holding, financed by the farmer himself, either from profits or by loans'. The 'celebrated class of yeomanry' rarely figures in Brenner's framework. The yeomen were the chief force behind peasant enclosures', concludes Barrington Moore.[27] The role of the big holders did increase later. 'Not until the last half of the 17th century did the concentration of landed property, characteristic of the 18th century, get under way, and by then agrarian capitalism was well-established'.[28] Brenner's formulation in regard to France i.e. the growing strength of small peasant property impeding potential agricultural growth on the basis of consolidation of holdings, has been found inconsistent with known evidence. Brenner, the rival argument goes, 'has exaggerated the so-called independence of the French peasantry', and misinterpreted the implications of the royal policy in France in terms of the status of the French peasantry. The monarchy had not bolstered up petty peasant ownership. In fact, together with the Church, seigneurs and landowners the monarchy 'depressed it brutally'. As a result, 'the country-side lost its most dynamic force—a class of truly independent peasants'. The peasantry and the bourgeoisie as well suffered from the activities of the monarch other than the normal taxation necessitated by the 'modernization' of the administrative apparatus and the massive conspicuous consumption of the crown. The incessant warfare in the 16th and 17th centuries abruptly added to the tax burden from time to time. The large-scale sale of offices by the crown toward mobilization of war finances diverted capital from productive investment and 'created a channel of upward mobility for those who wished to flee the uncertainties of commercial life and integrate themselves into the existing social hierarchy'.[29]

The relative agricultural backwardness of France cannot thus be blamed on the so-called strength of the peasant property. Barrington Moore[30] relates it partly to inadequate market stimulus. During the latter part of the 17th and the first decade of the 18th century 'the impulse towards commercial agriculture was weak in comparison to that in England'. The grain-trade thrived mainly in the neighbourhood of the big cities. Growing of wine, a very important commercial product, did not bring about the kind of changes, such as massive enclosures, that resulted from the commercialization of agriculture in England. Mainly a labour-intensive variety of agriculture it required a large amount of skilled peasant labour and relatively small amounts of capital, either in the form of land or equipment.

The economic thought on pre-Famine Ireland has not been faulted on logical grounds.[31] Given the economists' premises the inferences were valid. Critics found the economists guilty of treating 'landlords' and 'tenants' as abstractions, not as people. The majority of the landlords, including those handicapped by encumbrances' and 'settlements', utterly ignored their obligations as proprietors. Most tenants were poor and ignorant. Yet 'the standard economic prescription of the day required these men to be transmuted into responsible, active and affluent proprietors on the one hand, and thrifty and intelligent yeomen, or sober and industrious labourers on the other'. It was unrealistic of the economists to ignore altogether the attitudes of the people towards land and to assume that cottiers and small tenants would accept the status of wage labourers if it offered a better subsistence. The people felt in their bones they had a just claim to occupation of the soil, and would resist to the last any pressure to make they forgo it. Moreover, a heavily capitalised agriculture, even if it was feasible at all, would not necessarily benefit the mass of the population. The climate and soil over much of Ireland created ideal conditions for rich pasture and did not quite suit commercialised grain-farming. In fact even in the early 19th century the larger and wealthier farmers preferred grazing to tillage. The competitive state of the grain market after the repeal of the corn laws (1846) inevitably reinforced this preference. Marx noted how 'capital in Ireland has been devoted mainly to livestock production', with the consequent rural depopulation adding to the 'reserve army of labour'.

Let us indicate how we intend to examine Washbrook's reasoning. The background to the alleged protection of the small peasant property by the state is not discussed.[32] Nor do we account for the non-occurrence of 'capitalist development of agriculture', except in isolated pockets. We concentrate on some of the major assumptions and inferences of Washbrook.

First a problem of definition. Washbrook does not clearly define the phrase 'capitalist development of agriculture', which recurs in his essay. His plea was perhaps not for the elimination of small peasant farming altogether and its universal replacement by large-scale capitalist farming based on wage labour, the largest portion of the labour being provided by the dispossessed peasants. He was probably thinking in terms of a considerable investment of capital, in agriculture, mainly from sources external to the peasant community, with the small farmers left to fend for themselves against the intrusion of outsiders.

The major assumptions of Washbrook are as follows. The 'capitalist development of agriculture' was promised upon the operation of a free market system. His emphasis seems to be on an unrestricted circulation of capital, on the freedom of its owner to transfer it wherever he expected the highest return from its investment. Despite the availability of a plenty of capital this freedom was non-existent in India. Capital was consequently being diverted to unproductive channels, such as rentierism, commodity speculation and usury. Initially, the process had something to do with the monopoly control of the 'mercantilist state' over certain areas of trade and with excessiveness of its revenue demand. Far more crucial in the long run was the insistence by the state on the preservation of an 'archaic' rural property relations, of which protection of the small peasant property against the continuing inroads of 'rentier and mercantile capital' was particularly noted. Any measure of the state to limit indiscriminate rent increases by landlords, stabilise peasants' land rights, and control usury and unrestricted alienations of peasant holdings, Washbrook thought, amounted to 'protection'.

From the point of view of India's agricultural development this was a retrograde step for the state to take. Washbrook implicitly assumed that small peasant farming was incompatible with this development, and that the requisite capital and enterprise must come from sources external to the peasant community. He would not even trust the group usually called 'the rich peasantry.[33] We intend to examine two of these assumptions : the incompatibility of small peasant farming with agricultural improvement, and the effectiveness of the intervention by the state in the rural agrarian relations in scaring away capital from agriculture, and, consequently, perpetually starving it of the necessary capital.

Given favourable market conditions and the availability of the required inputs, either owned by farmers or borrowed, small farmers did show remarkable enterprise, particularly in two areas : expansion of acreage mainly through waste reclamation and allocation of resources to alternative crops.

Reclamation was of two broad types : a small-scale one more or less in the neighbourhood of settled village, which might have been temporarily deserted; and the other involving long-distance peasant migration. The first mostly resulted from the initiative of small farmers. The decision-making was theirs. Borrowing part of the necessary capital did not conflict with this control. Liberal terms of rent, where available at all, of course stimulated their initiative. Even in regard to the second, which required a large capital input and an elaborate organisation for mobilisation of labour, a notable development in very many cases, after the completion of the initial phase of the reclamation, was the increasing dissociation of the original entrepreneurs from direct supervision and control over the cultivation process.[34] Peasants, originally providing merely labour, gradually acquired some stable rights in the land they individually cultivated. The absentee entrepreneur rarely reasserted his control. He organised the first agricultural settlement; its eventual stability and expansion was largely due to the tenacity and skill of the small farmers.

Where the reclamation occurred in the areas owned by the Government it initially preferred to rely on 'capitalists' i.e. persons commanding enough resources for seeing the reclamation through over a fairly large area. Its motives in this regard in the Canal colonies of the Punjab were more ambitious. 'At the outset it was thought that a moderate infusion of the capitalist element would strengthen the colony, not only by providing natural leaders for the new society, but also by bringing in men of superior intelligence and wider outlook than the ordinary peasant proprietor'.[35]

Disillusionment came before long. It was the enterprise of the 'peasant proprietors', chosen mainly from fairly resourceful and skilful agriculturists,[36] that sustained the dynamism of the new canal colonies. Of the three categories of colonists in the large Lyallpur colony, for instance,—'small peasant proprietor'. 'The yeoman farmer', and the 'landlord, representative of the landed gentry'—the first was judged by Darling 'much the most important. He is the backbone of the colonies, as he is of the Punjab'. About 80 per cent of the land in the Lyallpur colony was controlled by him.[37]

Under the existing technological basis of agriculture acreage expansion seems to have been the most remarkable result of peasant enterprise. The growing food needs of an increasing population required cultivation of new land, since, apart from anything else the existing technology imposed a ceiling on the productivity of land, even assuming the unchanged quality of the additional units of land. Georges Duby's conclusion that from agronomical necessities alone the medieval peasant was first and foremost a coloniser'—largely applies to British India.[38]

Increasing cultivation of cash crops also introduced a certain dynamism in the peasant economy. The notion of 'forced commercialization' is at least, a debatable one.[39] Even the assumption of its validity does not conflict with the supposition that cash crop cultivation had a positive role to play in the peasant economy. Given the compulsions, such as payment of rent, revenue and debt, and also the non-availability of the required cash resources from any other source, the decision not to grow cash crops would surely have hurt peasants' interests. This was why cash crop cultivation largely increased over the years even in the absence of institutionalised compulsions (as in the case of indigo).

Cash crop cultivation necessitated reallocation of peasants' resources employed for long mainly in the growing of subsistence crops. This in most cases was the peasant's choice.

The cultivation of nearly all the important cash crops, except tea, was organised by small farmers. The decision in regard to the whole of the cultivation process, including occasional changes in the size of the cultivation of different cash crops, rested with them. Indigo was an exception. Its cultivation was a forced one, Indigo growers increasingly resisted it till they finally overthrew it through a combined movement. The opium monopoly of the Government also limited the opium grower's freedom to produce as much as he liked and to sell his product in the open market. However, except occasionally the government could not make peasants grow opium against their will, which flagged when the price they received from the government for their product did not please them. The awareness of the government about the limitations of its powers as a monopolist was evident from its readiness to increase the price whenever it intended to secure a considerable expansion of opium production. The peasants had also other devices to beat the monopolist.[40]

In regard to most other cash crops it was the peasants who decided whether they would grow them at all, and how much of their resources they would allocate to crops of their choice. The credit agencies on which farmers usually depended, for at least a part of their cash needs, seldom interfered with this decision: Acceptance of advances involved a obligation to hand over a portion of their product to the agencies offering the advances. Where the farmers just farmers just borrowed from the local moneylenders on the usual interest rates, they were presumably free to sell to any group. The size of the open market sales of raw jute, the most important peasant cash crop in Eastern India, suggests that advance from the jute traders or jute paikers constituted only a portion of the total capital input in the cultivation on jute.

Much, however, depended on the state of the market. A, favourable market normally created other favourable conditions : an efficient system of information, improved marketing facilities, easier availability of credit, and lesser opportunities for merchant creditors to control the disposal of the peasants crops. For instance, the monopolistic powers of the jute manufacturers could be more effectively exercised when the market demand for jute remained sluggish over a considerable length of time.

As in the case of England, concentration by historians and economists on the alleged virtues of large-scale farming has resulted in an underestimation of the role of resourceful and affluent farmers in the improvement of local agriculture. Studies on this rather heterogeneous group in India have generally stressed its origins, its relations with the poorer peasants of the village, its involvement in rural credit and the trade in agricultural produce and the factors in the relatively greater efficiency of small farming under certain conditions.[40a] Ravinder Kumar's study[41] with reference to some regions of Maharashtra suggests that apart from the stabilisation of the level of agricultural production investment by the rich peasantry created a sound base for a growing agriculture. It is sometimes assumed that the alleged attachment of this group in some regions 'to a traditional life-style', and its considerable expenditure on account of conspicuous consumption tended to frustrate its entrepreneurial potentialities.[42] We do not know enough about this type of expenditure to make any conclusive generalization. This however, seems to be an erroneous impression.

Washbrook's view that the legal constraints on landlords and moneylenders tended to scare capital away from agriculture, or to make these groups apathetic to investment in agriculture, is now examined.

The case of the landlords is taken first. We examine a counterfactual proposition : what did they actually achieve where their powers were largely unconstrained ? Oudh, where the superior landlord power, *talukdari*, was admittedly firmly entrenched, provides an illustration.

Thomas Metcalf has recently analysed the nature of the talukdars' involvement in the local agriculture. They had very little to their credit. Metcalf concludes : 'Apart from indigo no other crops benefited from active taluqdari encouragement.... The two most remunerative and widely grown commercial crops, sugarcane and poppy, were wholly the product of tenant initiative. Indeed, for the most part, they were grown in order to obtain cash to pay the landlord's rent'.[43]

Metcalf's explanation for this is, notably, similar to 'Washbrook's : the limited freedom of the taluqdars in exploiting the land resources. The growing interest of the talukdars, since about the beginning of the 20th century, in preserving and enlarging their home farms, (*sir* lands) resulted, Metcalf believed, from the much wider discretion which the law then allowed them in managing such lands. *Sir* lands, forming only a tiny portion of any estate, could not anyway be the base of a growing agriculture. Outside of such lands the major barrier to any effective enterprise of the taluqdars, Metcalf concluded, was the presence of 'settled' tenants. The unavoidable dependence on the latter' at once ruled out as impracticable much that might otherwise have transformed agriculture in Oudh'. He cited the English case as a contrast. Improvement there 'was dependent on enclosure... and relied for its success upon a capitalist farmer who controlled under the landlord the actual elements of production. No such transformation which in effect would have made a landlord's entire estate a *sir* holding, was possible on the thickly settled peasant-held lands'.[44]

Could the presence of 'settled' tenants and 'sub-proprietors' in any way effect potential capital investment by taluqdars? It conceivably could not. The proportion of the 'sub-settled' taluqdari villages of the total number of villages included in taluqdari estates was in general small. Furthermore, the sub-proprietors, too weak to resist the aggressive designs of the taluqdars even in pre-British Oudh, steadily lost their ground during British rule to their wily rivals.[45]

The taluqdari domination over the countryside, firmly entrenched during the nawabi days, consolidated itself under British patronage. The British government increasingly committed itself to be preservation of the taluqdar class in the context of the growing nationalist movement, regarding it as its best ally. 'Tenant right' remained fragile and insecure.

Indeed, till about 1886 the government ignored it altogether. Its protection, it was argued, would be inconsistent with the repeated pledges to the taluqdars since the Mutiny that the

Government would ever uphold their position.[46] Even the Act of 1886 put only a mild check on their powers. While forbidding them to increase a tenant's rent during a period of seven years, the Act left them free to evict the tenant after the end of the period. Nothing more was done till 1921, when the demonstration by the peasants of their political strength and will forced the Government's hands. An Act of that year gave every resident cultivator a life tenure.

Taluqdars had, therefore, no constraint whatsoever to face till 1886. Rent was indiscriminately increased. The means was simple : warning the tenants through ejectment notices that opposing the taluqdar's will would cost them the possession of their lands. These were not idle threats.[47] Even the check intended by the Act of 1886 was largely ineffectual.[48]

Inability of taluqdars to make tenants pay for any investment of their was, therefore, not the reason why they did not make any notable one. Given their enormous legal powers taluqdars could surely have persuaded the tenants to share the cost of investment.[49] In fact legal demands were seldom denied by peasants, let alone resisted. The ineffectiveness, even as early as the 1870s, of the traditional weapon of the tenants to baffle an overbearing taluqdar, i.e. threat to relinquish their holdings, weakened their will to resist. The taluqdar's main aim was to ensure his social domination even where the measures towards it would have depressed the productivity of lands, for instance, forbidding the construction of wells by tenants.[50]

Even the limited incentives taluqdars had during the nawabi days for improving agricultural resources gradually disappeared during British rule. Their enterprise in pre-British Oudh was largely a necessity. Mostly intruders, they had then to fix their priorities in the context of their recurring clashes with the old owners or rival intruders. The rapidly changing social composition of the new landowners as a result of the increasing reliance of the nawabs on the contract system for the collection of revenue complicated the scene.[51] These strifes made the intruders realise the dire need for a stable local agriculture and peasant support.[52]

Such incentives did not any longer motivate them during British rule. Show of might was not now necessary for securing their control. The British Government now saw to that. Indeed it went out of its way to stabilise the landed aristocracy in Oudh. Increase in rental income steadily occurred without any role of theirs in the peasant economy. Domination over the countryside, reinforced by the law and the increasing demand for land among cultivators, ensured it.

The way taluqdars spent their income shows that investment in agriculture was none of their priorities. They knew 'making good the position in the world they felt to be theirs' did not necessitate the role of an improving landlord. 'The Oudh taluqdars....devoted much of their time and energy to the prosecution of lawsuits, the patronage of poets and pundits, the pursuit of personal honours and titles and an ostentatious display in adornment and amusement....Much of the taluqdars' time and money, was consumed in protracted legal tussles over land and property'.[53] They, like most Irish landlords, did not fit the mould of an entrepreneur.

The argument that the local peasant economy was the worse off for the legal curbs on moneylenders seems to be based on two assumptions : The available rural credit included a considerable portion of non-rural and urban capital, and secondly, and replacement of destitute small peasants by moneylenders was a change for the better because of the greater resourcefulness and enterprise of the latter.

The nature of the legal restrictions on moneylenders widely differed from region to region. So did their effects.

In Bengal the law, notably, favoured the creditors till the depression. The attempt to impose ceilings on interest rates entirely failed. There were hardly any identifiable rates. The change that helped the creditors most was the eventual removal of all restrictions on free transfers of peasant holdings. The first hesitant step was taken by the Bengal Tenancy Act of 1885.[54] Its amendments in 1928 and 1940[55] completed the process. Occupancy peasants welcomed the changes, expecting an appreciable increase in the mortgageable value of their holdings and, consequently, in their credit-worthiness. Most zamindars consistently opposed the changes, and got the government to concede some demands of theirs. However, completely outwitted by the wily moneylenders and their destitute accomplices, they at last gave up the fight.

The unrestricted transfers of peasant holdings rarely led to any reorganisation of cultivation by the new owners, unless where it promoted their primary activities. In Dinajpur, for instance, several new owners, having grain trade as their primary occupation, preferred direct supervision over cultivation to sharecropping, expecting thereby an increase in their trade. The cultivation was normally left to the old owners, and the purchase of peasant holdings by the creditor merely amounted to a transfer of a portion of his saving with a view to securing a stable rental income.

In U.P. too the law did not do any significant extent constrain the creditor's freedom. Yet urban creditors were not necessarily attracted to purchase of peasant holdings. Indeed, as Musgrave's study[56] of the rural credit scene in U.P. (1860-1920) shows several considerations weighed with the creditors for not being keen on grabbing peasant holdings whenever possible. A major one, where a sizeable portion of the mercantile capital had been diverted to rural credit transactions, was that purchases of peasant holdings rendered largely immobile the capital that was actually sunk in the purchases. The primary activity of these creditors was not grain-trade alone.

In Maharashtra and the Punjab creditors had far greater restrictions to cope with.

In Maharashtra after 1878 debt contracts were not necessarily enforceable in the law courts. Before accepting the creditor's claims they would investigate the origins of a contract. No new contract would now be valid without the Court's approval. The court could even revise the interest rates. Alienations of peasant holdings, particularly to 'non-agriculturists', came under severer restrictions. This group could not attach or purchase peasant holdings unless they had been specifically pledged as security for debt repayment.

Such restrictions did bear on the level of credit circulation. The creditors felt threatened, and even alleged that the Act of 1878 was designed to undermine their position. Obligatory investigations into origins of debt contracts particularly alarmed them, since they feared even the legitimate contracts would now be questioned. The small *vanis* (creditors), mostly dependent on urban-based *sowkars* for their loan capital, suffered most. Uncertainty about recovery of loans made the *sowkars* hesitant to lend to the vanis, at least on the earlier scale.

Circulation of credit appreciably contracted as a result. This, however, did not continue for long. About 50% of the peasants could not do without a regular supply of credit. The creditors too had little opportunities of diverting their capital to alternative uses. The need for an outlet for the accumulated idle capital 'was reinforced through the rise of new social groups, like native civil servants and members of liberal professions, which had substantial capital to invest, and whose confidence in commercial channels of investment had been destroyed during the crisis which overtook so many houses in Bombay in the depression which followed the civil war in America'.[57] A leading Bombay businessman referred, as late as 1902, to a 'growing class of capitalists' which 'lacked the acumen to enter into business on its own', but 'desired a higher return on its capital' than that provided by the government securities.[58] Founding something like a central bank mainly with a view to widening contacts with the rural areas through provision of credit, was regarded by the leading *sowkars* as the best way of employing their capital. They, however, moved cautiously. They wanted the Government to be associated with their enterprise, insisting particularly on its help in recovering loans. The Government would not commit itself to going as far as that, fearing that its intervention on behalf of the *sowkars* would be a grossly partisan measure. The plan for founding a new credit institution failed. The growth of the cooperative movement provided an outlet for the employment of the *sowkars's* capital. The new rural credit societies considerably drew upon this capital.

The credit scene in the Punjab after 1901 had two striking features : withdrawal from agriculture of a considerable amount of capital belonging to non-agriculturists and urban groups, and replenishment of the loss as a result of the rise of agriculturist moneylenders.

The first development resulted from the ban imposed by the Act of 1901 on transfers on peasant holdings to groups other than 'agricultural tribes'. The systematic enforcement of the ban evidently created serious difficulties for non-agriculturist creditors. The bitterness of a cross-section of contemporary public opinion with the Act reflected the widespread discontent among them. The open letter addressed by the Indian Association of Lahore to all sahukars of the Punjab forewarned them by asserting that the Act would destroy the livelihood of the classes who, 'unable to compete with Europeans in commerce and manufacture; invested their money in land.[59]

The gloomy forecast that the abrupt fall in the availability of rural credit would hit agriculture did not eventually come true. The required credit came from an affluent peasantry that had been appearing everywhere and consolidating its position. The following is Darling's explanation of the phenomenon.[60] The widening of the market for agricultural produce tended to stabilise their prices. An increase in them also gradually occurred. A big spurt came with the First World War, and more or less continued till the depression. Cultivation of wheat for the market significantly increased. The boom continued till the 1880s. The rising land values and the increasing marketability of land reflected some of these trends in the economy. The savings of the agriculturists were not all generated within the rural sector. A considerable portion was derived from the earning of soldiers fighting in the First World War, and from the remittances of emigrants to Australia, America and other countries.

Such agriculturists contended for a position in the rural credit market and consolidated their sphere of influence at the cost of the old moneylenders, including the non-agriculturist ones, The Act of 1901 immensely helped them. 'The *sahukar*, deprived by the Act of the security of the land, can only lend up to the limit of what can be repaid from the produce; but the agriculturist moneylender, to whom the Act does not apply, can afford to lend upto the value of the land, and with the land selling at inflated values, as it was before the fall in the prices, this limit was considerably higher'.[61]

Investigation by the Punjab Banking Enquiry Committee revealed the extent of the steady replacement of the old non-agriculturist moneylenders by the new rural moneylenders. The latter 'are common all over the province, except in the Muhammadan north and west... Everywhere else the bulk of the usufructuary mortgage debt had passed into their lands, and so rapidly did they increase their operations during the period of prosperity which followed the war that probably ... half of the total agricultural debt of the province is now owing to them'.

Darling's surmise that the diminishing role of the urban and non-agriculturist credit groups would eventually ruin the peasant economy is strongly influenced by a preconception about the cruciality of urban capital in the regeneration of agriculture. He cites the English case. He generalised from his judgement that the Arora, a landlord group of non-agriculturist origins, was the 'only progressive influence' in such districts as Multan, Dera Gazi Khan, Muzaffargarh and Jhang. His inference that, therefore, 'the most progressive landlord is a non-agriculturist' is obviously fallacious. Given similar conditions, (such as those relating to quality of land, ecology and market), there is no reason why resourceful agriculturist ones. In fact they did not. Indeed, they were in a way in a position of advantage. The Act of 1901 scarcely anywhere reduced the number of alienations of peasant holdings. The number went on increasing, and the agriculturist moneylenders were the main beneficiaries. Their traditional involvement in agriculture would normally have helped them in making the most of their acquisitions. Redistribution of holdings would have made possible creation of more viable units of cultivation, where they were keen on improvement.

Aimed against certain credit groups, the Act of 1901 strengthened some others and also brought about some change in the composition of the creditors. The volume of credit circulation did not anywhere appreciably fall.

The ephemerality and the marginality of the contraction of rural credit following the Act of 1901 sharply contrasts with the freezing of rural credit during the Great Depression. Only a severe dislocation in the general economy could bring this about. What happened in the Madras Presidency may be taken as an illustration.[62]

With the slump in the agricultural prices the creditors, composed mainly of big landlord moneylenders, and normally lending on the security of the crop of the year nearly, lost the whole of their loan. Suits in the civil courts and seizure of lands were mostly useless, since the peasants' land, in the context of the sharp fall in the market price of land, was not worth even the half of what they owed. Moneylenders could not replenish either their loan capital through borrowing from their own creditors, the urban financiers and banks. The sharply weakened social control of the rural local boss as a result of the breakdown of the rural credit system resulted in a further contraction of rural credit, since the creditor facing an overt defiance of his authority by the traditionally submissive clients made him doubt the wisdom of continuing any credit transaction whatsoever. On the other hand, the prevailing conditions were favourable for the transfer of capital from agriculture. Drain of capital from agriculture of such a nature on any significant scale could occur under conditions when the terms of trade between agriculture and. industry turned sharply in favour of the latter.

Washbrook has not cared to test his assumptions empirically. Hence his erroneous inferences. His obsession with the notion of a 'free market system', of an unrestricted circulation of capital led him to exaggerate the availability of capital for investment in agriculture once the alleged impediment to it, i.e. the perpetuation of small peasant property through artificial measures, was removed. He has not ever indicated the composition of the group which would make this investment. In fact he does not seem to be quite sure about it. He has not established either his recurring theme—the persistence of an archaic property relations as a result of the intervention of the State. The fact that the system had been firmly entrenched for long did call for occasional interventions by the State. He has misconceived the casual relationship between the two phenomena. The non-occurrence of this intervention hardly made any difference to the long-term behaviour of the local agricultural economy. His implicit assumption that small peasant farming was incompatible with sustained agricultural development led him utterly to ignore the positive role of small peasants in the economy.

References

1. Washbrook D.A. 'Law, State and Society in Colonial India', in C. Baker, G. Johnson & A. Seal (eds) *Power, Profit and Politics: Essays on Imperialism, Nationalism and Change in Twentieth Century India* (Cambridge University Press, 1981), pp. 649-721.
2. Duggett M. 'Marx on Peasants', *Journal of Peasant Studies*, Jan 1975, p. 161.
3. Saraswaty Library Edition, Calcutta 1946, pp. 638-646.
4. *The Eighteenth Brumaire of Louis Bonaparte*. Two-Volume Selected Works (Moscow 1950), Vol. 1, pp. 302-308.
5. Marx notes the causes of the 'downfall' of small peasant property which 'show its limitations'. *Capital* Vol. 3, p. 641.
6. Brenner Robert, 'Agrarian Class structure and economic development in Pre-industrial Europe', *Past and Present* (Feb 1976), pp. 30-75.
7. Brenner's explanation is as follows: The extensive rural depopulation in the late 14th and early 15th centuries enabled landlords to establish control over the vacant holdings. A great deal of land was thus removed from the 'customary sector' to the 'leasehold sector'. The process later had much to do with the landlord victories in the conflicts with the peasants over the landlord's claims that in cases of transfers of peasant holdings the landlord could claim 'fines' from the new holders. Tawney observed that peasant victory in this struggle would have 'clipped the wings of rural capitalism' in England.
8. For an excellent survey of the ideas of this group, R.D.C. Black, *Economic thought and the Irish Question, 1817-1870* (Cambridge Univ. Press, 1960), Chs. 1 (sec 2); IV (Sec 1); V (Section 1) & VIII.
9. Bipari Chandra, *The rise and growth of economic nationalism in India* (P.P.H., New Delhi, 1969), pp. 486-493. John R. McLane, *Indian Nationalism and the early Congress* (Princeton Univ. Press, 1977), pp. 214-216.
10. The restrictions, Ranade thought, were particularly improper in view of the rapidity of the process of transition from the old order to new in India.
11. The State was then directly involved in trade. The India Trade was thrown open in 1813. The direct association with trade ceased in 1833. The major Government 'monopolies' were opium, salt and *abkari*.
12. During this period smooth functioning of the apparatus of British rule in India depended on the existence and expansion of an 'open economy'. For the characteristics of an 'open economy', B.R. Tomlinson, *The Political Economy of the Raj, 1914-1947'* (Macmillan, 1979), 157-58.
13. The State has been so called because of the increasing inclusion of indigenous elements in the administration.
14. The Settlement meant two things: fixation of the land revenue demand for ever, and entrusting of the collection of revenue to the group known as zamindars i.e. hereditary landholders.
15. Under the influence of the scriptures the law courts 'recognised and validated the caste system and the varna theory of social order'. p. 653. Washbrook, *op. cit*.
16. The revenue demand was fixed only in Bengal and Bihar. Even here the demand was admittedly excessive. A change in this regard came after the 1850s in several parts of India.
17. A kind of revenue-free land.
18. Under Act of 1859 a peasant qualified for the right through continual occupation of the same piece of land for 12 years. The Bengal Tenancy Act of 1885 simplified the process : continuous occupation of any land in the village would do. Increase of rent rates of an occupancy ryots was subject to specific conditions.
19. The Punjab Land Alienation Act of 1901 permitted transfers only to the groups called 'agricultural tribes'.
20. The Court of Wards managed the estates of minors, heavily-indebted proprietors etc.
21. A paper entitled 'Agrarian structure in pre-partition Bengal' by Partha Chatterjee introduces an argument similar to Washbrook's : *Three Studies on the Agrarian Structure in Bengal, 1850-1947*. (Oxford University Press, Delhi, 1982). The relevant passage is as follows : 'One consequence of the stabilising concerns of the colonial state was to foreclose any possibility in Bengal of landlord-based capitalist agriculture in which the landlord seizes the opportunities opened by a growing market for agricultural commodities and, by evicting the tenantry and consolidating his estate, assumes complete control over the labour process and the product', p. 203. Tomlinson observed, also rather casually, that the 'conservative social policy' of the Government impeded the growth of capitalist agriculture in India.
22. Duggett M. op. cit., p. 168.
23. *The Class Struggle in France 1848-50*. Vol. 1 of Marx-Engels, *Selected Works*, Moscow 1950, p. 159.
24. Marx has himself analysed 'peasant Bonapartism' in terms of the specific class interests of the peasantry. While the other ruling classes in France in the 19th century (the Bourbons and the Orleans) represented classes hostile to them 'memories of the First Napoleon suggested to them that Bonaparte was their man'. Marx concluded : 'Behind the emperor was hidden the peasant war'. *The Class Struggle in France* etc., p. 159.
25. The following elements have been noted by historians : (a) the growing pressure of population on the land. 'France's rural population reached its all-time peak in the late 1840's; (b) Decay of the rural industry, as urban factories began to displace the old system of home-spinning and weaving the consignment; a major source of supplementary income for peasants thus dried up by the mid-19th century; (c) the 'sporadic continuation' of the 18th century enclosure

movement, which challenged the peasants' ancient rights in the village common lands; (d) the continuing inclination of the urban bourgeoisie to buy rural property, primarily to gain social prestige, which drove up land values at a time when peasant land hunger was intense. Gordon Wright, *Rural Revolution in France* (Standford Univ. Press, 1964). ch. 1. Wright cites evidence that where industrial growth had taken place the pressure on land was much less severe, and that proximity of urban markets encouraged rapid advances in agricultural productivity. B. Moore Jr. concludes : 'the continued advance of capitalist industry tended to undermine small peasant property which was at a disadvantage to produce for the market'. (*Social origins of dictatorship and democracy*. Peregrine Books, 1977 edn.) p. 108.

26. For criticisms of the general Brenner thesis, *Past and Present*, Feb. 1978; June 1978. I have found particularly useful the note by Patricia Croot and David Parker criticising Brenner's view on the comparative growth of 'agrarian capitalism' in England and France. *Past and Present*, 1978 February; pp. 37-47
27. Barrington Moore Jr. *op. cit*. p. 11.
28. *Past and Present*, Feb 1978, pp. 44-45.
29. *Ibid*, p. 46. 'By contrast the virtual immunity of the English people from the taxation in the century or so before the Civil War facilitated the emergence of an independent group of prosperous yeomen, artisans and traders, thus contributing to the formation of a domestic market...'
30. Moore B. *op. cit*. pp. 45-46, 48.
31. For a critical appraisal of this school of thought, R.D.C. Black, *op. cit*., pp. 240-244.
32. Washbrook makes the point that the British tended to exaggerate the links between the nationalist movement and peasant unrest, and that the Raj misread the implications of this unrest in terms of its political security. op. *cit*., p. 685.
33. Neil Charlesworth's views on the role of this group may be quoted 'The rural agriculture structure and its evolution over the 19th century in India was admirably attuned to the encouragement of capitalist development'. He thinks the 'rich peasant elite' in India compared favourably with the Meiji landlord in Japan, who has been 'so vaunted for his alleged contribution to Japanese development'. *British rule and the Indian economy* (Macmillan, 1982), pp. 30-31.
34. Contemporary reports explain this dissociation mostly in terms of the leaseholders' aspiration to a landed status, with which direct involvement in agriculture was not traditionally compatible. Some reports do refer to the leaseholders' difficulties in continually supervising the growing cultivation over a large area. Delegation of the responsibility to intermediaries and relatively affluent farmers partly solved the difficulty.
35. Darling M., *The Punjab peasant in prosperity and debt* (Reprint, Manohar, New Delhi, 1977), p. 118. The Government had political motives too. 'In parts of the Punjab society was still semi-feudal in character and there were obvious advantages in propiating the landed gentry with valuable grants of land; and the hope was cherished that this would help to restore the influence of a class, which had been seriously impaired by partitions of family estates, and by the rise to power of a prosperous and educated middle class in the towns', p. 118.
36. The migrants, Darling tells us, were carefully chosen. *ibid*. p. 116 About the skill of the migrants settled in the Lyallpur Colony Darling observes: 'A colony could hardly have had better material, for Ludhiana, Jullunder and Amritsar represent the flower of Indian agriculture. They are the home of the Jat Sikhs, who had been described as 'the most desirable of colonists'. p. 117.
37. Darling, *op. cit*. p. 117.
38. Duby, G. 'Medieval Agriculture, 900-1500', in C.M. Cipolla (ed), *The Fontana Economic History of Europe*, Vol. 1 (Fontana Books 1972), p. 198.
39. In its simplest version it means that peasants changing over the cash crop cultivation were not responding to market stimulus, but that they could not help doing this because of the compulsions they had faced, such as payment of rent, revenue and debt. As far as India is concerned the existing literature on the question is a considerable one. The role of land revenue in the commercialization of agriculture in some parts of Africa has been stressed by Clark and Haswell : 'administrators has imposed taxes in Africa, not only because they need revenue, but also with the object of provoking transition from pure subsistence to a cash economy'. *The Economics of subsistence agriculture* (Macmillan 1967), p. 73.
40. Particularly clandestine sales of opium to smugglers.
41. Ravinder Kumar, *Western Indian in the Nineteenth Century* (London, 1968), pp. 299-300.
42. For example, Eric Stokes, *The peasant and the Raj* (Cambridge Univ. Press, 1978), pp. 262-263.
43. Metcalf, T.R. *Land, Landlords and the British Raj: Northern India in the 19th century*. (University of California Press 1979), South Asia Edition, p. 311.
44. *Ibid*. p. 307.
45. Siddiqi M.A. *Agrarian unrest in north India: The United Provinces* 1918-1922, (Vikas, 1978), pp. 11, 17-19.
46. Metcalf *op. cit*. p. 222. There was also a curious argument that tenant right would breed a fatal 'animosity' between landlord and tenant as 'each tried to increase his hold over the property'.
47. During the years 1879-1882 such notices affected about 25% of the area held by tenants-at-will. Metcalf, *op. cit*. p. 220.
48. Siddiqi, *op. cit*. Chs. 2 & 3; Metcalf *op. cit*. pp. 218-220, 224-225.
49. Musgrave seeks to refute the notion of taluqdari domination. He concludes: the taluqdar's estate was 'like a rather loose and vague clump of relationships ... like a superconnection, dependent on the cooperation of the lowest levels'.

'Landlords and Lords of the land : Estate management and social control in United Provinces, 1860-1920', *Modern Asian Studies*, 1972, No. 3, p. 272.

50. Siddiqi, *op. cit.* pp. 69-72; Metcalf, *op. cit.* p. 310.
51. The contract system enabled many resourceful aliens to acquire landed property. 'Wealthy men with pretensions to landed status would buy up numbers of these (village communities) ... The annals of rural Oudh for the years immediately preceding annexation provide several examples of these 'capitalist estates'. John Pemble, *The Raj, the Indian Mutiny and the Kingdom of Oudh 1801-1859* (Oxford Univ. Press, Delhi 1977), pp. 132-134.
52. Apart from protecting the peasants from the violence of rival taluqdars in the neighbourhood, taluqdars encouraged settlement in their estates of the skilful and industrious classes of cultivators (*Kachies* and *kurmies*), made advances towards construction of houses and wells, plantation of mango groves etc. Metcalf, *op. cit.* pp. 35-37.
53. Metcalf, *op. cit.* 341, 347.
54. The Act allowed transfers only where they were consistent with the local custom. Occurrence of transfers on a large scale would warrant the assumption that the 'custom' existed.
55. The Act of 1928 accepted the principle of free transfers. The only qualification made by the Act was that the local landlord, in exchange for the recognition of the transfers, could claim 20 per cent of the sale price. The Act of 1940 removed this qualification.
56. Musgrave, P.J. 'Rural credit and rural society in the United Provinces, 1860-1920', in C. Dewey and A. Hopkins (eds) *Imperial Impact* ... (Univ. of London, 1978), Ch. 12
57. Ravinder Kumar, *op. cit.* p. 228.
58. *Ibid.* p. 259.
59. John R. McLane, *op. cit.* p. 251.
60. Darling, *op. cit.* pp. 172-176.
61. *Ibid.* p. 198.
62. Baker, C.J. *The Politics of South India, 1920-1933.* (Cambridge Univ. Press, 1976), Ch. 3.

Aspects of Indian History and Historiography
Editor : P.K. Mishra
Kaveri Books, New Delhi, India.

The Congress Ministry in the Central Provinces and Berar, 1937-39 : The Communal Problem

2

K. Mojumdar

Hindu-Muslim relations touched a new low in the two-year Congress rule, 1937-39. Riots, for long held in check at most places in the province, increased both in occurrence and intensity; so did the activities of communal organisations; Muslim-baiting by the Hindu Mahasabha was matched by Hindu-bashing by the Muslim League; a virtual war of words raged in local media and public platforms addressed by political propagandists; acrimonious debates marked Legislative Assembly sessions; communal incidents in other parts of the country aggravated local tensions; even ministers were accused of covert involvement in communal activity, and charges levelled against law enforcing agencies of having been tainted with communal bias. Indeed, the times were out of joint, in so far as Hindu-Muslim relations were concerned. The Intelligence Branch noted a marked increase in communal tension in almost the whole of Berar, Nagpur, Jabalpur, Hoshangabad, Raipur, Sagar and Nimar districts as a result of the

> mutual sniping of the leaders of the Hindu Mahasabha and the Arya Samaj on the one hand, and the Muslim League on the other with their allied organisations at their back.[1]

The 1937 election was held in not too congenial an atmosphere. A serious riot took place at Jabalpur just before the election. Candidates sought to garner votes by playing up communal sentiments. Election-eve scene in Jabalpur, particularly, was marked by "occasional instances of intentional playing of music near mosques" by the Hindus, which were followed by "purificatory cow slaughter" by the Muslims.[2]

Both among ticket seekers of the Congress and the Hindu Mahasabha, there were history-sheeters, and gang leaders involved in communal riots. Some such men, having been denied the Congress ticket by the national leadership, inspite of local Congressmen's recommendation, contested the election as Hindu Mahasabha candidates. One such candidate, Gaya Prasad Sunar, who had the support of the local Hindu merchant community, threatened to engage toughs and use "their shoes on Congress speakers", particularly Pandit D.P. Mishra and Seth Govind Das, whose "immoral lives" he would expose.[3]

The local press gave coverage to such issues as the Communal Award, the prospects of the Congress victory in the forthcoming elections and its acceptance of office in case of victory.[4] While the Congress rejection of the Communal Award was generally praised in the Hindu press, Nehru was criticised for not suggesting a way out of the communal tangle.[5] The *Independent* commented that the Congress attitude to the Communal Award was "more out of consideration for the Muslims than for the Hindus", and that the Congress could "more easily be accused of pro-Muslim sympathies than of pro-Hindu", for with a view to "maintaining its representative character, it is more careful about keeping in tact the Muslim cooperation".[6] The Mahasabha controlled *Sawadhan* expressed satisfaction over what it viewed as Nehru's "ridding the Congress of the influence of Gandhism", which had so long harmed the Hindu cause.[7]

Jinnah came in for sharper attack in the local Hindu press for his tirade against the Congress. The *Maharashtra* strongly condemned Jinnah's fourteen points as being the main hurdle to Hindu-Muslim unity, while the *Nishpriha* declared that the League spoke in such a vein as to suggest that the Indian Muslims were "communalists first and nationalists afterwards".[8]

Of the total 112 seats, the Congress won 71, and Non-Congress Hindus, 10; the Muslim League won 5 and other Muslim groups.[9] Dissensions in the Congress camp[10] were matched by a keen rivalry between Muslim candidates who were broadly divided between supporters of S.W. Rizvi and Rauf Shah, League members, and their opponents, who rallied under M. Yusuf Shariff.[11] The latter's supporter, Iftikar Ali, won the prestigious Jabalpur-Mandla Muslim Rural Constituency by defeating the Congress candidate, Abdul Rahim, and Abdul Sattar, a supporter of the Rizvi-Rauf combine, which was backed by E. Raghavendra Rao.[12] Both Hindu and Muslim candidates resorted to mud-slinging and character assassination to win. While Seth Govind Das and D.P. Mishra were publicly reprimanded by Nehru at Jabalpur on the eve of the election,[13] Akhtar Hussain and Muhammad Asgar of Nimar Muslim constituency alleged that the winner, Khan Bahadur Hifazat Ali, had made use of servants of the local municipality and dancing girls to "foster his interests".[14] Shia-Sunni bitterness was another factor among Muslim candidates.[15]

The Hindu Mahasabha candidates contested some seats on their own and some under the banner of the Democratic Swaraj party, composed of Tilakites of Maharashtra and led by Ramrao Deshmukh. The party's main plank was its opposition to the Communal Award which was viewed as being grossly unjust to the Hindus in so far as their representation to the Central Legislative Assembly was concerned.

II

Riots and killings were both a symptom and a cause of the bitterness in Hindu-Muslim relations. Serious communal riots took place in Jabalpur in October 1937 and March 1938, during the Dussehra and Holi festivals respectively.[16] The town had been free from riots for about a decade.[17] Tensions prevailed in Sagar, Mandla, Nagpur, Hoshangabad, Bhandara, Akola and Amravati districts.[18]

Muslim public opinion traced the October 1937 riot at Jabalpur to the Hasina affair in which the Minister, D.P. Mishra, was involved,[19] and which the ministry was keen on drawing a veil over to prevent damage to the Minister's public image. The Government withdrew criminal cases against Hindus involved in the riots, and the Speaker of the provincial Assembly rejected Muslim legislators' demand for adjournment motion on the issue. The Speaker also rejected a motion moved by Abdur Rahman Khan that a non-official enquiry committee of an equal number of Hindu and Muslim members be appointed to enquire into the causes of communal disturbances in the province, to record the local religious rights, usages and conventions and past agreements between the two communities regarding religious practices, and to suggest measures to bring about a permanent settlement of communal disputes and check their recrudescence. Rahman also proposed the setting up of conciliation boards to keep "a permanent watch" over Hindu-Muslim relations and take measures for their improvement.[20]

Communal tension built up at Patansangi in Nagpur district on 21 November 1938 following the desecration of a local mosque. Mosque. Muslims picketed cinema houses in Jabalpur city to prevent their co-religionists from wasting their money.[21] In February 1939, at Rehli, a village in Sagar district, a communal fracas broke out immediately after a bye-election when anti-Congress and anti-Hindu speeches were made by the Muslim League candidate. A small temple was desecrated, and then in protest Hindu shop keepers boycotted the Muslims for a time.[22] Again, a month later, communal disturbances marred the celebration of the Muharram and Holi festivals in Nagpur, Jabalpur, Raipur, Murtizapur, Khamgaon and Malkapur.[23]

III

Political propaganda and incendiary speeches, besides news and views expressed in the press worsened the communal atmosphere. The Hindu Mahasabha and the Rashtriya Swayam Sevak Sangh, the Muslim League and Muslim voluntary organisations stepped up their activities after the 1937 elections. The growing estrangement between the Congress and the League at the national level had its natural repercussion on the province too where Hindu and Muslim public opinion tended to get sharply polarised. Happenings in towns and even villages of the province received immediate notice and drew acerbic comments in the media outside the province. The need to defend the common cause of the Hindus against the Muslims and vice versa was emphasised in both the Hindu and Muslim press.

Many Hindu Mahasabha political propagandists kept visiting the province after 1936; they made fire-eating speeches to incite anti-Muslim feelings in the local Hindu population who were treated to such outbursts as that the Hindus alone were the natural residents of the country and they alone should have authority in the country; if the Hindus become organised, they would see "ships full of Muslims leaving India".[24] The Muslim press lampooned the Hindus as *kafirs* and cowards.[25]

The Hindu Mahasabha, which had opposed the Congress in the elections, launched a virulent campaign against the Congress ministry, blaming it for appeasing the Muslims instead of safeguarding Hindu interests. A Hindu Mahasabhite of Nagpur, Balkrishna Wagh, sought the Governor's intervention to restrain Dr. N.B. Khare, the Prime Minister,[26] and his partymen from calculated harassment of Mahasabha leaders and workers. Khare was accused of hiring *goondas* and jail birds to disturb Hindu Mahasabha meetings, particularly those addressed by J.P. Verma, Secretary of the Nagpur City branch of the Hindu Mahasabha. He was also alleged to have taken assistance of Muslim anti-social elements to cause riots in which Mahasabha leaders had been falsely implicated.[27] But then, the tone of the Mahasabha papers changed to sympathy for Khare when he was unceremoniously replaced as the Prime Minister.[28] Now Gandhi came in for vitriolic and even vulgar attack, "Maharashtrian youth", supposedly hating him as the devil incarnate.[29]

The Government viewed such an attack on Gandhi as "shocking" and "irresponsible journalism". It demanded security deposit from *Sawadhan*, whose owner, having refused compliance of the Government order, was obliged to shut down the paper.[30]

In 1938, V.D. Savarkar, the Hindu Mahasabha President, toured C.P. and Berar, drawing large crowds in whom the Rashtriya Swayam Sevak Sangh volunteers were prominently present. He took the province by a storm. He was presented with civic addresses at Khamgaon, Dharwa, Yeotmal, Akola and Nagpur where Congressmen actively participated in his meetings.[31]

At the annual session of the Mahasabha in Nagpur on 28-30 December 1938, Savarkar lambasted the Congress, for having declared the Mahasabha as a communal organisation,[32] with which Congressmen were asked to have no truck. He threatened to launch a civil disobedience movement in the Bhopal state. Resolutions were passed supporting the Federation scheme in the Government of India Act, 1935, and the Hyderabad Satyagraha[33] which the Congress wanted to be suspended; demands were made for extension of military training to the Hindu youths, establishment of armament factories where the youths would be employed, and the setting up of a "Hindu National Parliamentary Board to fight the next elections." The Mahasabha urged the Hindus to patronise only Hindu shops.[34]

Resolutions were also passed condemning the Government's restrictions on the playing of music before mosques and calling upon Hindus "to assert and maintain their right in face of all opposition, whether private or official, ignoring all risks involved."[35]

A similar call was given to support the *Shuddhi* movement for it was "not only a cultural and religious, but a political necessity too", because, when the political strength of a community depended on the number of its representatives in proportion to its population, the decrease in the numerical strength of the Hindus caused by conversion to other religions "has told and must tell upon their political strength in the legislatures as well". The Mahasabha declared "*Sanskrit-nishtha* Hindi, and not Hindusthani" as the national language and devanagari as the national script. It condemned the Congress support for Hindusthani as its "craven fear of and with a view to placate the Muslim opinion".[36] Savarkar explained his concept of Indian nation as meaning "merely the English synonym for the Hindu nation," because, he added, "to us, Hindus, Hindusthan and India mean one and the same thing. We are Indians because we are Hindus and vice-versa."[36a] Nagpur University conferred a D. Litt. degree on Savarkar in recognition of his contribution to Marathi literature.

Mahasabha leaders, Dr. B.S. Munje, Dr. L.V. Paranjpe, Balashastry Hardas, M.G. Chitnavis, Pachlegaonkar and J.P. Mishra in their extensive tours in the province made both anti-Muslim and anti-Congress speeches. Many new branches of the Mahasabha were set up and people urged to unite and wrest power from the Congress.[37] On 17 December 1938, Munje, the most prominent Mahasabha leader of the province, warned the Nagpur public of a "Muslim Federation of India" and exhorted the people to "shed their last drop of blood to maintain India as one nation."[38]

In the annual meeting of the provincial branch of the Mahasabha, the Hindus were urged to derive inspiration from the life of Chhatrasal Bundela who had fought the Muslims. Speakers laid stress on the need for Hindu unity, the resolution of internal differences in the Hindu society and the abolition of caste exclusiveness. It expressed no confidence in the Congress for its "pro-Muslim actions" and its "partiality towards the Muslims both before and after the elections". The Mahasabha condemned the Congress party's "timid polity" which had emboldened the Muslims to cause communal riots. Such a policy was a "blot of cowardice and scandal on the administration"; even the Muslim government employees regarded themselves not as "servants of the provincial administration, but as loyal servants of the Muslim League". The Mahasabha leaders charged Muslim police men of helping their co-religionists in abducting Hindu women, and the Government took no action against them. Hindus were exhorted to exercise their right of self-defence by arming themselves against the Muslims.[39]

Equally active at this time was the Rashtriya Swayam Sevak Sangh, a militant Hindu organisation, which had been set up in Nagpur in 1925 by Dr. K.B. Hedgewar[40] and had received the patronage of Munje to serve as the militia of the Hindu Mahasabha. In 1927, Munje had reorganised the R.S.S. corps in the four Marathi speaking districts of the Central Provinces[41] to defend the local Hindus from Muslim attacks during communal riots. The object of the R.S.S. was to inculcate in Hindu youths a spirit of nationalism and make them the defenders of Hindu religion and culture. R.S.S. volunteers received physical and intellectual training and undertook an oath to "serve bodily, mentally and financially in the cause of Hinduism" and not to divulge secrets.[42]

The Government had kept a watch over the R.S.S as a "communal and political" organisation of "potential danger" inspite of Hedgewar's claim of it being "purely a defensive and national" organisation. In a speech delivered in 1932, Hedgewar and reportedly asserted that Hindusthan was for the Hindus, that they would dominate the country and its government, and it was they who would determine "what political rights and privileges were to be conceded to non-Hindu elements". Convinced that the R.S.S was "essentially an anti-Muslim organisation aiming at an exclusive Hindu supremacy in the country" and that the R.S.S volunteers would not be "slow to act in their individual capacity" when communal passions were roused by inflammatory speeches of Hindu Mahasabha leaders, the Government had issued an order in 1932 asking government servants to keep away from the organisation.[43] Although Hedgewar took strong objection to the Government's labelling it as a "communal and political organisation, Sir M.V. Joshi, a prominent liberal leader of the province,[44] not only admitted that it was a "communal" organisation, but justified its functioning in the interests of the Hindus. Both he and Munje frankly admitted that the R.S.S. did not believe in non-violence and rather advocated the "policy of strike first."[45] In 1934, Gandhi had visited the R.S.S. annual camp at Wardha and had been impressed as much by the discipline of the volunteers as by their freedom from caste feelings.[46]

The financial position of the R.S.S. was sound, the main source of income being donations from members and sympathisers; its funds were believed to have been kept with a private banker.[47] In October 1937, the R.S.S. took a prominent part in the Dussehra celebrations held in several towns in Nagpur and Berar districts. S.A. Sohoni, an R.S.S leader made at the time what the police reported as an "aggressively communal speech". The Hindu Mahasabha annual session at Nagpur in December 1938 was managed by R.S.S. volunteers. The Democratic Swaraj Party, dominated by the Tilakites in the Central Provinces and Berar, had close connection with the R.S.S., which it helped in setting up branches in the Bombay Presidency too.[48]

Military discipline was a feature of the R.S.S., the General Officer Commanding of the volunteers being one M.P. Jog, who was an ex-service man; many members of the R.S.S. had received military training in the University Training Corps. In 1939, the R.S.S. had 350 branches all over India, and 150 in C.P. and Berar, the total membership being between forty and fifty thousand. The Sangh had student representatives at Amritsar, Ludhiana, Sialkot, Kanpur, Lucknow and Poona. In 1939 "Jagatguru Shankaracharya of Kolhapur" visited the "demonstration of military drills" by R.S.S volunteers at Wardha and he urged them to undergo military training, for to him Gandhi's teachings were a "farce."[49]

Hindu and Muslim communalism fed on each other. The Muslims of the province, though politically aware, were a disunited community; they had ever been so until the 1937 elections when the Muslim League, with its two-nation theory and threat to Muslim identity as its main slogan, attempted to rally the local Muslims under its banner. Jinnah-Shafi clash at the national level had its reverberations in local Muslim politics, besides the traditional shia-sunni animosity. In pre-1937 elections, some Muslim political leaders had acted in close concert with Hindu leaders, and some had served as colleagues of Hindu Ministers; some had even been the beneficiaries of Hindu leaders' political patronage.[50] In fact what had so long determined the political behaviour of local Muslim leaders was the prospect of personal gain and not any overt concern for community interests.[51]

Such interests were highlighted by Muslim league propagandists during and after the 1937 elections, in course of which too, divisions among the Muslims came to the fore. In pre-1937 provincial legislature none of the seven Muslim members belonged to the Muslim League; some represented Muslim splinter groups and some others none at all, having won the elections as independents.[52] In fact, the Muslim League had then no organisation worth the name at all in the province, although Nagpur had hosted the party general session twice-in 1909 and 1920—and some Muslim leaders of the province had regularly attended annual meetings of the party in different parts of the country.

Before the 1937 elections, the Muslim League was not a force in local politics. It had no mass base, its leaders being wholly upper class men.[53] Even in the 1937 elections, it could capture only six out of fourteen Muslim reserved seats in the Assembly, the rest being shared by other Muslim groups; Muslim Independents and the Muslim United Party drew a blank in the elections.[54]

The Muslim League toned up its organisational structure at local levels following the Congress Muslim mass contact movement.[55] The Congress leadership was sore that out of a total 482 Muslim reserved constituencies in the whole country, the party, having contested for 58 seats, could only win 26; in the Central Provinces it had contested only two, and had lost both.[56]

In Berar the Congress mass contact movement among the Muslims made some progress, several local Muslim young men promising it their support.[57] Reacting strongly against this, the Secretariat of the Berar Muslim League issued a press statement, warning local Muslims "against the suicidal consequences of joining the Congress."[58] The central leadership of the League made good use of the C.P. and Berar Muslim attacks on the local Congress ministry and its educational scheme, in particular. The working committee of the League, meeting in Karachi, approved of the C.P. Muslims' programme of agitation against the Government's supposedly anti-Muslim policy. The League also spread its activities in both towns and villages of the province; branches of the party were opened at Yeotmal, Jabalpur, Katni, Patan, Panagar, Belhari, Katangi, Bhandara, Barsi-Takli, Hasud and Adgaon in Akola district. By 1938, the League had its branches in fifteen out of the nineteen districts of the province with a total membership of 25,000. The more active branches were at Jabalpur, Yeotmal, Buldhana, Akola, Amravati and Nagpur, each having a large Muslim population.[59]

At the meeting of the C.P. Muslim Political Conference in Nagpur in October 1936, the President, Maulana Shaukat Ali, exhorted the Muslims to unite under the banner of the Muslim League. He deplored what he called inadequate representation of the Muslims in the local legislature. At that conference, the Provincial branch of the Muslim League was formed with M.Y. Sheriff as President and Abdul Razaq as General Secretary. The conference adopted the League constitution and elected fifty members to the Council of the Provincial branch of the League. But then, over the composition of the office bearers of the provincial branch of the party, there were sharp differences among delegates, some fifty of them staging a walk out, passing a resolution expressing no confidence in Shaukat Ali and threatening to form a new party independent of the Provincial branch of the League—and all this when the venerable Begum Muhammad Ali kept appealing to the delegates for unity, urging them to "realise you are Muslims," and "you are Muslims first and last."[60]

A year later, with local Muslim political opinion better organised than heretofore, the C.P. and Berar Provincial Muslim league could be set up in November 1937, when the Congress ministry became the butt of the general Muslim attack. Abdul Rauf Shah, M.L.A., was elected the President of the Provincial branch of the League with twenty other members elected to the central council of the party.[61] Soon after, Jabalpur Muslims decided to picket toddy and liquor shops and to hoist the League flag wherever the Congress tricolour had been flying. League propagandists frequently visited the province while the tone of the Muslim press became provocatively anti-Congress and anti-Hindu.[62]

The Sirat Committee, a religious body, decided at its Nagpur conference to cooperate with the Muslim League. In July 1938, Abdul Majid Qureshi, the Editor of *Iman*, a Punjabi newspaper, and an organiser of the Naujawan Sirat Committee, made a tour of C.P. and Berar, and then were established League branches at Wardha, Arvi, Karanja, Daihanda, Kandheli, Deolaghat, Damoh, Yeotmal, Wun, Durg and Pandharkauda. Other branches were set up at Pusad, Kali, Jalgaon, Mehkar, Chikhli, Bina, Katol, Gotegaon, Chhindwara and Khandwa. There were reports of about one thousand Muslim volunteers of the National Muslim Guard, Urdu Lashkar and the Muslim League, besides the Sirat Committee, having received training in arms in several Muslim localities in Nagpur city. The Sirat Committee, under the pretext of celebrating the prophet's birthday, organised several meetings in which the Congress was attacked as an "anti-Muslim organisation and inimical to their interests and culture," as evidenced in its replacing Urdu by Hindi.[63]

Jinnah visited Jabalpur in early 1939, and the police reported his speeches as being "progressively unreasonable".[64] Many other League leaders from northern India visited the province "to maintain enthusiasm at fever heat" among the local Muslims. Palestine day and anti-Vidyamandir day were observed by the Muslims on 26 August and 14 September respectively at all important places in the province.[65]

The Muslim League held regular meetings at Jabalpur, often presided over by Tajuddin, the Vice-President of the city branch of the party. It condemned the killing of a Muslim boy by the police at Katangi and the Government's lukewarmness in enquiring into the incident. It charged the police with inability to protect Muslim lives in general. Ten thousand Muslim mourners attended the burial of the Muslim boy. Muslims condemned the Congress dominated Jabalpur Municipal Committee for having presented a civic address to Savarkar at the Provincial Conference of the Hindu Mahasabha in June 1939. Savarkar was criticised for having garlanded a man of Katni for killing a local Muslim.[66]

A League membership and fund collection drive soon followed. Maulana Burhan-ul-Haq addressed public meetings after returning from his tour through the North-West Frontier Province, Punjab and Sindh as a member of the League delegation to apprise the local Muslims of the Congress misrule in U.P., Bihar and C.P. and Berar.[67] Burhan-ul-Haq condemned Congress leaders, including Gandhi, Nehru and Subhas Bose, as *kafirs* and enemies of Islam. Azad and other Congress Muslim leaders were not spared either. He claimed to have met Jinnah and received instruction from him to enrol at least two crore Muslims for the League. He criticised the Congress government for having arrested 156 Muslims in the Biswa murder case and keeping them imprisoned in a small room which could hold at best 40 persons. Gandhi was accused of intending to make frontier Pathans cowards at a time when the Congress influence in the region was on the wane and that of the Faquir of Ipi on the rise.[68]

In several Muslim meetings, the Police Inspector of Nagpur, R.B. Tarachand, was the target of vitriolic attack; the police was blamed for being indifferent to reports of Hindus beating up even the children of their Muslim colleagues, Hindu boys being given rifle training in clubs and Hindu Mahasabhites distributing handbills, urging Hindus to patronise only Hindu shops and *tongawallahs*. The Muslims strongly opposed the Goonda bill with which the Government sought to deal with all anti-social elements. The Government was also blamed for setting Hindu criminals and some mahars on Muslims.[69]

In March 1939, following the hoisting of the Congress flag on the Kamania or Patel gate in Jabalpur, the Muslim league and the Mahasabha too hoisted their flags.[70] Jabalpur Muslims expressed their want of confidence not only in Congress ministry and the local police but even in the Governor for his cooperation with the ministry.[71]

Shriller became the tone of the provincial Muslim press, which hitherto had been far from influential.[72] The Muslim press in Delhi and U.P., in particular, widely publicised the Muslim agitation in C.P. and Berar. A series of articles appeared in *Jaddo Jehad*, a Urdu paper in Nagpur, in which the police was accused of inaction and even complicity in communal riots following abduction of Muslim women by Hindu ruffians. The police not only winked at the breach of peace by lathi-wielding Hindu hooligans but even took part in the desecration of mosques. The paper lampooned Shariff, the Law Minister, and other "Congressite Muslims" as the paid pipers of the Congress and as "Congress Maulavis" who "by appearance look Muslims though in reality ... Hindus".[73] What, in the meanwhile, had embittered the local Muslims greatly was the sight of Shariff having "walked into the Congress parlour"[74]: he had joined the Khare ministry, the apparent motivation being to somewhat improve his dire financial straits.[75]

Muslim voluntary organisations worked zealously to promote the cause of the community. The Khaksar movement spread to the province at the same time when the Muslim League stepped up its activities. Founded by Inayatullah Khan Mashrique of the Indian Educational Service at Amritsar in 1930, the movement aimed at uniting all Islamic powers and imparting military training to Muslims "with a view to making Islam the ruling power. "In 1936 three Khaksar branches were opened at Elichpur, Anjangaon and Kapus Talani, all in Amravati district, and one at Yeotmal. In 1937, another branch was opened at Jabalpur at the instance of Mirza Khadin Beg of Lahore; two more branches followed at Hoshangabad and Sohagpur. In 1938, a rally of about 150 Khaksars was held at Amravati and four branches were opened at the instance of Muhammad Ibrahim, a pleader of Elichpur.[76]

Abdul Rahman of Ludhiana inspected the Amravati branch of the Khaksars in January 1939, and later a membership drive followed at Ellichpur. A corps of 241 Khaksars, who pledged to lay down their lives any time, assembled at Itarsi and were daily drilled by the local Urdu school teacher. Some Khaksar volunteers of the province attended the all India Khaksar camp in the United Provinces whereafter two more branches were opened at Ner and Sirkhed in Amravati district, and then two more at Betul and Multai. The Khaksar rally at Ellichpur in April 1939 was attended by seven hundred volunteers from Napur, Berar and Betul districts, who drilled daily in khaki uniform and a spade in hand. The Muslim National Guard, the activities of which were "of purely communal nature" opened branches at Katni, Sagar and Burhanpur. Urdu Lashkar and Muslim League Volunteer Corps were two other organisations "redolent of communalism" in which members were given training more zealously than before. Mist of these Muslim volunteer corps were suspected to be receiving financial help from the Nizam's government.[77]

IV

The Muslim opposition to the Congress ministry was well reflected in the proceedings of the provincial Legislative Assembly where Muslim members strongly accused the ministry of a patently anti-Muslim bias. Minority interests being ignored and minority rights being "trampled upon" were the recurring refrain of the Muslim M.L.A.s' speeches as also the charge that the Congress represented Hindus alone, and that it was hand in glove with the Hindu Mahasabha.[78] Asserting that the Muslim League was the sole representative organisation of Indian Muslims, the M.L.As targetted their attack on the Congress mass contact movement among Muslims, the singing of Vande Mataram as the national song, the Vidyamandir[79] and the Wardha schemes of education and communal riots in the province. Muslim public opinion got increasingly hardened to these issues—a process accelerated by the strong reaction they evoked in League leaders at the national level, Jinnah and Liaquat Ali, for example.

Muslim M.L.As moved resolutions demanding separate Muslim electorates for local bodies and panchayats, alleging that under the existing joint electorate system, Muslims had been denied adequate representation.[80] In refuting D.P. Mishra's contention that separate electorates for Muslims would spread communalism to rural areas, Muslim M.L.As pointed out that communalism had, in effect, already spread to rural areas and that Congress interests had been harmed thereby. A Congress Muslim at a taluk in Jalgaon district had lost the local board election to a Hindu who stood as an independent candidate. Qazi Muhammad Ali of Jalgaon, a staunch Congressman of twenty years standing and a habitual khadi wearer, had to fervently appeal to the Congress High Command for a ticket to stand as a Congress candidate for the local municipal election.[81]

Of the inadequate Muslim representation in local bodies the Muslim M.L.As gave many examples. In the Akola municipal election, only four Muslims could win, contesting for 18 seats, although Muslims constituted almost one-third of the local population. In the same municipality there had been a long standing tradition for one Muslim being elected as the Vice President of the municipality. After the Congress had come to power, the tradition had been given a go by; so, in protest, all the elected Muslim members of the municipality resigned their seats.[82] Under the Congress regime no Muslim had been nominated by the Government to the Sagar municipality; earlier some Muslims used to be so nominated. To the Muslim M.L.As it was also suggestive that in the last local board elections in the Amravati district, which had a sizeable Muslim population, not a single Muslim could be elected.[83] Some Muslim M.L.As also charged the Congress party of having joined an organised boycott of local Muslims in several villages.

Muslim M.L.As also joined the chorus of anti-Gandhi pronouncements; Gandhi was blamed for fomenting Hindu-Muslim tension. He was condemned for having converted the Congress into a Hindu organisation and for holding the whole country under his dictatorship.[84] Rauf Shah, the leader of the Muslim League in the Assembly, averred

> Had there been leaders like the late C.R. Das ... or Lokmanya Tilak at the head of the Congress, Muslims would not have left the Congress.[85]

Gandhi's "over-Sanskritisation of Hindi" and his *charkha* had no attraction for the Muslims, while his Harijan uplift programme was but a "political stunt to check the Harijans being converted".[86] Several Muslim M.L.As asserted "separate national identity" for their co-religionists, claiming that Muslims were "Muslims first and Indians afterwards".[87] They regretted that the Congress rule had reduced the Muslims to "eight crores of touchable slaves".[88]

The Congress Ministry's rural education programme provoked among the Muslims the greatest controversy both at the local and national levels. From public platforms, from the press and from the floor of the Assembly, Muslim public opinion expressed its strong and consistent opposition to the programme. Called the Vidyamandir scheme, the programme was a means of providing free and compulsory mass education in rural areas within a fixed period. It would meet the requirements of 24000 villages which had no educational facilities and for which the Government was unable to set up schools of the existing type.[89]

Drawn on Gandhi's educational ideas, the scheme was formulated in August 1937 by a special committee set up for the purpose and then approved by the provincial Congress committee in December 1937, after officers of the Government Education Department and some prominent members of the public had expressed their views on it.[90] The eminent educationist and a Gandhian, Dr. Zakir Hussain, framed the course structure of the scheme.

The scheme provided for the establishment of schools, called vidyamandirs, in villages within a radius of a mile with no schools and where about forty boys and girls of school going age lived. The medium of instruction would be the main local language—Hindi or Marathi or Urdu. The object of the scheme was to ensure literacy "of such a type that it will not lapse after the pupils have left the schools." The curriculum was so designed as to enable pupils to address themselves to problems of rural life—hygiene, sanitation and agriculture, for example, and create in them a sense of involvement in community welfare and environment awareness. Some subsidiary handicrafts and cottage industries, such as spinning, weaving, rope and toy making would also be introduced in the schools to enable pupils to learn a trade to earn a living. The pupils, after completing a ten-year course, would devote themselves to free teaching and social service in a village for a year before receiving their school leaving certificate.[91]

The scheme would foster both local initiative and local involvement in the establishment and maintenance of vidyamandirs. Villagers would themselves donate land for the schools and maintain teachers with the yields of lands attached to them. All charities in the village on festive occasions would be diverted to the local vidyamandir, and local merchants and other well to do people would be specially requested to provide funds to the schools from local *panchayati kothis* or grain banks.[92]

Pupils would learn sitting in the verandahs of schools or in the open under the shade of trees. Local people would be encouraged to construct school buildings out of materials locally available.[93]

Each school was to have a maximum of fifty pupils and one teacher who would be specially trained before appointment. The teacher would sign a pledge to serve the school for twenty five years on a minimum remuneration of Rs. fifteen per month, paid out of the endowment fund created for the maintenance of the school. Besides teaching, the teacher would do village uplift work, look after the physical development of local children and instill in them "a national outlook to all the activities of a village." The teacher would be on a five year probation, whereafter he would be confirmed and "insured for Rs. five hundred or thereabout."[94]

The vidyamandir scheme would at first be launched on a voluntary basis, the schools being initially under the direct management and control of the Government Agricultural Department till local panchayats took them over. The vidyamandirs would, in fact, be the focal point of the activities of all Government departments and the main agency of village uplift and rural reconstruction. The Agriculture Department would ensure the best utilisation of lands attached to schools, so that they developed as model firms; the Medical and Health Departments would take care of sanitation and hygiene of villages, the vidyamandir teachers being trained in first aid and elementary medicines. The Cooperative Department would set up multi-purpose societies in every village having a vidyamandir while the Veterinary Department would attend to local cattle and live stock. Thus all Government departments would coordinate their activities for overall rural development with the vidyamandirs serving as nodal points. The scheme would thus "in near future ... make village life interesting and happy and relieve the people from the misery in which they are living today." Each vidyamandir would be more than just a primary school; it would be also an "important social centre" where teachers, parents, boys and girls would discuss "national, social, as well as educational issues." It would be a "radiating source of light and learning in a village" and "serve as a model for all round progress."[95]

Local Muslim opposition to the vidyamandir scheme soon became a national issue for general Muslim agitation. Since "mandir" meant a "place for idol worship", the name of the educational scheme itself went against the very grain of Islamic tenets and so was repulsive to all Muslims. Muslim M.L.As condemned the scheme as not only "anti-Muslim" but "anti national" too; no Muslim would accept it for it amounted to "negation of our existence as a separate cultural entity."[96] Abdur Rahman Khan referred to the opinion of Dr. Zakir Hussain, the author of the Wardha Scheme of Education, that Muslim feelings against the name vidyamandir were 'genuine and sincere", and the name had better be dropped.[97] Muslim M.L.As also quoted the Pirpur Report in charging that in theory only under the vidyamandir scheme Urdu would not be neglected, while in actual practice it would be. Urdu would be "entirely extinguished".[98]

The M.L.As further held that the Congress government's much-trumpeted rural education programme would not benefit the Muslims at all, for most of them lived in towns. While the Government's policy was to provide primary education through the main language of the area covered by schools, Muslim M.L.As demanded that Muslim children should be instructed through Urdu alone, irrespective of their number in schools. This stand was supported by E. Raghavendra Rao who charged the Congress ministry of "complete departure from and complete repudiation of the principles enunciated by the Indian National Congress—the principle being that minorities be given the right of education through their mother tongue.[99]

Abdur Rahman took strong exception to the omission from History text books of "all important personages of Islamic History", so that "we are refused to know ourselves, our God, or history and the basic principles of our religion." A Muslim boy educated under Gandhi's scheme implemented by the Congress ministry would come out of his school as

> anything but a Muslim, nourished with anti-Muslim ideas, nurtured in religious sentiments and with an absolutely inferiority complex.[100]

The Congress scheme of education, Rahman continued, was not aimed at "creating a united democratic society out of Indians but merging the minority Muslim community in the fold of Hindu culture." It represented

> another Macaulay trap under which Muslims would be Muslims only in name but Hindus in culture and ideology.[101]

Ghulam Hussain Khan, another Muslim M.L.A. condemned the vidyamandir scheme as impracticable; teachers were more likely to care for crops grown in lands attached to their schools than for their pupils' education.[102] Muslim M.L.As also alleged forcible acquisition of land from Muslims for setting up vidyamandirs. They also moved adjournment motions on several issues relating to the Government's primary education programme: non-recognition of Urdu as the medium of instruction for Muslim pupils in primary schools, abolition of the posts of Urdu Inspectors of schools, hunger strike by pupils and teachers of the vidyamandir training school due to "starvation and inadequate stipends paid to them", orders issued by the Chandur Local Board to the Urdu Girls' School at Talegaon Dashashor to celebrate the birthday of Gandhi and to garland his portrait by Muslim girls under the orders of the provincial government, and non-enforcement of an agreement between local Muslims and Hindus regarding the playing of music before mosques at the place. Muslim M.L.As staged walk outs, dissatisfied with the Government's answers to their querries.[103]

Muslim public opinion outside the province was stirred as never before. The Muslim League Working Committee meeting in Karachi in October 1938 noted its strong disapproval of the vidyamandir scheme and endorsed its full support to the C.P. and Berar Muslim agitation against it. In Nagpur, at a meeting, chaired by Nawab Bahadur Yar Jang of Hyderabad, a resolution was adopted to launch a civil disobedience movement. For the purpose committees were formed and volunteers enlisted. Muslims of the province resolved to observe 14 September 1938 as anti-vidyamandir day.[104]

In mid-December 1938, Liaquat Ali Khan, General Secretary of the League, was deputed by the central committee of the party to make an on the spot study of the Muslim agitation in C.P. and Berar and to assess the prospect of a direct action against the local Congress ministry. Liaquat Ali held a meeting with the Prime Minister, Ravi Shankar Shukla, in which the latter promised to "call a conference or to appoint a committee to consider the question of giving an impetus to Muslim education" in the province. This assurance was misrepresented by some local extremist Muslim leaders as the Prime Minister having undertaken to postpone the vidyamandir scheme till he could make the local Muslim leaders agree to a scheme acceptable to them and him. The Chief Secretary's note and the Government's press release made it clear that the Prime Minister had given Liaquat Ali Khan no such undertaking.[105]

The Government decided to launch the vidyamandir scheme on 26 January 1939, whereupon local Muslim leaders, condemning the Prime Minister of breach of promise, decided to stage a satyagraha, inspite of Liaquat Ali's advice for restraint till the Prime Minister had his promised meeting with local Muslim leaders on 7-8 February. The provincial Muslim League leaders also advised accordingly. However, on 26 January, Khan Bahadur Siddiqui Ali Khan, M.L.A. (Central Legislative Assembly), and Israr Ahmad, Corporator, Nagpur Municipal Corporation, took out a procession to the Secretariat and were promptly arrested. Siddiqui and some other members of the Council of Action formed for the satyagraha later met the Prime Minister to elicit from him an assurance that the Government would act in accordance with the decisions to be reached at his forthcoming meeting with Muslim leaders on 7-8 February before it could ask them to abandon the satyagraha. Such an assurance Shukla refused to give whereupon the satyagraha was continued.[106]

The Government, however, was not much worried as long as local leaders of the League, Rauf Shah and Abdur Rahman Khan, were against such direct action till they met the Prime Minister on 7 February.

The meeting took place between the Prime Minister and local Muslim M.L.As and Liauqat Ali on 7 and 8 February. Shukla assured the Muslim leaders that the object of the vidyamandir scheme was to remove illiteracy from rural areas irrespective of caste and creed, and the scheme rested on endowments of land and money by private donors. To allay Muslim suspicion about the Government's motive, the scheme would now be implemented by a private registered association open to all classes and creeds, which would find endowments needed to meet the recurring expenditure of schools. The Government would welcome any such association of Muslims for the same purpose. Muslim schools set up under the scheme would be named, as suggested by Liaquat Ali, "Anjuman tul-ilm" or "Medina-tul-ilm". The Government would use its good offices to procure funds from local Muslims to set up Muslim primary schools. The Prime Minister assured the Muslim delegation that Muslim pupils would not be compelled to attend vidyamandirs nor the syllabus as framed by the Dr. Zakir Hussain Committee be introduced in schools till the views of the Muslim League on it were obtained.[107]

Even this concession to Muslims did not ease the situation for the Shukla ministry. Muslim papers hailed the Government's climb down as a Muslim victory, and the Prime Minister having signed an agreement with Liaquat Ali as a certification that the League was indeed the only mouthpiece of Indian Muslims. Some papers made snide remarks on Shukla's inability to formulate a common educational scheme for the two communities and his having conceded virtually "an educational Communal Award"—and that when the Congress had consistently opposed Macdonald's Communal Award scheme and the Muslim demand for separate electorates for local bodies election.[108]

Muslim educationists too joined their voice against the Congress scheme of mass education. A sub-committee headed by Sir Azizul Haque, Vice-Chancellor of the University of Calcutta, and Speaker of the Bengal Ligislative Assembly, toured provinces to collect facts about Muslim educational backwardness. The report, which was published in 1942, condemned the Wardha and vidyamandir schemes and their author, Zakir Hussain. Hussain was berated as a "Congress Muslim" who was "credited with a desire to submerge the specifically Muslim culture in a single Indian culture."[109] Iftikar Ali too would not count a Congress Muslim as a "true representative of the Mussalmans, because he is pledged to support the Congress views at any cost."[110]

V

Hindu and Muslim public opinion in the province became increasingly influenced by happenings in neighbouring regions; excitement ran high among members of the two communities following reports of wrongs suffered by them. A typical example of this was the reaction of the Hindus and Muslims to the Hyderabad satyagraha in 1938-39, which the Arya Samajists converted into a national issue. Reports of the Nizam's government's atrocities on the Hindu population of his state had a communal fall out in C.P. and Berar. Batches of volunteers organised by the Arya Samajists and Hindu Mahasabhites left for Hyderabad to join the satyagraha by the local Hindus demanding cessation of the Nizam's anti-Hindu policy. Arya Samaj agitators, mostly outsiders, addressed meetings at several places in the province with a view to mobilising public support to the Hindu agitation in Hyderabad. Police kept watch on satyagrahis passing through Ballarshah railway station on their way to Hyderabad. There was some commotion at Ballarshah when six men were arrested by the Hyderabad police within the British territory. Local authorities took strong exception to such trespass of the British territory "in contravention of rules regarding extradition of offenders from British territory to Indian states". Chanda authorities were confident that the local people were disinterested in the satyagraha, although some of them had escorted Hindu volunteers as far as the Wardha river on the borders of the Nizam's dominions.[113]

In June 1939, in an Arya Samaj meeting at Jabalpur, the Nizam government's anti-Hindu policy was condemned as also its attempts at driving a wedge between the Arya Samaj and the Hindu Mahasabha. The Congress government of C.P. and Berar was accused of lukewarmness in regard to any effective measure to alleviate the sufferings of the Hindus in Hyderabad. Forcible conversion of jailed satyagrahis, torturing them in jails and abduction of their female relatives were the specific charges listed by the Arya Samajists. The C.P. government was urged to press the Nizam in favour of the satyagrahis.[114]

The R.S.S. did not participate in the satyagraha, but police reports had it that its members could do so in their individual capacity. This was in keeping with the cautious policy of the organisation—the policy of avoiding overt involvement in any political movement of the time for fear of inviting the Government's reprisal. The policy had naturally caused some misunderstanding between Hedgewar and Hindu Mahasabha leaders, Munje and Savarkar, in particular.[115]

The C.P. ministry's was really an unenviable position, it being criticised by communal organisations of both Hindus and Muslims. The Hyderabad satyagraha had indeed provoked strong Hindu feelings in the province, and the ministry naturally disliked being projected as utterly indifferent to the Hindu cause. Such an image had affected the ministry's stock in the public. The ministry then chose to make a representation to the Crown Representative in

Hyderabad against the anti-Hindu policy of the Nizam's government, of which conversion was the most pronounced feature.[116] Government notifications were cited to prove that Hindus were denied even "primary civil and religious liberty". Small Hindu children in schools were "subjected to influence favourable to Islam", "fanatic Muslims" had been "asking Hindus to embrace Islam or die"; restrictions had been imposed on Arya Samaj activity even in private houses, apart from ban on extension and improvement of Hindu temples and *maths* in Muslim populated areas. Public performance of Hindu festivals was also disallowed; all these were "unmistakable evidences" of the state policy of Hindu persecution. The policy had reportedly resulted in the closure of 2971 Hindu private schools out of a total of 4253 such schools, following the Government's restriction on Hindu pupils learning through their mother tongue.[117]

Reports of Hindu prisoners being forcibly converted and the Nizam himself writing poems with clear anti-Hindu bias were also brought to the notice of the Crown Representative, who was requested to intervene so that the Hindu community in the Hyderabad state could "enjoy the free exercise of its religion and the unhampered pursuit of its individual culture". The C.P. ministry even warned that if the "just religious and cultural grievances of the Hindus" were not redressed, a full scale civil war might rock the state when the British were already worried over the gathering war clouds in Europe.[118]

Although the Hindu Mahasabha and the Arya Samaj activists acted in close concert in the Hyderabad satyagraha, the Congress government sought to differentiate between the "political" aspect of the movement emphasised by the Hindu Mahasabha, and the "moral aspect" embodied in the "purely religious and cultural" movement launched by the Arya Samaj. The ministry disclaimed any sympathy with the Hindu Mahasabha while expressing concern over the plight of the persecuted Arya Samajists in Hyderabad. D.P. Mishra cited documents to show the Nizam's attempts to "convert Hyderabad into a Muslim state per excellence", where the proselytising zeal of the ruler reminded one of such zeal of Aurangzeb in medieval times. In a strongly worded note, Mishra, the Home Minister, urged the British government for the sake of "its reputation as a civilised government to put a stop to this recrudescence of medievalism" in a state under Britain's protection and paramountcy. Mishra suggested representing to the Viceroy himself to prevail upon the Nizam's government to "concede the just demands of the Arya Samajists"; that done, he was sure, the fear of a communal civil war would pass off, and the "political satyagraha" of the Hindu Mahasabha would collapse, for it had "evoked little support as compared with the Arya Samaj". In the meanwhile the All India Aryan League meeting at Sholapur had expressed concern over the satyagraha, of which a first hand description followed in the report submitted to the Congress ministry by Ghanashyam Gupta, the Speaker of the C.P. and Berar Legislative Assembly. The ministry gave Gupta full authority to negotiate with the Hyderabad government and to withdraw the satyagraha when he was satisfied that the Hindu grievances had been redressed by the Nizam's government.[119]

VI

The All India Muslim League appointed a Committee under Raja Syed Muhammad Mehdi of Pirpur to report on the condition of Muslims in all Congress-ruled provinces. The Report of the Pirpur Committee submitted in December 1938 listed more than forty charges against the Congress government in C.P. and Berar before concluding that "Muslims in no other province have suffered so much as in the Central Provinces and Berar".[120] And by then the ministry had completed just one year and a half in office. All the charges were endorsed by a later committee headed by Fazlul Haque, another prominent League leader, whose report came out in December 1939.[121] Both the committees made an on the spot study of the situation and collected written and oral evidences from a cross section of local Muslim population, of which the local Muslim M.L.As and League leaders were the most prominent.

The Pirpur Committee saw "something like an identity of purpose between the Congress and the Hindu Mahasabha",[122] creating thereby a feeling in the Muslims that a

> vast majority of the Congress members are Hindus who look forward, after many years of British and Muslim rule, to the reestablishment of a purely Hindu raj.[123]

An average Hindu was inclined to associate swaraj with Ramraj and Congress raj with Hindu raj. The Congress government was virtually the Mahasabha rule by proxy, there being an apparent nexus between the two parties. The Congress government was alleged to have given the Hindu Mahasabha a free hand in Muslim baiting while preventing the League from its legitimise activities as a political party. Thus, while J.P. Verma, the Mahasabha leader of Nagpur, went about freely denouncing the Muslim League and the Muslims in general, the police banned a League meeting where Nawab Siddiqui Ali Khan, a member of the Central Legislative Assembly, was to speak and another where Muslim League resolutions were to have been explained to the public.[124]

R.M. Deshmukh, a Minister, was conspicuously present at Savarkar's largely attended meeting in Nagpur in December 1938 while the Prime Minister Khare himself participated in the reception of the Hindu Mahasabha President, as though suggesting a "complete identification between the so-called communal organisation of the Mahasabha and the oft-claimed `National institution' of the Congress."[125] At a conference held under the Presidentship of Sarat Bose and attended by Nehru, a huge decorative arch was put up in the name of Savarkar.[126] The C.P. and Berar government had also provided a large sum of money to the Hanuman Akhara at Amravati, which the Pirpur Committee viewed as the "training ground for the Mahasabha".[127]

Both in the Pirpur and Fazlul Haq Committee reports, the Congress ministry was accused of discriminating against the local Muslims and subjecting them to political and economic disabilities. Hindu Bidi manufacturers of Sagar, for example, were alleged to have turned out of job hundreds of their Muslim workers as punishment for voting for Muslim candidates in the 1937 elections. Various restrictions had been imposed on the sale and slaughter of cattle "under cover of economic and sanitary grounds", hitting hard Muslim cattle traders and butchers. A bill had been moved in the provincial Assembly to amend the C.P. Slaughter of Animals Act which would render animal slaughter difficult not only for communal but even "socio-religious purposes". On the very day the Congress ministry assumed office, and D.P. Mishra became the minister for local self government, the Jabalpur municipality, of which he was earlier the Chairman, imposed extra taxes on trading in and slaughter of cattle. Soon thereafter, licences for cow slaughter were withheld from the Muslims in several other municipalities in the province.[128]

The charge of cultural onslaught on Muslims was a graver one, and the League made the most of it. The Congress ministry was alleged to have adopted an anti-Urdu policy as indicated by some municipal boards having either abolished Urdu classes altogether from schools or withheld grants to the existing Urdu schools. Municipal committees did not entertain applications in Urdu nor were speeches in Urdu delivered by Muslim M.L.As in the Assembly printed in that language in the Proceedings of the Assembly. There was want of Urdu schools in even Sagar and Mandla districts, both having large enough Muslim population to warrant the opening of more such schools. There were only Hindi medium schools in Betul, which had been declared "a compulsory education area" where the sizeable Muslim population wanted education through Urdu. Thus the whole Urdu speaking population of the district was "being systematically converted into a Hindi speaking population" by the Government.[129]

The singing of the Vandemataram song and obeisance to Gandhi's portraits and statues came in for sharp criticism in both the Pirpur and Fazlul Haq reports. The Muslim League took notice of this when passing a resolution at its Lucknow session condemning the Congress for "foisting Vandemataram as the national anthem upon the country" in callous disregard of the feelings of the Muslims. The song was "not merely positively anti-Islamic and idolatrous in its inspiration and ideas, but definitely subversive of the growth of genuine nationalism in India." The religious import of the song was "directed against the Muslim alone."[130]

It was alleged that at the Normal School at Wardha, Muslim students were not allowed to touch food in the school mess and were forced to stand with folded hands and bow when the Vandemataram was sung; they were also made to live on vegetarian food alone. At Sagar, the President of the local municipal school was alleged to have ordered Muslim students to either sing the song or leave the school. The Pirpur Committee condemned the local bodies for seeking to "systematically force Hindu culture and religion on Muslims". Impervious to Muslim religious sentiments, the Chairman of the Chhindwara local board had in a circular letter to the Head Master of the local Urdu school asked him to arrange the worship of Gandhi's image as a part of the latter's birth day celebration; and this was in wanton defiance of the Congress resolution itself at Karachi on safeguarding minority rights.[131]

Muslim religious sentiments were further affected by reports of *fakirs* having been turned out of villages and local *idgas* desecrated. At Murtizapur, Arya samajists held meetings condemning the Nizam when local Muslims had been celebrating the Prophet's birth day; stones had also been hurled on Muslim devotees. In violation of an earlier agreement between local Hindus and Muslims, Savarkar's procession, with the playing of music, passed by a mosque, and the police did not entertain the Muslim complaint about the incident.[132]

Economic boycott of the Muslims at Katangi affected their trade and business; Muslim shops were picketed following appeals through the local Hindu press and public platforms. Muslim *tongawallahs* and taxi drivers too suffered from boycott, while Muslim employees in factories and private firms were systematically weeded out. The Hinganghat municipality imposed a heavy licence fee on aerated water business which was mostly Muslim in ownership; there were also reports of Hindu patwaris persecuting Muslim tenants, and Muslim weavers discriminated against regarding financial assistance from the Government. Muslim contractors had been taken to task by responsible officers of local bodies for employing Muslim labourers. All Muslim Honorary Magistrates had been removed from their post. In the public services also, the Muslims were alleged to have lost their erstwhile favourable position, particularly noticeable being the progressive reduction of Muslim employees in district offices at Jabalpur where the Muslims constituted about twenty five per cent of the local population. The Government had also stopped giving printing orders to the Anjuman Printing Press at Jabalpur and stopped the funds with which it had so long maintained the only Muslim High school in the town.[133]

The Hindu Press was accused of virulent and provocative anti-Muslim propaganda while the Government had taken penal measures against Muslim League leaders and workers alone. Muslim papers alone had been proceeded against while Hindu agitators had been given a free hand. Muslims of Akola, Nagpur, Khamgaon, Malkapur and Khandwa protested against Arya Samaj leaders' violent outbursts, one of whom was booked by the police before being released when Hindus staged hartals and hunger strikes.[134]

Both Pirpur and Fazlul Haq reports made allegations about police indifference and even complicity in anti-Muslim activities by Hindus. The police winked at huge Hindu processions, playing loud music, passing by mosques and armed Hindu hoodlums harassing Hindu women converted to Islam and plundering Muslim houses in villages. The murderers of Muslims in Nagpur riot in 1927 undergoing long terms of imprisonment were released immediately after the Congress assumed office; cases against Hindu criminals in the Jabalpur riot in 1938 were also dropped. A Muslim Superintendent of Police and a Muslim Deputy Superintendent of Police were harassed because they followed up the Hasina case in which the Minister, D.P. Mishra, was involved. Another Muslim D.S.P., who had prosecuted the brother of a Congress M.L.A. for defalcation of municipal funds was also harassed after the ministry took office. While the Law Minister, Shariff, was dropped from the ministry for releasing a Muslim prisoner, the Congress government remitted the death sentence of a Hindu criminal of Hoshangabad convicted of a graver crime against a Muslim woman.[135]

The Congress ministry was also blamed for allowing local bodies coercing Muslim employees to become Congress party members while Muslim Ministers and Government officers had been openly warning people against taking part in League activities on pain of receiving no financial assistance from the Government whatever.[136]

In the Pirpur Report demand was made for separate electorates for Muslim representation in local bodies. In the 83 such bodies in the province, there were only half a dozen Muslim elected representatives out of some 15000 members. Muslim employees in the local bodies numbered only a dozen. Before the Congress came to power the Report pointed out, the Government used to "redress communal inequalities by means of nominations" to local bodies, but the Congress government nominated only part members, totally ignoring Muslim interests. The tahsil Debt Conciliation Boards were also now filled by influential Marwaris and Brahmins, while unlike before, poor and heavily indebted Muslims in rural areas remained unrepresented on such boards.[137]

What reinforced the Muslim charges against the Congress ministry and what served as grist to the Muslim League propaganda mill was the deposed Prime Minister Khare's own allegations that his erstwhile colleagues had anti-Muslim bias. Khare disclosed that within a fortnight of assuming office a Minister for Local Self Government, D.P. Mishra had requested him to transfer Niaz Ahmad Khan, D.S.P. of Jabalpur for "the only apparent reason ... that he was concerned in the investigation of the famous Hasina kidnapping case" in which Misra was implicated. Some of Khare's Mahakoshal colleagues in the Congress party wanted him not to confirm M. Imamur Rahman, then Deputy Commissioner of Yeotmal and the only Muslim ICS officer in the province. Khare also charged the Congress High Command of "deferential" treatment to Hindus against Muslims in dealing with apparently identical cases of M.Y. Shariff and D.P. Mishra. Shariff had released some Muslim prisoners after they had served a part of their sentence. The C.P. Congress legislative party had disapproved Shariff's act, but had later condoned it when Shariff tendered an apology. But then, both the Congress High Command and the Working Committee of the party overruled the decision of the C.P. Congress legislative party and appointed a tribunal to go over the case. Shariff had to resign when the tribunal's verdict went against him. In a parallel case concerning D.P. Mishra, when several local Congress partymen had complained against him, the party High Command gave an ex-parte decision in Mishra's favour and, without obtaining any explanation from the complainants, asked them to tender an apology to Mishra.[138]

Khare, in fact, shared the Muslim grudge that while Shariff, the Muslim minister, had to resign due to the tribunal's adverse verdict, the Hindu Minister's involvement in the panwallah case was not enquired into. Khare fully endorsed the League charge that "the Shukla ministry has more often than not sacrificed the interest of other communities also". He urged Nehru to come down to Nagpur to investigate the charges of Fazlul Haq, sure as he was that "he will be shocked to find what the C.P. ministry has done."[139]

It must, however, be understood that Khare, then expelled from the Congress party and having had scores to settle with the Congress High Command, was eager to even cut his own nose to spite his face. When in power, his attitude to the RSS and the Hindu Mahasabha was rather ambivalent; after his ouster from the Congress party, it became openly sympathetic to the Hindu communal organisations. His friendship with Dr. L.V. Paranjpe, the Mahasabha leader, remained unimpaired and he bore no annoyance for the RSS for having helped the Mahasabha in the 1937 election; on the contrary, he had admiration for the disciplined cadre of the RSS;[140] and all this when the Mahasabha had declared its opposition to the Congress, and its President Savarkar, had urged the Hindus to vote against the Congress, which had betrayed the Hindu cause.[141]

In fact, most Maharashtrian high caste men had avowed sympathy for the RSS and the Hindu Mahasabha until the Congress High Command declared the later as a communal organisation in 1938, which the party men were asked to have no truck with. Khare's own close links with the Hindu *sangathana* movement and its leaders, Munje and Hedgewar, in particular, were well known, and the fact that his colleague D.P. Mishra, had "dragged into the Congress" the Hindu Mahasabha leader, Kunjilal Dubey,[142] reinforced the Muslim league charge that the Congress ministry and the Mahasabha had a close nexus between them.

Khare was never a member of the RSS, but, on his own admission, he "liked and respected that organisation".[143] While a member of the Viceroy's Executive Council (1945-46), he opposed Feroze Khan Noon's demand to ban the RSS, but he suggested the banning of the Khaksar movement. As the Prime Minister of Alwar state, he rendered all help to the RSS in holding its annual camp in May 1947. He was conspicuously present at the reception of M.S. Golwalkar, the RSS chief, when he was released from jail after involvement in the Gandhi murder case.[144] Khare's close association with the Hindu Mahasabha climaxed when for two years he became its President.[145] As one who had seen the RSS and the Mahasabha acting in close concert in the 1937 elections, he was upset over the "concealed hostility" between the two organisations during municipal and other local bodies election in the 1940s. It came to him as the "eighth wonder of the world" as to how the two organisations could be estranged from one another when their "policy, flag and ideology" were identical.[146]

It would also seem that for Khare political expediency at times got the better of his ideological convictions. He would not hesitate to seek Muslim support to achieve his personal ambition while he would declare his strong anti-Muslim bias when it suited his political purpose. As long as he was not forced out of power as the Premier and the Congress party, he was not as pronouncedly anti-Muslim as he later became. In fact, after the Congress ministry resigned in November 1939, Khare made an attempt to form a ministry under his leadership with Muslim League M.L.A.s' support and wrote to Jinnah accordingly.[147] The attempt failed when a rueful Khare discovered that

> Jinnah was an irreconcilable person and it was impossible to bring about a compromise with him.[148]

Little wonder Khare would declare that he was "an enemy of the Muslim League" because he regarded "that organisation as treacherous to the country."[149]

The C.P. and Berar Congress issued to the press a point by point reply to the allegations made against the ministry.[150] As for the singing of vandemataram in schools, it was only permissive, not mandatory; in no Government school had the Muslim students been forced to sing the song. Muslim students in municipal schools were also free to absent themselves when it was sung. Enquiries established the baselessness of the charge that Muslim students were compelled to stand with folded hands when the song was sung in the vidyamandir training school.[151]

But then, the fact that not only police contingents but the Governor, Sir Hyde Gowan, himself used to stand up whenever the song was sung reinforced the Congress contention that even the Government respected vandemataram as the national anthem.

The Congress government denied any discrimination against Muslims in respect of nomination to local bodies, for which municipal acts had no provision for either separate constituencies or reservation of seats for Muslims and other minorities. In fact, in thirtynine municipal committees and Notified Area Councils, and in one District Council, the Government had nominated the same number of Muslims as done by the previous government. In two cases the number of Muslim nominees was more than before, and in twelve cases the number was less. In none of the twelve cases were the Muslims unrepresented; they had secured their seats either by election or selection.[152]

The Congress government disproved the League contention that the proportion of Muslim members on Debt Conciliation Boards had decreased. Under the previous government, there were forty three boards in the province with a total strength of 325 non-official members. Under the new government, there were forty one boards with 296 non-official members, of whom 32 were Muslims; eleven boards had no Muslim representatives on them.[153]

As for the charge that the Congress government had levied exorbitant fees on slaughter of animals, the Government press release explained that the fees were levied under the bye-laws of municipal committees, and that the model bye-laws had been framed long before the Congress assumed office in July 1937. As for the charge that the Government was apathetic to education of Muslims through Urdu, the press communique pointed out that there were seven Urdu primary schools in the urban areas of the Sagar district; in the rural areas of the district, the Muslim population was too small to justify exclusively Urdu primary schools. For the same reason no separate Urdu school existed in Mandla district, but it was taught as an optional subject in the municipal combined school of Mandla and the Railway combined school at Nainpur. There were ten Muslim teachers in Mandla district and two under municipal committee of Mandla. The Government had already asked the municipal committee, Mandla to consider the question of opening an exclusively Urdu primary school. The municipal Urdu school at Betul had not been abolished as alleged in the Pirpur Report, but amalgamated with a local Hindi school. The allegation that Urdu primary schools in Berar suffered from want of supervision was also without substance. In Berar there was one Muslim Assistant District Inspector for each of the four districts who inspected Urdu primary schools besides, Akola and Buldana had Muslim District Inspectors. Another Muslim District Inspector supervised Urdu primary schools in Nagpur, Wardha and Chanda districts. Of the total 69 Assistant District Inspectors, there were 12 Muslims and 9 Non-Muslims who possessed a thorough knowledge of Urdu—a clear enough proof that the Government had indeed provided for adequate supervision of Urdu primary schools.[154]

The press release explained that the grant to the Anjuman Islamia press at Jabalpur had been stopped because it had been incurring an annual loss of Rs.7500 as established by an enquiry in November 1935, eight months before the Congress ministry assumed office. It was also pointed out that the Congress government gave a grant of Rs.7227 every year to Robertson Ajuman High school at Jabalpur.[155]

Not any prejudice against the Urdu language as such but the want of type sets in Persian script in the Government Press and want of good knowledge of Urdu among the Press staff were the reasons for the Government's inability to print speeches delivered in Urdu in the proceedings of the Assembly.[156]

The press release said that the Government had ordered an enquiry into the circular issued by the Chandur local board asking Head Masters of local schools to get the image of Gandhi worshipped by all students, including the Muslims; the Government denied having asked the Head Master of any Urdu school to perform the ceremony of worship by students.[157]

The Government assured the Muslim community that the vidyamandir scheme had "no communal or religious or political significance whatever". It had already been made clear that any Muslim who donated land for starting a school was free to name it "Bait-ul-Ilm", which was an exact synonym of vidyamandir or give it any other name of his choice. The vidyamandir scheme in no way altered the existing policy regarding the medium of instruction. The scheme provided for a seven-year course, having adequate provision for the teaching of Hindusthani either in Nagri or Urdu script according to the choice of the pupils. Therefore, teachers under the scheme had been trained in both Urdu and Nagari scripts.[158]

The Government also disclaimed having been partial to Hindu communal organisations and soft to Hindu leaders. Action had been taken against some Hindu Mahasabha leaders like J.P. Verma and the Hindu communical press.[159] The Congress High Command had also asked partymen to keep away from the Hindu Mahasabha and other Hindu communal organisations. Nehru in his reply to Fazlul Haq's letter pointed out that the Hindu Mahasabha and its sympathisers blamed the Congress ministry as pro-Muslim and that it had crushed Hindus with a view to pleasing and placating the Muslims.[160] The Congress ministry in C.P. and Berar rejected the League charge that Congress rule had a definite correlation with the aggravation of communalism in the province, for Bengal and the Punjab, both having non-Congress governments, had also serious communal problems.[161]

The Government justified its release of prisoners convicted of communal riots, and they included both Hindus and Muslims. The release had indeed restored communal peace during the *dasserah* when Muslims had cooperated with local Hindus in maintaining a peaceful atmosphere.[162]

The Muslim M.L.As' and the Muslim League's charge that the ministry had either been unwilling or unable to tackle the communal problem was also unfounded. The Government had indeed viewed the situation with grave concern and the law enforcing authorities were instructed to take stringent measures, especially when Shukla assumed the Premiership. The activities of all communal organisations were monitored, all inflammatory speeches reported verbatim, all writings in the press, Hindu and Muslim, carefully scrutinised and movements of all propagandists, both local and outsiders, closely watched. The Government issued a warning to the press against publishing provocative speeches and demanded security as a preventive measure. Inflammatory and insulting slogans, both anti-Hindu and anti-Muslim were banned, while places of worship were brought under surveillance to prevent storage of arms in them.[163] The Government was willing to form peace committees to prevent recurrence of communal fracas. Government officers were warned against entertaining any communal fracas. Government officers were warned against entertaining any communal bias on pain of summary dismissal. In a press note the Government warned against making "any innovations in the celebration of festivals", such as bringing out a procession which earlier had not been the "established feature of a festival" or carrying lathis "contrary to custom".[164] Leaders of both the communities were urged to peacefully settle the routes of religious processions, with or without musical accompaniments. Arrangements were made to take into police custody anti-social elements during festivals, and to quarter police pickets at riot torn places; the Government decided to impose punitive fines to make good the loss suffered by innocent people during riots.[165]

Most of the charges levelled against the Congress ministry was but propaganda ploy of the League and its supporters. So it seemed was the view of the liberal paper, the *Hitavada* which, in dismissing the allegations against the ministry, criticised the League for "trying to manufacture an agitation out of vacuum". But then, while complimenting the provincial government for being actuated by "no communal virus against the Muslims", the paper asked the Government to beware of communal spirit growing in local bodies as indicated by their "unnecessary insistence on the worship of Mahatma Gandhi at schools", for instance; such insistence, the paper warned, was "likely to be made the spearhead of an agitation" by the Muslims.[166]

Lord Linlithgow, the Viceroy, by no means well disposed to the Congress, saw little merit in the Pirpur Committee's accusations against the Congress ministries; Governors of provinces under Congress rule had privately informed him of no complaints of unjust treatment of Muslims.[167] Years later, Sir F.V. Wylie, Governor of C.P. and Berar, noted that "the accusations of gross anti-Muslim bias on the part of the Congress ministry were ... moonshine."[168]

Not surprisingly, therefore, the Congress challenge to the League that the latter's charges against Congress rule be enquired into by Sir Maurice Gwyer, the Chief Justice of the Federal Court, was not accepted by the League.

VII

The politically active two-year Congress rule was also a politically troubled one, in so far as Hindu-Muslim relations were concerned. Increasing polarisation of political opinion on communal lines was a distinct feature of the two years. Local communal organisations, both Hindu and Muslim, came under increasing external influence, mainly the press and propagandists. Visits of national leaders and conferences of national parties and organisations helped the process of political articulation. Riots and communal disturbances both reflected and aggravated the bitterness between the local Hindus and Muslims, affecting small towns and even villages. The Congress-League discord at the national level percolated to the province too, where local League leaders made the fullest propaganda use of the connection of high caste Hindu political leaders of the Congress party with the RSS and the Hindu Mahasabha at some stage of their career.

The Muslim leadership, divided so long, tended to get united under the Muslim League which intensified its activities both during and after the Congress rule. By contrast, the Hindu political leadership continued to be divided, the RSS and the Hindu Mahasabha, in particular, having no love lost with the local Congress which had internal differences between Hindi and Marathi speaking leadership. The Muslim community, small as it was, could never pose a political threat to local Hindu leadership, but the British government viewed the local Muslim leadership as an important factor for political calculations.

Law enforcing agencies dealt with riots and disturbances with their accustomed impartiality although on occasions communal parties accused them of bias and prejudice. But then, under the Governor's rule after 1939, riots were fewer despite more intensified political propaganda and more widespread activities of communal organisations. The administrative machinery was then, as ever, free from communal taint, the police, in particular, having no concern over the likely political fall out of what they needed to do as their sheer official duty.

References

1. *Report on Police Administration of C.P. and Berar for the year 1936.*
2. Fortnightly Report (Political and Military Deptt.) for C.P. and Berar for the first half of May 1937, Linlithgow Papers, quoted in P.N. Chopra, Ed., *Towards Freedom* (New Delhi, 1985), p.515.
3. Sinha Papers, File No. 280121, p.30, 33, Notes from personal files of Deputy Commissioners. W. Grigson, Dy. Commissioner, Jabalpur, to Hyde Gowan, Governor, 1 Nov. and 1 Dec. 1936.

   Sinha Papers are typed copies of Political and Military Deptt. files of the government of C.P. and Berar which were used by the committee which the government of Madhya Pradesh set up for the compilation of the history of the freedom movement in the province, the Chairman of which was D.P. Mishra, the Chief Minister. Professor R.M. Sinha, sometime Professor of History at Morris College, Nagpur, and later Head, Deptt. of History, University of Jabalpur, was a member of the committee. He donated the files to Nagpur University. The Sinha Papers are hereafter cited as SP.

   In a private letter to Linlithgow, the Governor, Sir Hyde Gowan, wrote : "Both Govind Das and Mishra have so long combined sexual aberration with successful careers in politics that unless either goes to jail, the interruption would only be temporary." Gowan to Linlithgow, 6 July 1937, Linlithgow Papers cited in Chopra, *op. cit.*, p.723.
4. SP, File No.280060, Extracts from newspapers, April 1936.
5. *Ibid.*
6. *Ibid.*
7. *Ibid.* Both *Independent* and *Sawadhan* were published from Nagpur.
8. *Ibid.*
9. Khursheed Kamal, *A Documentary Record of the Congress Government, 1937-39 : Related to Muslims under Congress Rule* (Islamabad, 1988), Vol. I, p.35.
10. *The Central Provinces and Berar, 1935-36 : A review of the Administration of the Province,* p.1.
11. M. Yussuf Shariff was a prominent Muslim leader of the province. He was a Minister in 1933-4; he was a founder of the provincial branch of the Muslim League, which, however, split between two groups, one led by him, and the other, led by S.A. Rauf Shah and S.W.A. Rizvi. Shariff was elected to the Assembly in 1937 from Nagpur-Rural constituency. He was the Law Minister for a while in the Khare Cabinet before he had to resign.
12. Rao was a leading politician of the province. He belonged to Bilaspur, where he worked as the follower of Tilak and Annie Besant in 1917-18. He formed the Independent Congress Party and became a Minister in 1927-28; he also organised the Democratic Party which dominated the Assembly for some years before the 1937 elections when the Congress formed the ministry. Rao was the Home Member in the Governor's Council from 1930 to 1936, when he was appointed the Acting Governor, following the Governor's absence on leave.
13. SP, 280121, *op. cit.*, p. 38.
14. SP., 280061, p.14 : Deputy Commr., Nimar to Government, 6 Feb. 1937. The Dy. Commr., however, did not believe that the allegation was true.
15. The Shias were unlikely to vote for Iftikar Ali, so opined Grigson, Dy. Commr., Jabalpur. SP. 280121, *op. cit.*,
16. *Assembly Debates*, 13 Dec. 1937, p.269; 24 Mar. 1938, pp.772, 802; 29 Mar. 1938, p. 792.
17. *C.P. Legislative Assembly Debates*, 24-3-38, p. 772; 29.3.38, p. 808.
18. *Report of the Police Administration in C.P. and Berar of 1937*, p. 1.
19. It was alleged that Mishra, before becoming a Minister, had been involved in the abduction of a Muslim woman, Hassina, who was later married to his Hindu driver. Besides provoking a public scandal, the issue was raised in the Assembly too. *Assembly Debates*, Dec. 1937, Vol. II, pp. 276-78. Hassina was converted to Hinduism and then married to the driver, Naidu. D.P. Mishra, *Living an Era* (Delhi, 1975), Vol. I, p. 260-62.
20. *Assembly Debates*, Dec. 1937, Vol. II, pp. 274-75; September-Oct. 1938, Vol. IV, pp. 53-54, 139-44, 217-18, 607.
21. SP, 280068, p. 40, Extracts from fortnightly reports for C.P. and Berar for the second half of 1938.
22. *The Hitavada* (Nagpur), 10 Feb. 1939.
23. SP, 280070, pp. 90-96, Chief Secretary's Note on Communal Situation, 20 June 1939
24. Maharashtra Archives, Nagpur, Political and Military Department File No. 778 of 1937 : C.M. Trivedi to all Dy. Commissioners, 27 Oct. 1938.
25. *Ibid.*
26. Khare was the Prime Minister for a year from August 1937.
27. SP, 280067, File No. 82 to 197, pp. 29-33.
28. Khare, the Premier, and leading the Marathi-speaking faction in the provincial Congress, had strained relations with D.P. Mishra, his colleague, and the most dominant leader of the Hindi-Speaking faction of the provincial Congress party. The bitterness in the Marathi and Hindi factions in the party was a significant feature of the provincial Congress politics. For Khare episode and the Marathi-Hindi bitterness see D.E.U. Baker, *Changing Political Leadership*

in an Indian Province : The Central Provinces and Berar, 1919-1939 (Delhi, 1979), pp. 177-93. Also, Khare, *My Defence* (Nagpur, 1938).

29. SP, 280067, *Sawadhan* bitterly condemned Gandhi, pp. 34-39.
30. *Ibid.*, pp. 41-45, views of the Governor and the Chief Secretary on the attack on Gandhi by *Sawadhan*.
31. SP, 280066, pp. 3-4.
32. SP, 280066, pp. 3-4, Central Provinces and Berar, Police, Abstract of Intelligence, SP, 280068, pp. 40-41.
33. The satyagraha was a protest movement against the Nizam government's anti-Hindu policy.
34. SP, 280068, p. 41, Extract from fortnightly report for the second half of December 1938.
35. *Indian Annual Register*, 1938, Vol. II (Calcutta, 1939), p. 338.

35a. Kamal, *op. cit.*, Vol. II, pp. 126-27.

36. *Indian Annual Register*, 1938, Vol. II, p. 339.

36a. Kamal, *op. cit.*, Vol. II, p. 124.

37. SP, 280068, pp. 24-42, Report on the communal situation in the province by the Chief Secretary, the Inspector General of Police and Y.A. Oakley, Asstt. to the Dy. Inspector General of Police, Nov. 1938; Fortnightly report on the political situation in the province, No.-Dec. 1938.
38. *Ibid.*
39. SP, 280071, pp. 130-42.
40. Hedgewar was the RSS chief from 1925 to 1940, when he died.
41. The four districts were Nagpur, Bhandara, Wardha and Chanda.
42. SP, 280072, pp. 157-65, Special Branch report on RSS, 29 May 1939.
43. National Archives of India, New Delhi, Home Political File No. 88 of 1933, Note on the RSS by the C.P. and Berar government.
44. Joshi belonged to Berar. He was a government advocate in the court of the Judicial Commissioner before becoming the Home Member in the Governor's Council in 1921.
45. SP, 280072, Special Branch Report on the RSS, 29 May 1939, *op. cit.*
46. V. Deshpande, Militant Nationalism in Maharashtra, 1925-51 (Unpublished Ph.D. thesis, University of Jammu, 1989), p. 95.
47. SP, 280072, Special Branch Report on the RSS, *op. cit.*
48. *Ibid.*
49. Maharashtra Archives, Nagpur, Pol. and Mily. Deptt. Files, No. 28 of 1939, S. Sanyal, Dy. Commr., Wardha, to H. Greenfield, Commr. Nagpur, 13 April 1939.
50. E. Raghavendra Rao wielded influence among Muslims with whose support he formed his parties-The Democratic Party, the United Party and the Independent Congress Party. S.A. Rauf Shah and S.W.A. Rizvi, later prominent League leaders, were close allies of Rao. Hifazat Ali served as a member of the Swarajist ministry in 1923-24. M.Y. Shariff was a Minister in 1933. Baker, *op. cit.*, pp. 115-19, 143, 162, 164, 175, 177.
51. On Iftikar Ali, who contested and won the Jabalpur-Mandla Muslim Rural Constituency in the 1937 election, W.V. Grigson, the Deputy Commissioner of Jabalpur, wrote to the Governor, Hyde Gowan, on 1 Nov. 1936:

    > "If elected, he will support whatever party suits him best, but change sides whenever he sees any chance of getting something better for himself".

    Iftikar's mentor, M.Y. Shariff, won the Nagpur Rural seat as a member of one faction of the Muslim League, but he soon joined the Congress ministry to become the Law Minister. Sometime later, however he had to quit, following an adverse verdict of a tribunal set up to enquire into his role in the release of a Muslim convicted in a murder case.
52. In the first C.P. and Berar Legislative Council (1921-23), there were six "Moderate Muslims"; in the second Council, (1924-26), there were seven Muslims, of whom one was a Swarajist, four Independents and two Liberals; in the third Council (1927-30), there were seven Muslims, of whom none was a Muslim Leaguer, in the fourth Council (1930-37), there were six Muslims, of whom, five were Democrats and one Independent. *The Central Provinces and Berar, 1931-2 : A Review of the Administration of the Province*, Vol. II (Nagpur, 1933), p. 12.
53. Kamal, Vol. II, *op. cit.*, p. 93.
54. *Ibid.*, Vol. I, p. 35.
55. The movement was the result of the deliberations at an informal meeting of the members of the All India Congress Committee at Vithalnagar on 21 February 1938. It was "child of Nehru's brain". Kamal, Vol. I, *op. cit.*, pp. 223-29; Vol. II, p. 199. Also, *Indian Annual Register*, 1937, Vol. I, pp. 207-08.
56. Kamal, Vol. I, p. 198.
57. Chopra, *Towards Freedom*, *op. cit.*, p. 722.
58. *Ibid*, Gowan to Linlithgow, 6 July 1937, Linlithgow Papers.
59. SP, 280068, pp. 35-37, Inspector General's Note on Muslim Communalism, 13 Nov. 1938.
60. *Indian Annual Register*, 1936, Vol. II, pp. 273-74.

61. SP, 280068, pp. 31-33, 37-42, Chief Secretary's Note on Communalism, 10 Nov. 1938, Inspector General's Note, *op. cit.*, Report on Muslim Communalism, 8 Nov. 1938, by Y.A. Oakley, Assistant to D.I.G. of Police; Fortnightly report for the C.P. and Berar for the first half of 1938.
62. *Ibid.*
63. *Ibid.*
64. *Ibid.*, p. 25, Chief Secretary's Note, *op. cit.*
65. *Ibid.*, pp. 31-33, Oakley's report, *op. cit.*
66. *Ibid.*
67. SP, 280070, pp. 125-28.
68. SP, 280071, pp. 126-30, Muslim League meeting, 10 June 1939; 280072, p. 150, Growth of communal feeling, Speech of Siddiqui Ali Khan, 7 Aug. 39.
69. *Ibid.*
70. SP, 280069, pp. 54-56, Chief Secretary's Note, 22 March 1939.
71. SP, 280067, p. 47, Speech of Tajuddin, 26 Aug. 1938.
72. SP, 280068, pp. 24-29, Chief Secretary's Note on communal situation, 10 Nov. 1938.
73. SP, 280063, pp. 84-92, Extracts from *Jaddo Jehad*; 280066, pp. 6-11, Extracts from *Jaddo Jehad*.
74. Chopra, ed., *Towards Freedom, op. cit.*, p. 722, to Linglithgow, 6 July 1937.
75. *Ibid.*
76. SP, 20072, pp. 158-60, Note on Khaksar Movement, by Special Branch, 29 May 1939.
77. *Ibid.*
78. *C.P. Legislative Assembly Proceedings*, 7 Nov. 1939, pp. 401-09, 6 Nov. 1939, pp. 280-81, 26 March 1938, p. 899.
79. Vidyamandir was the rural education scheme launched by the Congress ministry in the province.
80. *Assembly Debates*, 12 April 1939, p. 1121.
81. *Ibid.*, pp. 1126-29.
82. *Ibid.*, p. 1128.
83. *Ibid.*; Sept.-Oct. 1938, Vol. IV, p. 535.
84. *Ibid.*, 6 Nov. 1939, p. 280.
85. *Ibid.*
86. *Ibid.*, 4 Nov. 1939, p. 227.
87. *Ibid.*; 7 Nov. 1939, p. 352.
88. *Ibid.*, pp. 357-58.
89. *Indian Annual Register*, 1937, Vol. I., p. 344. Also, p. 288.
90. Govt. of C.P. and Berar, *Vidya Mandir Scheme—A Way to the Spread of Free and Compulsory Mass Education within a Fixed Period* (Nagpur 1938), pp. 5-6.
91. *Ibid.*, p. 6.
92. *Ibid.* pp. 7-8.
93. *Ibid.*, p. 9.
94. *Ibid.* p. 15.
95. *Ibid.*, p. 12-13.
96. *Assembly Proceedings*, 14 Aug. 1939, p. 783.
97. *Ibid.*
98. *Pirpur Report, op. cit.*, p. 60.
99. *Assembly Debates*, Sept.-Oct. 1938, Vol. IV, pp. 58-59.
100. *Ibid.*, 14 August 1939, p. 786.
101. *Ibid.*
102. *Ibid.*, p. 787.
103. *Ibid.*, Sept.-Oct. 1938, Vol. IV, pp. 139-44, 217-19, 527, 607; 15 Mar. 1939, p. 5; Also, 19 Sept., 1938, pp. 214-16.
104. SP, 280068, p. 31, Oakley's report, *op. cit.*; Inspector General's report, *op. cit.*; Fortnightly reports for the first half of 1938 and second half of 1938, *op. cit.*
105. SP, 280069, pp. 43-46, Chief Secretary's note on Muslim Satyagraha at Nagpur and press communique by the Govt., 10 Feb. 1939.
106. *Ibid.*, pp. 43-50.
107. *Ibid.*, pp. 47-50.
108. SP, 280069, p. 68, *Jaddo Jehad*, 19 Feb. 1939.
109. Kamal, II, *op. cit.*, pp. 81-82.
110. *Assembly Debates*, 12 April 1939, p. 1137.
111. Maharashtra Archives, Pol. and Mily. Deptt. Files, No. 101 of 1939, K.N. Nagarkatti, Dy. Commr., Chanda, to P.S. Rau, Commr., Nagpur, 22 June 1939.

112. Chanda district bordered on the Nizam's territory. Ballarshah was under Chanda district administration.
113. SP., 280070, pp. 108-121.
114. *Ibid.*,
115. *Home Political File* (National Archives of India), 28 August 1942. Hindu Mahasabha and RSS differences surfaced when despite Hedgewar's objection, his name was included among the office bearers of the Ram Sena, the Hindu militia organised by the Hindu Mahasabha in March 1940. Deshpande, Ph.D. thesis, *op. cit.*, p. 110; Also, pp. 103-04.
116. SP, 280070, pp. 71-77.
117. *Ibid.*, pp. 73-76.
118. *Ibid.*
119. *Ibid.*, pp. 76-77, D.P. Mishra's note, 13 June 1939.
120. *Pirpur Committee Report* (Lucknow, 15 November 1938), p. 53.
121. Padmasha, *Indian National Congress and the Muslims, 1928-1947* (New Delhi, 1985, second Edn.), pp. 133-38, Correspondence between Fazl-ul-Haw and Jawaharlal Nehru, Nov-Dec. 1939.
122. *Pirpur Report*, pp. 11-12.
123. Kamal, II, *op. cit.*, p. 86. R. Coupland, *Indian Politics*, (London, 1943), pp. 206-07.
124. SP, 280063, *op. cit.*, pp. 88-89, Editorial in *Jaddo Jehad*, 10 Nov. 1937.
125. *Pirpur Report* p. 12, 61. Khare admitted that even after the Congress High Command had declared the Hindu Mahasabha as a communal organisation, "individual Congressmen" attended the meetings addressed by Savarkar. *Ibid.*
126. *Ibid.*, p. 61.
127. SP, 280072, p. 60. The Government, however, found "nothing communal" in the activities of the *akhara*.
128. Padmasha, *op. cit.*, p. 135, *Pirpur Report*, pp. 55, 7.
129. *Ibid.*, pp. 55-57.
130. *Ibid.*, p. 20.
131. *Ibid.*, pp. 53-4, 57, 59, 21-22.
132. Padmasha, *op. cit.*, p. 133-38.
133. *Ibid.*
134. *Ibid.*, p. 133.
135. Padmasha, *op. cit.*, p. 134.
136. *Ibid.*, p. 135.
137. *Pirpur Report*, pp. 54-55.
138. Kamal, Vol. I, *op. cit.*, pp. 134-35.
139. *Ibid.*, p. 135, quoting Khare's statement.
140. Khare, *My Political Memoirs or Autobiography* (Nagpur, 1959), p. 214.
141. Deshpande, Unpublished Ph.D. thesis, *op. cit.*, p. 127.
142. Khare, *op. cit.*, p. 246.
143. *Ibid.*, p. 213.
144. *Ibid.*, pp. 214-15.
145. 1949-1951.
146. Khare, *op. cit.*, pp. 215-16.
147. *Ibid.*, p. 435.
148. *Ibid.*
149. *Ibid.*, p. 249.
150. *The Hitavada* (Nagpur), 10 February 1939.
151. *Ibid.*
152. *Ibid.*
153. *Ibid.*
154. *Ibid.*
155. *Ibid.*
156. *Ibid.*
157. *Ibid.*
158. *Ibid.*
159. SP, 280068, p. 42, Fortnightly report for second half of 1938.
160. Padmasha, *op. cit.*, pp. 138-39, Nehru to Fazlul Haq, 26 Dec. 1939.
161. *Assembly Debates*, 29 March 1938, p. 81.
162. *The Hitavada*, 10 February 1939, *op. cit.*
163. Maharashtra Archives, Nagpur, Political and Military Dept. Files, 778/1937; C.M. Trivedi to all Dy. Commissioners, 20 June 1939, 5 Aug. 1938, Press communique, 30 Aug. 1938, 22 June 1939.
164. *Ibid.*

165. *Ibid.*, Confidential Instruction to all Dy. Commissrs. by the Chief Secretary, 20 Dec. 1937, 2 April 1938.
166. *The Hitavada*, 12 February 1939.
167. Quoted in Rajmohan Gandhi, *Patel* (Ahmedabad, 1990), p. 289.
168. *Ibid*. Wylie made the remark in 1968.
169. *Ibid*. Linlithgow knew that the charges made by the League were baseless. He too saw no point in the charges being investigated by the Chief Justice.

Aspects of Indian History and Historiography
Editor : P.K. Mishra
Kaveri Books, New Delhi, India.

Civil Disobedience Movement and Women in Midnapore District

3

Niranjan Ghosh

Now India is free. Many men and women sacrificed their lives for the country. At the first stage of the movement the women did not take part directly. Gradually the women of villages and towns were inspired by the revolutionaries. Many women leaving their happy life joined the movement. Their main motto was to free the motherland from the foreign yoke.

From 1920 the women began to take part directly in the Freedom Movement and from the announcement of the Civil Disobedience Movement by All India Congress at Calcutta and Nagpur a new phase of National Movement began and the women determined to take part in the movement in large scale.[1]

A new chapter was opened by Mohandas Karamchand Gandhi in the history of the Freedom Movement of India through his Civil Disobedience Movement—commonly known as 'Salt Satyagraha'. The idea was to challenge the British authority as embodied in the laws of the British Government through an ostensibly minor action of preparing salt out of saline water of the sea. It was aimed at also demonstrating to the Indian people how a mighty Government like the British could be challenged in an unarmed, peaceful and non-violent way and thereby boost up the morale of the people. To violate the salt laws the women of villages of Midnapore district began to manufacture salt on a large scale. They began to manufacture salt by digging the small tanks and began to use the tanks to preserve the salt water. When police got secret news about the salt-manufacturing in that way, they went to villages and destroyed the manufacturing articles and threw clay and dust into the tanks. Even the police began to set up camps at different places of the Midnapore district.

Many salt-manufacturing centres were set up at different places of Midnapore district.[2] Upto the 6th May, 1930 approximately 34 such centres were opened at Contai Sub-division. The most important centres of that Sub-division were Rangalput, Gopalpur, Mirzapur, Pichhabani, Kalinagar, Subarnadighi, Balataliya, Thakurchak, Jagannathpur, Rupnagar etc. At Tamluk, the Civil Disobedience Movement took a militant character from the very beginning. Narghat was selected as the main salt-manufacturing centre of Tamluk Sub-division as this place was situated on the bank of the river Haldi. Many minor salt-manufacturing centres were also stated at different places of the district.

Many 'Mahila-sabhas' were organised by the women of Midnapore district during the Civil Disobedience Movement to inspire the women of the remote villages to take part in the Civil Disobedience Movement. Many women of the district picketed before the liquor shops and against the non-payment of tax to the Government.

Report of the Commissioner of Burdwan to the Chief Secretary to the Government of Bengal regarding the disturbance in Midnapore during the Civil Disobedience Movement may be quoted here:

"D.O. No. 446. J.Y. The 12th June, 1930.

My dear Hopkins

I am very pessimistic regarding Midnapore. The whole area through which I travelled with Peddie appears to have been thoroughly impregnated with the seeds of Civil Disobedience and I feel that we shall only root out this evil by arresting every single volunteer that we can lay hands on. I had no idea that Congress Organisation could enlist the sympathy and support of such ignorant and cultivating people as those in the Ghatal Sub-division, but the fact remains that they have done so and that their organisation has been extraordinarily good.

Sd/-Illegible.
Commissioner of Burdwan."[3]

About the success of Salt Movement in Midnapore district Jawaharlal Nehru wrote a letter from Allahabad on 2.2.31 regarding the people of Midnapore. The letter is as follows:-

"Among the many places which have provided martyrs for the cause of Indian freedom, Midnapore district occupies an honourable position. It was a feeling that special mention be made of it in the Resolution of Remembrance passed on the anniversary of Independence Day. I should like to tender my respectful congratulations to the brave men and women of the district who have suffered so much for the cause. Freedom will come to us. Of that there is no doubt and when the dust of the struggle subsides we may forget many of the little episodes, connected with it. But we can never forget the shining examples of heroism and sacrifice which specially India's women have given and we cannot forget what has happened in Midnapore district.

Sd/- Jawaharlal Nehru"[4]

The spirit of the Civil Disobedience Movement can be best understood from the report of W.D.R. Prentice to the Bengal Legislative Council. Prentice said on the 12th August, 1930, "In Midnapore there was great disorder due to the Civil Disobedience Movement. They (Satyagrahis) started with salt-subsequently there have been attacks on the police, murders and an attempt to burn a house in which the police were, there has been boycotting of chowkidars and now there is no-tax campaign."[5]

Side by side with salt movement the people of Midnapore began no-tax campaign against the British Government. The inhabitants of Midnapore decided not to pay *chowkidari* tax and any other kind of tax. Police began suppression for non-payment of tax. Police looted the properties of the villagers and resorted to beating, lathi charge, setting fire to the domestic houses. When the public did not pay any kind of tax, Government imposed punitive tax and police were posted at the villages to collect punitive tax. Women of Midnapore took prominent part in the tax movement. Women were instructed by the leaders to leave the village when police would come to the respective villages. When police came to villages people fled away from them. Police saw that there was not a single man in the village. Thus the British Government was not able to collect punitive tax from the villagers of Midnapore.[6]

During the second phase of the Civil Disobedience Movement many training camps for women were started. In 1931 Rishi Nibaran Chandra Dasgupta started such training camp for women at Darna near Contai town. Many women from different places attended the camp. Under the guidance and supervision of Nibaran Chandra Dasgupta, and the daughter of Basanti Devi, the training camp was completed with great success. In the camp the women were given training and lessons of the freedom movement. During 1931-32 several training camps for women were started at different places of Midnapore.[7]

Many women of the Midnapore even donated their ornaments for the freedom movement. A few names may be mentioned here:

	Name	Articles
1.	Bijanbala Roy	One nose-ring
2.	Tilottama Dhara	One nose-ring
3.	Prafulla Kayal	One finger-ring
4.	Hiranbala Bag	One finger-ring
5.	Apurbabala Karan	One finger-ring
6.	Tarubala Giri	Two pairs of ear-ring
7.	Narmada Pal	One bangle
8.	Bhagabati Ghosh	One finger-ring
9.	Basantabala Maiti	Two Haslis[8]

During the second phase of the Civil Disobedience Movement at many places of Midnapore salt law was violated by the women. Even the women gave prior notice to the British Government for meeting at different places of the district. One example may be cited here. On the 4th April, 1932, Sukhadamayee Roychowdhury gave prior notice to the District Magistrate of Midnapore for a meeting at Balyagobindapur, Pataspur P.S. The subject matter of the notice addressed to the District Magistrate is as follows:

"To
The Hon'ble District Magistrate,
Midnapore

Sir,

Two emergency ordinances had been issued to me. India is not a free country. The British Government has been rendering oppression on Indian people.... I have become the member of the unlawful Congress Organisation and rendering all kinds of help to its workers. I shall follow all the directions of the Congress. I shall deliver lecture in a public meeting on 4th April, 1932 at Balyagobindapur village under Pataspur P.S. on the occasion of "Gandhi Divas." I am to inform you in this regard.

Yours faithfully,
Sd/-Sukhadamayee Roychowdhury, "[9]

A few names of women-workers who took active part during the Civil Disobedience Movement may be mentioned here.

1. Charusila Jana of Basudevpur village, Sutahata P.S.
2. Subodh Bala of Bar-basudevpur, Sutahata P.S.
3. Subhadra Giri of Chakdwipa, Sutahata P.S.
4. Lakshmani Hazra of Mahishadal P.S.
5. Charusia Devi of Kuapur village, Chandrakona P.S.
6. Suhasini Devi of Tamluk,
7. Kusum Bagdi of Midnapore
8. Pusparani Banerjee of Tamluk,
9. Lakshmimani Mukherjee of Tamluk
10. Induprabha Chakrabarti of Tamluk P.S.
11. Charusila Dutta of Tamluk
12. Suramadevi Hota of Kalyanchak
13. Nani Bala Das of Asnan of Moyna P.S.
14. Puti Bala Daloi of Asnan of Moyna P.S.
15. Prabhabati Sinha of Solat of Sutahata P.S.
16. Muktakesi Samanta of Dakshin Dhalhara village of Mahishadal P.S.
17. Saila Bala Shee of Sautanchak village of Mahishadal P.S.
18. Mayarani Bag
19. Indumati Bhattacharyya of Jorapukur, Panskura P.S.
20. Bhivarani Chakraborty of Kolaghat, Panskura P.S.
21. Sabitri Dasi (De) of Tamluk
22. Kamini Samanta of Jardoi Panskura P.S.
23. Mayalata Das of Nandapur village Nandigram P.S.
24. Usha Dutta
25. Shriramani Karan of Paschin Bhanganmari, Khejuri P.S.
26. Brajeswari Maity of Khagda village, Egra P.S.
27. Ranibala Maity (Das) of Gopinathpur village, Bhagbanpur P.S.
28. Kushum Kumari Mandal of Ektarpur village, Bhagbanpur P.S.
29. Matangini Hazra of Alinan of Tamluk P.S.
30. Urmila Bala Paria of Khutia village, Kespur P.S.[10]

There were also so many women whose names are not mentioned here, they also took active part in the Civil Disobedience Movement in the district of Midnapore.

The Government adopted various repressive measures to stop the Civil Disobedience Movement in Midnapore. The police had recourse to certain measures such as—slapping, lathi-charging, caning and kicking with boots. Inhuman torture on the participants in the civil Disobedience Movement, such as pushing of cane-ends into the rectum, forcibly pouring urine and thrusting night-soil into the mouths of the Satyagrahis would certainly have shamed the uncivilised barbarians. Women satyagrahis of the Midnapore district had also to face all this. The women participants were sometimes forcibly stripped of their clothes by the local police and were caned black and blue.

In Tamluk, repression was carried on with much greater intensity. The police had put under arrest more than two thousand satyagrahis and declared 33 Congress Committees unlawful. Houses of many villagers were burnt to ashes. Quite bravely the women of Tamluk fought with enthusiasm and even Mr. Peddie, the then District Magistrate of Midnapore, an ex-soldier and typical civilian of 'Steel Frame' group had to admit in his confidential report to the Political department of the Bengal that Tamluk was the worst Sub-division in his District.[11]

Thus, we see that during the civil Disobedience Movement women of Midnapore district took active part to free the motherland. Though the movement between 1930-33 did not achieve the goal, yet it had a great value and importance in India's struggle for freedom. It demonstrated the awakening of political consciousness among the masses on a large scale. It gave them the high moral inspiration and unflinching courage, infused an unrelenting spirit among the people and it gave strength to masses to endure sufferings for the cause of the country. Midnapore, for decades to follow, was the model to the rest of Bengal in matters of political activities.

References

1. Ghosh, N. *Role of women in the Freedom Movement in Bengal*, p. 6.
2. *Ibid*, p. 77.
3. File No. 434, 1930. Home Political Section, Government of Bengal, "Riots at Midnapore" (State Archives of West Bengal).
4. Ghosh, N. op. cit. p. 99.
5. *Bengal Legislative Council Proceedings*, Vol. XXXV., 1930.
6. Ghosh, N. op. cit. p. 100.
7. Facts collected from "Nihar", a journal published from Contai during 1930-31.
8. Ghosh N. op. cit. p. 125.
9. *Kanthi Congress Barta*, No. 19, 1932.
10. Ghosh, N. op. cit. p. 197.
11. "Civil Disobedience Movement in Tamluk" by Tamluk Sub-divisional War Council.

Aspects of Indian History and Historiography
Editor : P.K. Mishra
Kaveri Books, New Delhi, India.

Nature of Agrarian Discontent and the Origin of Peasant Movements in India During the Pre-Nationalist Era (1757-1857)

4

Debabandya Kabi

An attempt will be made in the paper to examine the roots and nature of agrarian discontent during the British period and to analyze their impact on the origin and outbreak of peasant movements in India. By way of introduction it may be stated that the East India Company, after coming to power in India, had worked primarily to increase its revenues, as clearly reflected in its land policy and settlements. As a result, practically all sections of agrarian classes had been affected due to huge revenue demands of the British. This had prompted the Indian peasantry to rise in revolt either against their oppressor landlords or against the British by joining hands with other agrarian classes. In the process a series of agrarian unrests had taken place in Bengal, Bihar and Orissa. During the Colonial Period (1757-1947) profound changes had taken place in almost all sectors of Indian society and especially in the realm of agrarian social structure. It is necessary, therefore, to analyze the agrarian structure in Colonial India with special emphasis on aspects like the structure of land, agrarian class relations and the response of the peasantry to radical changes introduced by the British. As regards the period, it is proposed to restrict it to the first phase of colonial period namely, the period of Pre-Nationalist Era (1757-1857). It may be mentioned that, the colonial period has been demarcated into three distinct-phases namely, the Period of Pre-Nationalist Era (1757-1857), the Period of Nationalist Resurgence (1857-1920) and The Period of National Movement (1920-1947). The present study will thus, seek to examine and highlight the factors and forces concerning the origin and outbreak of peasant movements in India during the period of Pre-Nationalist Era.

To begin with, the social scientists in India have a strong tendency to analyze the socio-political movements involving the peasantry in a class framework which is rooted in Marxism. But the position of Karl Marx in this regard has been somewhat complex and full of ambiguities. For instance, Marx described the peasantry as a secondary social class and as one essentially outside the class system of capitalist society. At the same time he hoped that the peasantry would work as an ally of the industrial proletariat during the course of its struggle against the bourgeoise.[1] But after the fiasco of 1848 Revolution, Marx had denounced the peasantry as a "sack of potatoes that lack inter-connections, common political identity and organization."[2]

A more balanced view, however, has been provided by F. Engels. According to Engels, "Farm labourers", rather than "tenant farmers" were the natural allies of the industrial proletariat.[3] his experience of Russian conditions had prompted him to envisage an alliance between the agrarian and the working classes.[4]

But such classical notions of peasantry have been challenged by other Marxist leaders who are of the view that developments in China, Mexico, Cuba, Algeria and Vietnam clearly indicated the revolutionary potential of the peasantry.[5] As regards the nature and role of peasantry, several scholars have given differing interpretations. According to Barrington Moore, "a previous history of subordination to a landed upper class recognised and enforced in the laws, sharp cultural distinctions and considerable degree of de-facto possession of the land are the distinguishing features of a peasantry".[6] Eric R. Wolf, is, however, of the view that the peasant is a "rural cultivator who raises crops and livestock in the country-side, but who does not operate his enterprise in the economic sense".[7] According to Teodor Shanin, the peasantry consists of "small agricultural producers who with the help of small equipment and the labour of their families produce mainly for their own consumption and for the fulfilment of obligations to the holders of political and economic power."[8] Henry A. Landsberger characterizes three attributes of peasantry namely, their legal subordination, and their cultural distinctiveness as well as their de-facto possession of the land.[9]

As regards the nature of peasantry, historical experience has already demonstrated the fact that given an opportunity, a peasant is as rational, perceptive and receptive as any other elements in rural or urban societies. But he is unable to take risks in adopting innovations required for participation in mass action due to oppressive agrarian structure of rural India.[10] For instance, the peasant is unable to participate in mass action due to his exclusive dependence on the rural elites (mainly, the money lenders and absentee landlords) in times of urgent personal needs.[11] Other distinguishing features of peasantry, according to Kathleen Gough, has been that they are deeply rooted in religion and ceremony-oriented in outlook.[12] Barrington Moore expresses the view that the peasantry serves as an agent of revolution and that all peasant movements, are based on agitations and upsurges.[13] Some academicians, however are of the view that peasant movements have sought to achieve their objectives not by overthrowing the existing social structure but by attempting to eliminate the ingredients that had contributed to the suppression as well as exploitation of the peasantry.[14]

With this background, an attempt will be made to analyze the various framework of studies concerning the peasant movements in India. To begin with, Barrington Moore has provided the model of the three "ideal type" routes to radical change and modernisation namely, the Bourgeoise Democratic Revolution, the Fascist Revolution and the Communist Revolution. According to Moore, while the peasantry elsewhere in the world have moved along each of these routes, the peasantry in India unfortunately have not done so.[15]

Daniel Thorner, in his study has divided the Indian peasantry into three well-defined social categories namely, *Maliks, Kisans* and *Majdoors*. While the *Maliks* consist of the big landlords and rich land owners, the *Kisans* include small landowners and substantial tenants. The class of *Majdoors* include the poor tenants, share croppers and the landless labourers.[16] Basing on Thorner's model, Arvind N. Das has provided a fivefold classification of peasantry consisting of landlords, rich peasants, middle peasants, poor peasants and the agricultural labourers.[17] Dhanagare has more or less adopted a similar model for Indian peasantry in his study entitled, *Peasant Movement in India*.[18]

The tribal, peasant and other lower class movements in India have been analyzed by a group of scholars under a new banner called the *Subaltern Studies*.[19] Analyzing the works on popular and peasant movements in India, Guha has made a scathing attack on the academic elitism" as well as the whole gamut of colonial writings "for their lack of appreciation" of problems involving the peasantry.[20] Analyzing the nature of agrarian movements, Guha points out that whenever the peasantry had risen in revolt it had done so in violation of a series of codes that had defined his existence as a member of the colonial or semi-feudal society.[21] Further, Guha has disputed the contention made by some western scholars that peasant insurrections were purely spontaneous in nature. He has argued, instead, that an uprising of any significant scale had been preceded by some militant type of mass mobilization, such as the revolts of Kols and Santals.[22]

In his study on peasant movements, A.R. Desai has provided a perspective on the dialectical development of the agrarian struggles in India during the British period. In his introductory remarks he had stated that the consensus among scholars specializing on peasant movements indicate the view that the Indian peasantry had degenerated itself to become "passive, fatalistic, docile, unresisting and bogged down in the quagmire of superstitions and other worldly fantasies".[23]

Finally, Kathleen Gough in her study has examined the origin and growth of social protest movements in India. After a detailed study she has classified all peasant struggles into five types of mass actions namely, the "Restorative Rebellion", "Religious Movements, Social Banditry, Terrorist Vengeance and Mass Insurrections. Gough has further categorized these into two major types namely, political and social movements. While political movements seek independence or for regional autonomy among the tribals social movements mostly consist of the peasant uprisings.[24]

By way of background it may be stated that the British Colonialism had brought about socio-economic transformation in India by the introduction of the new land and revenue systems, legal and political changes, the destruction of indigenous industries and disintegration of age-old union between agriculture and industry. Further, India's economy and agriculture had undergone a commercial revolution, that had not been accompanied by an Industrial Revolution in the country.[25] As a result, a new agrarian structure had come into being with new classes namely, absentee landlords, and landlords at the top and tenants at-will share-croppers and agricultural labourers at the bottom. The Colonial Period had also witnessed an unprecedented growth of tenancy and a hierarchy of intermediaries between the state and the actual cultivator.[26] It may be mentioned that under the old agrarian system the Zamindars and landlords had owned and controlled most of the lands in both the Zamindari and "raiyatwari" tenure areas. In course of time, however, the Zamindars, could not cope themselves up with the system due to high revenue demands of the British as well as their rigid and unfavourable legal and administrative structures. In the process many Zamindars were liquidated and replaced by an altogether new set of classes, consisting of the merchants, money-lenders, speculators, officials, professionals, as well as others belonging to the urban groups.[27] This period also witnessed the emergence of commercial bourgeoise in India. As a result there was pressure on the peasantry to sell his products compulsorily to the merchant in order to meet his payments to the state and the landlord. The colonization of the economy and increasing commercialization had, thus, created a favourable climate for the village money-lender to occupy a dominant position in rural economy.[28]

A major feature of the agrarian class structure was the high degree of internal differentiation within the peasantry. At the top emerged a distinct class of rich peasants, who benefitted from commercialization of agriculture as well as from money-lending and trade. Below the rich peasants were a class of middle peasants who were very close to the rich peasants in social and economic positions.[29] But the vast majority of them had been reduced to the states of landless agricultural labourers and petty landholders, due to pressures of colonial innovations.[30]

Finally, at the bottom of the ladder were the classes of landless labourers, the most exploited ones, who constituted more than half of rural population.[31]

With this general background, an attempt will be made to analyze the origin as well as outbreak of peasant movements during the Pre-Nationalist Era (1757-1857). To begin with, the East India Company after coming to power in Bengal had worked primarily to augment its revenue, which had been reflected in its land policy and settlement. For instance, under the Permanent Settlement of Bengal, Bihar and Orissa in 1793, the existing Zamindars had been declared as full owners with absolute proprietory rights over land. In the process the Zamindars had constituted a dominant class in rural society with substantial economic power and political importance.[32] Some scholars attribute this to the benevolent attitude of the British as the latter had perceived in the Zamindars a good potential for bringing about a commercial revolution in India on the English pattern.[33] To others, however, the Settlement had been so designed as to create a class of "loyal collaborators" of the British.[34] However, the British experiment had miserably failed because it could neither transplant the enterprise and dynamism of the English landlords to the Indian soil nor could it end the "parasitic landlordism" of the Zamindars in India.[35]

The British had further introduced a new system for the assessment, payment and collection of their revenues. Under the new system, the revenue assessment was based on the potential productivity of the land, with the revenue payment to be made by the individual assessee, the Zamindar or the "raiyat", but not by the village community as a whole. Further, the revenue was to be paid to the government in cash but not in kind. The necessity for cash, had prompted the peasantry to depend, increasingly upon the money-lenders and the traders, which eventually resulted in the process of sale, mortgage and transfer of proprietory rights as well as assets and crops of the peasantry. The alienation of land had thus become a powerful feature in peasant's life.[36]

These developments, had paved the way towards the growth of an intermediary between the Chief Zamindar and the actual cultivator. It had also generated a fierce competition between various categories of tenants for security of tenure as well as for occupancy rights. Further, it had created a chain of contractors, farmers money-lenders, traders and others who had taken the land on lease from the Zamindars to grow particular type of crops like jute, indigo and tea etc.[37] The British system in the process brought about a high degree of disruption and suffering to the rural peasantry and created a structure of underdevelopment which became endemic in course of time. These developments contributed later to Bengal Famine of 1770, in which a third of the population had perished.

The changed situation in the agrarian sector very soon resulted in a series of peasant revolts in India. For instance, the Zamindars who had been dispossessed for default in revenue collection under the Permanent Settlement had become the rallying point of peasant rebellions. This scenario was particularly true in case of tribal areas where the new tenure system had deprived the native population of their community rights over forests and lands and had thereby forced them to give up many of their vital and customary rights.[38] Further, the British system had encouraged an influx of Zamindars as well as their representatives such as the forest contractors, traders, money-lenders, administrators, and the educationists. These people, however, had exploited the tribals with the political and judicial support received from the British government. As a result the tribal people had felt greatly alienated as their economic status had degenerated into that of landless labourers.[39]

In this background, the first symptom of revolt by disgruntled peasantry had taken place as far back in 1763. This revolt known as "Fakir and Sanyasi" rebellion of Bengal has been described by Bhawani Sen as a peasant movement.[40] The next phase was a series of uprisings in tribal regions of India. In Bihar and Orissa, for instance, the introduction of the Permanent Settlement to the tribal areas had undermined the traditional authority of the chiefs, as those who had failed to comply with the revenue demands of the British had been dispossessed. Further, their tribal lands had been confiscated and auctioned to recover the government dues. The auctioned lands, however, had gone into the hands of upper class Hindus like Brahmins and Mahajans (urban money-lenders). These people, infact, had been provided with unlimited powers, to increase the rents of their tribal tenants. As a result a series of tribal insurrections had taken place in Bihar and Orissa. The prominent among them were the Kol and Bhumij Revolts of 1831-1833.[41]

The Santal uprisings of 1855-1856 constituted a part of the tribal and agrarian unrests. A strong tribal identity and wholesale appropriation of land for recovery of revenue dues as well as land transfers to urban money-lenders had affected the tribal interests gravely. The Santals, infact, had resorted to armed revolts and in the process several landlords, *mahajans* and police officials had been murdered. The British government, however, had suppressed the insurrection ruthlessly.[42]

The revolt of 1857 was yet another landmark in the history of agrarian unrest in India. For instance, a close examination in the affected districts of Oudh (UP) clearly indicates that all rural classes had been deeply affected by the British land revenue policy and administration.[43] Further, between 1840 and 1857, the transfer of land from the cultivators to the non-cultivating class of money-lenders, urban traders as well as imposition of levies and illegal taxes by corrupt revenue officials had eventually culminated in the Great Revolt of 1857.[44]

The agrarian aspects of the 1857 Revolt, however, have not been reflected adequately by the historians and scholars. Even Karl Marx in his commentary on 1857 Revolt had not taken sufficient note of it. For instance, he had maintained that the only class affected by the British land policy was the feudal aristocracy of Oudh (UP) and that the mutiny had not touched the actual cultivators, who had supported the landed aristocracy during the uprisings.[45] It may be true that there were many reactionary elements within the feudal and landed aristocracy who had spearheaded the uprisings. But to brand the revolt as an "out and out reactionary upheaval",[46] is to undermine the role of popular sentiments in the discontent of 1857. Infact, as stated by Dhanagare, the support provided to the feudal chiefs and landlords by the mass peasantry had reflected the stage of historical development, the pre-capitalist agrarian relations and the level of consciousness among the lower strata of Indian peasantry.[47]

The period from 1757 to 1857 had also witnessed the foundations of a nascent Indian nationalism through the "Bhakti" and "Brahmo Samaj" movements. Infact, Raja Rammohan Roy who had established the "Brahmo Samaj" in 1828, had faced the dilemma of how best to eradicate the evils of Indian society. In 1837, however, his disciple Dwarikanath Tagore had taken up this work by establishing the Landholders Society to preserve the class interests of Zamindars. Simultaneously, the Bengal British India Society had been set up in 1842 to express its sympathy and concern for the raiyats. These two associations, in course of time had decided to merge themselves to form the British India Association in 1851. Also, a series of semi-religious and political organizations had emerged in Bengal, contributing to the origin of political consciousness in India.[48]

As a result of these uprisings, there had occurred, strong anti-British feelings in India. These had reached serious proportions especially in Bengal, where the local people had resorted to the harassment of the Englishmen at different places like Jessore, Birbhum, Bankura, Calcutta,

Rangpur, Vishnupur etc.[49] These developments, no doubt, had perturbed the English Governor General, Lord William Bentick, but strangely enough, his public reactions had been quite mixed. For instance, while admitting that the failures of the Permanent Settlement and resulted in the mass upsurge of Bengal he had also expressed satisfaction over the emerging fact that the Settlement had created a vast body of rich landed proprietors who would be deeply interested in the continuance of British rule in India.[50]

Thus, during the first phase of Colonial Era (1757-1857), all sections of agrarian classes had been affected due to high revenue demands of the British government. This had resulted in great economic burden on the lower strata of peasantry. The British system of revenue had introduced a dominant class of land-holders and cultivating peasants as well as money-lenders. In the tribal areas, while the new tenure system had deprived the native population of their community rights over forests and lands, it had alienated them further by the encouragement of the influx of Zamindars, forest contractors, traders and money-lenders who exploited them thoroughly. Infact, the agrarian discontent as well as the attempt to bring about a total or partial dislocation of the tribal society and its economy had contributed to the outbreak of a series of peasant movements in Bengal, Bihar and Orissa.

References

1. Karl Marx, *The Class Struggle in France* (London, 1934), pp. 33-131.
2. Karl Marx F. Engels, *Selected Works*, Vol. 1 (London, 1968), pp. 174-8.
3. F. Engels, *The Peasant Wars in Germany* (London. 1969), pp. 15-6.
4. Lenin V.I., *What is To Be Done* (Moscow, 1969), pp. 78-93.
5. Wolf Eric R., *Peasant Wars in The Twentieth Century* (London, 1971), p. 289.
6. Moore, Barrington, Jr. *Social Origins of Dictatorship and Democracy* (London, 1966), p. 3.
7. Wolf Eric, op cit, pp. 289-93.
8. Sharin, Teodore, 'Peasantry As a Social Factor', in Teodore Sharin, ed *Peasant and Peasant Societies : Selected Readings* (London, 1971), p. 241.
9. Landsberger, Henry. A. (ed) *Rural Protest : Peasant Movements and Social Change* (London, 1974), p. 7.
10. Seth A.N., 'Peasant Movements and Organizations in India', Unpublished Ph.D. dissertation, Indian Council of Social Science Research (New Delhi, 1978), p. 15.
11. *Ibid.*, pp. 18-9.
12. Gough Kathleen "Indian Peasant Uprisings" *Economic and Political Weekly* Vol. 11, 1974, p. 1401.
13. Moore, Barrington, *op. cit.*, p. 83.
14. Surana P. 'Social Movements and Social Structure : A study in the Princely State of Mewar', Unpublished Ph.D. dissertation submitted to Jodhpur University, Jodhpur, 1976, p. 120.
15. Moore, *op. cit.*, pp. 314-5.
16. Daniel Thorner, *The Agrarian Prospect in India* (Delhi, 1956), p. 46.
17. Das Arvind N. *Agrarian Unrest and Socio-Economic change in Bihar* : 1900-1980 (New Delhi, 1983), p. 14.
18. Dhangare D.N. *Peasant Movements in India : 1920-1950* (New Delhi, 1956), p. 15.
19. Ranajit Guha, ed. *Subaltern Studies* Vol. I (Delhi, 1982), Preface.
20. Ranajit Guha, *Elementary Aspects of Peasant Insurgency in Colonial India* (Delhi, 1983), p. 1.
21. Guha, Ranajit, *Subaltern Studies*. Vol. II (Delhi, 1983), p. 1.
22. *Ibid.*, p. 2.
23. Desai A.R. (ed.), *Peasant Struggles in India* (New Delhi, 1980), p. xii.
24. Gough Kathleen, *'Indian Peasant Uprisings'* in A.R. Desai, *op cit.*, pp. 94-112.
25. Bipan Chandra, *Nationalism and Colonialism in Modern India* (Delhi, 1979), p. 329.
26. Patel S.J. *Agriculture Labour in India and Pakistan* (Bombay, 1952), p. 148.
27. Bipan Chandra, *op. cit.*, p. 330.
28. *Ibid.*, p. 332.

29. *Ibid.*, p. 335.
30. Patel S.J. *op. cit.*, p. 148.
31. Bipan Chandra, *op. cit.* p. 335.
32. Anstey V. *The Economic Development of India* (London, 1957), p. 98.
33. Moore Barrington, *op. cit.*, p. 354.
34. Sen Bhawani, *Evolution of Agrarian Relations in India* (New Delhi, 1962), p. 63.
35. Moore, Barrington *op. cit.*, pp. 246-7.
36. Desai A.R. *op. cit.*, p. 129.
37. *Ibid.*
38. Dhanagare D.N. *op. cit.*, p. 34.
39. A.R. Desai, *op. cit.*, p. 130.
40. Sen Bhawani *op. cit.*, pp. 61-2.
41. Jha J.C. *The Kol Insurrections of Chhotanagpur* (Calcutta, 1964), pp. 240-2 and *The Bhumij Revolt*, 1832-3 (Delhi, 1967), pp. 106-43.
42. Dutta K.K. *The Santal Insurrections of 1855-1857* (Calcutta, 1940), pp. 1-37.
43. Eric Stokes, 'Traditional Elite in the Great Rebellion of 1857' in E. Leah and S.N. Mukhej, eds. *Elites in South Asia* (Cambridge, 1970), pp. 16-32.
44. Dhanagare D.N. *op. cit.*, pp. 35-6.
45. The Views of Karl Marx as cited in S.A. Avineri, ed. *Karl Marx on Colonialism and Modernisation* (New York, 1969), p. 315.
46. Moore Barrington *op. cit.*, p. 36.
48. *Ibid.*, p. 43.
49. O'Malley L.S.S. *Bengal, Bihar and Orissa Under British Rule* (Calcutta, 1925), pp. 208-9.
50. Keith A.B. (ed) *Speeches and Documents in Indian Policy* (Oxford, 1972), p. 159.

Aspects of Indian History and Historiography
Editor : P.K. Mishra
Kaveri Books, New Delhi, India.

Protest Movement in Manbhum Against its Merger with Bihar, 1912

5

S.C. Mukhopadhyay

The district of Manbhum was formed in 1833 as a result of the Ganga Narayan riot in Barabhum, when the East India Company felt it necessary to have a tighter control over the areas of Jungle Mahals. At that time, there were a number of 'Bhum'—ending tracts in this area, and Manbazar became the first district headquarters, as it was known as Manbhum at that time.

The district of Manbhum was formed as a part of the division of South West Frontier Agency under the government of Bengal. Originally the district embraced large areas including the Western portion of Bankura and Dhalbhum. The South West Frontier Agency was renamed in 1854 as the Chotanagpur Division under a Commissioner, while Manbhum formed the eastern portion of the division under a deputy commissioner. The district was situated between 22°43[1] and 24°4[1] north latitude and 85°49[1] and 86°54[1] east longitude.

The birth of the Indian National Congress and the partition of Bengal, the two most eventful developments surcharged the atmosphere of Indian politics with hope and dismay at the end of the 19th and in the beginning of the 20th Centuries. By the partition of Bengal in 1905, the British government outraged the feelings of the people of Bengal. By the partition, Bihar and Orissa remained with West Bengal with headquarters at Calcutta, While East Bengal and Assam with headquarters at Dacca formed a separate province. This bifurcation was a step towards subjugation and political emascultation of the Bengali-speaking people, by merging them with non-Bengali people in both the newly created provinces. The young educated Bengalis on their own initiative, launched a campaign of killing the British Officers by using bombs and pistols. They urged the re-union of Bengal and thus tried to preserve their social, cultural, linguistic and geographical identity[1]

But in Bihar a different situation prevailed. The partition gave the people of Bihar a new opportunity for the creation of a separate province. This demand for a separate Bihar emerged due to various considerations. It was alleged that the people of Bihar had so long been receiving a step-motherly treatment at the hands of the government. It was argued that economic, educational and political progress of Bihar was retarded due to its artificial union with Bengal. The people of Bihar claimed that they were different from the Bengalis in language, social habits and culture. Culturally the Biharis were more akin to the United Provinces than Bengal. While Bengal marched towards progress, Bihar remained backward for a long time. So the educated people of Bihar launched a movement for the separation of Bihar from Bengal. This movement was given a momentum by a number of Bihari leaders like Mahesh Narayan, Sachidanand Sinha, Bisweshwar Singh, Saligram Singh, Nand Kishore Lall, Ali Imam, Hussain Imam and Mazharul Haq. Ram Sewak in his writings even points out that it was an "unholy alliance"[2] of

Bihar with Bengal. The British government also took the plea of separating Bihar from Bengal due to administrative exigencies. Due to the fear of Bengal revolutionaries as well as the zeal of the *Swadeshi* movement, the partition of Bengal was annulled in 1911. Though east and west Bengal united, but a separate province of Bihar and Orissa was created by the British. The Bengali leaders then failed to realise that a large tract of territories with a Bengali population in Manbhum and Dhalbum, had now formed a part of Bihar, which had remained with Bengal even ages part. Thus, when the Bengali leaders were in jubilant mood for the re-unification of Bengal, the people of Manbhum and Dhalbhum were in deep sorrow. They did not take this transfer calmly, instead they launched a protest movement during the whole year of 1912. This movement took the form of petitions to the Government of India requesting to undo the unholy decision, by keeping Manbhum and Dhalbhum within Bengal. The zamindars colliery-owners, merchants and some inhabitants of the district rose on this occasion and sent some memorials to the government in both English and Bengali. The Chief Secretary of the Government of India thus requested the governments of Bihar and Orissa, as well as Bengal, to consider the matter and furnish the Government of India their views about the people of the district.[3]

In the first two memorials the people of Manbhum prayed for keeping them in Bengal on considerations of geography, history, race, language, laws and tenures, administrative advantages and the like. In paragraph 2 of the memorial, it was stated that Manbhum and Dhalbhum formed a continuation of the plain of Bengal proper. In reply, Le Messurier—the Chief Secretary to the Government of Bihar and Orissa in his letter to the Secretary, Government of India, completely rejected this claim by remarking that "Bengal consists of the lower valleys of the Ganges and Brahmaputra rivers, and is a level alluvial formation. Manbhum on the other hand, is the first step of a gradual dissent from the table-land of Chotanagpur to the delta of lower Bengal and its general characteristics are those of an upland district. Its physical features resemble closely those of the adjoining districts of Chotanagpur".[4] Remarking on the geography of the district, the Chief Secretary to the Government of Bihar and Orissa pointed out that the soils of Manbhum "are entirely different from those of Bengal proper".

The memorials of the people of Manbhum further stated that although "Manbhum is a non-regulation district, the ordinary codes of judicial procedure and almost all the laws of Bengal are in force". In reply to such claim, the Chief Secretary to the Government of Bihar and Orissa replied that this was also true not only in Manbhum but also true for the other districts of Chotanagpur. He further pointed out that in respect of the legal position "Manbhum and Dhalbhum differ in no way from the rest of Chotanagpur. They are all scheduled districts; in all of them the District Officer is styled Deputy-Commissioner, and he exercises the special powers referred to in section 30 of the criminal Procedure Code". Besides Manbhum and Dhalbhum had the special Tenancy Act as well as the Chotanagpur Rural Police Act. The special provisions of this act were equally necessary for these tracts, but there was no provision for Bengal Rural Police Act. Therefore the Secretary to the Government of Bihar and Orissa in his note stated that to keep the tribals, of these tracts in good temper, it was necessary to keep the local laws in force. But the Bengal officers who had no experience of these local laws, would prove themselves unworthy in implementing these special laws—if the districts remained in Bengal.[5]

In replying to the claims of the memorialists that the land Tenures of Manbhum and Dhalbhum were the same as in the adjoining districts of Bengal Le Messuriar remarked in his note about the misleading claims of the former. That the land tenures were quite different from the districts of Chotanagpur were opposed to truth. The Chief Secretary cited the Settlement reports for Dhalbhum and Barabhum, remarking that the similar system of land tenures existed in other parts of Chotanagpur. But at the same time he admitted that in the adjoining parts of Midnapore, Birbhum and Bankura similar land tenures existed resembling those of Manbhum and Dhalbhum. He believed that it was due to the overflow of the aboriginal tribes in those areas, who carried the peculiar tenures with them.[6]

On the questions of race, religion and language of the people the Chief Secretary admitted that the majority of the people of both the tracts spoke Bengali. But Santhali and Hindi were also spoken. In Dhalbhum, half of the population belonged to two aboriginal tribes—Santhals and Bhumijs; While in Manbhum, four such tribes—Kurmi, Santhal, Bhumij and Bauri were strongly represented. Though many of these aboriginal called themselves Hindus, they had preserved their original manners and customs, which resembled more closely to the tribes of Chotanagpur than to the Hindus. About the court language of both Manbhum and Dhalbhum, the Chief Secretary admitted that though Bengali was the court language of both these tracts, but there would have been no serious difficulty on that account. Officers posted in these tracts were required to Pass in Bengali, when Bengali was not their mother tongue. At that time a great majority of officers in the provincial and subordinate services in Bihar were Bengalis. In many districts like Katak, Bhagalpur and Patna, large proportion of Bengalis existed with a good educational background, would always claim appointments in the tracts of Manbhum and Dhalbhum. So there would never be any dearth of Bengali-speaking Officers. The Chief Secretary stated categorically the intention of the government of Bihar not to substitute Hindi for Bengali. Moreover the youths of Manbhum might attend the colleges at Calcutta, Burdwan and other places as they had always done in the past. As English was the medium of instruction, many good students of Bihar Colleges had always been Bengalis.[7]

The people of Manbhum also expressed their desire to remain with the same Bengali—speaking people of Bengal fearing that in Bihar, they would get no sympathy from the Biharis and could not send their own representative to the Legislative Council. The Chief Secretary to the Government of Bihar and Orissa noted in reply that the fear of the memorialists was baseless. But on the other hand, if Manbhum remained with Bihar, the Bengali Colonies of other districts of Bihar would undoubtedly gain and could send their own Bengali representative to the legislature. In rejecting the demands of the people of Manbhum and Dhalbhum, the Chief Secretary concluded by observing; "I am to point out that it would in any case be impossible to draw the administrative boundary along the line of racial and linguistic cleavage... Moreover if the test of language were applied along one part of the common boundary, it would have to be applied elsewhere also.[8] ....For the above reason the Lieutenant-Governor-in-Council is wholly unable to support the prayer of the memorialists.... All sorts of rumours appear from time to time in public press which unsettle the minds of the people and tend to shake the public confidence in the permanency of the arrangement announced at Delhi by His Majesty the King-Emperor, and now that these memorials have been examined in details, it seems very desirable from all points of view that further agitation on the subject should be discouraged".[9]

References

1. Singh, Nahar, Bhai and Kirpal Singh, Bhai (Eds), *Struggle for Free Hindusthan*, Vol-III (New Delhi, 1987), pp. V-VI.
2. Sewak Ram, *History of Bihar between the two world wars*, (New Delhi, 1985), pp. XIII-XIV.
3. Butler's letter No. III—D.L. Dated 14 February, 1912.

4. Letter from H. Le Messurier, Chief Secretary to the Government of Bihar and Orissa to the Secretary, Government of India, No. 42-42-A, dated 7 October, 1912 (Proceedings of the Home Department, No. 40, Part - A).
5. Proceedings of the Home Department, November, 1912, No. 40.
6. *Ibid*, Para - 6.
7. *Ibid*, Paras 8 and 9.
8. Here Le Messurier referred to the districts of Midnapore and Malda, where, in the formers, a large number of Oriya people and in the latter, a large number of Hindi-speaking people existed.
9. Proceedings of the Home Department, November, 1912, No. 40, Paras 11 and 12.

Aspects of Indian History and Historiography
Editor : P.K. Mishra
Kaveri Books, New Delhi, India.

The Indian Reform and Awakening of the 19th Century : A Study of its Impact on Bihar

6

Sumanta Niyogi

The socio-religious reform movements which emerged in the wake of British rule in India can be divided into two major categories. In the first category fall the movements which called for reform and changes in socio-cultural practices and values of Hinduism on the pattern of the primordial tradition of the Vedas. The followers of such movements were 'fundamentalists' in the sense that they believed in going into the texts of original scriptures in order to seek the truth and wisdom in their pristine purity as bequeathed by seers, saints and scholars long time back. Only by going to the original religious texts, they felt, one can find the aberrations, distortions and misrepresentations that crept into our socio-religious tradition in course of centuries. And it was these aberrations in the mainstream Hindu socio-religious tradition (the Great Tradition) that they pledged to cleanse Hinduism and Hindu society off. The Arya Samaj, Ramakrishna-Vivekananda and Kabirpanthi movements fall within this category. However, in their quest for truth they sometimes clung too rigidly to the ancient wisdom. For example, the Arya Samajis put so much emphasis upon the *Vedas* as the supreme and ultimate source of truth that the concepts of the Vedic infallibility and 'back to the Vedas' have become their guiding principles.

To the second category belong those movements which advocated synthesis of new norms and cultural themes with the traditional themes and value system of the Hindu culture. The Brahmo Samaj movement belongs to this category. The pioneers of this trend in socio-religions reformation have been the apostles of modernization in a greater measure than those belonging to the first one.[1] The Brahmo Samaj leaders, for example, in their search for truth and wisdom delved deep into the *Vedas* and *Upanishadas*, but, at the same time, they looked into the sources of other religions and cultures like the medieval Sufism, English Unitarianism and Americal Transcendentalism. Of course, their roots were in India's ancient past, chiefly the *Upanishadas*. The remarkable point is that they did not close their eyes to the West. They were not inimical or averse to the qualities and strengths of the western culture and value system. The immortal lines penned by Rabindranath Tagore reflect the attitude:

> "The doors of the West have opened,
> Folks bring gifts to our land;
> Give and take, meet and be met
> On the shore of vast humanity
> That is India."

One recent study has categorised these socio-religious reform movements into 'transitional' and 'acculturative'.[2] The study employs the term 'colonial milieu' to indicate the interaction between the indigenous civilizations of South Asia and British culture. It views that conquest did not necessarily create the colonial milieu for all individuals or for a given region; that was determined by human interaction, by those who found it expedient or necessary to become part of the new colonial world and its culture. The uneven development of a colonial milieu and the persistence of indigenous forms of socio-religious dissent, according to the author, produced two distinct types of movements (transitional and acculturative) within the period of British rule.[3] The transitional movements had their origins in the pre-colonial period, and grew out of indigenous forms of socio-religious dissent with virtually no influence from the colonial milieu, either because it was not yet established or because it had failed to affect individuals involved in a particular movement. Its leaders were rooted to the indigenous soil and were free from any sort of western impact. They were least willing to make any sort of adjustment to the colonial world. However, the author admits, in course of time these movements made limited adjustments to the colonial world. The Arya Samaj and Kabirpanthi movements are placed in this category.

As regards the acculturative movements, they originated within the colonial milieu and were led by men who had grown out of interaction with the alien culture. These movements were based on the Indian tradition of socio-religious protest. The founder of such a movement might or might not have been drawn into the world of British culture, but his followers and later leaders were largely western-educated South Asians influenced by the specific culture of England. Acculturative movements accepted the facts of British supremacy, the colonial milieu and the privileged position of its members within the colonial world, the author adds.[4]

This categorisation has its limitations. Most of the so-called 'transitional' movements (Kabirpanthi being among the exceptions) became 'acculturative' to some extent in course of time. We must take into account the nature and extent of the process of acculturation. Again, the author himself admits that the acculturative movements were not "totally new or without roots" in the general high culture and South Asia and that the difference between the transitional and acculturative movements was mainly at their points of origin.[5] Moreover, he puts too much emphasis on the question of class privilege in the colonial situation. This appears to be a narrow perspective of looking at the formidable personalities of the nineteenth and twentieth centuries Indian awakening and reform who faced insurmountable hurdles and sacrified everything (including privileges that accrued from British colonial rule) to guide people towards new awakening, new learning and socio-religious reforms.

The brief foregone discussion gives us an idea of the nature and scope of the Indian socio-religious reform movements of the modern period. None of these movements associated with the nineteenth century Indian reform and awakening can trace their origin in Bihar. The Brahmo Samaj and the Ramakrishna movements came here from neighbouring Bengal, while the Arya-Samaj and Kabirpanthi movements entered the province from the Punjab and the United Provinces. Of course, they made remarkable impact on the development of man and society in Bihar, which was clearly evident in the first half of the twentieth century.

I

The Brahmo Samaj movement was the most significant aspect of the Indian reform and awakening. It was characterised by a reformist zeal in socio-religious sphere and an irresistible upsurge of educational and intellectual activities. The unprecedented intellectual and cultural efflorescence through protestant Brahmoism had a profound impact on the Bengali thought and society. It was bound to affect the neighbouring province of Bihar. The spirit of the *Nabajagaran* or the new awakening percolated into Bihar in a slow manner.[6]

A fairly large migration of Bengali *'bhadraloks'*[7] to Bihar for serving the needs of the British Indian bureaucracy and of the newly-built railways, postal and telegraph services started in the sixties of the nineteenth century. Many of them were engaged in legal and medical professions, and some were employed as school teachers.[8] This process of Bengali *bhadralok* immigration into Bihar continued well upto the first few decades of the twentieth century. A sizeable section of these Bengali youngmen, kindled with the spirit of the new age, embraced Brahmoism and settled down in Bihar. Along with these new converts, the Brahmo missionaries also gradually came over to this province, carrying with them the message of the new awakening.[9] With the help of this vibrant Bengali officialdom and dedicated missionaries, the Brahmo Samaj movement could make headway in Bihar.

The first Samaj mandir was setup in Bihar in the town of Bhagalpur as early as 1863.[10] Bhagalpur had already been a centre of educated Bengalis engaged in government employment and professions. It was followed by the establishment of Brahmo Samaj centres at Patna and Gaya in 1866.[11] The movement gained momentum with every passing year when new branches of the Samaj were set up at Hazaribagh, Ranchi, Giridih, Muzaffarpur and some other places and the existing ones expanded their sphere of activities. The noteworthy point is that the Brahmo Samaj in this province was confined mainly to the educated Bengali community residing in the urban areas. This trend continued in the first half of the twentieth century. The Brahmos here could not shake off their Bengaliness nor their English-knowing elitist complex. The few Bihari converts that it could attract to its fold belonged mainly to the educated Kayastha families.[13] The philosophical doctrine of the Brahmo Samaj, centering on the concept of one formless Almighty God, universal brotherhood and religious tolerance was beyond the comprehension of a common individual in this province.

For this reason large-scale proselytisation of Biharis to Brahmoism could not take place. The Brahmo missionaries never dared to resort to conversion through force or pressure. The meagre number of converts the Brahmo Samaj could make here were done through persuasion, not pressure, it contrast to those of the Arya and Christian Missions. It is also very likely that they never strained themselves in the work of proselytisation, thinking of it as a futile effort in a rigidly conservative society. Sivanath Sastri, the great Brahmo leader and an illustrious personality of the Indian awakening and reform, expressed his agony at the attitude of the Brahmos in Bihar:

> It is a sad reflection that the mission of the Brahmo Samaj has not touched even the indigenous population of this province. It can also be fairly said that no systematic efforts have ever been made to carry the new message to the native population. The Bengali settlers among whom the light was confined were contented with working amongst their own class and offering the new gospel to their own people.[14]

This attitude of seclusion continued in the first half of the twentieth century, and accounted for the decline of the movement.

Though the brahmo movement could not take roots in Bihar so far as the religious aspect is concerned, yet its work in the socio-cultural sphere was outstanding. The lasting legacies bequeathed by the samaj to the posterity in the province speak for the dedication, sacrifice and hard work of the members of the samaj in various parts of the province. It can definitely be said that the Samaj's accomplishments were far beyond its capacity in terms of number and resources.

It made noteworthy contribution in the field of education. The Brahmo Samaj was the only indigenous agency to pioneer modern and secular education in Bihar.[15] Its role was also pioneering in the sphere of female education. The highly reputed educational institutions like the Rammohan Roy Seminary, the Bankipore Girls High School, the Rabindra Balika Vidyalaya, and the Aghore-Prakash Shishu Sadan, all in Patna; the Chotanagpur Girls' High School and the Chotanagpur High School both in Giridh; the Jadunath High School of Hazaribagh and the Sundarwati Balika Vedyalaya of Bhagalpur, all are continuing the work of education with success. Interestingly enough, the constitution of Rammohan Roy Seminary drafted in 1910, envisaged the wishes of the pioneers to introduce "secular progressive education"—and objective hardly thought of or understood in the pre-Independence era.[16] Another contribution was the effort for spreading literacy among the downtrodden and the deprived sections of the society by setting up night schools for Shudras and labourers in Patna Monghyr, Jamalpur and Gaya between 1910 and 1945. Yet another contribution was the promotion of library movement in the province. The Rajnarain Bose Library of Deoghar, the Union Library of Hazaribagh and the Rammohan Library of Patna are among the libraries established by the Brahmos. Their educational work entitled them to the distinction of being recognised as the first potent indigenous modernising force in Bihar.[17]

The Brahmo Samaj also acted as the agent of transformation so far as the status of women in the Bihari society is concerned. The Brahmo personalities like Aghore Kamini Devi, Brajagopal Niyogi, Sris Chakroborty and Sushama Sen played a vital role in releasing the womanhood of Bihar from the *purdah* and initiating the work of rescuing widows from traditional bondage.[18] The Anti-*purdah* Agitation, organised by Sushama Sen in 1928, was a turning-point in the movement for female emancipation. It had the blessings of Mahatma Gandhi and Sarojini Naidu.[19] Gandhi penned a few memorable lines in Young Indian appreciating the agitation.[20]

It is indeed surprising as to how such a forward-looking movement gradually declined and has, except in a few urban areas, gone into oblivion. Several factors account for it. As already observed, it was confined mainly to the educated middle-class Bengali elite. Reluctance to shake off this elitism stalled the expansion of the movement among the common folks in Bihar. Closely related to this had been the linguistic and doctrinal hindrances. Prayers and discourses were conducted in Bengali and English. Though some missionaries tried to make wide use of Hindi in the 1930's and 1940's, the effort was not continued. Moreover, even the switchover to Hindi was only partially successful, because the common folks found the Brahmo doctrine too unorthodox to be accepted. The monotheistic and unitrarian ideas preached by the Brahmos were beyond the grasp of a common individual. In a place where hundreds of deities were worshipped and numerous local cults were followed with unshakable faith, the Brahmo move against idol-worship and religious intolerance was bound to meet with severe opposition. Therefore, the orthodoxy and conservatism of the Bihari society was as much responsible for the failure of the Brahmo movement to gain sizeable following as the elitism of the Brahmos.

Again, the Brahmo Samaj lacked an organizational structure, a paid monkhood and financial patronage. The success of the later movements like the Arya Samaj and the Ramakrishna Mission was due to their having not only an efficient organization but also a trained and dedicated band of monks. The Brahmos belonged to professional bourgeoisie, and so, a Brahmo youth's mentality was oriented towards professionalism. Career-building and search for lucrative job was of prime importance to him, and in this frame of mind the mission work had the least appeal. As a result, the Brahmo movement in Bihar in the 1940's and 1950's was devoid of dedicated fulltime workers and missionaries. Moreover, the Samaj did not enjoy the financial support of a group of affluent patrons as possessed by the Arya Samaj and the Ramakrishna Mission. The Arya Samaj enjoyed the financial patronage of the *Baniyas*, while the R.K. Mission that of the affluent Bengali Hindus.

Lastly, the Brahmo ceremonies and functions were marked with a seriousness and tranquility which was too strange to have a popular appeal. It did not encourage any festivity with lot of fun and frolic, nor any lavish procession and ceremony, nor any pomp and grandeur in popular style, nor any popular cult of miracle and vegetarianism. Sublimity and purity were its watchwords in prayers and religious observances.

At present, the Brahmo Samaj does not possess much in Bihar except a few *mandirs* and educational institutions, which stand as relics to proclaim the sage of sacrifice of some souls. Surprisingly enough, the need for Brahmo movement is as urgent now as before with the emergence of fundamentalist forces and revival of social evils. With growing cases of ill-treatment to widows, wife burning and dowry deaths, the woman still remains unemancipated. The caste-system and dowry system are taking deeper roots in society despite legislation against them. The untenable notion about the obsoleteness of the movement contributed to its decline.

II

The Arya Samaj movement can also be regarded as an exceedingly remarkable aspect of the nineteenth century Indian awakening and socio-religious reformation. The way the Brahmo Samaj ventured itself as a regenerative force and catalytic agent in Bengal in the nineteenth and early decades of the twentieth centuries, the Arya Samaj wielded more or less similar influence upon the society of northern India, extending from the Punjab to Bihar, in the late nineteenth and the first half of the twentieth centuries. Though the Arya Samaj's doctrinal base lacked the broad perspective the profundity of its brahmo counter-part, it possessed that clarity and simplicity to appeal to a much larger section of the people. The movement was both protestant and purificatory in character. It was protestant because it raised a note of protest against the orthodox Hindu establishment marked by Brahminical preponderance. It was purificatory as it intended to purify traditional Hinduism from within rather than forming a separate religious sect with a distinguishable doctrinal base. If a separate sect emerged, it was due to the historical factor that such a thing happened. In other words, the Samaj's continuous involvement in the battle against the traditional socio-religious order rendered it a sectarian complexion contrary to its intention. In fact, the Arya Samaj movement is so much oriented to Hindu reformism that some scholars have even described it as some sort of effort at "Hindu revivalism.[21] While it cannot be denied that the Samaj's leading motto "back to the Vedas" demonstrates its rigid adherence to and unshakable faith in the infallibility of the *Vedas*, but at the same time, it has to be admitted that the movement emerged as the most potent modernising force in a large part of India where religious orthodoxy and social conservatism reigned supreme. Bihar is one such area where the Samaj's role was one of catalytic agent contributing to the process of modernisation.

Its activities in the province was characterised by endless endeavour for the acquisition and dissemination of knowledge, the tireless struggle for the emancipation of women and the continuous battle against the time-honoured orthodoxy, backwardness and superstition. It epitomised the attitude of non-conformity. The spirit of the new age was reflected in the setting up of numerous schools, libraries and gymnasiums in all parts of the province. The reformist activities that began in the last quarter of the proceeding century continued with greater momentum in the present century.

The arrival and sojourn of Swami Dayanand Saraswati at Patna in October 1872 heralded the initiation of the Arya Samaj movement in Bihar.[22] The indefatigable Swami with his lecture tours and reforming activities had already created a stir in the Punjab and United Provinces. On his way from Benaras to Calcutta he made a halt at Patna on 1 October 1872 and was so impressed by his reception here that he stayed for a month, putting up at the mansion of Raja Bhup Singh at Kumharar. A fairly large number of people which included many pundits and scholars flocked to the Raja's mansion to have a 'darshan' of the founder of the Samaj.[23] This period witnessed a noteworthy accomplishment. Under the Swami's guidance, his great follower Munshi Manohar Lal of Patna City wrote the solemn Arya text Satyartha Prakash's thirteenth volume. This was indeed a happy beginning of the Arya Samaj movement in this province.

The first *mandir* of the Samaj was established at Danapur, Patna in 1885. The Chapra Arya Samaj also came into being in that year. The influence of the Chapra Arya Samaj spread in the neighbouring areas and the Siwan Arya Samaj was founded in 1898. The Siwan Samaj was destined to become one of the chief centres of the Arya Samaj activities in Bihar. The only college founded by the Samaj in Bihar, the Dayanand Anglo-Vedic College is located at Siwan.

Then followed the foundation of the patna Arya Samaj, better known as the Bankipore Arya Samaj, which later became the nerve-centre of the Bihar Arya Samaj movement, in May 1908. The period 1926-27 marked a turning-point in the history of the Arya Samaj movement in Bihar. The Arya Samajis of Bihar and Bengal, till now under a single management, were now bifurcated, and the management of the Bihar Arya Samaj was entrusted upon a members-elected Arya Pratinidhi Sabha with head-quarters at Patna. By that year the number of Arya Samaj mandirs in Bihar had risen to 35, and each possessed on an average 40 workers, including Acharyas, Pracharaks, Upadeshaks and Sudharaks. The development of the Arya Samaj in Bihar can be gauged from the fact that at present it has about 450 branches and a few lakh members.[24]

The Samaj worked to free man-his body, soul and thought—from the bondage imposed by tradition and authority, and to lead him to the realm of freedom. The attitude of non-conformity and defiance was reflected in its struggle against the traditional socio-religious customs and cumbrous ceremonies. This brought the Samaj pracharaks and members into direct confrontation with the orthodox society, which often took violent turns. On the religious plane it caused a great stir when it allowed the *Vedas* to be read by members of all castes.[25] It initiated the system of Shastrartha, a religious discussion often taking the form of dialectic. The Shastrartha discussions often turned into acrimonious debate due to the strong bias of individuals belonging to the orthodox section. In such discussion the acharya or pracharak first presented a discourse on a subject ranging from the Vedic philosophy to the religious doctrine of the Arya Samaj. The question-answer session followed in which Aryas as well as non-Aryas (including a few Christians and Muslims) participated. The Shastrartha proved so damaging to the orthodox establishment that they started hate-campaign, combined with threat and intimidation, against the Samaj in several parts of Bihar, which sometimes turned violent.[26] This sort of violent resistance, which was a common occurrence in the thirties and forties of this century, very much dampened the spirit of the Samaj workers. They now thought of putting more emphasis on social reforms than upon proselytisation and the propagation of the religious ideas of the Samaj.

However, in its milder form the Shastrartha continued because it was an essential means not only for the spread of Arya doctrine but also for the removal of age-old social evils. The Shastrarthas emphasised the Vedic infallibility and also stressed the point that the greatness of man depended upon his work (Karma), not upon his caste (Varna) or birth (Janma). This message had a special appeal for the members of the backward castes, who not only held an inferior social status but were subjected to many disabilities and restrictions in the traditional system. This resulted in a good number of the members of the Baniya, Kurmi and Koiri castes, a conglomeration of the Vaishya and high Surdras, joining the Samaj. These intermediary castes were doing well in trade and commerce. But they cannot be regarded as a sort of commercial bourgeoisie because in a tradition-bound and caste-ridden society they were straining under several deterrents. In Bihar's society the members of these lower castes were not allowed to sit or to eat together along with those of the upper castes. This custom continued well into the twentieth century and is still continuing so far as the scheduled castes or Harijans are concerned, if not the backward or intermediary castes in all cases. The significant point is that by joining the Samaj they primarily gained a higher social status and thus bridged the traditional gap with the upper castes to a recognisable extent. Here the Samaj effected the process of Sanskritisation or upward social mobility for intermediary castes. Thus the Samaj prepared to a large extent, the way for the entrance of these backward castes into the fold of the commercial bourgeoise. Broadening of the economic base was a potent motivation behind their joining the Samaj. Of course, the economic motivation must not be overemphasised. Many of these *Baniya* individuals were not very much eager to elevate their social status, inspite of possessing considerable fortune. The chief urge among the Bihari backward castes in joining the new movement was, besides spiritual satiation, their search for an egalitarian society that would recognise their status as man. They certainly received it. If commercial interest or economic motivation was on their part, it was equally there on the part of the founders and *pracharaks* of the Samaj. The Arya Samaj leaders wanted to enrol these backward caste individuals into the fold of the Samaj partly because they needed to be socially and culturally elevated and partly because they possessed wealth. And as already noted, it was on the land and money of these wealthy castes that the physical structure of the Samaj was built up in various districts of Bihar. This explains the fact that the members of the backward castes and business communities, particularly the Baniyas, played a prominent role in the Arya Samaj movement in the province. It is true that they rarely held the positions of acharya or *prachark* because of the lack of knowledge in the *Vedas* and *Shastras*, but they made the maximum contribution in material terms.

Besides upgrading the status of lower castes another outstanding contribution of the Arya Samaj has been the spread of education. In fact, education was itself a means of elevating the lower caste man as well as enlightening the upper caste men, and thus the Samaj helped the development of man and society in Bihar. The remarkable points about the Arya Samaj's work in the sphere of education are : firstly, the spread of education was not only an objective and ideal of the Samaj, but also a necessary means for its survival in the conservative Bihari society. The hold of the religious traditions was so strong that the Samaj could not make much of an impact with its religious doctrine. Rather it aroused strong opposition. So the Samaj had to get involved in the work of education in justify its existence. Wherever in Bihar the Samaj opened its Mandir, a school and a library became its essential parts. The schools did not arouse direct opposition of the orthodox people. At worst they did not receive children from these families. But children from liberal families and educationally backward lower caste families flocked to these schools in fairly large number. In course of time these schools proved their worth and children from orthodox families too were being sent there. This proved to be favourable to the Samaj in another way. A good number of students of these schools, influenced by the Arya ideals, their austere and honest life and good deeds, would later join the Samaj. Thus, the schools, besides spreading education, helped to augment the number of Arya Samajis.

The second noteworthy point about the Samaj's work in the sphere of education is that both the D.A.V. School pattern of Lala Hansraj and the Gurukul pattern of Swami Shraddhananda were applied without the slightest evidence of schism in the Samaj. The D.A.V. pattern put emphasis upon modern education and included study of science and English. But the Gurukul pattern emphasised upon the Vedic studies in the ancient Gurukul environment. However, the Gurukul system was gradually liberalised in Bihar and it later included study of other subjects too, even English and Science in some cases. The schools run on the D.A.V. pattern are overwhelmingly larger in number, the famous among them are, the D.A.V. High School Siwan, the D.A.V. School, Chapra, the Dayanand High School, Khagaria. Among the schools run on the Gurukul pattern the well-known ones are Gurukul High Schools of Deoghar, Chapra, Sitamarhi (Bairgenia) and Danapur.

Thirdly, an extremely important aspect of the Samaj's work in the field of education is its emphasis upon female education. This has been the most noteworthy aspect of the Samaj's endless endeavour for female emancipation. It, along with the Christian mission and the Bramo Samaj, played a vital role for the spread of female education in Bihar. This was done by it in the face of opposition from a conservative society which not only assigned woman's place in the kitchen, but also put her within the veil. The Samaj workers took this as a challenge and responded to it with courage and determination. Under their initiative and patronage female education made steady progress in the province. An interesting point is that the Samaj set up both middle and high schools for girls. In many areas where parents did not send their daughters to school after an advanced age, the middle schools proved very useful, and they attracted good number of girls from the outset. The girls' high schools, established and managed by the Samaj, were equally successful. In fact, female education made slow but steady progress and many of the Samaj's middle schools were upgraded to high schools. Famous among these high schools are the Arya Kanya Uchcha Vidyalayas of Siwan, Chapra, Patna, Gopalganj, Muzaffarpur and Khagaria. The accomplishment of the Samaj can be measured from the fact that none of the girls' schools set up by it proved defunct, rather their enrollment of students increased and new ones came into existence all over the province.

Lastly, the Samaj took the lamp of learning not only to women, but also to be downtrodden and the deprived sections of the society. At several place including Patna and Siwan it ran schools for the sole purpose of educating low-caste or Shudra children. Thus, in some respects it anticipated the Harijan uplift movement of the past. Independence period. The D.A.V. Dalitoddhar Pathshbalas of Patna and several other places had been very successfully managed by the Samaj. Many children, who had remained hated, neglected and deprived, chained in the age-old shackles of untouchability, entered a new and respectable life after receiving education from the Samaj schools. However, it must be noted that the Samaj had to establish separate schools for the lower caste children because of the upper caste insistence on segregation. It gradually brought the lower caste children in its unsegregated schools, but for doing this it again had to struggle hard against the orthodox section of the society.

The Arya Samaj made efforts to bring social reform in several other ways too. The Samaj mandirs solemnised numerous interests and intercommunal marriages. The Arya marriage ceremony is simple, clear and inexpensive. So, several individuals, who opposed caste conformity and dowry, have resorted to Arya system of marriage. The Arya Samajis set up Jatpat Torak Samiti to fight against caste and dowry systems. All these certainly helped to create feeling against caste system. However, the Samaj's success in the eradication of the caste system has been rather limited. In Bihar's society the individual's caste has been a dominant factor in his life. It decided several important issues of his life. It was, and still continues to be, a social platform, an identity badge and a communication point. It is a safety-value which offered him security and safeguard against competitors from other castes, and the amount of support he received from his castemen was often an index of his success or failure. In such rigidly discriminatory caste system, the Samaj's achievement obviously has been a meagre one. So, what the Brahmo Samaj could do in Bengal even in its limited role of linking the *Bhadralok* castes through education and marriage and thus initiating a process of social mobility, the Arya Samaj's record in Bihar fell for short of it. Several Arya Samajis regretingly told this researcher that the virus of casteism is so widespread that it is infecting the Samaj itself, though to a limited extent. In the Samaj's elections these caste prejudices sometimes appear on the surface. This is definitely shocking and shows the peak of irrationality that some Samaj members themselves are in the grip of the evil they are supposed to wipe out.

The Arya Samaj movement, undoubtedly, began as a force of non-conformity. But since 1940's its activities in Bihar were so much directed towards Shuddhi, Go Raksha and Hindi Raksha that it conveyed the impression of being the chief protector of traditional Hinduism. It launched the Shuddhi movement or the 'purification process' on a fair scale to bring back to the fold of Hinduism those individuals who had been converted earlier as Muslims and Christians.[27] It also set up the Go Raksha Samitis or cow protection societies which brought it close to communal organisations like the Hindu Mahasabha.[28] Again, the members of the Arya Samaj in all parts of the province actively participated in the country's freedom struggle. They helped the growth of nationalist spirit. The British authorities resorted to severe measures against the Arya Samaj members for their active participation in the Civil Disobedience Movement and the Quit India Movement.[29] But the brand of nationalism advocated by the Arya Samajis was basically religious in character. It glorified the ancient Indian cultural heritage and hinted at the supremacy of Hinduism. Thus, the Samaj gradually turned into a citadel for safeguarding the interests of Hindus, Hinduism and Hindi.

Yet, the Arya Samaj's role in the development of man and society in Bihar has been a positive one. The members of the Samaj worked with dedication and devotion to bring reform and change in several spheres of society. Its accomplishment in the sphere of education has been outstanding. Here it came not only as a regenerative but also as a modernising force. It is true that the Samaj's achievements in Bihar, when compared with those in the northern part of the country, appear to be less significant. But in making an estimate of its role, we must always keep in mind the hazards an obstructions it had to face in a conservative society like that of Bihar. Taking them into consideration its achievements in the province stand out as noteworthy.

III

Among other religious groups which left their reformist mark on the society of Bihar, mention may be made of the Ramakrishna Mission, Theosophical Society and Kabirpanth. The Ramakrishna movement was formally launched with the establishment of the Ramakrishna Math and Mission of Jamshedpur in 1920. The followers of the movement had particular attraction for Bihar because Ramakrishna Paramhansa, Swami Vivekananda and Sister Nivedita had visited the province several times, being fascinated by the natural beauty and devotional atmosphere of Bodh-Gaya and Deoghar.[30] In 1922, Mission branches were set up at Deoghar and Patna. The R.K. Mission Ashram of Patna gradually became the chief centre of the movement in Bihar. The ranchi branch of the Mission was set up in 1927, and very soon it became an active centre.[31] With the passage of time the movement spread it influence to other parts of the province. It was fortunate to enjoy the financial patronage, particularly of the Bengali Hindus in the province. Moreover its organizational structure was large and contained dedicate men. Again, unlike the Brahmo Samaj, it made extensive use of Hindi and thus attracted a much larger following.

Inspired by the ideals of Ramakrishna and Vivekananda, the Mission workers did constructive work in the fields of education and humanitarian service. The Ramakrishna Mission Vidyapitha of Deoghar and the Ramakrisha Mission Vivekananda Society of Jamshedpur are among the highly reputed educational institutions in Bihar. An outstanding work in the sphere of education has been Divyayan. It is a residential rural development institution set up with the objective of training rural youths in agriculture, dairy and poultry farming, horticulture and community service.[32] It is an excellent institution and stands as a model training centre for rural development work. It has trained a large number of rural youths, particularly of the tribal areas. Besides these, the Students' Home and the Turiyananda Library in the R.K. Mission Ashrama premises at Patna are among the great contributions of the movement. The Ramakrishna movement in Bihar can also be credited with humanitarian services for the poor peoples. It set up a good number of charitable dispensaries, hospitals and a T.B. sanstorium.

But the role of the movement in social reform is an extremely limited one. It hardly made any attempt to fight against social evils like caste-system and dowry system. It never took any initiative in arranging intercaste marriages. It devoted itself in preserving some traditional customs and conventions of the Hindu society. The Durga Puja, the Kali Puja and the Kumari Puja are celebrated with great enthusiasm at the Mission's ashramas, Regular discourses on the *Vedas* and *Ramacharit Manas* are conducted at the Ashrama halls. The Hindu revivalist trend is clearly visible. One scholar views the movement as the revival of the Sanatana Dharma.[33] Yet it deserves a noteworthy place in the province's modern history for its role in promoting modern education and for its humanitarian work.

The Theosophical movement began in Bihar with the establishment of the first Lodge of the Theosophical Society at Bhagalpur in 1882. The movement with its emphasis on pure life, attainment of wisdom, love for all human beings irrespective of caste, community, race or religion and religious tolerance[34] made great appeal to the educated section of the society. The movement in Bihar was fortunate to have the active involvement of eminent theosophists like Col. Olcott, Annie Besant, Dr. G.S. Arundale and his wife Rukmini Arundale.[35] Within a few months after the establishment of the Bhagalpur Lodge, the Theosophical Lodges came up at Gaya, Arrah and Patna. It attracted educated people of all castes and communities. Some Muslims also became members of the society.

The movement received a great impetus with the opening of branches at Deoghar, Monghyr, Jamalpur, Siwan, Muzaffarpur and Hajipur and the formation of the Bihar Theosophical Federation at Patna in 1900. It possessed activists and patrons like Tej Narayan Singh, Purnendu Narain Sinha and Maharaja Lakshmishwar Singh of Darbhanga. Tej Narayan Singh was a rich and influencial resident of Bhagalpur, and the guiding spirit of the Lodge there. He set up a school at Bhagalpur to educate children in true theosophic spirit. This school in course of time became the famous Tej Narayan Jubilee College and at present, known as the T.N.B. College. The theosophists set up schools in other places too. Purnendu Narayan Sinha, a government advocate of Patna, had established the P.N. Anglo Sanskrit School at Patna. The movement attracted a good number of educated Biharis, which the Brahmo Samaj had failed to do. This was mainly due to the importance it attached to a pure life guided by a moral code and the emphasis it put on the ancient Indian cultural heritage, plus its wide use of Hindi in lectures and discourses.

Inspite of having active and dedicated workers, the movement showed a definite decline since the 1940's. Like the Brahmo Samaj it depended upon the professional bourgeoisie for its sustenance. Again, like the former, it lacked an organizational structure with paid workers. Being elitist in character it survived so long as it possessed devoted leaders and rich patrons. Moreover, its commitment to social reform was a limited one. It certainly spoke against social evils, but never took up cudgel against the caste-system or dowry system. It taught against social evils, but cautiously. For example, one of its schools, the Hindu Collegiate School, had put restriction on the admission of married students: this was done to discourage child-marriages. Yet its contributions in the sphere of education and enlightenment are still remembered and a few institutions still stand as monument to the dedication and devotion of the early Theosophists.

The Kabir Panthi movement was the most populist in character. With inspiration and guidance coming from the Kabir Panthi headquarters at Kabir Chaurah, Benaras, the movement spread to all parts of Bihar and attracted mainly the lower caste people like Koiris, Kahars, Chamars, Dusadhs and Pasis. There were some upper caste members too, particularly Brahmins and Rajputs. The simple preachings of Kabir based on love, brotherhood, peace and fellow-feeling appealed to a large section of the people. If the Arya Samaj movement attracted the intermediary castes, particularly the Baniyas, the Kabir Panthi movement brought in large number of lower caste people within its fold. Kabir *Sangathans* were set up in Patna. Monghyr and Gaya initially, and later branches came up in other places. Prayers and discourses were regularly held. It definitely helped to bring different castes on a single platform. That is in itself a sort of silent social revolution at the grass-roots level.

To sum up, all the reform movements with difference of degree left their mark in the field of education. Education was the most fundamental and convenient means for effecting social reform particularly in the matter of female emancipation. The liberal, progressive and forward-looking movements like the Brahmo Samaj and Theosophical Society did not succeed for their limited appeal and elitist character. Their assimilative and synthetic attitude also proved a deterrent factor. The Arya Samaj and the Ramkrishna movements, on the other hand, could sustain themselves due to well-built organizational structure and steady patronage, but more due to their adherence to the main body of Hinduism. Without undermining their great contributions, it cannot be denied that they somehow fostered the revivalist forces and stalled the emergence of a broad composite unifying culture.

References

1. Singh Yogendra, *Modernization of Indian Tradition*, Faridabad, 1977 p. 43.
2. Jones, Kenneth W. *Socio-Religious Reform Movements in British India*, Cambridge, 1989, p. 3.
3. *Ibid.*
4. *Ibid.*
5. *Ibid*, p. 4
6. Niyogi Sumanta, *The Brahmo Samaj Movement and Development of Education 1870-1975 : A Case Study of Bihar*, Patna, 1986, p. 2.
7. A term used to indicate the educated middle class elite of Bengal consisting chiefly, if not essentially, of Brahmins, Kayasthas and Vaidyas, See J.H. Broomfield, *Elite Conflict in a Plural Society*, Berkley, 1968, pp. 1-20 and N.K. Bose, *Modern Bengal*, Calcutta, 1959, for the picture of the bhadralok society.
8. Majumdar B.B. "Religious Movements in the Hindu Community in Bihar 1869-61, "in K.K. Datta (ed.). *Comprehensive History of Bihar*, Vol. III, Part II, Patna 1976, p. 6.

9. Bhattacharya Sutapa, "The Brahmo Samaj Movement in Bihar " A Study of its Socio-religious Dimensions, "unpublished Ph.D. Thesis, Patna University, 1983, p. 53.
10. Sastri Sivanath, *History of the Brahmo Samaj,* Calcutta 1974 (new edition), p. 525.
11. Sophia Dobson Collet, *Brahmo Year Book,* 1868.
12. Bhattacharya Sutapa, *op. cit.,* p. 57.
13. Narain V.A. "The Role of Non-Bengalis in the Brahmo Movement in Bihar," In S. Niyogi (ed.) *The 94th All India Brahmo Conference Souvenir,* Patna, 1984, p. 55.
14. Sastri Sivanath, op. cit., p. 524.
15. Pandey S.N. *Education and Social Changes in Bihar 1900-21,* Varanasi, 1975, p. 167: P.N. Misra and N.K. Jha, "Social and Religious Reform Movements in Bihar in the 19th and 20th centuries "in S.P. Sen (ed), *Social and Religious Reform Movements in the 19th and 20th Centuries,* Calcutta, 1979, pp. 108-10.
16. Guha, Rajanikanta, *Atmacharit* (autobiography in Bengali), Calcutta, 1949, p. 304 also see the constitution of t' ? Seminary kept in the Old Files Collection of the school at Patna.
17. Bhattacharya, *op. cit.,* 276-82.
18. Sen Sushama, *Memoir of an Octogenarian,* New Delhi, pp. 311-36.
19. *Young India,* 28 June 1928; also see the *Searchlight* 11 July 1928.
20. Desai A.R. *Social Background of Indian Nationalism,* Bombay, pp. 136-7, 290-2; Sumit Sarkar *Bibliographical Survey of Social Reform Movements in the Eighteenth and Nineteenth Centuries,* ICHR, New Delhi, 1975, p. 42. Also read the presidential speech of Prof. K.N. Pandikkar in the Modern India Section, *Proceedings of the Indian History Congress,* Aligarh Session, 1975.
21. Singh Asha, "The Arya Samaj Movement in Bihar 1872-1950", unpublished Ph.D. thesis, Patna University 1985, p. ^7.
22. Niyogi S. "The contribution of Arya Samaj in the Development of Man and Society in Bihar", in Swami Vedantananda, (ed), *Religion in Bihar in Modern Age,* Patna, 1984, p. 76.
23. Singh Asha, *op. cit.* pp. 76-82.
24. *Ibid,* p. 57.
25. *Ibid,* p. 62.
26. Kenneth Jones, *The Arya Samaj,* New Delhi, 1978, p. 36.
27. *Ibid,* p. 280.
28. Prabhananda Swami "The Ramkrishna Movement in Bihar "in Swami Vedantananda (ed). *Religion in Bihar in the Modern Age,* Patna, 1984, pp. 85-86.
29. *Ibid,* p. 88.
30. *Annual Report of the Ramakrishna Mission Ashram,* Morabadi Hills, Ranchi. 1983, p. 2.
31. Chattopadhyaya Siddheswar, "Revival of the Sanatana Dharma in Bihar in the 19th and 20th Centuries and its Impact," in Swami Vedantananda (ed) op. cit. p-19.
32. Sinha, Ramjivan, *Hundred Years of the Theosophical Society and Theosophy,* Patna, 1982, p. 11.
33. *Ibid,* 13, *Ibid,* p. 12.
34. Misra P.N. and Jha N.K. *op. cit.,* p. 111
35. *The Searchlight,* 5 December 1918, also see Misra and Jha, *op. cit.* p. 112.

Aspects of Indian History and Historiography
Editor : P.K. Mishra
Kaveri Books, New Delhi, India.

The Quit India Movement and the Tamralipta Jatiya Sarkar

7

P.K. Maity

Introduction

In the history of India's freedom struggle the place of Midnapore (West Bengal) is undisputable.[1] The history of freedom movement in India is vast and varied. In order to free India from the autocratic British rule, two opposite methods—methods of violence (i.e., adoption of extreme measures) and methods of non-violence preached by Gandhiji—were followed by the Indians. The impact of both the methods fell on Midnapore district. The freedom struggle in Midnapore was nothing but an echo of the all India freedom struggle. Yet it must be kept in mind that in all the phases of freedom movement the people of Midnapore including women took the leading part.[2] Although in different times the people of Midnapore shed their blood and tears to keep their freedom and suffered in various ways, their love for freedom could not be curbed down. Thus Midnapore is a name to reckon with in India's struggle for freedom.

In the Quit India movement, the last massive anti-British movement in India, the people of Midnapore played a very important and historic role. The history of the twentieth century Midnapore is the history of sacrifice and valour for the national cause. Here an attempt is made to throw light on the Quit India movement at Tamluk sub-division[3] and on the *Tamralipta Jatiya Sarkar*.

Before we actually deal with the Quit India movement at Tamluk sub-division, we shall speak something about the Pre-movement condition of the sub-division to have a clear idea about the gravity of the movement in comparison with other places of undivided Bengal, nay India.

Second World War and its Impact

Immediately after the outbreak of the Second World War, the Defence of India act was brought into operation at Tamluk sub-division and meetings and processions were banned,[4] possibly considering the past role of the people in national movement especially in the Civil Disobedience Movement.[5] This prohibitory Order made it difficult for the Congress Organisations to make easy contact with the messes. However, when Gandhiji launched his individual *satyagraha* movement on the 17th October, 1940 as a moral protest against the Second World War, thirty six *satyagrahis* from Tamluk participated and were imprisoned.[6] Among the one thousand selected *satyagrahis* throughout India,[7] the participation of thirty six from Tamluk sub-division suggests the strength of the Congress organisation of Tamluk in all India perspective.

The participation of Japan as an ally of the Axis powers in the Second World War in December, 1941 made the British government worried. Further the fall of Singapore and Malaya (1942, February) and the rapid advance of the Japanese forces in Burma posed a serious threat to the security of India. Under these circumstances, probably in April, 1942 Tamluk sub-division along with other parts of Midnapore was declared 'an emergency area'[8] for fear of Japanese invasion from a Bay of Bengal. Against this political background the government withdrew most of the motor buses from the roads, destroyed or removed all types of boats from the banned area and *seized* all bi-cycles from the area of our study.[9] These caused great hardship to the people in regard to conveyance and earnings.

Boats were the most important means of conveyance in the estuarial area of Tamluk, export and import of goods in the area solely depending on boats. Export of paddy, rice and hay was the basis of the local cash economy. This solely depended on boats, since water transport was the only means of communication with areas outside especially in the Sundarbans in the district of South 24-Parganas. A large number of people including land-holders, cultivators and traders depended on agriculture and trade of the Sundarbans. The fishermen living in Tamluk were also entirely dependent on boats. Essential like kerosene, medicine, cloth, spices etc. were brought from outside by boats.[10] Thus the destruction as well as the removal of boats from the region caused hardship to the livelihood and prosperity of the people.

Besides, some parts of the area had already suffered from the failure of *aman* crops in 1940 and deficiency of food in the next year. As the year of 1941 was a deficit year so far as the food situation of the sub-division was concerned, the sub-divisional Congress committee (henceforth SDCC) decided to stop any export of paddy and rice from the area concerned. With this view in mind the Congress leaders of this sub-division sent a deputation to the District Magistrate but it was of no use. The government followed the policy of exporting paddy and rice from the region instead of importing food-grains from outside to meet the deficit in future.[11] Practically the government began to procure food grains to build up stocks for the army. Procurement of paddy and rice by force was done through agents of a Company named Ispahani and Co. from the end of 1941. This also enraged the people to a great extent.[12]

To cope with this reactionary governmental policy and to make close contact with the masses to mobilise opinion against the autocratic government, SDCC of Tamluk decided to raise a large band of volunteers known as *Svechchhasevak Bahini*. Among the six *thanas* under undivided Tamluk sub-division, Mahisadal and Sutahata *thanas* took the initiative in this matter. Later on, a *Svechchhasevak Bahini* was formed at Tamluk *thana*. At Mahisadal and Sutahata *thanas* two trained volunteer corps numbering about three thousand volunteers including fifty female volunteers were formed in the course of one month.[13] The number soon rose to five thousand. "Several camps were started to train these volunteers. "Bhagini Sena Sibir" (Sisters' Army Camp) was also started at Sutahata. These camps were especially meant for full-time workers. Many prominent leaders including Dr. Prafulla Chandra Ghosh, member of Congress Working Committee, Dr. Suresh Chandra Banerjee, S. Annada Prasad Chowdhury and Sj. Panchanan Basu, paid visit to the sub-division and inspired the people. Side by side with recruitment of volunteers a large sum of money and rice and paddy were collected. Our workers appealed to the people to be fearless and to organise themselves for resisting all sorts of oppression, and advised them to grow more food, to produce necessaries as far as possible, to use only indigenous article and to preserve food grains inside the sub-division and not to allow them to be exported."[14]

The Quit India Movement Till the Establishment of the Tamralipta Jatiya Sarkar

The Quit India movement radically different from other two earlier movements launched by Mahatma Gandhi, was organised on the basis of a programme already drawn up by the All India Congress Organisation. The twelve-point Programme which includes a day long *haratal*, fasting and prayer, processions in the villages, explanation of *satyagraha* through meetings, breaking of salt-laws, non-payment of taxes, etc.[15] is said to have been prepared by the All India Congress leaders under Gandhi's instructions or with his consent, before 9 August, 1942.[16] An additional note to this programme declared that the final phase of the movement would lead to the "breaking of salt laws on a large scale, picketing of foreign cloth and liquor shops, promoting industrial strikes, holding up of railways and telegraphs, calling army to come out, non-payment of taxes, setting up of a parallel government."[17]

It was decided by the All India Congress Committee (hereafter AICC) meeting that Gandhiji would lead the movement on the basis of the principle of non-violence on the widest possible scale.[18] It was further resolved : "A time may come when it may not be possible to issue instructions or for instructions to reach our people, and when no Congress Committee can function. When this happens, every man and woman, who is participating in this movement must function for himself or herself within the four corners of the general instructions issued. Every Indian who desires freedom and strives for it must be his own guide urging him on along the hard road where three is no resting place and which leads ultimately to the independence and deliverance of India".[19]

After the adoption of the historic Quit India Resolution on Saturday, the 8th August, 1942, Gandhiji urged the members present in the AICC meeting in Bombay that "everyone of you should from this moment onwards consider yourself a free man or woman and act as if you are free.... I am not going to be satisfied with anything short of complete freedom... We shall do or die. We shall either free India or die in the attempt."[20]

The British Indian Government did not remain silent; rather they made all preparations to crush the movement at the initial stage. Thus just after the termination of the AICC meeting late at night on 8th August, 1942, the Government started its operation before the dawn of the next day by arresting Gandhiji and many other Congress leaders and banning the AICC and all provincial Congress Committees except in North West Frontier Province.[21]

The Quit India resolution of 8 August and the arrest of Congress leaders including Gandhiji on the next day were "immediately followed by peaceful and non-violent popular demonstrations in the shape of *hartals* and processions over nearly the whole of India"[22] and Tamluk sub-division, in particular. Here also *hartals* were organised and numerous demonstrations were held after 9th August on many occasions before the government offices, police stations and law courts etc. Public meetings were also held in front of these places. The meetings and processions consisted of 5000 to 10,000 people irrespective of caste and creed.[23] In those meetings the Congress leaders tried to arouse national feeling among the masses and to unite them against the British oppression by reading and explaining the Quit India resolutions.[24] One such meeting held in front of Mahisadal *thana* and attended by about two thousand people, Mr. Wazir Ali Shaik, I.C.S., the Sub-divisional Officer of Tamluk, ordered Police constables to arrest the speakers of the meeting, but the crowd opposed the attempt. Mr. Shaik then asked the constables to make a *lathi* charge to disperse the demonstrations. But the constables refused.[25] This incident throws light on the solidarity of the freedom-loving masses as well as their faith on the leadership for the local congress organisation. It is well recorded that hundred of such meetings were arranged[26] possibly with a view to make close mass contact so that the movement would be successful.

In the meantime a new Sub-divisional Congress Committee was formed and Susil Kumar Dhara became the Secretary of the SDCC. The students of this sub-division had played a great role in this movement.[27] The student force appears to have strengthened the hands of the Tamluk SDCC.[28] Out of the volunteer corps known as *Svechchhasevak Bahini* already existed in Mahisadal, Sutahata and Tamluk *thanas*, a separate volunteer force, consisting of specially selected young men and students was set up first at Sundara under Mahisadal thana and then at Sutahata, Nandigram and Tamluk *thanas*. The students and the youths associated with separate volunteer force received primary military training in drill and attack on the line of guerilla tactics as well as basic training to attend the casualties under the guidance of Susil Kumar Dhara who commanded the volunteer corps of Mahisadal. Originally this corps had three branches, namely action, intelligence and nursing. The Mahisadal volunteer corps of specially chosen persons named *Vidyut Bahini* was formally inaugurated on 26 September, 1942 by the veteran Congress leader Sri Baradakanta Kuiti, though the said *Bahini* functioned from the middle of August. Women Volunteers were also recruited at Sutahata and Mahisadal *thana* to form a *bhagini Sena Bahini* (Army Organisation of Woman fighters). This *Bahini* scheduled to be inaugurated on the 17 October, 1942 was inaugurated on 19 October by Sri Susil Kumar Dhara at the village Dariberia under Sutahata *thana*. Thus the army organisation including men and women was formed under the able guidance of Susil Kumar Dhara who led the militia of Tamluk during the Quit India movement.[29] When the *Tamralipta Jatiay* Sarkar was established this army organisation i.e., both *Bidyut Bahini* and *Bhagini Sena Bahini* became the National Army of the Jatiya Sarkar, and then the total members of this *Bahini* rose to about five thousand.

Police-mass direct confrontation began in Tamluk sub-division on 8 September, 1942 when a crowd of two thousand five hundred persons tried to stop the export of rice by the mill-owners at Danipur under Mahisadal *thana*. The police opened fire and killed three people. The dead bodies were not handed over to the people and were burnt in one single pyre. This enraged the people to a great extent. On the other hand, to take revenge the District Magistrate raided the surrounding villages next day and arrested two hundred villagers. "They were made to sit in the sun the whole day. They were not given any food. Only thirteen persons were sent up and sentenced to different terms of imprisonment, ranging from 1 1/2 years to 2 years. The mill owners had to bow to public opinion. They were fined Rs. 2000 which was promptly paid. Out of this Rs. 1500 was paid to the families of the bereaved. The mill owners expressed regret for having exported paddy and promised not to do so in future."[30]

Another confrontation took place on the 27th September, 1942 at Iswarpur in Nandigram *thana* where the police had gone to arrest two persons in the local Congress office. A large crowd surrounded the police who at first set fire on the thatched house of the Congress Office and then opened fire in order to find an escape route. As a result four persons were dead and twenty five persons were injured. Yet the mob followed the police party upto Narghat police camp situated at a distance of about five km. from Iswarpur. To disperse the mob the police first used the *lathi* charge and then opened fire. The mob dispersed but they destroyed the Narghat ferry building. sub-register's office, boats, etc.[31]

Almost similar firing incident occurred next day, 28 September, 1942 at Brindabanpore, a nearby village of Iswarpur under Nandigram *thana*. As a result two persons died and three persons were seriously injured.[32] Commenting on the Police-mass confrontation the District magistrate wrote : "The villagers were roused to a state of fury ... They were ready for a sort of guerrilla warfare."[33]

Against this background the War Council (*Samarparisad*) of Tamluk subdivision had already been formed and the important Congress leaders in a meeting decided to organize mass action against the government.[34] In the history of India's freedom struggle, September 29, 1942 was a remarkable day because on that day a concerted move was taken by the freedom fighters of Tamluk sub-division to occupy the police stations and government offices at Tamluk, Mahisadal and Sutahata in a peaceful manner. On the next day similar attempt was made at Nandigram P.S. of the same sub-division. No such attempts were made at Panskura and Moyna Police stations—both belonging to Tamluk sub-division-due to the lack of proper Congress organisation.

Detailed preparations were made for raiding the police stations and steps were made to draw as many persons as possible and to insulate police-station buildings from any outside help. During the night of 28 September, the important link roads of Tamluk sub-division were cut off at several points and many culverts on the roads were broken. Big trees were felled to block the roads and big holes were dug on the road. Telegraph and telephone lines were cut off.[35]

Tamluk, Mahisadal and Sutahata Police Stations were raided on the afternoon of 29 September. At Tamluk town about twenty thousand people marched towards the police station in five processions from different connecting roads, and the seventy three year old woman *Satyagrahi*, Matangini Hazra,[36] a widow who was at the head of one such procession, was shot at and she died a martyr's death, still holding on the national flag in her hand. Besides Matangini, other nine persons including Lakshminarayan Das (13) and Purimadhab Pramanik (14) died martyr's death on that day at Tamluk town.

The Mahisadal police station was raided by a crowd of about 20000 people and heavy firing killed thirteen persons there, Whereas the Sutahata police station fell to the raiders numbering about 4000 persons. The O.C. of the Police Station and other constables were at once disarmed and the crowd led by the *Bidyut Bahini* set fire to the Police Station building.

The Nandigram police station was raided on the 30 September by a crowd of 10000 persons. As a result of the police firing four persons were dead on the spot and another person died later at the Tamluk Government Hospital.

Though heavy firing had beaten back the mob in three police stations, between 29 and 30 September the local civil administration collapsed in Tamluk sub-division. The region passed under the control of the Congress organisation which attempted to cut off the police stations from the sub-divisional headquarter. Even attempts were made to isolate the latter from the district headquarter i.e. Midnapore. This chaotic situation had been well recorded by the District Magistrate who writes that "large crowds of peasantry are roaming all over the countryside, ready to fall on and overpower any small government agency".[37]

The people of the Tamluk sub-division became so anti-government that they went on destroying the government offices of any kind roads, telegraph and telephone lines with a view to paralysing the British administration there. Referring to these disturbances M.M. Basu, I.C.S., Additional District Magistrate, Midnapore made the remark that "the attacks take place so suddenly and simultaneously that no preventive action could be taken beforehand. In many places information about threatened attacks was received extremely late owing to the fact that communication had been seriously sabotaged and information had to be sent by special messengers who had to select devious routes for avoiding molestation on the way."[38]

This national upsurge which was characterized by Herbert, Governor of Bengal, as a "large scale rebellion" made the government very much worried.[39] To cope with the situation military reinforcements were arranged very quickly. But still the people showed determined courage to oppose military move here and there. Such opposition often resulted in firing. Commenting on it M.M. Basu, A.D.M writes : "The mob in Tamluk sub-division is apparently not afraid of (Police or military) firing."[40] Almost a similar observation had been made by the Superintendent of Police who felt that "the troops who come should have automatic weapons (Brenguns and Tommyguns) and unlimited ammunition. One can never be sure as to what lengths they (the nationalist rebels) will go."[41] From these observations and from other Government sources it is known that the people in general were very hostile to the government. Only the Communists and a section of local Muslims supported the government.[42]

As the movement assumed a vigorous form in the Tamluk Sub-division, Gurukha and British soldiers were posted by founding camps in different parts of the sub-division to crush the movement. From these camps they used to go to the villages for raiding and they oppressed men and women in a manner which may be compared with Nazi methods. While raiding, the police did not hesitate to commit rape and it is well recorded that the police committed rape on 73 women also included the married, unmarried, widows and even women at advanced stage of preguamen. Among them one Sindubala Maity aged 21 was raped on 27.10.42 by two police men[43] and died after nine days. Besides raping, physical torture, arrest, burning of houses and similar other destructive measures were regularly carried out by the police.[44]

In spite of severe repression, the Congress leaders of the sub-division decided to carry on the movement. Repressive measures by the Government to crush the movement were followed as before. A cyclonic storm followed by tidal wave near the sea that swept over the district on October 16, 1942 with the aftermath of the famine immediately following it caused untold miseries to the people of this district, especially to the people of Tamluk and Contai Sub-divisions. The apathetic British Government took no steps to relieve the woes of the famine-stricken people fighting for freedom.[45] However, the local Congress leaders took a challenge and organised the 'Mahendra Relief Committee' at Tamluk. The Organisers of this Committee served the people in various ways and also infused patriotic spirit among them.

The Tamralipta Jatiya Sarkar and its Characteristic Features

The fire of patriotism burnt into leaping flames on the 17th of December, 1942 when India's first national government, *Tamralipta Jaitya Sarkar*, was established at Tamluk Sub-division with the aim of turning free India into a *Mahabharatiya Jukta rashtra*, of which this *Tamralipta Jatiya Sarkar* would form a part. This government was formed by the Tamluk Sub-divisional Congress Committee with a view to abolishing the British Government from the area and to offer better administration for fulfilling the aims and aspirations of the people. The constitution of this new government was in accordance with the following procedure : (1) one *Sarrbadhinayak* or Director and (2) several departments under their respective *Sachivas* or ministers. These departments were (i) Law and Order, (ii) Finance, (iii) Education, (iv) War, (v) Administration of justice, (vi) Home and Defence. There was also a provision for the formation of *Thana Jatiya Sarkars* of Tamluk Sub-divisions and on 26.1.43 *Thana Jatiya Sarkars* were established at Sutahata, Nandigram, Mahisadal and Tamluk. A *Thana Jatiya Sarkar* was set up subject to the control and supervision by the *Tamralipta Jatiya Sarkar*.

It is the noteworthy that on account of the exceptional circumstances of those days of turmoil, elections could not be held; so appointments were made by the sub-divisional Congress Committee. The *Sarbadhinayak* was to act freely within the limits set by the Congress Committee.

He himself was the War Minister. The first *Sarbadhinayak* was Satish Chandra Samanta, a veteran leader of the Sub-division. The successive *Sarbadhinayakas* were Ajoy Kumar Mukherjee, Satish Chandra Sahoo and Barada Kanta Kuiti, all veteran leaders of the Sub-division. Ajoy Kumar Mukherjee became the Finance Minister, Susil Kumar Dhara, the organiser of the *'Bidyut Bahini'* and *'Bhagini Sena'*, was in charge of the Home and Defence Ministry. The *Bidyut Bahini* and the *Bhagini Sena* became the National Militia of *Jatiya Sarkar* whose commander-in-chief was Sushil Kumar Dhara. Mr. Dhara, a legendary figure of the movement, also organised a *Garam Dal*, an action squad to take strong measures against those who were suspected of corruption, spying and anti-national activities. Besides the persons mentioned above, there were other persons who were in charge of the different departments of the *Tamralipta Jatiya Sarkar*. Under the able and efficient leadership the *Jatiya Sarkar* "gained wide popularity which it enjoyed undiminished till and after the day of its voluntary dissolution."[46]

The *Jatiya Sarkar* functioned from the 17th December, 1942 to 31st August, 1944 and it was dissolved on September 1, 1944 at the instance of Gandhiji. By 29th September, 1944, 150 congress workers associated with the *Jatiya Sarkar* surrendered to the government in obedience to the order of Gandhiji. Subsequently when Gandhiji came to Mahisadal on December 25, 1945, he praised the work of the *Jatiya Sarkar* as 'heroic and glorious'. On the 23rd January, 1973 when Srimati Indira Gandhi the Prime Minister, visited Tamluk, she paid glowing tribute to the martyrs of the place, especially to Matangini Hazra, for their sacrifice in the Quit India Movement.

Though the movement of 1942 was modelled as a non-violent movement, the arrest of Gandhiji and other leaders changed the character of the movement. In place of well-organised non-violent movement it appeared as an unorganised and a partly violent movement. The places where the movement turned to a violent one were Ashti and Chimur in Madhya Pradesh and Bhagalpur and Chhapra in Bihar. The reasons for the change of the character of the movement were the following—(i) lack of leadership believing in non-violent methods, (ii) repressive measures and denial policy followed by the British Government and (iii) the fear of invasion of India by Japan. Although this was the general picture of the Quit India movement of 1942 in India as a whole, yet there were some special characteristic features of this movement of tamluk sub-division which deserve special mention here.

First, as the other provinces or areas, the Congress leaders of Tamluk did not waste their power and energy by taking up disorganised and scattered armed revolts; they took sufficient time to organise the people with proper planning and patience and then started the movement. After the 'Quit India' proposal was adopted (9th August, 1942), the leaders of Tamluk sub-divisions took more than a month to organise and inspire the people. But in most places, the movement started in a scattered and disorganised manner.

Secondly the leaders of Tamluk had drawn up flawless plan and for its execution they depended much on the organisational side. As a result *Bidyut Bahini* (i.e. army organisation, formed on the 26th Sept., 1942) was formed and this *Bahini* became the National Militia when the *Tamralipta Jatiya Sarkar* was established at Tamluk Sub-division.

Thirdly, at that time challenging the British system of administration national governments were established in some places of India. At Contai and Tamluk Sub-divisions (Midnapore) similar national governments were established. Among all these national governments, the national government of Tamluk known as *Tamralipta Jatiya Sarkar* functioned for a longer period (from the 17th Dec., 1942 to 31st August, 1944).

Fourthly, what the *Tamralipta Jaitya Sarkar* did in its life time from the standpoint of performing duty, no national government of any other place could dream of. From the statements of the Government and of the then Chief Minister Fazlul Haque we know the role of *Tamralipta Jatiya Sarkar*. The government publication "Some Facts about the Disturbances in India (1942-43)" records : "in Midnapore in Bengal the operations of the rebels indicated considerable care and planning; effective warning system had been devised, elementary tactical principles were observed, for instance, encirclement and flanking moments clearly on pre-arranged signals. The forces of disorder were accompanied by doctors and nursing orderlies to attend the casualties and their intelligence system was efficient."[47] While addressing in the Bengal Legislative Assembly Fazluk Haque the then Prime Minister remarked : "Midnapore had a parallel government with its military and police forces and intelligence branch; it had its jails where people were imprisoned, and in some cases, the people had actually paralysed the government".[48] These observations throw light on the role of *Tamralipta Jatiya-Sarkar* which performed its duties very successfully as evident form its activities.[49]

Fifthly, in this movement the people of Midnapore in general and the people of Tamluk Sub-division in particular showed real enthusiasm and it became a mass movement in Tamluk Sub-division. In this context it is noteworthy that in August 1944 Richard Casey, Governor of Bengal, informed the Viceroy Lord Wavell, that the government's position in Tamluk was still 'difficult', indeed there had been a further 'deterioration' and "a high proportion of the inhabitants are in sympathy with the local 'National Government or Jatiya Sarkar' as it calls itself."[50]

Sixthly, the concerted move by the freedom-fighters of this sub-division to occupy the police-stations, government offices and so on in September, 1942 was peaceful and non-violent.

Seventhly, the *Bhagini Sena Bahini* (Army Organisation of woman fighters) that was formed (19th October, 1942) in connection with the Quit India movement was very significant. The *Bahini* was formed among the chosen female Congress workers with a view to saving the honour of women of the locality. As far as our knowledge goes no such women army organisation was formed in any part of India in connection with this movement.

Eighthly, the participation of the womenfolk in great numbers in this movement was also a speciality and their untold sufferings in various ways for the national cause deserve our admiration.[51]

Ninthly, the sacrifice of the camp-workers associated with the *Jatiya Sarkar* is also a point to be considered here. They lived in a very poor manner and the total quantity of food for an individual was prescribed only 200-250 grams per day.[52]

Lastly, the speciality in naming the National government at Tamluk Sub-division also draws our attention. The full name of this government was "*Mahabharatiya Juktarashtra—Tamralipta Jatiya Sarkar*". The Organisers of this *Jatiya Sarkar* had no parochial outlook as evident from the name of the national government of Tamluk Sub-division. They had a wider outlook.

Conclusion

On the basis of the above characteristic features of the Quit India movement of Tamluk Sub-division, it may be concluded that the people of this place by establishing a long-lived national government based on popular support earned a special place for themselves in the history of the freedom struggle of India.

References

1. Majumdar, R.C., *History of the Freedom Movement in India*, Vol.3, p. 653; Majumdar, R.C., *History of Modern Bengal*, Calcutta, 1981, pp. 339f. Commenting on the August Movement Prof. Majumdar writes : "The non-violent movement

of August 1942, marred by violence at many places was conducted almost all over the country but the most noteworthy struggle took place in the district of Midnapore in Bengal.... it can claim to be the greatest violent revolution in India during the British administration so far as objective, purpose and programme in political revolutions are concerned". (History of Modern Bengal, pp. 339-340); Maity, S.K., Freedom Movement in Midnapore, Vol. -1, p. 48.

2. For details the following works may be consulted : Bhattacharya, T.S., *Swadhinate Sangrame Medinipur*, Calcutta, 1973; Das, B.K., *Swadhinata Seangrame Medinipur*, 2 Vols., Calcutta, 1980 1984; Pramanik, P.K., *Swadhinata Sangrame Medinipur*, Calcutta, 1973; Goswami, G., *Banglar Haldighat Tamluk*, Calcutta, 1973; Brahmachari, B., *Mukti Sangramer Kahini*, Vol. -1 (History of Freedom Movement in Sutahata *thana*), Chaitanyapur, Midnapore, 1988; Bhakta, B.B., *Nandigrame Swadhinata Sangram*, Gopalpur, Midnapore, 1989; Maity, P.K., *Biyalliser Tamluk Of Tamralipta Jatiya Sarkar*, Calcutta, 1981; Maity, H. *Swadhinata Sangramer* Itihas, Moyna thana; Das, N.N., History of Midnapore, Part-2, Calcutta, 1980; Maity, S.K., Freedom Movement in Midnapore, Vol. -1, Calcutta, -1975; Ghosh, N., Role of Women in the Freedom Movement in Bengal, Calcutta, 1988; Das, Kanailal, *Alite Sangrami Nandigram*, Tamluk/Calcutta, 1994, etc.; Pal, R. & Maity, H., *Swadhinate Sasngrame Medinipur*, Vol. -3, 1992.
3. At present Tamluk sub-division was divided into tow sub-divisions—Tamluk and Haldia—with the creation of a few new *thanas* (police stations). The undivided Tamluk sub-division consisted of six *thanas*, i.e., Tamluk, Mahisadal, Sutahata, Nandigram, Mayna and Panskura.
4. Samanta, S. and Others, *August Revolution and Two years' National Government in Midnapore*, Part-I (Tamluk), Calcutta, 1946, p. 3.
5. Jawaharlal Nehru and Mahatma Gandhi expressed their views about the role of Midnapore in the C.D. Movement. Nehru writing from Allahabad on February 2, 1931 refers to the district of Midnapore as a land of martyrs and writes : "Among the many places which have provided martyrs for the cause of India's freedom, Midnapore district occupies on honourable position...We can never forget the shining examples of heroism and sacrifice which especially India's women have given, and we cannot forget what has happened in Midnapore district".

   Gandhiji also wrote on the same date and he writes : "I tender my congratulations for your courage and patience with which you have borne your sufferings. It is a matter of joy that you have preferred deprivation of those to that of your liberty...."
6. *Sangrai Purush Kumarchandra* (Like History of Kumarchandra Jana) Pub. by Tamralipts Swadhinata Sangram Itihas Committee, Tamluk, 1984, p. 97.
7. Dhara, Susil Kumar, *Prabaha*, Tamluk, 1390 B.S., p. 101.
8. Samanta, S. and Others, *op. cit.*, p. 6.
9. *Ibid.*, pp. 6-8.
10. Data collected through interviews with different aged persons.
11. Samanta, S. and others, *op. cit.*, p. 10; Pramanik, Prahlad Kr., *Swadhinata Sangrame Medinipore*, p. 33.
12. *Sangrami Purush Kumarchandra*; p. 99.
13. Samanta and others, *op. cit.*, p. 9.
14. *Ibid.*, pp. 9-10.
15. Tripathi, Amalesh, "*Biyalliser Bidroha O Tamralipta Jatiya Sarkar*", *Smarakgrantha*, (Souvenir), Nikhil Bharat Bangasahitya Sammelan, 46 Session, Tamluk, Medinipore January, 1974, p. 20.
16. Wickenden, T., "Report on the Disturbances of 1942-43" in Chhapra, P.N. (Ed.), Quit India Movement : British Secret Report, Faridabad, 1976, pp. 91f.
17. *Ibid.*, p. 93.
18. Majumdar, *op. cit.*, Vol. -3, p. 643.
19. *Ibid.*
20. *Ibid.*, p. 644.
21. *Ibid.*, pp. 644f.
22. *Ibid.*, p. 647.
23. Samanta and others, *op. cit.*, pp. 6-8.
24. Tripathi, A., *op. cit.*, p. 21.
25. Samanta and others, *op. cit.*, pp. 14f; *op. cit.*, p. 37.
26. Samanta and others, *op. cit.* p. 15.
27. *Ibid.*, pp. 15-16; For details Goswami, Gopinandan "*August Biplabe Kar-Ki-Bhumika Chhila*", `*Tamralipta*' (a weekly published from Tamluk), 30 September, 1977, p. 4 & 11 November, 1977, p. 3.
28. Maity, P.K., *Biyalliser Tamluk O Tamralipta Jatiya Sarkar*, Calcutta, 1981, pp. 31f.
29. Dhara, *Prabaha*, pp. 113-114; Goswami, *op. cit.*, pp. 36-38 Maity, P.K., *op. cit.*, pp. 35-37; Dhara, S.K., *Prabanda Guchchha*, pp. 25-46.
30. Samanta and others, *op. cit.*, pp. 10-12.
31. Bhakta, Bangabhusan, *Nandigrame Swadhinata Sangram*, Gopalpore, Medinipore, 1989, pp. 144f; The government records speaks otherwise. As per Govt. records : "When the police had reached at Iswarpur to arrest two Congress men, a

crowd of 5000 persons with *lathi* and choppers surrounded the police who opened fire the find an escape route. Two persons were killed." (Daily Report, 29 Sept. 1942 in Governor's Secretariat (Bengal) papers, Q/3/2/36, India Office Records) The mob did not carry neither lathi nor choppers and four persons were dead not two. (Data collected also from the interview with the local persons).

32. *Ibid.*, pp. 145f.
33. District Officers' Chronicles of Events, (Hereafter DOC), p. 20.
34. Bhakta, *op. cit.*, p. 147.
35. Samanta and others, *op. cit.*, pp. 18-19.
36. Born in a poor peasant family of Hogla, a small village under Tamluk P.S. in Midnapore, Matangini made her marks as an outstanding freedom fighter. She was popularly known as *"Gandhi Buri"* because she faithfully followed the ideals of Mahatma Gandhi. She took part in various demonstrations and agitations that were launched in her district to free the country from the yoke of the British rule. But finally she played the most glorious role in the Quit India movement of 1942 and sacrificed her life. As a mark of her sacrifice for the cause of our freedom the West Bengal Government had installed a 13ft. high bronze statue of her at the crossing of Red Road and Guru Nanak Sarani on the Calcutta Maidan on August 9, 1977 which, according to Sri Jatin Chakraborty, the then West Bengal's Minister for Public Works Department, "would always remind the people of the heroic role played by Matangini in the freedom struggle of our country" and he further adds that "she would continue to inspire the freedom-loving people throughout the World for all time to come". ("West-Bengal", a fortnightly journal of West Bengal Govt., Vol. -XX, No. 3, August 16, 1977).
37. Governor's Secretariat (Bengal) papers (Hereafter *GSP*), Report from. N.M. Khan, District Magistrate (Midnapore) to Additional Secretary, Home Govt. of Bengal, 30 September, 1942.
38. *GSP*, Report from M.M. Basu, A.D.M. (Midnapore), 2nd Octo., 1942.
39. *GSP*, Note by J.A.H. Herbert, Governor of Bengal, 1st Oct., 1942.
40. *GSP*, Report from A.D.M. (Midnapore) to J.R. Blair, Chief Secretary, Govt. of Bengal, 2nd Octo., 1942.
41. *GSP*, Report from Taylor, Suptd. of Police (Midnapore) to District Magistrate (Midnapore), 30 Octo., 1942.
42. Fortnightly Report (Henceforth FR), 2nd Sept., 1942 & Ist April, 1943; Report From District Intelligence Branch (Henceforth DIB), Midnapore, 2nd Feb., 1943, *GSP*; District Record, 4th Feb., 1943, *GSP*; The Communists are reported to have given 'effective assistance to the government' in crushing the movement here. (*FR*, 2nd Sept.) 1942. *FR*, Ist & 2nd Nov., 1943); A Few Muslims acted as government spies and helped actively to suppress the movement. (*FR*, 2nd Sept., 1942; *GSP*, D.M., Midnapore to Commissioner, Burdwan Division, 14 Nov., 1942; DR (District Record), 24 Nov., 1942, *GSP*; DM, Midnapore to Commissioner, Burdwan, 5 Feb., 1943, *GSP*).
43. Goswami, *op. cit.*, pp. 80-83; Samanta and others, *op. cit.*, pp. 62-64.
44. *Ibid.*, pp. 75-79; Samanta and others, *op. cit.*, pp. 57-62.
45. Tripathi, Banibrata, *"Sasrkari Banam Besarkari Relief Sanstha (1942)"* in *Ithihas Anusandhan* -7, ed. by Mahmud Abdul Weahab and published by Paschimbanga Itihas Samsad, Calcutta, 1993, pp. 546-556.
46. Samanta & others, *op. cit.*, p. 35.
47. *Ibid.*
48. *Ibid*, p. 49.
49. *Ibid*, p. 54.
50. Casey to Wavell, 14th August, 1944, Para -12, pp. 4-5, India Office Library, London.
51. Maity, P.K., *"Biyalliser Andolane, Tamluker Mahilader Bhumika"* in *Ithihas Anusandhan* -4, ed. by Chattopadhyaya, G., Pub. by Paschimbanga Itihas Samsad, Calcutta, 1989, pp. 521-531.
52. Dhara, *Prabaha*, p. 144.

Aspects of Indian History and Historiography
Editor : P.K. Mishra
Kaveri Books, New Delhi, India.

Western Poligars in Madras Presidency

8

Anies George

Introduction

My thesis entitled "Western Poligars in Madras Presidency" represents an attempt to the study of the history of the auxiliary powers in the Western region of Madras Presidency from 1690 to 1805.

The chieftains, from humble beginnings, emerged into a power to be reckoned with during the eighteenth century. Taking advantage of the political turmoils, they acquired territories, maintained their own armed establishments, developed an administrative system and extended their patronage to religion and art. However with the establishment of their political ascendancy in South India, the British found the existence of a parallel authority as a potential threat to their interest.

Accordingly, the British suppressed them and transformed them into Zamindars and Land Lords. This marked the eclipse of the Poligar System.

Origin of the Western Poligars

The term 'Poligar' is derived from the Telugu word "Pallegaru". Its original meaning is 'Palayakkaran', i.e. holder of an armed camp. *Palayam* means either an armed camp or a district under the control of a feudal chieftain. In early times, it was a common practice to set up camps or cantonments and that place was usually called *Palayam*. Depending upon the political situation of the time, the guards incharge of these military camps took possession of the areas around and established themselves. This trend gained strength in the period that followed the downfall of the Vijayanagar Empire.

The Poligars represented an order of auxiliary powers and played a significant role in the politics of South India since medieval times.

By tradition many of these chieftains claimed their origin from the ruling dynasties of ancient period. They came into existence as an order by mid Sixteenth century after the fall of the Vijayanagar Empire. They rose to prominence during the disorder that followed the collapse of the Vijayanagar Empire, the inroads made by the Bijapur and Golconda and the raids made by the Marathas. However, with the ascendancy of the English East India Company they suffered an eclipse by 1805. By 1805 they were suppressed and transformed into Zamindars. They combined in themselves the political, revenue and military authority. The Zamindars, on the other hand, exercised only revenue authority.

South India was the home of a large number of Poligars. Among them there were two major groups – the Western Poligars and the Southern Poligars. The Western Poligars had their territories in the north western region of the Carnatic which had its capital at Arcot. Many of them were in the Chittoor area. The Southern Poligars on the other hand had their estates in the Southern region of the Carnatic. Most of them had their territories in the Tinnevelly region.[1] Among the western Palayams the important were Venkatagiri, Kalahasty, Chittoor, Sydapoor and Bommarajapalayam.

Polity and Economy

After the decline of the Vijayanagar Empire, the Nayaks who established their authority at Madurai, Tanjore, Jinji, Chandragiri and Ikkeri associated the poligars with their government. Taking advantage of favourable circumstances created by political changes, the poligars extended their territorial limits and organised their own governments. By and large, they followed the traditions and patterns inherited from the Vijayanagar Empire.

Their territory of *palayam* varied in extent from one another. Venkatagiri and Kalahasty were the largest, when compared with the other *palayams* among the Western Pollams. The poligars were not permitted to construct forts and public houses without the permission of their overlords. But in practice, they never observed it strictly. As it was mentioned, irrespective of the extent and resources of his territory the poligar maintained a government of his own and observed those forms and ceremonies which were usually associated with the royal family.[2] With the decline of the central authority the poligars became practically independent; they deputed their agents in the *parganas* for revenue collection and took over political authority.[3] As they combined in themselves the functions of both the *jagirdar*[4] and the zamindar,[5] the poligars became the virtual rulers of their respective territories.[6] The poligars of Venkatagiri, Kalahasty, Chittoor, Sydapoor and Bommarajapalayam occupied principal positions, when compared to the other auxiliary power. Hereditary right guided successions as a rule.

Administration of the Palayam

The routine matters of each *palayam* were looked after by a governmental establishment, which resembled a monarchical form of government.[7] Every poligar maintained a government of his own and observed those forms and ceremonies which where usually associated with the royal houses. In fact, the functions of the poligars resembled those of a king.[8]

The poligar was assisted by a team of officers in administrative affairs, the principal of whom was called the *pradhan* or *dalaway*. On every important occasion, he held a *durbar*. He conducted official communications with his sovereign and other rulers through his ministers called the *staṇapathis*. Usually the matters like the construction of forts and fortress, capital penalty and mutilation were awarded only with the approval of his king.[9] The *pradhan* or *dalaway* assisted the poligar in the transaction of public affairs and exercised more or less the powers according to the nature of his calibre. Poligars' principal advisor, the *stanapathy* was stationed at the court of the ruler. It was through him that the poligar carried out official correspondence with the central government.

Each *palayam*, whether big or small, had its own commander of the forces, administrator of revenue, chief accountant, finance secretary and royal secretary,[10] named differently as *tasildhar*, *taluqdar* or even as *subedar*. Each sub-division of the estate had a principal administrator. It was the village headman who looked after the administration of the village. His rank and file included *kanakkapillais* or accountants, *silbendies* or revenue peons,[11] *daroghas* or superintendents,[12] *gomastas* or clerks[13] and *mahatadi peons* or messengers.[14]

The poligars maintained two categories of servants the *amuldars* or revenue officials and *sherogars* or military personnel.[15] In compensation for their services the public servants received allowances in the form of land or money. Grants of land, free of rent or on concessional rent and allotment of a share of the taxes, collected from the inhabitants or part of the customs, levied on goods passing through the particular places constituted the normal methods of remuneration.[16] Land given free of rent was called *inam,* while that on the concessional rent *shotirum*.[17] Allotted on favourable assessment, the land given in return for police or military duties was termed as *cuttubadi*.[18] The word *jagir* was applied to refer to any allowance of land. It was given in lieu of money payment to enable the servants to meet their public as well as private expenses.[19]

However, the administrative setup appeared defective. Because of the hereditary character of many of the officers, nepotism was the order of the day. Educational qualification or training was not the criteria of selection for appointments. Irrespective of their aptitudes or aspirations, they held their positions so long as they were in favour of the chief either through corrupt or fair means.

Administration of the Village

The village constituted the smallest unit of administration in the territories of the poligars. Each village was organised like small corporations and each village maintained its own administrative establishments, managed its own affairs and presented much of a united stand in its dealing with the *Circar*. The poligars did not leave the village communities altogether free although they permitted them to exercise powers of local interests and associated them with the administration so as to utilise their services for the collection of taxes and recruitment of troops. These simple institutions cherished a spirit of autonomy amidst autocratic forces of the time.

A village consisted of many parts like residential area which was divided into wards, cultivated lands, barren lands, water courses, burning ground and temple. The people constructed their houses and huts in the residential area which had been normally gained possession of free of cost from their ruler. Further allocation was effected at fixed times by lot, but the tendency was to retain a permanent possession of allotted fields. When waste lands were tilled and cultivated, consolidated shares were granted to the landholders or allotted to the new members of the village. When the season commenced, the *ryots* assembled together and determined the quantum of water in the tank and apportioned out to each according to the extent of the land that he possessed.[20] The poligar's village was skirted with thick woods. These jungles generally, of thorny bushes, served as barriers against invaders, supplied fire wood for the villages and served as pastures.[21] The temple was the centre of the cultural life. It was not only a place of worship but also a place of assembly during the mornings and evenings. Because of the vicissitudes of nature the worshippers adored the village diety for protection from calamities and for sustenance.[22] The community was the claimant of the village lands and institutions. It sought to assert its rights through the redistribution of land periodically and approbationed water for cultivation during the seasons.

The village communities preserved their territorial regime and communal character throughout the eighteenth century. They were usually of three descriptions. Firstly, there were the *agrahara vakai*—villages in which the Brahmins held the absolute property rights. Usually, it was awarded as charitable endowments by the prince. The Brahmin community of the locality held the village as its own common property. In these villages, the reallotment of land was effected periodically by a system of lot thereby excluding the right of any holder on any particular share.[23] But this did not appear favourable for the promotion of permanent interest on the fields, though it asserted the principle of communal claims. The *agrahara vakai* communities never allowed the non-Brahmins to settle in their respective villages.[24] In fact, these villages were preserved against the encroachments by other sections of the society which were commonly called as the Sudras.[25] The second division was the *pandara vakai* villages which were the settlements of the Sudras. The lands were distributed for cultivation generally with common consent. The third category consisted of all the villages which had gone into waste lands either because of war or natural calamity. The poligars took possession of such villages and allotted them to *ryots* for cultivation. The differences of these villages from *agrahara vakai* and *pandara vakai* were the absence of any sub division into *karai* or *pangu* and the denial of the right of a common ownership. However, the right of occupation was not disturbed so long as the peasants duly paid the revenue to the chief.[26]

The villages in the poligar's territory were divided into different parts in order to grant equal allotments to all the peons in the service of the poligar. If any differences existed, they were settled by the interference of the village-headman, if not by the poligar himself. In some villages, the original grant was never changed. In the absence of any male heir, the land fell into the possession of the poligar, though a portion of it might be given to the nearest female relative.[27] The existence of co-ownership marked a characteristic feature of most of the village communities, not only of the poligari but also the circar territories. In this case, land was regrouped and redistributed among the members of the village community.[28]

Village Communities

The village had a local council. Normally, the poligar did not interfere with its function. This village council was a representative institution as all land-holders were members of this local council. All the land-holders were members of the democratically constituted council's[29] while in other bodies they were only the representatives of different communities.[30] It was the poligar who appointed the village headman called *patel* on a hereditary basis. This headman had considerable influence among the villages. He was the intermediary between the poligar and the villages. He served as the collector of taxes, magistrate and judge. The *patel* was assisted by the village accountant known as *karnam*. He was keeping to perform his multifarious duties all details of land holdings in the village. There was a registrar to assist *Karnam*. The subordinates of these officers were the *Kavalkars* or watchmen and scavengers. There was no uniform system of remunerating the local servants. They were compensated for their services either in the form of land, grain or cash.[31]

It was the village headman who in consultation with the accountant decided the share of revenue to be paid by each land holder. He assessed the tax and collected it either in grain or in money. More than that, the village office supplied details about the land in the village to the circar servants and the information about government rules and regulations to the villagers. The services rendered by the community to the villagers appeared comprehensive. It looked after the maintenance of the temple, raised funds for festivals and supervised the performances of rituals. Because of the possibility of miscreant interventions, it constructed mud-walls or erected thorny fences to serve as barriers against encroachments.[32] If any potent party of free-booters appeared, it tried its level best to brush aside havoc by giving presents raised from the cultivated land among the holders, allotted uncultivated land for raising the crops, constructed and maintained water-courses and made equitable distribution of water for raising the crops.[33]

When the *amuldar* instituted judicial proceedings against any resident of the village, it deputed attorneys for the defence of his cause. As the judicial officials made no provision for the support of the persons in custody, the village community raised charitable endowment and furnished the means of sustenance. Thus the village communities performed manifold services.

As the *palayams* were situated in the hilly regions and were covered with jungles to a large extent, the poligars cleared the forest, set up new villages, constructed reservoirs and promoted cultivation.[34] They took keen interest in cultural activities too. In fact, the poligars, in general, identified themselves with the interest of the people of their territory. In the Rayalaseema area,[35] some of the poligars had been allowed to manage the affairs of other villages besides their *palayams*. Some of the poligars held vast areas of several miles while some others had a few. But each estate consisted of one or more forts, castles, temples, irrigation tanks, agricultural land and pastoral area.[36]

The poligars, in general, rendered an inestimable service to the community. Regularised in their *palayams*, these chiefs assumed constitutional responsibility as a second line of defence against external aggression and a guardians of public order and peace against internal commotion. They paid rent to the ruler for their lands and maintained bands of armed men for service with the troops of the State. They undertook to protect private property against robbery and to pay compensation in the event of their failure.[37] As guardians of public welfare, they performed police and judicial functions. As an intermediary authority, they did what the rulers normally neglected to do in the field of public welfare. While the common people found it beyond their reach to gain positions in the central administration, they experienced no such difficulty in the poligari-establishments. This created and nurtured a bond of affinity between the poligars and the villagers.[38]

The working of the local establishments like the village communities ensured to the inhabitants the basic requirements primarily local at a time when life had not become sophisticated as they felt essential for the promotion of their well being. Presided over by *patel* or *maccadam*, the village had its own local assembly and administrative system. The administrative establishment consisted of village guards, local jury, revenue-peons, accountants and scavengers. The village guards or *kavalkars* paid by the community, kept watch at night, noted all arrivals and departures, observed the movements of strangers and reported all suspects to the *patel*. They traced the culprits by keeping track of their footprints. If the stolen property could not be recovered, the village community paid compensation to the victim of robbery, as the poligars did, by a levy either on the village guards or on all members of the community.[39] Thus it shouldered full responsibility for protection of private property. The local jury called *panchayat* settled the disputes generally through arbitrations and occasionally by verdicts. The revenue peons of the village collected the taxes assessed by the *circar* for the village, remitted the amount to the public treasury and kept the residents regularly informed of rules issued by the administration from time to time. Endowed with its own revenue, levied on harvests, the village administration regulated the distribution of water for irrigation, kept the streets clean and looked after the welfare of travellers.[40] In fact, the village communities combined in themselves the characteristics of social welfare institutions and representative bodies. It appeared that the inhabitants were indifferent to political convulsions so long as the autonomy of their village was left undisturbed and its testimony to this conspicuous service rendered by the local institutions through the ages for he observed: "union of the village communities each one forming a separate little state in itself, I conceive, contributed more than any other to the preservation of the people of India through all revolutions and changes which they have suffered, and it is in a high degree conducive to their happiness and to the enjoyment of a great portion of freedom and independence".[41] The reasons for the mitigation of evils in the administration were the mutual restrictions imposed by the parallel working of the three orders, the distribution of powers, the importance attached to the observance of custom and the bond of union that existed between the poligari system and the village communities. If the village communities lacked the teeth of armament to resist, the poligari system supplied it. No wonder, the English administration itself had admitted that they (poligars) extended their protection to the victims of princely oppression[42] and the inhabitants looked upon them as the protectors of the defenceless cultivators.[43] J. Hodgeson, in his report on Tinnevelly, commented about the poligars that they considered themselves as defenders of *mamool* and they remained loyal to the rulers to the extent that the rulers remained loyal to the *mamool*.[44] They equally took part in prosperity as well as adversity of the common people. If the inhabitants were subjected to repression, they represented their grievances to the rulers for which they stationed their *stanapatis* in their courts and if no redressal could be had they guided the inhabitants in their subsequent dealings with the circar.[45] The integration of *kaval* system of the villages with the poligari system not only strengthened the bond of unity between the two institutions but accorded recognition to the poligars as the accepted leaders of the villages.

This polity, based upon division of powers, was a system of checks and balances and compromise of autocratic institutions at the higher level with representative institutions at the lower level of the social order. And it should not be confused with later political ideas on separation of powers. In the absence of anything better, it went a long way in safeguarding the rights and promoting the interests of the individuals in the community.

Administration of Justice

The administration of justice received no serious attention in poligar territories as in any other parts of the country. The important matters were settled by the poligar and the local *panchayat*. If it found difficult to ascertain and decide, some rude methods such as ordeals like boiled ghee were resorted too. The working of the *panchayat* had its irregularities such as bribery, nepotism, corruptions etc. Yet, it served as a catalytic agent in the prevailing system and if the litigants had no such body, they received no justice. They were also left free to appeal to the chieftain who served as higher court.[46] But the poligar could not award any death penalty or mutilation without the consent of the sovereign.[47]

The *quazi* who had his court in every chief town decided all cases in which the Mohammadans were concerned. The chiefs and the *amuldars* administered justice in their respective territories for the Hindus. Usually, the *pandits* helped in the interpretation of legal lore. In the poligar country, the administration of justice was not really a part of the duty of the *amuldar* or renter, yet he assumed this function evidently because it served his purpose. The relatives and dependents of the *amuldar* in each district were so numerous that in most of the cases, which came before him, their interests were involved. The *foujdar* and his deputies dispensed with criminal justice. Combining in himself the powers of a magistrate and those of a sessions judge, he tried cases and passed sentences upon the accused. His decisions were subject to an appeal to the sovereign and also to get his confirmation.[48]

There were established courts also. Normally, there was only one judge, who received regular salary. He decided the cases referred to him and permitted appeals to be taken to the king. The court sat daily and decided the cases according to the *sastras*. The fees and fines collected by the court formed a fund for defraying the salaries of the court officials. The litigants enjoyed the right of employing interpreters called *dubashies*[49] for the explanation of their cases to the judicial authorities. Criminal offences were usually atoned for by fines while disputes concerning properties were accommodated or settled by verdicts. The prisoners received no means of subsistence from the *Circar* but were left entirely to the charity of their villages.[50] Yet, they were frequently tortured.

The legal system was indeed marked by irregularity and abuse. The tendency was to overrate the pretensions of the superior castes, thus ignoring the principle of equality before the law.[51] The poor were refused protection against the despotic violence of influential people. In the absence of any respect for human rights, the administration of justice was tied to revenue.[52] Without any judicial training the judges were selected from all shades of life. *Jagirdars* mostly occupied the judicial offices though the Hindu jurisprudence required that the judges should be *pandits* well versed in law. The renters and *amuldars* with no knowledge of law decided cases in a rude and summary way. Sometimes, the judges became the object of displeasure of the authorities.[53] These corrupt practices exposed the inhabitants to tyranny.[54]

Sources of Revenue

The poligars for supporting their administrative and military establishments solely depended upon their own sources or revenue. Their sources of revenue were principally the rent from the lands, income from their personal possessions, customs and *kaval* dues. Their share of the produce was known as *pothuchilavu*. It was called *pothuchilavu* or common expense because it was a tax given by the inhabitants to the poligars for their common benefit; though the concept represented an ideal. The poligars were free to spend this amount for military and administrative purposes as they liked. The *pothuchilavu* usually came to about fifty per cent of the yield from the land. The revenue administration of the territory was solely shouldered by the followers of the poligars. The Vijayanagar Sovereigns handed over their administration to the poligar chieftains. The sub-ordinate poligars had to pay a fixed annual tribute to his superior.[55] He should also give a quota of cavalry and troops for the maintenance of law and order. Each poligar under this system had thus in his charge a number of villages with all manners of jurisdiction. The share of the chieftains was regulated by *mamool* or customs. However, there were instances when the poligari government proved oppressive to the peasantry who were squeezed by imposing high taxes on land, water, trade and salt.

The daily life of the poligar country was centered upon an agrarian economy based upon the possession of land. The poligars did not make any fundamental innovations in the rights of landed property. Usually, the peasants enjoyed the permanent right to till and own the land under his cultivation. Nevertheless, the usage and practice conferred on the occupants of land the right to possess, sell, bestow, devise and bequeath their property at their will. The holder of the land was known as *kaniatchikar* meaning an independent hereditary proprietor. In the villages where the land belonged to the community, the holder of an allotment possessed the right to transfer a certain portion of land corresponding to his share in the cultivated land together with his undefined interests in other properties. It was a common practice that the *kaniatchy* or the holder managed to own greater extent of land than what was found in the records. The additional area for which the peasant paid no tax varied from fifty to hundred per cent of the land for which he actually paid. Thus the system rested upon a state of conflict between oppressive exactions and attempted evasions.[56]

The *ryots* were not completely free from exaction and oppression. In the *palayam* the inhabitants had to pay tax only to the chieftain. At times, the poligars too collected taxes from Circar territories. If a comparison is made between the taxes of the *palayams* were lesser. The inhabitants of the poligar territories were required to shoulder much less burden of taxation than of Circar territories. During the poligar's regime, the economy appeared not rigid but it met with a drastic alteration by the close of the eighteenth century. It was mainly because of the alliance of the Nawab of Arcot with the British which resulted in the harassment for more presents and contributions which in turn resulted in the financial bankruptcy.

For the purpose of taxation the cultivated lands were classified into four categories; *kirsul*,[57] *Shuvul*,[58] pottul[59] and veppul.[60] This classification was applied only to wet lands while the dry lands were dealt with differently. Lushington's report states that a scientific analysis of land was attempted for deciding the criterion of taxation.[61]

The other sources of revenue were imports and *sayers* or customs. The land revenue was levied in three different modes namely by *teerva* or money assessment, by *warrum* or share of produce and *jodle* or quit rent. *Teerva* was a fixed money payment. It has its etymology from the Telugu word 'teerup' which means settled. According to *teerva*, when a *ryot* was desirous to cultivate a tract of waste or jungle land, it was handed over to him on *cowle* for a fixed term of years on the principle of a *nuseed* or progressive increase. Usually, the *karnam* fixed the percentage of taxation. At the expiry of the *cowle* when land was supposed to be brought to a state of improvement by successive cultivation and application of manure, assessment was raised to the normal level.[62] When *jodle* was once fixed it was never raised.

Excise duties were levied on the manufacture of salt and drugs. Duties were imposed on them at times. Apart from these taxes professional taxes contributed much to the revenue of the chief. The tax was collected on the basis of income. The taxes on the profession were paid once a year in cash. Military contribution was another source of income. For the maintenance of the army and forts in the *palayam* certain taxes were imposed on the people. It was known by the name *dalavi* and the *kottaipanam* respectively. Judicial income and fines too contributed fare share to the poligar's exchequer. They were imposed for faults, theft, adultery and injustice.

Customary payments were paid to the poligars at certain important periods of the year or on special occasions. Besides, there were a large number of dues generally customary which were demanded from the people. These were of a miscellaneous nature and were demanded in coins, grains and services. The poligars decided the rent based upon the accounts furnished by the persons called *anchandars*, employed in the revenue department to estimate the quality of the field and grain. They carefully prepared the accounts as they were personally held responsible in case of mistakes.[63]

When a *ryot* did not cultivate for a *teerva*, he can divide the produce with the *circar* or *warrum* basis. The Brahmins and other higher castes like Rachawar, Yelamawar etc. due to custom and religion never followed plough and it was entrusted to the people. Tradition permitted them to collect ten per cent of the total produce. The *warrum* on all arable land was in most instances registered in the *karnam's* accounts in the same manner as *teerva*. Religious institutions were exempted from any quit rent.[64]

Several types of coins were current in the Venkatagiri, Kalahasty and other *pollams*. They were : *star pagoda, kirkee, pulleput, cavery pank*, Company's rupee and the Madras *fanams*. The circulation of *pulleput* and *cavery pank* were confined to the Bommarajapalayam and the Chittoor country.[65] Their exchange value changed from time to time, though a *pagoda* was exchanged for three rupees and a rupee for four *fanams*.

Expenditure

The poligars spent the money collected from their subjects under different heads of expenditure. They paid tribute to the sovereign and used the rest for maintaining civil and military establishments in their particular area and also for their household affairs. The tribute was otherwise known as *peshcash* which was divided into two instalments called *kists*. And when the permanent settlement was effected with the British they demanded a third *kist* also. Usually, it was collected on 15 December, 15 March and 15 June. Every year the chief sent his representative to the headquarters to check the account of payments. In times to disorders payments were usually withheld.

Every year the chieftains spent large sums as charitable endowments for promoting public welfare. They paid the civil and military servants their remuneration either in the form of money or land. The Venkatagiri poligars, besides distributed grain from their own stores to the peons at uniformally advanced price for the whole year which, according to accounts, had usually been at sixtysix per cent above the bazaar rate. But the Kalahasty poligars made a practice of issuing grain from their stores at any rate which might suit their convenience which varied from 150 to 197 percentage above the bazaar rate. In Bommarajapalayam there was a peculiar wage system. It was to deduct two or three months' pay from every description of servants to make up any deficiency in the crops suffered because of drought or other causes. In these cases, the Venkatagiri and Kalahasty Poligars imposed sale of their grain on their dependents at a higher rate than usual in order to make the difference nearly equal to their loss.[66] The ill consequences of which worked equally alike not only in Kalahasty and Venkatagiri but also through out the Chittoor country.

The amarum assignment served a three fold purpose for it provided for remuneration to the servants, promoted cultivation and yielded additional revenue to the chief. Under *amarum* tenure whole villages were made over the peons in proportion for eight or ten to each village which were jointly bound to make up the demand of rent originally stipulated, which was never raised after. When any share of the village became vacant by death or otherwise, the son of the former occupant succeeded to it and his name was registered at the *huzur cutcherry* by the *karnam* of the village. If there was no, son, the next male kith or kin who obtained a *sanad* succeeded to the inheritance. The *amarum* peons were to attend on the poligar on receiving his summons.

The other mode of paying the peons by the poligars by assignments of land was termed *cuttubadi inams* for it implied gifts to bind. The *cuttubadi* peons were all *ryots* to whom spots of jungle and waste lands were assigned for cultivation on a stipulated money payment. The *cuttubadi* lands in respect to inheritance descended in the same manner as allotments in *amarum* villages from father to son and so on. The *amarum* and *cuttubadi* peons might be ranked among the productive classes of inhabitants from its being their interest to cultivate to their utmost. They proved of essential advantage to the general interest of the community.[67]

Collection of Taxes

The Western Poligars with the assistance of their overlords bestowed constant attention upon a vigorous collection of maximum possible revenue. They maintained complex organisation for the administration of revenue. The *amuldar* functioned as the principal administrator of revenue of the province under the poligars. A trustee, an arbitrator between the administration collecting the revenue and the subject paying it, enforced collections, promoted cultivation, prevented exaction and settled disputes.[68] Yet acting under the stress of the times and on personal greed, the administrator totally ignored the benevolent part of his duty. This system deteriorated further when Mohammad Ali, embarassed by his military expenses and demands from his ally the English East India Company, entrusted large area with the renters for fixed sum to the highest bidders.[69] In this manner, he raised collections to meet the demands of the ambitious adventurers.[70] The poligars with mounting debts, which the Nawab owed them to contract loans, found themselves unable to liquidate their financial liabilities. Further, Mohammad Ali made assignment of his revenue to private individuals. These grantees, usually European adventurers, superseded the public servants in the administration of revenue in the assigned territories and even interfered in the poligar territories. This created diversity of methods in the enforcement of collections. In fact, enforced by the *amuldars*, renters, assigners, tributaries and poligars, the revenue administration suffered for want of uniform system. Renters and *amuldars* in their endeavour to raise a large amount made an upward revision of the taxes. Many of these divisions were notorious for their conspicuous absence of any far-sightedness or humanitarianism. As a result, the *ryots* suffered.

Each poligar had a separate department of revenue. It was steered by the minister of revenue. He was assisted by a large staff of officers and clerks as they had to keep regular accounts of income from various sources. When the royal order was sent to the local governors, orders conveying the remission of taxes or the imposition of the new ones, it was communicated to the poligars by the royal governors.

The poligar governments remit taxes in favour of public institutions. Taxes due to the imperial government could be remitted with the approval and consent of the imperial authority. However, if the local authority remitted a tax due to the centre without the approval of the imperial authority it was to be done on his own responsibility. The central government did not suffer any loss of revenue because of remission as it was made good by the levy of higher rates of taxes on other sources. In the imposition of new local taxes or in their remission, the poligar's word was final. But the imperial taxes collected directly by the central government could be remitted only by the imperial government.

The financial year commenced in September-October, when the *Mahanavami* was celebrated for nine days and the accounts were cleared then. It began on the 12 September[71] and the new year commenced in the month of October. At the outset of the month of October, when eleven of its days had passed the new accounting year began. It was their new year day. They begin the year in this month with a new moon and they count the months always from moon to moon.[72] Within these nine days all the accounts in the interior kingdoms, *pollams* and villages, were settled.

The accounts of the period suggest that the poligars provided for a proper form of government and took much care for financial viability. The territories of the poligars were not so productive. The villages were isolated from each other with no means of proper communication. Inspite of the difficulties presented by nature and topography, the poligars developed and nurtured their own system of administration. No doubt, the poligars were feudal chiefs with autocratic propensity. Yet, what is significant is that they associated the villages and local communities with their own system of polity. Inadequate rainfall and droughts created obstacles to their smooth administration. Invasions and raids too added to their troubles. In spite of these, many of the poligars bestowed their attention for the improvement of cultivation, protection of the pilgrims and erection of rest houses. The choultries that they had erected for the care of the travellers and the stones that they put up for giving rest to the load-men have survived even to the present times.

References

1. Madras Council, Military Country Correspondence, 3 May 1753, Vol. 1, p. 94.
2. K. Rajayyan, *Rise and Fall of the Poligars of Tamil Nadu*, Madras, 1974, p. 23.
3. *Extract from the Proceedings of the Committee of Circuit in the Vizagapatam and Chicacole Districts*, Madras, 1915, p. 68.
4. Who rendered the service-civil or military or both as the primary duty in return for the possession of an estate.
5. Zamindars paid rent in return for the possession of an estate.
6. K. Rajayyan, *op. cit.*, p. 20.
7. Madras Council, Military Country Correspondence, 20 March 1795, Vol. 45, p. 30.
8. *Ibid.*, p. 36.
9. *Ibid.*, Vol. 46, p. 32.
10. Madras Council, Revenue Consultations, July 1801, Vol. 110, pp. 1401-1408.
11. Selections from the Records of Fort St. George, 1816, No. 11.
12. Sri Rama Sharma, *Mughal Government and Administration*, Bombay 1951, p. 243.
13. Madras Council, Military Country Correspondence, 1775, Vol. 24, p. 241.
14. Board of Revenue, Report on the Tiruvendipuram Farm, 1775, p. 7.
15. Madras Council Revenue Consultations, 14 December 1798, Vol. 91, pp. 4445-4450.
16. Madras Council, Military Country Correspondence, 10 April 1987, Vol. 36, p. 20.
17. B. Ramaswamy Naidoo, *Memoir on the Internal Revenue System of Madras Presidency*, Madras, 1908, p. 20.
18. A.C. Boswell, *Nellore District Manual*, Madras, 1933, p. 278.
19. Madras Council, Military Consultations, 23 October 1795, Vol. 199, pp. 3797-3798.
20. S.R. Lushington, Report to the Board of Revenue, 29 December 1800, p. 15.
21. C.S. Srinivasachari, *Village Organisation at the Time of the British rule in the Madras Presidency*, Madras, 1932, p. 51.
22. S.S. Raghavaingar, *Progress of the Madras Presidency During the Last Forty Years*, Madras, 1893, pp. 218-223.
23. S.R. Lushington, Report to the Board of Revenue, 29 December 1800, p. 16.
24. Madras Council, Military Country Correspondence, 12 July 1765, Vol. 23, p. 25.
25. *Ibid.*, 17 June 1778, Vol. 27, p. 278.
26. S.R. Lushington, Report to the Board of Revenue, 29 December 1800, pp. 16-18.
27. Madras Council, Board of Revenue, Consultations, 29 December 1800, Vol. 269, pp. 11099-11100.
28. *Journal of Indian History*, Trivandrum, 1960, Vol. 38, p. 176.
29. C.S. Srinivasachari, *op. cit.*, pp. 1-2.
30. Sewell's List of Copper Plates; No. 65A.
31. Correspondences Relating to the Revision of Village Revenue Establishments of the Madras Residency, 1866, pp. 6-8.
32. H.H. Dodwell, (ed.), *Cambridge History of India*, Vol. V, Cambridge, 1929, p. 463.
33. S.R. Lushington, Report to the Board of Revenue, 29 December 1800, p. 21.
34. T.V. Mahalingam, *Administration and Social Life under Vijayanagar*, Part I, Madras, 1969, pp. 200-201.
35. This area was otherwise called as the Ceded Districts.
36. Fifth Report of the Affairs of the East India Company, 28 July 1812, London, 1812, pp. 89-90.
37. Madras Council, Revenue Consultations, 4 September 1799, Vol. 97, p. 2246.
38. Madras Council, Military Country Correspondence, 14 April 1770, Vol. 18, p. 88.
39. Madras Council, Revenue Consultations, 4 September 1799, Vol. 96, Para 10-15.
40. Selections from the Records of Fort St. George, 13 May 1815, Nos. 2, 9 and 11.
41. Minutes dated 7 November 1830 (Quoted in Tara Chand, *History of the Freedom Movement in India*, New Delhi, 1961, Vol. I, p. 353).
42. Madras Council, Revenue Consultations, 24 July 1801, Vol. 110, pp. 1405-1406.
43. Madras Council Military Consultations, 27 August 1799, Vol. 257, p. 5678.
44. J. Hodgeson, Report on Tinnevelly, p. 22 and Madras Council, Proceedings of the Board of Assigned Revenue, 31 December 1785, Vol. 8, pp. 616-621.
45. Madras Council, Revenue Consultations, 24 July 1801, Vol. 110, pp. 1405-1407.
46. Selections from the Records of Fort St. George, 1816, No. 11.
47. Madras Council, Military Country Correspondence, 20 march 1795, Vol. 46, p. 32.

48. Madras Council, Proceedings of the Board of Assigned Revenue, 10 November 1783, Vol. I, p. 485.
49. The word *dubashi* means a translator.
50. Fort St. George, Military Sundry Book, Vol. 40, p. 93.
51. H.H. Dodwell, (ed.), *The Private Diary of Anandaranga Pillai*, Madras, 1928, Vol. XII, p. 191, (foot notes).
52. K. Rajayyan, *History of Tamil Nadu*, 1565-1982, Madurai, 1982, pp. 163-164.
53. Persian Records, State Archives Madras, Bundle 9, No. 67.
54. Madras Council, Revenue Despatches to England, 14 October 1775, Vol. I, pp. 13-14.
55. Report of the Tanjore Commissioners, 1799, p. 23.
56. S.R. Lushington, Report to the Board of Revenue, 29 December 1800, pp. 9-14.
57. Black Cotton Soil, free from stones and sand.
58. Land which was a mixture of red soil, stones and sand.
59. Ground with a mixture of black and white soil with stones.
60. Land of brown earth, clay and sand.
61. S.R. Lushington, Report to the Board of Revenue, 29 December 1800, p. 9.
62. Reports of George Straton, the Collector of Western Pollams to William Petric, President and Members of the Board of Revenue, 14 July 1801, para. 3.
63. Selections from records of the Nellore Collectorate, Nellore, 1919, p. 6.
64. George Stratton, *op, cit.*, para 12.
65. In 1730, Governor Morton Pitt had introduced a new *pagoda* called M.M. Pagoda. They proved to be a failure because they were not accepted in the Nawab's territory. After a trial of five years, the government decided to give them up. Then the *star pagoda* was used and later became the standard coin of South India until the early part of the nineteenth century. Besides *star pagodas*, Madras pagoda and North Arcot rupee were used in the government treasury. Gold mohors, silver dollars, etc. too were in circulation from time to time. *Fanam* formed the meditim of exchange in retail transactions. Twelve fanams were equal to one *pagoda*. Besides these coins, rupee was in circulation. It was first introduced in Carnatic by the end of the Seventeenth Century.
66. Madras Council, Proceedings of the Board of Revenue, Vol. 262, pp. 7830-7833.
67. *Ibid.*, Vol. 264, pp. 125-132.
68. J Sarkar. *The Mughal Administration*, Calcutta, 1952, p. 58.
69. B. Ramaswamy Naidoo, *Memoir on the Internal Revenue System of the Madras Presidency*, Madras, 1908, p. 21.
70. A.C. Boswell, *Nellore District Manual*, Madras, 1933.
71. Sewell Robert, *the Historical Inscriptions of Southern India and Outlines of Political History*, (ed. by S.K. Aiyangar), Madras, 1932, p. 263.
72. *Ibid.*, pp. 281-281.

Section II

Aspects of Indian History and Historiography
Editor : P.K. Mishra
Kaveri Books, New Delhi, India.

A Living Tradition of Tripura : An Ethno-Cultural Probe

9

Sumangal Sen

The sky in Tripura is cobalt blue now, slate grey at times, with stray floating clouds occasionally gathering into dark assemblies followed by *Kāla Vaiśākhi* storms (storms associated with the month of Vaiśākh, the first month of the Indian year). These storms are of short durations. It is the beginning of the South wind, and the end of the North wind.

The year begins in Tripura, as in many other parts of the country with the Sun's entry into the sign Aries, according to Indian Almanacs. For instance, in this year 1994 in Bengal, Tripura, Assam and the other North-Eastern States, the first month of the year, namely Vaiśākh, falls on 15th April, while in Punjab, Haryana and Orissa, it is on 13th April, and in Tamil Nadu on the 14th. This is a festive occasion for all the North-Eastern States of India. The hills are barren, water-level has gone down and food is scarce. Enjoyment, merry-making and festivals in otherwise eventless rural life depend on cultivation, harvest and prosperity. Harvest has been completed during winter, and now is the time to till the hills and the plains, to invite the rainy days, to propitiate the gods and welcome the New Year.

We are going to discuss the *Garia* festival of Tripura which is the greatest festival of the Kākbarak (a tribal language) speaking population of Tripura. This has assumed the dimension of an universal festival in Tripura. We will see how it synchronizes with the Bengali festivals of *Gājan* and *Chaḍak*, and *Vaishuva Saṅkrānti* (vernal equinox) and *Nava-Varsha* (the last day of the year and the New Year's day, respectively), the *Vijhu* (or Viju) festival of the Chākmas of Tripura, and *Vihu* (or Raṅgāli Vihu) of all the communities of Assam.

Vishuva Samkranti is the last day of the year. In Kākbarak or the Tripuri language Vishuva is called Visu, and the previous day is called Hari-Visu. We can trace the same origin or Vishuva here, and in Vijhu or Viju of the Chākmas and Vishu or Raṅgoli Vishu of Assam. They all seem to point at the same origin of Vishuva Samkranti, with more or less the same approach to inviting the New Year which is expected to be prosperous and full of agricultural products.

But in case of Garia Festival the days of Hari Visu or Visu synchronizes with another great event in the history of Tripura, with a strong flavour of legend.

In the shadowy lanes of this hilly kingdom of Tripura, legends are many. Some of them assume historical credence, and some of course have strong evidences as well. Before we proceed for a detailed discussion of Garia festival, let us for a while cast a glance at a legend-flavoured history related to Garia.

This episode in history can be named as *Climbing the High Kuki Hills*. It relates to Mahārāja Dhanya Māṇikya's (c.1490-1520) war with the Kukis. Kalia and Garia are the two brothers and war-lords of the Kuki Kingdom. Kukis believed that propitiating the deities before setting forth for a battle would ensure victory.

Mahārāja Dhanya Manikya had a dream in which the god Garia appeared before him and asked him to carry them (both Kalia and Garia) to his own kingdom since the Kukis had become *mlechchas* (savage or unclean). They were eating forbidden things.

Anyway, the Mahārājā waged war. Kukis were finally vanquished. Plundering followed. Jāmātiās (a major tribe in Tripura) captured the golden head of Garia and the other tribesmen in the regiment got the bamboo weapons etc. They were all brought home. Jāmātiās commenced worshipping the golden head, adding other parts of the body with bamboo. Tripuris, Hālāms, Noātias, Reangs and other Kākbarak speaking people make the deity with bamboo and worship Him. The army returned to Tripura on the Vishuva Saṅkrānti day, and the Garia puja started in Tripura on that very day and continued for a week. The return of the army also happened on the Vishuva Sankranti day, and this provided another reason of beginning of the celebration on this day, the last day of the year.

Another important thing: Garia was the war lord of the Kukis. To the people of Tripura, Garia is the Lord of agriculture, harvest and peace. We find a clear difference in the approach.

Garia festival, although comprises music and dance, is not just a dance festival though. It is not even a ritualistic tribal ceremony only. Kākbarak speaking people believe that the diety of Garia must be propitiated for plentiful of Jhoom Cultivation (shifting cultivation). Garia is also held to be the Lord of health and prosperity, and hence, according to some, is perhaps another name of Gaṇesa, the Lord of success and achievement. Some others hold that Garia is the Lord Siva, and Jamatias do worship the diety as Lord Siva.

Hari Visu, or the day previous to Vishu or Vishuva Saṅkrānti, is characterised by social gatherings and visits to friends and neighbours. People take early bath, wear new or washed clothes and collect wild flowers. Garlands are strung with flowers and buffaloes and cows are garlanded. Incenses are burnt and placed at the feet of them. This practice will remind us of the respect shown to the cattle from the early dawn of civilization of India, mention of which we find in *Srimadbhāgavata* in which Kṛishṇa is shown as a shepherd boy.

Male folks collect roots, leaves and fruits from forests and women collect various edible leaves and vegetables, and cook food. This practice is closely akin to the timeless tradition of the Bengalis of collecting 14 vegetable leaves (shak) and cook a food item on the 14th lunar day of the autumnal dark fortnight, previous to the New Moon day and *Kali Pūjā*. Certain similar rituals are also observed by some on the Vishuva Saṅkrānti day.

On the Hari Vishu day, the first thing to do in the morning is to worship the family deities. *Randhak* is worshipped first, and then *Nakchhumtai* is worshipped. *Nakchhumtai* is held to be the *Vastudevata* or the guardian deity. A *Lamfra* or a rectangular shaped bamboo image is inserted into the bamboo-wall of the main room before commencement of the celebration, and the old Lamfra immersed.

An earthen pitcher used for a sacred purpose is called a *Ghat*. A *Ghat* full with water is now placed on the cleaned and decorated compound of the house. This particular day for the beginning, and, in some respect, the rituals are typical of the Tripuri, Hālām, Noātiā, etc. communities, and are different from those practised by Jāmātiā community. Jamatias commence all these preparations even much earlier. We propose to come to this point later. Now, the head of the family who has already taken a bath and worn new or washed clothes, enters the forest and selects a faultless bamboo and brings it home. *Achai* is the priest, *Barua* is his assistant. *Jagalya* are the women who make the sacred sound of *Ulu* with their tongues in quick movement, signifying the commencement of the festival.

The piece of bamboo, brought by the head of the family is a chosen one, without defect, young and preferably of *Muli* variety. This piece of bamboo, when ceremoniously installed, symbolises the deity *Garia*. The bamboo is now erected on the eastern or southern corner of the courtyard at the directive of the priest. It is erected in a corner in order to safeguard against a careless trampling on the shadow of the deity by any devotee. The length of the piece of bamboo is between 72" and 90", corresponding to 4 to 5 hand measures.

Now about the details of the image and procedures of rituals. The bamboo which has knots all over the body at regular intervals, will now be decorated. Every alternate know will be decorated with flowers. All the thin branches and leaves of the bamboo up to the fifth or the seventh knot from the ground will be trimmed, leaving out the top leaves and the branches. The entire bamboo is now painted by the priest with parallel lines. This is called *Rikna*. The green skin of the bamboo is now shaven by making winding scratches. Flowers and pieces of cotton wool are now threaded and tied with the image to hang. The number of such flowers and pieces of cotton wool must be good. A sacred *Risa* (breast cover a tribal woman) is now wrapped around.

The priests having been satisfied with the details of the arrangement, proceeds for consecration of the idol. *Jagalya* women perform *Ulu* and all the members assemble to prostrate before the diety.

Only unmarried girls are held eligible for all the preparations and arrangement of the offerings like thread, risa, rice, drinks etc. A very special variety of rice, *Binny* is used for the purpose, and there is a striking similarity of this preference with that of the Chakmas during the Vijhu festival days, and the lyrics of the songs sung on the occasion repeatedly make mention of this item.

Other important items are a selected cock, some eggs and sacred drink, *Chuakma*, specially created for the occasion. This drink is called a sacred water.

The cock and the eggs are now sacrificed by the priest. He carefully examines the intestine of the sacrificed cock. If it is found without any defect, then the priest predicts allround happiness and prosperity of the family.

The above mentioned rituals relate to the Tripuri, Halam and Noatia etc. tribes' performing of the Garia festival. Jamatia people have a somewhat different and lengthy way of celebrating the occasion, and we propose to discuss this in brief.

To the Jamatia people, this festival is not just a family programme, but a programme which involves the entire community of a locality. About two and a half months previous to the festive days, the people go around the locality and collect subscription. The members who are authorised to collect such subscriptions are called *Matai Balnai*, i.e., the carriers of the deity. The subscriptions are generally collected from within the Jamatia community.

A carrier of the deity, *Matai Balnai*, the priest, *Achai*, and the drummer, *Daria* enjoy a special status in the community. This is a hereditary inheritance, and therefore an Achai's son becomes an Achai, a Matai Balnai's son a Matai Balnai and a Daria's son a Daria.

As we have already mentioned, Jamatias consider Garia as the Lord Siva, For them Garia Puja can begin on any weekday or Lunar Day. But the main festival centres around the Visuba Sankranti. The deity has only a head which, for the purpose of celebration, is joined with a bamboo-made body.

Bamboo can be seen in most of the art forms of Tripura and the adjacent States. Abundant growth of bamboo naturally contributes to its varied use, as stone did to the artists of Orissa and south India, and clay to the artists of Bengal.

Besides, in making the images of deities there is a striking similarity in approach among the tribes. They necessarily reflect or represent human shapes. Garia has his own appearance made out of bamboo pieces, springing out of the concept of the people who worship. It is rather a symbol. But there is a great problem in preserving any such piece of artwork. Apart from its own ritualistic practice of immersion, bamboo has a very short longevity.

A formal invitation to the Achai, Matai Balnai and Daria has to be extended by the organisers by appearing in person to their residences.

On the day previous to the commencement of the celebration, six senior members of the community bring three chosen bamboos. These are ways of selection of bamboos. The first, or the most important one, however, is called the *King Bamboo* and is chopped in one breath and at a single stroke of the chopper.

A big structure is constructed with bamboo and hand spun and handwoven clothes are placed on it. On the first day of the festival fasting is observed by all, and the Achai and the celebrities join hands in making the head of the deity which is later joined with other parts made of bamboo. The head is made with ground rice.

Consecration is performed by the priest. Sacrificial objects are placed before the deity. The feet of the deity are washed. A buffalo is sacrificed first, followed by goats of the individual members of the community. Remains of the food offered to the deity is then distributed to all.

Singing and dancing with the beating of drums (*Kham*) form an integral part of the festival. Every afternoon during this festive week, young boys carry the spear of the deity and sing and dance with the beating of the drums. They visit every house and sing and dance. Recently girls have begun joining the singing and dancing.

The idea or the message of the songs may be summed up as under :

> *Wake up, you master of the house. We are here with the Garia King who is going round. He loves to dance around, having heard of "Chaitra Parab" (Chaitra = the last mong, Parab = festival). He has crossed the hills, waded the streams. Come along to welcome Him. Come with water cans, sprinkle water on the ground, and offer Him a seat. He wanders day and night. If you accept Him as your Lord, He will graciously take His seat. Otherwise He will move away. Offer Him eggs, cocks and hens, offer Him gold and silver, offer Him thread, paddy and money.*

Asking for blessings follows and blessings are granted by those who carry the spears on behalf of the diety.

Visarjan or immersion follows after washing the feet of the deity with eggs.

One more thing. Even previous to Garia worship, *Randhak* is worshipped. Jamatias worship Randhak, whereas Tripuris worship two deities *Mailuma* — the Goddess of rice, and *Khuluma* - the Goddess of cotton. Separate earthen pots full of water are placed for worship of each of them.

Having discussed in brief the Garia festival of Tripura, we now propose to see how it coincides with, and can be conveniently linked to the Gajan and Charak of the Bengalis, the Vijhu of the Chakmas and the Vihu of Assam.

Gajan and Chadak are but varied rituals of the same festival-commencing and ending in the month of Chaitra, the last month of the year. Lord Siva is the *Nataraja* or the King of dance, the Lord of *Kala* or time or ending. The Bengalis celebrate Chadak — the festival and swinging or whirling on a post, with a person's back pierced with a hook and suspended on a rope. They celebrate Gājan in honour of Lord Siva. The overall idea is the end of the year, destruction of all the worn out and old things, a warm welcome to prosperous New Year, and with all these things in mind, people propitiate Lord Siva, the Lord of *Time, Destruction and Death*.

Now let us discuss Vijhu or Viju. It is celebrated by the Chākmas who generally are the residents around the southern part of Tripura and the adjacent Chittagong of Bangladesh and Burma. This festival begins on the day previous to the last day of the Bengali year. The first festival day is *Phool-Vijhu* or the Vijhu of flowers, the second, that is the Sankrānti day, is called *Mool-Vijhu* or the main Vijhu, the New Year's Day and the next day are called *Garja* and *Paraja*, respectively. Some believe that Garia of the Tripuris and Jāmātiās, Garja of the Chākmas and Karaiya of the Burmese have some link.

On the Phool Vijhu Day people go round the hills and forests, pluck flowers, assemble by the river, light lamps and worship *Mother Gangā*. Chākmās are Buddhişts, and therefore offerings are also made to Lord Buddha. On the Mool-Vijhu Day the celebrations are more colourful—the people go round and are Lord Buddha. On the Mool-Vijhu Day the celebrations are more colourful—the people go round and are offered sweets and food items prepared with *Binny* rice. *Garja*, according to general opinion, denotes the idea of home coming (Ghar = home, Ja = go), and *Parja* is meeting friends and neighbours (Par = others, like Parosi =neighbours). One very interesting thing to note is that the Chakma dialect is very close to the local Bengali dialect, much closer than Kākbarak is, and therefore many of the expressions and terminology are easily understood by the Bengalis.

Sweets and variety of dishes are prepared in every house, and the names of the items are very common with those of the Bengalis. They sing and dance with musical accompaniment and beating of the drums and the lyrics of the songs convey the idea of merry-making, mixing of younger people, boys and girls, and having a nice time.

Vijhu of the Chākmās is essentially a festival of agriculture, harvest, meeting friends, a celebration of *forget and forgive*, merry-making, end of the old year and the beginning of the New.

Raṅgoli or Raṅgali Vihu of Assam is very close to all these festivals. It is a festival of the year ending and beginning of a New Year. It is a festival of singing and dancing, merry-making and wearing exquisite dresses. Its essence is the idea of fertility of productivity, of cultivation and harvest. The word *Rangoli* or *Rangali* suggests colourfulness. Yes, it is very enjoyable and colourful.

In several respect, however, the Vihu of Assam is different from the festivals previously discussed. Firstly, Vihu of Assam is not a festival of a particular tribe or community. All the small groups or tribes gradually developed this greatest and the most colourful festival of Assam. Secondly, in Assam, they celebrate several Vihus, mainly three. When the fields become green with the appearance of crop, *Rangali Vihu* is celebrated. Another Vihu, named *Bahag Vihu*, is celebrated during harvest time, from the first day of Māgh (mid January) and continues for a week. Feasts, music and dance with close relations are held. Lighting lamps in the evening under the *Tulsi* plant (which is very sacred to Hindus) and singing devotional songs characterizes another Vihu called *Kangali Vihu* or *Kati Vihu*. But this Vihu is quite insignificant.

The most important Rangali Vihu is celebrated on the first day of the Bengali year. Spring, the Rituraj (King of seasons), comes to visit with abundant flowers. South wind blows. Rustling of the dry leaves and shiver of the new leaves join with the beating of the drums and music of the flutes and blowing of the horns. Male folk wear *dhoti* and *kurtā*, tie turban with a knot on the left side, girls mostly wear golden yellow saree and red blouse. Against the green topography and under the blue sky the Vihu dance begins.

Although adverse comments of disapproval of much of Vihu dance and songs are made by many of the writers of Assam, it is said that of late things have become more presentable, and

The Covered Area Garia Festival

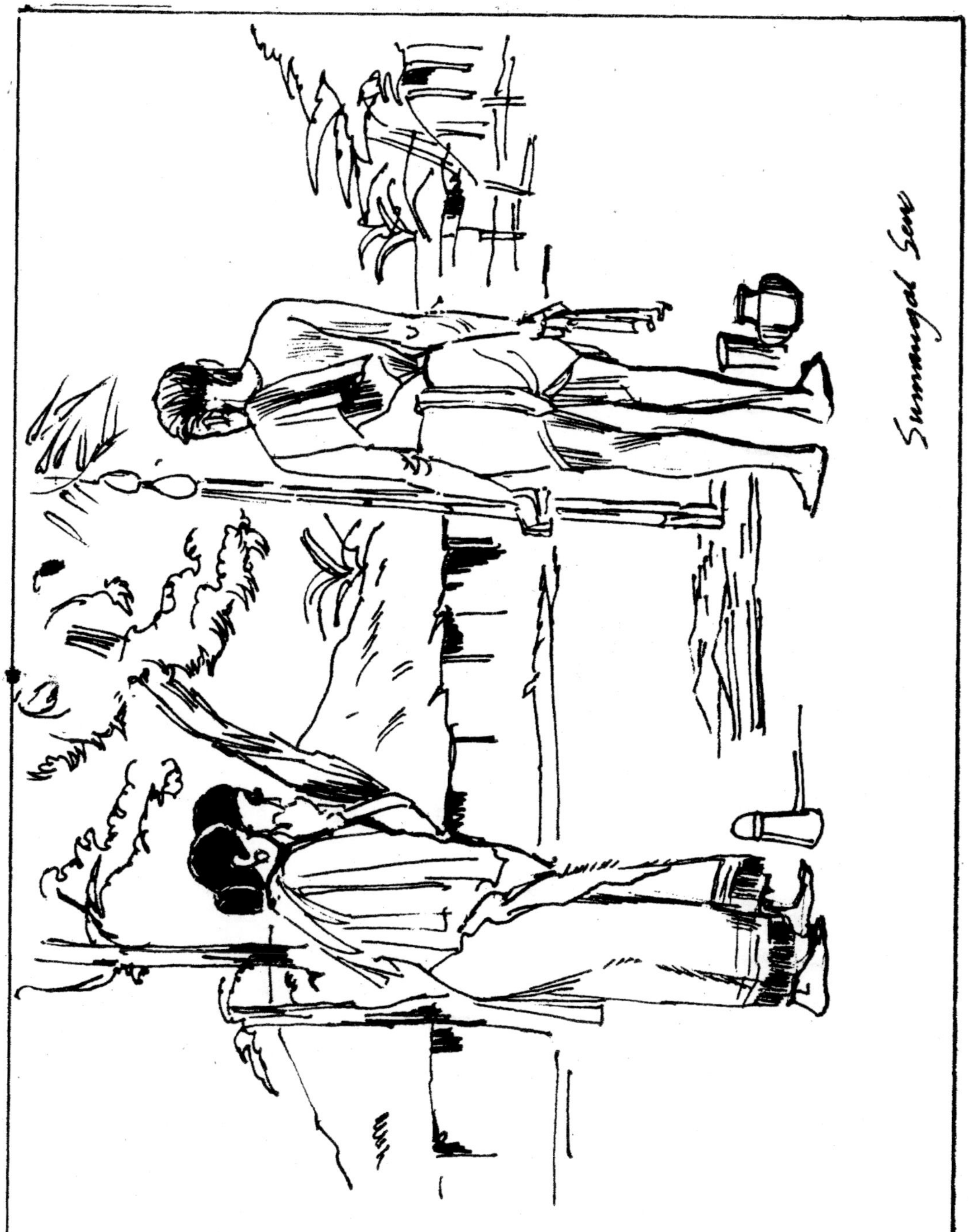

"Jagalyas" All performing "Ulu" while "Achai" is about to begin the rituals of Garia festival

Beating drum (Khām) during Garia Festival.

Bighu dance of Chakma community

Rangalu Vihu

there is no denying the fact that Vihu happens to be one of the most popular, colourful and vigorous folk dances of India. Besides, the great anthropologists hold that Vihu is Mother-worship and relates to fertility in nature and society.

In conclusion we return to what we originally proposed to explore. Garia is essentially the deity of agriculture, harvest and fertility, and is undoubtedly the greatest festival in Tripura. Besides the dates chosen for the purpose are the Hari Visu, the Vishuba Saṅkrānti and the New Year's Day, clearly suggest the end of the old and the beginning of the new, with renewed hope and aspiration. The victorious army of Tripura returned with the image of the deity on the Vihuva Saṅkrānti night, and celebrated the victory for seven days. And this particular event in history put an end to Tripuri-Kuki war.

We also have seen similarity among the festivals of *Gajan* and *Charak, Garia, Vijhu,* and *Vihu* of Bengal, Tripura and Assam. Certain findings also suggest similarities even across the border in Burma. In future, if a thorough probe is carried out, it may hopefully reveal further similarities with Far Eastern festivals.

References

1. *Garia Sanskriti,* Suren Deb Burman (ed.), Agartala. 1986.
2. *Garia Puja,* M. Damodaran (ed), IAS, Director, Directorate of Tribal Research, Tripura. 1976.
3. *A Cultural Profile-Tripura* (ed.), Deptt. of Information, Cultural Affairs and Tourism, Govt. of Tripura.
4. Music, Dance and Drama – Tripura, Deptt. of Information, Cultural Affairs and Tourism, Govt. of Tripura.
5. *Vijhu Smaranika* (Vijhu Souvenir) : Tripura State Vijhu Festival Committee. 1985.
6. *Cultural Theme of the Folk Dances of Tripura Tribes : A Short Study* : Suren Deb Burman
7. *Asamer Ujjwal Rangali Vihu Utsav* (Dazzling Rangali Festival of Assam): Anupam Gupta, Weekly *Vartaman* (A Bengali Weekly) 23 April, 1994.

Aspects of Indian History and Historiography
Editor : P.K. Mishra
Kaveri Books, New Delhi, India.

Endowments to Temples in Northern India (Early Medieval Period)

10

Puspa Niyogi

From the Gupta period onward many temples, both big and small were built in Northern India. Their architecture developed a distinctive regional style, but their ritualistic aspects bore a common trait. The temples became centre of religious activities which played a decisive part in social and economic life of the people.

The temples were supported and maintained by donations, gifts and endowments from different people, belonging to the different classes, starting from the king. The people, with their deep faith in religion contributed whatever they could and also accepted the imposition or order of the State (or guild, trading community) in regard to donations to temples. We have not come across a single instance against the State (or others) regarding any impositions for the maintenance of temples. This attitude and broad-mindedness of the people encouraged the Ruling class and also the higher classes of the society to built temples for their religious satisfaction.

Temples, whether big or small, had strong economic foundations. They constituted a major factor in the national economy as our evidences show and some of the temples were very wealthy institutions, amassed huge amounts of wealth composed of cash money, jewellery, precious stones and many other things. Some temples had large areas of land under their direct control and management. The lands under their supervision were in many cases more favourably taxe than private property. Of immovable property they owned house-sites and houses. Temples owned shops also and some of them possessed gardens where they grew their required fruits and flower tress. In short, the wealth of the temples were derived from rich gifts made by kings, dignitories, wealthy classes of the population, generous and religious members of society, as well as pilgrims and others. The immense wealth of the temples was one of the factors that encouraged the foreigners to invade India in the 10th and 11th centuries A.D. Besides rich gifts the temples received small donations as endowments from various sources for the daily rituals, and worship and maintenance of the temples. An idea about the different kinds and nature of endowments to temples may be found mainly from epigraphical records and some other sources. The different kinds of endowments received by some of the temples as are listed below:

1. Grants of land and villages in favour of temples which are ear-marked for meeting the cost of daily worship;
2. Grants of houses — these houses were either kept for the temple employees or they were rented;
3. Temples also received gardens which were utilised for growing fruits and flowers required for their everyday use;

4. Temples sometimes received shops as gifts;
5. Gifts from oil-millers;
6. Donations from Gardeners;
7. Endowments from Markets;
8. Endowments from the *Śulka-maṇḍapikā*;
9. Road cess for endowments;
10. Donation from horse-dealers;
11. Guilds as donors.

Gifts of Villages and Land

Inscriptions sometimes record grants of land in favour of temples. Lands were assigned not only by the king himself but by members of the royal family such as the queen, the queen-mother, the prince as well as others of high ranks, viz. ministers, *sāmantas*, and many others. Private gifts of land are also recorded, such as those made by merchants, land-lords, traders, artisans, members of guilds and others.

Most of the available land-grants of the period are found to have been assigned by kings. It is, therefore, needless to name inscriptions recording gifts by kings.

Gifts by Members of the Royal Family

In some cases gifts of land were made by princes and *yuvarājas* (heir-apparent) such as in the Karitalai stone inscription of the reign of the Chedi Lakṣmanarāja.[1] It is recorded that Śaṅkaragaṇa, the king's son donated the village Challipāṭaka in the district of Dhavalaharā and the village Antarapāṭa to the temple of Viṣṇu. It is interesting to note that in this grant we have a reference to gifts by the king himself and his wife, king Lakṣmanarāja and queen Rāhaḍā. Both of them donated villages to the temple of Viṣṇu. Many joint endowment by the king and his son are also found.

There are instances of land grants made by queens of the reigning kings. Thus from the Bilhari inscription of the Chedis, we learn that the Nohalā, the wife of the Chedi ruler Keyūravarsha erected a temple of Śiva and she endowed this temple with the revenues of the villages of Dhaṅgatapāṭaka, Pondi, Nāgabala, Khailapāṭaka, Viḍā, Sajjāhali and Goshthapali.[2] Similar evidence is furnished by the Bherāghāt inscription of queen Alhanadevi (dated in the Chedi year 907), where it is recorded that the queen Alhanadevi and Jayasiṁhadeva, founded a Śiva temple, with a *maṭha* or cloister, a hall of study and gardens attached to it, and for the maintenance of these buildings and their occupants, she assigned the income produced by the two villages of Nāmauṇḍi in the Jāuli *pattalā* and of Makarapāṭaka. Probably the queens assigned the shares of their income, which were due to them for the status they held.[3]

Not only did the queens endowed the revenues of the villages in favour of religious institutions but instances are also available of land grants by queens. Thus, the Barsur inscription of Gaṅgamahādevi, the chief queen of Someśvaradeva, granted a village named Keramaruka or Keramaṛuka to the two temples of Śiva.[4] Same kind of information is furnished by the Bayana inscription of Chitralekhā (V.S. 1012) where it is stated that Chitralekhā, built the temple of Viṣṇu and gave two villages named Gograpura and Nagapalli as well as certain fields to the deity. At the end of the record there is a supplementary verse mentioning the name of a village Aluvadraka by Indrajit may be to the same temple.[4a]

Donation by Others

Lands were also granted to religious institutions and temples by persons other than members of the royal family, such as feudatories, governors and others. The Pāṇāherā inscription of the time of Jayasiṁhadeva of Malwa (V.S. 1116)[5] records that the *Maṇḍalikā* (a Feudatory of king Jayasiṁhadeva), granted to the temple of Maṇḍaeśvara some lands and to the temple of Varuṇeśvarī some lands in the villages of Naṭṭapāṭaka, Pānāchhi and Maṇḍalodraka. From the Partabgarh inscription of the time of (the Pratihara) king Mahendrapāla II (V.S. 1003)[6] we learn that Mādhava, the great feudatory lord and Governor of Ujjayini, granted the village of Dhārā-Padraka for repair and maintenance of daily services at the temple of Indrāditydeva, a the request of the great feudatory Indrarāja, son of Durlabharāja of the Cāhamāna race.

A minister named Madoli received a gift from his master, king Jayāditya and he transferred the gift village Dummuddumāka to the goddess Durga.[7]

The Bhubaneswar inscription of Anaṅgabhima III records the grant of five *vātikas* of land situated in the villages of Tarallakshmi and Sāgarapaṭimā by Govinda Senapati, son of Garia-*Sēnādhyaksha*. The land was granted for making provision for sweeping the *Maṇḍapa* (which was repaired by Govinda) thrice a day, white-washing the walls once a year and repairing the roof once in every twelve years. Of the five *vātikas* of land two were allotted to the *kumbhakāra* (potter) for repairing the roof, two to the *chūrnakāra* (lime-washers) for white-washing and one to the sweeper. The grant was made for the repair of the *Maṇḍapa* in which the deity (Kirtivāsa i.e. Śiva) was installed. Govinda was an officer of the Gaṅga king Anaṅgabhima III.

Grant of land by a Senapati of the Gaṅga king named Īśvara (Ira) is recorded in the Bhuvaneswara inscription of Bhimadeva, for a lamp and other provisions. The inscription further records the grant of some pieces of land measuring 2½ *vāṭis* (about 45 acres); 6 *maṇas* (3/8 *vāṭi*) in Balabhadrapara; 3 *vāṭis* (60 acres) in Koṇtharāṅga *viṣaya* for *naivedya* or daily offerings to the deity and for the provision of *pāniyapatra (dhārā-patra)*.[9]

Two inscriptions of Durgarāja are found near Pushkara near Ajmer. The first inscription records certain gifts in favour of god Puṇḍarikāksha (i.e. Viṣṇu). The second inscription records certain gifts by Durgaraja in favour of the god Rannāditya (i.e. the Sun god), including land intended to provide for a lamp for the god as well as for the burning of incense, offering of food and white-washing the walls of the temple.[10] It is presumed that whatever was given by the pilgrims visiting the Pushkara *tirtha* became the gifts of the temple.

From a Vākārtaka inscription we learn that half a village was granted by a merchant named Chandra to a temple Rāmagiri, which was frequently visited by Prabhavatigupta.[11] Even the inhabitants of a village dedicated to the local temple whatever they could. Thus, the Kuruspal stone inscription of Śomesvaradeva states of that the inhabitants of the village dedicated a lamp to god Lokeśvara and paid eleven *gaḍyāṇikas* (coins).[12] The Mandkila temple inscription (V.S. 1043) refers to a banker named Nāgabari who built a Viṣṇu temple. His grandson is Nandana. He also built temples and tanks. Nandana erected a Viṣṇu temple adjacent to the temple built by his grandfather. He made provisions for the maintenance of these temples.[13] Similarly, in one of the plate of Lalitasūradeva (year 22) there is reference to grant of some land (which was in possession of a person named Dēnduvāka) in favour of the god Nārāyaṇa-bhaṭṭāraka. This gift was made for providing perfumes, flowers, incense, ointments, offerings and for repairing of what may be broken and for the maintenance of servants, attendants and others. In another plate from Pandukesvar mention is made of donation of land in favour of the god Badrikāśaram-bhaṭṭaraka for daily worship and for providing incense, flowers and other items of worship.[14]

Gift of land and money are recorded in some inscriptions. Thus, the grant of Mehra Jagamalla, dated V.S. 1264, records the grant of 55 *pāthas* of land in each of the two villages named Kambalauli and Phulasara for the maintenance of the gods. The inscription also records donations of annual grants of money (*drammas* and *rūpakas*).[15]

Besides, donations in cash was very common. Thus, the Jalor inscription of Cāhamāna Chachigadeva (V.S. 1331)[16] records the grant of 150 *drammas* to the god Mahāvira by Nāṁvai (Not clear), son of Dēdō and brother of Dhaṇasiṁha. The money was entrusted to the Superintendent of the Monastery (*Maṭhapati*) and the members of the Assembly (*goshṭhikas*). It is stipulated that the interest of the granted money, amounting to 15 *dramma* coins which should be spent on worship, offering and supervision. Apparently the interest was realised annually. Similarly, in one of the inscriptions of the time of the Guhilas, we learn that a lady named Vōṇṇā constructed a Śiva temple and granted 40 *drammas* for repairing, worship and cleaning of the same.[17] From a Gaya inscription (V.S. 1232) we learn that the *Gkuggulin* (one who burns *guggula* i.e. an incense-burner) Vidyādhara deposited 50 *kārshāpaṇas* for making provisions for feeding Brāhmaṇas at the Gadadhara temple on Āśvinasudi 5 every year. It is further stated in the inscription that 50 *kārshāpānas* was deposited as an endowment yielding an annual interest of 16 *kārshāpāṇas* at the rate of 32 per cent which was spent on the occasion.[18] From an inscription from Sonarpur we learn that the purpose of the grant was to record the grant of 12 coins called *Edaviya-paṇa* in favour of the god (coin of this name is yet unknown).[19] The Bhinmal stone inscription (I) of the temple of Jagaśvāmi records the grant of 40 *drammas* by Vilhāka, the *Vetaka* to the treasury. Similarly, another Bhinmal stone inscription (IV) registers two gifts of 55 *drammas* to the same god.[20] The Dariba temple inscription, dated V.S. 1359 records the gift of 16 *drammas* to the temple when the Mahārājakula Ratnasiṁha was ruling over Meḍapata.[21]

Temples also owned gardens which were utilised for growing fruits and flowers required for their everyday use. References to such gardens are to be found in some of the relevant inscriptions of the period.[22] Fields were also presented to temples.[23]

Houses

It was also customary to present house-sites and houses to temples on certain conditions. Thus we are told in the Ahar stone inscription that a house-site was granted as surety for a monthly payment of ten *viṁśopakas* to Kanakaśrīdevi, which had been acquired by the grandfather of the donee for a term of 99 years on which they had themselves constructed with burnt bricks, two *apavarakas* (inner apartments). It is further stated that the sons and other descendants, in succession, were to enjoy the rent of the above mentioned house after they had paid every month ten *viṁśopakas* to the temple.[24] Elsewhere we are told that the donees made over the entire rent and not ten *viṁśopakas* only, as previously arranged, by a deed of ninety-nine years, to the goddess in consideration of payments made out of the funds of the temple.[25] The object of this transaction would appear to have been the safe investment of the income of the temple by taking a lease of the house for ninety-nine years that it could be let out on rent, the entire amount thus realised being credited to the temple's account. From the same source it is learnt that by a deed of ninety-nine years the *goshṭhī* (i.e. the Managing Committee of the temple) also purchased the southern half of a building site with money belonging to the temple. A similar purchase was made by the *Sauvarṇṇikā Mahājanas* on behalf of the temple.

Grants of houses in favour of temples are recorded in some inscriptions, e.g. the Mathura Praśasti of the rein of Vijayapāla, the Siyadon inscription, the Bhāṭerā copper plate inscription and in many other grants.[26]

Some temples had shops, which were let out on a rental basis. From the Ahar stone inscription,[27] mentioned above, it is to be gathered that the money belonging to the goddess Kanakaśrīdevi, an *avārī* (shop) was purchased containing three rooms. Out of the rent yielded by the property, funds were to be provided for saffron, flowers, incense, lamps, for perpetual cleaning and plastering, white-washing and repair work in the temple. Similar other purchases are also recorded in the same inscription.

From the Kaman stone inscription[28] we learn that two *avārīs*, situated outside the fort, were donated by a *saṁkhika* (a worker on couchshell named Bhadra), by means of a written deed. It is further recorded in the same inscription, that some *drammas* were given by king, Bhojadeva to Pramanarasi, and after his death the amount was handed over to the *goshikas*. The latter purchased two *avārīs* with the *drammas*. The *vithīs* or shops in the *avārikas* were situated facing south in the *Kamballi-haṭṭa* i.e. where a cattle-market was held. The rent of these *vithīs* was to be utilised by the *goshṭhikas* in meeting the expenses of white-washing, vermillion and lights for the temples. Grants of shops in favour of temples are recorded in some inscriptions.[29]

Endowments from Oilmills

Endowments received by temples included assignments on trade. Endowments were made mostly for specific purposes in accordance with stipulated terms. Thus to provide oil for lamps, an inscription from Shergadh[30] records donations consisting of an assignment of the entire produce of two oil-mills owned by Thāiyaka, chief of the guild of oilmillers. Oilmills working in villages are mentioned in some cases to have contributed portions of their output, to religious endowments. Thus in the Mathura Praśasti[31] it is stipulated that from engine (i.e. an oil-mill) a *palī* was to be levied. The Jhanvara inscription[32] records that one *kalaśa* of oil, collected from the local oilmills, was to be used for the lighting of the lamp in a temple. From the Arthuna inscription of the Paramāra Chāmuṇḍarāja we come to know that a list of dues are given including on each *karsha* of oil a *panaka* was levied for the god.[33] From the Vāillabhaṭṭasvāmin Temple inscription[34] we come to know that the guild of oil-millers made donations in favour of a temple. In order to provide oil for the lamps, the chiefs of the oil-millers and the other members of the whole guild of oil-millers gave one *palikā* of oil per oil-mill. The Pratabgarh inscription of the time of (the Pratihara king) Mahendrapāla II (Samvat 1003)[35] records the donation of fields and many other items including 'one *palikā* of oil per oil-mill'.

Gardeners

It is interesting to note that the guild of gardeners, who dwelt on top of the Gwalior fort, made donation in favour of a temple. The chief with other members of the local guild of gardeners were required to provide fifty garlands (*mālās*) of daily market flowers for purposes of worship, as known from the second Vāillabhattasvāmi Temple inscription.[36] The Kaman stone inscription records similar information about donations and endowments, made from time to time, in favour of a deity, installed in a temple at Kamyaka. In document IV of the inscription it is stated that the guild of gardeners, living in Kamyaka, in consideration of a sum of money paid in advance, stipulated to supply permanently sixty garlands, of which thirty-four were be delivered at the temple of Viṣṇu and the remaining thirty-six at the shrine of Chāmūḍā.[37]

Not only members of guilds made gifts of garlands to the deities even others did not same. Thus in the Partabgarh inscription of the reign of Mahendrapāla II[38] records a permanent endowment in favour of the shrine attached to the monastery of Hari-Rishiśvara at Dasapura consisting of many items including hundred garlands of four strings each. Tasai inscription of Harsa (Year 182)[39] refers to the endowment in favour of a temple, consisting forty garlands, on the 12th day of the dark half of (every) month. Gardens were also gifted to temples. Thus, as in the Pāṇāharā inscription of the time of Jayasimha of Malwa we are told that the *Maṇḍalikā* granted a garden to the temple of Maṇḍaleśvara.[40] Similarly, we find the queen Alhanadevi founded a temple with a garden attached to it.

Endowments from Markets

Another source of revenue was the market. The evidence furnished by epigraphy in this connection, does not make the point clear whether gifts were made out of the State's due on sales and purchases or of specified levies collected at the market for religious purposes. Special levies were collected at the market for religious purposes. The Rājor inscription of Mathanadeva (V.S. 1016)[41] gives a list of taxes assigned to the temple of a god Lachchhukeśvara Mahādeva (Śiva) jointly with the god Viṇayaka (Ganeśa), consisting of the following items :

1. Three *viṁśopakas* on every sack of agricultural produce brought for sale to the market;
2. Two *palikās* from every *ghaṭaka-kūpaka* of clarified butter and oil;
3. Fifty leaves from every *chollikā*.

It appears that the particular market, mentioned above, dealt exclusively in agricultural products. No other kind of commodities is to be noticed in the list. It may not be unlikely that as appropriate levies had been already collected on such commodities at proper places, no further tax was imposed on them in the market.

The Arthuna inscription of the Paramāra Chānuṇdarāja (V.S. 1136)[42] gives an account of the endowment of the temple of *Maṇḍaleśa* (Śiva) by the king, as will be seen in the following :

1. One fruit out of every *bhāraka* of coconuts;
2. A *mānaka* on each *mūṭaka* of salt;
3. One nut from every thousand areca-nuts;
4. One *palikā* on every *ghaṭaka* of butter and sesam oil;
5. One and a half *rūpakas* on each *koṭikā* of clothing fabric;
6. Two *pūlakas* on a *jāla;*
7. Two *santas* on each *lagaḍā;*
8. A *panaka* on each *karsha* of oil;
9. A *vṛisha-viṁśopaka* on each load of cattle-fodder;
10. A *dramma* on every pile of sugar;
11. A *haraka* of barley on a water-wheel;
12. One *bhāraka* on twenty (packs) of loaded grain;
13. One *varnika* on each *bharaka* of candid sugar and jaggery;
14. One *rūpaka* on each *bhāraka* of Bengal madder,[42] thread and cotton.

It appear from this inscription that the local market dealt in all kinds of commodities, including agricultural products as well as industrial, such as clothing fabrics, also gold, silver and other metals. Endowments were both in cash and kind.

Another earlier inscription, the Ahar temple inscription of Allaṭa of Mewar (V.S. 1008 & 1010)[43] registers the construction of a temple of the god Murari and records various endowments for its maintenance. They are as follows :

1. One *dramma* on the sale of an elephant;
2. One-fortieth of a *dramma* on a horned animal;
3. Two *rūpakas* on a horse;
4. One *tūla* from a *lāṭa;*
5. One *chatuḥsar* from the flower-sellers every day.

These taxes like sales taxes, were collected on the sales taking place in the market; they were then given to the temple concerned. It is further stated in the same inscription that contributions were also levied upon various other traders of the locality, including even the gamblers. It is also laid down that the merchants of Karnata, Laṭa, Madhyadeśa, and Takka should pay contributions to the temple.

A permanent endowment made in favour of shrines attached to the monastery of Hari-Rishiśvara[44] as recorded in the Partabgarh inscription of king Mahendra-Pāla II includes :

1. One *palikā* of oil per oil-mill;
2. Five bundles of foliage;
3. One hundred garlands of four stringes;
4. Two *pālas* of saffron;
5. One pāla of betel-nuts

These items are to be given by the trading community in the month of Chaitra, in favour of the Vata-yakshini Devi.

It may be interesting to refer, for a comparative study, to the Bijapur inscription[45] which records a variety of donations made in favour of the Jaina temple of Rishabhanātha, as noted below :

1. One Rupee for each twenty loads carried for sale;
2. One 'Rupee' on each cart filled (whether going from or by the village or passing by it);
3. One *karsha* for a *ghaḍā* at each oilmill;
4. 14 (thirteen) *chollikas* of betel-leaves by the Bhaṭṭas;
5. *Pellaka-pellaka* (?) by the gamblers;
6. One *ādhaka* of wheat and barley from each *araghaṭṭa* (i.e. a well with a water-wheel;
7. Five *pālas* for pedda (?);
8. One *viṁśopaka* coin for each bhara (= 2,000 *pālas*);
9. Ten *pālas* from each *bhāra* of articles, such as cotton, copper, saffron, gum-resin (*pura* i.e. *guggulu*), madder and so forth;
10. One *mānaka* for each droṇa of wheat, *mung*, barley, salt, *rāla*, and such other objects as can be measured.

The Mathura Praśasti of the reign of Vijayapāla (V.S. 1207)[46] refers to the construction of a large temple of Viṣṇu and the endowments made to it which includes the following :

1. A *gonīprasriti* of rice (*anna*) 'possessing the proper weight, size and flavour;
2. A *palī* from each engine (i.e. oilmills);
3. '...a....from the flower-garland-maker; and
4. Fourth part from the *māpaka*. The literal meaning of the word *'māpaka'* is a 'measurer'. Probably the text refers to the *māpāri* i.e. the official who had to measure the grain brought into the market, the rate of which were fixed by the government. The *māpāka* may have been entrusted to levy a small tax on the dealers in grain. From the above it

follows that besides the king's normal share of the produce and other specific taxes, villagers were sometimes required to pay extraordinary taxes such as the one levied on the *māpaka*. Such demands were to be met in kind and the amount collected did not go to the coffers of the state but was regarded as a local levy to be used for religious purposes.[47]

Besides the state dues levied on the market, there were some other impositions on the buyers and sellers as noted below. There are some other items which were subject to taxation mainly for religious purposes and in most cases they were in kind. Thus, in the Patanarayana stone inscription of the Paramāra Pratapsiṁha, dated V.S. 1233[48] it is stated that for the maintenance of a temple the villagers of Kalhanavada were required to pay one *seer* of grain at each plough. The Sevādi stone inscription of Aśvarāja (V.S. 1176)[49] records the provision for the daily worship of Śrī Dharmanāthadeva in the temple of Samipati, of barley corn equal to one *haraka* for each of the wells (*arahata*) belonging to a group of four villages. The Sāṇḍērav stone inscription of Kelhaṇadeva (V.S. 1221)[60] records that Analadevī, the queen mother of Kelhaṇadeva granted one *hāele* (i.e. as much land as could be tilled by a single plough in one day) of *yagaṁdharī* (or jvīr corn) from the king's personal property to the god Mahāvīra. Similarly one *hāele* of *yugamdharī* was also granted by the *rathakāras* (i.e. cart builders). From the Lālrai stone inscription of Kelhaṇadeva (V.S. 1233)[51] we learn that the princes, Lākhaṇapāla and Abhayapāla together with the queen Mahibaladevī granted barley corn measuring one *haraka* from the machine-well (i.e. *araghata*) called Urahari for celebrating the festival of the god Sāmtinātha. The Dubkund stone inscription of Kachchhapaghāṭa Vikramasiṁha (V.S. 1145)[52] records that for the building of the temple, for keeping it in good repairs and also for the maintenance of worship assigned (a tax of) one *viṁśopaka* charged on each *goṇi* (of grain) of wheat and he moreover provided certain amount of oil for lamps, etc. The Bhinmāl stone inscription of Udayasiṁhadeva (V.S. 1306)[53] records the deposit of forty *drammas* in the treasury of the god Jagatsvāmin, out of which were to be defrayed the expenses of the '*divasa-bali*'. The inscription also gives us an idea about the provisions for the *balī*, which was to be composed of 2 *sēī* of wheat and 8 *kalaśa* of boiled ghee besides for *naivedya* or offering to the god, fixed quantities of pulse, rice and ghee, etc. From the Sasbahu Temple inscription[54] it is understood that a prince took necessary steps for the maintenance of the employees of a temple. Besides making donations of *naivedya* and for light, he also presented a number of valuable gifts such as a golden diadem, covered with precious stones and a large jewel in the middle, a frontal ornament made of emeralds, a golden ornament for the neck, a pair of arm-rings and four bracelets, all of which were studded with precious stones.

Endowments from the Śulkā-Maṇḍapikā

An attempt may now be made to focus our attention on that branch of taxation which was related to trade (i.e. *śulka*). Śulka used to be collected at the *Śulka-maṇḍapikā*. Inscriptions do not give any idea about the rates of taxation but some of them refer to *Śulka-maṇḍapikā* in connection with donations made out of the tax collected there for religious purposes in favour of temples. The Nadol plate of Ālhaṇadeva[55] mentions that the Cāhamāna ruler, granted to a Jaina temple a monthly sum of five *drammas* from the local *śulka-maṇḍapikā*. Here the amount to be paid to the temple authorities was specified, whatever might have been the actual collection at the *maṇḍapikā* in any month of the year. The same nature of information is available from the Praśasti of Baijnāth[56] which record that a local chief granted daily two *drammas* out of the income derived from the *maṇḍapikā*. The Nadol plate of Pratāpasiṁha (V.S. 1213)[57] similarly records a grant by a feudatory of Kumarapāla, consisting of a *rūpaka* per day, which was to be paid out of the collection at the *maṇḍapikā* in favour of some Jaina temples. The Bayana inscription of Chitralekhā (A.D. 955)[58] refers to the collection of three drammas a deity at the *maṇḍapikā* of Śripatha and of a similar sum at the *maṇḍapikā* Vasāvaṭa. Similarly, the Nanana grant of the Chaulukya king Kumarapāla (V.S. 1212)[59] mentions that Kumarapāla granted one *dramma* per day out of the collection at the custom-house of Nadol in favour of a temple. The information supplied by the Bilharī stone inscription, is of a different nature. It appears from the inscription that various manufacturers and traders as well as the inhabitants of a certain locality had to deliver or pay to the *maṇḍapikā*, for the benefit of a monastery and its occupants certain articles such as salt, oil, betel, pepper, ginger, vegetables, etc. and also fixed sums of money for every horse, elephant, and some other animals sold by them, evidently as taxes for religious endowments.[60]

Endowments from Roads-Road-Cess

From the inscriptions of the period it appears that road-cesses constituted a definite source of revenue out of which donations were sometimes made to temples and religious institutions. The Pānāherā inscription of the time of Jayasiṁhadeva of Malwa (V.S. 1116)[61] for instance records that king Jayasiṁha assigned to the god one *viṁśopaka* on every bull that passed on the road, for the maintenance of the worship of a deity. It is likely that in this case the assignment formed a part of the total collection of road-cess in a particular, the charge on the bull being a levy on the standard load carried by the animal. The Nāḍlāi stone inscription of Rājyapāla (V.S. 1195)[62] makes the point clear when recording that the king granted one-twentieth part of the income (*ābhāvya*) derived from the loads on bullocks going on their way or coming to Nāḍlāi for lamp, incense offering, flowers worship and so forth of Śrī Neminātha (Temple of Neminātha). The inscription, however, does not definitely show whether the donation in the recorded case was in cash or in kind. The Junā stone inscription of Samantasiṁhadeva (V.S. 1325)[63] refers to a grant of one *pāilā* from every incoming and outgoing caravan 'exceeding ten camels and twenty bullocks'. In default of this payment in kind, ten *Bhīmapriya viṁśopaka* were to be charged. The grant was to be distributed equally between the two gods at Bahadamaru, namely, Vighnamardana and Chaumdarāja, in the temple of Ādinātha. It appears that the cess in question was levied on inland commercial transport, either arriving at or departing from a certain station. One Nāḍlāi stone inscription (V.S. 1202)[64] furnishes similar information regarding cesses collected on highways. Here a distinction is drawn between bullocks and carts as carriers of loads in fixing the rates of the cess. There are also certain specific details in this record in regard to the schedule framed for the purpose of charging the levy, which are lacking in similar grants. Thus the inscription notes that there were two different rates for bullocks and carts, and that in the case of bullocks two *rupakas* were to be charged for each twenty *pāilās* of load, carried by the former, while one *rūpaka* was to be charged on each cart conveying commodities which came under the class *kiraṇas* (i.e. substance such as gum, dry ginger, black pepper, etc.). The charge per cart is mentioned without any specification as regards to the weight of the load carried, which implies that carts in all cases were approximately of the same size and type and that their maximum carrying capacity was of a known standard which was invariable. The donation was made in favour of a temple of Mahāvira.

The inscriptions, so far considered in connection with cesses collected on roads, show that these were either in kind or cash or in both. The amount of a donation was not fixed, for it depended upon the actual turnover, which may have varied, although it was quite possible to form an approximate estimate on the basis of past figures available to the donor. One inscription makes it definitely clear that the donation was out of the income from transport, but the other inscriptions do not mention this point specifically, from which it may be conjectured that the cess may have been an additional one which was levied for a religious endowment.

Taxes for Endowments from Horse-dealers

Like the oilmillers and gardeners the dealers in horse also imposed upon themselves taxes for endowments to religious institutions. The evidence of the Pehoa inscription (882-83 A.D.)[65] seems to suggest that when it concerned a religious institution it was possible even for private individuals to introduce a tax, the payment of which was obligatory on the part of all similarly placed, not excepting the king himself. This inscription records that certain horse-dealers, meeting at a *yātrā* held at Pehoa, agreed to impose upon themselves and upon their customers certain taxes or tithes, which were to be distributed among some temples. The taxes, thus voluntarily imposed were :

1. Two *dharmas*, which were to be collected by deducting from the sum received by the dealer in horse for each animal, sold at Prithudaka to the king or to any of his subjects.
2. One *Dharma*, to be paid by the buyer on each animal which was in excess of the stipulated price. Even if the king was a party to the transaction, he was equally liable to pay his share in conformity with the agreement, arrived at.

In the Harsha stone inscription[66] one *dramma* on every horse was assigned to a temple by the horse-dealers the occasion when this money is given is not stated. Similarly, the Bayana stone inscription of Chittralekhā (V.S. 1012)[67] shows that for a deity, one *dramma* was to be set apart, collected on every horse sold, or on every horse-load of merchandise. The Bāli stone inscription (V.S. 1200)[68] records that whenever a horse-fair was held, in which horses were sold, one *dramma* per horse was to be levied and assigned to a goddess; two *drammas*, similarly collected, to the *Saṁghapati*; one *dramma* each to other persons and for other purposes. The contents of the inscription are not clear with regard to these other beneficiaries.

Guilds as Donors

Sometimes members of guilds showed their interest in the maintenance of village temples by deciding to raise subscriptions from amongst themselves on a stipulated basis. Thus an inscription at Gwalior[69] states that in order to provide oil for lamps, chiefs of oilmillers and other members of their association agreed to give one *pālikā* or oil per oilmill. On the same day when this agreement was drawn up, it was also decided that the chiefs of gardens and other members of the entire guild of gardeners were to furnish for daily requirements of worship, fifty garlands (*mālā*) of seasonal flowers, etc. on a perpetual basis. Other people of the town also made a joint grant for the benefit of the same temple. A similar endowment is recorded in the Kaman stone inscription[70] which shows that a guild sometimes did not pay out of its common fund, but levied a small cess on every member working in a particular locality. The inscription mentions three such guilds, viz. those of potters, artisans and gardeners. We find that the members of the last named guild were to pay in kind, while those of the first two had to pay a small cess probably because the articles produced by them were not regularly required for the use of the temple. Our inscription explicitly states that every one of the potter who followed the particular profession in the place called Kamyaka, was to contribute one *pāṇa* per wheel every month; and likewise the guild of gardeners stipulated to supply permanently sixty garlands; and every artisan, who worked in the same place, undertook to pay one *dramma* per month. Obviously the different guilds could be trusted to collect the stipulated amounts from their respective members and pay them regularly to the beneficiary of the endowments. Further contact was maintained through the investment of endowed money with villagers, who agreed to pay the interests on the sums deposited, to the authorities of the temples concerned.

References

1. EI, II, pp. 174 ff; VIII, pp. 200 ff; XXXIII, pp. 82 ff.
2. *Ibid*, I, pp. 251 ff.
3. *Ibid*, II, pp. 7 ff.
4. *Ibid*, IX, pp. 162 ff.
5. *Ibid*, XXII, pp. 120 ff.
5. *Ibid*, XXI, pp. 32 ff.
6. *Ibid*, XIV, pp. 176 ff.
7. IA, XXI, pp. 169 ff.
8. EI, XXX, pp. 17 ff.
9. *Ibid*, XXX, pp. 232 ff; *dhārā-patra-pānīyapatra*- it is a water jar with a small hole at the bottom from which water trinkles down continuously on the Śiva *linga*.
10. EI, XXXV, pp. 239 ff.
11. Ed. by Vasudev Vishnu Mirashi, Inscriptions of the Vakatakas (CII, V), Ootacamund, pp. xi ff., Nos. 9 and 13.
12. EI, K, pp. 37 ff.
13. EI, XXXIV, pp. 77 ff; cf. XXXVI, pp. 39 ff.
14. EI, XXXI, pp. 277 ff; 284 ff; 290 ff.
15. IA, XI, pp. 337 ff.
16. EI, XXXIII, pp. 46 ff.
17. EI, XXXV, pp. 57 ff.
18. *Ibid*, XXXV, pp. 233 ff.; cf, SI, p. 150n 5.
19. BG, Vol. I, Part, I, pp. 474, ff; EI, XI, pp. 55 ff.
20. Rajputana Museum Report, 1927, p. 3.
21. EI, I, pp. 32 ff; 135 ff; II, pp. 232 ff; XIII, 283 ff; XXI, pp. 42 IA, VI, pp. 205 ff.
22. EI, XXXV, pp. 242 ff; XIV, 176 ff; XXII, pp. 283 ff; WZKM, XXI, pp. 14 ff.
23. EI, XIX, pp. 32 ff.
24. *Ibid*.
25. *Ibid*, I, 287 fff; pp. 162 ff; XIX, pp. 277 ff; XXXIII, pp. 112 ff.
26. *Ibid*, XIX, pp. 52 ff.
27. *Ibid*, XXIV, pp. 329 ff.
28. EI, I, pp. 287 ff.
29. *Ibid*, XXIII, pp. 131 ff; cf, the Chitorgarh inscription of the Chaulukya king Kumārapāla records the gift of a *ghanaka* or oilmill for lights, EI, II, pp. 421 ff.
31. EI, I, pp. 287 ff.
32. JASB, XII, pp. 101 ff.
33. EI, XIV, pp. 295 ff.
34. *Ibid*, I, pp. 154 ff.
35. *Ibid*, XIV, pp. 176 ff; cf, the Tasai inscription records the endowments to the temple for the proper performance of worship, namely 2 *palas* of oil for lamp. 2 *palas* of *guggula* (incense), 40 garlands and 80 *mashakas* of saffron and two *chattikas* (pitchers) of *varuna* (wine) on the 12th day of the dark half of every moth-EI, XXXVI, pp. 47 ff.
36. EI, I, pp. 41 ff.
37. *Ibid*, XXIV, pp. 329 ff.
38. *Ibid*, XIV, pp. 176 ff.
39. *Ibid*, XXXVI, pp. 45 ff.
40. *Ibid*, XXI, pp. 41 ff.

41. *Ibid*, III, pp. 263 ff.
42. *Ibid*, XIV, pp. 295 ff.
43. IA, LXIII, pp. 161 ff.
44. EI, XIV, pp. 176 ff.
45. *Ibid*, X, pp. 17 ff.
46. *Ibid*, I, pp. 287 ff.
47. *Ibid*.
48. IA, XLV, pp. 55 ff.
49. EI, XL, pp. 29 ff.
50. *Ibid*, pp. 47 ff.
51. *Ibid*, pp. 49 ff.
52. *Ibid*, II, pp. 232 ff.
53. *Ibid*, XI, pp. 55 ff.
54. IA, XV, pp. 33 ff.
55. EI, IX, pp. 63 ff.
56. *Ibid*, I, pp. 97 ff.
57. IA, XLI, pp. 202 ff.
58. EI, XXII, pp. 120 ff.
59. Annals of the Bhandarkar Oriental Research Institute, Poona, (Silver Jubilee Number), XXIII, pp. 29 ff.
60. EI, I, pp. 251 ff.; cf, the Sānchor stone inscription of Pratapasiṁha (VS 1444) informs us that Salha liberated the people of Bhinmal from the Turushkas. We are further informed that Kamalādevi, wife of Pratapasiṁha renovated the temple of Vāeśvara and also rebuilt the dilapidated temple of the god Vayeśvara. We are further informed that, for the daily offerings to the god, a gift was made of (1) a field, and (2) *two p[illegible]lās on every maund of each commodity from the custom house.*
61. EI, XXI, pp. 41 ff.
62. *Ibid*, XI, pp. 36 ff.
63. *Ibid*, XI, pp. 59 ff.
64. *Ibid*, XI, pp. 42; cf, cf, EI, X, pp. 17 ff (Some of the terms in the above account are left unexplained. No explanation has been offered in similar other cases also where satisfactory evidence has not been found.
65. EI, I, pp. 184 ff.
66. *Ibid*, II, pp. 116 ff; IA, XLII, pp. 57 ff.
67. EI, XXII, pp. 120 ff.
68. *Ibid*, XI, pp. 32 ff.
69. *Ibid*, I, pp. 154 ff.
70. *Ibid*, XXIV, pp. 329 ff.

Aspects of Indian History and Historiography
Editor : P.K. Mishra
Kaveri Books, New Delhi, India.

Modern and Secular Trends in Muslim Social Thought in Nineteenth Century Bengal

11

A.F. Salahuddin Ahmed

The great intellectual ferment which was created as a result of the impact of Western education in early nineteenth century Bengal came to be known as the 'Bengal renaissance'. It is generally believed that it was this movement that had led to the development of what may be called modern and secular outlook in the Indian subcontinent. A great deal of research has been done on the subject and much has been written on it during the last half a century.

In recent years, however, some historians particularly those belonging to the Marxist school have critically analyzed the character of the 'Bengal renaissance' especially emphasizing its limitations. Their main arguments are : (a) the phenomenon of the 'Bengal renaissance' had affected only a handful of *bhadralok*, that is, the urban middle class belonging to the Hindu community only; the great majority of people particularly of the rural areas remained totally unaffected by it. (b) This movement again had no role to play against British colonial rule or imperialism; on the contrary, its protagonists were close collaborators of the British *raj*. (c) And finally, no section of Muslim society had anything to do with this movement.[1] Without however denying the significance of these arguments it may be pointed out that in every age only a handful of men have dared to uphold new ideas which were never widely accepted by the people of their time. Nevertheless, it cannot be denied that these new, progressive and revolutionary ideas despite their limitations did in course of time promote the advancement of mankind.

With regard to the contention that the men of the 'Bengal renaissance' had collaborated with the British colonial power it is suffice to say that it was only through the establishment of British rule that medieval despotisms and feudal social order which had existed in the pre-colonial era were destroyed and the foundation was laid for the growth of modern bourgeois democratic system although imperialist constraints would not allow its full development. Karl Marx himself had noted that although the English colonial rulers had mercilessly exploited the Indian people, they had acted as the "unconscious tool of history" in bringing about social revolution in India.[2]

Until recently it was generally believed that the movement for intellectual freedom which the 'Bengal renaissance' had initiated did not at all affect the Muslim society and that conservative and backward-looking attitude and religious exclusiveness had stood in the way of progress of the Muslim community. This view was derived from a variety of sources among which the most important one was W.W. Hunter's book *The Indian Musalmans* published in 1871. In this book the English civilian had out of his somewhat extraordinary sympathy for the Muslims made certain sweeping statements which, however, were based mostly on inadequate and erroneous evidence. Nevertheless, most Muslim historians have since then accepted them as axiomatic truth.[3] Other works which testify to Muslim conservatism in the nineteenth century are all written in English and Bengali. It should be noted, however, that till the early decades of the nineteenth century the language of the upper class and educated Muslims of Bengal and Persian. And Persian was not cultivated by the Muslims only. Many Hindus particularly of the *bhadralok* class used to learn it with great interest. Raja Rammohun Roy (1774-1833) was an accomplished scholar in both Persian and Arabic. His first book *Tuhfat-ul Muwahhidin* which was published from Murshidabad in 1803-1804 had an Arabic title and preface but the text itself was in Persian. In 1822 Rammohun brought out from Calcutta the first newspaper published in Persian language. It was called *Mirat-ul Akhbar*. While visiting England in 1831 Rammohun Roy gave a written evidence before the Select Committee of the House of Commons constituted to enquire into the affairs of the East India Company. Referring to cordial relations existing between the Hindus and Muslims Rammohun pointed out that during his time, besides similarity in dress between upper class Hindus and Muslims, "the Mussulmans, as well as the more respectable class of Hindus chiefly, cultivated Persian literature, a great number of the former and a few of the latter also extending their studies likewise to Arabic."[4] It should be noted that till 1837 Persian was used as the official language of the East India Company's government. Therefore, in order to have an acquaintance with the intellectual history of the Muslims in the nineteenth century it is necessary to go through various sources that are available in Persian language. These include quite a number of Persian language newspapers, books and pamphlets as well as an unaccountable number of unpublished manuscripts. These are scattered in different parts of the country and are being destroyed for want of proper care. These, in fact, constitute invaluable source materials for reconstructing the intellectual and social history of the Muslim community in Bengal. If one would care to critically study and analyze these sources then many of the presumptions which had been made with regard to society and social thought of the Muslims in nineteenth century India would have to be substantially amended. Here we seek to discuss the subject highlighting one such source. But before we do that the historical perspective has to be taken into account.

By the end of the nineteenth century the Indian subcontinent faced a crisis of unprecedented magnitude. After the collapse of the Mughal central authority the economic and social structure which that authority sustained also began to crumble. This breakdown had also affected the realm of ideas. The possibilities of some revolutionary changes began to manifest in this scenario. In an age of political conflict and social turmoil there was a marked propensity in the intellectual circle to reexamine or revaluate and even question the age old traditional religious beliefs and social practices.

During the Mughal times social leadership was provided by feudal-military aristocracy. After the establishment of British colonial rule this leadership no longer existed. Its place was taken by a new middle class which had emerged as a result of close cooperation with the European mercantile interests and the patronage of British colonial rulers. This class along with the new zamindars created by the Permanent Settlement of 1793, now assumed the leadership of society. Thus was born the aristocracy under the British rule. One section of this class which had established close links with European business interests had not only become acquainted with the modern bourgeois ideas and practices, a considerable number of people belonging to this section had also come in contact with contemporary Western thought. The city of Calcutta, the metropolis of the new rulers provided the ideal cosmopolitan setting for the confluence, clash and convergence of ideas of all kinds. A spirit of inquiry and tolerance of different religious faiths formed the characteristic feature of the age. Thus the study of comparative religion had become popular among the intellectuals of the time. A seventeenth-century Persian treatise called *Dabistan-Mazahib* or Discourse on Religions written by a Zoroastrian scholar had gained wide popularity in contemporary learned circle. Francis Gladwin had translated it into English and it was published in 1797 by the Calcutta Asiatic Society. According to some scholars it was this work which had inspired Rammohun Roy to write his famous tract called *Tuhfat-ul-Muwahhiddin* or 'A Gift to Monotheists' which was published from Murshidabad in 1803-1804.[5]

In fact, the character of social thought in nineteenth century Bengal has to be viewed in this historical perspective. Three distinct trends in this field have been identified.[6] The first trend has been called conservative. Those who upheld it were vehemently opposed to any reform or change in the time-old traditional religious beliefs and social customs. This conservative trend was noticeable in both Hindu and Muslim social thought. However, the attitude of some conservative Hindus was somewhat practical. During the long period of Muslim rule when Persian was the court language, the Hindus did not hesitate to learn it well and were thus able to gain many advantages. But they saw no reason to bring about any change in the traditional Hindu religious and social order. Despite the prevalence of the ancient caste system and the rigidity of the various customs and rituals in Hindu society, there has always existed an element of openness and flexibility in Hindu religious and social thought which had provided Hinduism with an inner strength to survive and withstand any kind of external challenge by adjusting itself with the contemporary situation. As already mentioned, during Muslim rule the Hindus had not hesitated to cultivate Persian, the state language of the Muslim rulers and had thus been able to strengthen their position by securing many benefits from the Muslim rulers. After the establishment of British rule the Hindus had little difficulty to shift their loyalty to the new rulers. For sheer practical consideration they were now eager to learn English, the language of the new rulers. In 1816 some leading members of the Hindu community in collaboration with a number of enlightened European merchants and officials of the East India Company had taken the initiative to establish the Hindu College with the object of imparting education in English language and European science among the Hindu youth. Nevertheless, the hold of conservatism in Hindu society remained as strong as ever. On the other hand, the character of Muslim conservatism was somewhat different. There were two opposing elements in Muslim conservative thought. The first element was traditional and backward-looking whose proponents dreamt of taking the entire Muslim society of their time back to the classical age of the first four Caliphs of Islam (*Khulafa-i-Rashedeen*). Infact, their aim was to reconstruct the nineteenth-century Muslim society on the basis of principles and precepts that existed in the seven-century Arabia during the days of Prophet Muhammad. This romantic dream and mentality have deeply influenced and inspired some sections of Muslim society in every age. The other element of Muslim conservatism was somewhat practical and moderate. This element may be compared with Hindu conservatism of early nineteenth century. Its chief exponents were men like Raja Radhakant Deb (1784-1867). Sheer practical considerations had prompted them to collaborate with English rulers and acquire Western education, but they scrupulously avoided any contact with Western civilization which they feared would pollute Hinduism. They had vehemently opposed any move to change or reform the traditional Hindu religious and social order. During the latter part of the nineteenth century a new generation of Muslim leaders like Nawab Abdul Latif (1828-1897) were keen to promote English education among the Muslims for precisely the same reasons which had led conservative Hindu leaders like Radhakant Deb to advocate the cause of English education. But both Radhakant and Abdul Latif were strongly opposed to Western civilization and modern liberal thought. Both of them realized the need of promoting English education for serving the worldly needs of their respective communities. But they abhorred the idea that modern Western philosophy and practice would influence the life and thought of the people of this country. This attitude, however, was illogical and unrealistic. It was impossible for anyone to learn the English language and yet remain totally unacquainted with English ideas and institutions. In fact, in course of time quite a good number of Hindus and Muslims who had acquired a good proficiency in the English language had become well acquainted with contemporary Western liberal thought. And these were the people who were in the vanguard of the educational and social reform movements in the nineteenth century. In fact, it was this class which represented the second or reformist trend in our social thought.

During the early part of the nineteenth century Rammohun Roy (1774-1833) represented the reformist trend in Hindu society. Similarly, during the latter part of the century the reformist trend in Muslim society was represented by Syed Ahmed Khan (1817-1898) of upper India and Syed Amir Ali (1849-1928) of Bengal. Just as Rommohun's movement had aimed at reforming and reconstructing the traditional Hindu society in response to the contemporary challenge, so also Syed Ahmed Khan, Syed Amir Ali and the Muslim modernists had endeavoured to reinterpret and revaluate Islam in the light of the nineteenth-century Western liberal thought.

The third trend in our social thought may be called the radical trend. It was already manifested in the early decades of the nineteenth century in the age of the 'Bengal renaissance'. As is well-known, its principal exponent was the flamboyant Eurasian teacher of the Hindu College, Henry Louis Vivian Derozio (1809-1831) and his young band of students. They were so deeply influenced by European rationalist philosophy of the age that some of them went so far as to abjure their faith in Hinduism or for that matter in any conventional religion.

Despite the inflexibility of Islamic religious dogma an element of rationality has always existed in Muslim social thought. Most probably its early manifestation is found in the ninth-century Arab philosophy of the *Mutazila* school. The *Mutazila* philosophers were deeply influenced by the ancient Greek rationalist thought particularly by Aristotelian logic. They were chiefly concerned with the eternal question : how to reconcile religious faith with logical reason? But in face of stiff opposition from the Islamic religious fundamentalists this bold adventure in the realm of thought could not go very far. Nevertheless, it did not die out completely and has always remained as a distinct element in Muslim intellectual heritage ever since. In the liberal intellectual climate of the nineteenth century this rationalist trend seemed to have witnessed a revival.

Recent investigation has brought to our knowledge the existence of an extraordinary Muslim radical thinker Abdul Rahim (c. 1785-1853).[7] This man was a veritable genius. The education he had received was entirely traditional; but his intellectual interest extended to such varied subjects as astronomy, mathematics, physics and philosophy. Besides, he was a poet of considerable merit. He wrote in Persian and also produced some translations in Arabic. Unfortunately, most of his works remain unpublished and a great many of his writings are lost. The main source of information about his life is his autobiographical work entitled *Sheegraf bayan Ibrat Tawaman* in which he gives some details of his chequered career till he reached his thirty-eighth year.

Abdul Rahim was born around 1785 at Gorakhpur in upper India. His father Musahib Ali was a weaver by profession. He was a great admirer to the Persian language and he desired his son to acquire a sound knowledge of Persian in addition in learning Arabic. While a young boy Rahim had fallen from horseback which incapacitated his left hand. This accident proved to be a turning point in his career. Being considered unfit to take up his family profession Rahim was allowed to continue his education. By the time he had reached fifteen, he had mastered the

Persian language. Soon he acquired proficiency in Arabic. He also read the basic texts in both these languages. He was then taken by his father to a place called Tanda about forty-eight miles from Gorakhpur and placed under the tutorship of his spiritual guide. Here Rahim stayed for three years and though he suffered from much hardship he gained considerable knowledge in various subjects. In 1804 Abdul Rahim moved to Lucknow for obtaining higher education. He stayed for one year in this city. In the varied intellectual atmosphere of Lucknow Abdul Rahim's mental world underwent a transformation. The frequent religious bickerings between the *shia* and the *sunni* sects filled his mind with disgust. After spending a year in Lucknow he proceeded to Delhi and there he studied the religious texts of Islam under the guidance of Shah Abdul Aziz and Mullah Rafi-ud-Deen, two leading Islamic theologians of the time. Here one of his fellow scholars was Sayiid Ahmad of Rai Bareli.[8] Abdul Rahim also studied Oriental indigenous medicine from Hakim Sharif Khan. At Delhi Abdul Rahim had not only read the principal Islamic theological works but also the classical treatises on philosophy and science that were then available in Arabic and Persian languages. His poetic talent also found expression in this time. He began to compose poems on the lines of the classical Persian poets. In this early life Abdul Rahim had been a devout Muslim zealously performing the Islamic religious rituals and practices, and conducted his life strictly in accordance with the *sharia*. But in the cosmopolitan environment of Delhi and particularly after reading the sacred books of different religions and also treatises on different schools of philosophy, his mind was freed from all kinds of religious dogma. Completely shedding his former religious beliefs and prejudices he became a freethinker and a rationalist. Because of his heretical views he had now come to be known as *dahri*, that is, a materialist or atheist.[9] According to Abdul Rahim the idea of God or a Supreme Being was the innovation of the *imams* or priests. He believed in the law of nature. According to him the sun was the source of all creation.

In 1810 at the age of twenty-five Abdul Rahim came down to Calcutta where he spent the rest of his life. In Calcutta he seemed to feel quite at home because to this great city, the cosmopolitan metropolis of the new rulers, all kinds of people were drawn who brought with them new ideas and this great city provided a safe haven for conformists and heretics. It is learnt that when the fundamentalist Whabi leader, Sayiid Ahmad of Rae Bareli, had visited Calcutta in 1920, he tried to meet his old class-mate Abdul Rahim so that he could persuade him to return to the fold of Islam. But the latter did not see him nor did he give up his heresy.[10]

Soon after coming to Calcutta Abdul Rahim had started learning English. Within a few years he had gained such proficiency in that language that the Committee of Public Instruction employed him for translating various English works into Arabic and Persian. This had become necessary in order to implement the Government policy of introducing European science in the curriculum of the Calcutta Madrasa. Accordingly, Abdul Rahim translated an article on geometry into Persian from *Encyclopaedia Britannica*, also Hutton's *Course on Mathematics* and Bridge's *Algebra* into Persian.[11]

While in Calcutta Abdul Rahim for quite a number of years used to live in the house of Tipu Sultan's son, Sultan's Shukrullah, in Tollygunge and was appointed tutor of the prince's two sons. It was in this house that poets and literary lovers assembled periodically and Abdul Rahim became the focal point of a lively intellectual circle. Having stayed for sometime in Tollygunge, Abdul Rahim from some unknown reason moved to an area known as Tiljala where he began to live in a tent pitched in a park. Here he lived in seclusion devoting his time to study and teaching. He never married. Abdul Rahim died on 29 December 1853. Among his favourite pupils was Obaidullah el Obaide (1834-1885), the well-known Orientalist scholar, educationist and social reformer. According to Obaidullah's own testimony he received his first lessons in philosophy and the sciences from this great teacher.[12] Obaidullah also seems to have imbibed some of the rationalism of Abdul Rahim which impelled him to translate into English Raja Rammohun Roy's famous tract *Tuhfat-ul Muwahhiddin*. In this work Rammohun had not only denounced traditional Hindu idolatry; he was equally critical of the traditional Muslim beliefs regarding performance of supernatural acts and miracles. He even made the bold assertion that "falsehood is common to all religions without distinction". Maulana Obaide had agreed to undertake the translation of this remarkable treatise of Rammohun at the request of his friend Rajnarayan Bose (1826-1899), a leader of the Brahmo Samaj.[13]

In his personal life Abdul Rahim was a simple and king-hearted gentleman. He loved nature and animals. He was a vegetarian and considered it unlawful to kill animals and birds. He also thought it improper to pluck flowers or tear away branches or leaves from trees because he believed that trees and plants have life and, therefore, should not be hurt. He found pleasure in seeing birds flying in the sky. He would even purchase birds caught by hunter and set them free.[14]

This rationalist manifestation did not disappear with Abdul Rahim *dahri*. It continued to maintain its somewhat feeble existence in Muslim intellectual tradition. Thus during the later part of the nineteenth century we come across a new radical trend in Muslim thought which was secular, scientific and modern in character. Its chief exponent was Delwar Hussain Ahmed (1840-1915). His ideas are far more radical than those of his contemporary Muslim modernizers like Syed Ahmed Khan (1817-1898), Abdul Latif (1828-1897) and Syed Amir Ali (1840-1928). Unlike Abdul Rahim, who was an immigrant to Bengal, Delwar Hussain was a Bengali Muslim. He was born in a village in the Hoogly district of West Bengal. He was the first Muslim student of Calcutta Presidency College and took his B.A. degree from the Calcutta University in 1861; he was perhaps the first Muslim graduate of India. Delwar Hussain joined government service and was appointed Deputy magistrate and served is several districts of Bengal and Bihar. He ended his official career as Inspector General of Registration being the first Indian to hold this position. After retirement in 1898 he settled down in Calcutta. While in service Delwar Hussain used to write on various social problems affecting the Bengali Muslims of his time. In 1889 two volumes of his writings under the title *Essays on Muhammadan Social Reforms* were published by Thacker, Spink and Company, an English Publisher of Calcutta. He continued to write on current social and economic problems of the Muslim community. Most of his later writings appeared in contemporary English newspapers particularly *The Englishman, The Moslem Chronicle* and *Muhammadan Observer* and *The Mussalman*.

Delwar Hussain was deeply influenced by contemporary European liberal and rationalist ideas. As he himself observed :

> James Mill's *Dissertations in Liberty and Economical Science*, Buckle's *Outlines of the History of Civilization* and the *Essays* of Herbert Spencer on Politics and Sociology, early turned my thoughts to a consideration of the causes of the rise of nations and fall of empires. A careful study of these teachers convinced me that the decline of Mohammedan education is not the cause but the result of our social degeneracy, and that the cause of our national decay must be sought for in our past history, in our laws and institutions, in our domestic and social organization.[15]

In fact, compared to the views of two other contemporary Muslim leaders of Bengal, namely, Nawab Abdul Latif and Syed Amir Ali, Delwar Hussain's ideas were far more advanced and were completely different. As we know, Abdul Latif had been exerting to promote English education among Muslims out of sheer practical considerations.. But his social outlook was conservative. He was a patron of Maulana Keramat Ali of Jaunpur (1800-1873), who though an ardent supporter of the British *raj* and had issued a *fatwa* (religious proclamation) against the Wahabis, was himself extremely orthodox in his religious and social views. It was the Jaunpur maulana and his mostly non-Bengali and Urdu-speaking disciples who with the tacit support of men like Abdul Latif fomented communalism and religious exclusiveness in the social life of rural Bengal. Thus started a process which Rafiuddin Ahmed calls 'Islamizing the rural masses'. Bengali Muslim peasantry, ignorant and economically exploited by zamindars and moneylenders mostly Hindu, fell easy prey to the pernicious propaganda of these *maulvis* and *mullahs* who were mostly ill-educated and religious fanatics. Again, it was at the insistence of Abdul Latif that the outmoded madrasa system of education was perpetuated in Bengal despite the fact that his other contemporary Syed Amir Ali had advocated its replacement by a modern education system suited to the needs of the age. In fact, Amir Ali's views were relatively more advanced and progressive than those of Abdul Latif. In his book *The Spirit of Islam* (1891) Amir Ali had called for reinterpretation of Islam in the light of liberal and rationalist thought of the contemporary West. But his ideas were somewhat vague. He did not and perhaps could not spell out clearly which of the laws and practices of Islam had to be changed or modified to meet the requirements of the age.

In comparison, Delwar Hossain's ideas had a greater degree of clarity and they emanated from a keener sense of awareness of the reality of the situation. They were also more radical and somewhat revolutionary. Intellectually, Delwar Hossain regarded himself as heir to the Mutazilite philosophers of the ninth century Arabia who sought to explain the doctrines of faith in the light of reason. In fact, he used to write occasionally under the pseudonym "Mutazelah". Delwar Hossain was perhaps one of the first Muslim thinkers of modern times who stressed the need to modify, and even abolish certain institutions and practices of Islam which he believed were not directly connected with purely religious faith. This he argued, was necessary to meet the changing and practical needs of the time. Delwar Hossain believed that the economic backwardness of the Muslims was mainly due to their extravagant habits, indolence and also belief in predestination. According to him the Islamic prohibition on taking interest had prevented the accumulation of capital without which there could not be any industrial development. Similarly, he believed that the Muslim law of inheritance was not conducive to economic growth. He therefore maintained that laws and institutions relating to society should be secular and kept free from the influence of religion. In fact, Delwar Hossain believed that the material needs of changing society could not be met by static religious laws and practices. According to him:

> . . . . . union of religion with social customs and civil laws has done the most serious injury to Mohammadans in every part of the world and unless soon and timely dissolved there is every possibility of the name becoming a byword and the Mohammadan races a laughing stock among civilized nations.[16]

According to Delwar Hossain the decline of the Muslims was mainly due to their religious exclusiveness and lack of toleration. Referring to the prevalence of autocratic rule in most of the Muslim countries of his time he noted that it was due to want of self-confidence and self-reliance among the Muslims. He pointed out that :

> No Mohammadan nation has ever been able to provide any constitutional means of checking the immense authority and arbitrary power

> of kings. In the most advanced Christian countries the power of the Sovereign whether designated Emperor, King or President is more or less limited by law; but in Mohammadan countries the Sovereign is above the law and is responsible to none for what he may choose to do or not to do.[17]

In fact, Delwar Hossain was a firm advocate of secularism. He maintained that the union of religion with the state had done great harm to Muslim civilization. Again, according to him Muslims had failed to make substantial contribution to modern knowledge because of the lack of intellectual freedom in Muslim society.

During the time of Delwar Hossain the urban elite, mostly Urdu-speaking, held the leadership of Muslim society in Bengal. It was proud of its *ashraf*, that is, respectable and aristocratic background and looked down upon the Bengali-speaking rural population which in fact, constituted the majority of the Muslims of Bengal. They remained steeped in ignorance and poverty. On the one hand, they were economically exploited by Hindu zamindars and moneylenders; on the other, they fell easy prey to religious and social obscurantism nurtured by semi-literate village elders and mostly Urdu-speaking *mullahs*. No attempt was made by the urban elite to lift the common people from degradation and misery. Left to themselves the Bengali Muslim peasantry was led by illiterate and half-educated but strong willed men like Titu Mir, Haji Sharaitullah and Dudu Miyan, who had no understanding of the reality of the situation prevailing in nineteenth-century colonial India. Hence their movements failed.

Delwar Hossain, though he himself came from elitist background, did not fail to realize that to promote the general improvement of the Muslim community the existing gap between the urban elite and the rural population should be bridged. He believed that in order to achieve progress it was imperative for the Muslims to learn both English and Bengali. Advocating the introduction of modern system of education he demanded the abolition of the traditional madrasa education which backdated learning. Delwar Hossain pointed out that the neglect shown by the urban Muslim elite to the native language of Bengal had done great harm to the Muslim community. It had widened the gulf between the urban elite and the rural masses. He thought that it was only through the mother tongue that the common people could be acquainted with modern science and knowledge since it was not possible for everyone to learn English. Hence he recommended that those of his countrymen who had gained proficiency in English language should undertake the responsibility to translating into Bengali the basic books that were available in English on science, philosophy and other subjects. He believed that Western progressive ideas could be disseminated among the people through this process.[18]

Delwar Hossain also advocated changed in the Islamic law of succession. He recommended its replacement by a secular law applicable to all communities.[19]

There were, however, certain contradictions in Delwar Hossain's thoughts. While he upheld Western liberal ideas, he nourished almost pathological dislike for the Hindus. Perhaps this was due to the growth and impact of Hindu revivalist movement and the generally anti-Muslim attitude of the Hindu middle class. This class viewed with suspicion and hostility the emergence of the new Bengali Muslim middle class which seemed to threaten Hindu monopoly in government service and other avenues. This gave rise to communal tension which embittered the relations between the two communities.

Delwar Hossain's radical ideas, however, did not find favour in contemporary Muslim society. It rather tended to regard him with derision. The dominant trend of the time was conservative. Again, since Delwar Hossain wrote exclusively in English, his ideas did not reach the common people. This explains why Delwar Hossain is still relatively unknown in Bengali

Muslim society. Nevertheless, it is undeniable that in his thoughts were embedded the germs of revolutionary possibilities for the future. The tradition of modernizing radicalism which Abdul Rahim *dahri* and Delwar Hossain Ahmed had upheld was transmitted to a later generation of Bengali intellectuals who were able to make a significant contribution to bring about the political and cultural awakening of the Bengali Muslims in our time.

References

1. Sarkar Susobhan, *One the Bengal Renaissance*, Calcutta, 1979, pp. 70-71. Also Suprakash Roy, *Bharater Krishak Bidroha O ganatantrik sangram* (in Bengali), Calcutta, 1967, and Badruddin Umar, *Bidyasagar O Unish Sataker Bangalee samaj* (in Bengali), Dhaka, 1970.
2. Marx and Engels, *Selected Works*, Moscow, 1962, vol. i, p. 351.
3. Ahmed, A.F. Salahuddin, "Muslim Thought and Leadership in Bengal in the Nineteenth Century" in Barun De et al (ed.), *Essays in Honour of Prof. S.C. Sarkar*, Delhi, 1976, p. 634.
4. Written evidence of Rammohun Roy on the condition of India before the Select Committee of the House of Commons on the affairs of the East India Company, *Parliamentary Papers, House of Commons*, 1931, v. 302A pp. 739-41. See also A.F. Salahuddin Ahmed, *Social Ideas and Social Change in Bengal, 1818-1835*, Calcutta, 1976, p. 19.
5. Roy Ajit, '*Tuhfat-ul Mujahhiddin* and the seventeenth-century Persian tract *Dabistan-i-Mazahib*, Paper presented at the 28th International Congress of Orientalists, Canberra, 6-12 January, 1971.
6. For detailed analysis on the subject see Susobhan Sarkar, *op. cit*. and A.F. Salahuddin Ahmed, *op. cit*., pp. 29-58.
7. Muhammad Abdullah, *Paschim Bange Farsi Sahitya* (in Bengali), Unpublished research report submitted to the University Grants Commission, Bangladesh, Dhaka 1983. Dr. Abdullah gives much valuable information regarding Abdul Rahim's life from unpublished manuscript sources. An earlier reference to Abdul Rahim and some particulars about him are available in A.B.M. Habibullah, *Samaj, Sanskrit O Itihas* (in Bengali), Dhaka, 1974.
8. Habibullah A.B.M., *Samaj, Sanskriti O Itihas*, p. 129.
9. Muhammad Abdullah, *op. cit*., p. 12.
10. Habibullah A.B.M. *op. cit*., p. 129.
11. Ahmed, A.F. Salahuddin *op. cit*., p. 141.
12. Abdullah, Muhammad *Bāṅglādeśe Fārsī Sāhitya*, Dhaka, 1983, p. 145.
13. Roy, Rammohun *Tuhfat-ul Muwahhiddin* or A Gift to Deists, English translation by Obaidullah el Obaidi, (first published in 1884), reprint, Calcutta, *The Nineteenth Century Studies*, vol. 1, 1973, pp. 1-2.
14. Abdullah Muhammad *Paśchim Baṅge Fārsī Sāhitya*, p. 15.
15. Salik, Sultan Jahan (ed.), *Muslim Modernism in Bengal: Selected Writings of Delawar Hosaen Ahmed Meerza, 1840-1913*, Dhaka, 1980, p. 1.
16. *Ibid*., p. 20.
17. *Ibid*., p. 32.
18. *Ibid*., p. 114.
19. *Ibid*., p. 115.

Aspects of Indian History and Historiography
Editor : P.K. Mishra
Kaveri Books, New Delhi, India.

Tribal History of Ancient Bengal

12

Bhaskar Chatterjee

The reconstruction of the tribal history of Bengal is a difficult task due to dearth of materials, although the task deserves to be undertaken. There are tribes who have been accommodated within the social framework approved by the law-givers of ancient times, and there are tribes who have been assigned a place on the fringe of the society. The ethnographic records of contemporary simple societies indicate that there are tribes who remain still at the stage of hunting and food-gathering on the frontiers of Bengal. Despite the social changes that have taken place so far since primitive times, the continuity of the tribal societies even in modern times is an enigma. There is no denying the fact that the hunting and food-gathering economy, the sample of which is represented by the Kolas, Mundās, Sāntāls, Birhors, Khāriās and others inhabiting the western borders of West Bengal. Some of those tribes have taken to food-producing economy, involving themselves in primitive form of agriculture, and others are devoted to some handicrafts, depending mainly upon the resources available from the forests. Samples of tribal societies showing signs of socio-economic progress are few and far between.

Theoretical Framework

A model of tribal history has been set up by some western scholars in recent times. Leslie White (1948)[1] began the discussion on the evolution of society. Later, the discussion was further extended by Elman Service (1971)[2] and Marshall Sahlins (1972).[3] Their views are widely accepted. Ethnographic records of contemporary simple societies indicate, according to them, different organisations such as Bands, Tribes, Chiefdoms and State-organised societies.[4] *Bands* represent the most primitive form of human organisations. Each band consists of a group of people (25 to 60) related by kinship ties. The group co-operated in hunting and food-gathering activities without any form of permanent leadership. Men may have lived in band-society from early Paleolithic age till the beginning of agriculture. Abundance or scarcity of resources as also the density of population within an area can often bring about drastic changes in the band-formation. A band sometimes splits into a number of sub-bands spread over a large area or similar bands merge into a bigger one. *Tribes* are the kind of larger organization of early agriculturists. Several families or bands are grouped into a clan, tracing their origin to a common ancestor. These clans belong to a tribe that jointly owns the resources. It is in the Neolithic age that man attains the change in the basic economy, from foodgathering to food-production, along with sedentariness. *Chiefdoms* represent a complex form of tribal organization. Increase of population, grater prosperity, invasions by other society or even the natural growth of charisma of members of kin-group clan lead to the re-structuring of the group in families with hierarchical order. The chief with his family enjoys great respect and privilege. The social surplus is kept at the disposal of the Chief to create professional artisans who catered to the needs of the society. Although egalitarianism is replaced by a ranked society, the tribal chief looks into the proper distribution among the members of the society. Many early Bronze age societies in Europe may have lived in this kind of social organization. *State-organized societies* take birth with the early city-states. While in Chiefdoms the authority of the tribal chief is generally guarded by spiritual ascriptions, the ruler or the ruling class in state-organized societies is secular, although the king may seek religious sanction. Tools and implements made of iron are used in this kind of society to produce huge social surplus that was surrendered to the ruling class for maintenance of a full-fledged managerial system, military system, judicial system and even sometimes slave-system.

An attempt has been made by R.S. Sharma[5] to make an application of the above theory of social evolution in the Indian context. His study is based on suitable interpretation of the words contained in the *Vedic Index* and leads one to think that the social evolution occurred in India with the settlement and expansion of the Indo-Aryans. It has been suggested that there may have been some *relics* of hands in the Rig Vedic age, although pastoralism was the chief characteristic of the age. Nomadic pastoral Indo-Aryans evolved the tribal society, when they settled in their chosen territories and adopted agriculture, instead of cattle-rearing, as their chief occupation in the latter half of the Rig Vedic age. Further, towards the end of the Rig Vedic age, the tribal chief acquired more power and higher status with the amalgamation of tribes and territories. The process was accelerated kin the Later Vedic age with the expansion of the Aryans in the middle of the Gangetic plains comprising eastern part of modern U.P. and also Bihar. By the middle of the first millennium B.C., the rich iron-mines in the Chotanagpur plateau were exploited to develop iron-technology that revolutionised the mode of production and yielded higher social surplus with which the emergence of the full-fledged state-organised society was possible.

The application of the theory of social evolution on the basis of the literary data culled from the Rig Veda and the later Vedic texts does not take into serious consideration of the view. of the archaeologists[6] that the food-gathering economy characterised the Paleolithic age, the food-producing economy was begun in the Neolithic age and the surplus-production was realised in the age of metals. There is a consensus among the scholars that the surplus-production is a pre-requisite for the state-formation. In fact, the tribal history of a country or of a region included in it can be best judged, in the present state of our knowledge, on the parameter long established by the researches of the anthropologists and archaeologists. We propose to undertake the task of reconstructing the tribal history of ancient Bengal within the theoretical framework in which a tribal organisation is said to have been preceded by a band-society and succeeded by the tribal Chiefdoms and the state-organised society. It is presumed that the emergence of the state is a logical conclusion of the evolution of the tribal society. The tribal history means the history of the social evolution in which the tribal society has a pivotal role to play.

Archaeological Data

Considering archaeology as the index of social evolution, we may examine the data discovered so far by the archaeologist's spade.

Paleolithic Data[7]

Discoveries of V. Ball (1865, 1867, 1876) at Kunkune (Hooghly district), Gopināthpur (Bankura district) and Raniganj Coal-field area (Burdwan district) were mostly hammers and bi-faces. V.D. Krishnaswamy (1959-60) found Early Stone Age and Middle Stone Age tools on the banks of the rivers Kangsāvatī and Kumārī in Bankura district. B.B. Lal's (1958) discoveries at Birbhānpur (near Durgapur) and in the area between Malandighi and Jaydeb-Kenduli have yielded some Paleolithic data. A.K. Ghosh (1962) found choppers, hand-axes, cleavers and scrapers in the north-western part of Midnapur district. D. Sen (1963) made his discoveries in the valleys of the rivers Dwārakeswar, Kangsāvatī and Kumārī in the district of Bankura. A.K. Ghosh (1963-64, '64-65, 65-66, '68-69) again made some important discoveries in some parts of the districts of Midnapur, Bankura and Purulia lying on the fringe of the Chhotanagpur Plateau. The Directorate of Archaeology, West Bengal 1966-67), carried on explorations in Birbhum, Purulia, Midnapur, Bankura and Burdwan.

Most of the paleliths are surface-finds and the data are not sufficient to trace the sub-phases, namely, Lower, Middle and Upper. No palaeoliths are generally found in the deltaic Bengal, although some Middle Stone Age tools have been found at Deulpotā on the Bhāgirathī-Hooghly. Most of the paleoliths are found in those parts of West Bengal which are adjacent to the Chhotanagpur plateau.

Microlithic Data[8]

N.G. Majumdar (1939) found microliths at Durgapur on the northern bank of the Dāmodar. B.B. Lal (1958) and his discoveries at Birbhānpur and Gopālpur in Burdwan district and at Dejuri in Bankura district. V.D. Krishnaswamy (1958-59) found microliths in the valleys of the rivers Kangsāvatī and Kumārī in the districts of Bankura and Purulia. The explorations undertaken by the Department of Anthropology, Calcutta University (1961-1976), led to the discovery of lunates, flakes, blades, knives and scrapers in the north-western parts of Midnapur, Bankura, Purulia and Birbhum districts. The Directorate of Archaeology, West Bengal made its discoveries mainly along the rivers Damodar, Ajay, Kumār and Tārāpheni, besides Pāruldāngā near Śāntiniketan. The Department of Archaeology, Calcutta University (1975-76), had its findings at Silda on the bank of the Tārāpheni. Typologically, the microliths, mostly found in the districts adjoining the Chhotanagpur plateau, may be classified as of geometric and non-geometric patterns.

Neolithic Data[9]

Walsh (1904) found some neoliths at Kalimpong in Darjeeling district, where the Directorate of Archaeology, West Bengal (1966-67), made its explorations. N.G. Majumdar (1939) found some neoliths at Dinājpur. D. Sen (1948) and Krishnaswamy (1959-60) had their discoveries at the confluence of the Kumari and the Kangasāvatī. A. Ghosh (1962) made his explorations in north-western part of Midnapore. The Directorate of Archaeology, West Bengal (1965-68), worked at Susuniā in Bankura district and also in those parts of West Bengal which are adjacent to the Chhotanagpur plateau. Neoliths such as adzes, chisels, celts and ring-stones, so far discovered in West Bengal, are generally surface-finds except at Bāngarh, Tamluk, Pāṇḍu Rājār Ḍhibi and Bharatpur.

Chalcolithic/Iron Age Occurrences[10]

The site at *Pāṇḍu Rājār Ḍhibi*, lying near the south bank of the river Ajay, was excavated by the Directorate of Archaeology, West Bengal (1962-65). The excavation produced four major occupational deposits. *Period I* is characterised by the remains like the ruins of huts and floors of pellety laterite which have been occasionally burnt hard, burial of secondary nature with a headless skeleton, hand-made ware showing impressions of paddy husk, black-and-red ware and plain red ware with coarse fabric. *Period II* is represented by the structural remains of floors of pellety laterite with pot-holes and ovens, and different varieties of ware, viz. black polished, bright red, black-and-red, lustrous red, chocolate or buffish wares, painted in creamish white. The other collections comprised mocroliths, bone tools and copper objects like rings, bangles, antimony rods, a fish hook and a nail-parer. In addition to the evidence of burial practice, a red ware vase preserving a human tooth suggests an urn burial. However, this Period II represents 'the full blooded chalcolithic culture'. *Period II* is a continuation of Period II. The structural remains of this period include six 'elliptical ovens' in a row, flanked by a thick deposit of ash, bearing a fragmented sword-blade and iron-slag besides the ceramic. The remains possibly indicate iron-smelting at the site. Charred rice in large quantities were found from one of the levels of this period. The ceramic remains are red ware, black-and-red ware, black burnished ware. Besides, there are copper objects, bone tools, microliths, neolithic celts, beads, terracotta objects, gold pellets, a broken pin and iron objects. The remains of *Period IV* belonged to the early historic period.

The site at *Mahiṣādal* lying on the north bank of the Kopāi was excavated (1959-60, 1963-64). The stratification produced two periods. *Period I* is characterised by the habitation floor of 'beaten earth with a soling of rammed terracotta modules', red impressed clay-doubs, burnt husk impressed clay plasters and large quantities of ash. The pottery included plain and painted black-and-red ware, black-painted red ware, red ware with incised fillets. Besides, there were terracotta objects including a phallus, beads of semiprecious stones, bone artifacts, microliths, a copper celt and a large quantity of charred rice. *Period II* shows the continuation of the pottery belonging to *Period I* with the addition of buff and grey ware. This period also contained the evidence of iron ore, slag and artifacts. Iron specimens comprise arrow-heads, spearheads, chisels and nails. Besides, there were microliths, a small clay sealing with obscure symbols and a broken terracotta elephant.

Period I is dated between C.1300 and 800 B.C., while *period II* is datable to C. 750 B.C.

The site at *Nānur*, lying east of Mahiṣādal, was in occupation from the proto-historic period to modern times, according to the opinion of the excavators (1963-64). The cultural material of the site was mainly the pottery such as plain and white painted black-and-red wares.

The excavation at *Hārāipur* (1965-66), lying between the rivers Mayūrākshi and Bakreswar, yielded six layers of occupation. The site yielded plain and painted black-and-red ware and grey ware, iron objects and some burial remains.

The site at *Bharatpur* on the northern bank of the river Dāmodar, having been excavated, brought to light a four-fold cultural sequence (1970-1973). *Period I* (middle of the second millennium B.C.) shows the remains of a floor, plaster, reed-impressed burnt clay plasters. The pottery types found are plain and white painted black-and-red ware, black painted and white painted red ware and handmade pottery. The other finds were copper objects, tiny stone celts, microliths, bone tools, beads on steatite etc. *Period II* is marked by the occurrence of iron implements. The pottery of the earlier period continued. The N.B.P. deserves special mention.

Period III is represented by the baked brick structure which probably belongs to the Gupta period.

The site of *Tulasipur* near the confluence of the rivers Kumārī and Kangsāvatī has revealed three major occupations (1967-68). *Phase I* is characterised by some habitational floors, a pit and gritty red-slipped ware, black-and-red ware and the evidence of iron. *Phase II* has yielded a few chalcolithic gritty red slipped potteries and some black-and-red sherds. Iron was also found in this phase. *Phase III* is characterised by a bright red ware.

Bāṇeshwar Ḍāṅgā is located in the village Bara-Belun in the district of Burdwan. An excavation at the site (1972-73, 1981) has brought to light three prehistoric occupational levels. The lowest two (*Period I & II*) levels belong to the Chalcolithic period, characterised by the evidence of the black-and-red ware, and the next one (*Period III*) contains the iron remains. *Bāhiri* (Chandra Hāzrār Dāṅgā, located near Bolpur in Birbhum district, yielded three periods of occupation (1981). *Period I* (1000-500 B.C.) is represented by the remains of black-and-red ware (painted and plain), red ware, incised pottery, both in black and red, the structural remains of a mud floor, burnt, semi-burnt and unburnt pieces of clay with reed impressions, a kiln, a large number of iron-ore and slag, chunks of fossil wood, a plain copper ring, a reasonable amount of bone implements, animal bones, and some terra-cotta objects, *Period II* is dated C.500 - 200 B.C., while *Period III* is dated C. 4th - 6th century A.D.

From the above it appears that the Chalcolithic sites characterised by the black-and-red ware along with the evidence of the use of iron are located in the basins of the rivers Kunnur, Kopāi, Ajay, Bakreswar, Mayūrākshi, Dāmodar and Kangsāvatī in the districts of Burdwan, Burdwan and Bankura. Besides the excavated sites yielding chalcolithic and iron occurrences, a huge number of explored sites are recorded in the districts of Birbhum, Burdwan and Bankura. These less known chalcolithic sites are known only by the evidence of the black-and-red ware.

The archaeological data discovered so far in Bengal, either by exploration or by excavation, leave little scope of doubt that the original inhabitants of Bengal, the Pre-Aryans and the Pre-Dravidians, passed through the stages of culture indicated by the Paleolithic, Neolithic, Chalcolithic and iron occurrences in different parts of Bengal, especially those parts which are adjoining the Chhotanagpur Plateau.

Linguistic and Anthropological Data

On both linguistic and anthropological grounds it is held by scholars that the Pre-Aryans settlers in Bengal were the Negritos, Proto-Australoids, Dravidians and Mongoloids. An analysis of the Bengali language would show that besides the Indo-Aryan, it incorporated in its body the words derived from the Austric, Dravidian and Tibeto-Burman families of languages. The physical characteristics of the people belonging to different strata of the caste-structure in Bengal would indicate an admixture of the races represented by the above language-families. It would be worthwhile to examine whether the Negritos, Austrics and Dravidians belonged to the Paleolithic, Neolithic and Chalcolithic age respectively.

Negrito or Negroid

The Negritos had striking physical similarities with the Semang of Malay and Sumatra. The Negroid speech is related to the Andamanese. Such word as *bāduḍ* (bat) in Bengali is derived from *bād* which is related to *wāt* of the Andamanese.[11] The Negritos mixed up with the

Austrics and thus lost their separate identity. Such racial admixture explains the physical variations among the Austrics living in Central and South India and in Bengal. Again, the Negrito speech was covered up by two other linguistic strata, viz. the Austric and the Dravidian. The remains of the Negrito speech that may be traced in the Andamanese or in the aboriginal languages of Malay and Sumatra hardly provide any data related to a knowledge of agriculture or cattle-breeding. It may, therefore, be reasonably assumed that the Negritos were not food-producers but food-gatherers and lived at the hunting stage belonging to the Paleolithic age.

Proto-Austroloids or the Austrics

The Austric tribes who settled in Bengal are represented by the Kol peoples like the Sāntāl, the Muṇḍās, the Bhils, the Bhumijas, the Śavaras etc., known to the Aryans as *Nishādas*. Their physical characteristics are short stature, dark skin, long head, snub nose and copperish hair. Anthropologically, the Austric element is predominant among the tribes like the Mālpahāris, and the lower castes of Bengal like the Bānsphors, Namaśūdras, Pods, Bāuris, Bāgdis and Chaṇḍāls. The Austric-speaking people of Central and Eastern India are known as *Kolid*, while those belonging to South India and Simhala are called *Veddid*.[12]

The Austrics developed a primitive system of agriculture in which a digging stick (*lag, lang, ling*) was employed to till the hill-side. Terrace-cultivation of rice on hills and plains-cultivation of the same grain were introduced by them, as the word, *Dhān* (paddy) is derived from the Austric language. Again, as the names from their language would suggest, they introduced the cultivation of the coconut (*nārikela*), the plantain (*Kadala*), the betelvine (*tāmbula*), the betel-nut (*guvāka*), turmeric (*haridrā*), ginger (*śriṅgavera*) the brinjal (*vātingana*) and the pumpkin (*alābu*)[13]. It may, therefore, be reasonably surmised that the Austric-speaking people lived in the Neolithic age and developed the food-producing economy, depending mainly or agriculture.

Dravidian

Anthropologically, the Dravidians were round or short-headed people. This physical characteristic may be traced among the Brahmins and the *Uttama-Saṁkara* castes of Bengal known from the *Brihad-dharma Purāṇa*. Again, the long-drawn process of racial admixture led to the emergence of the long-headed Dravido-Muṇḍā people.

It is suggested that the Dravidians, known to the Aryans as *dāsa-dasyu*,[14] made their remarkable contribution to material culture. With the help of pure Tāmil words which were not connected with Sanskrit or any other form of Indo-Aryan, an attempt has been made to trace the Pre-Aryan Tamil or Dravidian culture. The evidence of words suggests that the Pre-Aryan Dravidians had 'hamlets' and 'towns', were acquainted with the ordinary metals, had 'laws' and 'customs', and 'kings' who dwelt in 'strong houses' and ruled over small 'districts of country'.[15] The Dravidians who were city-builders must have reached the stage of surplus-production that was the characteristic of the Chalco-lithic age. The words[16] *Karmār* (smith), *Rūp* (figure or form), *Kalā* (art), *Kulāl* (earthen pottery), along with *Taṇḍula* (rice) and *Vrīhi* (paddy) are some of the Indo-Aryan words derived from the Dravidian language. *Kulāl* along with *Rūp* and *Kalā* remind us of the painted black-and-red were of the Chalco-lithic age, which is associated not only with copper but also iron in the context of Bengal at least. The necessity of *Karmāra* to manufacture articles of copper or iron was obvious. The ethnographic study of the contemporary simple societies in the Chhotanagpur plateau shows that the iron-smelting was known to the

Kol-Muṇḍā group of people.[17] The Kol-Muṇḍās might have borrowed the technology from the Dravidians in the process of racial and cultural fusion.

Mongoloid

The Mongoloid Sino-Tibetan tribes, known to the Aryans, as *Kirātas*.[18] Anthropologically they were round headed people. Their physical characteristics are traceable among the Koches and the Rājbansis of North and North-east Bengal. The Austric tribes had mixed a good deal with other races including the Mongoloids. The process of such a mixture, tribal in nature, is so complex that it is difficult to trace its history without definite or positive information.

The Buddhist text *Ārya Mañjuśrīmūlakalpa* refers to the people of Vaṅga, Samataṭa, Harikela, Gauḍa and Puṇḍra as *Asura*-speaking.[19] One of the most prominent dialects belonging to the Kol-Muṇḍā group of language is known as *Asura-buli*. There is little scope of doubt that the primitive inhabitants of Gauḍa-Puṇḍra-Vaṅga were the Proto-Australoids or the Austrics. From this it appears that the Austrics were the most predominant element in the population of pre-Aryan Bengal and further that they preserved their language inspite of the long-drawn process of their admixture with other tribes speaking different languages, Dravidian and Tibeto-Burman or Sino-Tibetan.

From the linguistic data it appears that the material culture of the Austric tribes was dependent on agriculture, for which group-effort was essential. It would be reasonable to hold that the groups devoted to agriculture were organised into classes and settled in villages. *Pañchāyata*,[20] the village-assembly of five members, was probably introduced by them. Even today a Muṇḍā witness in the court takes his oath in the name of *Pañcho*. For the implementation of law and order, the clans in the villages elected from among themselves a clan-chief, later known as *mahattara* or *grāma-bhojaka*, to supervise the functioning of the village-assembly. The clan-chiefs-in-charge of respective villages owed their allegiance to a tribal chief. In the villages are maintained by the Muṇḍās and the Orāons the banners or flags stamped with symbols or signs of ruling authority. The tribal tradition appears to have remained unchanged since primitive times.

The material culture of the Dravidians was dependent on trade and industry centering towns and cities, for which surplus production in the hinterland of villages was supplied. Agricultural production was, no doubt, boosted up by employment of tools made of copper initially and later of iron. The supply of surplus resources from the villages maintained the city-dwellers, the merchants and the craftsmen. The ruler dwelling in the city exacted from the peasants a portion of the surplus in the forms of tributes and taxes. Consequently, the tribal chief of the earlier times attained higher status, as he was in a position to maintain a bureaucracy comprising the ministry and the bureaucracy and also a standing army. The tribal chief turned to be a full-fledged king.

Tribal Settlements

In the process of the emergence of state *Janapadas* had a vital role to play, as without a territorial jurisdiction the existence of a state was not possible. *Janapada* literally means 'a tribal settlement'[21] at the initial stage. An amalgamation of tribes occurs in a *Mahajanapada*, the bigger territory that marks the boundary of a state. However, we have both literary and epigraphic evidence testifying to the existence of *Janapadas* in ancient Bengal, presumably inhabited by some tribes (*Janas*) like the Puṇḍras, Vaṅgas, Rāḍhas, Gauḍas, Suhmas and Pra-Suhmas. The specific *Janapada* for a specific tribe indicates the latter's sedentariness implying a food-producing economy. As it has already been mentioned, ancient tribes of Bengal were non-Aryans and spoke a language (*Asura*) that was least understood by the Aryans.

It may be suggested on reasonable grounds that the nomenclatures of the tribes were according to the names of the *Janapadas* they settled in. The *Janapada* of Pauṇḍra was so named as its characteristic agricultural production was the sugar-cane (*Ikshu= Puṇḍra*).[22] The *Kārpāsa* type of cotton known as 'Vaṅga' was the most important product in the *Janapada* of Vaṅga.[23] *Guḍa* (molasses) was produced in abundance in a country which was known as Gauḍa.[24] Rāḍha seems to have been derived from *rūḍha* (rough and rude). It was divided into two parts, *Subhabhūmi* (i.e. *Śvabhrabhūmi*) the land of holes and pits and *Vajjabhūmi* (i.e. *Vajrabhūmi*, the land of hard story soil). Hence, for the Jaina monks, *Lāla* (i.e. Rāḍha) was *duccara* (i.e. duścara)[25] or difficult to travel in. The tribes living in the midst of the streams of the Gaṅgā were known as *Gāṅgeyāḥ*[26] (*Gangaridae* of the Classical writers). All the tribes of ancient Bengal were also covered by the term *Prāchyāḥ*, [27] the people of the East. It was not unreasonable that the tribes living outside the Aryandom were known to the Aryans in association with their habitat characterised by some physical features or agricultural, commercial products. However, the socio-cultural and political position of the tribes settled in ancient Bengal have to be examined from the Aryan point of view, as the available texts put on record that view only.

Transition from the Tribal to the State-Organised Society

Puṇḍras: The Puṇḍras are referred to as *dasyus* in the *Aitareya Brāhmaṇa* (vii). They are classed with the Andhras, Śabaras, Pulindas and Mutibas. Again, in the *Ādiparvan* of the *Mahābhārata*, the Puṇḍras are associated with the Vaṅgas and the Suhmas. In the *Manusaṁhitā* (x) the Puṇḍras are mentioned as degraded Kshatriyas. But in the *Sabhā-Parvan* of the *Mahābhārata*, they are well-born Kshatriyas. Again, in the *Tīrthayātrā*, section of the *Mahābhārata* (*Vana Parvan*), the valley of the river Karatoya within the land of the Puṇḍras is recognised as a place of pilgrimage.

It may be surmised that the Puṇḍras were accommodated within the *Varṇa*-based society of the Aryans following their political reverses and submission to the heroes of the *Mahābhārata* like Karṇa, Krishṇa and Bhima. It is said that the chief of the Puṇḍras had to bring tribute to the court of Yudhishthira.

The Mahāsthān fragmentary stone plague inscription[28] gives us an impression that as early as the third century B.C., the land of the Puṇḍras with its capital at Puṇḍranagara was most probably a part and parcel of the Maurya empire.

Vaṅgas: The Vaṅgas are mentioned jointly with the Vagadhas (probably Magadhas) and the Cheras in the *Aitareya Āraṇyaka* (II). In the *Ādiparvan* of the *Mahābhārata, Matya Purāṇa* (Ch. 48) and *Vāyu Purāṇa* (Ch. 99), they are placed in the category of the Aṅgas, Kaliṅgas, Puṇḍras and Suhmas. In Baudhāyana's *Dhamasūtra* (I), the Vaṅgas, along with the Āraṭṭas (in the Punjab), Puṇḍras, Sauviras (in Sindh) and Kaliṅgas, are located in the region outside the pale of Vedic culture.

In the *Sabhāparvan* of the *Mahābhārata*, the Vaṅgas are referred to as well-born Kshatriyas. The list of Aryan peoples occurring in the Jaina *Prajñāpanā* includes the Vaṅgas. The recognition was extended to them in course of their political contact over a long time with *Madhyadesa* in the heart of the Gaṅgā Valley.

The *Rāmāyaṇa (Ayodhyā Kāṇda)* records that the Vaṅgas maintained political relations with Ayodhya and acknowledged the supremacy of the king of Ayodhya. The *Digvijaya* section of the *Mahābhārata* (*Sabhāparvan*) informs us that they suffered reverses in the hands of Karṇa, Krishṇa and Bhima. The land of the Vaṅgas is said to have been joined with that of the Aṅgas under the authority of Karṇa. The Vaṅgas were also defeated by Krishṇa whose first strike was against the lord of the Puṇḍras. The Vaṅgas, the Puṇḍras and the Kirātas are said to have been united under the main adversary of Krishṇa, that is, Pauṇḍraka Vāsudeva. The Vaṇgas, like the Puṇḍras, had to pay tribute to the court of Yudhishthira. From the *Bhīshmaparvan* of the *Mahābhārata* it is learnt that the ruler of the Vaṅgas took part in the Bhārata war as an ally of the Kauravas against the Pāṇḍavas.

Apart from the tradition recorded in the Epics, we have an epigraphic evidence of the fourth century A.D. suggesting that the Vaṅgas attained statehood in the Gupta age. The Meherauli Iron Pillar inscription[29] informs us about the victory of king Chandra (probably Chandragupta II) against the ruler of Vaṅga. In the beginning of the sixth century A.D., as suggested by the Gunaighar Copper plate inscription,[30] Vaṅga was a full-fledged independent state.

Rāḍhas : In Jaina *Āchāranga Sūtra* is recorded the travel of Mahāvira in the pathless country of the Rāḍhas who used the expression *Chhu Chhu*,[32] while letting loose dogs against the monk. The expression is derived from the Austric language. The spread of Jainism most probably accelerated the process which ultimately led to the accommodation of the Rāḍhas within the Aryan fold. In the Jaina *Prajñāpanā* the Lāḍhas (i.e. Rāḍhas) are referred to as one of the Aryan peoples.

From the Susunia Rock Inscription[32] it is learnt that king Chandravarma, a devotee of Vishnu, ruled sometime in the fourth century A.D. with his capital at Pushkaraṇa, identified with Pakhanna on the southern bank of the river Damodar. The valley of the Damodar was, no doubt, included in Rāḍha. It may, therefore, be held that by the fourth century A.D. the Rāḍhas had the first taste of living in a state-organised society.

Suhmas : In the *Ādiparvan* of the *mahābhārata* and the *Purāṇas* (*Matsya*, Ch. 48; *Vayu*, Ch. 99), the Suhmas are mentioned along with the Aṅgas, Vaṅgas, Kaliṅgas and Puṇḍras. In the *Bhāgavata Purāṇa* (BK II), they are classed with the Kirātas, Hūṇas, Andhras, Pulindas, Pukkasas, Ābhiras, Yavanas and Khasas. In the *Sabhāparvan* of the *Mahābhārata* it is said that the Suhmas, whose neighbours were the Pra-Suhmas, had been settled near the sea-shore and bore the brunt of Bhima's invasion. They are mentioned as Sumbhas in the *Samyutta Nikāya* (V) and the *Telapatta Jātaka* (I. 96).

There is hardly any evidence indicating the social recognition given to the Suhmas. But from the available pieces of evidence it appears almost without any scope of doubt that the Suhmas were closely related to the Rāḍhas who were recognised as one of the Aryan peoples. Further, the maritime region of the Suhmas included Gaṅgāsāgara, (confluence of the Gaṅgā with the Bay of Bengal), one of sacred places referred to in the *Vanaparvan* of the *Mahābhārata*. It should, however, be noted in this connection that the list of degraded Kshatriyas contained in the *Manusaṁhitā (Ch. X)* includes the names of Jhalla, Malla, Licchavī, Naṭa, Karaṇa, Khasa, Draviḍa, Pauṇḍraka, Oḍra, Kāmboja Yavana, Śaka, Pārada, Pahlava, Cīna, Kirāta, Darada etc. But no mention is made of the Suhmas.

Gauḍas: The Gauḍas are known from Vātsyāyana's *Kāmasutra*, the Harahā Inscription (554 A.D.) of the Maukhari king Iśānavarman[33] and the *Anargha-Rāghava* of Murāri (latter half of the eighth century A.D.). The city of the Gauḍas, known as Gauḍapura, is mentioned in Pāṇini's *Ashtādhyāyi*. The products of the land of the Gauḍas are referred to in Kauṭilya's *Arthaśāstra*

(II.13). However, from the Harahā Inscription we have an impression that the Gauḍas lived on the sea-shore. If that be so, it is difficult to distinguish them from the Suhmas whose habitat was the maritime region and also from the Rāḍhas whose territory extended from the Gaṅgā or the north to the sea-coast on the south. Krishṇa Miśra in his *Prabodha Candrodaya* (11th-12th century A.D.) has indicated that *Gauḍa-rāshṭra* included Rāḍha.

From the territorial extent it appears that the Gauḍas represented not a simple tribe but an amalgamation of tribes like the Puṇḍras, Rāḍhas, Suhmas and even Vaṅgas. Such an amalgamation of tribes and territories was a sure sign of the emergence of a state. Because, in a state-organised society, no tribe is identified with a fixed territory. The first king of Gauḍa was, no doubt, Śaśāṅka who seized royal power and authority in the beginning of the seventh century A.D. and had his capital at Karṇasuvarṇa (Rāṅgāmāṭi in Murshidabad district). Śaśāṅka had his precursor in Pauṇḍraka Vāsudeva of the *Mahābhārata*, under whose aegis were united the Vaṅgas, Puṇḍras and Kirātas.[34]

The Puṇḍras, Vaṅgas, Rāḍhas or Suhmas might have developed tribal chiefdoms separately as it seems from their Epic accounts. In the historic period, the Puṇḍras were the people inhabiting a province or a part of a bigger kingdom like that of the Mauryas or of the Guptas. So also was the position of the Vaṅgas and the Rāḍhas (or Suhmas) in the Gupta period. A homogeneous political entity, accommodating almost all the tribes and tribal settlements, became a reality in the seventh century A.D. It is worth-mentioning that the Aṅgas and the Magadhas were often in close political contact with the tribes in ancient Bengal as suggested not only in the Epics and the Classical accounts but also in the epigraphs of the Maurya and the Gupta period.

From Tribal to Caste-society

Apart from the political transformation, one has to take into consideration the *Varṇa*-based social hierarchy that was sponsored by the Brahmin settlers in Bengal. The tribal society was gradually changed into a caste-society. The caste-society consisting of some social strata was, no doubt, a pre-requisite for the emergence of a state-organised society. The consolidated social structure in Bengal, as it appears from the *Brihaddharma* and *Brahma Vaivarta Purānas*, is found to have accommodated different professional and occupational groups and aboriginal tribes with the Brahmins at the apex. Besides the Brahmins, other castes are treated as either mixed (*saṅkara*) as in the *Brihaddarma Purāṇa*, or śūdra as in the *Brahmavaivanta Purāṇa*. The former *Purāṇa* identifies the *mlecchas* who are not found fit to be accommodated within the categories of mixed castes and the latter *Purāṇa* assigns the lowest position to the *antyajas* who are found unfit to be counted among even the Śūdras. Of course, the position of the lowest stratum of mixed castes (*adhama saṅkara*) in the *Brihaddharma Purāṇa* is equivalent to that of the *antyajas* in the *Brahmavaivarta Purāṇa*.

The tribes whose names occur in the lists of the above-mentioned Purāṇas are Bhilla, Malla, Ābhira, Kola, Koñca, Pauṇḍraka, Pukkasa, Pulinda, Khasa, Khara, Kāmboja, Yavana, Suhma and Śavara. In the Bhāgalpur copper plate inscription[35] mention is made of Meda and Andhra. The Naihāti Copper plate inscription[36] of Vallālasena refers to the Pulindas and Śavaras. Bhaṭṭa Bhavadeva in his *Prayaśchitta Prakaraṇa* mentions Meda, Bhilla and Pukkasa. The *Charyāpadas* refer to the Śavaras.

The Ābhiras have been assigned a place among the *Madhyama Saṁkara* or mixed castes of the middle stage (*Brihaddharma Purāna*). Although they were of foreign origin, *Manu* (X.15) recognised them as the offspring of a Brahmin father and Ambashṭha (Brahmin + Vaiśya) mother. The Bhillas are recognised as *Satsūdra* or purer among the Śūdras in the *Brahmavaivarta Purāṇa*, but Bhavadea includes them in the list of *Antyaja* or outcastes along with the Medas. In fact, the Medas were the original inhabitants of Mewar and the Billas represented a branch of the Meda tribe. The Pauṅḍrakas, Puṇḍras or Puṇḍras of Puṇḍras have found a place along with the Mallas in the status of *Asat Sūdra*, that is, Śūdra of the impure type. Puṇḍras and the Mallas are referred to as *Vrātya* (degraded) Kshatriyas in the *Manusaṁhitā* (X. 22). The Puṇḍras represented one of the most ancient tribes of Bengal, while the Mallas might have been the tribe from which the Ugrakshatriyas of Bengal derived their origin.

Among the *antyajas* we find mention of the tribes like the Kols, Koñcas, Medas and Andhras. Kol is a generic name applied to the Muṇḍā and Orāon tribes.[37] The Koñcas seem to have been the Koches, descended from the Tibeto-Burman stock. The Medas, original inhabitants of Medapāta or Mewar,[38] are said to be the offspring of Vaideha (son of Vaiśya father and Brahmin mother) father and Nishāda (Brahmin + Śūdra) mother in the *Manusaṁhitā* (X. 36). The Andhras, original inhabitants of the country between the Godāvarī and the Krishnā,[39] are considered as mixed caste descended from Vaideha father and Kārāvara (Offspring of Nishāda father and Vaideha mother) mother. From the *Manusaṁhitā* (X) it appears that the lower castes of the society arose out the union between mixed castes. Again, it may also be inferred that the theory of mixed castes as propounded by Manu was devised to accommodate the aboriginal tribes into the society. However, the expression *Medāndhra Caṇḍālaparyantān* occurring in the Bhāgalpur Copper plate inscription of Nārāyaṇapala[38] implies that the tribes like the Medas and Andhras who had been reduced to the position of Caṇḍālas were deprived of land-rights, social and political rights. However, their mention in the royal documents leaves no scope of doubt that they were given recognition as part and parcel of the society.

Immigration of Some Tribes from Outside Bengal

The Pala epigraphs give us to understand that the Pala army were recruited soldiers from different parts of India. In course of their military service, tribes of both indigenous and foreign origin came and settled in Bengal. Mention is made of Mālava, Karṇāṭa, Khasa, Lāṭa, Hūṇa and Kulika tribes in the Monghyr Copper plate of Devapāla,[40] Bhāgalpur Copper plate of Nārāyaṇapāla and Bānagaḍ Copper plate of Mahipāla I.[41] In addition to these, the Manahali Copper plate of Madanapāla refers to the Choḍas (Cholas).[42] Again, the invasions from outside Bengal, like those of Yaśodharman, king of Malwa, in the 6th Century, of the Śilas[43] from the Himalayan region in the 7th century, of the Pratīhāras[44] in the 9th - 10th Centuries, of the Chālukyas[45] from Karṇāṭa and the Cholas[46] from the Tāmil land in the 11th - 12th centuries, might have brought in Bengal some tribes along with them. Further, the rule of the Khaḍgas[47] in the 7th century, that of Bhāskaravarman,[48] king of Kāmarūpa, in the 7th century, of the Kāmbojas[49] in the 10th century and of the Varmans[50] from Orissa and of the Senas from Karṇāṭa in the 11th - 12th centuries A.D. leave little scope of doubt that there were channels more than one which paved the way towards immigration of different ethnic elements and their amalgamation in the population of ancient Bengal.

Among the *mlecchas*, referred to in the *Brihaddarma Purāṇa*, mention is made of the Pukkasas, Pulindas, Khasas, Kharas, Kāmbojas, Yavanas, Suhmas and Śavaras. The term *mleccha* seems to imply that the tribes in question were not at all ready to accept the Aryan or Vedic culture in any form. However, of the tribes mentioned above the Khasas and the Kharas seem to have been allied with the Hūṇas who had been settled in the north-western part of India since the sixth century A.D. The Yavanas might have represented the Arabs of Sindh, who are known from the Khālimpur Copper plate inscription[51] to have acknowledged the supremacy of Dharmapāla. The territories of the Huns and the Kāmbojas were adjacent to each other. The Bādāl pillar inscription[52] of Nārāyaṇapāla claims Devapala's victories against the Hūṇas. Again, the Monghyr Copper plate[53] records the victorious march of Devapāla's army as far as Kamboja lying most probably in north-west India.

The Pukkasas are described by *Manu* (X.18) as descended from Nishāda (Brahmin + Śūdra) father and Śūdra mother. This is another instance of Manu's scheme of accommodating the aboriginal tribes within the traditional society. The Pulindas[54] and the Śavaras are mentioned together in the Naihāti Copper plate grant of Vallālasena, while in the *Aitareya Brāhmaṇa* (VII.18) the Pulindas are associated with the Andhras, in the *Purāṇas* (*Matsya*, Ch. 114 *Vayu*, Ch. 45) they are mentioned with the Śavaras as *Dākshiṇā-pathavāsinaḥ* together with the Vaidarbhas and Daṇḍakas. The *Mahābhārata* (XII. 207) also refers to the people of *Dakshiṇāpatha*. Pulindanagara, the capital of the Pulindas, is located near Bhilsā in Jabbalpore district in Madhya Pradesh. The country of the Śavaras (*Śavaradeśa*)[55] extended as far southward as the Pennār river, as it seems from the location of Sabarai in Ptolemy's *Geography*. Lastly, the Suhmas represent one of the ancient tribes of Bengal. It is difficult to explain how, inspite of the Aryanisation of Bengal through centuries, the Suhmas, ally of the Rāḍhas, could remain outside the fold of Aryan culture.

Detribalisation : A Social Process

The *antyaja* status in the traditional society was held by some de-tribalised castes such as Vyādha, Haḍḍi (Hāḍi), Ḍom, Jolā, Bāgatit (Bāgdi), Chaṇḍāla, Malla (Malo), Dolāvāhi (Dulia, Dule), Ghaṭṭajīvī (Pāṭni) and Baruḍa (Bāuri). The Ḍoms and Chaṇḍālas are mentioned not only in the *Brihaddharma* and *Brahmavaivarta Purāṇas* but also in the *Charyāpadas*. Some sections of the aboriginal tribes living in the forests came in contact with the traditional society and gradually seceded from the original stock. The contact was necessitated by some economic factors.[56] Some groups of the aboriginal tribes were more dependent on crafts than on hunting. They used to sell their goods to the people of higher castes. Sometimes they served as day-labourers, being hired by the landed gentry. The higher castes and more affluent people found the goods produced by the tribal people cheaper and also sought to purchase their labour at a cheaper rate of wages. It was in this background that the tribals were accommodated within the society by according to them the status of the lowest caste. Some sections of the tribal people who were employed in agriculture seem to be referred to as *Karshaka* or *Kshetrakara* in the Pala records.

Trends in the Tribal History

The tribal history of ancient Bengal shows some major trends. First, there were some tribes who were quick enough to get themselves Aryanised. They crossed the stage of food-gathering and reached the stage of food-producing. The hunters were transformed into agriculturists. They also adopted the caste-hierarchy. Thus, the stage was set for the emergence of the state-organised society. The brahmanical law-givers were not slow to accord them social recognition and assign to them a status in the scheme of social stratification. Of course, the status was generally accorded on the basis of special occupations and religious beliefs held by a particular group of people. Second, there were some tribes who failed to cope with the social evolution and could not keep pace with the development of technology employed for living. Others could not be brought under the influence of either Vedic or Purāṇic religion, as they strictly adhered to their primitive religious beliefs and practices. The remains of such tribes may still be traced in those parts of West Bengal which lie adjacent to the hills and jungles of Santal Parganas. The Parganas. The process of give-and-take between the primitive tribal and elitist societies has, however, continued since time immemorial. The religious beliefs and practices of the Muṇḍās and Orāons have been allowed to enter with due sophistication into the Purāṇas. On the other hand, the Purāṇic religion,in some form or other, has left its influence upon the tribal people. Third, another distinguishing feature of the tribal history of Bengal is that although the history had its beginning with the *Nishādas, Dāsa-dasyus* and *Kirātas,* at a later period some aboriginal tribes from the western, northern, north-western and southern parts of India came and settled in Bengal. Ethnic elements of both indigenous and foreign origin were incorporated in the population of Bengal. Fourth, whatever might have been the languages used by the original inhabitants of Bengal, Indo-Aryan speech re-organised them into a homogeneous unit known as Bengali language, a sister of Maithili, Assamese and Oriya. The Origin and development of Bengali language gradually submerged the identity of different tribal peoples. Even to-day the use of Bengali language has made it more and more difficult to distinguish the people of tribal origin from those of the caste-society.

References

1. White, Leslie A., *The Science of Culture*, New York, 1948.
2. Service, Elman R., *Primitive Social Organisation*, New York, 1971.
3. Sahlins, Marshall D., *Stone Age Economics*, Chicago, 1972.
4. Bhattacharya, D.K., *An Outline of Indian Prehistory*, Delhi, 1989, p. 13-14.
5. Sharma R.S., *Material Culture & Social Formations in Ancient India*, Delhi, 1985, Chs. I-V.
6. Childe, Gordon V., *Man Makes Himself*, London, 1948, Ch.IV., Morgan Lewis H., Ancient Society, New York, 1907, p. 20.
7. Chattopadhyay, R.K., *Prehistoric and Early Historic Archaeology of West Bengal*, an unpublished M. Phil dissertation of Delhi University, 1982, pp. 15-42.
8. *Ibid*, pp. 43-62.
9. *Ibid*. pp. 63-75.
10. *Ibid*. pp. 76-100.
11. Chatterjee, S.K., *Indo-Aryan and Hindi*, Calcutta, 1969, p. 36.
12. Roy, N.R., *Bangalir Itihasa, Adiparva*, Calcutta, 1980, p. 38. Ref. to Von Eiexsted's view.
13. *Chatterjee, S.K., Op. cit.*, p. 38.
14. Chatterjee, S.K., *Op. cit.*, p. 47.
15. Caldwell, R., *A Comparative Grammar of the Dravidian*, Delhi, 1974, p. 113.
16. Roy, N.R., *Op. cit.* pp. 65-66.
17. Dalton, E.T. *Descriptive Ethnology of Bengal*, 1872.
18. Chatterjee, S.K., *Op. cit.* p. 50.
19. Vide Ray, N.R., *Op. cit.* p. 56.
20. Ray, N.R., *Op. cit.* p. 64.
21. Sharma, R.S., *Aspects of Political Ideas and Institutions in Ancient India*, Delhi, 1959, p. 18.
22. Sen, S., *Vangabhumika*, Calcutta, 1974, p. 9.
23. *Ibid.*, p. 8.
24. *Ibid.*, p. 9.
25. *Ibid.*, p. 9.

26. *Ibid.*, p. 11.
27. *Ibid.*, p. 11.
28. Sircar, D.C., *Select Inscriptions*, Vol. I, Calcutta, 1942, pp. 82-83;
29. *Ibid.*, p. 276.
30. *Ibid.*, p. 331 ff.
31. Bagchi, P.C. (trans.), *Pre-Aryan and Pre-Dravidian in India*, Calcutta, 1929. pp. XXV-XXVI.
32. Sircar, D.C., *Op. cit.* p. 341.
33. *Ep. Ind.* XIV. 117.
34. Majumdar, R.C. (ed.), *History of Bengal* (hereafter *HB*) Vol. I Dacca, 1943, p. 38.
35. Mukherjee, R. & Maity, S.K., *Corpus of Bengal Inscription* (hereafter *CBI*), Calcutta, 1967, p. 168.
36. *Ibid*, p. 259 ff.
37. Risley, H.H., *The Tribes and Castes of Bengal*, Vol. I, Calcutta, 1981, p. 505.
38. *Ep. Ind.* II p. 409.
39. Risley, *Op. cit.* p. 291, Law, B.C., *Historical Geography of Ancient India* (hereafter *HGAI*) Paris, 1967, p. 167.
40. *CBI*, p. 114 ff.
41. *Ibid.*, p. 197 ff.
42. *Ibid.*, p. 209 ff.
43. *HB.*, p. 82.
44. *Ibid.*, p. 129.
45. *Ibid.*, p. 147.
46. *Ibid.*, p. 137.
47. *Ibid.*, p. 86-87.
48. *Ibid.*, p. 80-81.
49. *Ibid.*, p. 133-134.
50. *Ibid.*, p. 197.
51. *CBI* p. 95 ff.
52. *Ibid.*, p. 150 ff.
53. *Ibid.*, p. 114 ff.
54. *HGAI*, p. 219.
55. *Ibid.*, p. 223.
56. Bose, N.K., *The Structure of Hindu Society*, Delhi, 1975, p. 46.

Aspects of Indian History and Historiography
Editor : P.K. Mishra
Kaveri Books, New Delhi, India.

The Cōḻa Army and the Royal Temple of Rājarājēśvaram

13

Geeta Vasudevan

Rājarāja I involved the Cōḻa army in several ways in the administration of the empire and the royal institutions. The active participation of the army in the civic life of the people was one way by which the kings ensured the support of the military to their government. The army officers were rewarded for their loyalty by being given high administrative positions in the government, as well as through land grants (māṇyams). With time, these military officers became powerful local chiefs, who in the last days of the Cōḻa empire, proclaimed their independence as rulers of petty kingdoms.

It was to the credit of Rājarāja that he realised the power of a large, standing army and gave it due importance. Apart from giving his military officers administrative responsibilities, Rājarāja encouraged them to participate in his religious institutions. During his reign and that of his successors, the army was involved in temple affairs in many ways: in administering some temples; managing endowments in others; helping the auditors to detect irregularities in the financial transactions in temples; acting as guardians by protecting the temples and their properties; making grants to temples, etc. In these and other ways, the Cōḻa kings brought about a close interaction between this important arm of the royal government and society through the medium of the royal temple.

The Cōḻa Army

First and foremost, we must establish the fact that the Cōḻa army was a standing one, stationed in garrisons or cantonments. A standing army was of vital importance of the Cōḻa kings, who were engaged in incessant wars against their neighbouring states to expand their frontiers. It was only with the help of a large regular army that control could be maintained over the conquered territories, which were often brought under the rule of a Cōḻa governor. The size of the Cōḻa army must have been considerable. A Western Cālukyaṉ inscription at Hottūr (in the Dharwar district of Karnataka State) states that the Cōḻa army which fought under Rājēndra I against Satyaśraya consisted of nine lakh soldiers. If this were so, then the total strength of the army must have been considerably greater, taking into account his engagements in other sectors such as the Pāṇḍya country, Malaināḍu, Vēṅgi and Śri Lanka.

This is contrary to the observation of Burton Stein that the Cōḻa army consisted of mercenaries or peasants and labourers, who fought when the occasion (vēlai) demanded. He states, "The conquests of Cōḻa rulers from Sundara Cōḻa (A.D. 956-73) to Kulōttuṅga I (A.D. 1070-1120) are real enough, but these conquests neither presuppose nor require a vast standing army. Military power was possessed by numerous chiefs, by itinerant merchant groups and others throughout the Cōḻa macro-region. These were locally recruited and controlled forces. It is one of the major flaws in the reading of Cōḻa evidence to see armed force was the monopoly of the Cōḻa kingship, and it is important to recognize that upon the specious notion of a vast, central and standing army, much of the justification for the Cōḻa bureaucracy rests...It can be shown that there existed neither a centrally controlled military organization nor centrally coordinated redistribution of what were regarded as state resources. Military needs and the support of religious institutions and Brāhmanās were met from resources allocated by those under whose control such resources were: locality chieftains, not the Cōḻa rulers, except as the latter were themselves locality leaders in the central parts of Kāvēri basin."[2]

However, an analysis of inscriptional evidence proves that Stein's ideas are not justified. The evidence of the existence of 'kāḍagams' or garrisons shows that army cantonments were established in different parts of the empire. These kāḍagams were also called paḍaiviḍus. There are references to the villigal (bowmen) of Ēnanallūr-kāḍagam,[3] as also to troops in the Tiruvidaimarudur.[4] The Captain of the troops is mentioned too, 'ivvūr-paḍait-talaivar'.[5] The importance of the delta region of Paḻaiyāṟu is seen in its growth as a temple-based urban centre under the Cōḻa, right from the time of Ādityā I[6]. A series of army cantonments surrounded the palace area. Several small villages and hamlets bear names ending in 'paḍaiyūr'or 'paḍaiviḍu' (meaning the place where the army is stationed). A section of the army is called 'pāṇḍippaḍai' and is mentioned in an inscription of Parāntaka I in the Nāgēsvara Temple. A whole group of army men, (śēṇaiyar) was entrusted with the protection of the temple endowments at Tiruviḍaimarudūr.[7]

The mode of remuneration of the army is not clear; however, it is likely that a sizeable quantity of the booty from war would have been distributed among the army units. Though the spoils of war must have been considerable, this mode of payment would have been erratic and made the army depend solely on loot. It is more likely that a regular mode of payment for the army would have ensured a disciplined, well-organised army.

The names of several regiments, units and divisions of the army give some idea of how and when they were formed. Though the methods of recruitment are not clear, nor is it clear that they were a highly trained professional outfit having little or nothing in common with the civilian population yet it can be stated that they were no mere rabble with little military training. The names of some 30 regiments mentioned in Rājarāja's inscriptions have been collected by Venkayya.[8] Many of them have royal titles incorporated in their names. Venkayya opines that they possibly distinguished themselves in some engagement or other. Mention is made of the different sections of the army, like the elephant corps (āṇaiyāṭkaḷ), the cavalry (kudiraccēvagai), bowmen (villigaḷ), etc.

The regiments were divided on territorial lines, like Pāṇḍi-paḍai,[9] Teṇ-Illaṅgai-Valañjiyar,[10] etc. That some of them had long and distinguished traditions and achievements to their credit is seen from the Tiruvāliśvaram inscription[11] near Ambāśamudaram in Tirunelveli district. This undated inscription is assigned to the period of Rājarāja I and Rājēndra I. The regiment is called the 'Mūṉṟukai-Mahāśēṇai' (the Great Army of the Three Arms or Sections). In the epigraph, it speaks with pride about its various conquests in several engagements, all under Rajarāja I and his successor, in which it distinguished itself. This army is also called the residents of Pāṇḍi-nāḍu. These armymen took under their eternal protection the temple of Tiruvāliśvaram with all its belongings, priests and servants. In another record[12] from Sēramādēvi in 1096A.D., this unit undertook to protect another temple and its properties, and calls itself, "the several armed thousands of the great army of the three divisions (kai).

The mention of the three divisions (mūṉṟukai) of the army is also found in record[13] from Polonnaruva in Śri Lanka. This record of Vijayabāhu I mentions the vēlaikāras, who consisted of the three divisions of the Mahātantra, the Valañjiyar and the Nagarattār, who were invited by the Śiṁhala king to protect the Buddhist temple for the tooth relic. The temple was renamed as Mūṉṟu-kai-tiru-vēlaikkāraṉ-daladay-perum-paḷḷi. They bound themselves to protect the temple, its lands, its serfs and properties, etc. The Mahāvamśa[14] states that these vēlaikāras were brought to the Śrilankan mainland by the conquering Cōḷa kings, and were left behind to protect the Cōḷa properties, including the temples built by them; that they were a powerful community who were wooed by the Śiṁhala kings and that they were quite capable of creating problems like revolting against their masters.

This velaikāra branch of the army has been described in several ways. Hultzch defined them as a troop of servants.[15] Venkayya states that they were volunteers when the occasion (vēlai) arose. In later times they migrated to Śri Lanka with the merchants under whom they served. This is attested by their association with merchant guilds such as the nagarattār and the valañjiyar; in one inscription they are mentioned as the valañjiyar of South Lanka (Teṉ-Ilaṅgai-Valañjiyar).[16] However, in course of time they developed into a powerful force to reckon with. Thus the interpretation of the term, 'mūṉṟukai' is varied and interesting. If this same unit is also mentioned in the Tiruvāliśvaram record mentioned above (as is quite likely, since they refer to themselves as the residents of Pāṇḍināḍu) then the transformation and conversion of bodyguards or soldiers associated with the merchant guilds into a powerful regiment of the army with a rich martial tradition was complete. In the Tañjāvūr inscription of Rājarāja I and Rājēndra I the regiments mentioned are Śirudānattu-vaḍuga-kkāvalar and Śirudānattu-Valaṅgai-Vēlaikkāra-ppaḍaigaḷ. Śirudānam was the title of army officers as well as honorary titles of officers and private individuals.

The Kaikkōḷas are another section of the army. The Kaikkōḷapperumbaḍai[17] or the great troops of the Kaikkōḷas, included all regiments known as Kaikkōḷar. Interpreted also as 'weavers',[18] Sastri feels that the term has a more literal meaning in the Cōḷa epigraphs.[19] He states that it indicates a class of men distinguished by the strength of their arms or soldiers of the infantry division in the army. Some regiments of bowmen and swordsmen were called 'Vāḷperṟa-kaikkōḷars'.

There are also references to another specialised regiment called 'nāṭṭuppaḍai-paḷiyili-ainnūṟṟuvar', who are involved in maintaining a charitable endowment.[20] Who these faultless 500 were and what their relation to the rest of the nāṭṭuppaḍai was, is not clear. Sastri points out that the two divisions of the army mentioned appear to have constituted two out of the four kinds of troops prescribed in the books of Indian polity-hereditary (maula), mercenary (bhrtaka), militia (śrēni) and tribal (atavi).

The Army's Role Vis-A-Vis The Temple

The army regiments had a corporate life of their own. Through the inscriptions we learn more about the role that the army units played in civil life than about their military exploits. By involving the army in temple matters the king ensured its commitment to the upkeep and protection of the royal undertakings. In the Tañjāvūr temple, the military was involved in several ways. Icons were set up by important officers and endowments made too them in the form of gold and silver ornaments and vessels Cash grants to the temple by the army officers were invested with the śabhās. Endowments for maintaining lamps were made by several important individuals.

Including army officers. Building activities and repair work were undertaken by the army. Finally, punishment was meted out to the erring officers by the king in the form of compulsory endowments for lamps.

Although army officers were not actively involved in the administration of the Tañjāvūr Temple, there were several temples where the army's role in managing them was encouraged by the rulers, as seen in the case of the temples at Tiruviḍaimarudūr and Tiruvāliśvaram, as mentioned earlier. Even in the case of the royal temple of Rājarājēśvaram, certain shrines were maintained and managed by the armymen. They made donations of gold and silver and ornaments and made cash grants. The cash thus granted was lent out on interest to the śabhās in Cōḻamaṇḍalam. Out of this interest, several services were conducted. An analysis of some of the army units attached to the Rājarājēśvaram and the cash grants made by them is given in the table below. The table shows the financial resources commanded by various army regiments and how they were actively involved in the management of various shrines within the Tañjāvūr temple. The Table 1 has been prepared from the following inscriptions: SII,II, 9, 12-19, 35, 54.

The active involvement of the highest officers in the royal temple is shown by the role played by Krishṇaṉ Rāmaṉ, the Commander-in-Chief of Rājarāja I. (The Larger Leyden Copper Plate tells us about him).[21] He became the Tirumandira Ōlaināyagam which was the highest position in the Cōḻa bureaucracy under Rājarāja I and Rājēndra I. Krishṇaṉ Rāmaṉ outlived Rājarāja and served his son and successor, Rājēndra I, under whom he took the title of Rājēndraśōla Brahmamārāyaṉ. He also had the title of 'perundāṇām'. It is significant that a Brāhmānā military officer rose to the rank of C-in--C and it is equally important to note that the top civilian posts were entrusted to high-ranking officers of the army.

Krishṇaṉ Rāmaṉ is among the donors of the royal temple of Tañjāvūr. He constructed the inner wall of the enclosure round the Rājarājēśvaram Temple as mentioned in three inscriptions.[22] This wall on the southern and western wings was called the 'Krishṇaṉ Rāmaṉ Tiru-churru-māḷigai' with the Rājarājatiru-vāśal, and immediately outer wall of enclosure with the Kēralāntaka-tiru-vāśal, i.e. the walls of fortification with the bastions and the moat around, are mentioned in the Tiruviśaippā of Karūr Dēvar, the guṛu of Rājarāja I. Incidentally, this seems to be the first example of soul defence works in any South Indian temple. A metal image of Ardhanāriśvarar was also set up by him in the temple before the 29th year of Rājarāja and he endowed it with jewels.[23]

Similarly, another important officer, Īrāyiravaṉ Pallavāyar, alias Mummaḍiśōla Pōśan set up and image in copper of Chaṇḍēśvara Dēvar and endowed it with ornaments. Pallavayar was a perundāṇam of Rājarāja.[24]

Military officers aided in auditing temple accounts. For e.g. in the 3rd year of Adhirājēndradēva and the 8th and 21st year of Kulōttuṅga, there were cases of embezzlement in the Aruṇājatēśvara Temple in Tiruppandal in Kumbakonam district. These cases of misdemeanour by the temple treasurers were inspected by Rājarāja Mūvēndavēḷāṉ Śēnāpati Pallavarāyar and Śēnāpati Nandiyarājar respectively.[25]

Apart from the cash grants (which by army officers and army regiments alone amounted to more than 56/9 kāśus), a number of inscriptions give details of donations of cattle to the temple of Rājarājēśvaram. This was made for the purpose of maintaining lamps in the temple. In most cases, cash was paid to the temple, which in turn paid the amount to the shepherd/shepherds, who entered into a service contract with the temple for supplying a stipulated quantity of ghee daily for the purpose of lighting different types of lamps.

Altogether there are four inscriptions which give details of the donations made for lamps. Of these two (SII, II, 63 and 94) were grants for lamps made by Rājarāja himself. Inscriptions 64

Table 13.1

No.	*Army Unit*	*For the Image of*	*To Sabha*	*Amount in Kāśu*
1.	Valaṅgai-Parambaḍai-gaḷilār (Right Hand Troops)	Bikśadēvar (set up by Queen Lōkamāhādēvi	Neḍumaṇal (Madanamañjari CVM in Nenmalināḍu	252
2.	Regiment Niyāyam Perundāṇattu Valaṅgai-Vēlaikkāra Paḍaigaḷ Contigents:	Main Deity		
	a. Paṇḍita-Śōḷa-terinda villāḷigaḷ		Paḷḷiyil (Nenmalināḍu)	31
	b. Rājavinōda-terinda-valaṅgai-vēlaikkārar		Pērumbalamarudūr (Puraṅgaranbaināḍu)	310
	c. Pandita-Śōḷa-terinda-villāḷiyar		Pērumbalamarudūr (Puraṅgaranbaināḍu)	267
	d. Chandraparākrama-terinda-valaṅgai-vēlaikkārar		Pērumbalamarudūr (Puraṅgaranbaināḍu)	223
	e. Nittavinōda-terinda-valaṅgai-vēlaikkārar		Paḷḷiyil (Nenmalināḍu)	13
3.	Niyāyam-Śirudānattu Valaṅgai-Vēlaikkāra-Paḍaigaḷilār	Dakshiṇa Mēru Viṭakar	a. Kalappal (Puraṅgarambai Nāḍu)	125
	Niyāyam-Śirudānattu Valaṅgai-Vēlaikkāra-Paḍaigaḷilār	Dakshiṇa Mēru Viṭakar	b. Kōri (Puraṅgarambai Nāḍu)	300
	Niyāyam-Śirudānattu Valaṅgai-Vēlaikkāra-Paḍaigaḷilār	Dakshiṇa Mēru Viṭakar	c. Vaṅganagar (same nāḍu)	500
	Niyāyam-Śirudānattu Valaṅgai-Vēlaikkāra-Paḍaigaḷilār	Dakshiṇa Mēru Viṭakar	d. Ariñjigai CVM	800
			e. Kundavai CVM	500
			f. Paṇaiyūr (Puraṅgarambai Nāḍu)	500
4.	Niyāyam-Uttama-Śōḷa-terinda-aṇdalagattāḷar	Chandēśvara (set up by a Perundaram)	Paḷḷiyil (Nenmalināḍu)	60
5.	Military Officers		Śri-Vīranārāyana CVM (taniyūr)	743
6.	Military Officers		Perumakkalūr (Kirār-Kūṟṟam)	120

and 95 give details of donations made by Rājarāja as well as by others. Among the individual donors are a group of 14 persons who appear to have made in contribution under special circumstances. Military operations were on at Kōḻi, i.e. Uṟaiyūr (ancient Cōḻa capital). A number of military officers were disgraced by the king for having lost the battle (or quell a riot). They vowed to put up lamps in the temple fearing that the wrath of the king would be brought on them and their fair names would be besmirched. "The supposed rationale behind the kind of penal provision was that the guilty should be imposed a monetary penalty and the sin be expiated by presenting cattle to the temple. This means that to them, a guilt was not only a crime but also a sin."[26]

Eight of them have the title, 'Perundāṉam', prefixed to their names indicating their high status. Three of these fourteen were arbitrators and were Brāhmaṇās. This is a fair pointer to the rich emoluments that these military officers received, or perhaps it indicates their share in the loot from wars which must have been quite substantial. For instance,[27] Perundāṉam Uttaraṅguḍaiyāṉ Kōṉ Vidiviḍaṅgaṉ (alias) Villavaṉ Mūvēndavēḷāṉ has made grants for the maintenance of several lamps. From nine records we get to know that he has given in all 342 ewes, which @ 3 ewes for each kāśu, works out to be 114 kāśus. This group of officers has given almost 800 ewes in all. The ancient idea of serving punishment for wrong doing through pious acts like maintaining lamps in temples seems to be behind the act of penance by the disgraced officers.

The donation of the other military officers and military units amounts to almost 512 kāśus (figures not complete due to certain inscriptions being obliterated). The following groups of men are also among the donors:[28]

(a) Udaiyaṉ-Śri-Rājarājadēva-Mummaḍi-Śōla-terinda-parivārattār;

(b) Jaṉanātha terinda-parivārattār;

(c) Palavagai-parampaḍaigaḷillār. These were royal retinues.

Apart from these officers, there were others who made grants for lamps purely for merit as well as to curry favour with the king. A list of some of these officers is given in the Table 13.2. Thus we have evidence of the manner in which the kings kept their military officers in check and in constant fear against any misdemeanour on their part. Fear of royal disapproval kept powerful military chieftains under control and discouraged personal ambitions from surfacing. Loyalty to the king and empire and to the royal institutions was the paramount guiding principle.

An interesting feature which comes to light from these inscriptions is that the temple served as a channel for the redistribution of funds from the military sector to the agrarian sector. Spencer highlights the temples' role as the major connecting link between the imperial activities of a small military elite on one hand and the agricultural sector of society which it served on the other. The inscription of the Tañjāvūr Temple "reveals that vital economic resources, contributed by the king and other individuals to provide endowments, passed through the temple to various villages in return for the payment of interest or the performance of specified perpetual services for the temple. The flow of taxes and military manpower from the countryside to the royal court was partially counterbalanced by a reverse flow into certain villages of money, livestock and other goods, obtained in part from carrying out plundering expeditions into 'enemy' territory. In this way, the remarkable temple at Tañjāvūr served not only as a means of redistributing resources, but also as a means of binding together court and countryside in politico-economic symbiosis."[29]

These records which give details of donations for lamps are just one aspect of the manner in which the military was involved in the affairs of the temple. This also shows how the booty

Table 13.2

No.	*Individual's Name*	*Belonged To*	*Title*	*Or Occupation*
1.	Ādityaṉ Śūryaṉ	Poygaināḍu	Headman	Śrikāryam of temple
2.	Karayileḍuttapādam	Rājakēśarinallūr	Headman	Royal Secretary Tirumandira Ōlai
3.	Śembaṅguḍaiyāṉ Tēvaṉ	Semabaṅguḍi (Āvūr Kūṟṟam)	Perundaram	Viruppaṟaiyaṉ
4.	Īrāyiravaṉ	Araiśūr (Pāmabuṇi Kūṟṟam)	Perundaram	Pallavarāyar
5.	Rājarāja Vaṇakōvaraiyar	—	Perundaram	—
6.	Pūdi Śāttaṉ	Miḍur	Headman	
7.	Nambaṉ Kūttāḍi	—	Perundaram	Jayaṅgoṇḍa-Śōḷa Brahmamahārājan
8.	Tirumalai Vēṅgaḍan	Vayalūr	Headman and Perundaram	—
9.	Kōṉ Śuṟṟi	—	Perundaram	Arumori-Pallavaraiyaṇ
10.	Nittavinōda Mahārāja	—	Perundaram	—
11.	Savur Parañjōdi	Tañjāvūr Suburb	Superintendent of temple women	—
12.	Achchaṉ Kōnūrkkāḍan	Tañjāvūr Suburb	—	Merchant
13.	Īśānaśiva Pandita	—	Guru of King	Chief priest of Rājarājēsvaram

acquired through wars was redistributed to the countryside (agricultural sector) and how the temple acted as a conduit in this redistributive process.

The participation of the military in certain aspects of civil administration is thus well attested. It ensured that the army was never idle. At the same time, Rājarāja and his successors kept military ambitions under control in the ways delineated above. The royal temple was thus a useful institution in engaging the army in various economic and welfare activities of the royal government.

References

1. Balasubramanyam, S.R. *Early Chola Art*, 1966, p. 5.
2. Burton Stein, *Peasant State and Society in Medieval South India*, 1980, p. 257-58.
3. 394 of 1921, South Indian Inscriptions.
4. 242 of 1907.
5. T.A.S. LV, p. 134-5.
6. Champakalakshmi R. "Growth of Urban Centres in South India : Kudamukku-Palaiyarai, the Twin-city of the Cholas", Studies in History, Vol.1, 1979, p. 18.

7. 239 of 1907; SII, XIII, 7.
8. SII, II, 5, Introduction by Venkayya.
9. 255 of 1911.
10. A.R. on Epigraphy for 1923, p. 106.
11. 120 of 1905.
12. 189 to 1895.
13. E.I., XVIII, 38.
14. *Mahāvaṁśa*, Ch. LX.
15. SII, II, p. 97.
16. Derived from the Sanskrit 'Vanij'.
17. 253 of 1907.
18. SII, II, p. 390, No. 6.
19. Nilakanta Sastri K.A. *The Cholas*, 1955, Ch. XVIII, p. 454.
20. 253 of 1904.
21. E.I., V, 34.
22. SII, II, 31, 33, 45.
23. SII, II, 39.
24. ASII, II, 55.
25. 46 of 1914.
26. Vasantha Bai T.R., *History of Thangavun Through The Ages*, p. 134.
27. SII, II, 95.
28. SII, II, 64, 95.
29. Spencer George W., "Royal Initiative Under Rajaraja I", IESHR, 1970.

Aspects of Indian History and Historiography
Editor : P.K. Mishra
Kaveri Books, New Delhi, India.

The System of Education in Ancient Orissa (6th Century A.D. to 13th Century A.D.)

14

Sanghamitra Dasgupta

Despite the deprecatory attitude of the Dharmaśāstrakāras to the 'unholy east,[1] the kingdom of Orissa, like its other eastern counter parts i.e. Bengal and Assam, had played a significant role as an important centre of education and culture during the period under review.

The modern state of Orissa evolved out of Oḍra or Utkala (Northern Orissa), South Kosala (Western Orissa) and Kalinga. Kalinga of the past, in its broadest sense, extended from the southern borders of Midnapur to the river Godavari.[2a]

Following the decline of the Imperial Guptas this region seldom witnessed political unity. Nevertheless the entire region proved itself to be within one cultural ambit; and inspite of political troubles educational activities in Orissa do not appear to have been substantially affected. The numerous donative records of the reigning kings and the feudatory chiefs of Orissa like the Māṭharas, Gaṅgas, the Bhauma - Karas, the Śailodbhavas, the Bhañjas, the Sulkis and the Imperial Gangas prove that they had actively patronised educational activities.

Education in ancient India being the handmaid of religion, all educational institutions seem to have drawn their guidelines from Buddhism, Jainism and Hinduism, the three prominent religions practised in this sector. Rivarly among the adherents of the three systems was common, but religious persecution was unheard of. Thus Bālārjuna, a Śaiva ruler made generous grants for building a Buddhist monastery and also made provisions for the *satra* atteched to it.[2b]

Of the three types of educational system; the British system seems to be the more organised one, Orissa played a significant part in the development of Buddhism and nourished it long after Muslim conquest. It contributed towards the development of Vajrayāna and Kālachakrayāna forms of Buddhism, and their varied forms of iconography. Tāranāth[3] refers to the preaching of esoteric Buddhism in Orissa by "Munindra" at the request of king Indrabhūti of Orissa. Elsewhere he refers to the centres of esoteric Buddhism in Kalinga.[4]

The main centres of Buddhist education were the Buddhist monasteries or the *mahāvihāras* which, under the patronage of the Gupta rulers, had developed into some thing like modern Universities equipped with the usual paraphernalia, viz. professor and students, graded course, approved syllabi, academic regulations, lecture halls and libraries. Though essentially centring round Buddhist canonical lores, later on the syllabi included secular subjects as well Hiuen - Tsang saw in the Wu-tu or Odra[5] country more than one hundred monasteries. (7th century A.D.)

Of these, *Ratnagiri Mahāvihāra* was a mahāvihāra of front rank. The Tibetan Chroniclers[6] attest to the fact that its fame had reached abroad. Excavations carried out at the top of the Ratnagiri hills in 1958 on the bank of the stream of kelua in Orissa have laid bare the remains of this monastery. The seals found among the ruins bearing the legend *Śrī Ratnagiri-Mahavihāriya-bhikṣhu* Saṁghasya has enabled the archaeologists to ascertain the site of the monastery which was a great centre of education.

Tāranātha[7] attributes the construction of the monastery to a king called Buddhapakṣha who ruled in *Odivisa*. He also speaks of a later king Balabhadra[8] who built many temples and monasteries in *Śrī. Ratnagiri*.

Excavations[9] unearthed the remains of an important monastic complex, the edifices consisting mainly of the stupas and the residence of the monks. Some slabs belonging to the Gupta period inscribed with the Buddhist text *Pratitya - Samutpāda - sūtra* have been found here. The votive stupas found here are decorated with images of Vajra, Buddha, Tārā, Lokeśvara and other Vajrayāna deities. The images of the divinities testify to the full sway of Mahāyāna and Vajrayāna forms of Buddhism. Another feature seems to be the presence of esoteric figures. The Ratnagiri copper - plate of the Somavaṁśi king Kornakeśarī records the grant of a village by Rāni Karpuraśri king Karnakeśarī records the grant of a village by Rāni Karpuraśrī who hailed from the Solanapura Mahāvihāra. The site, which is probably Solanapur near Jaipur, 13 miles from Ratnagiri, and interestingly enough the grant refers to the presence of the dancing girls in the Solanapura Vihāra. The system reminds of the later day of Devadāsis or dancing girls in the Hindu temples. It is suggested that the queen passed her retired Life in Ratnagiri. Obviously, the Vihāra had arrangements for the nuns or *bhikṣhunis*. The other charter found here also indicates that the monastery enjoyed royal patronage.

Tāranātha,[10] speaking of the Vihāra of Ratnagiri in the reign of Buddhapakṣha (probable identification with Narasimhagupta Bālāditya) of the Gupta dynasty, said that in this vihāra were kept three sets of *Mahāyāna* and *Hinayāna* śāstras and there were eight great groups of *dharma* (religious schools) and five hundred monks.

According to Sumpā,[11] Āchārya, Bito-pā went through magic to Sambala where he obtained Kālachakrayāna, brought it to Ratnagiri and explained it to Avadhuti-pā, Bodhiśrī and Nāro-pā. This legend proves that towards the end of 10th century A.D. *Tāntrik*, influence had penetrated here and that this vihāra was associated with the intellectual stalwarts of the Age. Hiuen-Tsang[12] refers to a debate between the scholars of Ratnagiri vihāra with those of Nālandā. The excellence of the vihāra is proved by the fact that one Prajñā,[13] and inhabitant of Kapiśa (near kabul) who came to India visited many monasteries including Nālandā, and atlast settled in ratnagiri which he found to be an unrivalled centre of yoga.

Another important centre of Buddhist learning seems, to be Tampralipti or modern Tamluk. Hiuen-Tsang[14] saw here ten monasteries with one thousand monks. Of them most important one seems to be the *Varāha monastery* mentioned by I-tsing.[15] He speaks of the high moral character and stern discipline of the monks of this Vihāra. Rāhulamitra of this vihāra was respected all over India for his excellent character and high learning. A register recording the names of the inmates of the vihāra was regularly maintained. The saṁgha was run on democratic lines; the assembly of monks used to run the affairs of the monastery. The learned monks who had mastered the *Tripitakas* were alloted the best rooms and servants. Those who delivered lectures were relieved of other duties. The priests had to confess their faults before the assembly. It seemed that the monasteries possessed considerable amount of land. I-tsing says that the residents of the vihāra did not themselves till the land but leased it out to the tenants who cultivated the land and gave one-third of the vegetables to the priests. I-tsing himself stayed here and studied sanskrit. Te-cheng-Tsang,[16] was another Chinese priest who stayed here for twelve years and studied the Buddhist—Sanskrit texts. On his return to China he explained the

Nidāna-Śāstra of Ullaṅga. Another Chinese scholar who stayed here for three years was Tao-lin.[17] He learned Sanskrit and entered into the orders of the *Sarvāstivāda* school.

Hiuen-Tsang[18] speaks of another monastery called the *Tamralipti Vihāra*. This vihāra was endowed with a rich library. The Chinese monk was so impressed by it that he stayed here to copy the *sutras* and to draw pictures, of Buddhist images. It appears that *Śilpavidyā* was also included in the curriculum of Buddhist education. I-tsing[19] too, visited this centre of education.

Tāranāth[20] refers to one Bhadrapālita who founded sixteen vihāras which turned into great centres of learning.

Another famous Buddhist monastery in Orissa seems to be the *Pushpagiri Mahavihara* or *Pu-sie-po-ki-li of*[21] Hiuen-Tsang. This has been identified by the scholars with one the two Jaipur hills, i.e. Lalitagiri and Udayagiri.[22]

From the foregoing account it appears that Orissa was an important centre of Buddhist learning and was visited by students from abroad.

Jainism too, appears to be a pivot round which grew up a definite system of education. The architectural and plastic remains as well as literary accounts including the account of Hiuen-Tsang[23] prove that Jainism gained foot hold in Orissa in the first century B.C. and survived till the 16 century A.D. Like its Buddhist counter-parts, the Jaina moanasteries also developed into centres of education infact. The Jaina church from the early period of its existence laid stress on 'knowledge' or *'jñāna'*.[24] Though at the early state of existence the Jaina curricula was entirely religious,[25] with the passage of time it shed its exclusively monkish character and included, besides Jaina religious lores, the study of such subjects as the *four Vedas, Vedāṅgas Vyākaraṇa, Dharama, Itihāsa, gaṇita, the Epics, metre, etymology* and many sciences.[26] It may be presumed that the Jaina monasteries in Orissa too acted as centres of education and imparted religious as well as secular learning.

The existence of a Jaina monastery in the Navamuni cave in the Khandagiri hills is proved by the archaelogical and epigraphical evidence. The bas-relief on the caves depict various Jaina images and icons. The cave inscriptions also point to the installation of Jaina image in the site.[27] The numerous small cells in the hills were presumably used to accommodate the Jaina ascetics. That this place was a centre of learning is proved by the cave inscription which states that the Jaina Saint Āchārya Śubhachandra, the disciple of Kulachandra taught here.[28]

The Bānpur plate of the Śailodbhava king Dharmarājā[29] (7th century A.D.) states that queen Kalyāna Devi made gift of land to the Jaina *muni* Prabuddhachandra, a disciple of Arhatāchārya Nāsichandra. The inscription of king Udiyatakeśari (11th century A.D.) refers to the repair and excavation of the tanks and Jaina temples in the Kumārapravat.[30] Orissa abounds in many such Jaina Shrines, images of deities belonging to Jaina pantheon, particularly those of the *tirthankaras* and the *Śāsanadevīs*. Among the other important Jaina sites, mention may be made of the districts of Koraput, Cuttack, Bhuvaneswar, Mayurbhanj, and Keonjar region, the Prachi valley, Charmula near Bhairvsinghpur.[31] Many of the relics and temples found in these places are datable to 11th century A.D. Most of the sites answer to the description in the *sthānanga* regarding the ideal place for the monasteries which should be situated in the lonely areas like sea shores, banks of rivers, slopes of mountains and hills; but at the same time in the vicinity of important cities to ensure accessibility to the lay devotees and students. The Jaina monks too, often under-took preaching tours. The *Prabodhachandradaya*[32] refers to wandering Jaina ascetics preaching Jaina religion and philosophy and at the same time trying to protect their faith from heretical attacks.

Paucity of source materials makes it difficult to construct a systematic account of Jaina education in Orissa. But the continuance of Jainism as a living force is proved by the three shrines of modern origin in the town of Cuttack.

Notwithstanding the popularity of Jainism and Buddhism, Brahmanical learning too seemed to have received a spurt during this period. It is true that Aryan acculturation had been rather late in this region, as in the other regions of the Eastern Sector. Moreover Tantrikism had found a congenial home here. Nevertheless as the numerous donative copper plates reveal, Brahmanical religion had struck too deep a root to be completely relegated to the background. Attempts were made even by the Buddhist Bhuma-kara kings to "put the castes in their proper duty".[33] The *Prabodhachandrodaya*[34] points to the influence of Kumarila Bhaṭṭa in Orissa.

The land grants of the ruling dynasties as well as the feudatory chiefs mentioning the Vedic Śākha and Charaṇa of the donees throw light on the flourishing state of Brahmanical education. To mention a few : The Jirjingi copper plate inscription of Eastern Gaṅga king Indravarman I[35] (537 A.D.) and the Ponnutur grant of Sāmantavaraman[36] record grants of land of Brāhmanas studying the Vedas. The Chicacole grant,[37] the Purle copper plate grant[38] and the Tekkali grant[39] of indravarman III record grant of land to Vedic Students (7th century A.D.). We come across numerous grants of the Eastern Ganga dynasty gifting land to the Brāhamṇa teachers and students. The Bhañja kings like Neṭṭabhañja,[40] Śatrubhañja[41] and,Raṇabhañja[42] too made gifts to lands to the teachers of Vedas. The inscriptions of the Śulki chiefs like Kulastambha[43] and Ranasthambha[44] (9th century A.D.) record grants of land to the Brahmin scholars. The *Paramasaugata* Bhauma-karas too actively patronised the study of the Vedas. Śubhakara I granted land to two hundred Brāhmaṇas.[45] The Terundia plate of Śubhakara II,[46] The Denkanal plate of Tribhuvana Mahādevi,[47] the Chaurasia plate of Śivakara II,[48] the Hindol plates of Śubhakara deva[49]—all these testify to this. Instances can be multiplied to prove that during this period generous grants were made to the Brāhmaṇa scholars and teachers by different ruling dynasties.[50]

In response to the changing times different types of Bhāhmanical Institutions came into existence during the period under review. But the old aśrama (hermitage) type institutions still existed in the outskirts of the villages or the towns. The charter of the Somavaṁśi King Bālārjuna refers to a *tapovana* in *Dvaitavana* where lived Śulapāṇi, the preceptor of the king. Relevant illustrations may be gleaned from Dandin's *Daśakumaracharita*[51] (6th century), and Krishna Misra's *Prabodhachandrodaya*[52] (11th century A.D.). The Sāmba Purāna[53] composed in Orissa also mentions one *'Thapavana'* by the sea-side (*lavaṇodadhi*). The Purāṇic stories as well as the injunctions laid down by the Dharmaśāstras prove the continuance of the *gurukula* system, under which the disciple stayed with the *guru* (preceptor) as a member of his household : and lived according to the injunctions of the Dharmaśāstras.

Apart from this, the temples had also emerged as centres of learning, and played a great role in imparting mass education. The religious discourses on the epics or the Purānas and the practise of dancing and singing devotional songs, particularly songs of Jayadeva had helped in the dissemination of culture among the mass.

The *āchāryas* of the temples appear to be erudite persons, adept in religious as well as secular subjects. The Megheśvara temple inscription[54] refers to Vishṇu Āchārya who was well versed in the *Vedas, Purāṇas, ethics, logic* and *political science*. The land grants testify to the residential arrangements in the temples for the teachers as well as students. The Simāchalam temple inscription[55] records grants of land by the king Anatavarman Chodagaṅga for the provision of scholars therein. Hindol plate of Śubhakara III 56 (9th century A.D.) records grant of a village for the maintenance of the temple of Pulindeśvara in Tośāli and the ascetics living therein. The Chicacole plate of Satya Varman[57] mentions Kamalāsaha Bhattāraka, a Devasthaniyi (Superindent of a religious institution) and indicates that there was residential arrangement for the students in the temple mentioned in the grant Patanga Śivāchārya the preceptor of the Ganga ruler Devendravarman lived in the temple of Yogeśvar with his śishyas (students) and parā śishyas (disciple of disciple)[58] (8th century A.D.) Bālārjuna of Somavaṁsi dynasty (9th century A.D.) built a Vishnu temple at Śripura with a Vedic college attached to it, and donated a village for the maintenance of the priests, the teachers, "the two bhāgavatas" and the other staff of the institution. Provision was also made for the maintenance of temples almshouses and repairing service.[59] The Śobhaneśvar temple inscription mentions the existence of a cloisture for vedic studies.[60] (12th century A.D.).

Another type of educational institution, designated as the *maṭhas*, emerged presumably in the neo-Vedantic period when Saṁkarāchārya and his disciple Kumarila Bhaṭṭa tried to re-establish Brahmanical religion. Tradition ascribes to saṁkarāchārya the establishment of four *maṭhas* in four different quarters. One of them was Govardhana Piṭha[61] in Orissa. The *maṭhas*, originally established to give shelter to the monks, gradually turned out into centres of education. Numerous inscriptions recording endowments of property or wealth have hailed from different parts of Orissa. Many of the early *maṭhas* were Saivite in origin. The earliest Śaiva *matha* in Orissa appears to be the one in Tribhuvaneśvar[62] (7th century A.D.), Lakulissa, its āchārya, is said to have organised mass preachings. We also hear of the Śaiya teachers of Mattamayūra cult who had established various *maṭhas* accommodating students.[63] One such was situated in Ranipur-Jharial region. Its āchārya Gagana Śambhu[64] (9th century A.D.) wrote a commentary on *Vaiśesika* Philosophy entitled *'Vyomavati'*. The Terundia copper plate inscription of Śubhākara deva II[65] records grant of land to a *maṭha* for the upliftment of the monasteries and the *maṇḍpas* established by the Brāhmaṇas. The inscription of king Śatrubhañja[66] refers to the grants of the said king to various *maṭhas*. Curiously enough one such maṭha is said to have been founded by a conch-shell worker of Ahichhatra. It appears from the donative records that alm houses were also attached to the *maṭhas*.[67] The Śobhaneśvar inscription[68] (12th century A.D.) refers to the construction of a *maṭha* accommodating teachers as well as students. The inscription of king Anangabhimadeva III[69] refers to a *maṭha* where *Vedas, Vyākaraṇas* and *Purāṇas* were taught. The plate gives the name of the scholars as donees who were attached to the *maṭhas* for the purpose of teaching. Thus, it appears that these *maṭhas* though originally imparted religious education later became centres of liberal education.

Finally, mention may be made of the *agrahāras* or the 'settlement of *brahmaṇas*'[70] which acted as centres of education. The *agrahāras* appear to be rent free autonomous villages free from the interference of royal officers.

Presumably the *agrahāras* furthered the cause of learning. The inscriptions refer to the Brāhamaṇas engaged in *"shatkarma"* (traditional sixfold duties) of which *adhyaponā* or teaching occupies an important part.[71]

A practised from the donative records it appear that land was given to renowned scholars and teachers. Brāhmaṇa scholars from different parts of India, i.e. Madhyades[72] Ayodhya[73] and Rāḍha[74] were encouraged to settle here. As tradition has it, the Soamvaṁśi ruler Yayātikeśari[75] brought in to Orissa. One thousand Brāhmaṇas well-versed in the Vedic lores.

The donative grants prove that numerous agrahāras were established by the ruling kings and also by the wealthy members of the community. The Godavari plate of Prithvimula[76] (7th century A.D.) records grant of agrahāra to forty—sixty vedic Brāhmaṇas with the object of establishing a colony of *Alharva vaidikos*. King Devendravarman of the same dynasty granted a village to three hundred Brāhamṇas of vājasaneya Śākha[77] (8th century). King Bhānudeva I[78] granted one hundred śāsanas (*agrahāras*) to Brāhamṇa Scholars. His son Narasiṁhadeva[79] II also donated land to the same number of Brāhmaṇas. Vajrahasta[80] granted land to as many as five hundred Brahmaṇas. (8th century A.D.) Agrahāras were also attached to temples and *maṭhas*. King Indravarman[81] donated land for the maintenance of an *agrahāra* and also for *Bali-Charu-Satra* of the temple attached to it. Donative grants indicate that alms houses were attached to the agrahāras. Education seems to be free in the *agrahāras* and there were also arrangements for *vṛitti*[82] or scholarships to learned Bhaṭṭa Brāhmaṇas.

The Agrahāras were sometimes, placed in charge of renowned scholars. Vattapallika (in Sambalpur) was a famous agrahāra in charge of Harisvami and Bappasvāṃi.[83] The Sumandala Copper plate in the reign of the Śailodbhava ruler Dharmarājā II[84] (8th century A.D.) records grants of land to many Brāhmaṇas, the chief of them being the Upādhyāya Muṭuśvāmi.

Regarding the details of education, though no systematic account is available, useful information may be gleaned from the inscriptions and other stray references. The system of free education in the agrahāras or in the temples seems to indicate that the teacher; student relationship was above financial consideration.

Regarding the method of education Halāyudha in his *Brāhmaṇ-Sarvasva*[85] indicates that the *Brāhmaṇaś* of Utkala learn the Vedas by rote. But the age old recommended steps of the Vedic Study are said to have included (1) *Śravaṇa* (listening to the teacher), (2) *Manana* (thinking of the subject heard) and *nididhyāsana* (constant thinking of the subject heard); and it seems improbable that the people of Utkala wholly depended on rote learning. In fact Krishna Misra in his '*Probodhachandrodaya*'[86] states that one who learns the Vedas without understanding its import, defiles it.

Regarding the curricula, it appears that Vedic studies, (or pursuit of *Parā Vidyās*) as well as secular subjects (*aparā Vidyā*) found their way into the curricula. The Neulpur grant[87] refers to persons well-versed in the four Vedas. But, as is known from the land grants, the study of One Veda or even a Śākha (branch) or Caraṇa (a portion) of the *Vedas* was permitted. The Bhuvaneś was inscription[88] mentions the study of *Siddhānta, Tantra, Phala, Saṃhitā, Vyākhyā* and *Hora Śāstra*. Epigraphic evidence[89] also proves that *Itihāsa, Purāṇa*, the *six Vedāngas*, i.e. *Sikṣhā* (science of pronunciation), *Kalpa* (science of ritualism) *Vyākarana* (grammar), *Nirukti* (etymology), *Chhanda* (prosody) and *Jyotisa* (astrology) were studied. The donative grants indicate that the study of Jyotisha[90] or astrology occupied a prominent place. The study of other practical sciences also seem to have been pursued.

Sādhāraṇa, another Brāhmaṇa scholar is said to have studied political economy and endless sciences.[91] We hear of Brāhamṇas adept in military science.[92] Reference to the many Brāhamṇa ministers[93] and military generals[94] indicate the importance given to the study of polity and military science. The gaṇeśā Gumphā cave inscription mentions the Brāhmaṇa physician (*Bhishaka*) Bhimata, thus proving that the study of *Ayurveda* was prevalent.

All these are suggestive of the high standard attained by the scholars of Orissa both in the sphere of religious and secular learning.

Orissa could also boast of reputed authors like Bhavadeva Bhaṭṭa whose three works on Dharmaśāstras enjoyed considerable reputation. Other celebrated writers of the period included Bṛihaspati Sūri, Viśvanāth Miśra, Śankhadhāra, Śambhukara, Yogiśwara patra. That creative literature was equally encouraged is proved by the works of Murāri Miśra, or Krishan Miśra. The donative records too, prove the spread of Sanskrit.

One significant aspect of Brahmanical system of education in Orissa was the advancement made in the field of female education. Women enjoyed the right to learn and also teach the Vedas. Pillikā Śvāminī was a teacher of renown.[96] Bhasābhattarakā, wife of Ganga ruler Danārṇava is described as a great scholar.[97] Śivarāṇi,[98] another Ganga queen is described as kaliyuga Sarasvati for her scholarly attainments. Chandrikā Devi,[99] a daughter of the Ganga king Anangabhima was adept in song, sports and music we also hear of women rulers like Tribhuvana Mahādevi which prove the high status accorded to women. Epigraphic evidence points to the appointment of Female Officers in the administration.[100]

Thus it may be concluded in all fairness that though the die-hard Pundits[101] of the Middle country (*Madhyadeśa*) were not much respectful about the intellectual capabilities of the scholars of the Eastern and South-Eastern sector, Orissa succeeded in giving a good account of herself in the educational activity and contributed to the growth of the cultural development in the early medieval period.

References

1. *Baudhayana, Dharmasūtra,* 1.1.2.14 (Translated by G. Buhler in Sacred Books of the East. II Oxford 1896.)

2a. Sahu N.K. Mishra P.K., Sahu J.K. *History of Orissa,* pp 18-19.

2b. Rajaguru S.N. *Inscriptions of Orissa,* Vol, IV, pp 44 ff.

3. Tāranātha, *Historyof Buddhism In India,* (ed. by D.P. Chattopadhyaya, Translated by Aloka Chattopadhyaya) (Simla-1970) p. 241.
(Henceforth referred as HBI (DPC)

4. *Ibid.,* pp 332-33.
5. Watters T., *On Yuan Chwang's Travels in India,* II, p. 193 (Henceforth referred as Watters, *Travels*)
6. *HBI* (DPC), p. 144
7. *Ibid.*
8. *Ibid.,* p. 333.
9. Mitra Devala, *Buddhist Monuments,* pp. 225-26.
10. *Loc. Cit.*
11. Sumpā, *Pag-Sam-Jon-Zang* (ed S.C. DAS) I, Index, CX; IXXI
12. Watters, *Travels, IIp. II,* 184-191
13. *Epigraphica Indica,* XV (1920), p. 364
14. Watters, *Travesl II,* pp 184-191
15. I-tsing, *A record of the Buddhist religion as practised in the Westsern World,* (Translated by Takakusu) pp. 62-65, (henceforth referred as *Records*)
16. *A Catalogue of the Chinese Transalation of the Buddhist Tripitakas, the Sacred Canons of the Buddhists in China and Japan (edited by B. Nanjio)* p. 1227
17. *Life of Hiuen - Tsang,* (Translated by S. Beal) Introduction, *XXVI,*
18. *Records of Buddhist Kingdoms,* (edited by J. Legge) p. 100.
19. Takakusu, *Records* p. 91.
20. *HBI* (DPC) pp. 184-85.
21. Takakusu *Record* p. XXX.
22. *Archaeological Survey of India Memoirs,* Vol. 44, p. 6.
23. Watters, *Travesl, II* p. 183.
24. *Uttarādhyāna Sūtra,* (ed by P.C. Shyamasukha, Calcutta 1960), XXIX, 59.
25. *Ibid.,* XVII, 17; *Uvagadasāo,* (ed by N.A. Gore, Poona 1953) 58, p. 76.
26. *Kalpasūtra* 1.10 (ed by B.K. Chattapadhyaya, Calcutta, 1953, Translated by H. Jacobi, in *Sacred Books of the East,* (Delhi, 1964). XIV. I.
27. *Epigraphica Indica,* XIII, (1915-16) pp. 159, 166 ff. (Henceforth referred as *EI*).
28. *Ibid.*
29. *Indian Archaeolgy, Review,* 1954 - 55 p. 29
30. *EI,* XIII (1915), pp. 166-67

31. Mahapatra R.P. *Archaelogy in Orissa*, I, pp. 240-247.
32. Krishna Misra *Prabadhachandrodaya* (ed and translated in Samskrita Sahitya Sambhār Vol VI) III. 4,9
33. *EI*, XV, (1920), pp. 1-8.
34. *op. cit*, II, 3.
35. *EI, XXV* (1940-45) pp. 281 ff; *Ibid*., XII (1913) p. 95.
36. *Ibid*, XXVII (1948), p. 216; *Ibid*, xxvii (1949), p. 171.
37. *Indian Antiquary*, XIII (1884) p 122-24 (Henceforth referred as *I.A.*
38. *E.I.*, XIV (1917-18) p. 360-63
39. *Ibid*., XVIII, (1925) pp. 307-11; *Ibid* XXIII p. 70
40. *Ibid*., XXVIII (1949) pp. 260 ff.
41. *Ibid*., XI, (1911 12) pp. 98-101 *Journal of Bihar and Orissa Research Society* II (1916), pp. 167 ff; pp 432 ff (Henceforth referred as JBORS).
42. *JBORS*, II, pt. II (1916) pp 171 ff.
43. *Ibid*., II, pt IV (1916) pp. 400 ff.
44. *Ibid*., pp 39 ff
45. *EI*, XV, p. 1.
46. *Ibid*, XXVIII (1949), p 211
47. *Journal of Bihar and Orissa Research Society*, II pt (VI) (1916) pp. 422
48. *Ibid*., XIV (1928) pp 292-306.
49. *JBORS, XVI*, pp 69 ff; B. Misra, *Dynasties of Medieval Orissa*, (1933), p. 16.
50. *Ibid*, p. 168; *EI, IX* (1911-12) pp. 185 ff.
51. Dandi, *Daśakumāracharita* (edited by Mr. Kale, Varaṇasi, 1966), p. 146 ff.
52. *op. cit VI*, p. 272.
53. Hazra R.C., *Studies in the Upapuranas*, II p. 91, 105
54. *Journal of Asiatic Society of Bengal*, Vol *LXVI*, pp. 18 ff.
55. *Soth Indian Inscriptions* Vol *VI*, No. 1096 *EI*, XXVI, (1941-42), p. 67.
56. Misra B. *The Bhauma kings of Orisa*, pp. 4-8.
57. Rajaguru, *Inscriptions of Orissa*, II, pp. 148 ff.
58. Rajaguru, *Inscriptions of Orissa* Vol II, pt. I pp. 69-73; (Henceforth Rajaguru, *Inscriptions*) *EI* XXVI (1941-42), pp 63ff.
59. *EI, XI* (1911-12) p. 184; Rajaguru, *Inscriptions, IV*, p. 77 ff
60. *Journal of Bihar Research Society, XVII*, pp. 124 ff.
61. Mukherjee P. *Medieval Vaishnavism*, p. 69.
62. Mahapatra R.P. *op. cit* p. 97.
63. Sircar D.C. *Silalekha-Tamra Sasanadir Prasanga* (in Benergali), pp. 86-87.
64. *Orissa Historical Research Journal*, Vol. III, pp. 66 ff.
65. *EI*, XVIII 91949) p. 211 ff.
66. *Ibid*., p. 189.
67. *Loc. cit*.
68. *Loc cit*.
69. *EI* XXVIII (1949), p. 246.
70. Mookerjee R.K. *Education in Ancient India* (Calcutta 1947) p. 372.
71. *EI, XXXIV*, part IV, p. 191.
72. *Ibid*., IX, pp. 194 ff
73. *Ibid*.
74. *Ibid*., XXXIV (1961) pp. 98 ff.
75. *Proceedings of All India Oriental Conference*, XXVIII, pp. 124.
76. Rajaguru S.N. *History of the Gangas*, p. 69.
77. *IA*, X, pp. 243-44.
78. *EI*, XXXI (1955) pp. 110 ff.
79. *JASB*, XVII, (1951) p. 34.
80. *EI, IX* (1907-8), p. 95.
81. *Ibid*., XXV, pp. 194-98.
82. *Journal of (Royal) Asiatic Society of Bengal, VI, pp. 189 ff.*
83. *EI*, IX, (1907-8) p. 342.
84. *EI*, XXVIII, p. 79 ff.
85. Halayudha *Brahmana Sarvasva*, (ed. by M. Bhattacharya, Calcutta 1960), p. 8-10.
86. *op. cit*., 1. 4.
87. *Loc. cit*.

88. Majumdar N.G. *Inscriptions of Bengal*, p. 54.
89. Rajaguru, *Inscriptions*, Vol, II, part I, pp. 187, 107.
90. *Indian Historical Quarterly* XX p. 247; *JBORS*, II p. 51. *EI* XVIII, p. 299.
91. *Ibid*, *III* p. 348.
92. *Ibid*, p. 355.
93. *South Indian Inscriptions*, Vol, *VI* NOS. 1009, 783, 900, 1037, 1118; Rajaguru, *Inscriptions*, IV, p. 210.
94. *EI XXIV*, pp 133, 137; *EI*, *XXVIII*, p. 226; *Orissa Historical Research Journal* Vol, II, p. 54.
95. Rajaguru, *Inscriptions* IV, p. 210, *EI XIII*, p. 160.
96. *Indian Historical Quarterly*, XI, p. 301.
97. *EI*, XXIV, (1937-38), p. 130 ff
98. *South Indian Inscriptions*, Vol VI No. 1180
99. *EI*, XIII (1915-16) p. 150 ff.
100. *EI*, XXVIII (1949) p. 385.
101. *Loc. Cit.*

Aspects of Indian History and Historiography
Editor : P.K. Mishra
Kaveri Books, New Delhi, India.

Widow Burning and the Madri Episode : An Analysis

15

Ashvini Agrawal

The origin and antiquity of the custom of burning the widow alongwith the body of the dead husband, popularly known as *satī* and referred to in the ancient texts and inscriptions as *anugamana, anumaraṇa, sahagamana* or *sahamaraṇa* etc., is a subject of controversy amongst the modern scholars. The general impression is that the custom of *sati* originated in India and its antiquity goes back to hoary past.[1] However, there is hardly any evidence to support such a view. A single hymn in the *Ṛgveda,*[2] often quoted as evidence of the existence of *satī,* is not only of doubtful nature and controversial, it does not even refer to the actual burning of the widow. Except for this verse which is repeated in the *Atharvaveda*[3] and refers to burning of the widow as a custom of by gone times there is not a single reference to this custom in the vast ocean of Indian literature upto the beginning of the Christian era.

However, a few instances of widow burning contained in the two great epics of India—the *Rāmāyana* and the *Mahābhārata*—are stressed upon time and again as a proof of the existence of the custom and require a close examination. The *Rāmāyaṇa* contains a solitary reference to the burning of Vedavatī's mother.[4] The story here is legendary and can in no way be connected with the custom of *satī.*[5] There is no other reference to widow burning in the entire epic. On the contrary we find all the three wives of Daśaratha living after his death and none of the ladies in Rāvaṇa's camp dies with her husband. In the *Mahābhārata* Draupadi as Sairandhri was ordered to be burnt on the pyre of Kīcaka, after the latter's death at the hands of Bhima.[6] Not only that Sairandhri was not actually burnt but the cause of such an order was said to be an ancient custom of burning slave or slaves with the ruler (not wives). There is no question of *Satī* in this case as the persons involved were not husband and wife and it may have been purely an act of vengeance. The *Mausala Parvan* contains two instances, first where four wives of Vasudeva, viz. Devaki, Bhadrā, Rohini and Madirā burnt themselves with him[7] and the second where Rukmiṇi, Gandhāri, Śaibyā, Haimavati and Jāmbvati amongst the consorts of Kṛṣṇa ascended the funeral pyre with him.[8] But all other wives of Kṛṣṇa survived him and those like Satyabhāmā retired to forest for penance. This passage in the *Mausalaparavan* appears to be a later interpolation and may have been added to remove the discrepancy between the accounts given in the *Bhāgavata Purāṇa, Viṣṇu Purāṇa* etc. which were composed in the Gupta period and those of the *Mahabhārata.* It is quite probable in the light of the fact that none of the ladies in the Pāṇḍava or Kaurava camp is shown to have burnt herself with her husband in the epic.

The most well-known instance contained in the *Mahābhārata* is that of Mādri ascending the funeral pyre of her husband Pāṇḍu after the latter's death in the forest.[9] This episode is always construed as a direct instance of *satī* in the great epic and the prevalence of the custom during this period is stressed on its basis. However, such a conclusion is unwarranted in the light of the circumstances under which the incident took place. The reasoning given for it is quite different from that of a *satī* custom. It is therefore, worthwhile to discuss it in some detail.

As the story goes, Pāṇḍu once killed a sage and his wife in the form of deer when they were copulating and was cursed by the *ṛṣi* that he would die as a result of the similar action. Aware of the curse and full of remorse, Pāṇḍu led the life of an ascetic with his wives Kuntī and Mādrī and their sons. One day when Kuntī was busy looking after the brāhmaṇas invited for sacrifice on Arjuna';s completion of fourteenth year, Pāṇḍu began to rove in the woods with his favourite wife Mādrī. Soon the sweetness of surroundings aroused desire in him and he copulated with Mādrī and died. Full of remorse Mādrī plunged into grief which was accentuated by the words of Kuntī who blamed her for not protecting their husband from his lustful behaviour.[10]

It was at this moment that Mādrī decided to end her life alongwith her husband Pāṇḍu. Kuntī is also made to express a similar desire but not so emphatically nor she talks of this as the' only *dharma'* for her. Mādrī gave two reasons for her resolve. Firstly, she said that since she was the cause of her husband's death she must die. Secondly, she told Kuntī that she (Mādrī) was not capable of treating all their sons alike and shall incur the sin of ill-treating her step-sons which she did not want. On the other hand Kuntī was capable to look after all the sons like her own, was wise and well protected by her parental family, so she alone should live.[11] Nowhere does she talk of any religious merit of the act or following any such tradition where a wife's *dharma* was to die on the funeral pyre of her husband. She does not even talk of any past or prevalent custom of this type which clearly establishes that the whole episode was a result of a peculiar situation and Mādrī's personal resolve to end her life alongwith her husband due to her attachment to him.

On the other hand the prevalent cultural ethos of the time are reflected in the words of the sages assembled by the body of Pandu who tried their best to dissuade Mādrī from her resolve.[12] They told her in no uncertain words that her resolve shall not only endanger the welfare of her sons which was insecure under the rule of Dhṛtrāṣṭra and his sons but a pious woman is she who leads the life of *brahmacarya* after her husband's death. Following the rigid rules of discipline, controlling her desires of heart and body and restraining her speech she bears suffering. Performing the vows and fasts like *Cāndrāyaṇa* etc. she sleeps on the ground, gives up salt and pungent foods and takes her meals only once a day. Therefore, it is proper for a noble woman to destroy her sensual and worldly feelings by observing these penances after the death of her husband. Such a lady who devotes herself to the memory of her (dead) husband causes the deliverance of her husband, her sons and herself.

Here in lies the essence of the prevalent tradition of the time. It did not permit the immolation of a widow, a custom which came into vogue at a much later date, but expected her to lead a pure and simple life after the death of her husband. The absence of the custom of *satī* during the epic period is also attested by numerous references to living widows contained there in. We have already referred to the survival of Kauśalyā, Sumitrā and Kaikeyī, the wives of Daśaratha after the latter's death. In the Mahābhārata war numerous heroes died in both the Pāṇḍava and Kaurava camps. None of their wives became *satī*. On the other hand we are told that they performed the last rites of their husbands after the war was over and offered the oblations of water on the banks of Ganga. This sets the stamp of certainty on the issue that the Mādrī episode can not be cited as an example of the custom of widow burning in ancient India.

References

1. For detailed discussion on the subject see the author's paper—Sati—How do? How Indian? Haryana Sahitya Akademi Journal of Indological Studies, Vol. III, 91-98. Also see Kane, P.V., *History of Dharmasastra*, Vo. II, Pt.I, 618-19; Altekar, A.S., *The Position of Women in HIndu Civilization*, 137-38.
2. Rg., X. 18. 7-8.

   इमा नारीरविधवाः सुपत्नीराञ्जनेन सार्पेषा सं विशन्तु ।
   अनश्रवो ऽनमीवाः सुरत्ना आरोहन्तु जनयो योनिमग्रे ।।
   उदीर्ष्व नार्यभि जीवलोकं गतासुमेतमुप शेष एहि ।
   हस्तग्राभस्य दिधिषोस्तवेंद पत्पुर्त्न नित्वमभि सं गभूय ।।
3. XVIII. 3.1.

   इयं नारी पतिलोकं वृणाना निपधत उपत्वा मर्त्य प्रेतम् ।
   विश्वं पुराणमनुपालयन्ती तस्यै प्रजां द्रविणं चेह धेहि ।।

   "Oh (dead) man! This woman choosing the world of the husband lies down by thee, the deceased, observing the old universal custom; bestow on her in this world offspring and wealth." P.V. Kane, op. cit., 618.
4. *Rāmāyana*, Uttarakāṇda, 17.15.
5. Some scholars have referred to Meghnāda's wife becoming *satī*, however, there is no such reference in the Rāmāyaṇa of Vālmiki.
6. *Mahābhārata*, Virāṭaparvan, IV. 23.
7. *Mausalaparvan*, VII. 18.
8. *Ibid.*, VII. 73-74.
9. *Ādiparvan*, 124.
10. *Ibid.*, 124. 18-20.
11. *Ibid.*, 124. 26-28.
12. *Ibid.*, This portion is missing from certain versions of the Mahābhārata but is contained in the Southern Version. It is also included in the Gita Press, Gorakhpur edition, V.S. 2013. We find no reason to omit it. It appears that the verses were removed from the Northern recenssion of the epic at a later date when *Sati* had become popular in northern India.

Aspects of Indian History and Historiography
Editor : P.K. Mishra
Kaveri Books, New Delhi, India.

Glimpses of Social Condition of India in the Aṅguttara-Nikāya

16

Gayatri Sen Majumdar

I

One of the five Nikayas (collections) of the Buddhist *Sutta Pitaka*, the *Aṅguttara-Nikāya* is supposed to have been compiled towards the beginning of the fourth century B.C. and together with the *Dīgha*-and others it is earlier than the *Khuddaka* and reflects the condition of the age of Gautama Buddha.[1] Although the *Aṅguttara-Nikāya (AN)* is primarily a religious book, it contains many matters of social import and on the basis of a critical analysis thereof a tolerably good picture of the social conditions of the people of the age it belongs to can be drawn. And in doing so one has to make use of collateral materials embedded in other Nikayas, and the Brahmanical and Jain texts.

II

The society during the period, the sixth-fifth century B.C., centred on the village (gāmay) the lowest unit of human settlement, and the economy was basically rural. Barring a small section consisting of *araññaka bhikkhus* or the mendicants who preferred to live in forests (*arañña*) a sizable section of the population lived in villages of varying dimensions, but without the fortifications of *nagara* (town or city) where the ruler or king used to reside. The *gāmas* consisted of *kulas* (families) which could vary from thirty to one thousand and the families then, unlike many of their modern counterparts, consisted also of father and mother, children, grandparents, and the wives and children of the sons. Besides *gāmas*, there were *nagaras*, *puras*, and *nigamas*, all these three denominations standing for towns and cities. Nigama probably signified the towns dominated by traders' guilds and the compound word *gāma-nigama* occurring in the *Aṅguttara-Nikāya* and elsewhere suggests a difference these two types of settlements. Some of the *nagaras* were designated *mahānagaras*, obviously in view of their large dimensions, geographically and demographically. Similarly, there were *janapadas*, that is, bigger settlement units or countries, and again, some of these *janapadas* were called *mahājanapadas* because of their still larger areas and populations. And the *AN* while supplying a plethora of data on different aspects of the society, economy and political conditions of the period under study, gives a list of sixteen such *mahājanapadas (solasa mahājanapadas)*, the most of which Magadha, Avanti, Vatsa and Kosala, gained importance in the course of time and our text also refers to their respective capitals or headquarters at Rajagaha (Rājagṛiha), Ujjeni (Ujjayinī), Kosāmbi (Kauśāmbī) and Savatthi (Śrāvati).[2] There were a few more cities of note, such as Champā (capital of another *Mahājanapada*

Aṅga), Vārāṇasī (capital of the *mahājanapada* Kāśdi) and Sāketa (of the Kosala *mahājapada*, along with Savatthi) and all these were *mahānagaras*. Presumably many of them were transformed from *gāmas* and came up in the fertile Gangetic valley after the discovery of iron and the introduction of the iron technology. It is to be noted that Pāṭaliputra (modern Patna) was yet to emerge as a great city and the key-place of later day history and culture of India. And its transformation from a jungle townlet (*nagaraka*) to a city began from the reign of Udayi, the successor of Ajataśatru (c. 462-30 B.C.). However, it appears from a study of the *AN* and other Buddhist treatises that the inhabitants, whether of villages or towns, lived a happy and peaceful life and in the context of the urban life the *AN* indicate the keenness of the townfolk to enjoy life in merry-making programmes.[3]

Social life during the period under review was marked by the age-old caste system and its concomitant feeling of superiority among the members of the first two *varṇas* or (vannas) castes to the members of the remaining two castes. Gautama Buddha accepted the caste system but was bold enough to challenge the caste superiority. In tune with the the *Chulla-Vagga*[4] states that the Master once observed that 'as rivers, after pouring their waters into the Great Ocean lose their identity, similarly all castes having entered the monastic fold renounced their lineage'. And that what he said was translated into reality is proved Upāli's becoming the chief of Vinaya. The Lord effected one noteworthy change in the contemporary caste structure: he gave precedence to the Kshatriyas over the Brāhmaṇas, and this is attested to by the *AN*,[5] among other texts. He argued that the Kshatriyas preserved the purity of blood and the lineage for seven generations from the mother's and father's sides, while the Brāhmanas failed to do so by intermarrying into lower castes and further the Brāhmanas of his time proved themselves unequal to their forefathers who were great seers and mantra-makers and ideal moralists. However, personally being a Kshatriya the Buddha seems to have had a soft corner for his caste and the *AN* claims the the purity of the lineage for kings,[6] although other texts lay similar claim for the Brāhmaṇas as well, and significantly enough, even for the Buddha.[7]

Gautama Buddha, as our text indicates, maintained his preference for the Kshatriyas and could not be expectedly liberal towards the Śūdras (Suddas); this is indicated by its references to Khattiya Parisā, Bāmhana parisa and Gahapati Parisā, that is, the councils of Brahmaṇa, Kshatriyas and Gahapati or Vaisya listeners.[8] The Vessas or the Vaiśays or the Vaiśyas, mentioned by the terms like *Gahapati, Kuṭumbika* and *Setthi*, were looked upon as a powerful community in the society evidently for their affluence, but the lower castes or the members of the Śūdra varṇa (*vaṇṇa*) suffered social indignation. The *AN* and the other texts do not speak much about these Śūdras, but indications are not wanting that peoples of lowly professions (*nīchakula*) like potters,carpenters and smiths as well as dancers, singers and acrobats, were included in the last or the fourth varṇa; and besides, there were also communities on the social periphery such as the Chaṇḍālas and the Pukkusas.[9] Among them the lot of the Chaṇḍalas was the worst, or at least worsened in the course of time as one can guess from the Jātaka literature of later days (it forms a part of the *Khuddaka Nikāya*, chronologically the last of the Nikāyas).[10] In later days they moved further from this periphery and were outcastes, living a life hardly better than the animals.

The *AN* together with other Nikāyas testify to the existence of slavery during the time of the Buddha and thereafter.[11] The *Dīgha-Nikāya (DN)* seems to have placed them under a separate category and they were procured in various ways, such as in the course of predatory raids and in conviction; sometimes men and women offered themselves as slaves.[12] Apparently they were engaged by affluent persons of cities and villages. But their fate was not as bad as their counterparts of ancient Greece and Rome. And that the Venerable One did not like the trade in human beings is spelt out in the text under study where he is seen as telling his devotees that they should not accept the gift of slaves, either male or female.[13] The *DN* states that a slave could have liberated himself or herself by accepting the life of homelessness, that is, by joining the Sangha.[14] Sometimes a slave could do so by paying off a ransom or by bringing good news for the master.[15]

The *AN* does not purvey much information about the marriage system, but indicates, like the kindred texts, that both polygamy and monogamy prevailed, and the former was presumably current more among the well-to-do persons than among those of weaker economic position. The *AN* speaks of one Nakulapitā, a disciple of the Buddha, who was content with one wife, while others had several wives.[16] The *DN* alludes to a certain Mahāgovinda (High Steward), of the Brāhmaṇa caste, who had as many as forty wives all enjoying the same status, and all of them were set free by him on the eve of his renunciation.[17] Kings like Bimbisāra and Ajātaśatru of Magadha had several wives and the *Mahāvagga*[18] has assigned five hundred wives; the figure may be an exaggeration, but that he contracted matrimonial alliances with the contemporary royal dynasties has been proved to be a historical fact.

The Pāli texts of later days suggest that marriages generally took place through negotiation by the elders of the families of the prospective bride and bridegroom and generally such marriages were endogamous.[19] *Anuloma* marriage (that is, taking bride from a lower caste) was permitted, but the *pratiloma* marriage (girl of a higher caste marrying a man of a low caste) was disfavoured, and in this respect the Buddhist attitude was similar to the Brahmanical one.[20] Marriage among the relatives was perhaps rare, and one well-known instance is furnished by Ajātaśatru's marrying the daughter of his uncle Prasenajit of Kosala.[21] A girl of sixteen years was an ideally suitable bride and it appears that the post-puberty marriage was the order of the day; and the bridegroom was a few years older than the bride.[22] Our text speaks of one Nakula who was a mere lad when he entered into wedlock.[23] It also refers to the practice of widow marriage in this context; Nakula's mother is seen here as assuring her dying husband that she would not marry after his death and would take up the job of spinning cotton and matting wool for rearing up their children.[24] it again appears from our work that issueless widows got husbands more easily than the widows with issues.[25] Sometimes husbands allowed their wives to remarry, particularly when they decided to renounce their worldly lives.[26] In addition to the case of the aforementioned Mahagovinda, was a certain Ugga-gahapati who on the eve of his renunciation advised his four wives either to remarry persons of their choice or go to the houses of their relatives.[27] The conjugal life was based on love and affection and reciprocal fidelity and the *AN* tells about a king who did not take food and attend the royal duties for a few consecutive days after the death of his wife.

The *AN* and other Nikāyas do not provide any clear picture about the status and the position of women during the period under review. But it will not be unreasonable to infer that it remained almost the same as it was in the earlier period. Women in India was regarded primarily as mother. She is expected to give birth to male children. In other words, the Indian tradition regards the necessity of keeping the continuity of the family lineage through the male child and an ideal Indian woman is the mother of male children. In spite of the preference for the male child, the *AN* gives the impression that the female child was not neglected during this period; once born, she used to get the affection of her parents and she was not discriminated from her brother, if any. The *AN* records that the Buddha once rebuked a lamenting couple for the birth of a daughter child by saying that a daughter may prove even a better offspring'.[28]

However, in the context of women the Buddhist view was similar to that of their Brahmanical brethren which preferred the image of a woman as mother and on account of her motherhood it gave women precedence over man or the father. This is perhaps reflected in the placement of the word *mātā* before ptiā compound expression *mātaro-pitaro* on many occasions.[29] In one place of our text it is stated that the power of children over their mothers lay in their tears.[30] The eternal relationship between the mother and her children is touchingly reflected in this statement. Although women in general enjoyed the prestigious position in the family, sometimes she used to get inhumane treatment from their husbands, some of whom did not hesitate to go to the extent of beating their wives on the ground of their alleged misbehaviour.[31]

The hallmark of Buddhism in contemporary social life lay in the emancipation of women from the male dominance. Women tasted, as it were, the sense of freedom for the first time by embracing the religion of the Master and entering his monastic Order. In other words, the Buddha opened the gates of the Buddhist Church for women, which he reportedly did at the request of his foster-mother. He believed in their capacity of comprehending his doctrines and told his devotees that a mother and her son can equally overcome the three terrors by following the eight-fold path.[32] He had, however, doubt in their capability of reaching the highest stage of Nirvāṇa of the Buddhist conception. The *AN* includes Ambapāli, Isidāsi, Khemā and Patachara among eminent *upasikās* or lay devotees.

Buddhist women during this period made more rapid strides than their Brahmanical and Jain sisters on the economic front. They could earn their own livelihood by taking up different jobs like weaving, spinning etc. and the afore-mentioned instance of Nakula's mother attests to the fact (*supra*, p. 4). But the Master did not favour their taking up independent business and entering into judicial service.[33]

It has been stated above that a certain Ugga-gahapati advised his wives before his renunciation that they should either remarry or go to the houses of their relatives. It is here that we come across a bright aspect of the Buddhist society of the period under review. It was the *ñātikula* or *ñātisaṁgha* (Sanskrit *Jñātikula* or *jñātisaṁgha*) consisting of persons of the same kin group. This *kula* or *saṁgha* used to take the responsibility of the kins in distress, providing them food and shelter to them. And thus this *ñātikula* uniquely stood for the social security for the people within the same family or caste and it was a great boon particularly to women facing financial difficulties. *Ñātikula* was a self-supporting organisation with a common fund to which all *ñātis*or kins used to contribute.[34]

The *ñātikula* prompts one to consider the question of the nature and character of individual *kula* which was different from the in-nuclear family of modern times. It consisted of father, mother as well as of other kins and relatives (*supra*, p. 1) and in general the relationship among these members was cordial. In different places of our text these relationships are alluded to and the Lord highlighted the do-s and don'ts of the numbers of the *kulas*. For example, he once told a monk that a parents should be highly regarded because they bring their sons to this world and do everything for their upbringing,[35] and they should be properly looked after by their sons in their old age. Similarly, the relationship between a nephew and his uncle (father's brother) or his aunt was cordial.[36] Classifying seven types of wives, the Buddha enjoins that an ideal wife should possess four qualities, namely, the capability to work, management of servants, ability to become lovely to her husband and the ability to protect wealth.[37] The slaves and servants were also looked upon as family members, as it were, and here an Indian slave enjoyed a position better than his or her Greco-Roman counterpart.

The daily fare of the Indian household at that time, as revealed by our text as well as other three Nikāyas, consisted mainly of rice, pulse, vegetables, milk, curd and butter.[38] Different varieties of rice are referred to in them and some Jātakas state that cooked rice called *bhatta* (modern *bhāta*) was normally taken with *sūpa* (pulses) and vegetables. Meat and fish were also preferred and the prevalence of practice of meat-eating is hinted at by allusions to cattle butchers and slaughter houses in the *Majjhima Nikāya*.[39] The injunctions of the Buddhist and Jain texts regarding non-injury to animals was thus virtually ineffective. Similarly, although addiction to liquors or drinking was not liked as a social habit, drinking was seemingly widely prevalent among common men, except the orthodox members of religious groups or monks. The *AN* mentions *surā* and *meraya* as intoxicating drinks.[40] *Surānakkhata* of the Jātaka literature specially stands for drinking festivals. In this connection festive gatherings and merry-making together with fairs were an important feature of the social life of the contemporary Indians and *samajja* is the Pāli word for festive gathering. And such *samajjas* were enlivened by dances, singing, instrumental music, acrobatic feats and the like.[41] Fairs, as now, were the occasions for selling of varieties of products, but were also noted for visual delights furnished by acrobats like tumblers, jugglers and rope-dancers as well as by snake charmers and drummers.[42]

Life in general, as indicated by the *AN* and other texts, was peaceful and the people liked to enjoy life. Imaginably the life styles varied according to the economic power and position of the people. Our text sheds light on the life style of an affluent section of the Koliyas of Rāmagāma near Kapilavāstu, in the modern Pipraw region in the Basti district of U.P. Describing them as a pleasure-loving and pleasure-seeking people, it says that they were 'cumbered with the bedmates and sons and wore Vārāṇasi muslins and decorated themselves with flowers, garlands, cosmetics, gold and silver'.[43] It appears from the *AN*, the other three contemporary Nikāyas and the Vinaya texts that during this period, sixth fifth the century B.C. (stretching the by a couple of centuries, the compilation of these texts being in the early fourth century B.C. in as much as they reflect the condition of the age of the Buddha social life was rich and variegated and marked by a wide outlook and in this receipt it showed an advance on that of the earlier days represented by the later strata of the Vedic literature. It is reasonable to assume that Indians during this period aimed at maintaining a balance between *dharma, artha* and *kāma*, the three ends of the later day Kautilyan paradigm.

References

1. T.W. Rhys Davids states that the four Nikāyas were compiled around 100 A.B. (after Buddha), and if it is assumed that the Buddha passed into *Parinirvāna* in 486 B.C. then their date would be 386 B.C. More specifically he holds that these collections, born out of older materials, were compiled at a period about half way between the death of the Buddha and the accession of Aśoka (c. 272 B.C.), that is, around 379 B.C. E.J. Rapson (ed.), *(The) Cambridge History of India*, I, London, 1922, second Indian reprint, Delhi 1962, pp. 174-75. Rhys David's view has since held the ground and the opinions of other scholars veer round it. Nalinaksha Datta, for example, states that roughly speaking, the bulk of the *Vinaya Piṭaka* and the first four Nikāyas of the *Sutta Pitaka* were compiled before 350 B.C., see B.C. Majumdar (ed)., *History and Culture of the Indian People*, II ('Age of the Imperial Unity), Bombay, 1951, p. 408.
2. For an account of these *mahājanapadas*, see *Age of the Imperial Unity*, pp. 2-16.
3. *Samyutta Nikāya*, Vol V, p. 157.
4. *Anguttara Nikāya (AN)*, IV, p. 202; *Chulla VAgga*, IX. 1. 4.
5. *Ibid.*, II p. 194, IV, 129-34; also *Majjhima Nikāya (MN)*, II, p. 128.
6. *Ibid.*, IV, p. 188; III, p. 151.
7. *MN*, II, p. 165, and *DN*, I, p. 113 (cf. Brāhmaṇas); *MN*, II, p. 166 and *DN*, I, p. 131 (cf. The Buddha).
8. *AN*, III, pp. 133, 183; also *DN*, II, p. 109.
9. *AN*, II, p. 85, III, p. 385; *MN*, II, p. 152, III, p. 119.

10. See for example, the *Jātakas*, vols. IV, 200, 376, 388 390, 397.
11. *DN*, I, pp. 60, 72, 92ff, 104 etc.
12. *Vinayapitaka*, I, p. 72; *Sumangalavilāsinī*, I, p. 168.
13. *AN*, II, p. 209.
14. *DN*, I. pp. 60-61.
15. *MN*, II, p. 62; *Jātaka*, VI, 546-47.
16. *AN*, II, p. 61.
17. *DN*, II, p. 239.
18. Among these queens Kosaladevi, the sister of Pasenadi (Prasenajit) of Kosala, Chellanā, the daughter of the Lichchavi chief Chetaka, Vāsabi of the Vedeha chief and Khemā, the daughter of the king of Madra (Central Punjab) were important. Kosaladevi was the chief queen.
19. *Jātaka*, III, 93.
20. *Ibid.*, III, 21. Even *Anuloma* marriage was the normal practice. For the marriage of a Kshatriya Lichchhavi girl marrying a low-caste barbarboy, see *Jātaka*, II, 5.
21. *Jātaka*, I, 457, II, 119, 327, IV, 342-43, VI, 436.
22. See *Therīgāthā*, 445, *Jātaka*, III, 93, IV, 484 etc.
23. *AN*, II, P. 61.
24. *Ibid.*, III, p. 245.
25. *Ibid.*, III, p. 295. The *Uchchanga Jātaka* (Jātaka, I, 307) indicates that widow marriage was more prevalent among the members of low castes than among those of the high castes.
26. *AN*, IV, p. 210.
27. *Ibid.*
28. *AN*, I, pp. 25-26.
29. I.B. Horner, *Women Under Primitive Buddhism*, pp. 5 ff.
30. *AN*, IV, p. 223.
31. *Ibid.*, V, 264.
32. The three terrors are: great fire break, heavy rainfall and forest raid of robbers (or in general robbery). *AN*, I, p. 26, III, p. 49, IV, p. 208.
33. *Samyutta Nikāya*, I, p. 86.
34. *AN*, I, p. 152.
35. See my paper (summary), 'Some Aspects of Family Life in Ancient India as depicted in the Anguttara Nikaya', 'Summaries of Papers, All India Oriental Conference', Calcutta, 1986, pp. 333-34.
36. *Ibid.*
37. *AN*, IV, pp. 269-71.
38. *AN*, II, p. 95; *Jātaka*, VI, 372.
39. *MN*, I, pp. 364; II, 193.
40. *AN*, II, pp. 53-54, IV, pp. 5, 246; *Chulla Vagga*, XII, XII. I. 3.
41. *DN*, II, p. 6. II. 267.
42. *Jātaka*, I, 430; IV, 324.
43. *AN*, IV, p. 281.

(Note: The numbers after *AN*, *MN* etc. refer to the volumes published by the Pali Text Society, London. The *AN* edition used here was edited by R. Morris and E. Hardy and was published in five volumes between 1885 and 1890).

Aspects of Indian History and Historiography
Editor : P.K. Mishra
Kaveri Books, New Delhi, India.

Medical Science as Known to the Chinese Pilgrims 17

Sukumar Sengupta

Let us deal with the evidence furnished by the accounts of the Chinese pilgrims from which we may have some idea of the condition of medical science and practice in India during the fifth-seventh centuries A.D.

During the reign of Chandragupta II, India was visited by Fa-hsien (399-411 A.D.), the Chinese traveller who spent six years on travel alone and another six years on study in India.

Fa-hsien noticed numerous charitable institutions throughout the Middle Kingdom established by the rich and prosperous inhabitants who were well-known for their charity and philanthropy for "setting up on the road-side houses of charity, where rooms, couches, beds, and food and drink were supplied to travellers, and also to monks, coming and going as guests, the only difference being in the time for which those parties remained" (Legee, Fa-hsien's Travels, p. 62).

Fa-hsien also describes the charitable dispensaries in the town of Pataliputra thus: "The nobles and householders of this country have founded hospitals within the city to which the poor of all countries, the destitute, cripple and the diseased may repair. They receive every kind of requisite help gratuitously. Physicians inspect their diseases, and according to their cases order them food and drink, medicines or decoctions, everything in fact that may contribute to their ease. When cured—they depart at their convenience." (Beal's Record, Vol. I, Introduction, lcii; Legge, Far-hsien, p. 79).

The next Chinese pilgrim was Hsuen-Tsang who followed Fa-Hsien after an interval of nearly two centuries. He travelled for sixteen years (A.D. 629-645 A.D.) through Central Asia and India (excluding the South and Ceylon). The account of Hsuen-Tsang also throws considerable light on some important points of medical interest, like foundation of hospitals, medical aid offered to travellers and poor persons, medical studies, etc.

Medical Aid Offered to Travellers and Poor Persons — Puṇyaśālās (Hospices)

We also learn from Hsuen-Tsang's account that King Śilāditya, who was inclined towards Buddhism, built stupas and "in all the highways of the towns and villages throughout India, he erected hospices, provided with food and drink, and stationed there physicians with medicines for travellers and poor persons round about, to be given without any stint" (Beal's Record, Vol-I p. 214).

He also mentions charitable institutions called "Punyasalas" which were founded at many places by Kings and nobles in those days. Thus he states regarding these hospices existing on the way from the Cheh-Ka (Ṭakka) Country: "on from this country there were numerous Punyasalas or free rest-houses for the relief of the needy, and distressed and these houses medicine and food were distributed and so travellers having their bodily wants supplied, did not experience inconvenience." (Watters on Yuan Chwang, Vol-I. p. 286).

Again he says: "Pious Kings erected Puṇyaśālā in the district of (Mo-ti-pi-lo or Matipura). This foundation is endowed with funds for providing choice food and medicines to bestow in charity in widows and bereaved persons, on orphans and the destitute". (Beal, Vol-I, p-198); Watters, Vol-I, p. 328). A similar Punyasālā or hospice also existed in K'ei-P'an-to or Kabandha (Beal, Vol-II, p. 303).

In describing Multan he says : "They have founded a house of mercy (happiness), in which they provide food, and drink, and medicines for the poor, and sick, affording succour and sustenance" (Beal, Vol.-II, p. 274).

Regarding Śilāditya again he says: "Every year he assembled the Śramaṇas from all countries, and on the third and seventh days he bestowed on them in charity four kinds of alms, viz. food, drink, medicine and clothing", (Beal, Vol-I, p. 214).

Place of Medical Studies in the Scheme of Education in the 7th Century A.D.

In spite of his chief interest in Buddhist life and thought, Hsuen-Tsang has recorded certain observations on Brāhmaṇical education and culture. As regards Brāhmaṇical education, the students had to study the four Veda treatises, viz. the Āyurveda, the Yajur-Veda, the Sāmaveda "why the first Veda is here not the Rig but the Ayur. It is reckoned as Veda, we learn, because its teachings have been found by experience to be wise and beneficial". (Watters, Vol-I, p. 159).

Regarding the method of education imparted in the Buddhist monasteries, Hsuen-Tsang gives a fair idea of the preliminary education that was followed in those days. According to Hsuen-Tsang the primary education began with a first book of 12 chapters entitled "Siddham" giving the Sanskrit alphabet and the combinations between vowels and consonants. Next after the mastery of Siddham, the child was introduced at the age of seven to the "great Śāstras of the Five Sciences", viz. Vyākaraṇa (grammar), Śilpasthānavidyā (Science of Arts and Crafts), Chikitsāvidyā (Science of Medicine), Hetu-Vidyā (Nyāya or Logic), and Adhyātmavidyā (Inner Science) which according to Watters, included the metaphysical and argumentative treatises of the great Doctors of Abhidharma" (Watters, Vol-I, p. 158). Thus we see that the study of medical science (Chikitsā-Vidyā), was made a compulsory part of the syllabus even at the stage of elementary education.

In stating the curriculum that was followed in the Nālandā University in the seventh century A.D., his biographer (Shaman Hwui Li, the Life of Hsüen Tsang, trans. Beal p. 112) says that "students at Nālandā study the Great Vehicle, and also the works belonging to the eighteen sects, and not only so, but even ordinary works, such as the Vedas and other books, the Hetuvidyā, Śabdavidyā, the Chikitsāvidyā, the works on Magic or Atharvaveda, the Sāṁkhya; besides these, they thoroughly. . . investigate the `miscellaneous works'. Thus Nālandā was the Centre of all higher in all its branches, including the Science of Medicine (Chikistsāvidyā).

Next we find a few particulars in the account of Hsüen-Tsang as to the ways in which the people of India treat their sick.

"Every one who is attacked by sickness has his food cut off for seven days. In this interval the patient often recovers, but if he can not regain his health, he takes medicine. Their medicines are of various kinds, each kind having a specific name. Their doctors differ in medical skill and in prognostication". (Watters on Yuan Chwang, Vol-I, p. 174).

I-tsing was another Chinese traveller who set foot on Indian soil in A.D. 672 within a few years after Hsuen-Tsang had left it (A.D. 645). His account gives us copious information regarding various aspects of medical condition and medical studies prevailing in the seventh century A.D.

More detailed information on the place of medical studies in the scheme of education is given by I-tsing. Ling Hiuen Tsang, he gives an account of the general and elementary education of the times prior to specialization and higher education in the monasteries and the universities. According to I-tsing, before the stage of specialization and advanced study was reached every student had to study the compulsory five subjects of study, viz. (1) Śabdavidyā (grammar and lexicography), (2) Śilpasthānavidyā (Arts and Crafts), (3) Chikitsāvidyā (Medicine), (4) Hetuvidyā (Logic), and (5) Adhyātmavidyā (Science of Universal Soul or Philosophy).

Thus the accounts of Hsuen Tsang and I-tsing clearly indicate that the study of Medical Science was made a compulsory part of the syllabus in the course of elementary and general education and every student was required to acquire a knowledge of the elements of that science. I-chsing seems to explain why Medical Science was a part of the compulsory of elementary studies for all, including the monks. "Is it not a sad thing", he asks, "that sickness prevents the pursuit of one's duty and vocation". He further says, "I desire that an established disease may be cured without expending much medicine, and that a fresh disease may be prevented, thus not necessitating a physician; — then a healthy condition of body (lit, the four elements) and the absence of any disease may be expected. It is not beneficial, if people can benefit others as well as themselves by the study of medicine?" I-tsing himself declares,- "I made a successful study in medical science, but as it is not my proper vocation I have finally given it up." (Takakusu-Records, p. 128).

Different Branches of Indian Medicine (Ayurveda)

I-tsing also mentions eight branches of medical science. The first treats of all kinds of sores, inward and outward; the second treats of acupuncture for diseases above the neck (i.e. all that is on the head and face); the third of the diseases of the body (i.e. any disease lower down from the throat is called a 'bodily' disease); the fourth, of demoniac disease due to attack of evil spirits; the fifth one is the Agada Medicine, i.e. antidote or medicine for counteracting poison; the sixth is the 'diseases of the children' from the embryo stage to the sixteenth year; the seventh treats of the means of lengthening one's life, (i.e. to maintain the body so as to live long); the eighth, of the methods of invigorating the legs and body. He further states that "these eight arts formerly existed in eight books, but lately a man epitomized them and made them into one bundle". It is very strange that I-tsing does not refer to the name of the man who epitomized them and made them into one bundle". The learned scholar Hoernle is inclined to identify the person with Vāgbhaṭa I. Thus be observes—"Seeing that Vāgbhaṭa I's Compendium bears that precise name of Epitome (or Summary, Saṁgraha) of the Octopartite Science", the conclusion seems warranted that I-tsing was referring to that Summary. It so, Vāgbhaṭa I can not have preceded I-tsing by any very long interval of time; nor may the interval be made too short, because time was necessary for the diffusion of the Summary as a standard work 'throughout India'. Accordingly Vāghaṭa I may be placed early in the seventh century or about 625 A.D.". (Hoernle, *Studies in the Medicine of Ancient India*, pp. 10-11). It may be pointed out in this connection that these 'eight arts' mentioned by I-tsing agree with the eight divisions of the Āyurveda (Medical Science) which are as follows:- (1) Śalya which may be equated with I-tsing's cure of sores (2) Śālākya, i.e. I-tsing's art of acupuncture; (3) Kāya-cikitsā, i.e. I-tsing's treatment of the diseases of the body, (4) Bhūta-Vidyā, i.e. I-tsing's treatment of demoniac diseases, (5) K aumāra-bhṛtya = I-tsing's treatment of the diseases of children; (6) Agada, i.e. I-tsing's Agada medicine; (7) Rasāyana, i.e. I-tsing's application of the means of lengthening one's life (the elixir that was to render health permanent and life perpetual) (Takakusu's Note in the Buddhist Records, pp. 222-223).

Position and Practice of Physicians

I-tsing tells us that according to the medical science in India, a physician examined the voice and face of the diseased and prescribed medicine for him in accordance with the eight sections of medical science. If he did not understand the secret of this science, he, though desirous of acting properly, fell into mistakes. The Indians greatly honoured physicians, as they did not injure life, but gave relief to the people.

Medical Herbs in India

The pilgrim also refers to some of the principal medical herbs that were used in India, viz. Haritaka (which is abundant in India), Kuṅkuma (saffron, found in North India), and the A-Wei (assafoetida) which grows in Persia and is also found in abundance in the Western limit of India. (Takakusu, pp. 128-129). He also points out the benefit derived from the regular use of Haritaka (Yellow myrobalan). If one is accustomed to bite "a piece of Haritaka every day and swallow its juice, one's whole life will be free from disease". (Takakusu, p. 134).

Fasting as a Method of Cure

I-tsing insists on fasting as an effective method of cure by practice of which "each man is himself the King of physicians, and anyone can be Jīvaka". In the words of I-tsing, "fasting is an effective cure, without any trouble of cauterising the head or rubbing the throat. This is in accordance with the general rule of the science of medicine, i.e. healing a disease without using a decoction or any medicine. The reason is that when the stomach is empty violent fever abates, when the juice of food is absorbed phlegmatic disease is cured, and when the internal organs are at rest and bad breath dispersed, a severe cold will naturally be over. There will be no failure in a cure if this method be adhered to.

Food should be abstained from in all other diseases, such as a sudden appearance of a carbuncle or a smaller boil; a sudden rush of blood causing fever; a violent pain in the hands and feet; any injury to the body caused by heavenly phenomena (such as lighting), climate, or sword and arrow; a wound inflicted by falling down, an acute febrile disease or cholera morbus; the half-day diarrhoea, a headache, heart-disease, eye-disease, or toothache". (Takakusu, pp. 133-134). We also learn from the Records of I-tsing that in the Country of Lāṭa in Western India, those who were taken ill, abstained from food, sometimes for half a month and sometimes for full month. They did not eat at all so long as the illness persisted. In Central India the longest period of fasting was a week. According to I-tsing, the period of long fasting it not harmful. He witnessed a person who abstained from food for thirty days and recovered again.

Physical Exercise

Along with the needs of mental and moral training, the monasteries were not unmindful of the needs of physical health for which regular exercises were prescribed. I-tsing tells us that in India both priests and laymen are generally in the habit of taking walks, going backwards and forwards along a path, at suitable hours, and at their pleasures.....The walking hours are in the forenoon and late in the afternoon. They either go away (for a walk) from their monasteries, or stroll quietly along the corridors".

Aspects of Indian History and Historiography
Editor : P.K. Mishra
Kaveri Books, New Delhi, India.

Medicine in Ancient India : A Review

18

Rakhal Chandra Nath

Primitive thought saw in every illness not readily susceptible of explanation, where the sequence of effect upon cause was not immediate, as in most illness, the influence of a strange malevolent will or a demonic power. Thus primitive man arrived at the conception that all not-readily explainable diseases were the creation of super-natural powers and thus came to formulate the most ancient theory in medicine, viz., demonism. These supernatural powers he conceived under two categories viz., those beyond his powers of control and those amenable to his control. By religious rites like prayers, incantations, and propitiation, he tried to appease the second group and bring them under his control. Thus the medicine of the men of the stone-age consist of religion and magic. Demonism formed their theory of medicine and magic practice.

The city dwellers of Mohenjo-daro and Harappa showed great maturity and a civic consciousness. The two cities between them represent the oldest samples of town-planning in the world. In those cities were baths, lavatories, drains, manholes with covers, fresh-water tanks, and handsome interior court-yards, comfortable bed-rooms etc. Their whole conception shows a remarkable concern for sanitation and health, without parallel in the orient in pre-historic past or at the present day. But, unfortunately we have no means of ascertaining the medical beliefs of the Harappan Civilization, as their script has not yet been deciphered. These beliefs have to be conjectured from a study of medical beliefs prevalent in the contemporary civilizations of Mesopotamia and Egypt, with which the Indus Civilisation had close contacts and about whose medical beliefs we have written records. The medicine of Mesopotamia was magico-religious. It was ancillary to religion. Here the art of divination attained a high degree of development. Astrology formed an important aid to prognostication of diseases. Oracles were sought on all occasions and the doctrine of the stars influenced deeply all phases of popular thought and religion. Egyptian medicine was magico-religious. Magic, incantations, spells, and prayers were freely employed in treatment. We shall see that in the *Atharva-veda* and the Buddhist canon, the Silas, divination of all sorts, astrology, oracles, auguries drawn from celestial phenomena and other signs, magical rites, incantations, spells, and charms, were very prevalent. It is reasonable to suppose that these beliefs were derived, as a result of permeation of these beliefs, from the Harappan Civilization, who shared these beliefs with contemporary civilizations of Mesopotamia and Egypt.

The question naturally arises from where the Indus Civilization derived these beliefs. There are many possibilities. They might have evolved from the primitive medicine of the people of the stone ages. They might have been borrowed from the older civilizations of the ancient world with which Indus Civilisation was in close communion. Finally, the possibility that these beliefs were common to the older civilizations and Indus Civilization shared these views with them. Medicine, based on an animistic hypothesis, has followed the same pattern of evolution all the world over. It either remains as primitive medicine or evolves into magico-religious medicine. The medicine of Mesopotamia and Egypt were magico-religious. So also the medicine of the Indus Valley must have evolved into magico-religious. The final answer to this question must wait till we know something more definite about the Indus Civilization medicine. But, on one point the excavations at Harappa and Mohenjo-daro provide positive evidence viz., hygiene and sanitation.

A perusal of Vedic literature shows that there was a keen interest in the medicinal plants and their application in various maladies. Scanty references to diseases and their cures are found scattered in the *Rg-veda*. There is a verse in the *Rg-veda* (1,3,6) which says that health is maintained when the three *dhatus* or humors (i.e., phlegm, bile, and wind) are in equilibrium. The Ausodhi-Sukta of the 10th Mandal in the *Rg-veda* describes in detail the various uses of plants in medicine. There are also references to the use of plants for counteracting the evil influence of demons. Plants were classified as trees, herbs useful to man, climbers, creepers and grasses.

It is to the *Atharva-veda* we are mainly indebted to our knowledge of Vedic medicine. "The oldest name of the *Atharva-veda* in Vedic literature, is *Atharvāngirasah*, i.e., the *Atharvans* and the *Aṅgirasah*. The two words denote two different species of magic formulae; *atharvan* is holy magic bringing happiness and *angiras* is hostile or black magic. The former included among others, formulae for healing of diseases, while the latter included curses against enemies, rivals, malicious magicians etc." "The hymns of the Atharva-veda comprise of incantations against demons sorcerers, enemies; of charms for expelling diseases wrought by demons or sent by gods as punishment of man's sins; of incantatious intended to impart health, longevity, success and victory, sex-attractiveness and manly vigour. In the Vedas these hymns are supplemented by amulets, medicines, philters and other devices of witchcraft and magic" (Zimmer 1948). In the *Atharva-veda,* religion and magic reign supreme.

Vedic medicine, however, was not primitive medicine. Sigerist distinguishes between primitive and magico-religious medicine. In primitive medicine, magical, religious and emperico-rational elements are inextricably combined, whereas in magico-religious medicine, though these elements are frequently combined, a separation takes place. In Vedic medicine, we notice this separation between the magical and religious elements and emperico-rational elements. Thus, we read in A.V. 11.9.3., that there are hundreds of medical practitioners and thousands of herbs but what can be done by these can be effected by binding an amulet with the particular charm of this verse. Thus, it would appear that the practice of pure medicine by professional medical men, apart from the priest-physicians, has already begun. Again, in A.V. 11.9.5., the *Atharvan* who binds the amulet is described as the best of all the doctors. In A.V. VIII. 7.20., we read, in how many herbs the human physicians find a remedy, so many, all remedial do I bring to thee. This would imply that even at the time of the *Atharva-veda* there were physicians and an elaborate pharmacopoeia treating diseases with drugs. The praise of the Atharvan as the physician per excellence, being superior to all remedies prescribed by the other physicians, implies the existence of two contending systems of medicine viz., the system of charms prescribed by the Atharvan, the priest-physician, and the system of drugs prescribed by the ordinary medical practitioners. This itself implies that vedic medicine was becoming magico-religious.

Numerous diseases like hysteria, leprosy, jaundice, gout, cholera, etc. were prevalent in vedic ages and there are clear references, especially in *Atharva-veda* to the cause and the method of treatment of these diseases. One hymn from the *Rg-veda* relating to a lung condition presents a fairly good description of pulmonary tuberculosis. Different kinds of T.B., originating due to different causes in the different organs of the body have been described. One of the causes was supposed to be the sexual excesses and abuses. The hymns show that psychological, natural and medical methods of treatment of T.B. were current. Malaria in the *Atharva-veda* is characterised by "Alterations between heat and cold delirium and the return of fever daily or every third day." The *Atharva-veda* contains a description of dropsy, and interestingly enough, associates this condition with heart disease. There are hymns to suggest that vedic physicians were aware of such conditions as epilepsy, tetanus and rheumatism. More than 150 herbal and other medicines have been described. Many of them are being used by Vaidyas even now. Even during these very early times there are references in the *Rg-veda* which point to a certain degree of development in the field of surgery. There are references to show that surgeons were employed on the battle-field to attend to patients suffering from injuries resulting from clan warfare. They extracted arrow shafts, amputated limbs, and substituted artificial ones. They removed eyes blinded by injury and assisted women in labour. To relieve pain, during surgery and child birth, the *Soma* plant was commonly prescribed. The Aswini Kumaras can definitely be called as the greatest Vaidyas of their times. They were famous for curing several diseases of different persons. *Śuktas* (Rg) 112 to 120 have exclusively been devoted to them and to their astonishing deeds. Following achievements of Aswin Kumaras in the realm of surgery are worth-mentioning, for, they show the advanced knowledge of Vedic Rishis in this branch. Aswini Kumaras replaced Vishpatas broken thigh by a metallic thigh. They took out Rebha Rishi from the well and joined his amputed organs. They treated the eyes of Rijaśwa who was made blind by his angry father. They joined the three parts of Syāva and made him alive. Anatomy was confined largely to descriptions of gross structure of the human body such as the limbs, the external part of the head, the ear, nose, and mouth. Likewise, any knowledge of Physiology or pathology was non-existent.

It needs to be mentioned here that the Vedic physicians had no knowledge about the nature of disease processes. Diseases were ascribed to the action of supernatural powers. They were looked upon as visitations by demons into the human body, and every disease process was attributed to one evil spirit or another. There was no rational therapy. Treatment was directed towards expelling from the body of the sick the intruding spirit that caused the trouble. This was attempted by various kinds of rituals. This was purely magico-religious.

Āyurveda has been translated as the science of life, and its exponents were medical men with a thorough grounding in the knowledge of the morphology and the properties of plants. Suśruta says it was an upāṅga of the *Atharva-veda*. It is regarded as a branch of Atharva-veda or as the fifth Veda. The Āyurveda was supposed to have consisted of eight divisions: Salya (Surgery), Śālākya (minor surgery), Kāya-cikitsā (medicine proper), Bhūtavidyā (demonology), Kaumāra-bhṛtya (children's diseases), Agada-Tantra (the science of poisons), Rasāyana-Tantra (the science of rejuvenation), and Vājikarana (the science of acquiring sex-strength). The subject of *Bhūtavidyā* and *Sarpavidyā* were contained in the *Ātharva-veda*. Besides these, we have in the *Atharva-veda* hymns dealing with the securing of long life and increasing virility. These were treated in the Āyurveda under the names of *rasāyana* and *Vajīkarana*. Four new subjects make their appearance in the *Āyurveda* viz., Salya, Sālākya, Kāya-cikitsā and Kaumāra-bhrtya. These must have come into existence at a later date and allied themselves to the *Atharva-veda*.

The sixth century B.C. was an important century in the history of humanity. From Athens to the Pacific the human mind was astir. About the sixth century B.C., there is evidence in older civilizations of Egypt, Mesopotamia and China, of a leap forward in speculative thought of a new birth in ethics, of a religion of conscience, threatening to take the place of the religion of custom and magic. In India also, this was a period of great intellectual ferment and spiritual revolt, leading to the establishment of new faiths like Jainism and Buddhism. It was also a period of a quiet philosophic movement which gave rise to the six systems of Indian philosophy.

The period of rational medicine in India began from this time and, in the thousand years than followed, it flourished with great vigour and dynamism. The emergence of Indian medicine during this period from its intimate association with religion and magic and its association with philosophy is closely connected with the rise of these schools of philosophy and its influence of medical thought. Medicine played a significant role in the scientific activities since alleviation of suffering and compassion towards one's fellow creatures was the duty of all following the Noble Eightfold Path taught by Buddha. Generally speaking, medical thinking, in analysing man and his environment, in diagnosing diseases and prescribing therapies, adopts a scientific non-theological view of the entities and energies concerned. The doctrine of the human body, as well as the greater part of diagnosis and therapy in classic Indian medicine, are based on the conception of certain constituents or elementary substances (*bhūta, dhātu* and *dosa*) which pervade the organism and maintain its functioning. These concepts were taken over from the cosmological speculations of Indian nature philosophers who considered matter as composed of certain elementary bodies called *bhūtas*. Even as early as the Upanisads this idea is traceable. The Upanisads speak of five elements (bhūtas) viz., Space (akāśa), Air (Vāyu), fire (agni), water (ap) and earth (prithvi). The two philosophical systems which have influenced the Indian medical writers are the *Nyāya-Vaiśesika* and the Saṃkhya. These two systems accept this classification.

Indian medical tradition traces medicine from a mythical, through a semi-mythical, to an historical beginning. According to this tradition, Indra taught the science of medicine to Ātreya and the science of surgery to Dhanvantari. This may be taken to mean that Ātreya, the physician, and Dhanvantari, the surgeon, were understood to have been the founders in their respective departments, of medicine as a science. From this time onwards the systematic development of Indian medicine proceeded, primarily, on two principal lines viz., one that of Ātreya and the other that of Dhanvantari. Under the leadership of Ātreya who lived around 600 B.C., medicine was taught at the famous University of Taxila. He is said to have had six pupils each of whom individually committed his teachings to writing. The works of only two of his pupils, Agnivesabhela and Hārita are known to have survived. Similarly Dhanvantari taught surgery to his six disciples who wrote treatise on surgery and that of Suśruta in surgery survived. According to D.C. Muthu, writing in the book entitled *Antiquity of Hindu Medicine, Ātreya Saṁhitā* is the oldest known medical book containing 4500 verses. About 800 years later these works were revised, edited and supplemented by Çaraka of Kashmir, a court physician of King Kanishka. The medical work of Çaraka contains 120 chapters and much scientific knowledge about medicine in all its aspects. Suśruta who also lived around 600 B.C. was the head of the Medical Section in the flourishing University of Varanasi and his compendium, largely dealing with surgery, is a remarkable piece of work in the scientific approach, breadth and comprehensiveness.

There were two periods in the early medical literature of India, the Tantra-Kalpa period and the Saṁhitā period. Tantras dealt with separate branches or special subjects and Kalpas are monographs on special subjects. The writings of the disciples of Ātreya were called medical tantras and those of Dhanvantari were called surgical tantras. Of the medical tantras we have the tantra of Agniveśa and of the surgical tantras we have the tantra of Śusruta on Salya. These tantras and Kalpas formed the early medical literature and the básis of teaching in the medical schools. Caraka refers to the existence of various schools of medicine and also to various treatise on medicine before his time. He also mentions that diversity of views with regard to medical theories existed. It was the existence of these diverse treatise, expressing diverse opinions on medicine, that called for the systematization of the then existing medical knowledge. This, the Saṁhitās attempted to do. Thus following the Tantra-Kalpa period, we have the Saṁhitā period.

The Saṁhitā period may be called the creative period of Indian medicine. We have three important Saṁhitās viz., Caraka, Suśruta and Bhela Saṁhitās. The Saṁhitās of Caraka and Suśruta form the classics of Indian medicine. Caraka, court physician to King Kaniska (first century A.D.) was the author of the *Caraka-Saṁhitā*, the second great work on medicine, which was actually a redaction of a much older medical work due to Agniveśa. The *Caraka Saṁhitā* consists of eight sections with 119 chapters-30 on general subjects, 8 on anatomy, 8 on physiology, 11 on the senses, 12 on pharmacology, 30 on therapeutics and 12 on purification. Careful instructions have been laid down for the identification and the application of 2,000 vegetable remedies. Caraka lays very great emphasis on correct diagnosis as the basis of any rational treatment.

In *Suśruta Saṁhitā* surgery achieves a leading position, as an indispensable element of general medical training. Suśruta recommends that every student of medicine must be taught both medicine and surgery. So also Caraka recognizes surgical treatment as an integral part of treatment in general. "Surgery", says Suśruta, "is the highest division of the healing art, least liable to fallacy, perpetual in its applicability, the worthy produce of heaven, the sure source of fame on earth."[1] At the same time he emphasized the unity of medicine, "He who knows only one branch of his art is like a bird with one wing."[2] Even in this early pre-Christian era he had the wisdom to propound some very fundamental educational principles and he laid great stress on the value of practical training in the field of medicine and surgery. "He who is versed only in books will be alarmed and confused, like a coward in the battle-field, when confronting active disease. The student who obtains his knowledge only from books is like an ass with a burden of sandal wood, for he knows the weight but not the value thereof."[3]

The writings of Suśruta give an undisputed pioneering position to the Hindus in many fields of surgery. Indian Surgeons of the sixth century B.C. excelled in plastic operations. Suśruta was perhaps the first surgeon to do rhinoplasty and plastic operations on the ear lobes. The need for these procedures was frequent because the nose and ears were often deformed or excised by the authorities as a legal punishment. Restoration was effected by bringing down flaps from the forehead and fastening the edges with pure wax or with sutures of linen, plant fibre, hair, or animal tissue.[4]

Suśruta was familiar with the clinical picture of Cataract[5] which he described as an opacity of the lens caused by the derangement of intra-ocular fluid. He was the first surgeon to do systematically and in great detail with the development and anatomic structure of the eye.[6] He studied the physiolgocial factors and the pathological changes of the ocular apparatus and the symptoms and treatment of ocular diseases. He described diseases of the eyelids,[7] Conjunctive,[8] Sclera,[9] Cornes,[10] Uveal tracts, lens,[11] retina and the vitreous. His account of Glaucoma is outstanding. He was probably the first Ophthalmic Surgeon, to do the classic couching operation for Cataract. He gave a most elaborate description of the several varieties of Pterygium[12] and his surgical treatment for this condition was as perfect as any modern procedure. According to Bidyadhar (Nabin Kishore, 1939 Arch. op. p. 550-574), Suśruta's views regarding the prognosis of various ocular diseases for example Uveitis and Glaucoma stand fundamentally unaltered even to-day.

Suśruta's compendium deals with various aspects of surgical operations[13] including extraction of solid bodies, excising, incising, probing, scarifying, suturing, puncturing and evacuating fluids. Many surgical procedures were carried out. Tonsillectomies[14] and operations on Anal fistula[15] were accomplished with skill. He described the operation of Laparatomy[16] and tells how to extract foetal head when it is blocked in the pelvis. He described the different kinds of version and Flexion[17] to be performed when the foetus was in an abnormal position, and discussed the application of forceps and operations such an Craniotomy[18] and Caesarean section[19] in difficult cases. The Hindu surgeon tapped the abdomen for Dropsy;[20] he repaired prolapse of the rectum[21] treated haemorrhoids,[22] incised the urinary bladder to remove the Stones,[23] carried out successfully amputations and set the dislocation of the long bones.[24] Even neural surgery was not unknown. The division of the Superaorbital nerve[25] was advised for Superaorbital neuralgia which did not respond to medicinal treatment. There is some evidence that intracranial explorations[26] were undertaken. His Saṁhitā deals at great length with the surgical techniques and the pre-operative and post-operative care.[27]

Surgical procedures attained a higher position and by way of pre-operative preparation, the skin was rubbed with a pledget of cotton saturated with a suitable medicament. Suśruta enumerates 101 varieties of blunt instruments[28] and 20 kinds of sharp instruments.[29] The instruments include scalpels, scissors, needles, saws, sounds, lances, hooks, probes, forceps, trocare, Catheters, bougies, syringes and speculums.[30] Suturing material[31] employed was mostly made from flax, hemp and bark fibres; occasionally hair was used. Two kinds[32] of needles were employed; straight ones for fleshy parts and curved ones for abdomen and scrotum. When operating on the temples, cheeks, eyelids, lips and axillae, the practice was to make a transverse incision; when cutting the palms a circular incision[33] was affected; when the anus and penis were incised a semi-circular cut was made. Dressing of wound was done in a most sanitary manner. The wounded on the battle-field were quickly picked up and carried to a tent, haemostasis was secured and then the wound was washed with an anodyne oil. Suśrutā knew how to ligate blood vessels and Cautery[34] was frequently used. Surgical techniques were demonstrated to the students on various objects such as the following :

Incisions were shown on fruits; scarification upon stretched skins with the hair still on them; punctures on distended bags; venesection on blood vessels of dead animals; opening an abscess, a lump of wax attached to wood; suturing on thick cloth and cauterizing on meats. Great emphasis was laid on the technique of bandaging and ligaturing.

Suśruta's surgery was based upon knowledge of anatomy studied from human cadaver. That the groundwork of the study on anatomy was well laid by Suśruta is clear from his writings on the subject. He emphasized that no accurate account of any part of the body including even the skin can be rendered without a knowledge of anatomy. Hence anyone wishing to acquire a thorough knowledge of anatomy must prepare a dead body and carefully examine all its parts. Suśruta listed 300 bones,[35] 500 muscles,[36] 900 ligaments,[37] 210 joints,[38] and 700 blood vessels in the human body. As compared with modern knowledge there are discrepancies in Suśruta's account of human anatomy. This may be partly due to lack of detailed observations but may also be due to differences in classification and the fact that the dissections[39] were principally made on bodies of children less than 2 years of age since older children and adults were cremated.

Even from this brief review of work of Suśruta the pioneering nature of scientific surgery among the Hindus in the days of Suśruta should be obvious.

On the medical side while advancements were not as remarkable as in the field of surgery, there is clear-cut evidence of the beginning of rational thinking. Attempts were made to classify diseases in accordance with their etiology and Suśruta recognised the following seven classes:[40]

1. Hereditary diseases,
2. Congenital diseases,
3. Diseases due to such causes as hunger or age,
4. Diseases due to atmospheric influence or to contagion,
5. Diseases due to injury,
6. Diseases originating from primary elements, and
7. Diseases caused by demonic influence.

Although the concept of the supernatural sin and Karma still figured heavily in causation of disease, there was at least a beginning of a rational approach. Many diseases were accurately described. Diabetes mellitus[41] was first recognised by observing flies and insects feeding upon sweet urine, Tertian and quartan malaria[42] as also pulmonary tuberculosis[43] were described in detail. Leprosy[44] was probably put on the medical map. Small pox[45] was unquestionably observed. Various diseases affecting the mouth,[46] ear,[47] nose,[48] throat,[49] many types of mental illness,[50] and several varieties of fever[51] and jaundice[52] were tabulated. Judged from modern knowledge, Hindu physiology of this period was primitive and all diseases were supposed to result from disequilibrium of three main humors[53]-air, bile and phlegm. The art of diagnosis was fairly well developed even in those ancient times. The diagnosis[54] was based upon careful observation of the patient by the use of special senses. In addition to inspection, palpation and direct auscultation, the senses of taste and smell were used as diagnostic aids. Aspects of tongue and skin were carefully scrutinized. Notice was paid to the crepitus produced by a fractured bone. Great emphasis was laid on volume, quality and nature of the pulse[55] in the diagnosis of disease. Suśruta recognized direct auscultation as a diagnostic method, as may be seen from the statement, "By the ear can be heard the sound of air, bubbling in the phlegm of the air passages." In the evaluation of disease and its outcome, careful attention was thus paid to the patient's age, mode of life, habits, pulse, body temperature, colour of skin, condition of the eyes, face, strength of the voice, respiratory sounds and specially to his intelligence. The last, according to Suśruta, is very important. "Stupid people are more easily cured than intelligent individuals, because the first are more obedient to the instructions of the physician."[56]

The *Materia Medica* of the time contains a large number of medicines which were classified according to the disease for which they were thought efficacious such as emetics, purgatives, laxatives, tonics and aphrodisiacs.[57] Drugs were dispensed in various forms such as infusions, decoctions, mixtures, pills, syrups, pastes, ointments, suppositories and powders.[58] The works of Suśruta and Caraka embrace an immense number of drugs belonging to the vegetable, mineral and animal kingdoms. The largest number of drugs were of vegetable origin. Suśruta[59] listed 700 plants and Caraka[60] enumerated 500 medicinal plants. The part of the plants used included fruits, blossoms, roots barks, leaves, juices, oil and resins.[61] Among the vegetable substances used were camphor,[62] Cinamen,[63] peppers,[64] cane-sugar, nuts, ginger[65] and garlic. Of the animal substances the most important was milk[66] from humans,cows, elephants, camels, goats and mares. Butter,[67] honey, meat,[68] bile, blood and urine,[69] were also used. Horns,[70] claws and nails were employed for various purposes. Numerous minerals[71] were used in treatment. Mercury[72] was known as the King of metals and was prescribed both internally and externally. Oxidised gold[73] was prescribed as a stimulant. Sulphate of Iron[74] or Copper[75] and Oxide of lead were prescribed as aphrodisiacs. Such drugs as arsenic[76] sulphur,[77] alum[78] and ammonium chloride[79] were also prescribed in the Materia Medica. Many remedies of modern pharmacopaeia were known. Dhatura-Stramonium[80] was used for asthma, arsenic[81] for intermittent fever and mercury for syphilis. A salt-free diet was employed for nephritis, and high protein, high caloric diet for tuberculosis.[82] The fumes of burning Indian hemp has been used by Hindus from remote antiquity as an anaesthetic.[83]

The ancient writings contained detailed discussion regarding personal cleanliness and other rules of hygiene, diet, exercise and prophylaxis.[84] Vaccination against small pox was known in India as early as 550 A.D.[85] Strict hygienic[86] rules were ordered, during pregnancy, delivery and the puerperal state. Instructions[87] for the care of the babies were definite. Hypnotism[88] originated in India and Briad, who introduced it in England, undoubtedly got the ideas while he practised his profession in India.

Many centres of higher education flourished in India during this period and the Universities at Benaras, Taxila, Ujjain and Nalanda were famous. Students desiring admission to these schools had to produce evidence of their family background and certificate of their physical, mental and moral qualifications.[89] Preference was given in the medical schools to the sons of the physicians and those who hailed from medical families.[90] Ethical standards[91] for the physicians were greatly emphasized. The hours of instructions, the number of students for each instructor, in fact, the entire curriculum was well regulated.[92] In addition to theoretical instructions, bed-side instructions[93] were very much in vogue and physicians were urged to broaden their knowledge through contacts and discussion with their professional colleagues.[94] Hospitals[95] were built in India as early as 226 B.C. The relative importance of the nurse in medical practice was clearly recognized. Physicians and surgeons generally observed high ethical standards in their dealings with the patients and commanded the respect of the public.

The creative period of ancient Indian medicine comes to an end with Caraka and Suśruta. Caraka accomplished the final synthesis of Indian medicine and Suśruta that of Indian surgery. The Indian medical writers, after Caraka and Suśruta were but their imitators and abstractors, and commentators. No real original contribution was accomplished after them.

One of the most important documents in connection with ancient Indian medicine is the Bower Manuscript discovered in 1890. The second part of this manuscript is called the "*Nāvanītaka*" and consists mostly of formulae. The date of the manuscript, which is a copy of the original, is about 350-375 A.D. But the *Nāvanītaka* belongs to an earlier date and Hoernle assigns it to late second century. It is not an original work. It is a compilation of the then existing medical tantras and Kalpas. It is of very great importance as a source book for ancient Indian medicine. It confirms the existence of the ancient medical classics of the classical period. It gives an idea of the growth of Indian medical literature. It confirms the existence of the Tantra-Kalpa period. It offers invaluable help in the fixing of the dates of the various medical classics. From a study of it, we learn, that the six tantras of the pupils of Atreya are the oldest, next come the Caraka Saṁhitā, that portion attributed to Caraka, the *Salya-tantra* of Suśruta, the Uttara-tantra of Suśruta, the Junior and last the Bhela Saṁhitā.

Caraka, Suśruta and Vagbhata form the famous 'Triad of the Ancients.' There were two Vagbhatas, viz., Vagbhata I and Vagbhata II. Vagbhata I is the author of *Aṣtaṅga Samgraha*, which is frequently quoted in commentaries. It contains much independent material and is therefore of the greatest value for verifying as well as supplementing Çaraka and Suśruta. Vagbhata must have probably flourished either late in the sixth century or early seventh century. Vagbhata II is best known as the author of *Astāṅga-hṛdaya-Saṁhitā*. There is nothing original in this work. As the name implies it is a compilation of existing medical works. He may be placed in the eighth century. Mention may be made of Madhavacharya, the author of a compendium of Pathology or Nidāna called simply Nidāna. A popular stanza assigns to him a rank equal to that of the "Triad of the Ancients." Mādhava is considered, the foremast authority an diagnosis. He may be placed in the eighth century A.D.

It is rather strange that ancient medicine with such a promising beginning, with such vitality and force behind it lost its dynamism and passed into obscurity after approximately 800 A.D.

References

1. Suśruta Saṁhitā, Sutrā-Sthānam : Chap. I, verses 18-19.
2. Suśruta Saṁhitā, Sutrā-Sthānam : Chap. 3, verses 48, 49, 50.
3. Suśruta Saṁhitā, Sutrā-Sthānam : Chap. 4, verses 3-4.
4. Jolly, Julius (1951) : Indian Medicine.
5. Suśruta Saṁhitā, Uttartantram, Chap. 7, verses 34-35-36.
6. Suśruta Saṁhitā, Uttartantram, Chap. 1, verses 1-19.
7. Suśruta Saṁhitā, Uttartantram, Chap. 3, verses 1-30.
8. Jolly, Julius (1951) Indian Medicine.
9. Suśruta Saṁhitā, Uttartantram, Chap. 49, verses 1-9.
10. Suśruta Saṁhitā, Uttartantram, Chap. 5, verses 1-10.
11. Suśruta Saṁhitā, Uttartantram, Chap. 7.
12. Suśruta Saṁhitā, Uttartantram, Chap. 15, verses 3-18.
13. Suśruta Saṁhitā, Sutra Sthānam, Chap. 25, verses 1-2.
14. Suśruta Saṁhitā, Cikitsā-Sthānam, Chap. 23, verses 49, 50, 51.
15. *Ibid.*, Chap. 6, verses 23-27.
16. *Ibid.*, Chap. 14, para 17.
17. *Ibid.*, Chap. 15, verses 9-11.
18. *Ibid.*, Chap. 15, verse 12.
19. *Ibid.*, Nidāna-Sthānam, Chap. 9, verse 14.
20. *Ibid.*, Cikitsa-Sthānam, Chap. 14, verse 18.
21. Gordon, B.L. (1949), Medicine Throughout Antiquity, p. 333.
22. Suśruta Saṁhitā, Cikitsa-Sthānam, Chap. 6, para 3.
23. *Ibid.*, Saṁhitā, Cikitsa-Sthānam, Chap. 6, verses 30-34.
24. *Ibid.*, Saṁhitā, Cikitsa-Sthānam, Chap. 3, verse 19.
25. Gordon, B.L. (1949), Medicine Throughout Antiquity, p. 330.
26. *Ibid.*, p. 330.
27. Suśruta Saṁhitā, Sutra-Sthānam, Chap. 5, para 17.
28. *Ibid.*, Sutra-Sthānam, Chap. 7, verse 3.
29. *Ibid.*, Sutra-Sthānam, Chap. 8, verse 3.
30. *Ibid.*, Sutra-Sthānam, Chap. 8, verse 3.
31. *Ibid.*, Sutra-Sthānam, Chap. 25, verses 20-21.
32. *Ibid.*, Sutra-Sthānam, Chap. 25, verses 23-26.
33. *Ibid.*, Sutra-Sthānam, Chap. 25, verses 27-28.
34. Suśruta Saṁhitā, Sharir Sthānam, Chap. 5, para 18.
35. *Ibid.*, Sharir Sthānam, Chap. 5, para 37.
36. *Ibid.*, Sharir Sthānam, Chap. 5, para 29.
37. *Ibid.*, Sharir Sthānam, Chap. 5, para 26.
38. *Ibid.*, Sharir Sthānam, Chap. 5, para 49.
39. Gordon, B.L. (1949), Medicine Throughout Antiquity, p. 338.
40. Suśruta Saṁhitā, Nidān-Sthānam, Chap. 6.
41. *Ibid.*, Uttaratantram, Chap. 39.
42. *Ibid.*, Uttaratantram, Chap. 41, verses 17-25.
43. *Ibid.*, Nidān-Sthānam, Chap. 5.
44. *Ibid.*, Nidān-Sthānam, Chap. 13, verse 38.
45. Suśruta Saṁhita, Nidān-Sthānam, Chap. 16, verse 3.
46. *Ibid.*, Nidān-Sthānam, Chap. 16, verse 3.
47. *Ibid.*, Uttaratantram, Chap. 21.

48. *Ibid.*, Uttaratantram, Chap. 22.
49. Jolly Julius (1951) Indian Medicine, p. 134.
50. Suśruta Saṁhitā, Uttaratantram, Chap. 46, verses 61-62.
51. *Ibid.*, Uttaratantram, Chap. 39.
52. *Ibid.*, Uttaratantram, Chap. 46.
53. *Ibid.*, Sutra-Sthānam, Chap. 31, verse 3.
54. *Ibid.*, Sutra-Sthānam, Chap. 10, para 4-5.
55. Gordon, B.L. (1949) Medicine Throughout Antiquity, p. 349.
56. Suśruta Saṁhitā, Sutra-Sthānam, Chap.. 39.
57. Jolly, Julius (1951), Indian Medicine, p. 42.
58. Suśruta Saṁhitā, Sutra-Sthānam, Chap. 38.
59. Caraka Saṁhitā, Sutra-Sthānam, Chap. 4, verse 8.
60. Suśruta Saṁhitā, Sutra-Sthānam, Chap. 38.
61. Sengupta, Kaviraj Nagendra Nath (1914), Ayurvedic System of Medicine, Vol. 3, p. 85.
62. *Ibid.*, Kaviraj Nagendra Nath (1914), Ayurvedic System of Medicine, Vol. 3, p. 157.
63. *Ibid.*, Kaviraj Nagendra Nath (1914), Ayurvedic System of Medicine, Vol. 3, p. 169.
64. *Ibid.*, Kaviraj Nagendra Nath (1914), Ayurvedic System of Medicine, Vol. 3, p. 42.
65. Suśruta Saṁhitā, Sutra-Sthānam, Chap. 38.
66. *Ibid.*, Saṁhitā, Sutra-Sthānam, Chap. 45, verses 92-93.
67. *Ibid.*, Saṁhitā, Sutra-Sthānam, Chap. 44, verse 90.
68. *Ibid.*, Saṁhitā, Sutra-Sthānam, Chap. 45, verses 217-228.
69. *Ibid.*, Saṁhitā, Sutra-Sthānam, Chap. 1, verse 31.
70. Suśruta Saṁhitā, Sutra-Sthānam, Chap. 38, verses 62-63.
71. Jolly, Julius (1951) Indian Medicine, p. 43.
72. Sen Gupta, Kaviraj Nagendra Nath (1914)—Ayurvedic System of Medicine, Vol. 3, p. 658.
73. *Ibid.*, Sen Gupta, Kaviraj Nagendra Nath (1914)—Ayurvedic System of Medicine, Vol. 3, p. 658.
74. *Ibid.*, Sen Gupta, Kaviraj Nagendra Nath (1914)—Ayurvedic System of Medicine, Vol. 3, pp. 467, 224, 629-30.
75. *Ibid.*, Sen Gupta, Kaviraj Nagendra Nath (1914)—Ayurvedic System of Medicine, Vol. 3, p. 529.
76. *Ibid.*, Sen Gupta, Kaviraj Nagendra Nath (1914)—Ayurvedic System of Medicine, Vol. 3, p. 149.
77. *Ibid.*, Sen Gupta, Kaviraj Nagendra Nath (1914)—Ayurvedic System of Medicine, Vol. 3, p. 339.
78. *Ibid.*, Sen Gupta, Kaviraj Nagendra Nath (1914)—Ayurvedic System of Medicine, Vol. 3, p. 509.
79. *Ibid.*, Sen Gupta, Kaviraj Nagendra Nath (1914)—Ayurvedic System of Medicine, Vol. 3, p. 268.
80. *Ibid.*, Sen Gupta, Kaviraj Nagendra Nath (1914)—Ayurvedic System of Medicine, Vol. 3, p. 529.
81. Gordon, B.L. (1949), Medicine Throughout Antiquity, p. 340.
82. Sen Gupta, Kaviraj Nagendra Nath (1914)—Ayurvedic System of Medicine, Vol. 3, pp. 144-5.
83. Jolly, Julius (1951), Indian Medicine, pp. 53-55.
84. Gordon, B.L. (1949), Medicine Throughout Antiquity, p. 345.
85. Suśruta Saṁhitā, Sharir-Sthānam, Chap. 39, verses 3-22.
86. Suśruta Saṁhitā, Sharir-Sthānam Chap. 10, verses 23-29.
87. Gordon, B.L. (1949), Medicine Throughout Antiquity, p. 348.
88. Suśruta Saṁhitā, Sutra-Sthānam, Chap. 2.
89. Jolly, Julius (1951), Indian Medicine, p. 30.
90. Caraka Saṁhitā, Sutra-Sthānam, Chap. 8, verses 18-28.
91. Ibid, Vimana-Sthānam, Chap. 8, verses 3-6.
92. Suśruta Saṁhitā, Sutra-Sthānam, Chap. 9.
93. Jolly, Julius (1951), Indian Medicine, p. 30.
94. Gordon, B.L. (1949), Medicine Throughout Antiquity, p. 350.
95. Suśruta Saṁhitā, Sharir-Sthānam, Chap. 10.

Aspects of Indian History and Historiography
Editor : P.K. Mishra
Kaveri Books, New Delhi, India.

Orissan Chronology : An Epigraphical Study

19

P.K. Nayak

Chronology is an essential feature of historical writing. Eras and dates are considered as the instruments for determining the historical chronology. The epigraphs are replete with the mention of various systems for reckoning dates. We come across a number of specified areas adopted by different dynasties of Orissa in their charters. The purpose of this paper is to present a profile of the various methods employed in the Orissan epigraphs for maintaining the chronology.

The early epigraphs of Orissa are undated. The Aśokan edicts,[1] Hāthigumphā Inscription of Khāravela[2], the charters of the Māṭharas and the Vaśisṭhas[3] are not dated in any specified era. Only the regnal year of the individual King has been mentioned for the purpose of the chronology. They do not furnish the details of a date like *māsa, vāra, tithi, nakṣatra* etc. However, the Aśokan Inscriptions supply us with the information about the seasons with the fortnight. In those days the year was divided into three seasons-each season consisting of 4 moths. This mode of reckoning was known as *Chaturmāsya* system.

The Māṭhara dynasty of Orissa was known to have followed the *Chaturmāsya* system. In three of their charters, namely, Korasaṇḍā grant of Viśākhāvarman,[4] Bobbili plates of Chaṁḍavarman[5] and Baranga plate of Nanda Prabhañjanavarman[6] are dated in this system. But in other charters we find mention of the names of lunar months and *tithis*. This suggests a phase of transition i.e. gradual abrogation of *Chaturmāsya* system and adoption of luni-solar reckoning. We do not find the use of Chaturmāsi reckoning in any Orissan record succeeding to those of the Māṭharas. It was supplanted by the luni-solar dating.

The earliest use of an era for reckoning dates in Orissan epigraphs is found in the charters of Eastern Gaṅgas of Orissa. The Gaṅga charters describe the era as 'Gaṅga Vaṁśa Vijaya Rājya Saṁvatsara' and as 'Pravardhamāna Vijaya Rājya Saṁvatsara'. About 42 grants of the Gaṅga kings are dated in this era. As many as sixteen scholars have examined the grants for fixing up the initial date of the epoch. All the views of the scholars have been examined by the author with the help of the internal corroborative evidences and it is found that except the proposition of V.V. Mirashi[7] (i.e. 498 A.D.) no one fits in with the astronomical details mentioned in the inscriptions. So the epoch of 498 A.D. is accepted as the initial year of the Gaṅga era. The starting point of the era is fixed at Chaitra Sudi 1 of 498 A.D.[8] It has been used both in expired year and current year. The era is in vogue for about five hundred forty eight years. The earliest mention of the Gaṅga era is found in Jirjingi plate of Indravarman dated in Gaṅga era 39 i.e. 537 A.D.[9] As it is first used by Indravarman, the first king of Eastern Gaṅga dynasty, it is generally accepted that he had founded the era of his dynasty. He has dated his charter in "Pravardhamāna Saṁvat 39" i.e. ever increasing year 39.[10] The extract suggests it to be regnal year of the king.

But his successor Sāmanta Varman in his Ponnuturu grant[11] transformed the regnal reckoning of Jirjiṅgi plates into an era of the kingdom. Sāmanta Varman dated his inscription in 'Pravardhamāna Vijayarājya Saṁvatsara' i.e. 'the year of the increasing victorious kingdom.' This tradition of reckoning was followed by his successors which later on was identified as Gaṅga era. In the later period the era was appropriated by the feudatories like Kadaṁbas and Kodalas. The former renamed it as Gaṅga-Kadaṁba era. The Kadaṁba chief Dharmakheḍi has issued the Simhipura grant[12] dated in Gaṅgakadaṁba era 520 and the Kodala chief Laxmana released Chicacole plates[13] in the year 526. But the use of Gaṅga era by the Gaṅga kings is also found in this period. The Rāmapuram plates[14] is dated in Gaṅga era 495, the Poṅḍuru plates[15] is dated in Gaṅga era 500 and the last known use of the Gaṅga era is noticed in Māliaputti plates of Anantavarman[16] which is dated in the Gaṅga year 550 i.e. 1048 A.D. This plate is unpublished and referred to by N. Makundarao in his work. Subsequently it was abandoned by the Imperial Gaṅga rulers who adopted the Śaka era in dating their charters. The Gaṅga era has enjoyed a longer life than any other epoch except the Śaka era in Orissan chronology. When the Gaṅga era was popular in South Orissa, the Gupta era was familiar with the ruling dynasties of coastal Orissa.

The Gupta era is used as a measuring unit of chronology in the charters of Vigrahas, Mudgalas and Śailodbhavas. The era is fixed at 319 A.D. As many as Seven charters of Orissa are accepted to have been dated in Gupta era though some do not contain explicit mention of the same epoch. The charters are Erbang charter[17], Sumanḍalla copper plate[18], Kaṇāsa copper plate[19], Soro copper plate[20], Paṭiākelā charter,[21] Āraṅg copper plate[22] and Gañjam copper plate.[23] The Orissan materials though not fix pinpointedly the year of the Gupta era, have provided a probable period during which the era was started. The Gañjam plate of Mādhavarāja II is dated in Gupta era 300. Mādhavarāja was a contemporary of Pulakeśin II, Harsha and Hiuen Tsang. Hiuen Tsang visited Kalinga, Koṅgada, Kośala etc. in about 638/39 A.D. So the starting period of Gupta era is definitely in the early part of 4th century A.D. (638/39-300 =338/39 A.D.). The Gupta era did not get the favour of the subsequent ruling families of Orissa. The later Śailodbhava rulers adopted Harsha era in their charters.

In the seventh century A.D. India witnessed the activities of three powerful personalities-Śaśāṅka, Pulakeśin II and Harsha. Among these Harsha had a long rule and an era in his name is known to have been instituted from the date of his coronation i.e. 606. Harsha, after the death of Śaśāṅka and Pulakeśin II had occupied Daṅḍabhukti, Utkala and Kaṅgoda and left an impression of his magnanimity and profound powers among the ruling dynasties who were his feudatories. They began to record their charter in the Harsha era. In the Soro plate,[24] Somadatta has reckoned the date in Saṁvat 15 which can be safely taken as Harsha era. The Śailodbhava charters like Pārikud plates of Madhyamarāja,[25] Nivinā charters[26], Chanḍesvar grant[27] and Puri plates[28] of Dharmarāja II are dated in Saṁvat 88, 100, 105 and 112 respectively. This Saṁvat mentioned in the charters very likely refers to Harsha era. If we take it as correct, all these dates synchronise well with the political events of Orissan history without disturbing the dynastic chronology.

The next important epoch adopted in Orissan epigraphs is Bhauma Saṁvat. This epoch is also used like Harsha era without any specific name. Because the era is found in continuous use by the Bhaumas in their charters it is named as Bhauma Saṁvat. Besides the Bhauma rulers, their feudatories like Bhañjas, Śulkis, Nandobhavas, Tuṅgas are known to have dated their charters in this era of their overlords. S.N. Rajguru by calculating the Aastronomical details mentioned in Gañjam and the Daspallā charters of Satrubhañjadeva, has fixed the epoch at 736

A.D.[29] K.N. Mohapatra[30] and D.C. Sircar[31] have respectively proposed 614 A.D. and 831 A.D. as the initial date of the epoch. Both are found unsuitable to the known facts of Orissan history. On the contrary, the date 736 A.D. satisfies all querries and suits well with the historical synchronisms. The foundation of the era is generally attributed to Śivakara I. But K.C. Panigrahi[32] thinks that Kṣemaṅkara was the founder of the Bhauma era. The epithets attributed to Kṣemaṅkara leave no trace of doubt that he had a royal status. Though Sivakara Deva I was a powerful ruler who played vital role in the kingdom, he was a successor of Kṣemaṅkara. So the attribution of the foundation of Bhauma Saṁvat is not an improbable hypothesis though nothing can be said conclusively unless definite information are available in this regard. The adoption of this era in epigraphs is first noticed in Neulpur charter of Śubhakaradeva I issued in Saṁvat 54.[33] The last known use of the era is noticed in Orissa Museum plate of Neṭṭabhanja[34] which records the date as Saṁvat 213 (736 A.D. + 213 = 949 A.D.). Thereafter the use of the era was discontinued. Probably, the use of the era was abandoned after the collapse of the Bhauma dynasty. The Śaka era, by that time, had already been accepted as a standard era and it was being adopted by the prominent ruling dynasties in reckoning dates, both in North and South India. The Gaṅga monarchs thought to adopt this era as it had gained All-India recognition and dropped the use of Gaṅga era having a local importance. The Śaka era probably came to Orissa through the Chālukyas who were contemporary to and whose territory was conterminous to that of Gaṅgas of Kaliṅga. The Madagrāma plates of Bhimakheḍi is dated in Śaka era 917.[35] V.V. Mirashi[36] reads and interprets the date as 888 S.E. (966 A.D.); on the other hand S.N. Rajguru[37] reads it as 988 Śaka era i.e. (1066 A.D.). If the reading of V.V. Mirashi is accepted, then Madagrāma plates will be the earliest epigraph to mention the Śaka era in Kaliṅga. Otherwise, the credit will go to the Manḍāsā plate[38] which records the date in Śaka 917 (995 A.D.). The first Gaṅga king of Kaliṅga to use this era was Vajrahasta V. After him it has been in continuous use in Orissa till date.

Unlike the Śaka Saṁvat, Vikram Saṁvat has a very limited use in Orissa. Vikram era was not popular among the ruling dynasties of Orissa. It has not got extensive employment in the Orissan epigraphs. Its introduction in Orissan epigraphs is very late and rare. Only one inscription of the Gaṅga period is found dated in Vikram era. The Kurmeśvara temple inscription of Risi dāsa[39] during the time of Narasiṁhadeva IV records the donation of hundred goats for maintaining a perpetual lamp in the temple in Śaka 1325 and Vikrama era 1459.

The Kaliyuga era (3101-02) has also been used sparingly in some Orissan Inscriptions. Only three inscriptions of Orissa contain the date in Kaliyugābda. The Polasarā plate of Arkeśvaradeva[40] and the Poṭṭeśvara temple Inscription of Bhānudeva III[t41] are dated in Yugābda 4248 (1147 A.D.) and Yugābda 4477 (1376 A.D.) respectively. The Warangal inscription of Raghudeva records the data in Kaliyuga era 4561 which corresponds to A.D. 1460 (4561-3101).[42]

Another important system of reckoning dates which was profusely used in Orissan epigraphs is the method of chronogram in which the year is expressed in words and sometimes in letters. In this system certain words denote some numerical value which are used in place of the numbers. This method of word numerals had gained wide popularity in medieval Orissa. Two words or more than that form a chronogram. The principle of *Aṅkānām vāmotah gatih* (turning round the number) is followed to transform a chronogram into a number. For instance "vyomeṅdu" is a chronogram. Here Vyoma stands for `O' and Indu stands for 1. The chronogram when converted into number would mean 10.

The earliest adoption of the chronogram is noticed in the Patna museum plate of Vijayā Mahādevi, the wife of Raṇabhañja,[43] The date runs as *'Indu Vāk visanti varise'*. Scholars have advanced divergent views regarding the interpretation of the chronogram. In the tradition of chronogram the word *Indu* stands for the number 1, *vāk* also for 1. R.D. Banerji[44] while editing the plates corrected the word 'visanti' as 'viṁsati' meaning 20 which made the chronogram 2011 (Indu-1, Vāk-1, Viṁsati-20). But, unable to adjust the date in the Orissan chronology, Banerji held that the rule of the chronogram i.e. turning the figure from right to left, is not followed and it should be interpreted as 22 (1 + 1 + 20) which was according to him, the regnal year of the king. Hirānanda Sashtri accepted the interpretation but he took the word 'vāk' to imply the number '4'. So the date became 25 (1 + 4 + 20). It is also suggested that the word 'visanti', may be corrected as 'viśveti'. As 'viśva' stands for 14 (*Chaturdaśa bhuvana*) Smt. Tripathy interpreted it to be Vikram Saṁvat.[45] So the date became 1411 V.S. i.e. 1353 A.D. But she rejected her date subsequently on the ground that Vikram era was not used in Orissan epigraphy during this period. Finally, she dismissed the word 'visanti' and took 11 to be the regnal year of the king. But it is not wise to dismiss the word which fails to provide a suitable date. The word 'viśveti' may also be interpreted as to represent the number 3 (tri bhuvana) instead of 14 (*Chaturdasi bhuvana*). Thus the chronogram would make the date 311. The Saṁvat may be taken as Gaṅga era. Vijayā Mahādevi was the daughter of Niyārnama or Niyārnava which is a very popular name in Kadaṁba family. The Kadaṁbas were using Gaṅga era. So the Saṁvat 311 very likely represents the Gaṅga era which would correspond to 809 A.D.[46]

If this be accepted then this is the earliest use of chronogram found in Orissan inscriptions.

The other type of this method is the expression of numbers through letters. In three of the Bhañja charters this method has been applied to reckon the regnal years of the rulers. This system is known as Kaṭapayadi system.[47] In this system the letters of the alphabet denote the numbers as shown in the table.

Numbers	*1*	*2*	*3*	*4*	*5*	*6*	*7*	*8*	*9*	*10*
Letters	ka	kha	ga	gha	na	cha	chha	ja	jha	na
Letters	ta	tha	da	dha	na	ta	tha	da	dha	na
Letters	pa	pha	ba	bha	ma					
Letters	ya	ra	la	va	sa	sa	sa	ha	la	

In case of a conjunct consisting of two or more consonants the value of the last consonant is counted. The Singhorā Plates,[48] the Orissa Museum Plate[49] and the Phulbāni plates[50] the University Museum plates of Raṇabhañjadeva[51] bear the regnal year in a chronogram of letters 'namāme' meaning '50' me' or in the 50th regnal year. However, this system was not familiar and was discontinued.

Among the other modes of reckoning in Orissa, the Vārhaspatyamāna and the Aṅka Śrāhi are worth mentioning. The Vārhaspatyamāna has two systems of counting-12 year cycle and 60 year cycle. Both are in vogue in Orissa since long past. But the former has scanty reference where as the latter has a fairly good circulation. The modern almanacs also contain the reckoning in 60 year cycle.

The Aṅka year is a unique chronographic feature of Orissa. It is a system of reckoning the regnal years of individual king in which number 1, 6, any number having zero (0) at the end except and any number ending in 6 are not counted. The year is stated on *Bhādra Śukla Dvādaśī*. The reference of Aṅka year can be traced to the time of Vajrahasta V. But the rules of the system were not followed rigidly. The Suryavaṁśi kings adopted this method of reckoning with exclusive adherence to the rules.

The above study reveals that the earliest inscriptions of Aśoka, Kharavela, Māthara and Vaśiṣthas record the date in regnal years of the individual rulers. Although the Gupta era is adopted by the Mudgala and Vigrahas in their charters in the 6th/7th century A.D., the Eastern Gaṅgas of Kaliṅga was the earliest known dynasty to have employed an era named after their family as Gaṅga era. It was in continuous use from 6th century A.D. to 10th century A.D. and in intermittent use up to the 1st half of 12th century A.D. The Śailodbhavas used Gupta era and Harsha era in some of their charters. Somadatta, of Uttara Tośali also is known to have adopted Harsha era in his Soro charter. In the 8th century A.D. the Bhauma-karas of Utkala had promulgated an era known as Bhauma Saṁvat. It was initiated in 736 A.D. This era was used upto 949 A.D. by them and by their feudatories like Bhañjas, Śulkis, Tuṅgas and Nandodbhavas. The Śarabhapuriyas and Somavaṁśis of South Kośala have never dated their charters in any specific era. They preferred to reckon the dates in the regnal years of the individual kings. The Śaka era was introduced by the Kadaṁbas, the feudatories of Eastern Gaṅgas in their charters, and this found ready recognition by the Gaṅga rulers who employed this era in their copper plate grants abrogating their family era i.e. Gaṅga era. Further, they started a new system of reckoning dates in chronogram. They initiated a unique system of dating to reckon regnal years known as Aṅka Śrāhi years which got royal acceptance by the Suryavaṁśi Gajapatis who succeeded them. As shown in the discussion, the Kaliyuga era and Vikram Saṁvat were used sparingly and rarely. The most familiar dating systems in Orissa are Gaṅga era, Bhauma era, Śaka era and AṅKa Śrāhi out of which the former two are obsolete and the latter two are still current for dating.

References

1. D.C. Sircar, *Select Inscriptions, bearing on Indian History and Civilisation*, I, 1965, Calcutta, pp. 15-75.
2. N.K. Sahu., Utkal University *History of Orissa*, I., Bhubaneswar, 1964, pp. 397-404.
3. S.N. Rajguru, *Inscriptions of Orissa*, I, Pt. II, Bhubaneswar, 1958, pp. 1-80.
4. J.B.O.R.S., XIV, Pt. II, pp. 282f.
5. S.N. Rajguru., op. cit., pp. 25-27.
6. *Ibid.*, pp. 78-80.
7. E.I., Vol. XXVI, pp. 326f.
8. P.K. Nayak. Eras and Dates in Orissan Epigraphs, Un-published Ph.D. thesis, Sambalpur University, 1982, p. 98.
9. JKHRS, III, pp. 49-53.
10. JAHRS, III, pp. 49-53.
11. EI., XXVII, pp. 216-20.
12. JAHRS, III, pp. 171-80.
13. JBORS, XVIII, pp. 272ff; JAHRS, VIII, pp. 168-80.
14. JAHRS, 35, (Hyderabad 1976), p. 177 ff.
15. JAHRS, IX, p. 23 ff.
16. N. Makundarao, *Kalinga under the Eastern Gangas*, (Delhi, 1991), p. 6.
17. OHRJ, XII, No. 3, pp. 113-121.
18. *Ibid.*, I, pp. 66-69.
19. JKHRS, II, pp. 261-66.
20. EI, XXIII, pp. 197-202.
21. *Ibid.*, IX, pp. 285-288.
22. *Ibid.*, pp. 342-45.
23. *Ibid.*, VI, pp. 143-146.
24. EI, XXIII, p. 202.
25. S.N. Rajguru (ed), op. cit., pp. 199-205.

26. EI, XXI, pp. 34-41.
27. JKHRS, II, No. 1, pp. 59-72.
28. JBORS, XVI, pp. 176-88.
29. OHRJ, I, No. 3, pp. 208 ff; EI, XXXVII, p. 257.
30. M.N. Das (ed.), Sidelights on History and Culture of Orissa, Cuttack, Vidyapuri, 1977, p. 542.
31. EI, XXIX, p. 189.
32. K.C. Panigrahi, *Chronology of Bhaumakaras and the Somavaṁśis of Orissa*, Madras, 1961, p. 23.
33. EI, XV, pp. 1-8.
34. *Ibid.*, XXVIII, pp. 272-78.
35. *Ibid.*, XXXI, pp. 45-52.
36. V.V. Mirashi, *Studies in Indology*, Vol. II, 1971, p. 141.
37. S.N. Rajguru, op. cit., Vol. II, 1960, pp. 217-220.
38. JBORS, XVII, pp. 175-88.
39. SII, V, No. 1176.
40. EI, XXVIII, pp. 63-67.
41. JAHRS, VI, Pt.I, p. 51f.
42. EI, XXXIII, III, No. 23, pp. 125-130.
43. *Ibid.*, XX, p. 100-104.
44. *Ibid.*
45. Mrs. S. Tripathy, *Inscriptions of Orissa*, VI, Bhubaneswar, 1974, p. 84.
46. P.K. Nayak, op. cit., pp. 40-42.
47. D.C. Sircar, *Indian Epigraphy*, 1965, Delhi, p. 222.
48. JBORS, VI, pp. 481-486.
49. OHRJ, XI, pp. 155-159.
50. S. Tripathy, *op. cit.*, pp. 268-275.
51. N.A.H.O., Vol. II (Sambalpur, 1978), p. 7.

Section III

Aspects of Indian History and Historiography
Editor : P.K. Mishra
Kaveri Books, New Delhi, India.

Jagannath Cult of Orissa and the Rajas of Nepal

20

P.K. Mishra

Introduction

Nepal being the only Hindu Kingdom of the World the Rājā (of Nepal) is an object of profound reverance among the Hindus. It is amazing to observe that he is considered as the Living Vishnu and high respect commensurating with his sacred status is ungrudgingly offered to him. In Orissa the Jagannāth Temple at Puri has been the epicentre of Vaishnavite worship since the eleventh century. Puri is one of the four *Dhāms* (sacred places) which every Hindu wishes to pay a visit during his life time. The Rajas of Nepal at times come to Puri on pilgrimage. When they visit the Puri temple no other pilgrim is allowed entry to the temple premises except the Rajā and his family members. He enjoys the rare privilege of worshipping the three Deities himself without being assisted by the Priest/Priests. He is authorised to touch the deities while offering worship. The privilege is not enjoyed by any other Hindu Rājā of India.

The Jagannāth Temple at Puri was built by King Anantavarman Choḍagaṅga of the Imperial Gaṅga dynasty during 1135 to 1147.[1] But it took about a century or so of consistent royal patronage for the Cult revolving Lord Jagannath to evolve and grow. King Anaṅgabhimadeva III, the great grandson of Anantavarman Choḍagaṅga popularised the concept of 'Rāṣṭra devatā' and called Jagannath the synonym for Orissa empire.[2] With his support the Cult of Jagannath spread far and wide. Orissa was a powerful kingdom then, which withstood the dangers of Muslim invasion from Bengal. There are epigraphic evidence to prove that King Narasimha Deva, the son and successor of Anaṅgabhimadeva III and the builder of the famous Sun temple at Konarak near Puri had inflicted a decisive defeat upon the Nawab of Bengal.[3] Orissa was well protected in the North and South to promote the cause of Jagannath cult.

It is difficult to ascertain the exact date or time when the Cult of Jagannath spread to Nepal. There is a two storey Jagannath Temple facing the multi language Inscription of Hanumān Ḍhokā in Kathmandu. The temple was built in the 17th century by Raja Pratap Malla. It is famous in Nepal as Jagannath Devala. It is a solid structure, thought not quite graceful as compared to other temple in the square. But its plan is unusual and the sculptures are excellent. Dedicated to Jagannath and Guhyesvari and having a large complex involving a brick covered circumambulatory plinth extending six feet beyond the building on all sides. There are four miniature shrines at the four corners of the plinth which exhibit the basic features of a standard Nepalese temple.[4]

The main temple has three doors on each side of the first floor with a torana over each centre door. The wooden frames which extend over each door are quite large with four niches on each frame holding small divine figures. On the brick walls are seen small wooden shrine frames. The waterjars or *Purna ghatas* are painted over the wooden doors. The strut supported roofs are made of tiles and heavy cement with white flowers painted on the borders/edges. But the upper cornice is not painted. There is no painting of birds. The pinnacle is of stipulated design, simple but large and gilded.[5]

Although the above temple of Kathmandu is not architecturally identical with the Jagannath Temple at Puri the depiction of gods and goddesses and the erotic scenes have some resemblance with the Orissan temples. It is not known if along with the worship of Lord Jagannath King Pratapa Malla also induced a group of priests to migrate to Nepal to ensure similar ritual practices as prevailed in Puri. It seems that except the introduction of Jagannath as a deity to be worshipped by his people Pratap Malla did not bother to follow/introduce the ritual details of Puri Temple.

About thirty years ago the Public Relations Department of the Government of Orissa had published a brochure entitled "Lord Jagannath and Nepal" on the occasion of the visit of His Majesty King Mahendra and Her Majesty Queen Ratna to Puri on 17 December 1965.[6] A copy of the above brochure was available with the Lalmoharia Panda which revealed further details of the age old relationship between the royal family and the deity. The brochure was prepared by the Government on the basis of traditions and the Temple chronicle. It says that only the Gajapati King of Puri as custodian of the Temple and the Royal Highness of Nepal are respected as the moving figures of Lord Jagannath. The Queen of Nepal is equally respected as the moving figure of Lakshmi, the consort of Vishnu. When the King of Nepal visits the Temple he has the right to be carried in a palanquin and proceed in procession accompanied by bands and music to enter the temple. He is welcomed at the Lion Gate by the *Sevāyats* and other important persons. If the queen is there, she can be carried to the *Kalpavaṭa* (Sacred banyan tree). Before the entry of the royal couple all others have to vacate the temple and the four gates have to be closed. This ritual is called `Mandira sodha' (clearance of the temple). The Royal visitors will then keep their Royal Insignia under the *Kalpavata* tree and thereafter they will be welcomed by the Lalmoharia and the Pratihari *Paṅḍā*. Then the second *Parichha* or the Patjoshi Mahapatra will recite the following welcome *Mantra* called the *Mudala siddhi* (Traditional right of worshipping Jagannath).

The welcome *mantra* is quoted below:

Swasti Śri Anshumāli Kulodbhava
Lichhāviya Navakoṭa Kailāsha Kuṭādhipati
Saptagaṅduki Mahābhaṭṭāraka Manḍala
Nārāyaṇi Sarita sevita
Matsyendra ghanṭākarṅa Bhairava rakṣhita
Paramabhattāraka paramasaugata Śankaradeva
Sankaradeva Mahendra pari kushali
Shankarshana Vāsudevaṅka Lakṣhana thivā
Vishnuśilā ubhayamukhi suvarnagarbha
Arpaṇa Karithibāku Āpane Purusottama Kshetra
Āpaṇara Vaṁśaku Ujjala Karithivāku Āpane
Purusottama Kshetra Ādya Samvatsare
Gajapati Mahārājāṅkara Aṅke dina
Mudalasiddhi sevaku Alpanā Kari
Abadhana Karivā huantu

Translation

Hail you, the scion of the Solar dynasty, the descendant of the Lichhavis, the Lord of Navakota and Kailasakuta. Your country which is known as Bhattarakamandala is served by the rivers, the seven Gandukis, and Narayani. Your country is protected by Lord Matsyendranath and Ghantakarna Bhairava. You are a great Saiva. You are a great devotee of Lord Buddha. When your predecessor Maharajadhiraj Sankaradeva was ruling as the great Indra, he presented Vishnuśila representing the symbols of both Sankarsana Vasudeva and Ubhayamukhi Kundalini from the holy river Ganduki and thereby he had made his dynasty spiritually famous. Being the scion of that great King Sir, you may kindly accept the traditional honour of worshipping Lord Jagannath).[7]

The palmleaf manuscript recording the above welcome address is dated on the 23rd regnal year of Raja Divyasimha deva III of Puri corresponding to 1880 A.D.[8] From the language also it appears to be of the late 19th century. Though this palmleaf is dated 1880 A.D. the practice of welcoming the Royal family of Nepal appears to be much older.

There are two episodes which bear evidence to the close relation between the Jagannath Cult and the ruling family of Nepal. *Firstly*, King Yayati I, of the Somavamsi dynasty is traditionally believed to be the builder of the first temple of Jagannath at Puri. He is known to have migrated from Dakshina Kosala (Raipur-Bilaspur-Sambalpur region) to Utkala along with the Jagannath faith and the tribal priests (Daitapati) associated with the worship.[9] *Secondly*, the King of Nepal had donated the sacred *Vishnuśila* for the deities in Puri temple. These points are further elaborated in the following paragraphs:

The Temple Chronicle (Mādalāpāñji) of Puri records that the first temple for Purusottama-Jagannath was built by King Yayati I of the Soma dynasty whose original homeland was South Kosala in the Upper Mahanadi Valley with Capital at Sirpur (near Raipur). After some years this temple became dilapidated for lack of proper maintenance. This is possible because the Soma Kings being Saivities they concentrated the Cultural activities at Bhubaneswar for which the Vishnu temple at Puri was neglected. In the 12th century the present temple for Jagannath was built by Anantavarman Choḍaganga (1075-1147 A.D.).[10]

The early Soma dynasty had great patrons of Vaishnavism like King Tivaradeva.[11] His Copper plate grants issued from Rajim and Baloda mention him as a great Vaishnava (Period 545-590 A.D.). His brother Harshagupta was the 9th King of the Soma dynasty (590-615). He had married Bāsaṭā, the daughter of King Suryavarman of Magadha. The beautiful Vishṇu temple of Sirpur (Lakshmaṇa Temple) was built by Queen Bāsaṭā.[12] It is interesting to note that Princess Rajyamati, the daughter of King Harshadeva (or Harshagupta) and Qeen Bāsaṭā was married to Raja Joydeva II, the Lichhavi King of Nepal. The Stone Inscription of Joydeva II found in Nepal is of great historical significance for it describes Harshadeva as the Lord of Gauda (Bengal) Oḍra (Orissa), Kaliṅga, Kośala and many other places. Hence the Somavaṁśi kings (who later founded the first Vishnu temple of Puri) had matrimonial relation with the Lichhavi Kings of Nepal in the Sixth-Seventh century A.D., a relation which was lovingly cherished in later centuries. Therefore, the Kings of Nepal received a place of honour in the religious Institutions built by the Soma Kings in Utkala.[13]

About the Vishnuśilā episode the tradition records that Rājā Śankaradeva donated Vishnuśilas from the river Ganḍuki which bore the necessary symbols of Śiva, Vishnu and Kunḍalini with gold inside, both living with insects. Vishnuśilā is commonly known as the Śālagrāma Stone, the symbolic representation of Vishnu. These are rare objects of great veneration by the Hindus. The two Vishnuśilās sent by the king of Nepal had the unique value of being living stones. The Purāṇas state that Vishnu cursed by Vrindāvati assumed the form of an insect and lived in the river Ganḍuki. He was ordained and lived out Vaishnava symbols on the Vishnusila.[14]

The Padmapurāṇa in Uttarākhanda, Chapter XI, states :

> *'Ganḍakyāmeva deśe tu Śālagrāmasthalam Mahat*
> *Pasanastadbhavo yastu Śālagrāma iti Sthitam".*

The following passage from Dharmasaṁhita may be quoted as relevant in the present context :

> *Hiraṇyagarbha Bhacabanaddouh nārāyaṇam svayam*
> *Vajrakiṭah Prabhurbhutvā Chāchara dharaṇitale*

Therefore, the gift of Vishnuśilā by the Raja of Nepal enshrined in the deities of Puri Temple was respectfully acknowledged by the King of Puri by according special privileges to the former in the ritual ceremony of Lord Jagannath. The privilege is being enjoyed by the Rājās of Nepal for several centuries since Śankaradeva (end of 7th and early part of 8th century).[15]

On the occasion of the *Navakalevara* which falls once in every twelve years the wooden idols are remade with fresh timber and the old ones are consigned to fire. During the rituals of change the Chief Priest or his family member removes the sacred object from the old idol and puts it inside the new idol of Lord Jagannath. This work is performed hereditarily by the Panda's family in a secret ritual which is not allowed to be witnessed by any body else. The object that is transferred from the old image to the new is called *Brahma Padārtha* (spiritual material) and is considered the quintessence or soul of the deity.[16] This mysterious object has so far baffled the scholars who have no access to the transfer ceremony. But it is widely believed to be the Śālagrāma or Vishnuśilā of the remote period of history gifted by the Rājā of Nepal.[17]

Visits and Donations

From the records and statement of the Lalmoharia Panda it was ascertained that in the recent past the following Kings and members of the Royal family of Nepal came on pilgrimage to Puri. Records earlier to the 19th century were destroyed by fire in 1912. Even the Sanands granted in favour of the Panda were destroyed. He has, however, retained the royal seal which is produced as Appendix-A. The visitors in 1912 were Commander-in-Chief Bhim Samser Jung Bahadur and his brother Colonel Ram Samser Jung Bahadur. In 1923 Genéral Kesar Samser Jung Bahadur Rana with Baḍā Mahārāṇi and others came for the *darshan* of Lord Jagannath. On 15 January 1941 Sri 3 Kanchha Baḍā Mahārāni and her entourage came on pilgrimage. The entry made on 30 November 1944 shows that His Majesty Sri 5 Tribhuvan Vir Vikram Shah Dev the King of Nepal, Sri Yuvarajadhriraj Vikram Shah Dev and others paid their obeisance to the Lord. The next distinguished visitors were Sri 5 Jetha and Kanchha Suma Baḍā Mahārāṇi who came to Puri on 7 February 1957. In 1959 had come Śri 5 Mama Jethā Baḍā Mahārāṇi and Śri 5 Mama Kanchha Baḍā Mahārāṇi including the Rāni Saheba of Kasipur.

The Lalmoharia Panda has in his possession the Copper plate Sanad granted to him in 1833 by His Majesty Śri Śri Mahārājā Rajendra Vikram Shah Bahadur Samser Jung. It records the right of Śri Jagannāth Panda, his brother Sri Ganes Prasad Panda and his son Sri Gangadhar Panda to be *Panḍās* for the country of Nepal. They have been assigned with the duty of making arrangements for the stay and *darshan* of Lord Jagannath for all people coming from Nepal and to pray for the welfare of the royal family.

Another Sanand was granted by Maharajadhiraj Tribhuvan Vir Vikram Jung Bahadur Shah Bahadur Samser Jung in 1911. It records that consequent upon the death of Sri Gangadhar Panda, Sri Bhimsen Sri Krishna was appointed as the priest for Nepal. The Panda receives an annual salary of Rs.500 from the Majesty's Government of Nepal.[18]

The Royal visitors from Nepal liberally granted donation to the temple. It was revealed by the present Lalmoharia Panda (Sri Bhuvan Mahapatra) that the Royal family had donated 275 *bighas* of land in Sarlai district of Nepal for the temple of Lord Jagannath. Further details of the land grant were not immediately available. A big brass bell was presented by one Sri Jitgovind of Nepal sometime in 1903 which bears a Nepalese Inscription and remains suspended from a big and decorated iron beam pitched near the Storehouse.[19]

Conclusion

Today Nepal is the only Hindu country in the world. It has not only preserved the cultural heritage of Hinduism but has served as complimentary force of Pan-Indian culture. The spirit of religious syncretism as the outcome of a synthesis of Hinduism and Buddhism can be best appreciated there. In the context of promoting the glorious Hindu tradition one is highly impressed by the role played by the rulers of Nepal. It is most manifest in the relation between Nepal and Orissa, especially the link between the royal family of Nepal and the Jagannath cult. Besides the ancient matrimonial relation between the Lichhavis of Nepal and th e Soma Kings of Dakṣhina Kośala who had migrated from the Upper Mahanadi Valley to the coastal region of Orissa along with the cult of Jagannath and had built the first Vishnu temple at Puri, the gift of two Vishnuśilās by KIng Sankaradeva in the 7th century played significant role in promoting the Institution of Jagannath at Puri. The Kings of Nepal have time and again made munificient contribution for its sustenance. They have assiduously maintained the link with one of the four Dhams of Hinduism for the pilgrimage and spiritual upliftment of their devoted countrymen. The frequent visits of the Kings and the Nepalese people to Orissa have resulted in the acceptance of worshipping Ghanṭākarna Bhairava in every household (in Orissa) on the occasion of Rekhāpañchami (fifth day of the dark fortnight of the month Bhadrava). This is a national festival both in Nepal and Orissa when during the ritual ceremony one common *mantra* is recited for the safety of the house. Thus, Hindu religion and kingship have facilitated the social and cultural evolution of the two centres of Hinduism-Nepal and Orissa since time immemorial.

References

1. K.C. Panigrahi, *History of Orissa* (1981), pp. 406-07.
2. H.Kulke & Others, (ed), *The Cult of Jagannath and the Regional Traditions of Orissa*, (1978), pp. 199 ff.
3. K.C. Panigrahi, *op. cit.*, pp. 166-67 and P. Acharya, *Studies in Orissan History, Archaeology and Archives* (1969), pp. 28-43.
4. Ronald M Bernier, *The Temples of Nepal* (1970), pp. 125-26.
5. *Ibid.*
6. Monograph entitled "Lord Jagannath and Nepal" published on 17 December 1965 by the Home (Public Relations) Department, Government of Orissa.
7. *Ibid*, pp. 2-3.
8. *Ibid.*

9. K.C. Mishra (ed), *Studies in the Cult of Jagannath* (1991), pp. 92-93.
10. H. Kulke & Others (ed), op. cit., pp. 139 ff.
11. N.K. Sahu & P.K. Mishra, *History of Orissa* (1981), pp.168-69.
12. S.K. Patel, *Hinduism in India* (1983), p. 56.
13. Monograph (1967), *op. cit.*, p. 16.
14. *Ibid*, p. 15.
15. Netra Bahadur Thapa, *A Short History of Nepal* (1990), pp. 177. Appendix-A.
16. K.C. Mishra, *op. cit.*
17. Monograph, *op. cit.*
18. As stated by the present Lal Moharia Panda Sri Jagannath Mohapatra (Western Gate, Puri Temple).
19. Monograph, Appendix-R.

श्री श्री जगन्नाथ स्वामी जीऊ

श्री ५ सरकार नेपालके व

भरराजके पुरहित

स्वर्गीय भिमसेन श्री किशनजिके बेटा

लालमोहरिआ पण्डा

लोकनाथ | PHONE-3194
S. T. D 06752 | जगन्नाथ

बेटा
गङ्गाधर अनन्तराम
दामोदर

बेटा
बलभद्र
भुवनमोहन

ठिकाना

मन्दिरका पश्चिमद्वार हातिभुण्डका

दरबाजा, पो-पुरी जिल्ला-पुरी

APPENDIX

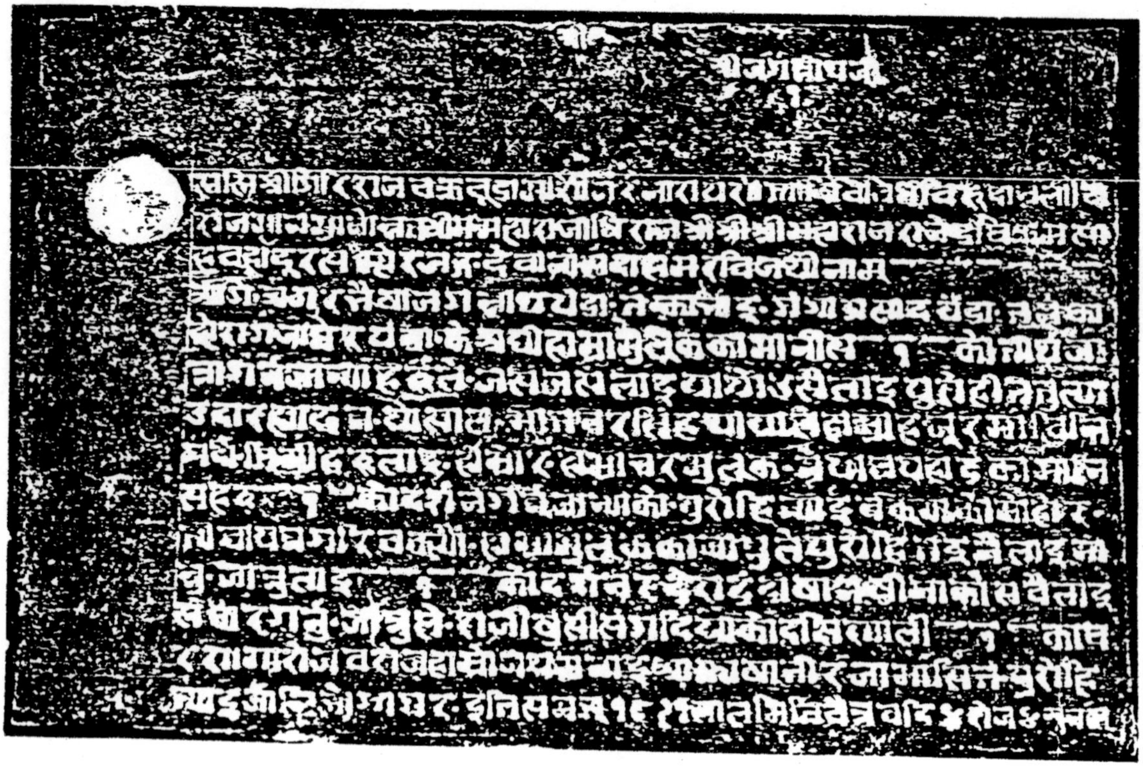

Sanand 1833

Aspects of Indian History and Historiography
Editor : P.K. Mishra
Kaveri Books, New Delhi, India.

Indians Around the Pamir Plateau in the First Decade of the Nineteenth Century : A View of Contemporary Russians

21

Surendra Gopal

By the seventeenth century several European countries had established sea-trade with the Orient especially with India. The Tsarist Russia could not do so because of her geographical location. As the century advanced, she felt increasingly hurt because of her inability to share the profits of Indian and Eastern trade with the western European nations.

The Russian contacts with India were older than that of the nations of the north-western Europe, be it England, France, or Holland, etc. They had their own distinguishing features. Afanasi Nikitin had visited India in 1469[1] and by 1630s the Indians had appeared in the Russian capital Moscow[2] and its other cities.[3] Soon a colony of Indians emerged in Astrakhan.[4] No Indian was present in any other European country such as England, Holland or France, etc., despite their continuously increasing and intensive trade contact with India. The presence of Indians on the Russian soil further stimulated the Tsarist desire to have direct access to India, Indian commodities and Indian trade.

Aware that they could not reach India by the sea-route because of geographical constraints, the Russian authorities tried to collect authentic and detailed information about India, Indians and routes to India from Indians, from Russian merchants and officers in touch with Indians or working in areas bordering Persia and Central Asia. They appointed envoys to the Mughal court in the hope that they would bring in first-hand information about India. One managed to travel to the peninsular India where the last Great Mughal Emperor Aurangzeb was holding his court.[5] Diplomatic relations were not established and the Russian quest for direct access to India through Central Asia/Iran continued.

Peter the Great persisted with this dream in the beginning of the eighteenth century. He decided on a route which would emanate from the shores of the Caspian and the Aral Seas and enable Russian ships to sail down the Oxus river (which emptied into the Aral Sea) and then reach India via Afghanistan.[6]

With this end in view the fortress of Orenburg, established in the Kazakh steppe on the banks of river Ural[7] in 1735, was sought to be developed as as centre for trade with Central Asia and further on to India. But here again they did not meet with the expected success. The Russian search for a route to India via Central Asia had now a new dimension.

The Russians in the eighteenth century even tried to find out a sea-route to India but geography thwarted their efforts.[8] Russian entry into the Black Sea at the cost of the Ottoman empire was thwarted by the European powers who felt Russian competition would threaten their interests.

ministry called them to St. Petersberg and the Foreign Minister N.P. Rumyantsev asked them to proceed once again and they left Semiplatinsk on 4 August 1808. In course of three years they visited Kulja, Aksu, Kashgar, Yarkand and Kashmir and returned to Semiplatinsk in March 1811.[23]

Rafailov submitted his first report to Glazenag, the local military commander which was forwarded to the Russian Foreign Minister and he was asked to proceed to St. Petersberg along with his goods.[24] Glazenag in his second letter forwarded the detailed account given by Rafailov of the cities and regions which he had visited.

The Report of Rafailov enhanced the confidence of the Russian government in him and convinced them that India could be reached by this route. He was again asked to lead another caravan along with goods worth 110306 roubles and 90 kopecks.[25]

The government had so much confidence in him that he started his visit to the region with goods worth 160,000 roubles and was given a letter for the ruler of Tibet.[26] He intended to go to Kashmir but returned without visiting Kashmir as he was able to sell all his goods procure Kashmiri goods in 'Tibet'.[27] He returned via Kulja to Semiplatinsk.

For all that he was doing for Russian trade, Rafailov wanted reward and recognition from the Tsar, who made him a commercial counsellor in 1817.[28] In 1819 he was honoured by the Tsar; he was made a Court Counsellor.[29] His stock at the court of St. Petersberg remained high and he was asked in 1819 to undertake another journey to deliver a letter to Maharaja Ranjit Singh, the ruler of the Punjab from the Russian Foreign Minister, Nesselrode.

This time it was to be more than a commercial expedition. He was to carry a letter for the ruler of 'Tibet'.

The Tsarist government sought an alliance with Ranjit Singh and wanted to develop bilateral trade relations. This letter never reached Ranjit Singh as Rafailov died during his trip before reaching the Punjab.

The Reports of Rafailov shed interesting light on the commercial activities of Indians in the region of Eastern Turkistan and Tibet, the importance of this trade and the routes that the traders followed.

In the report which Rafailov submitted after completing the first trip in 1808, he says that in the city of Aks or Aksu, he found merchants from Tashkent, Bukhara, Kashmir, India and also the 'wild Kirghizs'.[30] All the merchants were taxed at the rate of 'one piece out of thirty' and 'one animal out of thirty' but the Kashmiris were required to pay 'one piece out of forty-one' an 'one animal out of forty-one'.[31]

Obviously there was a long tradition of the Kashmiri and Indian merchants undertaking this long and arduous trip to Aksu, otherwise they would not have been given these concessions. Probably this was the northern most point reached by them. We do not get any idea of the religious persuasion of these Kashmiri and Indian merchants.

The road to Aksu from Kashmir ran through the intervening areas of Laddakh, Yarkand and Kashgar.

Yarkand was another city frequented by traders from Kashmir. In course of a subsequent visit to the city in 1813, Rafailov met with a Kashmiri merchant from whom he purchased Kashmiri shawls and spent all the money he had.[32] As a result, he had to cancel his proposed visit to Kashmir since his requirements had been met and he had no more money to invest.

The Kashmiri merchant was prepared to visit Russia in his company but had to give up the project as we was called back to Kashmir.

We come across another interesting fact. Rafailov after Yarkand fails to identify a place by its name. He describes the places by the name of the region to which they belonged. Thus Leh in

Laddakh and other contiguous places are described as Tibet all through. When he left Laddakh and entered the Kashmir valley, he does not mention the name of any city. All through he gives his impression in terms of the region. The description shows how rudimentary the knowledge of the geography of this region was among the Russians and also among the merchants visiting this area of Laddakh and the Kashmir valley.

He spoke of Tibet. We are not clear about the exact place he visited. But it seems he was referring to Laddakh.[33]

It took him thirty-four days to reach Laddakh.[34] From Yarkand to Laddakh a distance of about 100 versts was flat but thereafter he crossed several mountains, Karakuram (Black stone), Muzdaban (mountain of snow), Karaul Dabam (mountain of watchmen), Aktan (white mountain), Karatan (black mountain) and Kizyltan (red mountain). These mountain ranges were very high and 'some of them were perpetually covered by snow'. There were hardly any forests. Those that existed lay along small rivers and were met only after a day's or two journey. There was no grass and hence travellers carried 'barley and fodder for their horses'.[35]

According to him the entire area between Yarkand and 'Tibet' was full of mountains and was uninhabited.

The 'city of Tibet' was free, not subservient to any power and the ruler was called 'Raja'.

The people of 'Tibet' professed a religion which believed in idol-worship. They were Buddhists.

There were very few villages around 'The City' and there was very little cultivation because of unavailability of cultivable land.

The air was heavy and harmful. As a result, according to Rafailov, the people were weak and did not have a good colour on the face.' The local people agreed that the climate of the land where they lived was not healthy.

The city itself was economically in very bad shape. It was economically sustained because of the export of valuable wool to Kashmir. Similarly, the people earned some money because of the visits of traders from 'Kashmir, Hasa, Yarkand and India.'[36]

The wool was purchased by Kashmiris for the manufacture of shawl. The quantum of wool thus sold amounted to 7000 puds each year.

The government charged customs duties from traders who passed through the city. The people arranged for the stay of the traders in their houses.

The people were not war-like. According to Rafailov 'they did not know even the meaning of war.'[37]

Rafailov left for Kashmir after staying for eight days in Laddakh and after obtaining a pass-port from the local ruler.

The journey to Kashmir took seventeen days and he passed seventeen villages. Up to the place 'Drast', the people belonged to the Tibetan race and thereafter they were all Kashmiris.

The people in general were poor. They were either farmers or were engaged in animal-husbandry. Each place contained between 20 and 30 houses.

The route from 'Tibet' to Kashmir was hilly, full of forests, cultivated land and plenty of orchards.

He correctly stated that the valley was under the sovereignty of the Afghans but on account of the civil war raging among them, 'the local governor withheld the payment of the annual tribute of 15,000,000 roubles'.[38] The figure was only a guess-work.

Then he goes on to say that this region was divided into two by the 'river Vernak'.[39]

The valley had a number of cities which had '1,00,000 houses', out of which '20,000 houses' belonged to 'people of the Indian law'.[40] He obviously means non-Muslims, i.e. Hindus.

The houses were small, each meant for only one family and these could not be compared to the large European houses.

The population here consisted of people from 'Turkey, Persia, India, Afghanistan, Yarkand and Bukhara'. Rafailov's observation was perfectly correct in this regard as merchants from all the adjoining regions frequented the Kashmir valley.

Without naming the chief city in the valley, he went on to say that it had '20,000 looms.'[41] The government received an income of '1,200,000 roubles' from taxes levied on them.[42]

The city itself was not fortified. But the place where the governor lived was surrounded by a brick-wall. The army consisted of cavalry, numbering between ten and twelve thousand and infantry between eight and ten thousand. They had fire-arms but 'these were locally made after the Asian fashion and were without locks into wicks'.[43]

The majority of the Kashmiris were Muslims and some of them professed the 'Indian faith', i.e. Hinduism.[44]

The cities and other areas of Kashmir were surrounded by high mountains.

The people of the country were 'beautiful, healthy, clever and enterprising'. They were hospitable.[45]

There were no factories for making any variety of metal.

The local authorities charged the same customs duties on all goods either imported or exported by the merchants.[46]

They did not charge any duty on either the import or export of gold and silver.[47]

Rafailov returned to Semiplatinsk from Kashmir by the same route by which he came. In all he calculated the distance to be 2010 versts to be covered in sixty-seven days.[48]

He described this route running through the towns of 'small Bukhara' i.e. eastern Turkistan as the suitable one because one could easily find food and also because there was peace and 'no disquiet' among the local population'.[49]

He was keen that Russia should bring all these areas under its protection.[50] He averred that the task was easy as the 'Chinese authorities lacked courage'.[51]

After subsequent visit in '1813 to Kashmir Rafailov presented another detailed account of the various routes which could be taken by the merchants going from Russia to India.

He also analysed the political situation in the area. His aim was to assure Tsarist authorities that the advance of the Russians would be welcomed and the local rulers would submit to the protection afforded by the Tsar. He dangled the hope of large profits accruing from the unhindered and increased trade with the region.

In a subsequent note on the routes to India, which were fairly detailed he again dwelt upon the importance of Indian trade and the activities of the Indian traders in the area.

For example, when he wrote in detail about Laddakh (called by him 'Tibet'), he clearly stated that the route from Bukhara to Kashmir lay through Laddakh. The Raja, out of fear for the might of the ruler of Kashmir and also because of the advantages he gained as a result of transit trade passing via the territory to Kashmir, submitted to the governor of Kashmir.[52] His income consisted solely of customs duties imposed on caravans passing through his territory and on fine wool carried by the Kashmiris for the manufacture of shawls and other woolen clothes.

He pointed out that the Laddakhis knew nothing about warfare and did not possess fire-arms. The ruler of Kashmir who kept friendly ties with the Laddakhi ruler, however, would not come to his aid in the event of any external attack.[53]

Rafailov was very clear about the fact that the roots of prosperity of Kashmir lay in

Laddakh since three-fourth of the Kashmiris was engaged in weaving shawls and other woolen garments and one-fourth earned profits from selling them.[54] The wool came from Laddakh.

Rafailov was sure that if Russia extended it hands of friendship to the Sikh ruler of the Punjab, he would welcome it.[55] He expressed the fear that Britishers, who had already occupied a major portion of India, were preparing in the near future to extinguish the freedom of the Punjab.[56] He even mentioned Delhi, the fate of the Marathas, who had been driven out by the Britishers.

Rafailov suggested that imperial Russian authorities should enter into correspondence and establish friendly relations with 'the Afghans, the Marathas and the successors of Tipoo Sultan'.[57] Obviously impressed by the description and analysis of the prevailing political and economic situations, the imperial Russian authorities entrusted him with a latter for Maharaja Ranjit Singh. As stated earlier, Rafailov died in course of the journey before reaching the Punjab and the letter could never be delivered.

Rafailov's accounts of his journeys and the circumstances surrounding it clearly show that the imperial Russian authorities were extremely keen to establish stable trade contacts with India by the overland route even by passing the oft-used road running through Bukhara, Balkh, Kabul, Peshawar, etc., if that was feasible in spite of the barriers of high mountains surrounding Laddakh and Kashmir and the barren terrain through which it passed. The caravans carrying merchandise would be, in future, escorted by armed contingents if such a course suggested itself after the failure of diplomatic overture.

The Russian advances drew appropriate response on the part of the British authorities safely ensconced on the Indian subcontinent. 'The Great Game on High Pamirs' now began.

The Malcolm mission was the precursor of a series of diplomatic missions and agents in the guise of merchants or travellers sent by the British throughout the century to gauge the Russian designs. Like the Russians they also used local Indians (both Hindus and Muslims).[59]

To justify their actions the British portrayed the growing Russian interest directed against the 'jewel in the crown'. For the whole of the nineteenth century, British policy in India was determined and influenced by Russophobia.

The search for markets culminated in imperial and colonial rivalry which in the nineteenth century wrote the history of Central Asia, Eastern Turkistan, Tibet and other adjoining regions of India.

References

1. Khalfin N.A. and Shastitko P.M. (eds), *Rossiya i Indiya*, Moskva, 1980, p. 35. Some scholars believe that Nikitin arrived in India in 1471.
2. Goldberg N.M. (ed.) *Russko-Indiiskiya Otnosheniya V XVII v.*, Moskva, 1958 (henceforth cited as R-I. OV XVIII v.)
3. *Ibid.*, doc. no. 38.
4. Yukht A.I., "Indiiskaya koloniya v Astrakhani, "*Voprosy Istorii*, 1957, no. 3.
5. In the seventeenth century the Tsars sent four diplomatic missions to India. *Rossiya i Indiya*, p. 45; *Ibid.* p. 63. Aurangzeb received the Russian envoy Semen Melenki.
6. *Rossiaya i Indiya*, pp. 75-76.
7. The river falls into the Caspian Sea.
8. *Rossiya i Indiya*, p. 77; Antonova (ed), *R.I.O. v XVIII V.*, Moskva, 1965 docs. 175-77.
9. Hopkirk Peter, *The Great Game*, OUP, 1991, pp. 21, 26, 27.
10. Hopkirk, pp. 31-2.
11. *Rossiya i Indiya*, pp. 80, 98, 99.

12. *Rossiya i India*, p. 101. He thrice went to India.
13. *Ibid.*; During, his third journey (1822-23) he spent 'five years in India'. He returned via-Lahore, Kashmir, Kabul and Bukhara to Orenburg and dictated his memoirs. Ibid.
14. *Ibid.*, p. 101.
15. *Ibid.*
16. Shastitko P.M. (ed), *Rossiskiye Puteshestvenniki v Indii v XIX-nachalo* XX v., Moskva, 1990, p. 14.
17. *Rossiya i Indiya*, p. 101.
18. *Rossiiskiya...*, pp. 15, 16.
19. *Ibid.*, p. 14; *Rossiya i Indiya*, p. 12.
20. *Rossiskiye ....*, p. 14.
21. *Rossiya i Indiya*, pp. 101-102.
22. *Rossiskiye ....*, p. 22. His companion Mohammed Zugur, however, reached Kashmir and spent there ten months and purchased shawls and spent all the money left by Rafailov.
23. *Rossiskiye, ...*, p. 14.
24. *Ibid.*
25. *Ibid.*, p. 15.
26. *Ibid.*, p. 18.
27. *Ibid.*, p. 19.
28. *Ibid.*, p. 20.
29. *Ibid.*
30. *Rossiskiye....*, p. 33.
31. *Ibid.*, p. 33.
32. *Ibid.*, p. 75.
33. *Ibid.*, p. 35, f. n. 10.
34. *Ibid.*, 35.
35. *Ibid.*, p. 35.
36. *Ibid.*, p. 35.
37. *Ibid.*
38. *Ibid.*, p. 35.
39. *Ibid.*, p. 36.
40. *Ibid.*
41. *Ibid.*
42. *Ibid.*
43. *Ibid.*, p. 36.
44. *Ibid.*
45. *Ibid.*
46. *Ibid.*, p. 36.
47. *Ibid.*
48. *Ibid.*, p. 39.
49. *Ibid.*
50. *Ibid.*, p. 40.
51. *Ibid.*
52. *Ibid.*, p. 44.
53. *Ibid.*
54. *Ibid.*, p. 44.
55. *Ibid.*, pp. 44-45.
56. *Ibid.*, p. 45.
57. *Ibid.*, p. 45.
58. Shastitko, "Missiya Mekhti Rafialova k Ranjit Singhu", *Sovetskoye Vostokovedeniye* 1957, No. 4.
59. Indian agents such as Meer Izzatullah and Hafiz Mohammed Fazil Khan had been sent. Later on, Moorcroft went to Leh and Kashmir. He could not journey to Yarkand, Hopkirk, pp. 92-95. He was in Leh when Rafailov unexpectedly died. He reported the event to his superiors in Calcutta.

Aspects of Indian History and Historiography
Editor : P.K. Mishra
Kaveri Books, New Delhi, India.

India's Foreign Policy in the Post-Cold War Era : Can it be Reconstructed to Build a South Asian Community

22

Jayanta Kumar Ray

When we think of India's foreign policy in the post-cold war era, we have to point to actualities as also potentialities, to what has been happening, and what can happen, in pursuit of the familiar goals of regional/world peace and stability, economic prosperity, environmental upgradation, and reduction of inequalities between the rich and poor states. Before we attempt this analysis, however, we have to deal with the widely held view that the end of the cold war heralds a fundamental change in the conduct of international relations. In my opinion, this is a vital but not a fundamental change. For, the fundamental feature of international relations remains largely intact: it is the pursuit—sometimes half-hearted, sometimes determined— by the ruling circle of a state of its perceived self-interest (rightly or wrongly equated to national interest), by means, fair or foul, and with mixed results of success and failure. The international military action in Kuwait in the 1990s amply demonstrates the persistence of this fundamental characteristic of international relations: if Kuwait produced only dates (as in the 1940s), and not oil (an article of vital interest to big powers), the United States would not have dispatched its troops to Kuwait, whereas Japan and Germany would not have agreed to supply the financial prop för this military operation. In sharp contrast, there is virtually no international action in Myanmar of Fiji, where human rights are being violated for years in the most ruthless fashion.

In these circumstances, India has to conduct its foreign policy with that unemotional pragmatism, dynamism and resilience, which were often missing in the cold war days, when, contrary to the principal tenet of nonalignment, India could not afford to exercise much of independence of opinion (far less of action) in response to such major world issues as Afghanistan or Kampuchea. Just as the reaction of two super powers to such issues was almost predetermined, the Indian response too (of course verbal) was nearly prefabricated. There was not much scope of exercise of diplomatic skills/innovations on specific occasions—except that of the well-cultivated command over the comfortably elastic English language. It was an easy—if at times dull—world of habit forming stereotypes, of reassuring predictability. This expectedly gave way to a sense of unease at the termination of the cold war—perhaps also to a sense of distress among pro-Soviet decision makers, which recoiled on India by creating a diplomatic mess at the time of the failed anti-Gorbachev coup in Moscow.

Fortunately, the Indian diplomatic establishment could recover itself at an early date, provided examples of pragmatism and innovativeness, and aroused hopes for the future. Take, for instance, the extension of full diplomatic recognition to Israel by India. India had full diplomatic relations even with countries with whom (unlike Israel) she had direct conflicts of interest as also wars. In fact, this non-recognition of Israel was one of the most outrageous components of India's foreign policy in the cold outrageous components of India's foreign policy in the cold war era, that could not be defended even by an unqualified concern for the fate of Palestinians. After all, the Indian policy was irrelevant to any solution of the Palestinian problem. In contrast, complete diplomatic relations with Israel could have enabled India to play a useful part in shaping a solution to this problem. Moreover, India missed the opportunity to utilise Israel's services for mitigating the adverse impact upon India of America's South Asia policy in the cold war days.

This leads conveniently to an analysis of India's relations with the United States. This was one of inevitable but distasteful dependence, and, in the cold war days, we sometimes failed to restrain our inferiority complex, and indulged in intemperate criticisms of the US, which only hurt our interests. In the post-cold war era, apparently, India has been able to overcome this diplomatic immaturity, and adopt the path of low tension and high cooperation. So, when Cuba asked for 500,000 tons of wheat and 100,000 tons of rice, whereas the USA desired that India should send nothing, India wisely dispatched ten thousand tons of rice. The amount was too small to arouse the hostility of the United States. But it pleased Cuba, a great champion of the enormous bandwagon called the Nonalignment Movement. It also placated some opposition parties in India, to whom Cuba is the sole surviving idol. At the Earth Summit in Rio De Janeiro, where the USA was almost totally isolated, the Indian Prime Minister ciriticised the USA in a firm but restrained manner. In the pre-cold war days, India probably would have grabbed this opportunity to lash out at the USA with vituperative scorn, and enjoyed the satisfaction accruing to a successful college debater. When, again, the United States imposed a five per cent tariff on Indian pharmaceutical exports to the USA, and clamped some restrictions on the Indian Space Research Organisation for a rocket technology deal with Russia, India's response was critical but dignified. Despite provocations by some opposition parties, India refused to cancel Indo-US military exercises, and laid an institutional foundation for future interaction.

These currently visible signs of maturity, pragmatism and resilience in India's foreign policy embolden me to expect that in the near future India may—or should—be able to take some significant steps whereby India could build a wide ranging economic-strategic consensus/ cooperation with the USA as also other members of Group of Seven, and use this umbrella to accelerate the formation of a South Asian Community on the model of the European Community. If India can achieve this cooperation/understanding with the G-7, it can reduce its defence budget, prompt other South Asian countries to follow suit, and replace mistrust by trust, confrontation by fraternity.

The accomplishment of comprehensive accommodation with the Group of Seven may necessitate some policy initiatives by India, notably in the field of nuclear policy and external/ internal economic policy. In order to win the confidence of the G-7, India can agree to full-scope safeguards for its nuclear installations. This will not require as much of psychological-political adjustment as in the case of signing the Nuclear Nonproliferation Treaty. Moreover, acceptance of full-scope International Atomic Energy Agency safeguards will entitle India to play an important part in reshaping the NPT, e.g. in stopping the trade in bomb-grade plutonium. Currently, the critical time for India in the exercise of real nuclear option is estimated at 6-12 months. Acceptance of full-scope IAEA safeguards will only add a few days to this critical time. On this issue, India can learn from Russia, which has dismantled its mammoth apparatus of nuclear terror. Russia now may take several weeks to launch missiles (and not 15 minutes as before). America can now launch missiles in a week (and not in 15 minutes as in the past). China too has taken missiles off the alert status. Russia has had to undergo a severe pain of comprehensive adjustment. In contrast, India's strain in adjustment to full-scope IAEA safeguards will be somewhat insignificant.

In this connection, it is interesting to recall that Iraq, an NPT signatory, could go ahead with a nuclear weapons programme till it committed the indiscretion of occupying Kuwait. South Africa confessed, before it decided to sign the NPT, that, despite 115 visits by IAEA inspectors, it could manufacture six nuclear devices. Evidently, therefore , acceptance of full-scope IAEA safeguards by India will not have any adverse impact on India's civilian nuclear programme in which it has made enormous investments, and which is now attracting the belated (if grudging) support of some environmentalists on account of the dangerous depletion of the ozone layer. On the contrary, once India wins the trust of the G-7, its civilian nuclear programme (as also many other programmes) are likely to receive a big technological boost. To take just one instance, in the United States, 70 per cent of computer software are prepared by Indians. But these can be sold to India only after India revises its nuclear policy.

The change in economic policy has of course to accompany the change in nuclear policy if India has to make rapid advances towards building a state of mass prosperity instead of mass poverty. True, India has made some adjustments towards economic liberalisation, and, for instance, permitted 51 per cent equity participation by foreign investors. But the habits of Indian state bureaucracy die hard. The red tape is very strong. Foreign investors cannot commence operations without middlemen or fixers who have developed mutually profitable contacts with bureaucrats over decades. Consequently, India cannot even attract foreign investments worth $ 1 billion annually, whereas countries like Malaysia, Singapore and Thailand can attract $ 3 billion plus. Even Sri Lanka, amidst a largescale civil conflict, attracts more of foreign investment than India, because, among other things, it has cut down the red tape, offered off-shore banking facilities, so that one does not have to go as far as Switzerland to open numbered bank accounts. China, too, has abolished the red tape in coastal regions, and permits 100 per cent equity participation by foreign investors. But India lags behind, probably dreaming of a socialistic pattern of mass poverty postulated in the middle 1950s.

I would have been personally happy if India relied upon its own resources to replace mass poverty by mass prosperity. It is, however, not possible to do so because India cannot reform the huge state enterprises, which have worshipped the trinity of wastage, inefficiency and corruption. Without largescale reforms of these dinosaur enterprises, adequate resources cannot be generated. But it is dangerous even to attempt this largescale reform, because the Indian state bureaucracy, e.g. the nationalised bank bureaucracy, may be provoked to disrupt the entire economy by the nonviolent means of strikes and go-slow tactics. We are, therefore, compelled to permit the Indian state bureaucracy to wallow in its "socialistic" or "state capitalistic" privileges, and allocate as much as 100,000 crores of rupees for public sector undertakings during the eighth five year plan. If one can get rid of doctrinaire fanaticism about keeping the state strong, and read audit reports on state undertakings, one will be struck by the utter absence of accountability of state enterprises (barring a notoriously few agencies, which deserve, but will not receive, much greater patronage). Many social scientists, who are on the periphery of the state bureaucracy, and share some of its privileges (minus monitoring), do not allow their conscience to be stirred by the phenomenon that the Indian state is so powerful that it can keep the economy weak, perpetuate mass poverty, and preserve the privileges of a tiny minority.

It is in these circumstances that I plead for assigning a priority to economic diplomacy in India's foreign policy in the post-cold war era, and to attracting foreign investments, especially investments by foreign institutional investors. It is a pity that the Indian Government is deeply pleased to receive a few hundred million dollars from the World Bank, and considers it a great achievement. But this sum is insignificant, if one considers the resources at the disposal of the FIIs. In case FIIs allocate even 1 per cent of their resources for investment in South Asia, the available sum will amount to $ 200 billion. If India can attract a substantial portion of this sum, it can not only transform mass poverty into mass prosperity, but also undertake vast projects for the generation of electricity, flood control, navigation, pisiculture and environmental upgradation, which will enormously benefit other countries, e.g. Nepal, Bangladesh, and bring nearer the goal of a South Asian Community.

Evidently, FIIs may not take the risk of investing immense sums in enormous multi-country projects of South Asia without being assured of a strategic stability. That is an important reason (apart from the need to curtail defence expenditure for the generation of developmental resources without any adverse impact on security) why I have advocated strategic proximity between India and the G-7. To embrace this notion of strategic proximity is possibly to show a disrespect for that sacred but elusive, that undefinable yet unchallengeable, hymn called nonalignment. Acceptance of this notion may be interpreted as a sort of defeat by some Indian decision makers and social scientists. Yet, in terms of potentialities for good, to borrow the title of a book by an Oxford philosopher-cum-novelist, Iris Murdoch, it will be a 'a fairly honourable defeat'.

Actually, the Government of India (and other South Asian countries) should pay more attention to retrieving their honour in other ways. For instance, they should stop dishonourable practices in the shape of undue restrictions on commerce which compel South Asian businessmen to fulfil the legitimate needs of the people by astonishingly largescale unofficial trade. It does not shame the votaries of strong Government in India to note that businessmen in South Asia are far ahead of Governments in promoting the goal of a South Asian Community. Let Governments try to catch up, and prove themselves worthy of honour. Let the Indian and other South Asian Governments also contemplate that largescale collaboration with the G-7 may enable us to accelerate a cultural revolution in South Asia by means of the revolution in high speed communications and transportation (as argued succinctly by Japan's Murata Keijiro, and as evidenced already in Japan).

Nevertheless, initiatives by India (and other South Asian countries) may not suffice. The G-7 countries should also exercise realism (if not generosity) in developing the poverty-ridden regions of the world, and lessening rich-poor disparities. Otherwise, such unwelcome phenomena as environmental degradation and terrorism may rise, in spite of restrictions on migration from poorer regions. Terrorism by migrants may exacerbate indigenous terrorism, and multiply such ghastly incidents as the April explosion in London's financial centre. If the nervous reactions of the people working in this area of London, and discussions on preventive measures are indicators, the affluent in the G-7 countries may have to live in fear, almost in a state of lifelessness, like the rich South African Whites in Nadine Gordimer's novel. The Late Bourgeois World, unless they do what they are able to do, i.e. take determined steps to diminish rich-poor disparities at home and abroad.

Aspects of Indian History and Historiography
Editor : P.K. Mishra
Kaveri Books, New Delhi, India.

Origin and Development of the Arakanese Settlements in Bangladesh : A Study of Arakan-Bangladesh Relations (1760-1825)

23

Abdul Mabud Khan

Although a state of the union of Burma, now known as Myanmar[1] situated in its western parts, Arakan considerably influenced the south and south eastern parts of Bengal, now included in Bangladesh since the earliest time both politically and culturally. At different stages of history, several groups of people[2] from Arakan migrated to this region and settled down permanently in this area of Bangladesh. Among the migrants, the *Maghs* constitute one of the major tribes comprising two groups the *Marmas* of the hill regions and the *Rakhaines* of the plains.

The *Maghs* are chiefly found in three districts namely Cox's Bazar, Banderban and Patuakhali but a small section is met with also at Khagrachari.[3] The total population of the *Maghs*[4] is about 35, 348. In this paper, an attempt has been made to trace the origin and development of the Arakanese settlements in Cox's Bazar District.

Cox's bazar, noted for its scenic beauty, is the head quarters of the district of the same name which on the east is surrounded by Banderban district and the Naaf river and on the south and the west by the Bay of Bengal and in the north it is attached to Chittagong district. The total number of the *Maghs*[5] of this district is about 7, 167.

Tribes in general have two names; one is given by the neighbours of the areas in which they live and the other is used by themselves for self-identity. Both types of names generally signify certain characteristics or qualities of a given tribe. There are also some appellations which are resented by the tribes as un-complimentary. The Arakanese of Cox's Bazar district have two names (a) *Magh* (b) *Rakhaine*.

Magh

The Arakanese of Cox's Bazar district are generally known as *Maghs*. As to the generic nomenclature *Magh* which is of uncertain origin,[6] it is to be noted that it is applied to the Buddhists of Arakan and those residing in south eastern parts of Bangladesh. According to Phayre, the name *Magh* originated from the ruling race of Magadha and relying on a Burmese oral tradition he says that they were originally a Kshatriya tribe of northern India and migrated from Magadha to Burma through eastern Bengal. Subsequently, from Burma they spread over Arakan.[7]

In ancient time, several groups of Hindu and Buddhist missionaries went to Arakan for preaching their respective faiths and in course of time, some of them settled there.[8] In the struggle among different religious groups that followed, only Buddhists survived with the support of the ruling class of the land. Probably, a section of the Indian imigrants who were merged into the local population were from Magadha, the land of Buddhas Enlightenment. And they asserted themselves as superior in status to the rest of the population of Arakan; most of whom were animists by faith. It is not unlikely that the imigrants from Magadha gave rise to the ethnic nomenclature *Magh* which ultimately became a generic appellation of the people of Arakan. A cultural intercourse between south-India and the coastal regions of Arakan is also believed. Harvey, for example, says that Indian immigrants in Lower Burma came by sea from Madras and seeks to connect Talaing form Telingana, a region of Andraprades.

The movement of Indian culture to the coastal regions of Arakan seems to have started before the Christian era. Among the old testimonies regarding Arakan's association with Magadha is that of Daulat Kazi (1622-38), a well Known Poet, according to whom, the rulers of *Rosnga* (i.e. Arakan) belonged to the Magadha dynasty and were Buddhists by faith. The poet in his *Sati Moyna* frequently uses the terms *Magadhar Pati* and *Magadha-rajya* to signify the kings and the Kingdom of Arakan respectively.[9] Alaol another Bangalee poet of the 17th century who spent most of his time in Arakan used *Moghi* Era to point out the date of his work. All these show that Arakan was known as *Mogh* Kingdom in medieval times.

The Kings of Arakan might have traced their ancestry from Magadha but the connection of the whole population of Arakan with Magadha is uncertain. The Arakanese were primarily of the Mongolid origin and lately had intermixture of the Austroloid and other ethnic elements but not any element which can ethnically be called *Magh*. Hence, perhaps, the Arakanese residents of Bangladesh argu that as there was no race in Arakan called *Magh*, their ancestors who came from Arakan can never be termed as such. They further protest to be designated as *Magh* which they regard as highly derogatory on its being synonymous with piracy, depredation and lawlessness. They point out that a small segment of the Arakanes in the middle ages adopted piracy as a means of piracy with the Portuguese collaborators but not the entire people. And viewed as a whole, the Arakanese are among civilised nations of the world. Historically, this claim of the Arakanese is attested by cultural attainments and monumental relics that exist in Arakan. Besides, the Association of the Arakanese with marauding activities extends from about the beginning of the fourteenth century to the first quarter of the eighteenth century i.e. upto the death of Mushid Qulikhan in June,[10] 1772. And further as said above, only a small segment of the Arakanese participated in practical activities.

It may be pointed out that some appellations given by the outsiders to a tribe is misunderstood. For example, the Indian immigrants residing in Burma known as *Kola* (i.e. *Kula*) derived from Indian (sanskrit and Sanskritie) word *Kula* which the Burmese take to mean a man of higher status.[11] But the Indian immigrants donot liked to be called *Kola* since they take this word as associated with the black (kāla) complexion of their body. Similarly, the Arakanese residents of Bangladesh, as noted above, take the term *Magh* as derogatory although originally it denotes a person of higher status having its Kshatriya and Mayadha origin.

Rakhaine

The *Magh* residents of Cox's Bazar identify themselves as *Rakhaines*. It has been held by Phayre that the name, *Rakhaine* comes from that of a tribe in Arakan Known as *Rakhaing* and from that of their country designated as *Rakhainepray*; the said tribe supposedly being the aboriginal of the land.[12] Phayre further says that during his stay in Arakan he saw a group of people at Pegu known as *Rakhaine* who according to an oral tradition protected their aged-hold culture with zeal and sincerity and had no connection with Buddlistic faith. These *Rakhaines* (Sanskrit *Rakshapura*),[13] and so, he is inclined to trace the derivations of the term "Arakan" from *Rakhaing*, the archaic form of modern *Rakhaine*.

According to Muslim tradition, the ancient mane of Arakan is *Arikhongpray*, (i.e. land of wealth)[14] which in its turn comes from the Arabic word "*Al-Aukun*.[15] On the basis of this oral tradition, some Muslims seek to designate Arakan as *Arikistan*.[16] Historically, Muslim settlements in Arakan are not traceable before the eight country. While Philologically, *Arikistan* is a corrupt from of *Rakhaing* and hence, some Muslims of Arakan want to disignate themselves as *Rohangya* claiming a separate indentity from the Buddlists who call themselves as *Rakhaings*. The facts remains that the Muslim nomenclature *Rohangya* is derivable from the Buddlist designation *Rakhaing* and in support of this, it may be mentioned that *Rohang* a Tibeto-Burman word, itself denotes Arakan, the land of both *Rakhaings* and *Rohangyas*.[17] Incidentally, the people of Chittagong district even to day use the term *Rohang* and *Rohangya* to mean Arakan and the Arakanese Muslims. Words like *Rohang, Rosanga* and Rokam denote Arakan or its part are siginificant.[18] Thus, *Rakhainepray* the original name of Arakan whose inhâbitants were older than *Rohang* seem to be the known *Rakhaine* Country. On the basis of this historical background, the Magh residents of Cox's Bazar district like to introduce themselves by the ethno-cultural designation `*Rakhaine*'.

Some scholars argu[19] that Arakanese colonies grew up in Bangladesh when south and south-eastern parts of Bengal, present day Bangladesh was under the Arakanes rule (1459-1666 A.D.) But they donot give any positive historical evidence in support of their argument. There might have developed some Arakanese settlements during that period but these settlements are not historically traceable. However, for the main Arakanese settlement in Bangladesh we have definite historical evidence pointing to a much later date i.e. by the end of the 18th century.

After the battle of Plassey, in 1760 a treaty was signed between the East India Company and Nawab Mir Kasim. According to the provisions of this treaty, the tracts later known as the districts of Burdwan, Midnapur and Chittagong were ceeded to the East India Company. Henry Verlest took the charge of the administration of Chittagong district and decided *interalia* to develop friendly relations with Arkan and to put a stop, to the depradation of the Arakanese pirates. Verlest was not fully aware of the limits of the territory under his jurisdiction; Ramu and Teknaf were parts of the British territory and this came to be known only in 1790.[20] During the time of Natial Bateman (1775-77), the successor of Verlest, a group of about two thousand Arakanese arrived at place called Borpholaung near to the later day Cox's Bazar; Bateman allowed them to settle at *pargana* Anandapur, *Mouza* Chambal, Puichari, Sonaichari, Lolakota and Manikpur under the leadership of Taj Mohammed, Atikullah, Takur Chand, Sadullah, Azizullah, Fakir Mohammed and Rosan.[21] Bateman invited the refugee leaders at Chittagong town in order to know the real cause of their migration. They told him that the political instability forced them to leave their mother land. While he allowed them to stay at the above noted place included in the Joynagar Mahal (i.e. a revenue unit); he added at the same time that the leaders would be treated as the sub-ordinate Zaminders of the said mahal. This order of the collector Bateman did not satisfy them because, in Arakan they were in a better administrative position and hence, with the exception of Taj Mohammed all left Chittagong while some died meanwhile. Taj Mohammed also revised his decision and followed his friends. The common immigrants also followed their leaders expectedly. The important cause of the en masse departure, if we rely on the English collector was the infertile soil which was covered with stones and other hard materials, as well as their failure to enlist the support of the local population.[22]

From 1775 to 1784 there was no exodus of the Arakanese population. By the end of 1784 the second phase of the Arakanese migration began when Arakan was subjugated by the Burmese monarch Bodawpaya (1782-1819).[23]

The main reason of this migration was the tyrannical Burmese rule in Arakan.[24] Indeed, at one stage the Arakanese found it better to leave their country and to settle in the not far off British territory where they would at last, live the life of human without fear. As a result, migration began in different weaves making Arakan a desolate country. Being in geographical proximity, Chittagong become a land of preference and from 1784 to 1794 nearly two-third population of Arakan settled in the south-eastern part of Chittagong now known a Cox's Bazar district. In one year we are told, a body of not less than ten thousand entered Chittagont.[25] And according to the testimony of captain Cox' in 1799 forty to fifty thousand Arakanese entered this district.[26] The British government, however, granted them asylum and provided food partly on humanitarian ground and partly to increase the population of the sparsely populated areas. By 1814 the Arakanese refugees within eighteen kilometers of Ramu near Cox's Bazar was estimated[27] at about 100,000. Thereafter another phase of migration is heard of Hlawa Morang, a relative of the last Arakanese king Tamada with 3500 followers crossed the river Naaf and took shelter in the British territory; in course of time, his descendants became the Zaminders of Neela and Teknaf; his grandson Charipru Chaudhury acted as an Honorary Magistrate for some time. During the period (1784-1814) five thousand refugees who had taken shelter at Harbang moved to Taknaf for settlement[28] under the leadership of Nga Chin Pyan popularly known as king Berrig. The British government granted ninety sp. kilometers of land to them as a reward for their services in the First[29] Anglo-Burmese War (1824-25).

One of the earliest account of Cox's Bazar informs us that Mr. Pechell, Magistrate of Chittagong in 1817 recommended to the government the town of Cox's Bazar should be freehold of the Arakanese refugees in perpetuity. Since then the Arakanese refugees enjoyed it rent free; each person occupying as his own property.[30] Besides, the Arakanese were also allowed to buy land from the local inhabitant as will be evident from Waymo, a refugee leader and his followers.[31]

Intrepid and freedom-loving as the Arakanese were, they rose against the Burmese rule whenever they found their independence in peril.[32] All these unsuccessful risings of the Arakanese including the one led by Nga Chin Pyan and the grant of asylum to him by the British may be regarded as one of the causes of the First Anglo-Burmese war of 1824-25 in which Burma was defeated and had to sign a treaty at Yandaboo (1826) by the provisions of which Arakan and

Name of the Place	*Year*	*Total Rakhaine population*
Cox's Bazar town	1799	10,000 (a)
	1872	3,205 (b)
	1982	1012 (c)

Sources (a) Quoted by Pearn, P.R. *op. cit.* p. 68.

Sources (b) Quoted by Hunter, W.W. in his *Statistical Account of Bengal* VI, London, 1876, p. 152 from the *Census Report* of 1872

(c) Khan, A. Mabud: 'Chattagrām Jelār Arakāni Sampraday' a project sponsored by Bangladesh University Grants Commission, 1982, Report, p. 12. The *Rakhaines* have been enumerated in Bangladesh census under the head of the Buddhists but there are several Buddhist groups. Hence, there is no separate population figure of the *Rakhaines* in Cox's Bazar district.

Tenassarim were annexed to the British dominion. As a result, the Arakanese refugees got a permanent foothold in the areas of Chittagong and because of the geographical proximity between Arakan and Chittagong, trade and commerce too considerably developed.

Demographically, the main concentration of the Arakanese in the district of Cox's Bazar which is called by the Arakanese as *Phalaung* shey (i.e. residence of the Prince) is found in the following areas: Harbang, Manikpur, Ramu, Cox's Bazar, Kuruskul, Chawfaldandi, Maheshali, Kharangkhali, Neela, Chaudhury para and Teknaf. And their total population has been estimated[33] at 7172.

The table shows a sharp fall in the member of the *Rakhaine* population. And the phenomenon can be explained by a number of causes. First, the southern part of Bangladesh. Particularly its coastal areas, have always been exposed to cyclones and inundation; consequently, the *Rakhaines* of the coastal regions, for instance, have suffered most at the cruel hands of nature. Of late 1960 to 1994 several cyclones and tidal weaves in this district are known to have killed numerous tribe. Secondly, in the pre-partition days, some *Rakhaines* of Cox's Bazar district had considerable income from trade and commerce which they used to carry on with Burma.[34] But the occupation of Burma by Japan in 1942, partition of India in 1947 and the ultimate emergence of the Union of Burma in 1948 stopped the trade relations between Burma and erstwhile East Pakistan leading to the deterioration of their economic condition and their eventual migration elsewhere. Thirdly, the *Rakhaines* were simple in nature and habit and failed to combat the local rogues and land grabbers and eventually evicted from their land. A couple of example is cited here.[35] In such circumstances, most of the *Rakhaines* of the region had no alternative than to migrate from the farmer East Pakistan and present day Bangladesh to Burma. The asylum in Burma was but natural in as much as a vast tract of land remains uncultivated and the population of Burma is less than half of the total population of Bangladesh. Fourthly, for the *Rakhaines* the scope for employment in areas they lived in was always limited because of the absence of factory or mills or even of small cottage industry establishments. In addition, comes the language bar which made them socially and economically isolated from the majority of the neighbours. Feeling of such socio-economic isolation among them were then intensified in the post-independence era. Finally, the *Rakhaines* experienced a feeling of insecurity when Pakistan's relation with Burma deteriorated. For example, they could not easily visit their relatives in Arakan and Burma who were linguistically and culturally close to them. Further, Pakistan's denial of the right of the minorities to participate in the political life of the country by declaring the state an Islamic Republic and denying a non-Muslim to be the president of the Country relegated the *Rakhaines* to the position of the second class citizens.[36] Although the Hindus were the principle victims; communal riots that broke out at Narayangonj and Khulna in 1960's greatly alarmed also the Buddhists including the *Rakhaines* as a religious community. All these factors collectively contributed to large scale exodus of the *Rakhaines* to Burma. The political status of the minorities and their integration into the mainstream of national life a fundamental question has yet to be solved. Initially in the constitution, Bangladesh was declared as a secular state. But after the political change in 1975 the term secularism was withdrawn from the constitution and some Islamic provisions were introduced in it and indeed, the declaration of Islam as the state religion of Bangladesh generated some sense of insecurity and mistrust among different minority groups. This attitude which the Ershad Government had shown to the minorities gave them an impression of their being 'a Protacted Minority'. And subsequent amendment of the constitution have not substantially effected the former position of the minorities. Their status remains the same as it was in the past. Unless the fundamental issues are solved, it is likely that the *Rakhaine* population in this region would continue to decline.

References

1. For the sake of convenience the most familiar expression *'Burma'* in place of *'Myanmar'* has been retained throughout the paper.
2. Chākma, Chāk, Kumi and Mro belong to this Arakanese group. They spread over throughout greater Chittagong Hill Tracts (henceforth CHT).
3. The sub-division of Chittagong Hill Tracts, namely Banderban Rangamati and Ramgarh have recently been raised to the status of the district. The headquarters of Ramgarh district has been shifted to Khagrachari after which the district is so named. Cox's Bazar a sub-division of Chittagong district was also made a district. So also is Patuakhali, formerly a sub-division of Barisal district, it is now a separate district.
4. The figure is the result of my investigation.
5. I Conducted a survey on the Magh population of this district in the year 1982. No separate census of this ethnic group is available.
6. Scholars hold divergent views about the etymology of the term *Magh*. Some scholars take it to be a Persian word which denotes fire worshippers. According to others, the word *Magh* is derived from *Magdu*, a Sanskrit word which means a sea-bird and by implication therefore, the term *Magh* denotes pirates. Yule and Burnel (ed.) *Hobson-Jobson*, London-1903, Reprint, Delhi, 1969 pp. 594-95.
7. Phayre, A.: *History of Burma*, London,-1883. p. 3.
8. Sharif, A. : 'On Arakan and Arakanese' Habibullah, A.B.M. (ed.) *Nalinikanta Bhattasali Commemoration volume*, Dacca, 1966. p. 358.
9. Sharif, A.: *Op. cit.* p. 358.
10. Karim, A.: *Murshid quli khan and His times, Dacca* 1963, p. 58.
11. Fytche, A.: *Burma : Past and Present*, London-1878, P. 268.
12. Phayre, A.: 'on the history of Arakan' *Journal of the Asiatic Society of Bengal XIII*, 1844, p. 24. The race of a hateful group of men in the coastal regions of Arakan is called in the local vernacular *Bee-loo* which means monster or cannibal in human shape. It is from these animals the country received its Pali mane *Rakkhaik* and hence, its present name is *Rakhaine*. Phayre, A. 'on the history of Burmah race' *Journal of the Asiatic society of Bengal, XXXIII*, 1. 1864. p. 21.
13. On this issue I interviewed a group of people at Cox's Bazar and their views agrees with that of A. Phayre.
14. *Rohangyar Daak*, a Pamphlet published by the Rohangya Patriotic Front, I, January, 1981. p. 11.
15. Ibid.
16. It is an enthusiastic religion-linguistic attempt to present a Buddhist monk in Arabic garb. Indeed, this attempt is connected with the Pan-Islamic Movement set afoot by Jamal Uddin Afghani (1839-97). This movement although made considerable impact on the Muslims all over the world, ultimately, failed.
17. The *Rohangas* are mainly concentrated in the north-western parts of Arakan. They were numerous compared to the other Muslim groups. With the exception of the *Rohangyas* all of them introduce themselves as Rakhainkola i.e., Arakanese Muslim.
18. Quoted by Sharif, A. *Op. cit.* pp. 335-65.
    a. Rosāngā sahar ēk grām Monohar.
    Punthi parichiti, 1957. p. 242.
    b. Karnafuli Naḍi Pūrbe acche ek puri
    Rosāngā nagar nam śvarga avatari
    Ghosal, S.N. (ed) Daulat Kazi, *Sati Moyna*, p. 45
    c. *Rosāngā* desete ācche Yāto Mussalman.
    Sharif A. (ed.) *Sikandarnama, Tofa*, p. 115.
19. Sattar, A.
20. Mohammed Sirajuddin, Alamgir; *The Revenue History of the East India Company in Chittagong*, Chittagong University press, 1971. p. 120
21. *Ibid.*
22. Mohammed Sirajuddin, Alamgir, *op. cit.* p. 127.
23. With the death of Tsanda Thudamma (1652-84) Arakan entered into a period of chaos and turmoil. Insecurity and social instability reigned there; assassination, intrigue in the court become natural situation. Tamada (1782-84)., the last king of Arakan was hated by all. And one of the nobles named Hario invited the Burmese king to attack Arakan who did so immediately. The Arakanese offered stubborn resistance against the Burmese but without any success. Tamada was captured and sent to Pegu together with his family and the Mahamuni image. Thus Arakan lost her independence.
24. In fact the Burmese rule in Arakan is associated with persecution and reign of terror. The Arakanese were occasionally called at the headquarters of various garrisons on the pretext of surrendering arms and when they arrived, the

Burmese rounded them up and massacred them. Even the infants were not exempted from the poll tax; three thousand Arakanese were requisitioned to work for the re-constructions of the Meiktila lake and none of them returned. Again, six thousand were dragged away (1790) to serve against Cheingmai expedition where many of them died. It was not known when one would be killed in the morning by the orders of the Burmese officials. Years after years this sort of tyranny continued in Arakan. Pearn, P.B. 'King Berring' *Journal of the Burma Research society XXIII*, I, 1933. p. 35.

25. When one party of the refugees was ordered by the officers of the British government to return to Arakan, the leader repeatedly replied that they would rather die and dwell in the jungles but would never go back to Arakan.
    Malcom, John: *The Political History of India*, Calcutta-1826, p. 549.
26. He was one of the British envoys in Burma and later on, superintendent of the Arakanese settlement in Chittagong and from whom the name of the settlement Cox's Bazar arose. The road which runs between Ramu and Ukhiaghat was built under his supervision.
27. Walter, H. *Geographical, Statistical and Historical Description of Hindustan and Adjacent Countries*, London, 1820, reprint, Delhi, 1971, 1. p. 168.
28. Late Kamra U Chaudhury of Teknaf and Chantowa Chaudhury of Neela claimed that they were the descendants of Nga chin pyan.
29. Pearn, P.R. *op. cit.* p. 73.
30. O'Malley, L.S.S. : *Eastern Bengal and Assam District Gazetteer : Chittagong*, Calcutta, 1908, p. 182.
31. At Edgaon near Ramu they purchased land from one Shib-Charan and settled down there. Subsequently, Regulation XI of 1812 confirmed the ownership. Kha, M.S. 'Captain George Sorril's Mission to the Court of Amarapura 1823-39. An Episode in the Anglo Burmese War' *Journal of the Asiatic Society of Pakistan*, II, 1957, p. 140.
32. Pearn, P.R. *op. cit.* pp. 55-84.
33. No separate censes of the Arakanese of the Cox's Bazar district is available. In conducted a survey on the Arakanese population of this group in 1982.
34. U Scin, a leader of the *Rakhaine* community in Cox's Bazar town informed me of Fathe Chaudhury and Do Aung Ḍalal of Ramu who became important business magnates in the early forties.
35. The forceful occupation of *Zedi Pāhār* and the burial ground in the neighborhood of Cox's Bazar town and *Zedi Pāhār* at Neela by the non-*Rakhaines* clearly démonstrate their helplessness. I visited those places on a number of occasions.
36. A person shall not be qualified for election unless he is a Muslim Article 32 (2) of 1956 constitution of the Islamic Republic of Pakistan. The 1962 constitution also retained this clause.

Section IV

Aspects of Indian History and Historiography
Editor : P.K. Mishra
Kaveri Books, New Delhi, India.

Craft of History Writing: An Early Indian Perspective

24

Sukla Das

There is no branch of knowledge which in course of intellectual evolution has exhibited more varied modalities and answered to more contradictory conceptions than history.[1] There is in fact none which has had and continues to have more difficulty in determining its definite status. The perspective of history changed and will change with the widening of knowledge horizon.

What is history and what are the basic principles of a historian's craft and what is the philosophy of history are the three vital points that generated scholarly debates and controversy. Theories advanced by scholars are multifarious and highly academic. Generally speaking however, composition of history is essentially the accomplishment of two operations. First, to establish the facts and second, to work them up. The historian's craft invariably involves the process of selection of facts. All history therefore is selection.[2] In fact the historian (1) discovers facts (2) assesses them (3) sifts them (4) co-relates them into homogenous series (5) classifies facts in chronological order and above all (6) examines the reciprocal relationship within this series : action, reactions and interactions.[3] In this process the historian is expected to remain impersonal and be no partisan in the disguise of a scholar.[4] Within this conceptual framework history writing any undergo phenomenal changes to be more streamlined.[5]

From mythology and miraculous events to history is a long way and there is a knowledge gap at various points. Real historiography began with the Greeks. Early Greek historiography reached its flowering in Herodotus,[6] Thucydides[7] and Polybius.[8] The models of historography worked out by the Greek historians were followed by the Romans first in Greek language and subsequently in Latin[9] but they evolved their own, distinctiveness.[10] The tradition of historical compositions in China is of remote antiquity. The office of Shih or archivist is almost as old as the Chinese history. He was a keeper of detailed day to day chronicles.[11] The composition of Shih-Chi (Historical Records) by Ssū-ma-Chi'en, the father of Chinese historiography around 100 B.C. is a major breakthrough. In Egypt history writing can be traced back to Manetho the priest who composed in Greek the history of Egypt in the third century A.D. with a preference for narration and record of events to historical analysis.[12]

In the backdrop of flowering of the craft of history writing in ancient civilisations the mode of historiography in early India would appear rather rudimentary. Romila Thapar has rightly pointed out that we should acquire the confidence of critically assessing our own culture and history.[13] The dearth of true historical literature in ancient India has given rise to contrary theories about early Indian knowledge of history. There are scholars who suggest that th e early Indians lacked correct appreciation of the true ideas and methods of history[14] which has been strongly refuted by R.C. Majumdar.[15] His view of high watermark of historical knowledge by the ancient Indians was however primarily based on the evidence of the Rājataraṅgiṇī of Kalhaṇa. But in view of the time (twelfth Century A.D.) and place (Kashmir) of the composition of this Chronicle D.K. Ganguly suggests that some influence of the Chinese and Arab historians on it cannot be brushed aside and as such the evidence of this text may not genuinely reflect the historical concept and methodology of the early Indians.[16]

A pertinent question centred round the issue of influence naturally arises. India's contact with the Graeco-Roman world is of remote antiquity. So is with China. What precluded Graeco-Roman or early Chinese influence in initiating true history writing in early India? The early Indians penetrated in all conceivable branches of literature and excelled in many of them so paucity of pre-Kalhaṇa historical texts certainly appears a very strange phenomenon.

Alberuni in the eleventh century A.D. observed that the "Hindus do not pay much attention to the historical order of things, they are very careless in relating the chronological succession of their kings, and when they are pressed for information and are at a loss, not knowing what to say, they invariably take to tale-telling."[17] In the backdrop of comparative abundance of Islamic historical records this paucity of the historical texts of the early Indians might have bewildered Alberbuni, a contemporary of Sultan Mahmud of Ghazni. It is still a popular belief that the Indians were a-historical people and they kept no records of their history.[18] A critical survey of scattered source materials however indicate that the ancient Indians did keep records which they felt were significant and worth-preserving. But they are more in the nature of legends, genealogies, monastic chronicles-all legitimate constituents of a historical tradition but not history.[19] Absence of real historical texts of ancient India therefore needs to be reconciled keeping in view the Indian situation. Various suggestions have been advanced by scholars.

Firstly, they have been summed up as lack of curiosity in mundane affairs. "The notion of other-worldliness of the Indians" demands a logical analysis and reappraisal[20] because the ancient Indians were no less materialistic as proved by recent investigations and findings and their spiritual affiliations if any did not negate their mundane interest and involvement.

Secondly, lack of scientific approach and critical outlook is also attributed to the paucity of genuine historical texts.[21] This theory however does not stand historical scrutiny in the light of Indian intellectual attainments, analytical acumen and logical approach.

Thirdly, a preponderence of fatalist doctrines is also considered a vital reason that discouraged accurate record of historical facts in their proper sequence.[22] The events were considered predestined hence mere recording of them would in no way affect their occurrence or otherwise.

Fourthly, it is assumed that the doctrine of Māyā which propagated the illusory status of the phenomenal world or the concept that entire creation is unreal hardly allured to record events for posterity as the early Indians considered these as accounts of unreal and transitory life.[23] Consequently, the texts meriting the title of history had not been produced in early India.

Fifthly, the concept of totality which evolved out of India's religio-philosophical system precluded development of the craft of historical writing as history history distorts the totality and highlights the part of a whole. In the Indian context the concept of time-span is endless. This concept is not conducive to the development of the sense of history. Evidently, in this framework the chronological form of time as dates and years would have been simply redundant.[24]

Sixthly, R.N. Dandekar pinpoints that non-individualistic attitude is a basic Indian approach. Man is regarded as just a part of the cosmic whole in this universe. No unique position is ascribed to man in the cosmic scheme of things. It is on account of this that India has failed to produce any real work of history as we understand it today. That is also the reason why in India one speaks not in terms of individual philosophers but of Schools of Philosophy. All interest here revolved round ideas and not on individuals, on principles and not on personalities. In India individuality has indeed been never regarded as a problem worthy of serious consideration.[25]

Seventhly, slow development of history writing in early India has also been attributed to the legacy of Śruti-Smṛti. Tales of past events were orally transmitted and were retained in memory instead of preserving them in writing.[26] Moreover, in India history became a part of religious literature incorporating many religious legends and anecdotes. This religious content was a bar to the proper development of objectivity in the craft of history writings.[27]

Eightly, the four element theory (Bhūtacaitanyavāda) advanced by the advocates of Lokāyata/Cārvāka philosophy was an attack on the theological determinist approach to history. Here as Pratima Asthana notes, we find the potentials for salvaging history from supernatural.[28] Unfortunately the craft of history writing in an objective manner emerged rather slowly as the Lokāyata views had to pass through persistent persecution[29] and the idealistic philosophy primarily stimulated all our conceptude developments.

Ninthly, a possible factor seems to be the apathy of the Brāhmaṇa intelligentsia towards recording bare facts which provided less scope for imagination, exaggeration and creativity.[30]

Tenthly, some protagonists believe that the ancient Indians did possess historical sense and historical literature did exist and they explain its non-availability by the theory of total destruction,[31] which is rather a far-fetched explanation.

It would thus appear that the reason for lack of historical spirit of the early Indians lay in the innate and deep-rooted traits of ancient Indian ideal, outlook and psyche. History is a prosaic idea. It aims at knowledge of facts in bringing out larger principles governing the human affairs and it demands objective accuracy. It is thus entirely out of tune with the ethos of early Indian literature and could not be disciplined by its formal concept of art and aesthetics. The idea of composing history for its own sake was thus slow to emerge and when it did emerge in its small way it could not delink itself of its legendary and poetic associations. Consequently the historian was submerged in his poetic identity.[32]

Slow emergence of the concept of history writing is thus most closely connected with the inherent traits of Indian thought and culture[33] and it would be impractical to assess the Indian craft of history writing against alien models. It is significant to note Alberuni's striking remark that "they differ from us in everything which other nations have in common."[34] This difference notwithstanding it has to be admitted that the word Itihāsa though without a definite connotation finds its mention as early as the Vedas.[35] We come across the word Itihāsa Veda in the Brāhmaṇical literature and the Upaniṣadas.[36] Etymologically the word denotes Iti-ha-āsa or so it was. Monier Williams interprets the word as traditional account of former events and heroic history.[37] The Vedic word Itihāsa thus had a remote antiquity but it is rather difficult to determine its actual meaning and scope. In an attempt to survey the growth of early Indian historiography, U.N. Ghoshal refers to "the mixture of mythology and folklore" in the Vedas.[38] In fact here was an effort to bring the historical tradition to the mytho-religious fold.

The Vedic words Gāthā[39] and Nārāśamsī[40] are of great significance in this context as they are classed with Itihāsa.[41] They imply songs in praise of human beings and are sharply distinguished from religious songs or hymns. The institution of the Sūtas[42] and Māgadhas[43] or bards[44] from most ancient times selected heroic achievements as the theme of their ballads to be recited or sung to entertain the elites and the public. These oral traditions rather fluid in nature need not be taken for history. R.G. Collingwood however suggests that certain residue of elements which we should outright dismiss as non-historical also have elements of history.[45] The Gāthās and Nārāśamsis are to be viewed in this perspective and can be considered as the nucleus stage of the concept of history or rudimentary specimens of history.[46] The Vedic materials thus provide an approach to history preserving fragments of tradition.[47] This oral tradition was also adopted by the Jainas and Buddhists intermingling elements of history with legends and dogmas.[48] Thus the growth of a trend was set in motion.

Connotation of Itihāsa acquired a new dimension under Kauṭilya. It embraced within its purview—

(a) Purāṇa (which had existed from the past)
(b) Itivṛtta (past occurrence of event)
(c) Ākhyāyikā (Historical tale rooted in authentic tradition)
(d) Udāharaṇa (examples)
(e) Dharmaśāstra (legal literature) and
(f) Arthaśāstra (work on polity).[49]

Kauṭilya's comprehensive concept of history thus incorporated besides historical chronicles in their widest significance law and legal institutions and social, moral and economic theory and practice. Kauṭilya highlighted the need of regular study of history by the Kings.[50] At least from the time of the Mauryas royal archives were organised and maintained.[51] The trend persisted over a long period and the Gupta inscriptions allude to the office of Akṣapaṭalādhikṛta or the imperial record keeper.[52] Hiuen-tsang also noted the existence of archives and records during the time of his visit to this sub-continent in the seventh century A.D.[53]

The vast mass of the Purāṇic literature which might have existed in its embryonic form at a fairly early date and had attained its final shape between the second and the sixth century A.D. has also some link with history. Conceptually the Purāṇas belong to the ancient Puāṇa-Itihāsa tradition which can be classified into three broad groups :

1. Itihāsa or epic history represented by the Mahābhārata,
2. Kāvya or epic poetry represented by the Rāmāyaṇa which is considered as an allegory,
3. Purāṇas or epic legends represented by the Purāṇic literature.[54]

Contents of the Purāṇas are varied and extensive. Their mytho-religious and cultural significance apart, surprisingly they also contain genealogical accounts which ended with the period of the Guptas in the fifth century A.D. probably on account of proper organisation of royal archives which rendered these lists unnecessary.[55] It is therefore difficult to dismiss or bypass them in the study of the craft of history writing in India. In fact, the Purāṇic genealogies stimulated the trend of genealogical recordings of the subsequent phase in the form of the Vamśāvalis.[56] A formative phase of history writing was thus reached.

The next significant phase of historical tradition blossomed in the milieu of royal court under the designation of Carita literature. The wandering Sūta-Māgadhas gave way to paid court poets or panygyrists. The genesis of the Carita literature can be traced to the Praśastis or eulogies, the main aim of which was to create a piece of aesthetic literature with a harmonious blending of historical facts. Inscriptions written in Prākṛt and Sanskrit like the Hātigumpha inscription of Khāravela,[56a] Nānāghāṭ inscription of Sātakarṇi I,[57] Nasik inscription of Pulamāyi,[58] Junagaḍh inscription of Rudradāman,[59] Allahabad Praśasti of Samudragupta written by Hariṣeṇa,[60] Mandasor stone pillar inscription of Yaśodharman written by Vatsabhaṭṭi,[61] or Aihole Praśasti of Pulakeśin II written by Ravikīrtti[62] may be treated as miniature historical Kāvyas in their narrow canvas. A definite turn in the style, diction, language and thought emerged which influenced inscriptions of the subsequent periods like Bādal pillar inscription of the time of Nārāyaṇapāla (ninth century A.D.) composed, by Bhaṭṭa Gaurava Miśra in the Vasantatilaka metre[63] or Deopārā Praśasti of Vijayasena (eleventh-twelfth century A.D.) written by the reputed poet Umāpatidhara.[64]

The Carita literature however found its initial expression in the Buddhacarita written by Aśvaghoṣa who was probably a contemporary of the Kuṣāṇa monarch Kaniṣka. Written in epic style the text narrates the life history of the Buddha where influence of the Rāmāyaṇa is unmistakable.[65] The Buddha-bhakti was already latent in the popular cult received mature support under the patronage of the Kuṣāṇa rulers.[66]

The Carita literature trend attained a new complexion in the Harṣacarita of Bāṇabhaṭṭa written in the seventh century A.D. which initiated writing of biographies of intimately known contemporary monarchs. The Harṣacarita called Ākhyāyikā or historical tale rooted in authentic tradition thus has the distinction of being the first attempt at writing a prose Kāvya on historical theme.[67]

The biggest lacuna of ancient Indian literary works is that many of them do not bear the names of the authors, not to speak of any other personal details. In this respect the Harṣacarita is a notable exception. The first two and half chapters of the work may be considered to a certain extent an autobiography of the celebrated author.[68] Thus we know about his parents Citrabhānu and Rājyadevi, his brothers and relatives, his ways of living, adventurous spirit, unbridled youth, his scholarship and varied experience through extensive travels and his close association with the Puṣyabhūti ruler Harṣavardhana and the courtly circle.

Bāṇa however began his narrative with a prior indication that he would devote his attention on partial projection of Harṣa's attainment instead of a full biography. Consequently, the historical focus is confined to certain events only making the work rather fragmentary.[69] In its premeditated framework the broad spectrum of history is thus narrowed and chronological sequence sacrificed.

Neeta Sharma has aptly highlighted Bāṇabhaṭṭa's over-embellished, difficult and pompous style[70] for which he was repeatedly accused and criticised by the scholars. Bāṇa evolved a new ornate poetic prose style which was characteristic of Bāṇa in form and content.[71] Admittedly, we have here not an abundance but a riot.[72] But in Sanskrit prose style Utkalika prāya variety of prose marked by long compounds was characterised by the quality called Ojas or force.[73] This enabled Bāṇa to place greater emphasis as and when he desired. He could equally be brief and simple. His use of Cūrṇaka or Simple prose was calcuted to evoke the desired emotion.[74] This expertise both ways has added a new dimension to literary art. It appears that the Harṣacarita was composed to display the literary excellence of the author rather than to work out a sober history. Hence it eventually turned out to be a mere historical romance. Belief in fate, supernatural elements and miracles and mingling of legends and myths contrived here to keep concrete facts far away and this precluded crystallisation of critical historiography.[75]

Notwithstanding its limitations composition of a prose Kāvya on a historical theme and that too embracing contemporary events itself has to be viewed as breakthrough. The model of a new genre thus set up by Bāṇabhaṭṭa was followed for a few centuries. In spite of its ornate style admittedly the Harṣacarita is less imaginative[76] and not totally devoid of historicity. Some of its informations are of utmost importance in restructuring the life and time of Harṣavardhana as they corroborate well with other archaeological and literary evidence.

Study of the Harṣacarita is historically rewarding if one could overcome his prejudices against bāṇabhaṭṭa. E.B. Cowell justly assesses that Bāṇa was not a mere rhetorecian, his descriptions provide "a mirror of time".[77] The Harṣacarita is very rich in its social content. Despite his position at Harṣa's court or his close association with Harṣa, his work displays a refreshing, almost saucy boldness.[78] Bāṇa vividly describes the tyranny and oppression of the royal officers,[79] apathy of the monarch and discontent of the common people.[80] It is his strength of thought to ridicule monarch's surrender to sycophancy.[81]

Significantly, Bāṇa's affluent milieu was no bar to his intense sympathy and concern for the helpless and the deprived. The glaring contrast between affluence and poverty is so convincingly portrayed in his narration that this fundamental realism gives the Harṣacarita a new contour. The text provides a clear picture of Bāṇa's social attitude which projects sharp deviation from accepted social norms. In fact in this area he ventured to walk where the Śāstrakāras feared to tread.[82]

Political history and dynastic studies remain an important aspect of historical interpretation but other aspects also need to be viewed[83] because sense of history is not essentially single dimensional.[84] Situating the Harṣacarita in its proper perspective it may be said that Bāṇabhaṭṭa had aptly compensated for the lacuna in political history by his faithful presentation of prevailing socio-economic conditions and his unconventional assessment. The infra-structure of history writing was thus laid.

From the genre of Carita literature to the Rājataraṅgiṇi is a long stride forward in the craft of history writing in India. Production of uninterrupted series of written records of its history seems to be an outstanding phenomenon of Kashmir[85] and the twelfth century Kashmir produced the famous chronicle of Kalhaṇa, the Rājataraṅgiṇi a work of quality that displays a remarkable maturity in historical analysis.[86] kalhaṇa himself testified to the existence of at least eleven earlier compositions on the history of Kashmir which he consulted to write his chronicle.[87] We further learn from him that there had been extensive works of ancient date containing the royal chronicles of Kashmir which were reported to be lost.[88] It is suggestive that writing of history had been a traditional art of Kashmir and in Kalhaṇa's chronicle the craft attained a high watermark. The evidence of this text does not reflect the historical concept and methodology of the earlier works of India for Kalhaṇa was not a mere reporter but a critical narrator.[89]

The Rājataraṅgiṇi written in Sanskrit verse in A.D. 1148-49[90] contains eight Taraṅgas (Books) covering various dynasties from the earliest period down to the time of the author. The name of the author occurs in the colophon of each Taraṅga along with the name of his father Caṇpaka who was a minister of King Harṣa. The dynastic war cost Harṣa's life and throne and Caṇpaka lost limelight. It appears that Kalhaṇa himself held no state office and enjoyed no favour from the court.[91]

Kalhaṇa was a scholar with knowledge in various branches of traditional learning, thorough and extensive.[92] His close knowledge of topography reveals that he was a man of wide travels. Though belonging to the Brāhmaṇa elite group and attached to Śaiva creed Kalhaṇa was singularly free from narrow sectarianism[93] and this eclectic mental make up stands out prominently in his writing.

Kalhaṇa wrote in the milieu of feudal social frame work. The Rājataraṅgiṇi thus chronicles court intrigue, wars of succession, domination of the Ḍāmaras or feudal landlords who systematically oppressed the peasantry, tyranny of the Kāyasthas or clerical officials,[94] political acumen of the Brāhmaṇa priests who even resorted to hunger-strike (Prāyopaveśana[95]) to force weak rulers to act in the manner they wanted, moral degeneration of the nobility and the soldiers as well as progressive decline of the merchant class. He made specific mention of forced labour[96] and sale of men to the Mlecchhas.[97] All round corruption, fallen standard of morality and erosion of royal authority and allied feudal traits are well-documented by him.[98] D.D. Kosambi thus points out, importance of Kashmir to historians lies in that "it shows the true motive force of Indian feudalism."[99]

R.C. Majumdar gives Kalhaṇa the credit for anticipating the modern critical method of historical research in India which was not fully developed till the nineteenth century.[100] A perusal of the text indicates that Kalhaṇa initiated the line of historical research. The method of his data collection is a novel feature in Indian craft of history writing. For collection of materials he not only consulted literary sources[10] but also handled archaeological sources like inscriptions, coins, monuments and buildings.[102] Moreover, he utilised oral history and eye-witness accounts.[103] This methodology is a sharp departure from the conventional concept of chronicle writing.

Kalhaṇa's knowledge of geography was strikingly vast. Role of geography in history writing finds its proper significance in the Rajataraṅgiṇi. He was the master of accurate topography of Kashmir. Numerous references made by him regarding the origin of towns, villages, estates, shrines and their exact location are of great topographical interest. It is a pointer not only to his theoretical knowledge but also to his experience attained through travels.

In his writing not only the neighbouring Indian principalities but also distant alien peoples like the Turks, Persians, Arabs, Afgans and the like have found their places. Kashmir was the cross-road where multiple races met and many entered into the indigenous social mainstream. Many Kashmiris even adopted alien names also.[104] Kashmir in relation to India and Kashmir in relation to neighbouring foreign lands, this twin perspective indeed has added a new dimension to this chronicle.

Kalhaṇa's impartiality as a historian and honesty of purpose are remarkable. He admits dispassion as a quality of a historian "whose words like that of a judge free from love and hatred records facts of the past."[105] His objective approach is striking as he made no attempt to conceal the failings and weaknesses of the king even in whose time he wrote. In fact he highlighted the later activities of king Harṣa that evoke condemnation in spite of his family gratitude for the king. This boldness can in no way be underrated.

History, according to Kalhaṇa was not something to learn only but to make people live and understand life. He portrayed both sides of all issues and pointed out the failings of the virtuous and virtues of the faulty monarch. Hence he restricted the language to the exposition of facts which is a new phenomenon in the development of Indian historiography.

Though the author of a regional history, Kalhaṇa was free from narrow regionalism and sectarianism. His glowing tribute to the brave men of Gauḍa who travelled all the way up to Kashmir and avenged at the cost of their lives the death of their king who had been treacherously murdered by the whimsical king Lalitāditya of Kashmir[106] is a unique instance of his historical approach. Similarly the Rājataraṅgiṇi is an eloquent testimony to his religious tolerence and eclectism.[107]

Romila Thapar has pointed out that the study of institutions did not receive much emphasis in historical writing even of recent times.[108] In Kalhaṇa's writing nucleus of this concept can be detected. His observations indicate that personal achievements of the great are merely answers to certain needs in society and hence he did not cover up the limitations and failures of an individual ruler or group of men. In his chronicle there is no trace of hero-worship as they are only functionaries. Instead of personal failings thus drawbacks and discrepencies of the institutions have been highlighted by him to understand the real operative forces.[109] This institutional perspective of Kalhaṇa is remarkable as being far in advance of his time and milieu.

History is not confined to the rigid framework of political and dynastic studies. In this respect Kalhana's qualities as a historian are unsurpassed. The Rājataraṅgiṇi is a rich storehouse of information, political, social and to some extent economic.[110] It is impossible to peruse the chronicle particularly in later portions without realising that the author had an observant eye and an open mind for the affairs around him. It appears that what had been accurately seen and genuinely felt were fairly recorded. Moral degeneration of the society in a feudal background, customs, manners and position of respective groups have all emerged very forcefully.[111] In the mirror of this work we also get a reflection of the status of women in the valley of Kashmir.[112] Description of famine, food price, taxation, currency system and other economic factors and features throw considerable light on the facets of the economic system.[113] The iconoclasm without theology and violation of temple property for expropriation of accumulated wealth by the central power to combat financial stress[114] is indicative of a degenerating process in economy. Kalhaṇa's approach to reality is unchallengeable.

The Rājataraṅgiṇi is not only a valuable contribution to history writing but also to the domain of Kāvya literature. Usually the eight rasas or sentiments comprise the essence of a Kāvya. Surprisingly, Kalhaṇa added the ninth, the Śānta rasa or inner calm and resignation[115] which remains the prevailing sentiment of his chronicle. It determines his approach because he requests the reader to be calm and not to pass any abrupt judgement and jump to hasty conclusion. S.K. De calls him a poet with originality.[116] In Kalhaṇa's own view his work was not a mere history but pre-eminently a work of art and he looked upon himself as a Kavi.[117]

One can in no way miss his sense of philosophy of history a quality rare among the past chroniclers. Kalhaṇa the narrator of events and Kalhaṇa the thinker who explains the facts by causes and effects and exposes the principles which underlie them are one and indivisible self who did not marshal the facts to substantiate the thesis much less did he manipulate them to fit in a doctrine of his own. His philosophy waits upon facts and does not govern them.[118] The Rājataraṅgiṇi thus strikes a new note in the area of history writing.

It is also another scholarly opinion that Kalhaṇa is not a great historian but only an author of a remarkably flowing and forceful narrative.[119] Though it is difficult to subscribe to this contention in the context of reappraisal of the work, we have to take into account discrepencies of Kalhaṇa's chronicle in the perspective of modern historical technique.

The Rājataraṅgiṇi is a comprehensive work but its accomplishment is rather uneven. Kalhaṇa has mixed up legend with history. Though he explored primary source materials, his handling was defective. M.A. Stein pinpoints want of critical estimate of his sources.[120] kalhaṇa's work displays lack of historical criticism. he had limitations as a critical investigator.

Kalhaṇa's unquestioned acceptance of myth and legend, witchcraft and miracle, fanciful anecdotes, belief in omens, inability to withstand the distant glamour of ancient glory, his reckoning of fate or destiny, sins of previous birth, intervention of gods and demons as sufficient explanation of human action is difficult to accept in proper appreciation of historical events and motives.[121] Here the traditionalist Kalhaṇa could not wriggle out of his conventional steelframe. Consequently history suffers.

The Rājataraṅgiṇi also suffers from serious shortcomings in chronology. In the first three Taraṅgas while duration of individual reigns is mentioned, to precise dates are given. According to the scheme of chronology adopted by Kalhaṇa, nearly the whole of the Gupta period is covered by the reign of a single king of the Gonanda dynasty who is said to have rule for 300 years. Such an absurd regnal period renders the chronolgy defective and misleading.[122]

Several scholars have devoted attention to a study of Kalhaṇa-chronology in the light of recent archaeological and numismatic discoveries but nothing significant has emerged.[123] Proper dates are indicated only from Jayāpiḍa's reign in 813 A.D. beginning with the verse 703 of the fourth Taraṅga. These are indicated in the Laukika era customarily in use in Kashmir from ancient times. There is no doubt that Kalhaṇa's history after this date is more or less accurate and the defective chronology of the earlier period is due to errors of early chronicles. But exact dates are conspicuous by their absence even when Kalhaṇa is writing about his own time. Sometimes he mentions just months only leaving the year a guess-work.[124]

Selection of verse for a historical narrative is rather injudicious. Metaphor, similes, puns, poetic figures and ambiguities have thus rendered the flow of his history sluggish.[125]

In spite of some vital flaws, it has to be admitted that the Rājataraṅgiṇi bears a remarkable historical individuality and has become a class by itself. Indeed in this chronicle the craft of history writing in India went a long way to attain its maturity.

References

1. *Encyclopaedia of Social Sciences*, Macmillan, 1957, Vol. 7-8, p. 356.
2. *Ibid.*, p. 363.
3. *Ibid.*
4. *Ibid.*, p. 367.
5. *Ibid.*, p. 368.
6. M.I. Finley, *The Greek Historians*, New York, 1971, p. 5.
7. J.B. Bury, *The Ancient Greek Historians*, New York, 1909, p. 147.
8. *Ency. of Soc. Sciences, op. cit.*, p. 370.
9. *Ibid.*
10. H.E. Barnes, *A History of Historical Writing*, New York, 1963, p. 38.
11. Burton Watson, *Ssu-Ma-Chi'en. The Grand Historian of China*, New York 1956, pp 70-71, *The New Encyclopaedia Britannica*-Macropaedia Chicago 1986, Vol. 20, p. 624.
12. Robert C. Denton (Ed.), *The Idea of History in the Ancient Near East*, London 1955, p. 32. D.K. Ganguly, *History and Historians in Ancient India*, New Delhi 1984, pp. 8-9.
13. Romila Thapar, *The Past and Prejudice*, New Delhi 1975, p. 2.
14. S.K. De, *A History of Sanskrit Literature* Vol.I, Calcutta 1947, pp. 347 ff; A.K. Majumdar, *Concise History of Ancient India*, New Delhi 1977, Vol.I, N. Subramanyam, *Historiography*, Madurai 1973, pp. 327 ff.
15. C.H. Philips, *Historians of India Pakistan and Ceylon*, London 1961, p. 25.
16. D.K. Ganguly, *op. cit.*, p. 7.
17. Alberuni, Kitab-Ul Hind, trans E.C. Sachau, Vol. 2. London Reprint 1983, pp. 10-11.
18. Romila Thapar, *op. cit.*, p. 2.
19. *Ibid.*
20. *Ibid.*
21. D.K. Ganguly, *op. cit.*, p. 7.
22. *Ibid.*
23. *Ibid.*, p. 8.
24. V.S. Pathak, *Ancient Historians of India*, Bombay 1966, pp. 28-29.
25. R.N. Dandekar, *Exercises in Indology*, Delhi 1981, p. 315.
26. Bratindra Nath Mukhopadhyay, *Itihāsa: Ekṭi Prācina Bhāratiya Cetanā* (in Bengali), Calcutta 1967, p. 29.
27. *Ibid.*, p. 30.
28. Pratima Asthana, *The Indian View of History*, Agra 1992, pp. 89-90.
29. Debi Prasad Chattopadhyay, *Lokāyata: A study in Indian Materialims*, New Delhi 1968, p. 31. Hemanta Gangopadhyay, *Cārvāk Darśan* (in Bengali) Calcutta 1993, p. 12 ff.
30. D.K. Ganguly, *op. cit.*, p. 8, D.D. Kosambi, *An Introudction to the Study of Indian History*, Bombay 1985, pp. 279-80.
31. R.C. Majumdar and A.D. Pusalkar ed. *The Vedic Age*, Bomaby 1988, p. 47. Pratima Asthana, *op. cit.*, p. 23.

32. S.K. De, *op. cit.*, pp. 346-347.
33. Kalhaṇa's Rājataraṅgiṇi (R.T) ed., M.A. Stein, Reprint Delhi 1961, Introduction p. 3.
34. E.C. Sachau, *op. cit.*, Vol. I, p. 17.
35. Atharva Veda 15.6.4. B. Bhattacharya, Yāska's Nirukta, Calcutta 1958, 2.10.24, 10.26, 12.10.
36. Śatapatha Brāhmaṇa 13.4 3.12,
    Chhāndogya Upaniṣad 7.1.2., 7.11.4, 8.1.7.
37. Monier Willians, *A Sanskrit English Dictionary*, Delhi 1986 p. 165.
38. U.N. Ghoshal, *Studies in Indian History and Culture*, Calcutta 1957, pp. 37-38.
39. Ṛg Veda 10.85.6.
40. *Ibid.*, 10.86.42, 10.64.3,
41. Atharva Veda 15.5. 11-12, *Śatapatha Brāhmaṇa*, 10.5.6.8., Taittiriya Āraṇyaka 2.9.11.
42. Atharva Veda 3.5.7., Yajur Veda 30.6, *Taittiriya Saṁhitā* 1.8.9.1.
43. Yajur Veda, 30.5-6.
44. A.A. Macdonell and A.B. Keith ed. *Vedic Index*, Vol. 2, London 1912, p. 462.
45. R.G. Collingwood, *The Idea of History*, London 1961 p. 18.
46. *The Cultural Heritage of India* Vol.5, Ramakrishna Mission Institute of Culture, Calcutta 1978, p. 283.
47. Pratima Asthana, Op.Cit. p. 22.
48. *Ibid.*, V.S. Pathak, *op. cit.*, p. 19.
49. Kauṭilya's Arthaśāstra, trans. R. Shamasastry, Mysore 1929, I. 5.
50. *Ibid.*
51. *Ibid.*, 2.7.
52. Epigraphia Indica Vol. 25, p. 52, D.C. Sircar, *Select Inscriptions bearing on Indian History and Civilization*, Vol.I, Calcutta 1942, p. 7, 264.
    J.F. Flect, *Corpus Inscriptionum Indicarum* Vol. 3. London 1888, p. 256.
53. T. Watters, *On Yuan Chwng's Travels in India*, Vol.I. London 1904, p. 154.
    S. Beal, Si-Yu-Ki, Vol.I London 1884, p. 78.
54. *The Cultural Heritage op. cit.*, p. 40.
55. *Ibid* p. 284.
56. *Ibid.*, p. 285.
56a. D.C. Sircar, *op. cit.*, p. 206 ff.
57. *Ibid.*, p. 186 ff.
58. Epigraphia Indica Vol. 8, pp 60 ff.
59. *Ibid.*, pp 42 ff.
60. J.F. Flkeet, *op. cit.*, pp 6 ff.
61. *Ibid.*, No. 33.
62. *Epigraphia Indica*, Vol. 6. p. 10.
63. A.K. Maitreya, Gauḍalekhamālā (in Bengali) Vārendra Research Society, Rajshahi 1319 B.S., p. 70.
    Epigraphia Indica, Vol. 2. p. 160.
64. N.G. Majumdar, *Inscription of Bengal*, Vol.3.
    Varendra Research Society Rajshahi, 1929, pp. 42 ff.
    Epigraphia Indica, Vol.I. p. 305.
65. Sarla Khosla, *Aśvaghoṣa and His Times*, New Delhi 1986, pp 14-15, R.C. Majumdar and A.D. Pusalkar e.d *The Age of Imperial Unity*, Bombay 1990, pp. 266-267.
66. Biswanath Bhattacharya, *Aśvaghoṣa, A. Critical Study*, Santiniketan 1976, p. 12.
67. S.K. De, *op. cit.*, p. 227.
68. Bāṇabhaṭṭa, *Harṣacarita* ed. K.P. Parab, Nirnaya Sagara Press, Bomaby 1925, Chapters 1,2.
69. S.K. De, *op. cit.*, pp. 226-227.
70. Neeta Sharma, *Bāṇabhaṭṭa a Literary Study*, Delhi 1968, p. 193.
71. *Ibid.*
72. S.N. Dasgupta and S.K. De, *History of Sanskrit Literature*, Calcutta 1947 p. 237.
73. *The Cultural Heritage op. cit.*, p. 265.
74. *Ibid.*, p. 266.
75. S.K. De, *op. cit.*, p. 228.
76. *Ibid.*, p. 227.
77. Bāṇabhaṭṭa, Harṣacarita, trans, E.B. Cowell and F.W. Thomas, Delhi 1961, Introduction.
78. Sukumari Bhattacharji, Bāṇabhaṭṭa, *A Reappraisal of Some values*, Journal of the Asiatic Society, Vol. 32, No. 1-2, 1990, p. 66.
79. E.B. Cowell and F.W. Thomas, *op. cit.*, pp. 79-80.

80. *Ibid.*, pp. 208-209.
81. D. Devahuti, Harsha-A political study, Oxford 1970, p. 12.
82. Sukumari Bhattacharji, *op. cit.*, p. 69.
83. Romila Thapar, *A History of India*, Pelican 1966, p. 22.
84. A.C. Boquat, *The Valuation of Historical*, W.R. Inge ed. Radhakrishnan-*Comparative Studies in Philosophy*, printed in Honour of his 60th Birthday, London 1951, pp. 155 ff.
85. P.N.K. Bamzai, *A History of Kashmir*, Delhi 1962 p. 30.
86. Romola Thapar, *A History of India*, p. 226.
87. *Kalhaṇa's Rājataraṅgiṇī*, (R.T.) ed. R.S. Pandit, Sahitya Akademi edition New Delhi, 1968. Taranga I. 15.
88. *Ibid.*, I 11-12.
89. Sunil Chandra Ray, *Early History and Culture of Kashmir*, Delhi 1957, pp xxi-xxii.
90. R.T.I. 51.
91. P.N.K. Bamzai, *op. cit.*, p. 33.
92. *Ibid.*
93. Kalhaṇa's Rājataraṅgiṇi, tr. M.A. Stein, Reprint Delhi 1961, preface.
94. T.T. VII. 39-40.
95. *Ibid* IV. 82, 90. V. 468, VI. 25,336, 343, VII. 13, 1088, 1157, 1611, VIII. 51, 110, 658, 707, 768, 808, 939, 2224, 2733, 2739.
96. *Ibid.*, V. 172-174.
97. *Ibid.*, IV. 397.
98. Somnath Dhar, *Makers of Indian Literature: Kalhaṇa*, Sahitya Akademi, New Delhi 1978 pp. 22-26.
99. D.D. Kosambi, *Origin of Feudalism in Kashmir*, D.N. Jha ed. *Feudal Social Formation in Early India*, Delhi 1984, p. 143.
100. *The Vedic Age*, pp. 49-50.
101. R.T.I. 17-18 ff.
102. *Ibid.*, I. 15
103. Sunil Chandra Ray, *op. cit.*, pp. xxi-xxii.
104. R.S. Pandit, *op. cit.*, pp. xxxiv, xxxviii.
105. R.T.I. 7.
106. *Ibid.*, IV. 322-30.
107. M.A. Stein, Op. Cit, Preface.
108. Romila Thapar, *A History of India* p. 19.
109. P.N.K. Bamzai, *op. cit.*, p. 36.
110. .R.S. Pandit, *op. cit.*, foreward by Jawahar Lal Nehru.
111. D.N. Jha, ed. *op. cit.*, pp. 130-144.
112. Sukla Das, *Position of Women as reflected in the Rājataraṅgiṇī of Kalhaṇa*, Anvikṣā Research Journal of the Sanskrit Department Jadavpur University, Vol. 3. part-2. Vol. 4. part 1, pp. 58-70.
113. D.N. Jha, *op. cit.*, pp. 130-144.
114. R.T.IV. 617, 621, 623, 631-639, V. 168-170, VII. 1089, 1090-1092, 1095-1098, 1100-1107.
115. *Ibid.*, I. 23.
116. S.K. De, *op. cit.*, p. 358.
117. R.T.I. 3-7.
118. Sunil Chandra Ray, *op. cit.*, p. 358.
119. S.K. De, *op. cit.*, p. 358.
120. M.A. Stein, *op. cit.*, p. 4.
121. S.K. De, *op. cit.*, p. 356.
122. R.C. Majumdar and A.D. Pusalkar ed.
    The Classical Age, Bombay 1988, p. 132.
123. P.N.K. Bamzai, *op. cit.*, p. 62.
124. Somnath Dhar, *op. cit.*, pp 45-46.
125. *Ibid.*, p. 35.

Aspects of Indian History and Historiography
Editor : P.K. Mishra
Kaveri Books, New Delhi, India.

A Lost Book on Politics in Ancient India

25

Pratap Chandra Chunder

Many books on politics or political economy were lost in Ancient India. Even the famous *Arthaśāstra* of Kautilya had been lost. In the early years of this century, thanks to an unknown priest of Tanjore in South India, who brought a Sanskrit manuscript with incomplete commentary to the Government Oriental Library in the native State of Mysore, R. Sharma Sastry, the Librarian discovered the long-lost text of Kauṭilya's *Arthaśāstra*. The discovery was as thrilling to the Indologists as schliemann's discovery of the Homeric city of Troy to classical scholars or the chance discovery of the Dead Sea Scrolls to Butical authorities.

Of all the lost books on politics in Ancient India, one stands out prominently. This was the book on *Rājadharma* (royal duties) said to have been written by the mythical Supreme God (*Brahmma-Sanātana*) mentioned in the Mahabharata. Although the text is lost detailed contents are described in the Great epic are illuminating. We propose to examine the contents.

From the *Vedas* came various branches or appendices and specialised compositions. At the outset rules on *dharma, artha and Kāma* are found mixed up in many compositions on *dharma* or human duty. "It will be noted" says P.V. Kane, "Āpastamba (writer of ara early dharma sūtra) covers the whole field of *Rājadharma*." (HDS. III. 2). Further specialisation produced the *Arthaśāstras* and the *Kāmaśāstras* to meet the need for wise guidance. The process seems to be illustrated by the mythical origins of *daṇḍanītes, Kāmasūtra, āyurveda* and so on, all attributed to some god or other mythical persons to command the respect of human believers. A summary of the origins of *daṇdanīte* (i.e. *Arthaśāstra* according to some) is narrated in the *Mahābhārata* (*Śānti*, 59).

In a state of nature (*kṛta yuga*) men were pious, though without a king or *daṇḍa* (coercive power). Soon they succumbed to greed and other base passions. The gods were afraid. They approached the creator (Frahmadeva), who came to their rescue. He wrote a comprehensive manual with 1,00,000 chapters for man's guidance. It dealt with *trivarga* of *dharma, artha* and *kāma* and comprised four distinct subjects for study viz. the (Vedic) trial, *anviksiki* (rational philosophy), vārtta (economics) and *daṇḍanite* (law of punishment or coercion). Incidentally, Kauṭilya mentions all these four subjects for the education of the king (I. 2). obviously *Brahmasanātras* all-comprehensive book was too bulky. So samkara (Siva the god of welfare) abridged the text into the *Vaiśālākṣa śāstra* with 10,000 chapters; Indra, the king of gods, into the *Bāhudantaka* with 5,000; Bṛchaspati, the chief priest of the gods, into the *Bārhaspatya* with 3,000 and Kāvya or Śukra (alias Uśnas), the chief priest of the demons, into the *Auśanasa* with 1,000 chapters. Interestingly, Kauṭilya acknowledges all of them (except the Creator) as his earlier teachers (*pūrvācāryas*).

Earliest texts of the *Arthaśāstra* are all lost. But apparently they were available to Kauṭilya, as he said (I. 1), "This single *Arthaśāstra* is composed after collecting most of the *arthasastra* which have been propounded by earlier teachers for gaining (*lābha*) and protecting (*pālana*) the world." He cites the views of these teachers collectively or individually from time to time. Most of the teachers or their schools have been identified. He mentions *Viśālakṣa (Śiva), Parāsva, Piśuna* (the backbiting sage Nārada author of a *dharma Śāstra*) *Bāhudantibutra (Bhiṣma,* the exponent of the *Rājadharma* in the *Mahābhārata* and grandgive of the Kuru elan). *Vātavyādhi (Akrura* the teacher of the *Yādava* alone to which *Krṣṇa* belonged). *Kātyāyana, Kaminka Bharadvājen* (probably Kanika the adviser of king *Dhrtrāṣtra* of *Kuru* clan), *Bharadvāja* (*Droṇa,* the Brāhmma strategist or the *Kure Dirga Cārāyana* (the scheming adviser of *Virūḍhaka* who deposed his old father *Prasenajit,* King of *Kośala,* a protaype of Kauṭilya,) *Ghotakamukha* (also mentioned in the *Kāmasūtra*), *Kiñjalka,* and *Piśunaputra*. These are individual teachers, some apparently bearing nicknames. The schools mentioned by Kauṭilya are the Manavas (of Manu, the first mythical man to whom the foremost *dharmaśāstra, Manu Saṁhitā* has been later attributed; the *Bārhaspatya,* the *Auśansa* (both already noticed) and the *Āmbhīyas*. This is a formidable list of specialist on the art of Government. There were also some unknown teachers cited by Kauṭilya. They show the keen interest taken by ancient Indians in political science as a whole. Later *Dharmaśāstras* of *Manu, Yājñavalkya Nārada* and others contain large quantities of political instructions, and some have traced the influence of Kauṭilya on them, and *vice versa*.

In this background the mythical *Brahma-samātaras* treatise on political science is to be noted. According to the Mahābhārata as we have seen, the first treatise on the art of Government was composed by the mythical eternal Supreme Being (*Brahmasanātam*), at the instance of the gods who were perturbed in the fall of mankind from the right path. The epic briefly lists the contents of this *magnum opus* in Chapter 59 Verses 29 to 74 of the *Śānti Parvan*. A translation of this important passage set out below will be instructive for comparison:

"Then in his own wisdom he composed one hundred thousand chapters in which were specially described the spiritual, and then the material and the sensual goals of life. This group made by the self-born. One became famous as the threefold group (*Trivaja*). The fourth was salvation. Thus they have indeed different imports and different merits. Even of a salvation another threefold group is said to be *Sattva, rajas* and *tamas* (divine, human and animal qualities). And the threefold group arising from punishment is stagnation, growth and loss. Self, country, time, policies duties and aids are thought to be the sixfold group arising from the art of government (niti). O Bull among the Bharatas, in it were indicated the broad fields of learning (such as) the (Vedic) triad, rational philosophy (*ānvikṣiki*), economic (*Vārtta*) and politics (*daṇḍanīt*); the protection from and the regulation of the principal officers, the nature of a prince, spies and different secret agents pursuing different policies; conciliation, dissension, gift and then punishment, O King, and fifthly indifference (upeksa) were elaborately mentioned here. And deliberation and deception for (causing) dissension were described; (so also) the results of the success and the failure of deliberation. Treaties said to be three types viz. lower, medium, and best (respectively) for causing fear, honour and monetary gain were elaborately described, four occasions for offensive action threefold goals, just conquest, and a conquest for wealth and demonic conquest were described there extensively. Three features of the fivefold group (of principal officers, state, fort, armed forces and treasury) were described there. Open and secret armed forces were then mentioned. Open forces were of eight types, and secret spread far. O Pāṇḍava, chariots, elephants, horses, infantry, forced labour, boat spies and local guides being the eighth. O *Vaurvya,* there were eight open limbs of the armed forces. And moving (insects) and fixed (herbal plants) are mentioned for use in powders such as poison. Diverse secret punishments by means of touch and food were kept in mind. The enemy, the ally and the neutral,—such as there were also described; (as also) extensively the excellence of the paths (of the stars) and the excellence of the ground, self-defence, assurance and the supervision of transport. And also diverse planning about men, elephants, chariots and horses, military formations of different designations and peculiar war strategies, creating troubles, destructions, proper encounter and proper retreat, preserving and knowledge of weapons. O Bull among the *Bharetas*, relief in calamity of the armed forces, (their) troubles, dangerous moments and knowledge about infantry; O *Pāṇḍava*, the provision against unknown factors, deception and movement; troubling the enemy state with the help of thieves, forest tribes and ruffians and by others such a arsonists, poisoners, and causing adverse situations, rousing to rebellion of the chiefs of guilds, cutting off plants, injuring and threatening the elephants; honouring the devoted and earning confidence, growth and decline and proper condition of the seven limbs of the state. The deception practised on the enemy, the intermediate power and the allies were said to be proper, likewise (causing) oppression and counterattack on the superior power; very subtle judicial administration and the removal of (social) thorns; exertion, exercise, investment, grants and the procurement of goods; maintenance of those not maintained and caring for those maintained; the gift of money in time and the avoidance of calamity. In this were (mentioned) the excellences of the king and the excellences of the general, the grounds of the threefold group (of goals of life), likewise their qualities and defects; various misconducts of and the practices of the dependents; gaining what is not gained, augmenting what is gained, the grant of what is augmented to proper persons according to rules; the gift of wealth for spiritual, material and sensual objects had been mentioned and fourthly, (that) in tackling a calamity had been described here. O the best among the *Kurus*, here were mentioned ten types calamities arising from anger and excessive desire; O Bull among the Bharatas, hunting, gambling, drinking and women arising from excessive desire, as the teacher stated, were mentioned by the self-born; (so also here) abuse, also defiance, and assault, self-mortification and self-abnegation and financial offence (six arising from anger). Various machines and their functions were described there. Causing damage, counterattack and destroying the flat, causing damage to sacred mounds and trees, siege and direction of works, parts of vehicles (*avaskara*), industry and also the policies were described (so also) procuring drums, kettledrums, conchshells and trumpets and destroying things, these six (being gems, animals, land, houses, slaves and gold. Pacification of the conquered territory, specially honouring the good people, becoming one with the learned and learning the rules of gifts and fire cult. Taking auspicious measures, securing the remedy of the body, making provisions for food and constant belief in God; what is to be upheld by one truthfulness sweet speech, works in festivities and social gathering arising from home; constant watch over open and secret matters and practices in all departments. O Tiger among the *Bharatas*, the immunity of the *Brāhmaṇas* from punishment and penal (banishment on proper ground), (recruiting) dependents from one's own race and promoting on merit. And protecting citizens and enlarging the state, and thought on the circle of states. O King, consisting of twelve kings; seventy two types of (medical) remedies for the body, and the laws of the country, races and clans were properly described there. Here were described spiritual material and sensual goals and salvation, policies and diverse desires for wealth, O Too-generous One; here were described the performance of basic actions such as practising magic and tricks; polluting streams and running waters. Due to patience and policies people do not deviate from the way of the Aryas (elite). All this, O Tiger among kings, has been described in this treatise on political science." A comparison between the contents of *Brahma-Sanātana's* lost treatise and of Kauṭilya's *Arthaśāstra* will show that the former was wider in scope than the latter. The former discussed philosophical topics including salvation, while the latter was more concerned with the practical art of government. But there were many remarkable similarities between the two works. Both stressed the political, economic and social functions of the government. Deception, punishment (open or secret), the use of poison and magic (for which—Kauṭilya alone has been wrongly criticised) were common to both. Military organisation, formations and strategies, types of conquest, and international relations were discussed by both. It thus appears that these topics were the common heritage of the Indian people.

(This article contains extracts from the writer's new annotated English translation of Kauṭilya's—*Arthaśāstra* to be published by the M.P. Birla Foundation).

Aspects of Indian History and Historiography
Editor : P.K. Mishra
Kaveri Books, New Delhi, India.

Perspectives of Pāli and Buddhistic Studies and Bimala Churn Law

26

Dipak Kumar Barua

Introduction

The terms *Buddhistic Studies* coined by Dr. Bimala Churn Law (*b.* october 26, 1891-*d.* May 3, 1969) for one of his edited works may be viewed along with Pāli Studies as a necessary adjuncts of *Indological Studies*—words used by him also for one of his books, through the perspectives relating to philsoophy, religion, history, geography, and linguistics. Indeed because of his sundry writings and positive outlook for the promotion of such a branch of human learning, he is almost identified with this discipline which has gradually been popular among the scholars as well as general readers.

Before embarking on any discussion on the topic mentioned in the title of this paper it is prudent at the outset to present a resume of the background history of Pāli and Buddhistic Studies in India during the 19th and early 20th centuries.

Probably for the first time in India with a humble beginning at the under-graduate level in 1880-1881, introduction and post-graduate stage in 1889, arrangement for teaching on a small scale and ultimately establishment of an independent Department of Pāli in 1917 for teaching and research in Pāli and Buddhistic Studies, the University of Calcutta, becomes the pioneer in the promotion of learning in this area. "The objective of the University in undertaking this venture was to open out to its advanced students an opportunity for a comprehensive study of that distinct and widespread civilization which is represented by Buddhism. The fact should not lost sight of that from the 5th century B.C. to the 12th century A.D. Buddhism moulded thoughts, ideals and literatures of the entire Far East. The history of Buddhism is also a story of cultural contacts between different groups of people in South, South-East and East Asia. The Department of Pali was intended to provide opportunities for the study of the cultural contacts between all these different regions."[1] Being inspired, as if, by this objective Bimala Churn Law undertakes courses in Pāli and Buddhistic Studies both at the undergraduate and post-graduate levels. He is the first alumnus of the Department of Pāli to obtain the higher academic degree of Ph.D. (Arts) from the University of Calcutta as early as in 1924 for his research work on *Some Kshatriya Tribes of Ancient India* which is mainly based on Buddhist sources.[2] This is auspicious beginning of Pāli and Buddhistic researches in India. later on, however, he has written several books on Pāli and Buddhistic Studies from various standpoints. For the volumes and variety of his works in this displine Dr. Law will ever be remembered. Through his labour and munificence he has left no stone unturned and opened up a new vista of Pāli and Buddhistic researches as is evident in his writings and lectures.

There is no denying the fact that The Asiatic Society, Calcutta, has been the first organisation in India to initiate researches on Pāḷi and Buddhistic Studies, while later on for some obvious reasons the University of Calcutta has become th first institution to conduct both teaching and research in this discipline in the country. Thus mainly due to the influences of these two great seats of learning Bimala Churn Law has been prepared to choose some aspects of this discipline for his academic pursuits.

Bimala Churn receives higher education at the Presidency College, Calcutta, and at the University College of ARts of the University of Calcutta having secured the first position in the first class among the successful candidates both of the B.A. Examination with Honours in Pāli in 1914 and of the M.A. Examination in Pali with specialisation in Buddhist Sanskrit, Epigraphy and Palaeography in 1916. Mention has already been made about his doctoral disseration submitted to the same University in 1924—a year which again brings for him Sir Asutosh Mookerjee Gold Medal from the University of Calcutta for his thesis on *Heaven and Hell in Buddhist Perspective*. From the University of Lucknow he obtains the Degree of Doctor of Literature and Bonnerjee Research Prize in 1940 for his research work on *India as described in Early Texts of Buddhism and Jainism*. Because of his 'Buddhistic' outlook he has put the word 'Buddhism' first in the title of his D. Litt. thesis, although 'Jainism' appears to precede the former one. In this connection it should be noted that while presenting Dr. B.C. Law to the Chancellor Srimati Sarojinit Naidu to confer on him the degree of Doctor of Literature *Honoris Causa* Dr. Tarachand, Vice-Chancellor of the University of Allahabad, cities: "I present to you Dr. Bimala Churn Law, who has long been acknowledged as a leading scholar in Buddhism and early Indian history." In recognition of his scholarship the Bomaby Branch of the Royal Asiatic Society of Great Britain and Ireland awards to him Campbell Memorial Gold Medal in February 1947. But unfortunately he cannot go to Bombay to receive it personally at its Annual Meeting. So the Medal has to be despatched to the Royal Asiatic Society of Bengal, now called The Asiatic Society, Calcutta, for presenting the same to Dr. B.C. Law. On February 3, 1947 at its Annual General Meeting His Excellency Sir Frederick Burrows, the then Governor of Bengal and Patron of the Society remarks : "It is with great pleasure that I hand over to you, Dr. Law, this medal (i.e. Campbell Memorial Medal). And I feel that the Bomaby Branch of the Royal Asiatic Society could not have made a worthier choice." In the meantime, the Vidyālaṅkāra Piriveṇa, now called Vidyālaṅkāra University, of Sri Lanka confers upon him the title "Bauddhāgamaśiromaṇi"—a rare honour with which a few Indians have been respected by the Sri Lankans in recognition of his distinctive service for the cause of Pāli and Buddhistic learning.

Works on Pāli and Buddhistic Studies

Turning back to the main theme of the present discussion Professor Benimadhab Barua's observation may be noted as follows. Professor Barua opines that the researches of Dr. Bimala Churn Law "are mainly directed to Buddhism, Pāli literature, History of Ancient Kṣatriya Tribes, History of India in the 5th century B.C., Geography of Ancient India, Jainism, and the Vaṁsa literature of Ceylon."[3] In fact, as already mentioned, almost all the efforts of Dr. B.C. Law have been mainly applied to the study of Pāli and Buddhistic themes. Mention may be made of his works on *A History of Pāli Literature*, Vols. I & II (London, Kegan Paul, Trench Trubner & Co. Ltd., 1933; *The Buddhist Conception of Spirits* (Calcutta, Thacker Spink, 1923); *A Study of Mahāvastu* with notes by A.B. Keith (Calcutta, Thacker Spink, 1930); *Concepts of Buddhism* (Leiden, Kern Institute, 1937); *Saundarānanda-Kāvya*, a Bengali Translation with notes;[4] *Buddhistic*

Studies [5] (Calcutta, Thacker Spink 1931), ed; Dr. *D.R. Bhandarkar Volume* (Calcutta, Indian Research Institute, 1940) ed; *The Debates Commentary* (London, Oxford University Press, 1940), an English translation of the Pali *Kathāvatthuppakarana-Aṭṭhakathā* for the first time; *Ancient Mid-Indian Kṣatriya Tribes*, Vol. I; *Ancient Indian Tribes*, Vols. I & II; *Historical Gleanings; Geographical Essays*, Vol.I; *Gautama Buddha; Aśvaghoṣa* (Calcutta, Royal Asiatic Society of Bengal, 1946); *Cariyāpiṭaka* (Poona, Bhandarkar Oriental Research Institute, 1949); *ed.* in Devanāgari Characters with Introduction in English; *Dipavaṁsa: A Historical Poem of the 4th century A.D. ed.* with a Introduction (*Ceylon Historical Journal*); *Kauśāmbī in Ancient Literature (ASI Memoir* No. 60); *Holy Places of India (CGS Bulletin* No. 3); *Thūpavaṁsa; Buddha Sahitye Pretatattva; Mountains of India; Rivers of India; Ujjayinī in Ancient India* (Archaeological Department, Gwalior State); *Bhārater Puṇyatīrtha; The Legend of Topes*, an english Translation of the *Thūpavaṁsa; The Magadhas in Ancient India (R.A.S. Monograph* No. 24); *Buddhaghosa* (Bomaby Branch of the *R.A.S. Monograph* No. 1 1946); *Panchālas and their capital Ahichchtra (A.S.I. Memoir* No. 68); *Avantī* (Pracyavani Mandir Publication); *Tirukkural et Dhammapada étude comparative* (Prais, Imprimerie Nationale, 1952); *Early Indian Monasteries* (Bangalore, Indian Institute of World Culture, 1958); *Geography of Early Buddhism* (London, Kegan Paul, Trench, Tribner & Co. Ltd., 1933); *Heaven and Hell in Buddhist Perspective* (REprint Varanasi, Bharatiya Publishing House, 1973); *History of Buddha's Religion* (*Sāsanavaṁsa*) (London, Luzac & Co., 1952); *A Manual of Buddhist Historical Traditions (Saddhamma-Saṅgaha)* (Calcutta, University of Calcutta, 1941); *The Life and Work of Buddhaghosa* (First *ed.* Calcutta, Thacker Spink, 1923, Reprint : Delhi, Nag Publishers, 1976); *Pali Selections for B.A. Honours ed.* (Calcutta, University of Calcutta, 1936);[6] *M.A. Pali Course*, 2 Pts. *ed.* (Calcutta, University of Calcutta, 1941);[7] *On the Chronicles of Ceylon* (Calcutta, Royal Asiatic Society of Bengal, 1947); *A Study of the Mahāvastu-Supplement* (Calcutta, Thacker Spink & Co., 1936), *Designation of Human Types tr* of the *Puggala-paññatti* (London, Pali Text Society, 1922), *Bauddha-ramaṇī* (Calcutta, G.D. Chattopadhyay, 1929); *Dāṭhāvaṁsa (A History of the Tooth-relic of the Buddha)* (Text & *tr.* together with a Note on the position of the *Dāṭhāvaṁsa* in the history of Pali Literature) *ed.* With a W., Stede (Lahore, Motilal Banarsidas, 1925); *Bauddha Yuger Bhūgol* (Calcutta, G.D. chattopadhyay, 1934); *Women in Buddhist Literature* (W.E. Bastian, 1927); *Kṣatriya Clans in Buddhist India* (Calcutta, Thacker Spink, 1922); *Licchavi Jāti* (Calcutta, R.N. Seal, B.S. 1331); *Rajagṛiha in Ancient Literature* A.S.I. Memoir No. 58); *Minor Anthologies of the Pāli Canon*, Pt. III : *Buddhavaṁsa : The Lineage of the Buddhas and Cariyā-Pitaka or the Collection of the Ways of Conduct* (London, P.T.S., 1938); *Srāvastī in Indian Literature* (Delhi, Manager of Publications, 1935).

Comments on Dr. B.C. Law's Works

Radhakumud Mookerji comments on a monograph on *Ancient India (Sixth Century B.C.)* written by Dr. Bimala Churu Law and published from Calcutta by the Indian Research Institute in 1948 in its "Popular Series" as follows: "... (the book draws) predominantly a picture of Buddhist India on the basis of its sources in Pali literature supplemented by the evidence from Jain and Brahmanical sources. It is a most useful handbook for the study of this unique period of Indian history. The book is made up of five sections dealing with geographical background, which contains much new material not so known: kings and peoples, social and economic life, religion and culture (including education and learning)." The reviewer further remarks : "...(it) in condensed writing, which has its own merits, not to be missed by readers, who are unable to undertake the study of specialised and extensive treatises...."[8]

A History of Pali Literature in two volumes written by Bimala Churan Law is indeed a comprehensive pioneer work on Pali literature. Because of its unique character it may be treated as *magnum opus* of the author who ill ever be remembered and revered by the Pali scholars. The French scholar Finot frankly notes: "It seems to be extremely well-devised to provide tillers of Buddha-*Ksetra* with an invaluable stock of information and references. The author has worked hard for this result and undoubtedly he will reap in return much *puṇya* with the gratitude of the whole *paṇḍitajana*".[9] This history of Pali literature is a voluminous compendium—the first volume dealing with the Pali Canonical literature and the second volume treating of the Non-Canonical Pali literature. Wilhelm Geiger, Professor of Indo-Iranian Languages, Munchen University, Germany, in the *Foreword* dated 16.2.1932 to the first Volume of this book writes: "I was very much pleased...when I heard that Dr. Bimala Churn Law had intended to publish a comprehensive work on Pali literature. We all know his former publications on Buddhist topics and their intrinsic value, and I repeatedly congratulated him on the happy choice of his themes and on the clever manner in which he had accomplished his task... It will prove to be extremely useful to all the Pali scholars by the sober and impartial judgment of the author and by the clear and exhaustive exposition of the various problems. Above all I wish to point at the important discussion of the relative chronology of the canonical texts, which means a considerable progress beyond what Rhys Davids has said on the subject, and at the ample and very clear summaries of the *Tipiṭaka* books which will be welcome to those who are unable to read them in the original language but with to become acquainted with their general plan and contents. I frankly say that I found all I could read extremely suggestive and I am convinced that I shall learn much from the book even where my opinion may perhaps differ from that of the author." The Contents of the first volume of this *History* are as follows: Chapter I: Chronology of the Pali Canon; Chapter II: Canonical Pali Literature Section I Vinaya Piṭaka, Section II Sutta Piṭaka—A. Digha Nikāya, B. Majjhima Nikāya, C. Saṁyutta Nikāya, D. Aṅguttara Nikāya, E. Khuddaka Nikāya, Section III Abhidhamma Piṭaka; Chapter III: Pali counterparts of the Seven Abhidhamma Treatises of the Sarvāstivāda School. On the other hand, the Contents of the second volume of the same work contains the following topics: Chapter IV-Extra Canonical Works presupposed by Pali Commentaries; Chapter V-Pali Commentaries; Chapter VI-Pali Chronicles; Chapter VII-Pali Manuals; Chapter VIII-Pali Literary Pieces; Chapter IX-Pali Grammars, Lexicographies, and Works of Prosody, etc.; Conclusion followed by Appendix A, Appendix B, Index. The first volume also consists of a Foreword, Preface, Introduction; while while the second volume contains an Introduction. In the Preface dated 22nd May 1933 to the first volume of *A History of Pali Literature*, Bimala Churn Law himself notes: "Scholars interested in Buddhism have no doubt felt a great want of an exhaustive treatment of Pali literature. I have, therefore, attempted for the first time to supply the need of a detailed and systematic history of Pali literature in two volumes...But my treatment of the subject is entirely different from those of my predecessors. The first volume deals with the chronology and general history of the Pali Pitakas. In the Introduction to this volume I have briefly discussed the origin of Pali and the importance of the study of Paly as one of the Indian languages....An attempt has been made to collect the parallel passages by way of comparison from other literatures wherever found. The second volume which treats of post-canonical Pali literature is devoted to the study of extra canonical works presupposed by the Pali commentaries, the Pali chronicles, the Pali manuals, the Pali literary pieces, the Pali grammars, lexicographies, and works on rhetoric. In the concluding chapter I have tried to give a general survey of the whole book and traced the development of Pali poetry. I have given two appendices dealing with the Historical and Geographical references in the Pali Piṭakas and the Pali tracts in the inscriptions, which, I believe, will be found useful". At the end of this *Preface* the author expresses his gratefulness with the following words: "I am grateful to

Mrs. Rhys Davids and Dr. B.M. Barua for their valuable suggestions for the improvement of this work. Dr. W. Geiger has really laid me under a deep debt of gratitude by writing a Foreword". About B.C. Law's Historical Gleanings (Calcutta, Thacker Spint & Co.) which contains a *Foreword* by Professor B.M. Barua, Mrs. C.A.F. Rhys Davids remarks: "It is all useful work", Lord Ronaldshay writes: "I have found much interest in it". According to J.N. Farfuhar: "They are a most useful set of essays setting for the material of genuine historic interest, and of special value for the student who doe snot read Pali". And Mahamahopadhoyay Dr. Ganga Nath Jha has commented as follows: "The articles are stimulating and sometimes provocative. I hope they will prove useful". A learned paper on *Slavery as known* Early Buddhists contributed by Bimala Churn Law tot he first part of the Diamond Jubilee Volume of the Bharatiya Vidya, Vol. IX, 1948 published from Bombay by the Bharatiya Vidya Bhavan in 1949, is important.

On the *Preface* to the *Buddhistic Studies* Dr. B.C. Law writes (in July 1931): "An attempt has been made in this volume to collect and publish some contributions to the study of Buddhist thought from eastern and western scholars various topics relating to Buddhism and Buddhist history have no doubt been dealt with here and I shall consider my labour amply rewarded if this treatise is found useful to those for whom it is intended".

Bimala Churn Law has also rendered into English the *Thupavamsa*, one of the *Vamsa* texts, with the title *The Legend of the Topes* (*Thupavamsa*) under the Bibliotheca Indica series (No. 268 : 1945) from the Royal Asiatic Society of Bengal. The translator aptly comments on the original Pali text as follows: "The *Thpavamsa* is undoubtedly one of the products of the decadent period of Pali literature in Ceylon. It is lacking in originality and the atmosphere of life it creates is dull and monotonous. Its English translation may, nevertheless, help the reader to understand and appreciate a Pali traditional work of the late medieval period, to crack the hard nut of the stereotyped and highly, conventionalized prose of scholastic writings". In fact, this English translation of a Pali *Vamsa* text is one of the many scholarly works done by a great scholar like B.C. Law.

The following contents of Dr. Bimala Churn Law's *Geographical Essays*, Vol.I, reveal that this work is primarily concerned with Buddhist Studies, namely, (1) Geographical data from Sanskrit Buddhist Literature, (2) South India as a centre of Pali Buddhism, (3) Geographical data from the *Mahāvaṁsa* and its Commentary, (4) Damila and Damilarattha, (5) Mountains and Rivers of India, (6 & 7) Countries and Peoples of India and Appendix to the same, (8) Kapilavastu, (9) Buddhist cave temples in India, (10) Sacred places of the Jains, and (11) Sacred places of the Vaisnavas. Except two or three out of the topics discussed in this work deal with Buddhistic themes. In fact, for the period of Buddha almost all geographical references concerning India are very carefully collected herein. About this book *The Hindu* reviews: "Dr. law, who is already known to the world of scholars as the author of a 'History of Pali Literature', 'Geography of Early Buddhist....deals at some length with the history of the Madhyadesa so far as it relates to the Buddhistic period....Of interest to the Puranic geographer is the reference to the places like Bamagrama in the land of the Koliyas where the eighth stupa and a caitya were erected by Asoka....An entire chapter is devoted to Kapilavastu bringing together in one place all that is Buddhistically connected with it". Although a very ancient city is Rajagrha, Dr. B.C. Law in his *Rājagriha in Ancient Literature* utilises mainly the Buddhistic sources in his discussions on (i) Different names : Their origin and significance, (ii) General description and topography, (iii) Antiquity and history of Rajagriha, (iv) Antiquity and location of five hills, (v) Rajagriha in religious history, and (vi) Architecture of Rajagriha. The *Oriental Litreary Digest* in its No. IX, 1939 issue reviews the work at length and concludes: "...an exhaustive and systematic account of Rajagriha from all available literary sources, Brahmanical, Jaina and Buddhist, which coupled with the map of Rajagriha...brings out in full historical relief this hallowed place so rich in historical and religious associations...It is difficult in this short notice to indicate the importance of the geographical and historical date recorded in this monograph about Rajagriha, the birth-place of Buddhism. If Lord Buddha praised the sombre beauty of Rajagriha with its hills and retreats with the words : "Elightful, Andand, is Rajagriha", we have no hesitation to say : "Delightful is *Rajagriha in Ancient Literature*".

About Dr. Bimala Churn Law's *Śrāvastī in Indian Literature* (Archaeological Survey of India Memoir No. 50, Government of India) the well-known scholar Dr. F.W. Thomas addressing the author writes : "I have persued your excellent memoir on Śrāvasti. You have collected a large amount of information, and the paper shows that with careful examination the Pali texts may still shed further important light upon the condition of India during the early period". Dr. E.J. Thomas also notes : "From an archaeological standpoint it is one of the most important steps taken since Rhys Davids' researches in Buddhist India". On the other hand *The Hindu* in its review published on 9.1. 1936 remarks as follows : "The author has brought to bear on his task the literary materials that lie imbedded in Brahmanical, Buddhist and Jaina texts, as well as the intineraries of the two celebrated Chinese pilgrims Fa-Hien and Yuan-Chwang. The result is an exhaustive account of an important centre of religion and art, that had a continuous period of activity from the time of the Buddha to the 12th century after Christ. This book by Dr. Law is certainly welcome addition to the already rich stock of Buddhistic literature".

Dr. B.C. Law's *Kauśāmbi in Ancient Literature* (A.S.I. Memoir No. 60) deals with the (i) Antiquity and origin of the name, (ii) General description and topography, (ii) The Vasas or Vatsas and their land, (iv) Political history of Vatsa, (v) Udayana, his parents, queens and children, (vi) Vatsa and Kausambi in religious history. It also contains an index, three plates and a well-drawn map. This work is also mainly based on Buddhistic sources, although the Brahmanic and Jaina texts have been consulted wherever necessary. The *Hindustan Standard*, in its issue dated August 6, 1939 reviews this book as follows " "...Based on literary sources, Brahmanical, Jaina Buddhist, and the itineraries of the Chinese piligrims, the monograph gives an account of the ancient historic city of Kausambi, the capital of the Vatsas, important alike because of its political and religious associations...use has been made of considerable original material hitherto unused."

Regarding *The Buddhist Conception of Spirits* (revised edition)_ of Dr. B.C. Law opines Dr. L.D. Barnett : "It is an excellent work illuminating a side of Indian mental life which is really important and yet has been much neglected by previous scholars". *The New Review* in its September 1937 issue records : "In this short but substantial book Dr. B.C. Law tells us all that is known about the Buddhist belief in *pretas*, the spirits or ghosts of the unhappy dead. The origin of the belief, its definition and description, the *pretas* and their state, stories about them, and the moral purpose of these stories—nothing has escaped his scholarship. The result is a volume which no anthropologist, and especially no student of India's popular religion, can afford to neglect."

Dr. B.C. Law has written some books in Bengali. One of them is the *Bauddha-ramaṇī* (Buddhist Women)[10] dedicated to his father and grandfather contains the following seven chapters, namely, *Prathama Pariccheda : Bauddhayuge Udbāhatattva* (First Chapter—Marriage System during the Buddhist period), *Dvitiya Pariccheda : Bauddhayugo Kṛtadāsī* (Second Chapter-Female Slaves in the Buddhist Age), *Tṛtiya Pariccheda : Bauddhayuge Narttakī O Bārabanitā* (Third Chapter-Female Dancers and Prostitutes during the Buddhist Period), *Caturtha Pariccheda : Naricaritra* (Fourth Chapter-Female Character), *Pancama Pariccheda : Bauddayuge Stri Siksa* (Fifth Chapter-

Female Education during the Buddhist Period), *Sastha Pariccheda : Gautam Buddha O Ramanigan* (Sixth Chapter-Gautam Buddha and Women), and *Saptama Pariccheda : Khyatanama Bauddharamanigan* (Seventh Chapter-Famous Buddhist Women), which is followed by a *Nirghanta* or Index of Proper Names

Bimala Churn Law has also creditably edited B.M. Barua Commemoration Volume of the Indian Culture (Vol. XV, Nos. 1-4, July 1948-June 1949). The first two articles of this volume are written by Dr. H.C. Raychaudhuri of the University of Calcutta and Ven. A.P. Buddhadatta of Sri Lanka on Porfessor Benimadhab Barua. However, this Volume contains thirty papers, nineteen book-reviews and three obituary notes on C.E.A.W. Oldham, batakrishna Ghosh and D.R. Bhandarkar. Dr. B.C. Law has himself written a very interesting paper on *Ancient Indian Flora* for this volume. The source-materials of it comprise mainly the Pali texts. But Brahmanical and Jain books have also been fully utilised by the author. Besides, he has supplied also the botanical terms for trees and flowers. In the second part of it he remarks and actually does accordingly : "Indian literature mentions various kinds of trees, plants, shrubs, fruits, flowers, etc., arranged in an alphabetical order in the subsequent pages. An attempt has been made to elicit information regarding them as far as available from the literature concerned. It mentions many medicinal plants, water plants, royal trees (*rāja-rukkhā*)[11], and fragrant grass (*bīraṇaṃ*). It refers to trees, the flowers of which have the colour of collyrium (*añjana*). Fiver kinds of leaves (panna) recommended for medicinal purposes, namely, *nimba-kūṭaja, paṭota, sulasī,* or *tulsī,* and *kappāsika* are mentioned in the *Vinaya Piṭaka*. There are trees which cannot be identified such as *somarukkha*.

In the sixth century B.C. India saw several groves of *anjana* (name of a tree, 'black tree', *Jat* I. 331) *amba* (mango) and *sala* at Upavattana and Kusinara." In order to attract the attention of the botanists, bio-chemists, and medical practitioners only one entry found in this learned paper may be mentioned as an illustration as follows: *Haritaka Terminalia Chebula,* Retz.)-A large tree; flowering time—hot season; flowers small, its fruits form the commercial chebulic myrobalans. It is used as a purgative. Myrobalan plants grow in the Himalayas. They are known as *Terminalia Chebula,* Retz; *Phyllanthus Emblica,* Gaertn and *Emblica officianlis*. It fruits and seeds are used for medicinal purposes. They give relief to those suffering from piles, rheumatism, eye-disease, stone in the gall bladder and smallpox. Its fruit acts as a good purgative. It should be first taken and then a drink of tepid water according to the *Susruta Samhita* (Chap. I)." There are more than 240 entries of trees, plants, and flowers arranged in an alphabetical order and properly identified with modern terminology along with their medicinal uses in this paper which is, in this perspective, really a useful one. Bimala Churn Law commenting no Nalininth Das Gupta's *Bangalay Bauddha-dharma* (Buddhism in Bengal) Published from Calcutta by A. Mukherjee & Co. writes : "Mr. Das Gupta has made an attempt for the first time in this book to give a connected and comparative account of Buddhism in Bengali in seven sections. He has given a very readable account of Buddhist images in the Pala period and latter. His section on Buddhist *viharas* in Bengal is interesting but in some places there are inaccuracies...In the *Introduction* (P. 13) we are astouned to find his wrong statement that no systematic account of Buddhist philosophy is found in the *Abhidhamma-Pitaka*... Mr. Das Gupta is specially requested to read these books (of the *Abhidhamma-Pitaka*) before making any such misstatement. In pages 14 and 15 of his book he has made a confusion between Sanskrit and Pali words...In page 32 Mr. Das Gupta says that there is a reference to Lalha or West Bengal in one of the *Jatakas* (*Jat*.I, p. 447). There is no such reference in the said *Jataka* in which occurs the word *lala-manavo* meaning a dull young Brahmin. I must invite the attention of the learned author to the serious mistake committed by him. Can he find at any reference to Lalha in the whole *Jataka* book? He will surely by disappointed..."

This is how a serious reviewes like Dr. B.C. Law reviews a book and does not compromise in case of academic excellence. Still he never discourages the author. So he writes ultimately : "This book will be welcome, if the author takes particular care in correcting all these errors in the second edition... The book contains some good illustrations and a serviceable index." Such constructive criticism is really meaningful to any author.

Addresses and Lectures on Pali and Buddhistic Studies

Dr. Bimala Churn Law while addressing to the scholars or to the general public has always been aware of his own subject of specialisation. Thus in his address as the President of the Buddhistic Section of the Indian Cultural Conference held in Calcutta in 1936 Dr. B.C. Law points out : "It is encouraging to find many people of Asia and Europe interested in the study of Buddhism and Buddhist thought...We must always remain grateful to the Pali Text Society of England and especially to the late T.W. Rhys Davids and his talented wife Mrs. C.A.F. Rhys Davids for the indefatigable labours done by them for printing and publishing a major portion of the Pali texts and commentaries and making them accessible to the public". Dr. Law also reminds : "in order to arrive at a real significance of Buddhism we have to study carefully Mahayàna Buddhist Sutras". Next in the same lecture he has dealt elaborately with Tibetan and Chinese forms of Buddhism and concludes with the following remarks : "I must record here our indebtedness to the late lamented Sir Ashutosh Mookerjee, the greatest and the ablest Vice-Chancellor of the Calcutta University, who fostered and furthered the study of Pali and Buddhism...His death has been a great loss to the Buddhistic studies in India."

At the inaugural meeting of the Bharati Buddha Parisat held in May 1943 as the President Dr. Bimala Churn Law says about the *Dhammacakkapavattana Sutta* : "In his first discourse the Buddha was required not only to state his own doctrine but to contrust it with those of others that held the field. His was that of a golden mean (*madhya*)as contrasted with the position held by other teachers of the age. As regards the thought, the mean was represented by *pratītyasamutpāda* or formula of causal genesis and as regards the path, the mean was represented by the noble tenfold path...The first point is the basic idea of Buddhism as a system of thought....It is interpreted as a theory of *Uppāda* (genesis, evolution) other than that which was contemplated by the Samkhya doctrine of *Puruṣa* and *Prakṛiti*. The celebrated Pali commentator, Buddhaghosa, has advanced four arguments to refute this, two of which are noteworthy: (1) that there is no *sutta* to lend support to this view and (2) that the view goes against the purport of authorotive texts, e.g. those stating that when the Buddha had revolved the law of causal genesis in his mind for the first time, he did it in both *anuloma* and *patiloma* modes embracing the *samudaya* and *nirodha* aspects of *dukkha*, and those (e.g. the *Kaccāyana Sutta*) presenting the law in the very same two modes with a view to meeting the two extreme positions of *atthi* and *n'atthi*, *sassata* and *uccheda*." In the same speech Dr. law opines : "In short, the Buddha's life was a life of action, earnestness, wakefulness, simplicity, frankness, sincerity, perfection and order" and concludes : "The more we have Buddha societies in India and abroad, the better".

The Presidential Address which Dr. Bimala Churn Law delivers at the Maha Bodhi Society, Calcutta, on the occasion of the Vaisakha Purnima Celebration in 1944 may also be taken care of in th is connection. He says : "The importance of the Vaisakha (Vesak) purnima day in the history of Buddhism is very great as this day witnessed three important events in the life of the Buddha, viz., his birth, his attainment of enlightenment and his `pari-nirvāṇa' or his passing away". This long but throughout provocating speech ends with the undernoted words : "The religion which he (Buddha) preached spread far and wide in India and abroad and moulded the civilization of the countries and nations of the world. It is still followed by millions of people in all parts of the globe. His religion has served to raise India in the estimation of the civilised world and I think it is now the time when we should remember the famous sayings of the Master who was the first to proclaim to the world:

Na hi verena verāni sammantīdha kudācanaṁ
averena ca sammanti; esa dhammo sanāntano.
"hatred does not cease by hatred,
it ceases by love — this is the good old rule".

It is interesting to not that at the Annual Meeting of the Royal Asiatic Society of Bengal, now called The Asiatic Society, Calcutta, held in February 1948 Bimala Churn Law revealing his awareness and drawbacks in the field of Pali and Buddhistic Studies remarks : "Now we have broad outlines of literary history of Jainism and Buddhism. No attempt broad outlines of literary history of Jainism and Buddhism. No attempt has yet been made to publish : (1) *A concordance of the Pāli and Ardhamāgadhī canonical texts,* and (2) *a good comparative study of their contents.* The Pali Text Society has rendered an immense service to indological studies by publishing the Pali texts, commentaries, and manuals, along with a few English translations. Laudable attempts have subsequently been made in Ceylon, Burma, Siam and also in India to make them accessible to the reading public. But they are mostly edited uncritically, there being a very few examples of high standard as maintained in Fausboll's edition of the Jātaka...The discovery of several fragments of Buddhist literature in Eastern Turkisthan and that of the Gilgit manuscripts of several Buddhist works in Sanskrit have helped us a good deal in restoring the Buddhist compilations made in the schools other than the *Theravāda*. The restoration of the *Sarvāstivāda* version of the *Vinayapiṭaka* completely preserved in a Tibetan translation, on the strength of the Gilgit manuscripts, is a definite gain to Indology. The Korean representative to the Asian Relations Conference informs us that the complete set of a Sanskrit version of the *Piṭakas* exists in Korea. But more startling than these is the discovery of some of the original Indian manuscripts of Buddhist works on logic and other subjects in Tibet by Prof. Rahula Sanskrityayana...The Tibetan Buddhist literature should be thoroughly and systematically studied". He is also aware of the fact that "The Japanese scholars have made a distinct improvement in some respects at least on the pioneer works done by Csoma De Koros and Coedier...The Sino-Indian Studies by S. Beal, Watters, Paul Pelliot, Chavannes and Sylvain Levi have acquired much importance since the discovery of the remains of Buddhism and Buddhist literature in Central Asia....The historical chronicles in Pali, Sanskrit, Sinhalese, Burmese, and Tibetan, are being critically studied for reliable materials". Having discussed many points of indological studies in general and Buddhistic studies in particular in his long presidential address Dr. B.C. law has at the end submitted : "My interest, however, is just to draw your attention to some of the salient points. In doing so it is no less my intention to emphasize the fact that India can ill afford to neglect the investigations concerning her and Asia, if she really aspires to take her rightful place in the comity of nations, nor is it to be supposed that the scholars and researchers, who have silently devoted themselves to the pursuit of knowledge about India and Asia, are in any way lesser patriots than those who have publicly fought for freedom."

Conclusion

In the foregoing pages an attempt has been made to reveal the fact that in the broad spectrum of indological studies Dr. Bimala Churn Law has focussed his spotlight on Pali and Buddhistic Studies. Throughout his life in his writings, popular lectures and learned addressed he has shown that without the background knowledge of Pali and Buddhistic Studies it is hardly possible to have an idea of the heritage of India, of which the scholars have been now-a-days more and more conscious for rewriting the incomplete chapters of Indian history and culture.

References

1. C.U. *Annual Report*, 1954-55.
2. *Journal of the Department of Pali* (University of Calcutta), Vol. I : 1982-83, p. 195.
3. Barua, Benimadhab, *Asoka and His Inscriptions* (Calcutta, New Age Publishers Ltd., 1946), p. XIV (*Dr. B.C. Law—A Memoir*)
4. *See* at the end of the Bengali translation of Aśvaghoṣa's *Saundarananda Kavya*, by B.C. Law.
5. Law, Bimala Churn *ed. Buddhistic Studies* (Delhi, Indological Book House, 1983), p. iii.
6. Law, Bimala Churn *ed. pali Selections For B.A. Honours* (Calcutta, University of Calcutta, 1936), p. i.
7. Law, Bimala Churn *ed. M.A. Pali Course* Part I (Calcutta, University of Calcutta, 1941), pi. iii.
8. *Indian Culture*, Calcutta, Vol. XV, Nos. 1-4, July 1948-June 1949, pp. 240-241 (*Reviews*)
9. *Indian Culture*, Calcutta, Vol. XV, Nos. 1-4 (July 1948-June 1949), pp. 242-244 (*Reviews*).
10. Chattopadhyay & Sons, 2nd edition, 1923. Laha, Bimala Charan. *Bauddharamaṇī*. Calcutta, Gurudas Chattopadhyay & Sons, 1929.
11. Cathartocarpus fistula, V.A. 43.

Aspects of Indian History and Historiography
Editor : P.K. Mishra
Kaveri Books, New Delhi, India.

Some Illusionistic Thoughts in History Writing

27

Rasesh Jamindar

The purport here is to examine some of the false perceptions prevalent amongst the world of teaching about history writing. They are : repetition of history, problem of periodization, concept of Golden Age and wrong notion of comparing historical facts. The meaning and scope of the word history, its main characters and interdisciplinary approach have also been discussed as prelude.

Meaning of History

At the outset it is imperative to make clear the meaning and scope of history. Many historians, then and now, western and eastern, have been defining the word history. But we should bear in mind that even the careful exercise of defining this word will remain tentative and therefore, we will have to change the definition when conceptual complexion of the subject itself changes. Viewing through this criterion, history means an outward expression or activity of human mind or thought. Rabindranath Tagore has, therefore, rightly stated that : There is only one History—The History of Man.[1]

Why Human History?

Amongst the inanimate and animate substances man has a different and unparalleled significance for two reasons : (1) Man is a social animal, for individual constitutes society and in the society individual gets developed. Thus man and society are mutually dependable. Man is not valued just because he is a man, but he is considered only in the context of the society. This is not found in other animals except man, who is the most dignified animal in the animate world.

What is Dignifying a Man?

The gift of Intellect is the answer. This special element is positively not found in other animals. This is the reason why their activities normally go unnoticed. Contrary to this, the activity of a man with the help of the special gift (i.e. intellect) has, therefore, acquired much significance, Man, alike this sanskrit maxim, क्षणे क्षणे यन्नवक्षामुपैति । goes on doing things, tries to modify them and thus sets on the path of development. Man's totality of all these efforts is but history.

Man is the Centre History

Many incidents take place on the earth, of which not all are inspired or created by man's intellect. Thus, incidents taking place without man's efforts are termed as natural actions, while those produced by power of thoughts are called actions of history. Only the special element of intellect, the monopoly of man, is entitled to be a part of historical process, for 'man is regarded as the only animal that thinks or thinks enough and clearly enough, to render his actions the expression of his thoughts.....and is the only animal whose conduct is, to any great extent, determined by thought instead of by mere impulse and appetite'.[2] So to say, and as already noted earlier, the outward expression of mind or thought is the subject matter of history.

History's Main Characteristics

History consists of three main characteristics : Time, Space (Place) and Society (or individual or circumstances). All these three have their own settings. They are distinctly original; but even then each one of them is crippled, that is to says, their seperate existence or entity is meaningless. The importance of their existence is meaningful only in mutual nearness. Thus, these three characteristics are interwoven and interdependent. Absence of any of these ceases one's own importance and so also the probability of history. This means history conceives its form on the cross-roads of Time, Space and Society.

Trio is Dependable

For inanimate substances Time is least concerned. Its proper consideration takes place only in context of animate world; but it is much more valuable to man or society. Man cannot do without time, for it is motionable. To remain in constant motion is the very nature of time. Consequently, days, nights, seasons etc. are possible. These are must for human beings to live a life. If time stands still, human life is not possible. Thus, the relation between time and man is like a warp and woof.

Let us now examine the relation of time and society to place. Because of earth man gets every necessary item for smooth living. Without the earth animate world is impossible. Inasmuchas, the place is also a must for man as time.[3]

Scope of History

Closely interwoven with the problem of meaning of history is the question of its scope. Many of the historians even today consider history as only political history i.e. narration of kings and their kingdoms, their palaces and daily activities, their wars and achievements etc. This is onesided observation of the word history. 'The real connotation of the term does not include only political events. This was a history in which common people had no place. This narrow view of the word has gradually withered away. History, notwithstanding, is no longer a mere catalogue of political events, but includes in its fold the achievements of the common people in every walk of life'.[4] History of any country, in this sense, has therefore to be a history of social and cultural growth and development as well as of thought processes, and not as commonly believed a political history.

To sum up, history means any kind of inquiry in the field of human past. 'It is, therefore, not limited to what is ordinarily taught as history, but includes the history of art, language, literature, institutions, science, religion, philosophy, textual and a esthetic criticism, interpretation of works and movements, research of artistic poetical, political and religious forms, their first appearances, their withering away and their rekindling'.[5]

Definition of History[6]

Let us now study some of the definitions in corroboration of the foregoing discussion : They are : (1) History is the story of the deeds and achievements of men living in the societies.[7] (2) History is the science of men in time.[8] (3) Human activities, to be proper material for history, must be concrete, that is, restricted in time and place.[9] (4) History is concerned with men in time. The essence of history rests on time factor.[10] (5) History, the most inclusive and many sided of all the social sciences, may be defined as the science which first investigates and then records, in their casual relations and development, such past human activities as are (1) definite in time and space, (2) social in nature and (3) socially significant.[11]

All these five definitions have to say the same thing regarding history; that is according to them history; that is according to them history consists of three characteristics : Time, space and society. We have discussed earlier these characters : *Samaya* (time), *Sthāna* (Place) and *Samāja* (Society).

To sum up, history is the Diary of Man. (*Mānavikī Rajanishi Te Itihās*).[12]

Does History Repeats ?

Time is one of the prime characters of history. Rather it is the soul of history. Then what is Time ? Time is but change. In other words, time cannot stand still. if time stops human life is impossible, and therefore, history, whose centroid constitutes nothing but human activities, ceases by itself. Thus, change is a must for history. Garraghan advocates the same thing : Anything that changes will have a history; God who is unchanging and unchangeable can have no history .....Any true conception of history necessarily posits the idea of change.[13]

If any individual or an ideal given by an individual or an institution founded by anybody does not go with the passage of time, then he or it ceases to be progressive. Therefore, change is plainly necessary for progress, rather say, progress is the result of change. The only difference lies here is in the sense of degree.

Time moves in a definite direction. To step back is not possible for it. Time has an element of continuity and that is why it shows the continuity of events. Alike time, historical events also do not go back. History, is nothing but chain of events inspired by human intellect. One event follows another and this process goes on non-stop for ever. But every event takes place at a definite point of time. Hence, any event, which has taken place at a particular time, does not repeat or find the same place again.[14]

Thus it is quite obvious that history-made of warp and woof of Time, Place and Society (i.e. *Samaya, Ṣthāna* and *Samāja*)-does not, at all, repeat itself.[15]

Let us narrate some historical facts in support of this statement : History never repeats.

Ashoka Maurya, Kushaṇa Emperor Kaṇishka and Harshavardhana all had propagated for spreading the message of *Bhagawan Buddha*. Now if one says that the propagation committed by Kaṇishka is nothing but a mere repetition of what Ashoka did for spread of Buddhism or what Harshavardhan undertook for the development of Buddism is merely, a repetition of Kanishka's propagation, is very far from historical truth. Efforts for religious propaganda are universal. Therefore, repetition is least possible for universal thing, which has an attribution of continuity.

Secondly, all the three kings were unidentical in their Buddhist mission. After the bloodshed of Kalinga war Ashoka, to repent for his barbarous act, accepted the Buddha's teachings and tried his best for its spread. Kaṇishka was a foreigner. He was acquainted with doctrines of many religions known to the then Asia. Establishing his supremacy over most part of north India he also became a follower of Buddhism after reading thoughts of Ashvaghosha and Vasumitra, the great philosophers of Buddhism of that age. Harshavardhana was attracted towards Buddhism after rescuing his sister from firebath and after having an opportunity of hearing Buddhist Monk.

Thirdly, Ashoka propagated Buddhism on moral basis. He put ban on wars and preached to go for *Dharma*. For this very reason he engraved edicts on rocks, put ban on violence and killing of animals and worked whole-heartedly for the welfare of mankind and animal world. Contrary to this, Kaṇishka called the 4th Buddhist conference and collected the scattered religious literature. He also established the Buddhist doctrines. It was during this very *Sangiti* that the split in Buddhism became evident. Though Harsha built many big monasteries on the bank of the river *Gangā*, he did not offer his entire life to Buddhism.

The foregoing discussion obviously proves that there is no possibility of any kind of repetition in their propaganda.

Let us narrate another example. *Rushabhadev*, the first *Tirthañkar* of Jaina faith, as we know, advocated to practise Non-violence for religious preachings and welfare of human being; while Gandhiji, the prophet-activist of our times and the father of our nation, did preach *Ahimsā* as a political weapon for getting freedom from British yoke. Thus, both gave the message of *Ahimsā* but with different and distinct means as well as at a different time. Therefore, instead of viewing repetition in their efforts, it is rather proper to label it as a continuous and universal process, which is one of the basic characters of Indian Culture. No two events are identical as no two individuals are. So it is not fair to define the latter event as a repeated process of the former one; for time is not the same, place is also different and so is also the society or individual.

Let us refer to one more example regarding three big revolutions of the world. The root cause of American revolution was colonial settlements of the European countries and their shabby activities. It was a revolt against predomination of king George, the 3rd. Boats loaded with tea-leaves parcels arrived at Boston port. Colonists had thrown those parcels away into the sea and the war sparked out. French revolution centred around the middle class. Social inequality was its inspiring force. During the reign of Louis the 16th, political situation in France went worse. To bring the situation under control Louis took the help of military. Meanwhile people attacked the fort of Bastille and got the prisoners relieved, which resulted into a war. The labourers were responsible for the Russian revolt. This effort was mainly to uproot the age-old social system. Industrial revolution brought mechanism in Russia, which had a far reaching effect on the farmers. This was the prelude for Russian revolution. More than half a million defeated, oppressed and tired labourers took shelter of strike and started movement against the terrorism of Czar. Russia thus got entrapped into the mud of revolt.

Thus it positively seems from the foregoing discussion that history, particularly human history, does never repeat itself, though it does change, which is its prime function.[16]

Concept of Golden Age[17]

What do we understand by the term Golden Age? Generally when a particular age of history of any country marks the summit of prosperity in every sphere of human life we designate that period as Golden period. It is high time to appraise the problem of the concept of Golden Age; for it is customary that almost all of the historians, when they describe the Golden period either praise the ruling king or kings, or the dynasty during whose rule or reign the peaks of prosperity become evident. Is this not a wrong concept? Is this term not a misnomer? Let us take stock of this problem.

Is it logical to subscribe the so-called prosperity and all sided progress to the only credit of those kings or that dynasty during whose rule the quantum of success reaches its highest point? No doubt, partly, it is true to some extent that when a particular period enjoys the fruits of growth and development almost in every walk of life we call it a golden age. But development does not depend only on one factor, nor is it a result of the labour of the kings and people of that period.

Nevertheless, we should bear in mind that progress is not an overnight business, nor it is a process of magic. Fruits of the progress can be obtained after a hard labour for a long time. Rather it is a result of the hard labour of the multiracial and multi-dynastical work multiplied together for years together. While th Golden period is the form of the highest performance achieved by the people and ruler of that age, it is equally true that it is the result of the inlaid labour of the people and kings of the preceeding age or ages. Therefore it is not advisable to designate only that period as golden period during which the all sided progress and prosperity has become evident in its highest form. We should not fail to put on record the work done or hard labour put in by the earlier people with the help of contemporary rulers. In fact, the real credit should go to those people and dynasties who were predecessors of the people and royal dynasties to whom we attach this misnomer term. No matter, if progress in any field does not reach its highest peak at once or overnight.

Hence, how far is this term golden age correct? There are other factors to be looked into, such as, when the people breathe a free air without being worried about any external aggression or internal conflict of any nature, when people live their day-to-day life without a bit of state interference of any kind, when people get their household commodities at reasonable price without much labour, when social and cultural activities get grants or monetary help from the Government very frequently, when rulers the wedded to the welfare activities for the cause of the better and smooth life of their subjects, when we observe all sided economic progress and stability, when we feel both social and economic equality amongst all creeds and colours of people and when normally people live a peaceful life; then people get inspired to put together their head, hands and heart for all sided growth and development. Thereafter progress becomes the progress of the people.

Keeping this requirement in mind in its strict sense, can we really term Gupta period and Baburi dynasty of India, or Solanki period of Gujarat, or Periclean age in the history of Greece or Augustus, period of the Roman history as Golden Ages of World History?

it will not be out of place to narrate and analyse the Gupta period as a Golden Period in the light of the foregoing discussion about the concept of Golden Age.

Gupta administration was not at all original. Gupta rulers have adopted in toto the principles of state-administration of the Mauryas; which were founded and put into practice by Chandragupta Maurya and his Prime Minister Chāṇakya. No doubt, Gupta rulers were able to introduce their own and original principles for running the state, but they did not waste their time and energy; instead they used their precious times in the growth in other fields. Thus, it is imperative to note the contribution of the Mauryan period in the stable and strong administration of the Guptas.

It is true that *Brāhman Dharma* did reach its peak during the Gupta period, but the counchshell of the rise (*Abhudaya*) of *Brāhman Dharma*, was blown during pre-Gupta period by the king Pushyamitra, the founder of the Sunga dynasty. he was Brāhmin and hence revived the sacrifices and became responsible for the resurrection of *Brāhman Dharma*. His son Agnimitra continued the very efforts of his father. Rulers of Kāṇva and Bhārashiva dynasties contributed their might to the development of *Brāhman Dharma*. Andhra-Sātavāhanas also made their share in the growth of the said faith. The Vākāṭaka kings also did not lag behind. Thus, during the three-four centuries prior to the Gupta period, the process of the re-installation of *Brahman Dharma* had already started and its advantage was swallowed by the Gupta rulers. That is why we see the resurrection of this faith during Gupta period.

Likewise, in the field of economic growth both Maurya and post-Maurya periods have their due shares. Maurya Kings showed their enthusiasm in the growth of agriculture and its products. They initiated irrigation and provided various kinds of good seeds, agricultural implements and such other facilities. The Sudarshan lake of Girinagara, built by Chandra Gupta Maurya, is the best example in this direction.[18] The international trade, especially with that with Roman Empire, did grow during Post-Maurya times; i.e. during the first three centuries after Christ. This period showed tremendous increase in export than import. Therefore, in exchange for import items Romans had to pay the equal amount in Gold and Silver. Hence, the economic prosperity of India did set on growing, which ultimately, by all means helped the Gupta period in increasing its prosperity.

Thus, in the spheres of administration, religion, agriculture, trade and economy Gupta period witnessed prosperity which was due to the earlier efforts made by both Maurya and post-Maurya periods. This is no doubt visibly evident.

In this view we can also evaluate other Golden periods of Indian and world history. Such evaluation will disprove the thesis of Golden Period.

Periodisation in Indian History

The most pertinent question, which requires comprehensive discussion, is that of periodization in Indian history. This is really a baffling task for historians. Not much attention has been given to this problem. Viewing through the catholic nature of Indian history it needs thorough investigation.

Unfortunately, historians have divided world history into three periods viz. ancient, medieval and modern on the basis of the advent of Muslims and Europeans, overlooking the basic fact that history is an everflowing continuous stream of human activities since his first appearance on the earth. nevertheless, we have divided Indian history either into ancient, medieval and modern or as Hindu, Muslim and British. These are not logical and scientific divisions. Can we prove that during Hindu India only Hindu or Brāhmin Kings ruled over us? There were also Buddhist and Jaina Kings; such as Ashoka, Khāravela, Kanishka and others, ruling during Hindu period. Generally, we end our ancient period with the death of Harshavardhana. Then, what about the centuries between Harsha's death and the establishment of Muslim rule in India? Can we lable this lacuna either as Hindu or Islamic? There were Rajput kingdoms even during this gap. Can we designate this gap as Rajput period? Even these princely states were ruled by both Hindu kings and Muslim rulers. There were princely states of both Rajputs and Muslims during the British supremacy. Therefore, how can we call medieval India and modern India as Muslim India and British India?

This is a very erroneous belief. neither ancient, medieval and modern terms nor Hindu, Muslim and British words convey specific and correct concept and meaning regarding the problem of periodization. All these terms are misomer.

Did Muslims rule over India in the middle of our history? Cannot we consider medieval period as ancient period? Certainly the muslims ruled over India earlier than the British. Is twentieth century Indian Society is as catholic in nature and secular in outlook as Vedic Society of earlier times? People of Lothal Civilizations were enjoying the facility of drainage system as anterior as third millenium B.C., Can we boast now-a-days that every town of India is equipped with such bare amenities? Can we say Lothal Society was backward? Youths were free to choose their betterhalf during Vedic India. Society of that time approved of this system. Is this freedom we have given to them in so called modern times? In this sense, are we modern or the Vedic Society? All these terms-old and new, ancient and modern-are erroneous.

From the foregoing discussion, it seems that, if we want to classify history at the most for the study purpose, we can refer to past history and present history or early history and contemporary history. There are some modern elements in ancient and medieval times and old elements in modern period. To have progressive or backward elements is not the monopoly of this age or that age. Every age enjoys both types of elements with differences in degree only. That is to say, in some sphere ancient period is modern and modern period is an ancient one. Hence, it is not logical to divide the continuous flowing stream of history artificially. It is not logical to divide history on the basis of political events only; for man does not live only on politics. He also imparts his activities in other walks of life. So it is better to classify political history on the basis of political events and royal dynasties and geneologies, religious history on the basis of religious dogmas and principles as well as movements, art history on the basis of its styles, so on and so forth.[19]

Comparison of Historical Facts

If we go through the three important elements of history, viz. *Sasmaya, Sthala* and *Samāja* and keep them in view while writing history, it seems that any sort of comparison either of events or personalities always goes against this concept. But it is our experience that quite often we find examples of comparison of historical facts and figures. As we have already noted that time does not stand still, how is it possible to compare two things taken place at a different point of time? Background and environment of any two individuals, even they are brought up as members of the same family, are certainly not the same. Not only this, their ways of life and system of work are also different. This is also good for any two events. In short, we cannot ignore the co-existence of those three elements of history. Hence comparison, is not at all logical, of historical facts.

Let us explain this by sighting an example. It is our common experience of saying that Kalidas is Shakespear of India. This is against the very concept of history; for Kalidas lived in the 4th century after Christ while Shakespear lived in the 16th century A,D, Timewise Kalidas is far earlier than Shakespear. So even if we desire to compare both these personalities, though comparison is not logical, we must say that Shakespear was Kalidas of Europe. Is it ever logical to compare an individual of earlier time with that of the later one? Are we not committing anachronism?

It is true that we do not commit any sort of anachronism while saying that Sardar Patel was the Bismarck of India. But there is a basic difference between the iron will and ability of both Sardar Vallabhbhai of India and Bismarck of Germany. Method of working for integration of the states were certainly varied. Even their circumstances were not identical.

It is not at all so easy to solve the most excessively selfish problems of princely states and protect the integration of a nation of a large country like India in a year or so; which has variegated elements such as multi-speaking population, multi-religious society, different cultural background, particular geographical features than a small country like Germany whose language is one, religion is one, culture is one, style of dressing is one. Integration of Germany cannot be equated with the integration of India and hence Sardar Patel, the iron man, cannot be designated as Bismarck, the iron chancellor, of India. Looking through the magnitude and multitudity of our problem, if we so desire, we can say Bismarck was Sardar of Germany.[20] It is not at all scientific and logical to compare one thing or person with another as advocated earlier.

Interdiscipliamry Approach[21]

Often we see history books written with one bias or other, or with singular approach. This is very harmful for the cause of the development of knowledge while accepting the view of having a deep, specific and thorough knowledge of one discipline. It is equally necessary to have introductory and basic information of the disciplines as well. Lack of dialogue and communication with other disciplines go against the very nature of research needs. Rather it is the prime necessity for acquiring sound knowledge; for knowledge is not a monopoly of any discipline.

Therefore, the political historian, the social historian, the religious historian, the economic historian, and the art historian together with archaeologists, epigraphists, numismatists, archivists should work hand in hand for achieving the best of results. Sometime when the social historian comes across a particular difficulty, the antropologist or the sociologist may come forward to help him. When political historian stops somewhere, the social analyst or demographer may clear his path. When art historian ponders, the religious historian or an archaeologist may open a new vista.

As the nature and purpose of history is to reveal the ultimate consequences of actions and movements of the human past, it is for the historian to accept the interdiscipliamry approach and outlook for writing history books.

Any sort of writing always remains subjective and hence it is foolishness to boast to write history book objectively. At the most, with the help of interdisciplinary approach, one can be able to be as objective as possible in writing history.

Few More Thoughts

There is nothing like a national history or world history. There is only one history and that is human history. It is true the human history may be multi-national, multi-racial and multi-religious.

History is meant both for synthesis and interpretation. Its sole purpose is not to impart this fact or that one. But it aims at developing to the spirit of inquiry into past human affairs, an ability to question the facts and competency to challenge what is written as historical facts. This means history is interpretative and not only descriptive. If there is no interpretation, then there is no history.

The continuity of historical process is an important feature of history. Therefore, history never remains static; rather it moves in time. History goes on changing the nature and scope of its interest to man as time passes. That is why change is the synonym of the word history.

The style of writing history is as important as the collection of data and analysis of material. History is a delightful creation. it is not just a mere post-mortem of facts and documents to determine the truth that was then and there. Therefore the presentation of historical material should be as lucid and flowing as possible. It basis would be *satyam, Shivam* and *Sundaram*.

There should be no two opinions about that history books be written and rewritten from time to time. As our outlook and concept go on changing, so our historical writing have to be revised.

In the end, the submission would be : (1) History does not repeat at all itself, (2) Periodization of historical age of any country is not logical, (3) Use of the phrase of Golden Age is a misnomer, (4) Comparison of two things goes against the concept of history, (5) To adopt interdisciplinary approach, (6) History is nothing but man's diary i.e. man is the centroid of history.

References

1. *A Vision of India's History,* Calcutta, 1962.
2. R.G. Collingwood, *the Idea of History,* London, 1946, p. 216.
3. For detail discussion see Rasesh Jamindar, *Itihās Samshodhan,* Ahmadabad, 1976, ch. 2.
4. Rasesh Jamindar, *Itihas Samshodhan,* 1976, p. 3-4.
5. *Deadalus,* Spring, 1970, P-241. New York
6. For discussion see Rasesh Jamindar. *Itihās : Sankalpanā AnੴSamshodhano,* Ahmadabad, 1989, pp 1 to 6.
7. G.J. Remier, *History, its purpose and method,* London, 1950, p. 35.
8. Marc Bloch, *The Historians Craft,* Manchestor, 1954.
9. G.J. Garraghan, *A Guide to Historical Method,* Uni. of Wisconsin, 1957, p. 7.
10. R. Vajreswari, *A Hand Book for History Teachers,* Bombay, 1966, p. 19.
11. G.J. Garraghan, *A Guide to Historical Method.*
12. Rasesh Jamindar, *Itihās : Sankalpanā AnੴSamshodhans,* Ahmadabad, 1989, p. 6. (*Mānavike RojbarojkੴKāryonkā Arthapurṇa Mulyāṅkan hi Itihās Hai*).
13. *op. cit.,* 1957, p. 4.
14. Compare : If time were to stand still, history would soon cease, once the existing evidence was fully sifted, (V.H. Galbriath, *The Historian at work,* B.B.C. Publicaiton, 1962, p. 5).
15. Let us quote Toynbee : The histories of civilizations are nothing but strings of historical facts; that every historical fact is intrinsically unique and that history does not repeat itself (*A Study of History,* 1962, p. 43). also see Rasesh Jamindar, *Itihās Samshodha* 1976, p. 17 to 22.
16. Rasesh Jamindar, *Itihās Samshodhan,* Ahmadabad, 1976, p. 20-21. 'There is no certainty that future will repeat past. Every year is an adventure' (will Durant, *The Lessons of History,* new York, 1968, p. 88)
17. *Ibid,* pp. 23-38.
18. *Ibid,* pp. 4 to 5.
19. *Ibid,* pp. 4 to 5.
20. Rasesh Jamindar, *Itihās : Sankalpanā AnੴSamshodhano,* pp. 14-15.
21. Rasesh Jamindar, *Itihas Samshodhan,* 1976, p. 5-6.

Aspects of Indian History and Historiography
Editor : P.K. Mishra
Kaveri Books, New Delhi, India.

Swamikannu Pillai's Indian Ephemeris : A Reconsideration

28

Mahesh Sharma

Even as debates rage about serious issues like hermeneutics and deconstruction, as positions are constantly being taken and shifted, historians need perhaps to remind themselves that it is useful to cast a look, from time to time, even at humbler matters like the conventional tools they use. This note is about one such tools: the conversion tables of dates and eras that, in the Indian context, are most elaborately tabulated in Swamikannu Pillai's *Indian Ephemeris*.[1] It is designed to verify its accuracy.

First published in 1922, the *Ephemeris* has been of invaluable help to researchers working in a whole range of fields. Keeping in view the difficulties presented by the multiplicity of systems of reckoning and dating prevalent in our country-carying as they do, from region to region, period to period, dynasty to dynasty—the *Ephemeris* sets out to provide extremely useful tables which give equivalences and add other valuable data. In its organization it gives the equivalence, in the Gregorian calendar, of Solar as well as Lunar reckonings; correspondences with the *Saka* era, *Kaliyuga* (S. Circle). *Kollam, Hijra, Vikrami* and *Bengal Samvat* (N. Circle). In these broad categories are incorporated the cyclic sidereal year, month and day; Lunar reckoning of *tithi* ending moment; *Nakshatra*; and *Hijra* year, month and date. the Lunar and Solar eclipses and the phases of the moon are carefully pointed out. The month equivalences of Tamil, Telugu and North Indian tradition are also given, along with the Muhammaden months, as well as solar *samvatasāras* like *Prabhava, Vibhava, Rishabha*, etc.

No other work quite compases into the rich and text meshed information that this *Ephemeris* provides. It is for this reason that it has been relied on for generations. Almost as a matter of chance, the accuracy of the information it gives has been taken for granted.

However, it would seem that there is some reason for doubt in the matter of the precision of the information it contains. There is little question about its general accuracy, and turning to its pages is always rewarding when we are converting dates from an era to another; an engagement in similar exercises while working with inscriptions, colophons and the like. But if an argument brings almost exclusively the information the tables of the *Ephemeris* contain, some caution appears to be called for.

It is useful to work with some examples. While dating them, one presumes that the information provided in an inscription, an epigraph, a colophon, in respect of the day of the work, phase of the moon, day of the month and year, etc., if recorded by a contemporary, would be factually correct and unless, of course, there is doubt about the authenticity of such inscription, epigraph or colophon.

I draw attention here to three colophons of illustrated manuscripts and series of paintings. The colophon of an important *Shahnama* in the New York Public Library, reads"[2]

> "Written (and completed) at the time of *Chasht* (the hour between early breakfast and noon), on Monday, the 7th of the auspicious month of *Ramazan*, of the year (A.H.) 906, in the hand of Muhammad Mutabar Badakshi....".

The *Ephemeris* gives the equivalence of A.H. 906 in this month as A.D. 1500, and the day is worked out as Monday, the 6th of April. This seems to present no problem. The colophon of a Mewar *Gīta Govinda* reads as:[3]

> "Thus ends the *Gīta Govinda*. This book was got written by Maharajadhiraja Maharana Sri Sangram Singhji on Sunday, 13th day of the bright half of *Ashadha* in *Samvat* 1771..."

According to the *Ephemeris* this date, the 13th of the bright half of *Ashadha* corresponds to 24th June, 1714 A.D. However, the day of the week as worked out is Monday, *not* Sunday.

Yet another colophon of a series of paintings of the *Sat Sai* of Bihari reads:[4]

> "In the *samvat* 1776 on Thursday, the 5th of the black half in the month of *Chaitra* this manuscript was written and painted by Jagannāth kavirāja...." W.G. Archer works the year out as A.D. 1720;[5] while Andhare takes it to be A.D. 1719.[6] According to the *Ephemeris* the year is A.D. 1719. However, in this year the 5th of the dark half of the month of *Chaitra* works out to Sunday, instead of Thursday, as mentioned in the colophon.

The disparities that have been noticed in these examples are of interest, even if they are essentially of no great consequence. No argument concerning the date of these manuscripts or series of paintings is effected. No doubt has been cast on the authenticity of the colophons, as the dates are reasonably well established through these tables. However, the matter takes on a different shape when, as said before, the argument regarding the dating of a work brings upon the accuracy-or otherwise-of the calculations contained in the *Ephemeris*. This seems to have happened in the case of the celebrated *Devī Mahātmya*, in the *Chaurapañchāśikā* style, that surfaced a few years back, and is now in the Himachal Pradesh State Museum at Shimla.

The manuscript in question, written in Sanskrit in the Devanagari script, has been the subject of considerable disagreement among scholars, chiefly on account of the date to which it is variously assigned. That it is an unusual work in the Pahari context, painted as it is in what is called the *Chaurapañchāśikā* style-which is not firmly located anywhere but has certainly never been associated with the hills up to now, admits of little doubt. External criticism of the manuscript persuades one to place it anywhere between A.D. 1500 and 1600, keeping in view the temporal dimensions associated with this style till now. Ordinarily, one would have thought that the fact of the manuscript having a full, elaborate colophon would place the matter beyond doubt. But this is precisely where the problem arises, for the colophon has, as is usual, a date but such as is not easy to decode, for the author/scribe has put it in the form of a chronogram. This is where recourse to the *Ephemeris* comes in. But, first, the bare facts.

This is how the colophon reads, in Sanskrit:

> *'Śrīdevyei namah. Dṛvdhaṃ yadṛṣimārkaṇḍaya sudhiyā śrīdevīsaṃtuṣṭaya māhatamayaṃ vyalibhat sudhī sumanesā saṁsmṛtyā rāmaṃ hṛdi śāke tvaṣṭaguṇarasendu tulite māse tapaśye śubhe sukṣetre jayasiṃhadevanagare śrī bhavānīśarmādrutaṁ. Purṇimāṃ jīve samāptaṁ.*

This is how it has been rendered in English by Goswamy et.al.[7]

> 'Obeisance to the Goddess. As composed with his superb intellect by Risi Markandaya, this *Mahātmya* has been written, in order to propitiate the Devi, by Bhavani Sarma, remembering Rama in his heart, with good intellect and mind, having been completed with speed in *Śāka* equivalent to (indicated by words) *aṣtha, guṇa, rasa* and *indu* in the month of *Tapaśya* (*Phālaguṇa*) in the auspicious region of Jaisingh Deva Nagar. Completed (on) Thursday, the day of the full moon'.

The words used to indicate the date seem, initially, to be clear but do admit of different readings or interpretations. The numerical values of the four words involved: *ashṭa, guṇa, rasa* and *indu* can be taken as, respectively, 8, 3, 6 and 1, which yields the number 8361 when read in this order. However, following well-established convention, the order of the digits in the chronogram needs to be reversed: when this is done, according to this reading, the figure reads 1638. If this is the year, the era of the year needs to be determined. if the word "*Śāka*" used in the chronogram is interpreted literally, the year in the Christian calendar would work out A.D. 1716. While this should ordinarily be acceptable, the style of the paintings in the manuscript militates strongly against this date, for it is not consistent with the general styles we associate with the 18th century. Even more than this, the day of the week mentioned in the colophon, and the fact of that day being a full-moon day of the month of *Phālaguṇa*, need to be reconciled with the year mentioned. The tables given in the *Indian Ephemeris*, however, state that this day was a Sunday, not a Thursday as the colophon mentions. The date, 1716 A.D., is therefore discounted on two grounds.[8]

Another possibility has been considered: that the word *Śāka* used for the era in the colophon is not to be taken literally, and that it is used in the generic sense of "a year". If the year is taken to be 1638, then the era has to be determined. If the *Vikṛamī* era is assumed to have been meant, then the year works out to A.D. 1581. However, in that year the corresponding day of the week happens to be a Saturday. This possibility is also, therefore, abandoned, for it is inconsistent with the information otherwise contained in the colophon.

Another possibility has been suggested: that of reading the chronogram as referring to a year in the local era. This is how it has been argued: "The word *ashṭa* in a chronogram stands out as unusual in usage because it is a figure in itself and not the equivalent of one, like *guṇa* which is equivalent of three, and *Indu* the equivalent of one, in accepted usage. If we are willing to take this view that the chronogram is even more complicated then it appears at first, we could interpret this part of the verse as saying `the year indicated by 8 (*ashṭa*) multiplied by (*guṇa*) 6 and 1 (reversed to read 16)'. This gives us the reading 128".[9] In the era popular in the hills, like *Saptarishīkāla*, or the *Pahāri Samvat* also called the *Kacchā Samvat*, the figure arrived at, 128, can be converted into a year of the Christian era by adding 24, getting the figure 152, dropping the 1, representing a hundred in this figure, following convention, and adding a century to the two digits remaining: turning it in this case to 1452 or 1552 or 1652 etc. The most likely of these years is 1552, keeping in view the style of paintings in the manuscript. What is more, in that year, the full moon in the month of *Phālaguṇa* falls on a Thursday, exactly as the colophon mentions.

As far as the dating of the *Devī Mahātmya* is concerned this is not where the matter ends. Other possibilities have been considered and examined. Even the above calculation, that is based on taking the word *ashṭa* as truly a digit in itself and multiplying it with 3 representing *guṇa*, is possibly open to question, as the authors observe themselves: "....according to one opinion, in the Pahari area, after the middle of the month of *Pauṣa*, the new year is taken into reckoning. That would make the year as A.D. 1553 instead of 1552, and this could throw the whole calculation out of joint."[10] Again, Losty, who has taken the manuscript into account, reads the chronogram as representing the year 1361, taking the first word to be *tvashṭa* which could stand for one, and not reversing the order of the digits. Then, assuming that this year 1361 is of the *Śāka* era, he arrives at the data A.D. 1439-40.[11] Glynn treats the year given in the chronogram as standing either for 1631 or 1638, arrived at through reversing the order of the digits, as required, but reading the first word in two different ways, as *tvashṭa* or *ashṭa*. This gives the year in the Christian era as either 1709 on 1716 A.D., if the era is interpreted literally as *Śāka*, or as 1574 or 1581, if the era is treated as the *Vikṛamī Samvat.*[12]

For the art-historian, the range of these dates present a real problem, for not only has sense to be made of the information contained within the tersely phrased colophon, but the date finally arrived at, or preferred, has to be reconciled with the time-parameters of the style of the paintings. The dates worked out by different scholars[13] alone make for a baffling situation, as the Table 1 would show.

If, as would initially be natural, the conversion tables in the *Ephemeris* were to be taken as accurate in all respects, then all years in which the full-moon day of the month of *Phālaguṇa* does not fall on a Thursday would have to be left completely out of reckoning. This would certainly help in narrowing the range of dates down, but only if the information in the tables of the *Ephemeris* were completely beyond doubt; which, as one has seen from other examples, is not the case. However persuasive, therefore, the reasoning might be, as at present offered by different scholars in favour of the dates preferred for this *Devi Mahātmya* by them, a considerable space for doubt would remain, or creep in. In the final analysis, in this case atleast, the art-historian would have to rely more on the evidence of style than on the precise information contained in this problematic chronogram. The *Ephemeris* would afford little help.

Clearly, what is being said here is not that the *Ephemeris* is of no value: it emphatically is. But it is necessary to know that of pin-point accuracy is what a situation involving conversion of dates requires, the information in this most valuable work has to be regarded with a degree of caution.

Finally, I would like to append two tables that contain a comparison of the information concerning dates available to us from a range of inscriptions and as converted in the tables given in the *Ephemeris*. The selected inscriptions, it needs to be stated, may appear random, but care has been taken to have a representative sample of dates taken from different geographical regions and known eras so as to make the 'test-check' reasonably broad-based.

A tentative conclusion that one can arrive at from this comparison is that the 'errors' in the calculations as given in the *Ephemeris*, assuming that the information given in the contemporaneously composed inscriptions is accurate, are approximately to the extent of 31 per cent i.e. every third entry may be 'inaccurate'; which means here that it is off by a couple of days or so. It is to be noted that the rate of error is strikingly higher in the calculations involving the phases of the moon (50%). However, our conclusion, at least in the case of the eclipse years, does not hold good. In two cases the details tally with the succeeding year and, in one case, the sidereal month also tallies with the succeeding year, even though the details available are somewhat laconic in nature. One needs to add that the possibility of the contemporary composers of inscriptions having made error can not be altogether ruled out, one should also consider that the days in the Indian system do not begin at the same time as those in the Gregorian calendar, the first taking into account *ghaṭas* and *palas* and the second beginning from midnight. Therefore, in the data presented above, any calculation being off by a day, over or less, has been considered

Table 28.1

Reading of Devi Mahātmya Manuscript							As in Ephemeris				
Sr. No.	Place of Inscription	Era	Year	Day	Date	Month	Gregorian year A.D.	Day	Date	Month	Remarks
1.	Jaisimghapur (in District Kangra)	Śāka	1361	Thursday	Full Moon day	Phālaguṇa	1439	Sunday	1st	March[14]	Error-3 days Lunar Eclipse
							1440 (Śāka 1362)	*Thursday*	*18th*	*February*[15]	*No error in day but Lunar Eclipse*
2.	Jaisimghapur (in District Kangra)	Śāka	1631	Thursday	Full Moon day	Phālaguṇa	1709	Sunday	13th	February[16]	Error-3 days
3.	Jaisimghapur (in District Kangra)	Śāka	1638	Thursday	Full Moon day	Phālaguṇa	1716	Sunday	26th	February[17]	Error-3 days
							1717 (Śāka 1639)	*Thursday*	*14th*	*February*[18]	*Error-1 year*
4.	Jaisimghapur (in District Kangra)	V.S.	1631	Thursday	Full Moon day	Phālaguṇa	1574	Sunday	7th	March[19]	Error-3 days
							1575 (V.S. 1632)	*Thursday*	*24th*	*February*[20]	*Error-1 year*
5.	Jaisimghapur (in District Kangra)	V.S.	1638	Thursday	Full Moon day	Phālaguṇa	1581	Saturday	18th	February[21]	Error-2 days
6.	Jaisimghapur (in District Kangra)	Loka-kāla	152	Thursday	Full Moon day	Phālaguṇa	1552	*Thursday*	*10th*	*March*[22]	*No Error*
							1553	Tuesday	28th	February[23]	Error-2 days

Table 28.2

Sr. No.	Place of Inscription	As in Inscription: Era	Year	Day	Date	As in Ephemeris: Month	Gregorian Year A.D.	Day	Date	Month	Remarks
1.	Baijnath[24]	Lokakala Śāka	80 726	Sunday	1st of the bright half of moon	Jyestha	804	Tuesday	14th	May25	Error - 2 days
2.	Pattana-[26] Kudi	Śāka	910	Monday	5th	Kartika	988	Monday	29th	October[27]	No error
3.	Sravan-Belagola	Śāka	1050	Sunday	3rd of the dark half of moon	Phalaguna	1129	Monday	10th	March[29]	Error + 1 day
4.	Patna[30]	Śāka	1128	Full moon	Lunar Eclipse	Sravana	1206	Friday	21st	July[31]	No Lunar Eclipse
							1207 (Śāka 1129) Lunar Eclipse	Thursday	9th Full moon day[32]	August	Error 1 year
5.	–	Śāka	1151	Sunday	9th	Chaitra	1129	Saturday	3rd	March[34]	Error-1 day
6.	South(?)[35]	Śāka	1304	Thursday	10th	Dundhubi Magha	1382	Monday	3rd	February[36]	Error 1 day
							1383 (Śāka 1305)	Monday Dundhubi	5th Magha[37]	January	Error-3 days & 1 year
7.	Panugallu[38]	Śāka	1319	Sunday	11th	Pausa	1397	Saturday	6th	January[39]	Error-1 day
8.	Nallur[40]	Śāka	1321	Wednesday	Lunar Eclipse	Karttika	1399	Wednesday	15th	October[41]	No error
9.	Sonda[42]	Śāka	1530	Wednesday	10th	Karttika	1608	Wednesday	9th	November[43]	No error
10.	Bayana[44]	Vikrama (V.S.)	1012	Monday	12th of the bright half	Magha	955	Monday	8th	January[45]	No error
11.	South[46]	V.S.	1117	Solar Eclipse	5th Bright half	Jyeshtha	1060	Thursday	1st	June[47]	No error
							1061 (V.S.118)	Wednesday Solar Eclipse	20th	June[48]	Error 1 year
12.	Jodhpur[49]	V.S.	1174	Monday	5th	Ashadha	1117	Tuesday	29th	May[50]	Error + 1 day
13.	Vadnagar[51]	V.S.	1208	Thursday	5th	Ashvina	1208	Tuesday	2nd	October[52]	Error 2 days
14.	Dhanta[53]	V.S.	1277	Monday	2nd	Magha	1220	Monday	28th	December[54]	No error
15.	Baijnath[55]	V.S.	1296	Sunday	5th of the	Phalaguna	1259	Thursday	25th	February[56]	Error - 3 days
16.	Mala[57]	V.S.	1353	Sunday	15th of the dark half	Vaishakha	1286	Thursday	25th	April[58]	Error - 3 days

(contd. . .)

Sr. No.	Place of Inscription	As in Inscription: Era	Year	Day	Date	As in Ephemeris: Month	Gregorian Year A.D.	Day	Date	Month	Remarks
17.	Gujarat[59]	V.S.	1462	Sunday	7th	Marge	1405	Friday	4th	December[60]	Error - 2 days
18.	Maharashtra[61]	V.S.	1597	Tuesday	13th	Phalaguna	1540	Wednesday	24th	March[62]	Error + 1 day
19.	Gujarat[63]	V.S.	1616	Monday	12th	Chaitra	1559	Thursday	9th	March[64]	Error + 3 days
							1560 (V.S. 1617)	Monday	8th	April[65]	Error + 1 day and 1 year
20.	Mewar[66]	V.S.	1771	Sunday	13th of the bright half	Ashadha	1714	Monday	14th	June[67]	Error + 1 day
						Adhika Ashadha					
21.	Mewar[68]	V.S.	1776	Thursday	5th of the black day	Chaitra	1719	Sunday	15th	March[69]	Error + 3 days
22.	Rajasthan[70]	V.S.	1792	Monday	10th	Asuja	1735	Monday	9th	June[71]	No error
23.	Rajasthan[72]	V.S.	1804	Friday	11th	Jyeshtha	1747	Wednesday	10th	June[73]	Error - 2 days
24.	Rajasthan[74]	V.S.	1805	Monday	15th	Kartika	1748	Sunday	2nd	October[75]	Error - 1 day
25.	Rajasthan[76]	V.S.	1822	Wednesday	14th	Savana	1765	Friday	26th	July[77]	Error - 2 days
26.	–	Hijra[78] (A.H.)	906	Monday	7th	Ramazan	1500	Monday	6th	April[79]	No error -1 day
27.	–	A.H.	1011[80]	Friday	4th	Rabi-ul-awwal	1602	Thursday	12th	August[81]	Error - day
28.	–	A.H.	1014[82]	Monday	20th	Jummada-al-awwal	1605	Monday	23rd	September[83]	No error
29.	–	A.H.	1026[84]	Thursday	11th	Sawwal	1617	Thursday	2nd	October[85]	No error

Table 28.3

Sr. No.	Calculations based upon	Total Entries	Error (nos.)	Error Split			
1.	Era	29	20				
	a. Śāka	9	6	+ 3	days	=	1
			(22.2%)	+ 2	days	=	1
				+ 2	days	=	3
				+ 1	Year	+	1
	b. Vikṛami	16	13	+ 3	days	=	3
			(43.7%)	+ 2	days	=	4
				+ 1	days	=	4
				+ 1	Year	=	2
	c. Hijrā	4	1	+ 1	day	=	1
2.	Phases of Moon	8	7	+ 3	days	=	3
			(50%)	+ 2	days	=	1
				+ 1	days	=	2
				+ 1	Year	=	1
3.	Eclipse	3	2	+ 1	Year	=	2
4.	Dates	19	11	+ 3	days	=	1
			(20%)	+ 2	days	=	3
				+ 1	days	=	7
	Total	29	20	+ 3	days	=	4
				+ 2	days	=	5
			(31%)*	+ 1	day	=	8
				+ 1	Year	=	3

* If an error by year is considered to be the mistake of the author of the inscription and + 1 day as a conversion anomaly then *the rate of error* (i.e. more than one day, *in ephemeris* = 9 x 100 = 31%

a 'non-error'. Only the disparity involving more than two days, on either side of the frame of reference, has been considered as an 'error'.

There are no startling conclusions, perhaps. The value of the *Ephemeris* as a tool will continue to remain enormous. But it might be in the interest of the historian to be aware of these slight limitations from which it suffers.

References

1. Pillai, L.D. SwamiKannu, *Indian Ephemeris: A.D. 700 to A.D. 1799: Showing the Daily Solar and Lunar Reckoning According to the Principal Systems Current in India with their English Equivalents,* Vol. I. Part I and II, Vols. 6., Madras, Govt. Publication Press, 1922.
2. Goswamy, B.N., 'A Pre-Mughal Shah Nama from Jaunpur' in *An Age of Splendour': Islamic Art in India,* ed., K.J. Khandalavala and S. Doshi, Bombay, 1983, p. 122.
3. Andhare, Shridhar, 'Three New Documents of the Reign of Rana Sangram Singh of Mewar (A.D. 1710-34)', in *Lalit Kala* no. 19, p. 60.
4. *Idem.*

5. Archer, W.G., *Rajput Miniatures from the Collections of Edwin Binney 3rd*, Portland, 1968., Fig. 8., p. 23.
6. Andhare, *op. cit.*, p. 60.
7. Goswamy, B.N.; V.C. Ohri and Ajit Singh, 'A "Chaurapanchasika Style" Manuscript from the Pahari Area'. in *Lalit Kala*, no. 21., p. 16.
8. *Ibid.*, p. 17; Mankodi has purposefully used the *Ephemeris* to date it A.D. 1717, which coincides with the information of the *Ephemeris*. The objection is more pronounced because he falls into the same trap which he criticises while considering A.D. 1581 or 1574—the other dates coinciding with the *Ephemeris*. He, however, shows no awareness of Goswamy's date- 1552, A.D.; Mankodi, K.L., 'A Note on the Devi Mahatmya of Saka 1638 in the Shimla Museum', in *Dimensions of Indian Art*, ed. L. Chandra and J. Jain, Vol. I., Delhi, 1986, p. 278.
9. Goswamy, et. al., *Op. cit.*, p. 18.
10. *Idem.*
11. Losty, J.P., *The Art of the Book in India*, London, 1982, pp. 50-51.
12. Glynn, C.A., *A Sixteenth Century Devi Mahatmya Manuscript from Kangra*, Ph. D. Dissertation, Los Angeles, University of Southern California, 1979, pp. 114-15; also 'Early Painting of Mandi', in *Artibus Asiae*, XLIU, 1983, where she dates these as 1581 or 1574 A.D., p. 23.
13. The manuscript has been widely commented upon and scholars have been more circumspect in their treatment of the colophon, generally dating it between 1550-1600 A.D. Goswamy, B.N. and Eberhard Fisher, *Pahari Masters: Court Painting of Northern India*, Zurich, 1992. They emphasise A.D. 1552 as the most probable year but as a caution add, with certainty, that it was completed in the third quarter of the sixteenth century; p. 16. Karl Khndalavala as an editor of *Lalit Kala* assignes 1574-75 A.D. as the date, as he does to the plates of Goswamy's publication in no. 21: Dr. T.S. Maxwell in his catalogue on 'Mythology of Siva and the Goddess' dates it c. 1550-70, in *In the Image of Man: The Indian Perception of the Universe through 200 years of Painting and Sculpture*, London, 1982, pl. no. 448; p. 219. R.K. Tandon avoids the chronogram though obliquely hints that the manuscript should have been composed before 1585, in 'Mediaeval Miniature paintings-11th to mid 16th century: And a Reappraisal of the Mandu and Jaunpur Kalpasutra vis-a-vis Origin of the Chaura-pancasika Style', *in Dimension of Indian Art*, p. 501. More recently, B.N. Goswamy, re-emphasis the third quarter of the 16th century, 'Studies of Pahari Paintings: A Review', (Mimeograph, 1994), Forthcoming in *J.S. Grewal Felicitation Volume*, p. 45.
14. *Indian Ephemeris*, V., p. 80.
15. *Ibid*, V. p. 82.
16. *Ibid*, VI, p. 220.
17. *Ibid*, VI, p. 234.
18. *Ibid*, VI, p. 236.
19. *Ibid*, V, p. 350.
20. *Ibid*, V, p. 352.
21. *Ibid*, V, p. 364.
22. *Ibid*, V, p. 306.
23. *Ibid*, V, p. 308.
24. Buhler, G., 'The Prasastis of Baijnath', *Epigraphia India (E.I.)* I, Calcutta, 1892; Delhi, 1983 (Rep.) pp. 98, 103, 112.
25. *I.E.* p., II, p. 10.
26. Gopal B.R. and V.S. Subrahmanyam, 'Pattanakudi Plates of Silahara Avasara II, Saka 910', *E.I.*, 37, Part I, Delhi, 1967, p. 58.
27. *I. Ep.*, II, p. 379.
28. Hultzsch, E., 'Sravana-Belgola Epitaph of Mallishena; after Saka Samvat 1050' *E.I.*, III, Calcutta, 1897; Delhi, 1979 Rep., pp. 185, 207.
29. *I.E.*, III, p. 260.
30. Kielhorn, F., 'Patna Inscription of the Time of the Yadava Singhana and his Feudatories Soideva and Hemadideva', *E.I.*, I, pp. 240-41.
31. *I. Ep.*, IV, p. 15.
32. *Ibid.*, IV, p. 17.
33. Sarkar, D.C., 'Nagari Plates of Anangabhima III; Saka 1151 and 1152', *E. I.*, 28, Delhi, 1958, p. 244.
34. *I.Ep.*, IV, p. 60.
35. Sarma, K.H.V., 'Two Grants of Undiraja III', *E.I.*, 37, Part I., p. 92.
36. *I.Ep.*, IV, p. 366.
37. *Ibid.*, IV, p. 368.
38. Subrahmanyam, V.S., 'Panugallu Inscription of the Time of Hanihara II', *E.I.*, p. 50.
39. *I.Ep.*, IV, p. 396.
40. Vankayya, V., 'Nallur Grant of Harihara II', *E.I.*, III, p. 119.

41. *I.Ep.*, IV, p. 401.
42. Desai, P.D., 'Two Nishidhi Inscription from Sonda', *E.I.*, 28, p. 292.
43. *I.Ep.*, VI, p. 17.
44. Banerji, R.D., 'The Bayana Inscription of Chittralekha: V.S. 1012', *E.I.*, 22, Delhi, 1935, p. 122.
45. *I.Ep.*, II, p. 312.
46. Gai, G.S., 'Two Grants of Chalukya Bhimadeva-I', *E.I.*, 37, I, p. 38.
47. *I.Ep.*, III, p. 122.
48. *Ibid.*, III, p. 124.
49. Gai, G.S., 'Jodhpur Museum Inscription of Paramara Visala: Vikrama 1174', *E.I.*, 37, I, p. 202.
50. *I.Ep.*, III, p. 237.
51. Ojha, V.G., 'The Vadnagar Prasasti of the Reign of Kumarapala', *E.I.*, I, p. 296, 304.
52. *I.Ep.*, III, p. 305.
53. Suri, C.L., 'Dhanta Image Inscription of Parmara Somasimha: Vikrama 1277', *E.I.*, 37, I, p. 209.
54. *I.Ep.*, IV, p. 92.
55. Buhler, G., 'The Jaina Inscription in the Temple of Baijnath at Kiragrama', *E.P.*, I. p. 119.
56. *I. Ep.*, IV, p. 80.
57. Haldar, R.R., 'Mala Plates of Vikrasimhadeva: V.S. 1343', *E.I.*, 22. p. 192.
58. *I.Ep.*, IV, p. 174.
59. Shah, U.P., ed., *Treasures of Jaina Bhandaras*, Ahmedabad, 1978, Entry no. 574, p. 95.
60. *I.Ep.*, V, p. 13.
61. Khandalavala, K.J. and Moti Chendra, *New Documents of Indian Painting-A Reappraisal*, Bombay, 1969, p. 69.
62. *I.Ep.*, V, p. 282.
63. Shah, U.P., *Op. cit.*, Entry no. 576, p. 95.
64. *I.Ep.*, V, p. 320.
65. *Ibid*, V, p. 322.
66. Andhare, *Op. cit.*, p. 60.
67. *I.Ep.*, VI, p. 230.
68. Andhare, *op. cit.*, p. 60.
69. *I.Ep.*, VI, p. 240.
70. Topsfield, Andrew, *Paintings from Rajasthan in the National Gallery of Victoria*, Melbourne, 1980, no. 211, p. 92.
71. *I.Ep.*, VI, p. 272.
72. Topsfield, *op. cit.*, no. 117, p. 94.
73. *I.Ep.*, VI, p. 296.
74. Topsfield, *op. cit.*, no. 126, p. 100.
75. *I.Ep.*, VI, p. 299.
76. Topsfield, *op. cit.*, no. 27, p. 47.
77. *I.Ep.*, VI, p. 333.
78. Goswamy, B.N. 'A Pre-Mughal Shah Nama from Janupur', in *An Age of Splendour*, p. 122.
79. *I.EP.*, V, p. 202.
80. 'Akbar-nama', in Elliot and Dowson, *The History of India as Told by its Own Historians*, Delhi, 1964 (Indian Edition), VI, p. 3.
81. *I.Ep.*, VI, p. 7.
82. 'Takmila-i-Akbar-nama', in Elliot and Dowson, VI, p. 115.
83. *I.Ep.*, VI, p. 13.
84. 'Waka'yat-i-Jahangiri' in Elliot and Dowson, VI, p. 351.
85. *I.Ep.*, VI, p. 37.

Aspects of Indian History and Historiography
Editor : P.K. Mishra
Kaveri Books, New Delhi, India.

Voices of Protest and Dissent in the Works of Bāṇa

29

Shankar Goyal

'Progressive' Aspects of Bāṇa's Social and Political Thought

Bāṇa was an orthodox Brāhmaṇa of the Vātsyāyana *gotra*. he gives an eulogy of the four generations of his ancestors which may be compared with the similar praise of three of them in the introductory verses of the *Kādambarī*. The eulogies convey that they were all great teachers and diligent sacrificers, thus fulfilling all of the main duties of a Brāhmaṇa householder after the Smṛti standards. Bāṇa himself was brought up in orthodox Brāhmaṇical atmosphere. Among his teachers mention is made in the *Kādambarī* of a certain Brāhmaṇa teacher, Bhatsu, whose feet were worshipped by Maukhari rulers. When he went to meet Harsha he proformed Brāhmaṇical sacrifices and worshipped lord Virūpāksha (Śaṅkara). When he met Harsha for the first time and the latter accused him of being a great rogue (*bhujaṅga*), he made the submission that he was a Brāhmaṇa born in the family of the Soma-drinking Vātsyāyanas. Every ceremony of his was duly performed when its time came and he had thoroughly mastered the Veda with its six aṅgas and had as far as possible heard lectures on the *śāstras*.

Bāṇa was also a great admirer of Harsha. According to him, Harsha's achievements were of epic proportion[1] and greater than those of the great *Chakravartis* of the Vedic age.[2] Both these facts-that orthodox Brāhmaṇical background and his admiration for Harsha-have created the impression that he was a firm believer in the Brāhmaṇical ideas and customs and did not anywhere view the contemporary polity and administrative system with a critical eye.[3]

But that is not true. There are some passages in both of his works which certainly echoe his voice of protest and dissent against some traditional beliefs and institutions and contemporary administrative system. Of course, it must be conceded that as a member of the orthodox Brāhmaṇa class and a court-poet of Harsha, he could not raise his voice of protest or dissent at a very high pitch; but he certainly made it clear that he did not approve some of the traditional beliefs and customs and did not like some aspects of the contemporary administrative system. To that extent he may be regarded as a progressive intellectual of his age.

Bāṇa's Criticism of the Custom of Sati

First of all, Bāṇa was highly critical of the custom of *satī*. The custom of *satī* goes back to the Ṛgvedic age.[4] In the historical period its earliest notice occurs in the Greek accounts of Alexander's invasion.[5] It became popular during the age of the Imperial Guptas and continued afterwards. The Chāṅgunārāyaṇa inscription of Mānadeva[6] and the Eran stone pillar inscription of king Bhānugupta[7] offer first epigraphic evidence of the *satī* custom. When king Prabhākaravardhana was on the death-bed, overcome with excessive and unbearable sorrow, queen Yaśomati plunged into fire to avoid widowhood.[8] It seems that several other wives of king Prabhākaravardhana also committed *satī*. After the assassination of Grahavarman, Rājyaśri, his devoted wife, prepared to enter the funeral pyre.[9] Her decision was changed only after the persuasions of the Buddhist sage Divākaramitra. In the *Nāgānanda* of Harsha it is said that after Jimūtavāhana's death Malayavati asked for the crown of her deceased lord so that "clasping it to her heart she might enter into the funeral pyre." In the *Kādambarī*, when Mahāśvetā found that Puṇḍarīka was dead, she asked her friend Taralikā to rise and collect the wood to make a funeral pyre so that she might follow her lord.[10] In the same work, Kādambari decided to embrace death, "honoured the feet of Chandrāpiḍa with bent head and placed them in her lap.[11]

In the accounts of the self-immolation by Yaśomati and attempt for the same by Rājyaśri, Bāṇa does not say anything by way of his own opinion. Obviously he could not make any adverse remarks against the actions of the mother and sister of his patron. But in the *Kādambarī*, he does make Chandrāpiḍa, the hero of the work, criticise the *sātī* custom in no uncertain terms. Almost in the language of a modern critic of the sati custom, Chandrāpiḍa persuades Mahāśvetā not to commit *satī* by arguing that :

> life is easily resigned by those whom sorrow has over-whelmed, but it needs a greater effort not to throw away life in heavy grief. This following another to death is most vain! It is a path followed by the ignorant! It is a mere freek of madness, a path of ignorance, an enterprise of recklessness, a view of baseness, a sign of utter thoughtlessness, and a blunder of folly, that one should resign life on the death of father, brother, friend, or husband. If life leaves us not of itself, we must not resign it. For this leaving of life, if we examine it, is merely for our own interest, because we cannot bear our own cureless pain. To the dead man it brings no good whatever. For it is no means of bringing him back to life, or heaping up merit, or gaining heaven for him, or saving him from hell, or seeing him again, or being reunited with him. For he is led helplessly, irresistibly to another state to meet the fruits of his own deeds. And yet he shares in the guilt of the friend who has killed himself. But a man who lives on can help greatly, by offering of water and the like, both the dead man and himself; but by dying he helps neither.[12]

To convince Mahāśvetā that the *satī* was not a time-honoured custom, Bāṇa makes Chandrāpiḍa give several instances in which wives of great men, semi-divine beings and gods did not give up their lives after the death of their husbands though their fidelity to their husbands was quite well-known:

> Remember how Rati, the sole and beloved wife of Love, when her noble husband, who won the hearts of all women, was burnt up by the fire of Shiva, yet did not yield her life; and remember also Kunti of the race of Vṛihṇi, daughter of Sūrasena, for her lord was Pāṇḍu the wise; his seat was perfumed by the flowers in the crests of all kings whom he had conquered without an effort, and he received the tribute of the whole earth, and yet when he was consumed by Kindamma's curse she still remained alive. Uttarā, too, the young daughter of Virāṭa, on the death of Abhimanyu, gentle and heroic, and joyful to the eyes as the young moon, yet lived on. And Duḥshalyā, too, daughter of Dhṛitarāshṭra, tenderly cared for by her hundred brothers; when Jayadratha, king of Sindhu, was slain

> by Arjuna, fair as he was and great as he had become by Shiva's gift, yet made no resignation of her life. And others are told of by thousands, daughters of Rākshasas, gods, demons, ascetics, mortals, siddhas and Gandharvas, who when bereft of their husbands yet preserved their lives.[13]

Thus, here Bāṇa raises his voice of protest against a social evil which was quite prevalent in his times and was recognised of 'honourable' even in the family of his patron. It must have required some courage indeed.

Bāṇa's Criticism of the Divinity of Kings

Like the custom of *satī*, Bāṇa was also opposed to the theory of the divinity of kings-a theory which was widely current in ancient India. For example, *Manu Smṛti* (VII. 4-5, V. 96) says: "the Creator created the king with the essential parts taken from Indra, the Wind god, Yama, the Sun, Agni, Varuṇa, the Moon and Kubera, the lord of wealth and, therefore, he surpasses all beings by his majesty; one should not disrespect a boy-king with the thought `he is a human being (like others)', for it is a great diety that stands (before people) in human form as a king." (VII.8). Kauṭilya (I. 13) makes a spy say among *pauras* and *jānapadas*: "kings are (in) the place of (perform the functions of) Indra and Yama, since they visibly inflict punishment and bestow favours. Even divine punishment affects those who despise them (kings). Therefore, kings should not be despised." The *Matsya Purāṇa* (226.1) says that the king was created by Brahmā by taking portions of gods for wielding the power of punishment for the protection of all beings. According to the *Agni P.*(226. 17-20), as the king exercises the functions of nine deities viz. the Sun, the Moon, Vāyu, Yama, Varuṇa, Fire, Kubera, the Earth and Vishṇu, he has the form of all these deities. The *Śukranītisāra* (I. 73-79) echoes similar ideas. The *Nārada Smṛti* (Prakīrṇa Section, 20-31) argues that in the form of the king it is really Indra himself who moves about on the earth, that a king even when devoid of qualities deserves honour from the people, that kings exercise the functions of five deities, namely, Agni, Indra, Soma, Yama and Kubera. The *Mārkaṇḍeya P.* (27.21-26) mentions the same five deities. The *Mbh.* (Śānti Parvan, 69) states that all the gods are invisible, but the king is a deity that can be seen. The *Vayu P.*(57.72) remarks that in all past and future *manvantaras* universal emperors (*Chakravartīs*) are born on the earth with parts of Vishnu. The *Bhāgavata P.* (IV 14.26-27) says that Vishṇu, Brahmā, Śiva, Indra, Vāyu, Varuṇa-these and other gods-exist in the body of the king and that the king is full of (the parts of) all gods. It is to strengthen this conception that ancient Kshatriya dynasties and their panegyrists tried to trace for those dynasties descent from the Sun or the Moon and in later times from Fire. The *Pañchatantra* (I. 120) states that `Manu has declared that the king is made up (of parts) of all gods.' The *Rājanītiprakāśa* points out that the idea of the king having in him parts of the deities applies only to the independent Mahārājas while the idea of a ruler doing the functions of five deities applies to vassal kings. The practice of addressing the king as "*deva*" in Sanskrit plays was originally the result of the same tendency of the deification of the royal office.

The theory of the divine nature of kingship finds mention in the epigraphs also. Of king Samudragupta, we are told by Harisheṇa that 'he was the incomprehensible spirit that was the cause of protection of good and destruction of evil,' that 'he was equal of the gods Dhanada, Varuṇa, Indra and Antaka', that 'he was Apratiratha (=Vishṇu) roaming in the world' and that 'he was a mortal only in celebrating the rites of the observances of mankind, but otherwise a god dwelling on the earth.[14] The later genealogists usually describe Chandragupta II as Vishṇu himself' (*svayam-cha-apratirathaḥ*).[15] In the records of North Bengal the Gupta kings are given the trilogy of titles (*Paramadaivata, Paramabhaṭṭāraka, Mahārājādhirāja*) which, with the slight change of *Paramadaivata* into *Parameśvara*, became the distinctive designation of paramount rulers in later times. With the object of claiming superhuman excellence for them, the coin legends of the Gupta rulers attribute to them the conquest of heaven by good deeds following their conquest of the earth.[16]

Bāṇa was also quite familiar with the theory of the divinity of kings but in his *Kādambarī* he expresses his opposition to it quite explicitly, In this work at one place Śakunāsa, the minister of Tārāpiḍa, teaches Chandrāpiḍa, the crown-prince, some basic principles of pragmatic politics. It is quite a lengthy discourse and may be regarded as representing the ideas of Bāṇa himself on the subject. In this discourse at one place Chandrāpiḍa is taught that only utterly foolish kings believe that they are god incarnate on earth:

> . . . .though subject to mortal conditions, they look on themselves as having alighted on earth as divine beings with a superhuman destiny; they employ a pomp in their undertakings only fit for gods and win the contempt of all mankind. They welcome this deception of themselves by their followers. From the delusion as to their own divinity established in their minds, they are overthrown by false ideas, and they think their own pair of arms have received (like the four arms of Vishṇu)* another pair; they imagine their forehead has a third eye (like the third eye of Śiva)* buried in the skin. They consider the sight of themselves a favour; they esteem their glance a benefit; they regard their words as a present; they hold their command a glorious boon; they deem their touch a purification.[17]

This is obviously another instance of Bāṇa's dissenting voice against current political beliefs.

Bāṇa was also critical of some aspects of the administration of his patron though due to obvious reason he expresses his disapproval only in a guarded language. For example, he gives a picture of people's sufferings and their lamentations when the huge army of Harshavardhana was on march. At that time some persons, contented with the *Paripālaka* officers, were praising the ruler by saying that 'The king is Dharma incarnate'. But there were others who:

> . . . .despondent at the plunder of their ripe grain, had come forth wives and all to bemoan their estates, and to the imminent risk of their lives, grief dismissing fear, had begun to censure their sovereign, crying 'Where's the king?' 'What right has he to be king?' 'What a king!'[18]

Such observations made by despondent people at the risk of their lives, were indeed a great censure on the administration and it is to the credit of Bāṇa that he mustered sufficient courage to present a true picture of people's sufferings in the biography of Harsha himself.

Bāṇa's Diatribe Against Government Service

Another instance where Bāṇa becomes quite critical of the 'Establishment', so to say, occurs when he makes Haṁsavega, the Kāmarūpa envoy to Harsha, enter upon a diatribe against government servants. It is a bitter invective unparalleled anywhere else in Sanskrit literature. The flattery of the royal courtiers, the royal servant socked in utter selfishness and the haughtiness and proud demeanour of king who behaved with utter contempt have been painted here with a rare fidelity.[19] In his view the government servants hardly deserved to be called human beings:

* Brackets ours.

> ....if a wretch of a servant belongs to the world of men, then a *rājila* snake is a cobra, and a withered stalk the best of rice. Better for a manly man is a moment of manliness; at the price of bowing the wise deem not even the joy of a world-sovereignty worth a bow.[20]

According to Bāṇa, a penitent government servant pours contempt on himself thinking that:

> ....to hell with such wealth, perdition seize such advancement, hail to such worshipful enjoyments, my service to such grandeur, away with such glory, joy go with such pomp, for the sake of which my head must seek the earth.[21]

A government servant has no independent personality. He is:

> An eunuch whose love is but words, a worm of inodorous carrion, a mannikin of no account, a walking footstool all grey atop with the dust of feet, in coaxing notes a human cuckoo, in gratifying cries a peacock, in bosom rubbing a land tortoise, in mean fawnings a dog, in modulated notes a pipe, in strainings of body a harlot's person, in the rice-fields of manliness a straw, a jerkings of head a lizard, in curling himself up a hedgehog, in rubbing of feet a very footstool, in slapping with hands a ball, in beatings with sticks a lute board,[22]

According to Bāṇa, such a person has nowhere to go:

> Wither shall he go to find peace? What is his life like? What manly pride is his? What possible pleasures? What dream of enjoyment? This dreadful name of servant, like a torrent of mud, lays everything low.[23]

Why a normal goodly person becomes inclined to service? And what are the feelings which drive him to accept such a situation? These questions are answered by Bāṇa thus:

> When towards servitude inclined by overwhelming calamity, like a wicked mother, old in years; spurred on by greed like an unsatisfied wife; harassed by ill imaginings with their manifold cravings, begotten of youth, like bad children; beholding circumstances over-ripe, like an elderly daughter in his house, and suggesting recourse to another man; urged to exertion by all planets of distress, like poor kinsmen; persued by foul deeds, like aged servants, of long standing and not to be shaken off: when thus, cherishing in his heart in vain the desire of grasping the whole round of delights, as though the power of all his senses were blighted, a man makes up his mind to enter a palace, as a malefactor a cowdung fire, to the burning torment of all his frame,[24]

The diatribe of Bāṇa against government service is quite unique. He has analysed the mental feelings of those in service. He had himself made close observation of palace-life during his wanderings and also at the court of Harsha and had noted the peculiarities of the conduct of the government servants, their greed and lowly demeanour. His observations throw a flood of light on the nature of the bureaucracy of the age of Harsha. As he could not criticise this aspect of Harsha's administration directly, he has put his observations in the mouth of the Kāmarūpa envoy. In a way it is an elaborate commentary on the line of his own thinking as revealed in his musings on receiving the message of Kṛshṇa, the brother of Harsha, to come to the royal court at once:

> I have indeed been misunderstood by the king, and this advice has been given by my disinterested kinsman Kṛiṣṇa; but all service is hateful, and attendance is full of evils, and a court is full of dangers.

Thus, it is apparent that though an orthodox Brāhmaṇa and a great admirer of Harsha, Bāṇa was in no way blind to the evils of contemporary society and polity. One can hear the voice of protest and dissent in his works quite clearly if one lends one's ears to them.

References

1. *Harshacharita*, Eng. trans., by E.B. Cowell and F.W. Thomas, 2nd ed., Delhi, 1968, p. 76.
2. *Ibid.*, p. 74 f.
3. For a critical appraisal of the reliability of the *HC* of Bāṇa cf. my *History and Historiography of the Age of Harsha*, (Jodhpur, 1992) and my paper in the *ABORI* Vols. LXXII and LXXIII, 1991, 1992, pp. 331-61.
4. *The Vedic Age*, p. 390.
5. A.L., Basham, *The Wonder that was India*, p. 187.
6. D.C., Sircar, *Select Inscriptions*, 2nd ed., pp. 378-79.
7. S.R., Goyal, *Guptakālīna Abhilekha*, pp. 317-22.
8. *HC*, p. 154 f.
9. *Ibid.*, p. 254.
10. *Kādambarī*, Eng. tr. by C.M. Ridding, London, 1896, Indian reprint, 1960, p. 152.
11. *Ibid.* p. 217.
12. *Ibid.* p. 156.
13. *Ibid.*, pp. 156-57.
14. Goyal, *op. cit.*, pp. 42, 45.
15. *Ibid.*, p. 135.
16. Cf. my paper 'Political Ideology of the Early Imperial Guptas' in *Reappraising Gupta History for S.R. Goyal*, eds. B.Ch. Chhabra, P.K. Agrawala, Ashvini Agrawal and Shankar Goyal, New Delhi, 1992, pp. 215-23.
17. *Kādambarī*, tr. of Ridding, p. 95.
18. *HC*, p. 208-209.
19. V.S. Agrawala, *The Deeds of Harsha*, Varanasi, 1969, p. 207.
20. *HC*, p. 223.
21. *Ibid.*, p. 222.
22. *Ibid.*, p. 222 f.
23. *Ibid.*, p. 222.
24. *Ibid.*, p. 219 f.

Aspects of Indian History and Histography
Editor : P.K. Mishra
Kaveri Books, New Delhi, India.

A List of Select Writings of Professor K.K. Dasgupta

Appendix

Compiled by Dr. Korak K. Chaudhuri

Books and Monographs

1. *The Audumbaras*, Govt. Sanskrit College Research Series No. XLIV, Studies No. 26, Calcutta, 1965.
2. *The Mālavas*, Govt. Sanskrit College Research Series No. L, Studies No. 29, Calcutta, 1966.
3. *A Tribal History of Ancient India : A Numismatic Approach*, Calcutta, 1974.
4. *Indian Historiography and Rajendralal Mitra*, Sachchidananda Prakashani, Calcutta, 1976.
5. *Catalogue of Wood Carvings in the Indian Museum*, Indian Museum, Calcutta, 1981.
6. *Wood Carvings of Eastern Indian*, Firma K.L. Mukhopadhyay, Calcutta, 1990.
7. *Indian Art : Past and Present* (In press).
8. *Naṭarāja in Bengal Art* (In press).

Books and Journals Edited

9. H.M. Dasgupta, *Studies in Western Influence on 19th Century Bengali Poetry* (Edited with notes and Annotations), Calcutta, 1969.
10. *The Topographical List of the Brihatsaṁhitā* by J.F. Fleet, Calcutta, 1973.
11. *Ānanda Coomaraswamy : A Centenary Volume*, Calcutta University, Calcutta 1981.
12. *The Comprehensive History of India*, Vol. III, Pts. 1 & 2, (Edited jointly with R.C. Majumdar), Indian History Congress, Peoples Publishing House, New Delhi, 1981 and 1982.
13. *Journal of Ancient Indian History*, Vol. XIII, Pts. 1-2, 1980-82 (Benoy Chandra Sen Memorial Volume), Calcutta University, 1983.
14. *Journal of Ancient Indian History*, Vol. XIV Pts. 1-2, 1983-84 (Nihar Ranjan Ray Memorial Volume), Calcutta University, 1984.
15. *Buddhism : Early and Late Phases*, Centre of Advanced Study in the Department of Ancient Indian History and Culture, Calcutta University, 1985.
16. *Orissa and Her Remains* (by M.M. Ganguly), Patna, 1987.
17. *Śraddhāñjali : Studies in Ancient Indian History* (D.C. Sircar Commemoration Volume, edited jointly with P.K. Bhattacharya and R.D. Chowdhury, Delhi, 1988.

A List of Select Papers and Articles

A. Iconography

1. A Unique Image of the Buddhist Goddess Kurukullā, *Proceedings of the Indian History Congress*, Vol. XXIII, Aligarh, 1960, pp. 84-86.
2. Brahmanical Iconography : Prospective Lines of Research, *Bulletin of the School of Historical and Cultural Studies*, Vol. I, Pt. 2, 1965.
3. Vaṭuka Bhairava and Vedic Rudra, *Journal of the Asiatic Society*, Vol. IX, Nos. 3-4, Calcutta, 1967, pp. 260-261.
4. Iconography of Tārā, Opening Paper read in the Seminar on Tārā in the Deptt. of A.I.H.C.C.U., *The Śakti Cult and Tārā*, (Ed. D.C. Sircar), Calcutta University, 1967, pp. 115-127.
5. The Hāyaśirṣa Pāñcharātra and the Chaturviṁśati Vyūha of Viṣṇu, *Journal of Ancient Indian History*, Vol. X, 1976-77 (Ed. K.K. Ganguly), Calcutta University, 1977, pp. 172-179.
6. Iconographical Notes, *JAIH*, Vol. XII, 1978-79, (Ed. S.K. Mitra), Calcutta University, 1980, pp. 111-117.
7. An Iconographical Approach to the Study of the History of Ancient Assam, *Sources of the History of India*, Vol. III, (Ed. N.R. Ray), Calcutta, 1980, pp. 3-9.
8. Indian Iconography (A.D. 300-985), *A Comprehensive History of India*, Vol. III, Pt. 2, (Ed. R. C. Majumdar and Jt. Ed., K.K. Dasgupta), Indian History Congress, New Delhi, 1982, pp. 856-944.
9. An Image of the so-called Śiva-Lokeśvara, *Buddhism : Early and Late Phases* (Ed. K.K. Dasgupta), Calcutta University, 1985, pp. 103-107.
10. Benzai-Ten in Indian Perspective, *Vājapeya : Essays on Evolution of Indian Art and Culture* (Prof. K.D. Bajpai Felicitation Vol.), (Eds. A.M. Shastri, R.K. Sharma, Agam Prasad), Vol. I, Delhi, 1987, pp. 285-288.
11. Origin of the Buddha Image, *Śraddhāñjali : Studies in Ancient Indian History* (D.C. Sircar Commemoration Volume), (Eds. K.K. Dasgupta, P.K. Bhattacharya and R.D. Chowdhury), Delhi, 1988, pp. 148-155.
12. The Pāñcharātra Tradition and Brāhmaṇical Iconography, *Shāstric Traditions in Indian Arts* (Ed. Anna Libera Dallapiccolar), Vol. I, Stuttgart, Germany, 1989, pp. 71-91.
13. Two Unique Viṣṇu Icons (co-author Gopal Chandra Chauley), *Culture, Tribal History and Freedom, Movement* (Dr. N.K. Sahu Commemoration Volume), (Ed. P.K. Mishra), Delhi, 1989, pp. 137-140.
14. Śaivism in Bengal: An Icono-historical Survey, *Cultura Indica* (Tributes to an Indologist Professor Dr. Ashoke Catterjee Sastri), Delhi, 1994, pp. 269-297.
15. A Study of Early India-Iran Kelation : An Art-historical Approach, *Indo-Iranica* (Golden Jubilee Volume), 1995, pp. 75-102.
16. A Unique Icon of the Śiva-Naṭarāja of the Bengal School, *Viśvambharā : Probings in Orientology* (Prof. V.S. Pathak Festschrift), (Eds. Ajay Mitra Shastri, Devendra Handa, C.S. Gupta), Vol. II, New Delhi, 1995, pp. 289-291.
17. A Rare Type of Śiva-Liṅga from South Bengal, *Swarup-Saurabham* (Lakshman Swarup Commemoration Volume), 1995 (in press).
18. A Naṭarāja Image from South Bengal, (*Prof. Lallanji Gopal Felicitation* Volume), (Ed. T.P. Verma), (in press).

19. Maurya Sculpture, *Encyclopaedia of Indian Art*, (Ed. R.P. Srivastava) (in press).
20. Gupta Sculpture, *Encyclopaedia of Indian Art*, (Ed. R.P. Srivastava), (in press).
21. A Rare Pañchamukha Śiva-Liñga from Bengal, *Prof. Kalyan Kumar Ganguly Felicitation Volume*, (Ed. S.S. Biswas), (in press).
22. Buddhism in Eastern India, *Buddhism* (Ed. K.C. Mishra), Bhubaneswara, (in press).
23. Ādhunik Bhāratiya Bhāskarya (Translated in Hindi), (Ed. J.K. Sadani), *Bhāratīya Mūrtikalā* (in press).

B. Art, Architecture and Painting

24. Foreign Trade and Gandhāra Art, *Quarterly Review of Historical Studies*, Vol. V, No. 4, 1965-66, Ed. S.P. Sen. Institute of Historical Studies, Calcutta, pp. 199-202.
25. Indian Wood Carvings, *Indian Museum Bulletin*, Vol. III, Pt.1, Indian Museum, Calcutta, 1967, pp. 14-18.
26. Aśokan Art : Why and How far Buddhist *P I H C*, Varanasi, 1969.
27. Budhnāth Temple : An Unnoticed Rekha Deul near Bhubaneswar, *Summaries of Papers read in All India Oriental Conference* (Silver Jubilee Session), Jadavpore University, 1969.
28. Drawings and Paintings of Rabindranath, *Review*, No. 2, Indo-German Association, 1976, pp. 22-23.
29. Sources of the History of Mysore : Monumental Remains, *Sources of the History of India*, Vol. I, (Ed. S.P. Sen), Institute of Historical Studies, Calcutta, 1978, pp. 27-46.
30. Architectural Data in the Hayaśirṣa Pāñcharātra, *Āchārya-Vandanā* D.R. Bhandarkar Birth Centenary Volume, (Ed. S. Bandyopadhyay), Calcutta University, Calcutta, 1982, pp. 229-232.
31. Modern Painting and Sculpture, *Bhāratīya Saṁskriti*, Vol. II, (Ed. Prabhakar Machwe), Calcutta, 1983, pp. 91-104.
32. Wood Carvings of Arunachal Pradesh and Nagaland, *Indological Studies* : Essays in memory of Shri S.P. Singhal, (Ed. Devendra Handa), Delhi, 1987, pp. 287-293.
33. Wood Carvings of Bihar, *Nalinī Kānta Śatavārṣikī : Studies in Art and Archaeology of Bihar and Bengal*, (Dr. N.K. Bhattasali Centenary Volume, 1888-1988), (Eds. Debala Mitra and Gouriswar Bhattacharya), Delhi, 1989, pp. 249-254.
34. Abanindranath Tagore : The Spirit behind the Bengal School, *Lalit Kalā Contemporary-38*, Special Issue, Lalitkala Akademi, New Delhi, March, 1993, pp. 52-63.
35. Wood Carvings of Orissa, *Heritage of India : Past and Present* (Essays in honour of Prof. R.K. Sharma), (Eds. P.K. Mishra and S.K. Sullerey), Delhi, 1994, pp. 285-296.

C. Numismatics

36. Kushāṇa Influence on the Apratigha Coins, *Indian Historical Quarterly*, Vol. XXX, Pt. 2, 1958, pp. 264-270.
37. A Note on the Viśvāmitra type of Coins of the Audumbaras, *J S*, Vol. III, No. 1, 1961, pp. 4-19.
38. A Rare Variety of the Coins of the Audumbaras, *IHQ*, Vol. XXXVIII, Pt. 1, 1962-63, pp. 76-79.
39. The Vemakas and their Coins, *Our Heritage*, Vol. IX, Pt.2, July-Dec., (Ed. Gaurinath Sastri), 1961, pp. 73-76.

40. Some Curious Legends on the Mālava Coins, *PIHC*, (Allahabad Session), Vol. XXVII, 1965.
41. A Note on a Class of Mālava Coins, *Journal of the Numismatic Society of India*, Vol. XXVIII, Pt.1, (Prof. J.N. Banerjea Number), 1966, pp. 52-54.
42. A Note on Vachchaghoṣa on some Early Indian Coins, *J N S I*, Vol. XXVIII, Pt. 1, 1966, pp. 50-52.
43. Mālava and Senāpati Coins, *J N S I*, Vol. XXIX, Pt. 2, 1967, pp. 79-80.
44. Legends on the Agra Coins, *J N S I*, Vol. XXXII, Pt. 1, 1970, pp. 19-24.
45. A Note on the Attribution of Mahādeva Coins, *J N S I*, Vol. XXXII, Pt. 2, 1970, pp. 150-153.
46. Devices and Symbols on the Kuluta Coins, *J N S I*, Vol. XXXIV, Pt.1, 1972, pp. 23-30.
47. The Numismatic Society of India, *Numismatic Studies* (Special Monthly Bulletin), Conference of the N S I (LXII Session), Calcutta, 1974, pp. 12-15.
48. Rare Tribal Coins of the Lingen Collection, *J N S I*, Vol. XXXVI, 1974, pp. 50-56.
49. New Light on a Solitary of the Vrishnis, *J A S*, Vol. XVI, Nos. 1-4, 1974, pp. 50-56.
50. Coins of the Mālavas, *Research Journal of the University of Indore*, Vol. IV, No. 2, October, 1975, pp. 35-36.
51. The Ujjain Symbol : Genesis, Development and Allied Issues, *Summary of Papers read in the 63rd Conference of the N S I*, Indore, 1975, p. 3.
52. A Unique Silver Coin of the Ārjunāyanas, *J.N.S.I.*, Vol. XXXIX, Pts. 1-2, (C.R. Singhal Commemoration Volume), 1977, pp. 49-51.
53. Vāyuvarmā, a hitherto unknown king of Kausambi, *J N S I*, (Ananda K. Coomaraswamy Centenary Volume), Vol. XL, Pts. 1-2, 1978, pp. 96-97.
54. Ananda Coomaraswamy and Indian Numismatics, *J N S I*, Vol. XL, Pts. 1-2, 1978, pp. 7-8.
55. The Numismatic Source of the History of Uttar Pradesh, *Sources of the History of India*, Vol. II, (Ed. S.P. Sen), Calcutta, 1979, pp. 310-333.
56. Vāsudeva-Krishṇa on Early Indian Coins and Seals, *Journal of the Varendra Research Museum*, Vol. VI, 1979-80, Rajshahi, pp. 31-32.
57. New Varieties of the Audumbara Coins, *J.N.S.I.*, Vol. XLV, Pts. 1-2, 1983, pp. 23-26.
58. Indian Coins and Coin-Symbols, *J A I H*, Pts. 1-2, (Nihar Ranjan Ray Memorial Volume), 1983-84, pp. 41-70; *J N S I*, Vol. XLVI, Pts. 1-2, 1984.
59. Tribal Coins of Ancient India, (c. 2nd cent. B.C.-4th cent. A.D.), *Mudrā* (Journal of the Numismatic Society of Calcutta), Vol.I, December, 1987, pp. 10-19.

D. Historical Geography

60. The Sindhu in Early Indian History and Culture, *Great Rivers of India*, (Ed. Swami Vedantananda), Ramakrishna Mission, Patna, 1982, pp. 35-42.
61. Paśchim Baṅga to Baṅga : From the Unreal to the Viable, *The Telegraph*, 3 July, 1987.
62. Ancient Geography of India : Problems and Perspectives, *Indian Geographical Review* (in press).

E. Society, Economy, Religion, Science and Aesthetics

63. The Bauls and Pasupatas of Bengal. *J.N. Banerjea Volume*, Calcutta University, 1960, pp. 339-352.

64. Spread of Brahmoism in the Khasi and Jayantia Hills, *Sources of the History of India*, Vol. II, (Ed. S.P. Sen), Calcutta, 1979, pp. 268-274; *The Indian Messenger*, 112, Nos. 15 & 16, Calcutta, 1994, 164-168.
65. Vaishnavism in Eastern India, *J A I H*, (Ed. S.C. Bhattacharya), Calcutta University, (in press).
66. The Bauls of India, *Encyclopaedia of Art and Culture*, (Ed. R.P. Srivastava), (in press).
67. Expansion and Orientalism : The Asiatic Society of Calcutta and the Sanskrit Colleges of Benaras and Calcutta, *The Indian Renaissance in the Nineteenth Century*, (Ed. Swami Lokeswarananda), The Ramakrishna Mission Institute of Culture, Calcutta (in press).

F. History and Historiography

68. Antiquity of the Audumbaras, *P I H C*, Vol. XXIV; Delhi, 1961, pp. 44-47.
69. Rajendralal Mitra, *Q R H S*, Vol. II, Nos. 3 & 4, 1962, pp. 127-132.
70. Early Territory of the Guptas, *Summary of the papers read at the Conference of the Indian History Congress*, 1963.
71. Early Indian Historians, *Q R H S*, Vol. III, Nos. 1 & 2, 1963-64, pp. 24-28.
72. The Audumbaras, *Our Heritage*, Vol. X, pt. II, July-Dec., 1962, pp. 1-26.
73. The Puranas on Audumbaras, *Purāṇa*, Vol. VII, No. 1, January, Varanasi, 1965, pp. 186-190.
74. The Malavas, *O H*, Vol. XIII, Pt. II, July-Dec., 1965, pp. 1-22.
75. The Agras; An Ancient People of the Punjab, *Vishweswaranand Indological Journal*, Punjab University, Vol. IX, No. 1, March, 1971, pp. 139-150.
76. The Arjunayanas : An Ancient Indian Tribe, *Journal of the Oriental Institute*, Vol. XX, No. 4, June, 1971, pp. 431-441.
77. Dwarakanath Tagore : A Nineteenth Century Pioneer, *Indo-Asian Culture*, Vol. XX. No. 3, New Delhi, 1971, pp. 34-88.

77A. Kakhaidas Banerji (1886-1930), *Dictionary of National Biography*, Vol. I (A.D.)

78. (Sir) Asutosh Chaudhuri (1860-1924), *Dictionary of National Biography*. Vol. I (A-D), (Ed. S.P. Sen), Institute of Historical Studies, Calcutta, 1972, pp. 291-293.
79. The Aśvakas : An Early Indian Tribe, *East and West* (New Series), Vol. XXII, (Ed. Guiseppe Tucci), Nos. 1-2, March-June, 1972, pp. 33-40.
80. Rakhaldas Bandyopadhyay, *Hostorians and Historiography in Modern India*, (Ed. S.P. Sen), Calcutta, 1973, pp. 15-26.
81. New Light on the Audumbaras and the Sage Viśvāmitra, Communicated in September, 1973, *J A S*, Vol. XV, Nos. 1-4, 1973, p. 217.
82. The Rajanyas : An Early Indian Tribe, *Annals of the Bhandarkar Oriental Research Institute*, Vol. LIII, 1973, pp. 41-50.
83. Surya Kumar Sarvadhikary (1832-1904), *Dictionary of National Biography*, Vol. IV, (S-Z), (Ed. S.P. Sen), Institute of Historical Studies, Calcutta, 1974, pp. 76-77.
84. Gopinath Saha, (1901-1924), *Dictionary of National Biography*, Vol. IV, (S-Z), (Ed. S.P. Sen), Calcutta, 1974, pp. 4-5.
85. History in Bengali Literature (19th-20th Centuries), *History in Modern Indian Literature*, (Ed. S.P. Sen), Calcutta, 1975, pp. 25-40.
86. The Kulutas : An Early Indian Tribe, *Journal of Indian History*, Vol. LV, Pts. 1 & 2, April-August, 1977, University of Kerala, Trivandrum, pp. 11-23.

87. Ananda Coomaraswamy : His Contributions to the Studies in Brahmanical Iconography, *Bharat Pratibha*, Vol. I, No. 9, Independence Number, August, 1977, pp. 48.
88. Historical Biography in Sanskrit Literature, *Historical Biography in Indian Literature*, (ed. S.P. Sen), Institute of Historical Study, Calcutta, 1979, pp. 3-28.
89. Coomaraswamy and Indian Iconography, *Ananda Coomarswamy : A Centenary Volume* (Ed. K.K. Dasgupta), Calcutta, University, Calcutta, 1981, pp. 55-68.
90. Akshaya Kumar Maitreya : A Pioneer in the Historiography of Bengal, *Journal of the Varendra Research Museum*, Vol. VII, Rajshahi University, Rajshahi, Bangladesh, 1981-82, pp. 37-41.
91. Ananda Coomaraswamy (Editorial), *Ananda Coomaraswamy : A Centenary Volume*, Calcutta University, 1981, pp. vii-xvi.
92. Bengali Literature in Colonial Bengal (Early Nineteenth Century), *Western Colonial Policy*, Vol. I, (Ed. N.R. Ray), Institute of Historical Studies, Calcutta, 1981, pp. 472-490.
93. Radha Gobinda Basak : An Eminent Historian, (1885-1982), *J I H* (Golden Jubilee Number), Kerala University, 1982, pp. 265-276.
94. Niharranjan Ray, *JAIH*, Vol. XIII, Pts. 1-2, 1980-82, (B.C. Sen Memorial Volume), (Ed. K.K. Dasgupta), Calcutta University, 1983, pp. 333-338.
95. Ramesh Chandra Majumdar, *ibid*, pp. 325-330.
96. Radhagobinda Basak, *JAIH*, Vol. XIV, Pts. 1-2, 1983-84, (Nihar Ranjan Ray Memorial Volume), pp. 318-322.
97. Radhagobinda Basak, *R.G. Basak Commemoration Volume* (Ed. M. Banerjee); Basak, Radhagobinda, *Dictionary of National Biography* (Supplement), (Ed. N.R. Ray), Vol. I, Calcutta, 1986, pp. 128-129; Radhagobinda Basak (1885-1982); An eminent Historian, *JIH*, (Diamond Jubilee Volume), (Ed. T. K. Ravindran), Kerala University, 1982, pp. 265-275.
98. S.B. Chaudhuri (Editorial Note on), *JAIH*, Vol. XIV, Pts. 1-2, 1983-84, (Ed. K. K. Dasgupta), (Niharranjan Ray Memorial Volume), Calcutta University, 1984, pp. 325-326.
99. The Audumbaras : Ancient and Modern, *Festschrift for Syed Ali Ahsan* (Eds. M. Moniruzzaman and M.S. Quoreshi). Dhaka, 1985, pp. 314-316.
100. Indian Tradition and Communal Harmony, *Indian Medical Association Souvenir*, 1991.
101. History and the Disputed Water, *The Statesman*, February 22, 1992.
102. Judgement of Cambay, *The Telegraph*, 16 December, 1992.
103. Rajendralal Mitra : An Avantgrade Historian, *The Statesman*, March 1, 1992.
104. Indian Synthesis-Ideal of Universal Goodwill, *The Statesman*, January 17, 1993.
105. 1400 Bangabda and all that, *The Telegraph*, Wednesday, 14 April, 1993.
106. Last Days of the Maukharis, *IHQ*, Vol. XXXVIII, Pts. 2 &3, pp. 242-246.
107. Dr. S.P. Sen : A Historian and a Friend of Historians, *Q R H S* (Dr. S.P. Sen Commemoration No.), Vol. XIX, No. 4 (1979-80) pp. 74-77.
108. Bio-Sketches-cum-Critical estimates of 'R.C. Majumdar', 'O.C. Ganguly', and 'Niharranjan Ray', *Dictionary of National Biography* (Supplement), (Ed. N.R. Ray), Institute of Historical Studies, Calcutta, (in press).
109. Ancient Indian Geography : Problems and Perspectives, *Indian Geographical Review* (in press).

G. Book Reviews

1. *Nana on Lion* by B.N. Mukherjee (*Search Light*, January, 1972).
2. *Vishnudharmottara Purānam (Chitra Sutram)*. Edited by Asoke Chatterjee Sastri with a Hindi translation, Varanasi (*J A S*, Vol. XVI. Nos. 1-4, 1974, pp. 175-76).
3. *India as seen in the Bṛihatsaṁhitā of Varāhmihira* by Ajay Mitra Shastri (*J N S I*, Vol. XXXVII, Pts. 1-2, 1975, p. 187).
4. *Central Asia and South Asian Documents on the Old Saka Era* by B.N. Mukherjee, 1973 (*The Indian Historical Review*, Vol. II, No. 1, July, 1975. Indian Council of Historical Research, pp. 173-174).
5. *Ananda Coomaraswamy*, ed. S. Duraí Raja Singham, Petaḷing Jaya, Malayasia (*The Hindu*, June 1, 1976).
6. *Ancient Indian Rituals and their Social Contents* by N.N. Bhattacharya (*The Hindu*, July 19, 1977).
7. *Historical Geography of Madhya Pradesh* by P.K. Bhattacharya, Delhi, 1977 (*J A I H*, Vol.XI, ed. S.K. Mitra, 1977-78, Calcutta University, 1979, pp. 144-147).
8. *India and Indology, Selected Articles* by W. Norman Brown, ed. Rosanne Rocher, Delhi, 1978 (*Bulletin of the R.K. Mission Institute of Culture*, Vol. XXXIII, No. 3, March, 1982, pp. 89-70).
9. *Hindu Philosophy* by Theos Bearnard, Delhi, 1981 (*Bulletin of the R.K. Mission Institute of Culture*, Vol. XXXIV, No.2, February, 1983, p. 45).
10. *Hindu Divinities in the Japanese Buddhist Pantheon-A Comapartive Study* by D.N. Bakshi. Benten Publishers and Firma K.L. Mukhopadhyay (*J A I H*, Vol. XIII, Pts. 1-2, 1980-82, Calcutta University, 1983, pp. 306-309).
11. *Remains of the Bhārhut Stupa in the Indian Museum : Part 1* by Arabinda Ghosh, Indian Museum, Calcutta (*J A I H*, Vol. XIII, Pts. 1-2, 1980-82, ed. K.K. Dasgupta, B.C. Sen Memorial Volume, Calcutta University, 1983, pp. 313-316).
12. *Chālukyan Temples of Andhra Deśa* by Rajendra Prasad, Abhinav Publications, Delhi (*The Statesman*, Sunday, 11th November, 1984).
13. *Message of Tantra for the New World*, by Sachchidananda, Calcutta, 1982 (*J A I H*, Vol. XIV, Pts. 1-2, 1983-84, Calcutta University, 1984, pp. 308-310).
14. *Indian Buddhism*, by A.K. Warder, 1980 (*Bulletin of the R.K. Mission Institute of Culture*, Vol. XXXVII, No. 8, August, 1986, p. 190).
15. *Pinnacles of India's Past : Selection's from the Rigveda*, translated and annotated by Walter H. Manner, Amsterdam, Philadelphia, 1986 (*Bulletin of the R.K. Mission Institute of Culture*, Vol. XL, No.5, May, 1989, p. 135).
16. *The Comprehensive History of Assam, Vol. I*, ed. H.K. Barpujari, Guwahati (*The Sentinel*, Saturday, October 10, 1992).
17. *The Role of Feudatories in Pallava History* by M.S. Gobindasamy, Annamalai University, (*QRHS*, Vol. VI, Pt. 2 (1966-67), Ed. S.P. Sen, pp. 112-113)
18. *Studies in Indian History* by Chidambara Kulkarni, Bombay, (*Q R H S*, Vol. XVII, 1977-78, pp. 122-123).
19. *Index to Indian Culture (1934-1949)*, compiled and edited by Sibdaṣ Chaudhuri, Firma K.L. Mukhopadhyay, Calcutta (*QRHS*, Vol. XVII, 1977-78, pp. 123-124).
20. *Sri Chaitanya Charitāmṛita Madhyalilā*, *QRHS*, Vol. XVII, 1977-78, pp. 251-52.

H. Forewords and Prefaces

1. *The Concept and Iconography of the Goddess of Abundance and Fortune in Three Religions of India*, by Dr. Niranjan Ghosh, Burdwan University, 1979.
2. *Punjab Painting* by Dr. R.P. Srivastava, New Delhi, 1983.
3. *Political History of Tripura* by Dr. Ramanimohan Sarma, Calcutta, 1986.
4. *Art and Archaeology of Punjab* by Dr. R.P. Srivastava, Delhi, 1990.
5. *A Comprehensive History of Arunachal Pradesh* by Dr. Subid Chattopadhyay, Calcutta, 1991.
6. *Sculptural Art of Ancient Bengal* by Dr. Krishna Biswas, Delhi, 1995.

IVA. Lectures Delivered

1. Sarbeswar Sarma Kataki Memorial Lecture at Mangaldoi in Assam in 1991 on *Eastern Indian School of Medieval Iconography*.
2. The First N.N. Law Lecture at the Iran Society in Caluctta in 1992 on *A Study of Early India–Iran Relations : An Art Historical Approach*.
3. Alice Bonar Lecture at Varanasi in 1993 on *Wood Carvings of Orissa and Alice Boner's Principle of Composition*.
4. Lecture in the Asiatic Society, Calcutta on *Origin, Antiquity and Evolution of Brahmi Script* on January 19, 1995.

IVB. Convocational Presidential and Inaugaural Addresses

1. 'Draviddan in Bengal', Presidential Address, Section III, South Indian History Congress, 5th Annual Session, Mysore, Feb. 9-11, 1985.
2. 'The Tribal Peoples of Ancient Punjab (c. 200 B.C. - c. 300 A.D.)', Presidential Address, Section 1, (Ancient Punjab), Punjab History Congress, 20th Session, Punjab University, Patiala, Feb. 28 - March 2, 1986.
3. Sixth Convocational Address as the Vice-Chancellor of the University of Kalyani, 9th May, 1989.
4. Inaugural Address delivered on the occasion of the opening of the Post-Graduate Folk-Lore Department at the University of Kalyani, January 15, 1990.
5. Seventh Convocational Address as the Vice-Chancellor of the University of Kalyani, 4th April, 1990.
6. Eighth Convocational Address as the Vice-Chancellor of the University of Kalyani, 22nd April, 1991.
7. Address while inaugurating the Dakshini Purakirtti O Barenya Smriti Kaksha, Jaynagar-Majilpur, South 24 Parganas on 9th December, 1994.

Review of Professor K.K. Dasgupta's Books

1. Indian Historiography and Rajendralal Mitra, Calcutta, 1977-K.K. Ganguly, *Journal of Ancient Indian History*, Vol. IX (D.R. Bhandarakar Centenary Volume), 1975-76, pp. 261-263; also by Arati Guha, *Amrita Bazar Patrika*, 1977.
2. Ithihasa O Samskriti (in Bengali), Sachchidananda Prakashani, Calcutta, 1977-Anup Matilal, *Uttarsuri*, 1386 B.S., p. 103.

3. A Tribal History of Ancient India : A Numismatic Approach, Calcutta, 1974-B.P. Mazumdar, *Journal of the Bihar Research Society*, Vol. LXII, Pts. 1-4, 1976, pp. 266-269.
4. Ananda Coomaraswamy : A Centenary Volume, Calcutta University, Calcutta, 1981-R.P. Srivastava, *ABORI*, Vol. LXII, 1981, pp. 325-327; Kapila Vatsyayana, *JAIH*, Vol. XIV, Pts. 1-2, 1983-84, Calcutta University, 1984, pp. 289-294; *The Statesman*, 3rd January, 1982.
5. Catalogue of Wood Carvings in the Indian Museum, Indian Museum, Calcutta, 1981-A.N. Lahiri, *JAIH*, Vol. XIII, Pts. 1-2, 1980-82, Calcutta University, 1983, pp. 304-306; *The Statesman*, July 26, 1983.
6. Nijasva Nirjan (Ed. K.K. Dasgupta), Calcutta, 1982-Bijit Kumar Datta, *Desh*, 27th November, 1982; also by Aloke Ranjan Dasgupta, *Yugāntar*, Thursday, December 1, 1983; also by Sastyendranath Ray, *Ānanda Bāzār Patrikā*, 2nd April, 1984.
7. Wood Carvings of Eastern India, Firma K.L. Mukhopadhyay, Calcutta, 1990-Asish Sanyal, *The Statesman*, 18th August, 1991; also by Sunil C. Ray *Gaṇaśakti*, 21 January, 1991.

Publications in Bengali

Books and Monographs

1. *Sonaṭa* (Book of Poems), Calcutta, 1961.
2. *Itihāsa O Saṁskṛiti*, Sacchidananda Prakashani, Calcutta, 1977.
3. *Pratimāśilpe Hindu Devadevī* (in Press).

Books Edited

4. *Hālkā Megher Melā* (A compilation of Personal Essays of different authors), Pustak, Calcutta, 1956.
5. *Dvārakānāth Ṭhākur* (Kiśori Chānd Mitter), Beng. trans. Dvijendra Lāl Nāth, Sambodhi Publications, Calcutta, 1962.
6. *Nijasva Nirjan* (A compilation of Personal Essays of different authors), Navana, Calcutta, 1982.
7. *Śatavarṣer Āloy Rākhāldās Bandyopādhyay*, Sarat Samity, Calcutta, 1990.

A List of Select Papers and Articles

1. Gitisāhitye Nazrul, *Janasevaka Sāptāhiki*, May 29, 1955.
2. Śri Hema Chandra Roy Chaudhuri, *Māsik Basumatī*, Śrāvaṇ, 1363 B.S. (1956), pp. 583-585.
3. Rabin Rāyer Śilpavaichitrya, *Sundaram*, year 1, Nos. 2 and 3, Bhādra and Āśvina, 1363 B.S.(1956), pp. 145-152.
4. Āminā Āhmed, *Sundaram*, Year 1, Nos. 6-11, Pauṣ-Jaiṣṭha, 1363-64 B.S. (1957-57), pp. 393-398.
5. Śilpi Sunilamādhav, *Sundaram*, Year 1, Nos. 4 and 5, Kārtik and Agrahāyan, 1363 B.S. (1957), pp. 279-285.

6. Rathin Maitra, *Sundaram*, year 1, Nos. 12 and 13, Āshādh and Śrāvaṇ, 1364 B.S. B.S. (1957), pp. 510-519.
7. Śilpi Hemendranath, *Sundaram*, Year 2, Nos. 2 and 3, Bhādra and Āsviṇa, 1364 B.S. (1957), pp. 123-132.
8. Śilpi Indra Dugār, *Sundaram*, Year 2, Nos. 4 and 12, 1364-65 B.S. (1957-58), pp. 181-194.
9. Sarkār O Sāhitya, *Sāhityer Khabar*, Paush, 1364 B.S. (1957), PP. 5-7.
10. Bhāratiya Pratnatattva O Sir John Hubert Marshall, *Yugāntar*, 1958.
11. Tājmahal, *Dainik Basumatī*, 18 May, 1958.
12. Śilpi Pranakṛishṇa Pāli, *Sundaram*, Year 2, No. 13, 1365 B.S. (1958), pp. 242-251.
13. Kavi Sthapati Frank Lyed Wright, *Sundaram*, Year 3, Nos.1, Āśvin, 1365 B.S. (1958), pp. 68-82.
14. Bāluchar Śāḍi Pradarśani, *Samakālīn*, 1365 B.S. (1958).
15. Prāchin Baṅglār Śaharer Galpa, *Mafahsval*, Phālguṇa 11, 1365 B.S. (1958).
16. Gata Ek Bacharer Kabitā, *Sāhityer Khabar*, Jaiṣṭha, 1365 B.S. (1958), pp. 7-12; Āshaḍh, 1365 B.S. (1958), pp. 19-24.
17. Sāmpratik Prabandha, *Sāhitya*, Śrāvaṇ, 1365 B.S. (1958), pp. 17-23 and 19-25.
18. Pratnatattve James Prinsep, *Yugāntar*, 12 April, 1959.
19. Dhokrā Kāmār: jāti O Śilpakṛiti, *Yugāntar*, 5 January, 1959.
20. Pather Śilpi, *Sundaram*, Year 4, No. 1, 1366 B.S. (1959), p. 52.
21. Duṭi Svārthak Chalachhitra, *Sundaram*, Year 4, No.2, 1366 D.S. (1959), pp. 165-170.
22. Prāchin Bāṅglār Kayekṭi Śaharer Kathā, *Kathāvārtā*, April 1, 1959, p. 513.
23. Tāmralipta, *Kathāvārtā*, 1959.
24. Prāchina Bhārater Lipikalā, *Māsik Basumatī*, 1960.
25. Ispāter Ālpanā, *Sundaram*, Year 4, Nos. 3-12, 1367 B.S. (1960), pp. 249-279.
26. Rabīndrottar Chitrakalā, *Ekatā*, Rabīndrajanmaśatavārṣiki Biseś Sankhyā, Calcutta University, 1961, pp. 181-189.
27. Prāchina Bhārate Lekhār Upādān, *Māsik Basumatī*, Paush, 1369 B.S. (1961).
28. Ṭhākurbārir Ādikathā, *Sanskrit College Patrikā*, 1368 B.S. (1961).
29. Rabīndranāther Chhabir Bhāṣā, *Yugāntar*, 25th Baisakh, 1368 B.S. (1961).
30. Aitihāsik Rājendralāl Mitra, *Chaturaṅga*, Vaiśākha-Āshaḍha 1370 B.S. (1963).
31. Bāṅgāli Vidya Jāti Prasaṅge, *Amṛita*, December, 1964.
32. Ugrasena, *Bhāratkoṣa*, I, Calcutta, 1964, p. 558.
33. Ujjaini, *Bhāratkoṣa*, I, Calcutta, 1964, p. 558-560.
34. Indraprastha, *Bhāratkoṣa*, I, Calcutta, 1964, p. 520.
35. Akshaya Kumār Maitreya (in disguise of Chandra Śekhar Dāsgupta), *Chaturaṅga*, Śrāvaṇ-Āśvin, 1372 B.S. (1965) (later included in *Itihāsa O Saṁkṛiti*).
36. Hindu Klej D David Hare, *Chaturaṅga*, Baiśākha, Āṣāḍha, 1372 B.S. (965), pp. 63-71.
37. Kālikṛishṇa Deva, *Bhāratkoṣa*, III, Calcutta, 1966, pp. 305-306.
38. Kinnara, *Bhāratkoṣa*, II, Calcutta, 1966, p. 331.
39. Nibir Ghana Āndhāre, *Sāptāhik Basumatī*, 17 August, 1967.
40. Gaṇesha, *Bhāratkoṣa*, III, Calcutta, 1967, pp. 81-82.
41. Chāmuṇḍā, *Bhāratkoṣa*, III, Calcutta, 1967, pp. 315-316.
42. Tilak, *Bhāratkoṣa*, III, Calcutta, 1967, pp. 724-727.
43. Nirvāker Guhā, Svapner Jhāṅk (Rabīndra Chitrakalā Prasaṅge), *Sāptāhik Basumatī*, 15, Baiśākha, 1374 B.S. (1967).
44. Bāro Bhuiyār Āmale Bāṅglā, *Betār Jagat*, Issue 39, No.1, January 1-15, 1968, p.7.

45. Naṭarāja, *Bhāratkoṣa*, IV, Calcutta, 1970, pp. 148-149.
46. Bāṅgāli Kavi Nazrul, *Rabīndranāth, Nazrul O Bāṅglādeśa* (Ed. Raghuvir Chakraborty), Calcutta, 1971, pp. 262-270.
47. Bhāratiya Mūrtikoṣa, *Māsik Basumatī*, Phālguṇ, 1378 B.S. (1971), pp. 561-564; Chaitra, 1378 B.S., pp. 816-820; Vaiśākha, 1379 B.S. (1972), pp. 465-472; Śrāvaṇ-Bhādra, 1379 B.S. (1972), pp. 647-652; Āśvin-Kārtik, 1379 B.S. (1972).
48. Najir Nei, najir thākve nā, *Sāptāhik Basumatī*, 1971, pp. 1832-1833.
49. Itihās Indirā O Bāṅglādeśa, *Sāptāhik Basumatī*, 27 January 1972, pp. 1165-67.
50. Vishṇu, *Bhāratkoṣa*, V, Calcutta, 1973, pp. 119-121.
51. David Hareer Dharmamat, *David Hare Samraṇe*, David Hare Svaraṇ Saṁkhyā, year 7, February, 1976, pop. 33-36.
52. Kāli-Kalam Sekāle, *Ānandabāzār Patrikā*, December 12, 1976.
53. Lekhālekhi Prasaṅge, *Ānandabāzār Patrikā*, November 28, 1976.
54. Bhārat śilper Ādiparva, Videś-Vāṇijyer Saṁyoge, *Itihāsa O Saṁskṛiti*, Calcutta, 1977, pp. 175-178.
55. Prāchīna Mudrāy Hindu Devadevī, *Udbodhana Kārtik* 1384 B.S.(1977), pp. 566-72.
56. Bhārat-Saṁskṛiti, Mūrtitattve, *Itihāsa O Saṁskṛiti*, Calcutta, 1977, pp. 101-112.
57. Sekāleo Nirvāchana Chila,*Ānandabāzar Patrika*, February, 27, 1977 and March, 123, 1977.
58. Aitihāsik Haraprasād Śāstrī, *Ānandabāzar Partikā*, January 16, 1977.
59. Sarasvatī, Aitihya O Itihāse, *Anandabāzār Patrikā*, 12 February, 1978.
60. David Hare, *Udbodhan*, Āśviṇ, 1385 B.S. (1978), pp. 479-482.
61. Vanyā: Purāṇe O Itihāse, *Anandabāzār Patrikā*, 1978.
62. Pratimā-Śilpe, Mahiṣamardinī: Kayekṭi Smaraṇīya Tathyam, *Udbodhan*, Year 81, No. 9, Āśvin, 1386 B.S. (1979), pp. 438-440.
63. Worship of the Goddess Durgā: A Historical Outline, *Maināk Śāradīyā Souvenir*, Octo., 1980.
64. Bhāratīya Bhāskarye Naṭarāja, *Udbodhan*, Āśviṇ, 1387 B.S. (1980), Pūja Issue, pp. 502-504.
65. Rājnaitik Itihāse Prāchīna Tāmralipta, *Itihāser Prekṣāpaṭe, Tāmralipta*, Pūrvādri, Tamluk, 1982, pp. 109-126.
66. Bāṅglār Vāstuśilpe Poḍāmāṭir Bhāṣkarya, *Udbodhan*, Kārtik, 1389 B.S. (1982), pp. 572-574.
67. Ki nāma deva Vaṅga nā Vaṅgadeśa, *Gaṇaśakti*, June 5, 1987.
68. Prāchīna Bhāṣkarya Samakālīn Mānuṣer Mane Kona birūp pratikṛiyā Sṛiṣṭi Kareni, *Purvayan*, November, 1987.
69. Prasaṅga: Tathākathita ekṭi Śiva-Lokeśvara Mūrti, *Jagajjyoti* Buddha Jayyanti Annual 1988, Calcutta, May, 1988, pp. 15-17.
70. Prasaṅga : Lokaśilpa, *Śāntipur Public Library, Special Number*, 1989.
71. Bhārat Śilper Itihāsa charchāya Rākhāldās, *Śatavarsher Āloy Rākhāldās Bandypādhyāy*, Calcutta, 1990, pp. 174-208.
72. Ekjan Sampurṇa Mānush: Satyajit Ray, *Gaṇaśakti*, June 21, 1992.
73. Prasaṅga: Matuā, *Matuā Samarṇikā*, (ed.) Birāṭkumār Bairāgya, Calcutta, 1993, pp. 8/2-8/4.
    Rabīndranāth: Itihāsa-Viveker Darpaṇe, *Gaṇaśakti*, Baiśākha 25, 1401 B.S. (1995).
74. Mahiṣāsuramardinī, Bhārat Śilpe, *Mainā k, Śāradīyā Souvenir*.
75. Kalabau, *Mainā k Durgotsaver Smārak Patrikā*.
76. Bismṛita Samraṇiya : Hons Sloyan, pp. 44-47.

77. Bāṅglā Sāhityer Goḍār Kathā, *Śāradīyā Sabujpātā.*
78. Mudrāsaṁgraha O Mudrācharchā : Adeśe, *Ānandabāzar Patrikā.*
79. Mudrāsaṁgraha O Mudrā charchā : Videśa, *Ānandabāzār Patrikā.*
80. Kiśori Chānd Mitra, *Basumatī.*
81. Vaṅga-Bāṅglā-Bāṅglādeśa, *Souvenir of Padmapukar Institution,* Calcutta.
82. Hindu Chaḍaka Utsay, *Jugāntar.*
83. Chālchitra, *Lokasaṁskṛiti Abhidhān* (In press).

IV. Book Review

1. Antaḥśilā, Dhūrjaṭi Prasād Mukhopādhyāy, *Chaturaṅga,* Māgh, 1363 B.S. (1956).
2. Pūrva Bāṅglār Sreshtha Kabitā (ed.), Abdur Rashid Khan and Muhammad Mamun, Dhākā, *Chaturaṅga,* Kārtik, 1366 B.S. (1959).
3. The House of Ādaṃpur, Anand Lall, London, *Chaturaṅga,* Māgh 1366 B.S. (1959).
4. Ūnaviṁśa Śatābdir Prathamārdha O Bāṅglā Sāhitya, Asit Kumar Baṇdyopadhyay, *Chaturaṅga,* Māgh, 1366 B.S. (1959)_.
5. Ee aṅge eta rūp, Achintya Kumar Sengupta and Chirarūpā, Santosh Kumar Ghosh, *Sanibarer Chithi,* 1366 B.S. (1959), pp. 188-90.
6. Rabindranath, Devipada Bhattacharyya (ed.), *Chaturanga,* Karttick, 1368 B.S. (1961).
7. Rankurar Mandir, Amiya Bandyopadhyay, *Visvabharati Patrika,* 1369 B.S. (1962).
8. Modern Bengali Poetry : A Few Books (A discussion), *Chaturaṅga,* Śrāvan, 1369 B.S. (1962).
9. Bey and the Blues (African Poetry), Selected and Introduced by Rosey and Pool, *Chaturaṅga,* Māgh 1369 B.S. (1962).
10. Pṛithivī O Pāśchātya Jagat, Arnold Toynbee (The World and the West, 1952), *Chaturaṅga,* Śrāvāṇ, 1372 B.S. (1965).
11. Muralidhar Bandyopadhyay, Amalendu De, *Rabindra Bharati Patrika,* Year 4, Number 2, 1965, pp. 57-59.
12. Penguin Modern Poets, 1, 2 and 3 (Penguin Books), *Chaturanga,* Kartik, 1377 B.S. (1970).
13. Kalhana birachita Rajatarangini, Bengali translation by Ajay Kumar Mukhopadhyay, Calcutta, 1378 B.S. (1971), *Grantha Parikramā,* Āṣāḍha, 1379 B.S. (1972), pp. 2-3.

Index

Abhayapāla, 119
Achāranga Sutra, 141
Act of 1886, 15
Act of 1901, 17-18
Adhirājendradeva, 150
Āditya I, 148
Agni, 271
Agnimitra, 255
Agniveśa, 181
Agrarian discontent and origin of peasant movements in India during pre-nationalist era, 53-69
  Agrarian class structure, 55-56
  Anti-British feelings, 57-58
  British revenue system, 56
  Changed situation in, 57
  Colonial era, 58
  Farm labourers, 53
  Indian nationalism, 57
  Peasants movement during pre-nationalist era, 56
  Peasants movements in India, 54-55
  Peasantry challenged by Marxists, 54
  Revolt by disgruntled peasantry, 56-57
  Revolt of 1857, 57
  Risks in adopting innovations, 54
  Roots and nature of, 53-54
  Santhal uprisings, 57
  Social protest movement in India, 55
  Socio-economic transformation in British colonialism, 55
Agrawal, Ashvini, 164
Ahar stone inscriptions, 116
Ahar temple inscriptions of Allata, 117
Ahichhatra, 159
Ahmad, Isral, 33
Ahmad, Sayiid, 128
Ahmed, A.F. Salahuddin, 124
Ahmed, Delwar Hussain, 129-32
Ahmed, Rafiuddin, 130
Aihole Praśasti of Pulakesin II, 228
Ajataśatru, 168, 169
Akṣapaṭalādhikṛta, 228
Alberuni, 226, 227
Alexander, 269
Algeria, 54
Alhanadevi, 113, 117, 119
Ali, Keramat, 130
Ali, Khan Bahadur Hifazat Ali, 23
Ali, Mohammad, 95
Ali, Musahib, 127
Ali, Syed Amir, 127, 129, 130
Allahabad Praśasti of Samudragupta, 228
All India Aryan League, 35
All India Congress Committee, 78
All India Muslim League, 35
Amravati, 29
Anangabhimadeva III, 159, 161, 197
Anatavarman Chodagaṅga, 158, 197, 199
Andhare, 260
Andhra-Sātavāhanas, 255
Anglo-Burmese war, 218
Aṅguttara-Nikāya, 167
Anjuman Islamic Press, 40
Aṅka Śrāhi, 191
Anti-purdah agitation, 67
Arakanese settlement in Bangladesh, 215-21
  Against Burmese rule, 218-19
  Ariknongpray, 217
  Magh, 215-16
  Migration, 218
  Population of, 219
  Rakhaine, 216-19
Ārang Copper Plate, 189
Archar, W.G., 260
Ardhanāriśvarar, 150
Arora, 17
Artemor, 205
Arthuna Inscription of Paramora Chāmundaraja, 116-17
Aruṇājateśvara Temple in Tiruppandal, 150
Arundala, G.S., 73
Arundale, Rukmini, 73
Arya Samaj, 22, 34, 35, 64, 65, 67-72
Asgar, Muhammad of Nimar, 23
Ashoka, 252, 253, 255
Asokan edicts, 188, 192
Asthana Pratima, 227
Astrakhan, 203
Asvaghosa, 229, 253
Aswini Kumar, 180
Atharvaveda, 164, 178, 179, 180
Athens, 180
Atikullah, 217
Atreya Saṁhita, 181
Aurangzeb, 203
Avadhuti-pā, 156

Ayodhya, 159
Āyurveda, 160, 174, 175, 180
Aziz, Shah Abdul, 128
Azizullah, 217

Badabhadra, 156
Badakshi, Muhammad Mutabar, 260
Bādal pillar inscriptions of Nārāyanapāla, 229
Badrikēśarambhaṭṭaraha, 114
Baduri dynasty, 254
Bahudur, Bhim Samser Jung, 200
Bahudur, Ram Samser Jung, 200
Bālārjuna, 155, 158, 159
Ball, V., 135
Bāṇabhaṭṭa, 229-30
Bana works-voices of protest and dissent, 269-74
  Criticism of Divinity of Kings, 271-72
  Criticism of sati custom of, 269-71
  Diatribe against government service, 272
  Progressive aspect of social and political thought, 269
Banerjee, Suresh Chandra, 77
Banerji, R.D., 191
Bangladesh, 216, 219
Banpur plate of Śailodbhava king Dharmarāja, 157
Bappasvami, 160
Baranga plate of Nanda Prabhañjanavarman, 188
Barsur Inscription of Gaṅgamahādevi, 113
Bāsatā, 199
Basu, M.M., 80, 81
Basu, Panchanan, 77
Bateman, 217
Battle of Plassey, 217
Bayana Inscription of Chitralekhā, 113, 120, 121
Beal, 173, 174
Bengal, 15, 60
Bengal partition, 60
Bengal renaissance, 124
Bengal Tenancy Act of 1885, 16
Bentick, William, 58
Berrig, 218
Besant, Annie, 73
Bhadraloks, 66
Bhadrapālita, 157
Bhāgalpur copper plate inscription of Nārāyanapala, 143
Bhāgavata Purana, 271
Bhagiṅi Sena Bahini, 79
Bhagini Sena Sibir, 77
Bhakti, 57
Bhānudeva I, 160
Bhāra Shiva dynasties, 255
Bhasābhattarakā, 161
Bhaskaravarman, 143
Bhātera copper plate inscriptions, 115
Bhatsu, 269
Bhatta Bhavadeva, 142
Bhattarakamandala, 199
Bhauma Saṁvat, 189-90
Bharadeva Bhaṭṭa, 160
Bhela Saṁhitas, 182
Bherāghāt inscription of Queen Alhanadevi, 113
Bhimata, 160
Bhinmal stone inscription, 115, 119
Bhojadeva, 116
Bhubaneswar Inscription of Anarigebhima III, 114
Bhuma-kara, 158
Bhup Singh, 69
Bhutacaitanyavāda, 227
Bhuvanes inscriptions, 160
Bidyut Bahini, 79, 82
Bihar, 60
Bijapur inscriptions, 118
Bilhari stone inscriptions, 120
Biswa murder case, 28
Bisweshwar Singh, 60
Bito-pā, 156
Bobbili plates of Chandavarman, 88
Bodawpaya, 218
Boddhisri, 156
Bonaparte, Louis, 10
Bonaparte, Napoleon, 204
Bourgeoise Democratic Revolution, 54
Bose, Rajnarayan, 129
Bose, Sarat, 36
Bose, Subhas, 28
Bowar Manuscript, 185
Brāhman Dhārma, 255
Brahma Samātaras, 237-39
Brahmavaivarta Purāna, 142-43
Brahmo Samaj, 57, 64-67
Brenner, Robert, 5, 10
Bridge, 128
Brihaddharma, 142
British Indian Association in 1851, 57
Buckle, 129
Buddha, 105, 156, 167-70, 181, 199, 229, 252
Buddhacarita, 229
Buddhapakṣha, 156
Buddhism, 155-56, 181, 252-53
Buddhist missionaries, 215
Bundela, Chhatrasal, 25
Burhan-ul-Haq, 28
Burma, 215, 216, 219

Calcutta Asiatic Society, 126
Caraka of Kashmir, 181-82
Caraka-Saṁhita, 182-84
Casey, Richard, 83
Central Provinces and Berar, 22
Central Provinces Slaughter of Animal Act, 36
Chakroborty, Sris, 67
Chāṇakya, 250
Chandesvar grant, 189
Chandra, 114, 141
Chandragupta, 141, 255

Chandragupta II, 271
Chandrā pride, 270
Chandravarma, 141
Chandrika Devi, 161
Chāṅgunārāyana Inscription of Mānādeva, 269
Chatterjee, Bhaskar, 133
Chaturmāsya system, 188
Chaudhuri, B.B., 3
Chaudhuri, Korak K., 275
Chaudhury, Charipru, 218
Chaurasia Plate of Sivakara II, 158
Chayanov, 9
Cheh-ka (Takka), 173
Chicacole grant, 158
Chicacole plate of Satyavarman, 159
Chowdhury, S. Annanda Prasad, 77
Chowkidari tax, 49
Chunder, Pratap Chandra, 236
Citrabhānu, 229
Civil disobedience movement and women in Midnapore dist., 48-52
  Commissoner of Burdwan report, 49
  Mahila-sabhas, 48
  No tax campaign, 49-50
  Prentice report to Bengal Legislative Council, 49
  Repressive measure to stop, 51
  Salt satyagraha, 48-49
  Training camps for women for, 50
  Woman donated ornaments, 50
  Women participation in, 48, 52
  Women workers active part in, 50-51
Cōla army and the Royal Temple of Rajarajeśvaram, 147-54
  Army's role vis-e-vis temple, 149-53
    Cash grants by, 150, 152
    Grants for lamps, 150, 152
    Highest officers involvement, 150, 152
    Military officers auditing temple accounts, 150
Cōla army, 147-49
    Inscriptional evidence, 148
    Kaikkōlas, 149
    Mode of remuneration, 148
    Pāṇdi-Padal, 148
    Regiments, units and divisions of, 148-49
    Ten-Illaṅgai-valanjiyar, 148
    Velaikāra branch, 149
  Rājarāja I involved the, 147
Collingwood, R.G., 227
Communal problem to Congress Ministry in Central Provinces and Berar, 22-47
  Anjuman Islamic Press, 40
  Anti-Urdu policy, 36, 37, 40-41
  Cause of, 23-24
  Communal sentiments in 1937 elections, 22
  Congress attitude to communal Award, 22-23
  Congress govt denial of Muslim charges, 40-41
  Congress Muslim mass contact movement, 27
  Economic boycott of Muslims at Katangi, 37
  Election results, 23, 26
  Fee on slaghter of animals, 36, 40
  Hindu and Muslim communalism feed each other, 26
  Hindu Mahasabha threatened, 24-25
  Hindu Muslim relations, 22
  Hindu Press accused of anti-Muslim propaganda, 37
  Hindu Youths spirit of nationalism, 25
  History sheeters and gang leaders involved in, 22
  Hoisting of flags, 28-29
  Hyderabad Satyagraha, 34-35
  Influence on neighbouring regions, 34-35
  Oinnah attack on local Hindu Press, 23
  Killing of Muslim boy by, 28
  Law enforcing agencies dealt roots impartiality, 42
  Local bodies coercing Muslim employees, 38
  Local press coverage to, 22
  Mahasabha condemned Congress Party, 25
  Muslim in elections, 27-28
  Muslim charges against N.B. Khare, 38-39
  Muslim MLA joined anti-Gandhi pronouncement, 30
  Muslim MLA-PM meeting, 33
  Muslim MLA resolution on separate Muslim electorate, 30, 33
  Muslim opposition to Congress Ministry, 29
  Muslim opposition to Vidyamandir Scheme, 31-34
  Muslim press, 29
  Muslim religions sentiments, 37
  Muslim representation in local bodies, 30, 38
  Muslim schools, 36-37
  Pirpur Committee report on conditions of Muslims in all Congress ruled province, 35-36
  Police indifference to Muslims, 38
  Police inspector target at Muslim meeting, 28
  Political propaganda, 24, 28
  Release of prisoners convicted of communal riots, 41-42
  Riots and killing in Jabalpur, 23
  RSS and Hindu Mahasabha as Communal organisation, 26, 29
  Tension at Patansangi in descration of local mosque, 23-24
  Vandematram song, 37, 39-40
  Vidyamandir education programme, 30-33
Communist Revolution, 54
Corn laws, 11
Cowell, B., 229
Cox Bazar of Arakenese, 215-19
Cuba, 54
Czar, 253

Danārṇava, 161
Dandekar, R.N., 226
Dandin, 158
Danibegor, Rafail, 205
Dariba Temple Inscriptions, 155
Darling, M., 12, 17
Das, Arvind N., 54
Das, C.R., 30

Dasgupta, K.K. writings, 275-86
  Book reviews by, 281
  Books and Journals edited, 275
  Books and monographs by, 275
  Convocational, Presidential and Inaugaural address, 282
  Forwards and prefaces by, 282
  Lectures delivered by, 282
  Papers and articles by, 276-80
    Art, architecture and painting, 277
    Historical geography, 278
    History and historiography, 279-80
    Iconography, 276-77
    Numismatics, 277-78
    Society, economy, religion etc, 278-79
  Publications in Bengali, 283-86
    Books and monographs, 283
    Books edited, 283
    Books review, 286
    Selected papers and articles, 283-86
  Review of books by, 282, 83
Das, Lakshminarayan, 84
Das, Sukla, 225
Dasgupta, Niparan Chandra, 50
Dasgupta, Sanghamitra, 155
Daspallā charters of satrubhañjadeva, 189
Daulat Kazi, 216
Dayanand Saraswati, 69
Deb, Radhakanti, 126
Defence of India Act, 76
Democratic Swaraj Party, 23
Denduvākā, 114
Denkanal, Plate of Tribhuvana Mahādevi, 158
Deo, 115
Deopārā Prasasti of Vijayasena, 229
Desai, AR, 55
Deshmukh, RM, 36
Deshmukh, Ramrav, 23
Devadāsis, 156
Devendravarman, 159
Devi Mahatmya, 260, 261
Dhanagare, D. N., 54, 57
Dhanasimha, 115
Dhanvantari, 189
Dharmapāla, 144
Dharmaraja II, 160
Dharmeśāstrakāras, 155, 158, 237
Digha-Nikāya, 168
Divākaramitra, 270
Divyasimhadeva III of Puri, 199
Dubey, Georges, 13
Dubey, Kunjilal, 39
Dubkund Stone Inscription of Kachchhapaghata Vikramasimha, 119
Dudu Miyan, 131
Durgaraja Inscription near Pushkara, 114
Durlabharaja, 114

Earth Summit in Rio De Janeiro, 212
  Education system in ancient Orissa, 155-63
  Brahmanical education, 158
  Brahmanical institutions, 158-61
    Agrahāras, 159-60
    Curricula, 160
    Mathas, 159
    Method, 160
    Military science, 160
  British system of, 155
  Buddhist education, 155-57
  Buddhist learning centres, 156
  Buddhist monastery, 156
  Handmaid of religion, 155
  Jain education system, 157-58
  Jain monastery, 157
  Jain source material, 158
  Tantrik, 156, 158
Egypt, 178-80
Ellichpur, 29
Endowments to temples in Northern India, 112-23
  By royal family members, 113
  Donations by others, 114-15
  Economic foundations of, 112
  Endowment from markets, 117-19
  Endowment from oil mills, 116
  Endowment roads-road-cess, 120-29
  Endowment from S'ulkē-Mandapika, 119-20
  Gardeners, 116-17
  Gifts of villages and land, 113
  Guilds as donors, 121-22
  Houses, 115-16
  Kinds of, 112-13
  Supported and maintained by donors, 112
  Taxes for endowments from horse dealers, 121
Engels, F., 53
England, 5, 9-11
Eran Stone Pillar Inscription of Bhānugupta, 269
Erbang charter, 189
Ershad govt, 219

Fa-hsien, 173
Fakir Mohammed, 217
Faquir of Ipi, 28
Fascist Revolution, 54
Festivals of Tripura, 101-11
  Garia festival of, 101-04, 111
    Bambo piece, 102-04
    Climbing High Kuki hills, 101-02, 111
    Cock and eggs and sacred drink, 103
    Gajam and Chadak rituals, 104, 111
    Hari Visu, 102
    Image and ritual procedure, 103-04
    Immersion, 104
    Singing and dancing in, 104
    Vishuva Sankranti, 101, 102, 111
  Rañgoli or Rañgali Vihu of Assam, 105

Vijhu celebration by Chākmas, 105, 114
Festival of agriculture, 105
Phool Vijhu Day, 105
Year begins in, 101

France, 4, 5, 9-11, 204, 253

Gagana Sambhu, 159
Gandhi, Mahatma, 23, 24, 26, 28, 30, 32, 37, 39, 42, 48, 67, 76, 78, 82, 253
Ganeśā Gumphā cave Inscriptions, 160
Ganga charters, 188
Ganga era, 188-90
Gaṅga Kadaṁba, 189
Gāṅgamahādevi, 113
Ganguly, D K, 226
Ganjam copper plate, 189
Ganjam Plate of Madhavaraja II, 189
Garia festival, 101-04
Garraghan, G.J., 252
Gaya Inscription, 115
George, Anies, 86
George III, 253
German, 9, 256, 257
Ghantakarma Bhairava, 199, 201
Ghosh, A.K., 135
Ghoshal, V.N., 227
Ghosh, Niranjan, 48
Ghosh, Prafulla Chandra, 77
Gita Govinda, 260
Gladwin, Francis, 126
Glynn, C.A., 262
Godavari Plate of Prithvimula, 159
Golwalkar, M.S., 39
Gopal, Surendra, 203
Gorbachev, 211
Gordimer, Nadina, 214
Goswamy, B.N., 261
Gough, Kathleen, 54, 55
Goverdhana Pitha, 159
Government of India Act of 1935, 25
Govinda Senapati, 114
Gowan, Hyde, 40
Goyal, Shankar, 269
Grahavarman, 270
Great Revolt of 1857, 57
Gregorian Calendar, 259
Group of seven, 212-14
Guha, Ranajit, 54, 55
Guhyesvari, 197
Gupta inscription, 228
Gupta period, 156, 254, 255

Halāyudha, 160
Hansraj, 71
Hanuman Akhara at, 36
Haq, Mazharul, 60
Haq ul, Azizul, 34
Haque, Fazlul, 36-39, 41, 83
Harappa, 178-79
Hardas, Balashastry, 25
Harijan uplift programme, 30
Hari Rishisvara monasty, 118
Harisena, 228
Harisvami, 160
Harsavardhana, 229, 252, 272
Harsha, 189, 192, 229-30, 269-70, 273-74
Harshagupta, 199
Harsha stone Inscription, 121, 141, 142
Harvey, 216
Hasina affair, 23, 38
Hāthigumphā Inscriptions of Khāravela, 188, 228
Hazra, Matangini, 80
Hedgewar, K.B., 25, 26, 34, 39
Herbert, 80
Herodotis, 225
Himachal Pradesh State Museum at Shimla, 260
Hinayana, 156
Hindol Plates of Subhakaradeva III, 158
Hindu Mahsabha, 22-25, 34, 35, 36, 39, 41
Hindu National Parliamentary Board, 25
History writing, 225-35, 250-58
Carita literature, 228-30
Charateristics of history, 251
Comparison of historical facts, 256-57
Connotation of, 228
Craft of, 225
Definition of history, 250-51
Dignifying a man in, 250
Does history repeats, 252-53
Early Greek historiography, 225
Golden age concept, 253-55
Illusory status of phenomenal world, 226
India contact with Graceco-Roman world, 226
India's religio-philosophical system, 226-27
Interdisciplinary approach, 257
Kalhana works, 230-33
Lack of historical spirit, 227
Lacuna of, 229
Limitations in composition of prose Kavya on, 229-30
Man is centre of, 250-51
Meaning of history, 250
Non-individualistic attitude, 226-27
Notion of other worldliness of Indians, 226
Periodisation in, 255-56
Political history and dynastic studies, 230-31
Puranic literature, 228
Scientific approach to, 226
Scope of history, 251
Selection of facts, 225
Slow development of, 227
Songs in praise of human beings, 227-28
Thoughts on, 257-58
Trio is dependable, 251

Why human history, 250
Hiuen Tsang, 155-57, 173-75, 189
Hodgeson, J., 91
Hoerule, 175, 185
Hopkins, 49
Hultzch, 149
Hunter, W.W., 124
Hussain, Akhtar, 23
Hutton, 128
Hyderabad Satyagraha, 25, 34-35

Iftikar Ali, 23, 34
Imam Ali, 60
Imam Hussain, 60
Imperial Ganga, 197
India, 6
Indian ephemeris by Swamikannu Pillai, 259-68
Accuracy in, 259, 262
Colophons, 260-61
Conversion tables of dates and eras, 259, 262
Errors in calculations, 260, 262
Solar and lunar reckonings, 259
Value of, 266
Words used to indicate date, 261-62
Year in local era, 261
Indian National Congress, 60
Indian religion and awakening of 19th century, 64-75
Arya Samaj movements, 68-72, 74
Activities of, 68-69, 72
Branches of, 69
Education spread by, 70-71
Female education by, 71
Jatpat Torak Samiti by, 71-72
Mandir of, 69
Removal of social evils, 69-70
Socio-religious reformation by, 68-71
Upgrading status of lower castes, 70
Bengali Bhadraloks migration to Bihar, 66
Brahmo Samaj movement, 65-68, 74
Anti-purdah agitation, 67
Ceremonies and functions of, 68
Female education, 67
Lacked organizational structure, 67
Modern and secular education, 67
Movement declined, 67
Proselytisation of Biharis to Brahmoism, 66
Transformation of status of women, 67
Kabirpanth, 72, 74
New norms and culture themes with traditional and value system movements, 64
Ramakrishna Mission, 72-74
Socio-religious reform movements, 64-65, 74
Theosophical society, 72-74
Indians around Pamir Plate, 203-10
British more in Iran, 204
Colonial rivalry in, 209
Kashmiri and Indian merchants trip to Aksu, 206
Laddakh, 207-09
Merchants picked up for loyality, 206
Rafailov report to Glazenog, 206
Rafailov returned to semiplatinsk, 208
Raifailov visit to, 205
Rise of France in world politics, 204
Route to India via Eastern Turkistan, 205
Rumyantsev visit, 206
Russian contracts with, 203
Russian entry into Black sea, 203-04
Russian friendship with Punjab, 209
Russian search for route to, 203-05, 208
Russian trade across Tien Shan mountains, 205
Tsarist govt alliance with, 206
Yarkand city trade from Kashmir, 206-07
India's foreign policy in post-old war era, 211-14
Actualities in, 241
Afghanistan or Kampuchea issue, 211
Diplomatic establishments, 211-12
Economic policy, 214
Group of seven, 212-14
International military action in Kuwait, 211
Non-alignment, 212
Nuclear policy, 213-14
Own resources to replace mass poverty, 213
Relations with USA, 212
Indrajit, 113
Indraraja, 114
Indravarman, 188
Inscriptions at Gwalior, 121
Inscriptions of Hanuman Dhokā in Kathmandu, 197
Inscriptions of Udiyatakeśari, 157
International Atomic Energy Agency, 212, 213
Iran, 204
Irish agrarian situation, 5-6, 11
Iśānavarman, 141
Iśvara, 114
Itsing, 156, 175, 176

Jabalpur, 22, 23, 28
Jagannath cult of Orissa and Rajas of Nepal, 197-202
Evidence of close relations, 199
Gods and goddesses depiction identical, 198
Jagannath cult in Nepal, 197-98
Jagannath Temple at Puri, 197
Builders of, 197
Doors of, 197-98
Nepal Hindu kingdom, 197
Nepali Royal visit to, 198
Temples in Kathmandu, 198
Translation, 199-200
Vaishnavism, 199
Vishnu sila episode, 199-200
Visit and donations, 200-01
Worshipping method, 198-99
Jagannath Kaviraja, 260
Jagaśvāmi Temple grant, 115

Jagatguru Shankaracharya at Amritsar, 26
Jaina temple of Rishabhanatha, 118
Jain education system, 157
Jainism, 157, 181
Jalor Inscription of Cāhamāna Chachigadeva, 115
Jamindar, Rakesh, 250
Jātaka literature, 168
Jayadeva, 158
Jayāditya, 114
Jayapida, 233
Jayasimhadeva, 113, 114, 120
Jhanwara Inscription, 116
Jimutavāhana, 270
Jinnah, 23, 28, 30, 39
Jinnah-Shafi clash, 26
Jirjingi copper plate Inscription of Eastern Ganga King Indravarman I, 158, 188
Jitgovind of Nepal, 201
Jog, M.P., 26
Joshi, M.V., 26
Joydeva II, 199
  Stone Inscription, 199
Joynagar-Mahal, 217
Junagarh Inscription of Rudradāman, 228
Junā Stone Inscription of Samantasiṁhadeva, 120
Jungle Mahals, 60
Junker aristocracy, 9
Jyotisha, 160

Kabi, Debabandya, 53
Kabirpanthi, 64, 65, 72, 74
Kacchā samvat, 261
Kadambari, 269, 270, 272
Kakulissa, 159
Kālachakrayāna, 155, 156
Kalhana, 230-33
Kalidas, 256
Kalinga, 155, 189, 190, 199, 252
Kalipuja, 102
Kaliyugābda, 190
Kaliyugābda era, 190, 259
Kalpas, 181
Kalyāna Devi, 157
Kaman Stone Inscriptions, 116, 121
Kamasastras, 236
Kamatasaha Bhattarāka, 159
Kamini Devi, Aghore, 67
Kampuchea, 211
Kamyaka, 121
Kanakasridevi, 116
Kanāsa copper plate, 189
Kanchha Badā Mahārāni, 200
Kanchha Sumā Badā Mahārani, 200
Kane, P.V., 236
Kanika, 237
Kaniska, 181, 229, 252, 253, 255
Karitalai stone Inscription of Chedi Laksmanaraja, 113
Karnakeśari, 156
Karpuraśni, 156
Kashmir, 230-32
Kautilya, 141, 171, 228, 236-38, 271
Kazakh, 203
Keijiro, Murata, 214
K'ei-P'an-to, 174
Kelhaṇadeva, 119
Khaskar rally, 29, 39
Khālimpur Copper Plate Inscription, 144
Khan, Abdul Mabud, 215
Khan, Abdur Rahman, 23, 32, 33
Khan, Ghulam Hussain, 32
Khan, Liaquat Ali, 30, 33
Khan, Niaz Ahmad, 38
Khan, Sharif, 128
Khan, Siddiqui Ali, 33, 36
Khan, Syed Ahmed, 127, 129
Kharavela, 192, 255
Khare, N.B., 24, 29, 36, 38, 39
Kongada, 189
Korasandā grant of Viśākhāvarman, 188
Kośala, 189, 199
Kosambi, D.D., 231
Krishna, 102, 164
Krishna, Bhimsen Sri, 201
Krishnaswamy, V.D., 135
Ksemankara, 190
Kuiti, Baradakanta, 79, 82
Kulachandra, 157
Kumarapāla, 120
Kumārapravat, 157
Kumarila Bhatta, 158, 159
Kurmeśvara Temple Inscription of Risi Dāsā, 190
Kuruspal Stone Inscription of Somesvaradeva, 114
Kutottuṅga I, 147
Kuwait, 211, 213

Lakhanapāla, 119
Lakmana, 189
Lakshmana Temple, Sirpur, 199
Laksmanarāja, 113
Lal, B.B., 135
Lalitāditya, 231
Lalitagiri, 159
Lall, Nand Kishore, 60
Lal, Munshi Manohar, 69
Lamfra, 102
Landsberger, Henry A, 54
Lalrai Stone Inscription of Kalahanadeva, 119
Larger Leyden Copper Plate, 150
Latif, Abdul, 126, 129, 130
Laukika era, 233
Lichhavis, 199, 201
Linlithgow, 42
Lokeśvara, 156
Lost book on politics in ancient India, 236-39

Arthaśāstra of Kautilya, 236-39
Brahma-Samātaras, 237-39
Kritayuga, 236
Mehābhārata, 237
Rājadharma, 236
Vedas, 236
Louis, 253

Macdonald Communal Award, 33
Madagrāma plates of Bhimakhedi, 190
Madator, 205
Mādhava, 114
Madhavacharya, 185
Madhavaraja, 189
Madoli, 114
Madri episode, 164-66
Mahābhārata, 140-42, 144, 164-66, 236-37, 271
Mahapatra, Patjoshi, 191
Maharashtra, 14, 16
Mahāsthan Fragmentary Stone Plague Inscription, 140
Mahāśveta, 270
Mahāyana, 156
Mahendra, 198
Mahendrapala II, 114, 118
Mahendra Relief Committee, 81
Mahesh Narayan, 60
Mahibaladevi, 119
Mahmud of Ghazni, 226
Maity, P.K., 76
Maity, Sindubala, 81
Majumdar, N.G., 135
Majumdar, R.C., 226, 231
Makundarao, N., 189
Malayavati, 270
Malcolm Mission, 204, 209
Māliaputti Plates of Anantavarman, 189
Manahali Copper Plate of Madanapala, 143
Manbhum protest movement against merger with Bihar, 1912, 60-63
Bengali population, 61
Bihar different from Bengal, 60
Bihar opportunity for creation of separate province, 60-61
Feer of Bengali speaking population, 62
Formation of district, 60
Ganga Narayan riot in, 60
Land tenure of, 61-62
Manbhum for keeping in Bengal, 61
Non-regulation district, 61
Partition of Bengal, 60-61
Santhali and Hindi speaking in, 62
Special Tenancy Act in, 61
Mandāsā plate, 180
Mandasor Stone Pillar Inscription of Yaśodharman, 228
Mandkila Temple Inscriptions, 114
Mānikya, Dhanya, 101-02
Manu, 237, 271
Manusaṁhitā, 143
Markandaya, 261
Mārkandaya Purana, 271
Marx, Karl, 3-5, 9-10, 53, 124
Matai Balnai, 103
Materia Medica, 184
Mātharas, 188, 192
Mathura Prasasti Inscriptions, 115, 116, 118
Matsya Purāna, 271
Matsyendranath, 199
Maurya period, 255
Medical Science known to Chinese pilgrims
Branches of, 175-76
Chinese travellers during Chandragupta II, 173
Fasting as method of cure, 176
Medical aid offered to travellers, 173-74
Medical herbs, 176
Medical studies, 174-75
Position and practice of physicians, 176
Medicine in ancient India, 178-87
Astrology for, 178
Athurveda on, 178-79
Āyurveda, 180
Beliefs in Indus civlization, 178
Cataract, 182
Causation of disease, 184
Classification of disease, 184-85
Education on, 185
Herbal medicine, 180
Hymns for, 180
Illness, 173
Knowledge of vedic physicians, 180
Magico-religious, 178-79
Medical literature, 181-82
Medicine from mythical, 181
Numerous diseases, 179-80
Primitive medicine, 179
Rational medicine, 181
Saṁhitā period, 182
Surgery, 182-84
Vaccination, 185
Witchcraft and magic, 179
Megheśvara Temple inscripitions, 158
Meherauli Iron Pillar Inscriptions, 141
Mehra Jagamalla grant, 115
Mesopotamia, 178-80
Messurier, Le, 61
Metcalf, Thomas, 14
Mexico, 54
Mill, James, 129
Mirashi, V.V., 188, 189
Mir Kashim, 217
Mishra, D.P,, 22, 23, 30, 35, 36
Mishra, J.P., 25
Mishra, P.K., 3, 197
Mishra, Bhatta Gaurava, 229
Mishra, Krishna, 142, 158, 160

Misra, Murari, 160
Misra, Visvanath, 160
Modern and secular trends in Muslim social thought in Ninteenth century Bengal, 124-32
Arabic language, 127-28
Bengal renaissance, 124
Character of social thought, 126
Conservative trends, 126
During Mughal times, 125
English language, 126-28
Ignorance and poverty among, 131
Inflexibility of Islamic religious dogma, 127
Islamic law of succession, 131
Middle class patronage of British rulers, 125
Movement for intellectual freedom, 124-26
Muslim conservative, 126, 131-32
Muslims to learn English and Bengali language, 13
Openness as flexibility, 126
Persian language, 125-28
Radical trends, 127
Reformist trends in Muslim society, 127
Religious exclusiveness and lack of toleration, 130-31
Mohapatra, K.N., 190
Mohenjo-daro, 178-79
Mojumdar, K., 22
Monghyr copper plate of Devapāla, 143-44
Moore, Barrington, 10, 11, 54
Morang, Hlawa, 218
Mo-ti-pi-lo, 174
Mudgalas, 189
Muhammad, 126
Muhammad Ali, Begum, 27
Mukherjee, Ajoy Kumar, 82
Mukhopadhyay, S.C., 60
Munjee, B.S., 25, 26, 34, 39
Mūṉru-Kai-tiru-nelaikkāran-daladay-perum-palli, 149
Musgrave, P.J., 16
Muslim Federation of India, 25
Muslim League, 22-24, 26-28, 32, 39
Muslim National Guard, 29
Muslim Political conference in Nagpur, 27
Muslim United Party, 27
Muslim voluntary organisations, 29
Mutazila school, 127, 130
Muthu, D.C., 181
Myanmar, 211, 215

Nabajagaran, 66
Nabin Kishore, 182
Nadir Shah, 204
Nādlā I stone Inscription of Parāntaka I, 148
Nadol plate of Ālhaṇadeva, 119
Nadol plate of Pratapasiṁha, 119
Nāgabari, 114
Nāgānanda, 270
Nager, Jaisingh Deva, 261
Nagēsvara Temple Inscriptions of Parāntaka I, 148
Nagpur riots, 38
Naidu, Sarojini, 67
Naihati copper plate Inscriptions of Vallālasena, 142, 144
Nakehhumtai, 102
Nālandā, 156
Nāmvai, 115
Nānāghat Inscription of Setakarni I, 228
Nanda grant of Kumarapala, 120
Nandana, 114
Nandiyarājar, 150
Napolean, 4
Nārada, 237
Nārada Smrti, 271
Narasimha Deva, 197
Narasimhadeva II, 160
Narasimhedeva IV, 190
Narasimhagupta Bālāditya, 156
Nāro-pa, 156
Nāsichandra, 157
Nāsik Inscription of Pulamāyi, 228
Nataraja, 104
Nath, Rakhal Chandra, 178
National Muslim Guard
Muslim volunteers, 28
Naujawan Sirat Committee, 28
Narakota, 199
Navamuni Care in Khandagiri Hills, 157
Navanitaka, 185
Nayak, P.K., 188
Nehru, 22, 23, 28, 39, 49
Nepal, 197
Nepalese Inscriptions, 201
Neṭṭabhañja, 158
Neulpur Charter of Subhakaradeva I, 190
Neulpur grant, 160
Nga chin Pyan, 218
Nidāna-Śāstra of Ullanga, 157
Nikitin, Aganasi, 203
Nivedita, 72
Nivinā charters, 189
Niyārnama, 191
Niyogi, Brajagopal, 67
Niyogi, Puspa, 112
Niyogi, Sumanta, 64
Nizam govt atrocities on Hindus, 34-35
Non-alignment movement, 212
Noon, Feroze Khan, 39
No-tax campaign, 49
North-west Frontier Province, 28
Nuclear non-proliferation treaty, 212, 213
Nyāya-Vaiśesika, 181

Obaidullahel obaide, 128, 129
Odra, 155
Olcott, 73
Orenburg, 203
Orissa, 155

Orissa Museum plate of Nettabhanja, 190, 191
Orissan chronology, 188-93
  Aṅka year, 191
  Character of Eastern Gaṅga, 188, 192
  Chronogram method, 190-91
  Epigraphs in Bhauma Saṁvat, 189-90, 192
  Gupta era used measuring unit of, 189, 192
  Kāliyuga era, 190
  Orissan epigraphs, 188
  Saka era, 192
  Use of era for reckoning dates, 188-89
  Vikram Saṁvat in, 190, 192
Ottoman, 203
Oudh, 14, 15, 57

Pachlegaonkar, 25
Pakistan, 219
Palestinians, 212
Pallavāyar, Īrāyiravan, 150
Palmleaf manuscript, 199
Pānāhara Inscription of Jayasimhadeva, 114
Panāhara Inscription of Jayasiṁha of Malwa, 120
Pañchatantra Rājanitiprakāśa, 271
Panda, Ganes Prasad, 200
Panda, Gangadhar, 200, 201
Panda, Jagannath, 200
Panda, Lalmoharia, 198, 200, 201
Pandukesvar plate, 114
Panigrahi, K.C., 190
Pānini, 141
Paranjpe, L.V., 25, 39
Parāntaka I, 148
Parikund plates of Madhyāmaraja, 189
Patancrayana stone Inscriptions, 119
Patanga Śivachārya grant, 159
Patansangi in Nagpur, 23
Patel, Sardar, 250
Patiākele charter, 189
Patna Museum plate of Vijayā Mahādevi, 190
Pechell, 218
Persiā, 203, 204
Persian literature, 125
Perundānam, 152
Peter, the Great, 203
Petty peasant production and agrarian capitalism in colonial India, 3-21
  Agrarian structure in France, 5
  Allocation of resources to alternative crops, 12
  Archaic system of, 3
  Beneficiaries of states generosity, 9
  Capitalist development of agriculture, 11-12
  Cash crop cultivation, 13
  Ceillings on interest rate in Bengal, 15-16
  Condition of market competition, 7-8
  Conflict between land lords and peasants, 8
  Co-operative credit movement, 9
  Corn law, 11
  Criticism of washbook work on, 3
  Elimination of small peasants or providing capital, 3
  England peasantry, 13-14
  Expansion of acreage through waste reclamation, 12-13
  Failure of small peasants in France, 5-6
  Free market system, 18
  Free ownership of land, 4
  Govt failed to provide capital with instruments to subordinate production, 9
  High colonial state, 7-8
  Inadequate market stimulus, 11
  Inception notion state, 8
  Incompatibility of, 5-6
  India's agricultural development, 12
  Intervention of state protecting, 6-9
  Landlord right, 8
  Landlord and tenent as abstractions, 11
  Legal constraints on landlords and moneylenders, 14-17
  Marx formulation to specific historical studies, 9-10
  Marx idea on, 3-5, 9
  Mercantilist state, 7
  Monopoly control of mercantilist state, 12
  Obstacle to development of capitalism, 10
  Occupancy rights, 8
  Permanant settlement, 7
  Peasants proprietors, 12
  Pre-famine Irish agrarian structure, 5-6, 11
  Protection by state, 11
  Public laws, 7-8
  Reclamation, 12
  Rent, 15
  Rental rights and obligations, 89
  Restrictions on credit circulation, 16-18
  Settled tenants and sub-proprietors, 14
  Slumps in agricultural prices and credit, 18
  Small farmers in India, 6
  Social imperatives of market capitalism, 8
  Study of post revolution French peasantry, 4, 18-19
  Talukdari, 14-15
  Talukdar's investment in agriculture, 15
  Tax burden, 10
  Technical basis of acreage expansion, 13
  Unrestricted transfers of peasants holding, 16-17
  Urban and non-agriculturist credit groups, 17-18
  War finances diverted capital from productive investment, 10-11
  Welfare and security of Irish population, 6
Phayre, 215
Phulbāni plates, 191
Pillai, Swamikannu, 259
Pirpur committee report, 35-38, 42
Polasarā plate of Arkeśvaradeva, 190
Polybius, 225
Ponnutur grant of Samantavaraman, 158, 189
Potteśvara Temple of Bhānudeva III, 190
Prabhākaravardhanā, 269, 270
Prabhavatigupta, 114

Prabuddhachandra, 157, 158
Prajnā, 156
Pramanarasi, 116
Pramanik, Purimadhab, 80
Prasenajit, 169
Pratab Malla, 197, 198
Pratihari panda, 198
Pratitya-Samutpāda-Sutra, 156
Pravardhamāna Vijayaraja Saṁvatsara, 189
Prentice, WDR, 49
Ptolemy, 144
Pulakeśin II, 189
Pulindesvara Temple, 158
Puṇḍarika, 270
Punjab, 12, 16, 17
Punjab Banking Enquiry Committee, 17
Punyasālas, 173, 174
Puri plates of Dharmaraja II, 189
Purla copper plate grant, 158
Purusottama-Jagannath Temple, 199
Pushpagiri Mahavihara, 157
Pushyamitra, 255
Pu-sie-po-ki-li, 157

Qazi Muhammad Ali of Jalgaon, 30
Quit India Movement and Tamralipta Jatiya Sarkar, 76-85
  Characteristic feature of Tamralipta Jatiya Sarkar, 81-83
  Freedom struggle at Midnapore, 76
  Second world war and its impact, 76-77
  Svrechchhasevak Bahini, 77
  Till the establishment of Tamralipta Jatiya Sarkar, 78-81
    Arrest of congress leaders, 78
    Govt offices destroyed, 80
    Hartal and processions, 78
    National upsurge, 80-81
    Police confrontation, 79
    Police firing, 79-80
    Police stations raided, 80
    Students role in, 79
    Sub-Divisional Congress Committee on, 79-80
Quli Khan, Mushid, 216
Qureshi, Abdul Majid, 28

Rafailov, Mehti, 205-09
Rafiud-dean, Mullah, 128
Raghavendra Rao, E., 23, 32
Rahim, Abdul, 23, 127-29, 132
Rahman, Abdul, 29
Rahulamitra, 156
Rajaraja I, 147, 148, 150, 152
Rajaraja Inscription, 148
Rajarajesvaram, 150
Rājatarangini of Kalhana, 226, 230-33
Rajendra I, 148, 150
Rajendra Vikram Shah Bahadur Samser Jung, 200
Rajguru, S.N., 189, 190
Rajor Inscription of Mathanadeva, 117
Rajyadevi, 226
Rajyamali, 199
Rajyaśvi, 270
Ramakrishna Mission, 64, 65, 67, 72, 73
Ramakrishna Paramhansa, 72, 73
Raman, Krishnan, 150
Rāmapuram plates, 189
Rāmāyana, 141, 164, 229
Rammohan Roy Seminary, 67
Ram Sewak, 60
Ranabhañja, 158, 190
Ranade, 6, 9
Rana, Samser Jung Bahadur, 200
Randhak, 102
Ranjit Singh, 206
Rangoli festival of Assam, 105
Rashtriya Swayam Sevak Sangh, 24-26, 34, 39
Ratna, 198
Ratnagiri Copper plate of Somavaṁsi king Kornakeśari, 156
Ratnagiri Mahāvihāra, 155
Ratnasimha, 115
Ravinder Kumar, 14
Ravikirtti, 228
Ray, Jayanta Kumar, 211
Razaq, Abdul, 27
Rebha Rishi, 180
Revolt of 1857, 57
Rig Vedic age, 134, 164, 179, 180, 269
Rijaśwa, 180
Rizvi, S.W., 23
Rosen, 217
Roychowdhury, Sukhadamayee, 50
Roy, Raja Ram Mohan, 57, 125-27, 129
Rumyantsev, N.P., 205, 206
Rushabhadev, 253
Russia, 203-05

Sādhārana, 160
Sadullah, 217
Sahlins, Marshall, 133
Sahoo, Satish Chandra, 82
Sailodbhavas, 189, 192
Saiya teacher of Mattamayūra, 159
Sakunāsa, 272
Saligram Singh, 60
Salt Satyagraha, 48-49
Samanta, Satish Chandra, 82
Samanta Varman, 189
Sāmaveda, 174
Sambala, 156
Samba Purāna, 158
Sambhukara, 160
Saṁhitā period, 182
Saṁkarāchārya, 159
Samkhya, 181
Samundragupta, 271
Saṇḍerav stone Inscription of Kalhanadeva, 119

Sangram Singhji, 260
Sankaradeva, 199-201
Sankarsana Vasudeva, 199
Sankhadhara, 160
Santhal uprisings, 57
Saptarishikāla, 261
Sarasvati, 161
Sarma, Bhavani, 261
Śaśaṅka, 189
Sasbahu Temple Inscriptions, 119
Sashtri, Hirananda, 191
Sastri, Sivanath, 66
Sati, 164
Satrubhāñja, 158, 159
Sat sai of Bihari, 260
Sattar, Abdul, 23
Satyartha Prakash, 69
Satyaśraya, 147
Sawadhan, 24
Semiplatinsk, 205
Sen, Bhawani, 57
Sen, D., 135
Sengupta, Sukumar, 173
Sen, Majumdar, Gayatri, 167
Sen, Sushama, 67
Sen, Sumangal, 105
Śeramādevi record, 148
Service, Eleman, 133
Seth, Govind Das, 22, 23
Sevadi Stone Inscription of Asvaraja, 119
Shah, Abdul Rang, 23, 27, 30, 33
Shahnama, 260
Shaik, Wazil Ali, 78
Shakespear, 256
Shaman Hwui Li, 174
Shanin, Teodor, 54
Shārailullah, Haji, 131
Shārgilor, 205
Shariff, M.Y., 27, 29, 38
Sharma, Mahesh, 259
Sharma, Neeta, 229
Sharma, R.S., 134
Sharma Sastry, R., 236
Shaukat Ali Maulana, 27
Shergadh, 116
Shia-Sunni bitterness, 23
Shraddhananda, 71
Shriller, 29
Shuddhi movement, 25
Shukla, Ravi Shanker, 33, 39, 41
Shukrullah, 128
Sigerist, 179
Sircar, D.C., 190
Śilāditya, 173, 174
Silpavidyā, 157
Simāchalam Temple Inscriptions, 158
Simhipura grant, 189
Singhora plates, 191
Singh, Lakshmishwar, 73
Singh, Tej Narayan, 73
Sinha, Purnendu Narain, 73
Sinha, Sachidanand, 60
Sirat Committee, 28
Sivakara I, 190
Śivarāni, 161
Siyadori Inscriptions, 115
Śobhaneśvar Temple Inscriptions, 159
Social conditions of India in Aṅguttara-Nikaya, 167-72
  Buddhist Nikayas, 167
  Caste System in, 168
  Daily fare of Indian household, 170-71
  Marriage system, 169
  Nature and character of individual Kula, 170
  Settlement during, 167-68
  Slavery, 168-69
  Social life, 168, 170-71
  Society during, 167-68
  Status of woman, 169-70
Sohani, S.A., 26
Solanapura Vihāra, 156
Somadatta, 189
Soma kings, 199
Somavamsi dynasty, 199
Somesvaradeva, 113
Sonarpur Inscriptions, 115
Soro copper plate, 189
Spencer, Herbert, 129
Sri Lanka, 147, 149
Srimadbhāgavata, 102
Śripatha, 120
Śri Ratnagiri-Mahavrihāriyabhikshu, 156
Śsu-ma-chie'n, 225
Stein, Burton, 147, 148
Stein, M.A., 232
St Petersberg, 206
Subhachandra, 157
Subhakara I, 158
Sufism, 64
Sukranistisara, 271
Sumandala copper palte, 160, 189
Sunar Gaya Prasad, 22
Sundara Cola, 147
Sun Temple at Konarak, 197
Suri, Brihaspati, 160
Suryavaṁsi, 191
Suśruta, 180, 182-85
Susunia Rock Inscription, 142
Svechachhasevak Bahini, 77
Swadeshi movement, 61
Syed Muhammad Mehdi of Pirpur, 35

Tagore Dwarikanath, 57
Tagore Rabindranath, 64, 250
Taj Mohammed, 217

Tajuddin, 28
Taka Kusu, 176
Takur Chand, 217
Talukdari, 14, 15
Tamada, 218
Tampralibti, 156-57
Tamralipta Jaitya Sarkar, 76-83
Tañjavūr Inscription of Rājarāja I and Rājendra I, 149
Tañjavur Temple, 149, 150, 152
Tantra-Kalpa, 181, 182, 185
Tantra of Susruta, 181
Two-lin, 157
Tara, 156
Tarachand, R.B., 28
Taralikā, 270
Taranath, 155-57
Tārāpida, 272
Tasai Inscription of Harsa, 117
Te-Cheng-Tsang, 156
Tekkali grant of Indravarman III, 158
Temple Chronicle (Mādalāpānji) of Puri, 199
Terundia plate of Śubhakara II, 158, 159
Thaiyaka, 116
Thapar, Romila, 225, 231
Theosophical movement, 72-74
Thorner, Daniel, 54
Thucydides, 225
Tibetan Chroniclers, 155
Tilakites of Maharashtra, 23
Tipu Sultan, 128, 204
Tiruvāliśvaram Inscriptions, 148
Tiruvālisavaram Temples, 150
Tiruvidaimarudūr Temples, 150
Tiruviśaippā of Karūr Dēvas, 150
Titu Mir, 131
Tivaradeva, 199
Tośāli, 158
Transandentalism, 64
Tribal history of ancient Bengal,
  Archaeological data, 134
  Chaleolithic/Iron age occurrences, 136-37
    At Baṇeswar Daṅgā, 137
    At Bharatpur, 136-37
    At Harēipur, 136
    At Mahisēdal, 136
    At Nānur, 136
    At Pāṇdu Rājār Dhibi, 136
    At Tulasipur, 137
  Detribalisation, 144
  From tribal to caste society, 142-43
  Immigration from outside Bengal, 143-44
  Linguistic and anthropoligical data, 137
  Microlithic data, 135
  Negrito or negroid, 137-38
  Neolithic data, 135
  Paleolithic data, 135
  Proto-Austroloids or austrics, 138-39
    Dravidian, 138-39
    Mongoloid, 139
  Reconstruction of, 133
  Theoretical framework, 133-34
  Transition from tribal to state organised society, 140-42
    Gauḍas, 141-42
    Rāḍhas, 141-42
    Suhmas, 141-42
    Vaṅgas, 140-41, 142
  Trends in, 144-45
  Tribal settlement, 139-40
Tribhuvaneśvar, 159
Tribhuvan Vir Vikram Jung Bahadur Shah Bahadur Samser Jung, 201
Tribhuvan Vir Vikram Shah Dev, 200
Tripathy, 191
Tripura, Ethno-cultural problem, 101-11
Tsarist Russia, 203

Ubhaya Mukhi Kundalini, 199
Udayagiri, 159
Udayasiṁhadeva, 119
Umāpatidhara, 229
Unitarianism, 64
University Museum Plates of Ramabhānjadeva, 191
Upādhyāya, Mutuśvāmi, 160
Upanishads, 64
Utkala, 155, 199
Uttar Pradesh, 16

Vāgbhata I, 175, 185
Vāgbhata II, 185
Vaillabhattasvāmin Temple, Inscription, 116
Vaisēlaksa Sāstra, 236
Vaiśesika philosophy, 159
Vajra, 156
Vajrahasta V, 190, 191
Vajrayana, 155, 156
Vākārtaka, inscriptions, 114
Vākātaka, 255
Vande Mataram, 29, 37
Vārhaspatyamāna, 191
Vasisthas, 188, 192
Vasudevan, Geeta, 147
Vastudevata, 102
Vasumitra, 253
Vata-yakshini Devi, 118
Vatsabhatti, 228
Vatsyayana, 141
Vattapallika, 160
Venkayya, 148, 149
Verlest, Henry, 217
Verma, J.P., 24, 36, 41
Viceroy's Executive Council, 39
Vidyādhara, 115
Vidyamandir educational scheme, 29-33
Vidyut Bahini, 79

Vietnam, 54
Vigrahas, 189
Vijayabāhu I record, 149
Vijayā Mahādevi, 191
Vijayanagar, 86, 87
Vijayapāla, 118
Vijhu festival, 104-05
Vikram Dev, 200
Vikrama Samvat, 190
Vilhāka 115
Vishnu Āchārya, 158
Vishnuśila, 199
Vivekananda, 64, 72, 73
Vōṇṇā, 115

Wagh, Balkrishna, 24
Warangal Inscription of Raghudeva, 190
Wardha, 28
Wardha scheme of education, 29-30, 32
Washbrook, David, 3, 6, 7, 9, 11, 14, 18
Wavell, 83
Western Poligars in Madras Presidency, 86-97
  Administration of Paliyan, 87-88
  Auxiliary powers in, 86
  Collection of taxes, 94-96
  Expenditure, 94
  Justice administration, 91-92
  Origin of, 86-87
  Polity and economy, 87
  Sources of revenue, 92-93
  Village administration, 88-89
  Village communities, 89-91
White, Leslie, 133
Widow burning and Madri episode, 164-66
  Epics on, 164-65
  Immolation of widow, 165
  Mādri asconding funeral pyre, 164-65
  Origin and antiquity of, 164
  Sati custom, 164
Williams, Monier, 227
Wolf Eric, R., 54
World War II, 76
Wu-tu, 155
Wylie, F.V., 42

Yajñavalkya Nāradā, 237
Yajur-veda, 174
Yendaboo Treaty, 218
Yar Jung, 32
Yarkand, 206
Yaśodharman, 143
Yaśo mati, 270
Yayati I, 199
Yayatikeśari, 159
Yogiswara patram, 160
Yuan Chwang, 174
Yugābda, 190
Yusuf Shariff, M., 23

Zakir Hussain, 31, 32, 33, 34
Zimmar, 179